Compensation Management: Rewarding Performance

Third Edition

Richard I. Henderson

Reston Publishing Company, Inc.
A Prentice-Hall Company
Reston, Virginia

Library of Congress Cataloging in Publication Data

Henderson, Richard I., 1926–
   Compensation management.

   Includes bibliographies.
   1. Compensation management.   I. Title.
HF5549.5.C67H46   1982   · 658.3'142 81-22698
ISBN 0-8359-0913-1   AACR2

© 1979 by Reston Publishing Company, Inc.
A Prentice-Hall Company
Reston, Virginia 22090

10 9 8 7 6 5 4 3 2 1

Printed in the United States of America

Dedication

To my wife Jean, whose consistent efforts and attention have significantly influenced the production and development of the three editions of this book.

Contents

Part 2 Identifying Job Content and Determining Pay . . . 115

Part 3 Completeing the Compensation Package . . . 303

Preface

Even as the last quarter of the twentieth century begins, work-related problems caused by unsatisfactory levels of productivity and ever-increasing demands of workers continue to plague American organizations. Although many experts have been consulted and many solutions proposed, the panacea has still not been discovered. This text does not pretend to be that panacea. Rather, it is an attempt to seek solutions to problems in one small facet of our very complex organizational life—the compensation component of the reward system.

In reality, the concepts underlying the compensation system are simple and easy to understand. Employers provide money and in-kind payments to employees in exchange for employee-provided availability, capability, and performance. Problems arise in systems design when attempts are made to relate the many and varied concepts that identify and describe what employers can do to establish motivating workplace environment. It is here that complexity becomes an issue. Satisfying varying and frequently divergent individual, group, and organizational demands makes implementation of any system a most difficult assignment.

A century ago, the rapid expansion of the Industrial Revolution and its worker-related productivity laid the foundation for a rather simplistic approach to organizational compensation systems. The basic approach to employer-provided compensation in the industrial setting was to establish quantitative performance standards and pay incentives based upon those standards for workers who performed beyond predetermined output requirements. In most other organizations, employers paid a subsistence wage that provided for physical survival and little else.

Over the past 100 years, a constant increase in labor's share of the economic pot has caused the compensation system to become increasingly complex. Even a cursory analysis of why people work reveals a complex set of demands with an even more complex set of opportunities for satisfying these demands. This text attempts to describe some of the major issues that revolve around the "work ethic," the employee-employer exchange process, and the basic components of the compensation system.

This text views compensation primarily from the point of view of the employer. It also recognizes that a properly designed and skillfully managed compensation system can establish a workplace environment that stimulates employee performance. Although compensation payments are extrinsic rewards, they assist in providing the intrinsic or psychic rewards many employees seek from their workplace efforts. The ability to separate compensation from noncompensation rewards is, at best, a difficult assignment. Interaction between these two components of the reward system is both continuous and complex. The strength of the interaction varies according to individual perceptions, expectations, and aspirations. Recognizing employee demands and workplace behavior and linking them to the compensation provided by employers enable modern organizations to meet the productivity improvement challenge in these last decades of the twentieth century.

From the first edition to this third edition of *Compensation Management,* the ideas and efforts of hundreds of authors and organizations who contributed to the concepts and procedures developed in the text are deeply appreciated, although I accept full responsibility for the interpretation of their views.

I deeply appreciate the opportunity to have had a role in the exciting rebirth of the compensation field during the decade of the 1970s and I hope to continue to play a part in the advancement of the field of rewards management in the decade of the 1980s.

I would also like to express my deep thanks to Kitty Clark and Peggy Metz who helped put together parts of this book.

Dick Henderson

Introduction:

From earliest days, human survival and growth have depended on the ability of each person to adapt to and improve upon the environment—a process that has at times been a duty, at times an accomplishment, and frequently drudgery. More often, it has been a combination of all three. This is work. According to Webster, *work* is an "activity in which one exerts strength or faculties to do or perform something . . . sustained physical or mental effort to overcome obstacles and achieve an objective or result." However, the highly complex, somewhat nebulous nature of work has created a barrier that has led to a consistent misunderstanding of its relationship to the survival and the growth of the human race.

True, people gain satisfaction from their work, but the types and the strengths of satisfaction have been difficult, if not impossible, to identify, define, and measure with any degree of precision. Furthermore, the individual performer may gain one set of satisfactions from work efforts whereas the group with which the same individual identifies gains another. And as the individual and the group coordinate their needs and efforts, a third set of satisfactions

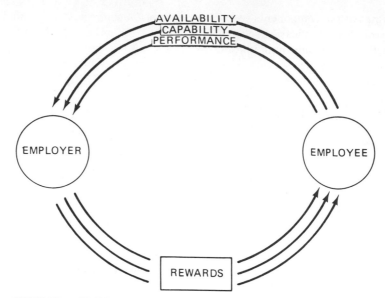

FIGURE I-1   THE EMPLOYER-EMPLOYEE EXCHANGE PROCESS

develops. The enigmatic issues related to work have defied simplification, but a better understanding may be gained by analyzing the process in which employers provide rewards in exchange for the availability, capability, and performance of the employee as described in Figure I-1.

THE REWARD SYSTEM

An organization is formed to accomplish a specific mission. To accomplish its mission, it must attract and hire people who have certain knowledge, skills, aptitudes, and attitudes. To attract and retain such people, the organization provides rewards. An organization designs and implements a reward system to focus worker attention on the specific behaviors the organization considers necessary to achieve its desired objectives and goals. The behaviors range from simply arriving at work at the scheduled time to meeting specified performance standards and providing innovative contributions that lead to improved organizational productivity. If rewards are to be useful in stimulating desired behaviors, they must meet the demands of the employees whose behaviors they are intended to influence. Because of the almost endless varieties of human qualities, job requirements, and situational demands, the design and the management of a reward system that produces such results are a most difficult and complex undertaking.

The reward system of the organization includes anything an employee may value and desire that the employer is capable or willing to offer in exchange for employee contributions. A rather broad classification scheme that improves the identification and the recognition of various kinds and qualities of rewards and increases the usefulness of this text is to separate rewards provided by employers into *compensation* components and *noncompensation* components. The underlying logic of this classification scheme is to place all reward components that act as monetary payments and in-kind payments into a compensation system. Monetary payments can be either tangible (coins or paper money) or intangible (checks or credit cards). They have value in use and simplify exchange transactions. In-kind payments are goods or commodities used in lieu of money that provide an equivalent value for what has been offered or received. All other reward components fall into the category of the noncompensation system. Figure I-2 is a simple representation of this process.

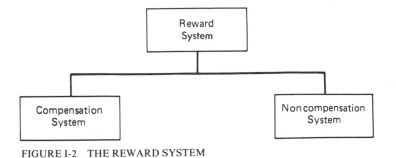

FIGURE I-2   THE REWARD SYSTEM

COMPENSATION REWARD SYSTEM

The compensation system results from allocation, conversion, and transfer of the income of an organization to its employees for their monetary and in-kind claims on goods and services.

Monetary claims on goods and services are wage payments received by an employee that come in the form of money, or payments that are quickly and easily transferable to money at the discretion of the employee. As a medium of exchange, money enables an employee to purchase certain types and amounts of the wide variety of goods and services available in the marketplace. The actual kinds and quantity of purchases made by the employee depend on the individual mechanisms that motivate choice behavior. Wage payments in the form of money may be further subdivided by payments earned and acquired in the present and payments earned but not paid until some future time—deferred payments.

In-kind claims are claims on goods and services made available and paid for either totally or in some percentage by the employer. Employees normally have little or no opportunity for immediate monetary gain from an in-kind payment. Many employer-provided in-kind payments, however, replace monetary payments of some amount of the employees' income were the employees to obtain similar goods and services elsewhere. Organizations purchase these required and usually desired goods and services for their members to take advantage of (1) economies of scale available through group purchasing, (2) the benefits available through tax laws and regulations, and (3) government laws requiring certain services.

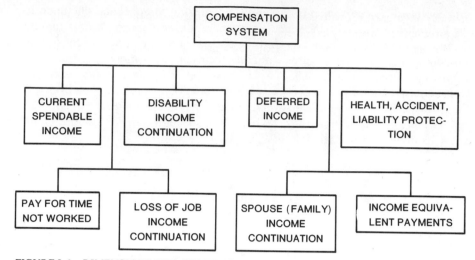

FIGURE I–3 DIMENSIONS OF A COMPENSATION SYSTEM

The value any one in-kind payment has to a specific employee depends directly on how the employee perceives its worth. Individual perception relates to a range of demographic characteristics (i.e., age, sex, marital status, education, number and age of dependents, length of service, level in the organization, other income, etc.), as well as to the physical and emotional state of the employee.

The total compensation package may be described in many ways, but the one recommended and used in this book includes eight compensation dimensions. Within each dimension are a number of compensation components. Each component has a variety of features. Because of different features, one component may relate to more that one dimension. The structuring of features, components, and dimensions into a compensation system is a job for the compensation specialist. Figure I-3 models the eight dimensions of a compensation system.

This book will discuss in detail the first compensation dimension, current spendable income. The other seven dimensions will be discussed briefly. An analysis of each compensation dimension must include a discussion of the many components comprising that dimension.

COMPENSATION DIMENSIONS

A brief description of the eight compensation dimensions and some of their components may assist the reader in gaining a better understanding and appreciation of the complexity of a compensation system in a modern organization.

Current Spendable Income

Current spendable income includes money provided in the short term (weekly, monthly, and annual bonuses/awards) that permits employees to pay for and contract for the payment of desired goods and services. The amount of money payments provided to employees normally depends on specified job requirements; outputs that meet or exceed quantity, quality, or timeliness standards; innovations that may lead to improved productivity; dependability; loyalty; and some combination of these items. Typical components within this dimension are base pay, premiums and differentials, short-term bonuses, merit pay, and certain allowances.

Pay For Time Not Worked

Over the years, not only has there been a decrease in hours worked per week but also in the number of days worked per year. During the past 35 years, workers have enjoyed more days off with pay for holidays, longer paid vacations, and paid time off for a wide variety of personal reasons. These pay-for-time-not-worked components significantly increase labor costs and also enhance quality-of-work-life opportunities for most employees.

Disability Income Continuation

The possibility always exists for a worker to incur health or accident disability. Because of these disabilities, employees are frequently unable to perform their normal assignments—or, for that matter, any assignment. Even so, individual and family living expenses continue; and medical, hospital, and surgical bills create additional burdens. Social Security, Workers' Compensation, sick leave, and short- and long-term disability plans are examples of disability income continuation components that provide funds for employees who are unable to work for health-related reasons.

Loss-of-Job Income Continuation

Job security is and has been for most workers their number one consideration. Workers want assurance that their jobs and the income derived from working will continue until they are ready to retire. Workers also know that few, if any, jobs are guaranteed to continue to retirement. Not only may accident and sickness problems occur, but economic conditions, technological changes, and personal performance or interpersonal dynamics problems arise that result in temporary layoff or termination of employment. A variety of components such as unemployment insurance, supplementary unemployment benefits (SUBS), and severance pay help unemployed workers to subsist until new employment opportunities arise.

Deferred Income

Most employees depend on some kind of an employer-provided program for income continuation after retirement. Some employees who are normally in the higher-income brackets are granted compensation opportunities that provide income at some future date. There are two basic reasons for these programs. First of all, most employees do not have sufficient savings at retirement to continue the life-styles they enjoyed while working. Here, various kinds of programs such as Social Security, employer-provided pension plans, savings and thrift plans, annuities, and supplemental income plans provide income after retirement. Second, tax laws and regulations make deferred income plans more appealing compensation components for both employers and employees. Because of tax regulations, employers can take immediate deductions and employees can defer tax obligations until income tax rates are more favorable. Stock purchase, option, and grant plans are commonly used components for achieving tax deduction and deferral goals.

Spouse (Family) Income Continuation

Most employees with family obligations are concerned with what may happen if they are no longer able to provide money that will allow their families to maintain a particular standard of living. Certain plans are designed to provide dependents with income upon the death of an employee or the inability of that employee to work due to total and permanent disability. Specific features within life insurance plans, pension plans, Social Security, Workers' Compensation, and other related plans provide income for the families of employees when these conditions arise.

Health, Accident, and Liability Protection

When a health problem occurs, employees must be concerned not only with income continuation but also with payment for the goods and services required in overcoming the illness or disability. Organizations provide a wide variety of insurance plans to assist in paying for these goods and services. In recent years, the cost of medical-related goods and services has increased at a greater rate than almost any other good or service desired or required by employees. Medical, hospital, and surgical insurance plans and major medical, dental, and vision insurance form only a partial list of an extensive group of compensation components designed to provide such protention for workers.

Because of savings available through group purchasing, organizations are now providing various kinds of liability-related insurance plans for their employees. These plans include group legal, group automobile, group umbrella liability, employee liability, and other insurance plans.

Income Equivalent Payments

A final set of compensation components may be grouped under the title of income equivalent payments. Many of these components are frequently called perquisites or "perks." These are usually highly desirable to employees, and both employers and employees find them to have certain tax benefits. Some perks are tax-free to employees and tax deductible to employers. In recent years, the Internal Revenue Service (IRS) has required that employer costs for a specific portion of certain perks be considered as earned income to employees. In most cases, when this occurs, the earned income charge to employees is significantly less than the amount an employee would have been required to pay if he or she had purchased the good or service at the marketplace. Some of the more desirable perks are use of a company car or a company credit card, payment for expenses to professional meetings, tuition reimbursement for educational programs, and subsidized food services.

NONCOMPENSATION REWARDS

The other major part of the reward system includes noncompensation rewards. The classification of noncompensation rewards is much more difficult to develop and the identification of noncompensation components far more complex than the classification and the identification of compensation rewards and components. Noncompensation rewards include all the work situation-related rewards not included in the compensation package. These rewards include an almost infinite number of components that relate to the work situation and, emotionally and psychologically, to each worker. Any activity of the employer that has an impact on the intellectual, emotional, and physical well-being of the employee and is not specifically covered by the compensation system is part of the noncompensation reward system. Figure I-4 models noncompensation rewards.

Within the noncompensation reward reside many of the reward components that behavioral scientists have been identifying and describing for the past 50 years as most critical for improving employee workplace performance. An in-depth analysis of the seven noncompensation dimensions identified in Figure I-4 soon reveals a strong interrelation between compensation and noncompensation rewards. The delineation between these two major reward segments that at first glance appear to be a black-white segmentation soon blurs into a gray area as they interact and blend together.

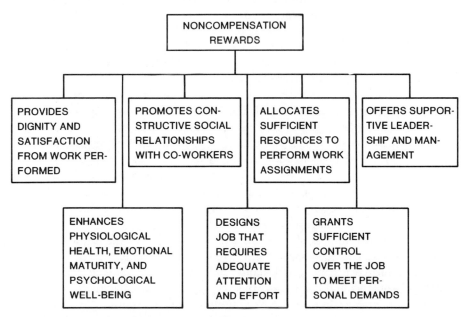

FIGURE I-4   NONCOMPENSATION REWARDS

Provide Dignity From Work Performed

Possibly the least costly and one of the most powerful rewards any organization can offer to its members is recognition as a useful and valuable contributor to the organization. This kind of employer recognition leads to employee feelings of self-worth and pride in making a contribution. Few people truly want to be given anything. They would much prefer to know that, through their own efforts, they have earned and deserved the rewards they receive. Every compensation and noncompensation reward component should carry with it a message that "we need you and appreciate your efforts." Enhancing the human dignity of each employee must, at all times, be a major organization concern.

Enhance Physiological Health, Psychological Well-Being, and Emotional Maturity

Considering the number of waking hours a person spends on the job, traveling to and from the worksite, and off-the-job time spent in attempting to resolve job-related problems, the influence work can have on the health of employees becomes apparent. Health-related problems frequently receive minimal attention until such problems occur. Once this happens, however, these problems override all other employee concerns and activities. Modern health practices recognize the direct relationship between the psychological and emotional well being of each individual.

A safe working environment has always been a thorny issue between employers and employees. Providing safe equipment, working in as risk-free an environment as possible, minimizing the impact of noxious fumes, avoiding extreme heat, cold, and humidity conditions, eliminating contact with radiation, cancer-causing, and other disease-related materials and substances are requests made by all employees. The clean work station, the cheerfully decorated wall and floors, and the reduction of noise to a tolerable level provide an enjoyable work environment that enhances employee health.

As important as these physical conditions are, more and more attention focuses on the emotional and psychological strains resulting from the extreme specialization of work assignments and the complex interactions resulting from this specialization. Additional stress is caused by technological advancements that require rapid changes in knowledge and skills of workers. Over these issues hovers the syndrome of ever-expanding aspirations and expectations of people throughout the world. Demands for a greater share of the limited resources of the organization and society as a whole result in further disharmonies that cause additional emotional and psychological problems.

It is almost impossible for management to overcome these universal problems, but it can recognize their existence and take actions to limit their negative influence on the performance of each employee. Understanding of employee problems and communication to employees of what the organization can provide to maintain a secure and stable life-style can assist in minimizing emotional and psychological stress. Training employees to perform current jobs in an acceptable manner and offering training opportunities that will assist employees in attaining their potential are noncompensation components that can influence this health-related dimension in a positive manner.

Promote Constructive Social Relationships With Co-Workers

An old adage states that "One man is not man." Although there are constant reminders of the results one dedicated person can achieve, there are even more reminders that one human alone is a weak animal.

However, together in concerted action, people can accomplish almost anything. Today, in this world of extreme specialization, more than ever before people need and must rely on other people. One of the most valued rewards gained from working is the opportunity to interact in a socially constructive manner with other people—to enjoy the comradeship of workplace associates.

The chance to communicate and interact with others is another inexpensive but valuable reward employees can offer. A workplace environment where trust, fellowship, loyalty, and love emanate from the top level of management to the lowest levels of the organization promotes the kinds of social interaction that most people need in order to live and grow. All parts of the reward system can further the establishment of a trusting workplace environment; or they can provide barriers where suspicion, jealousy, and intrigue can destroy any opportunity for widespread, productivity-promoting, social relationships.

Design Jobs That Require Adequate Attention and Effort

Over the past 30 years, organizational scientists have discussed problems arising from the boredom related to work. Specific attention has focused on "scientific management" efforts developed in the early days of the twentieth century to specialize work assignments. Jobs were designed so that workers could quickly be taught how to perform a few highly repetitive tasks. They were then required to perform these few tasks for as long as they remained on the job. What first appeared to be an efficient way of melding the human resources and the ever-improving machine technology proved to have serious drawbacks.

Many employees quickly became bored and dissatisfied while performing these easily learned, highly repetitive tasks. Work-related anxieties and frustration resulted in numerous kinds of employee behaviors that led to declining performance rather than the improvements sought. Turnover, absenteeism, tardiness, minimal concern for quality or productivity, waste of physical resources, and even theft and malicious damage were employee behaviors attributed to unacceptable workplace and job design.

Recognizing these problems, behavioral scientists and managers at all levels have been searching for and implementing new approaches to improve the quality of work life. On both an individual and group basis, employees are receiving more opportunity to have a voice in how their jobs should be performed. The restructuring of job tasks and job responsibilities is receiving top attention. Flexibility in job requirements is being provided by rotating work assignments and giving employees more opportunity to schedule their workdays and workweeks. Managers are being taught how to instruct workers to do their jobs and then to leave them alone to perform their assignments in their own unique ways. This does not mean that managers must abdicate their supervisory responsibilities, but rather that they must recognize when they should be available to provide needed support, be able to tell employees what they are doing right, and assist them in correcting their errors.

Allocate Sufficient Resources To Perform Work Assignments

Requiring employees to perform assignments for which they have neither the knowledge nor the skills necessary to achieve desired results and to meet performance standards opens the door for workplace problems. Not only is the organization likely to suffer because of outcome failures, but employee job-related interest and satisfaction break down because of the great likelihood or inevitability of failure. Most employees want to feel a sense of accomplishment from their work. They want some degree of challenge from their work, but they also want to feel reasonably sure that they can succeed.

Also, when employees are told that they must produce certain kinds and quantities of output within a specified time, they want to know that resources are available to help them meet these demands. Possibly the most critical resource is simply sufficient time available to accomplish an assignment. Does the employee have the time to perform the specific assignment? Are other assignments making demands on the employee's time that preclude or jeopardize successful job performance? Has the organization assisted or enabled the employee to gain the knowledge and the skills necessary to perform the assignment? Are the necessary human technical or physical resources available to support and aid the employee in accomplishing the specific assignment? These and many other similar questions must be answered by supervisors as they identify subordinate assignments and review the performance by these subordinates on their assignments.

To make work a satisfying, even exhilarating experience, employees must not be facing a no-win situation. This does not mean an employee should not be expected to stretch and put forth sufficient effort to meet workplace obligations. It does mean, however, that, with the proper interested effort, success is likely. The organization recognizes the support necessary and does everything possible to help the employee complete his or her work successfully.

Grant Sufficient Control Over the Job to Meet Personal Demands

From the 1950s to the present, behavioral scientists have discussed the need to grant employees a greater opportunity to participate in the organizational decision-making processes.

A problem with this participation concept is that there are all kinds of people in organizations with all kinds of decision-making desires. Some people simply want to be told what to do, shown what is considered to be an acceptable level of performance, and then left alone to do their jobs. A few people at all levels in the organization want to tell top management how to run the organization. Between these two extremes is a wide variety of demands for greater voice in determining how to perform given work assignments.

Possibly one of the most important decision areas being made available to more and more workers is that of scheduling work activities and, in a few cases, of choosing the location of assignments. Over the past two decades, flexible work schedules have been implemented that range from compressed workweeks (e.g., four-day, 40-hour schedules) to the flexitime programs where workers can work a 7½- to 8-hour day within a 12- to 14-hour interval.

Another advancement in this area has allowed two people who are full-time employees to share one job. Each of the two may work only from 15 to 25 hours per week, but together they share and perform all job responsibilities. Like many other noncompensation rewards, the benefits gained by granting such scheduling privileges frequently far outweigh the costs of having an additional employee on the payroll.

Offer Supportive Leadership and Management

It is difficult to separate this dimension from all other noncompensation rewards. It is so important, however, that it must be recognized as a unique dimension of the noncompensation rewards and not just as a component of the other dimensions. Nearly everyone looks to certain individuals for guidance and support. They want to recognize and respect individuals who can assist them achieve life-style goals. They want leaders who have influence and can bring about desired changes. Followers must have faith in and abide by the actions taken by leaders, and the leaders must heed the requests of the followers.

Employee faith and trust in management assist in establishing a workplace environment where job security becomes accepted, where social interaction thrives, and where work satisfaction is possible. Supportive leadership is shown in many ways. Some of the more common are interest demonstrated in coaching and counseling, praise for a job well done, and constructive feedback leading to improvement of job performance. Leaders must be sufficiently flexible with policies, rules, and regulations so that an employee can meet both job and nonjob responsibilities without infringing on the rights and the opportunities of other employees. Here again, the costs related to these rewards are minimal compared to the benefits received. The selection, the training, and the promotion of those individuals who will be effective leaders and managers are the cost components of this dimension.

EMPLOYEE DEMANDS

What do employees in modern organizations expect and demand from their jobs? Are there differences between the demands of employees at the beginning and at the end of the twentieth century? If so, what are these differences and what impact do they have on the reward system in general and the compensation system in particular?

Although human desires for freedom, self-determination, and fair treatment have remained unchanged throughout history, political and social reforms have had enormous impact on the design and the management of reward systems. Such reforms as those in the following list have guaranteed survival for most members of society.

1. Government endorsement of union activities and the collective bargaining process that provide the worker with a strong voice in decisions concerning workplace relationships.

2. Minimum wage and hour requirements that establish minimum pay standards for performing work activities.

3. Income security programs that protect the aged, the disabled, and the unemployed from complete financial disaster under conditions in which they have little or no influence.

4. Food, housing, health care, clothing, and educational allowances for those unable to work or find work opportunities.

Even with this government protection, the first demand most employees make of their jobs is *security*. Once the employee is on the job and past the probationary period, the need for job security quickly appears to recede in importance. Anything that happens that has any potential impact on job security, however, will dominate all other considerations.

Base Standard of Living

Job security ensures the continued flow of wages and the wide variety of in-kind payments that form the compensation system. The employee translates these compensation expectations into standard-of-living spending patterns that establish the amount and the quality of food, housing, clothing, transportation, health care, and other requirements of life. Through their jobs, the great majority of employees are able to enjoy incomes that exceed those designated by government statisticians as a poverty income for a nonfarm family of four ($8,450/year—1981)[1] or a lower-budget income for a nonfarm family of four ($14,044/year—autumn 1980).[2] The current standard of living enjoyed by most workers is, in their estimation, the minimal life-style that they accept or require; and the current job is what makes it all possible in most cases.

[1]*Poverty Income Guidelines for All States Except Alaska and Hawaii, 1981,* Office of Management and Budget Memorandum.

[2]*A Guide to Living Cost* (Atlanta, GA: U.S. Department of Labor, Bureau of Labor Statistics, 1980), p.3.

Life-style demands for modern workers exceed poverty and austere subsistence requirements and are always changing. The industrial state predicates future growth on increases in consumption of its products and services. Just as national survival and growth depend on ever-increasing consumption, the members of the industrial state measure their own growth and development through opportunities for increasing consumption choices. Marketing experts whet the appetites of the modern workers with a vast array of available goods and services. Workers can choose among these desirable goods and services (luxuries) with their discretionary income (that income available after paying for the necessities of their current life-style).

Influence

In addition to maintaining present life-style and being able to purchase luxuries, employees demand *influence*. Like that of practically every other aspect of the reward system, the definition of influence depends on individual perception and on the object of the influence activity. In general terms, *influence* is the ability to change the behavior of another for some personal gain or satisfaction. The compensation system provides many influence opportunities.

The absolute dollar amount of the paycheck is in itself an influence opportunity. A particular, conspicuous purchase (a car, house, or clothing), a donation to a favorite charity or religious organization, or a gift to a family member, friend, or associate of something desired or needed—all are examples of influence opportunities made possible through job-provided compensation.

Life-style and influence opportunities have future as well as current requirements. Government income and security programs provide a minimal base for future living standards. However, many employees, given the opportunity, will allocate some percentage of their discretionary income to savings and investments to provide for the continuation of their current standard of living, security, and influence opportunities beyond those offered through present employment or by government security-oriented programs.

The analysis of life-style demands and the opportunity for maintaining a current life-style and improving it in the future underscore the importance of job-earned compensation. It is no wonder that a major union leader made this statement, "A job is a job; if you don't pay enough, it is a lousy job." Or that another union leader has stated, "The most sensitive artery in the human body is the one going from the heart to the pocketbook."

Part 1

Work and Rewards: Concepts and Process

M ajor challenges and opportunities for change occur at the workplace. Albert Camus, a French author, once wrote, "Without work all life goes rotten. But when work is soulless, life stifles and dies." Although it may not be universally accepted, a basic concept of this part of the text is that people not only need to work, they *want* to. From work, they provide for their physical and emotional survival, but to achieve these goals, work must be meaningful. One of the primary ways by which to measure the value of work is through the rewards gained at the workplace.

Part 1 is a brief overview of some of the fundamental concepts and ideas that lay the foundation for designing and managing an understandable, meaningful, and workable compensation system. The compensation system is but one component of the exchange process in which employees provide a package of abilities, skills, desires, and vitality in exchange for a package of rewards provided by the employer. The intent of these rewards from the perspective of an employer is to encourage and channel employee behavior into activities that lead to successful operations of the organization.

It is possible for a reward system to channel or modify employee behavior through either a positive or a negative approach. A positive approach creates a motivational environment by providing incentives that employees see as being fair and just. Such an environment recognizes individual rights, stimulates high levels of individual effort, and promotes a willingness to cooperate in group activities.

On the other hand, a negative approach creates a reward environment based on fear and manipulation. A work environment based on negative rewards communicates to employees that the failure to behave in a prescribed manner can imperil their very survival.

It is all too easy for the reward process, either by design or through negligence, to achieve its immediate goals through intimidation and fear. Fear of losing a job, a promotional opportunity, or a desired reward can cause employees to conceal for some time behaviors that are unacceptable to employers. Is it in the best interest of the modern organization to design and operate a reward process that handcuffs employees to jobs and stifles human emotion and expression? Rather, is it not preferable to provide an open environment that promotes individual freedom of expression and recognizes each worker as a vital contributor whose interest, concern, patience, and skill assist the organization in realizing its goals and objectives? To achieve both its short-run goals and long-run objectives, the modern organization must develop an environment that generates employee cooperation and, at the same time, encourages and maintains the individuality of each member.

In many ways, the job performed by the modern worker requires less physical effort and fewer manual skills than those required a generation or even a decade ago. A more thorough understanding of the technical process and of the operation of complex subsystems is replacing manual skills. The highly complex technical and interactive systems in which the employees of today work require greater use of their intellectual faculties than ever before. Job requirements undergo constant change. Learning to improve job understanding and performance is no longer a one-time thing. Rather, it is a never-ending demand on every employee.

The change in workplace demands on human labor is having a dramatic impact on the type and the use of rewards for modifying or changing human behavior. Throughout history, most available human energy has been channeled into physical labor. The results of physical labor are usually observable and amenable to analysis and measurement. But the introduction, first, of machinery not powered by humans and then of instruments that direct, monitor, and regulate this machinery has resulted in the demand for different methods for rewarding individuals who display desired workplace behavior. Methods and procedures used for modifying human behavior have, at times, been called "the carrot and the stick." (The "carrot" is a reward offered to an individual who behaves in an acceptable or preferred manner. The "stick" is the negative motivator to coerce a demonstration of a certain behavior.)

The roots of the carrot-and-stick concept lie in human endeavor to change animal behavior. Although many experts now believe that the carrot and the stick are no longer useful for changing human behavior, the approach is as viable today as it has ever been. The difference is not one of philosophy but rather one of design and use procedures. Even a positive approach to behavior modification requires the use of the stick as well as the carrot. For example, the failure to provide a carrot can, from a recipient's point of view, have the impact of a stick. Within a positive approach to behavior modification, the use of rewards and punishment depends on the definition and the establishment of work standards and workplace behaviors that are acceptable to the employer and understood and recognized by the employees as just and fair.

The use of the carrot and the stick to channel human energy into certain physical activities takes one form whereas using the carrot and stick for channeling human energy into sets of intellectual activities takes another. The reason for this difference in the design and the implementation of reward and punishment is that results of physical effort are usually well defined and observable whereas the results of intellectual effort are at best often difficult to define and measure. Over time, the results of intellectual effort may even demonstrate that initial observations of these activities were inaccurate and possibly invalid. This is the major barrier in designing and implementing a reward system for employees of the modern organization. Developing understandable, workable, and meaningful workplace standards is a difficult, costly, and time-consuming activity. Since jobs are not static, standards for them must vary within changing job requirements, adding yet another dimension to the setting of job standards.

Although human demands may have changed over the years, the foundations of human behavior remain constant. There is still the need for the carrot to stimulate acceptable and desired behavior and the stick to limit or eliminate unwanted, unacceptable behavior.

Today, the emphasis on workplace behavior relates to individual desire and willingness to accept job responsibilities. Key concepts involved in this change in directing the activities of people at work are *involvement* and *commitment*—a self-dedication to performing job assignments and duties in an acceptable manner. To promote these valuable attributes of involvement and commitment, the modern organization must provide rewards that stimulate the desire of workers to achieve, to be constructive, to enhance self-growth, and to be productive.

1

Establishing A Motivating Workplace Environment

CONTENT

Chapter 1 discusses the complex nature of human behavior, including a number of theories and models developed by behavioral scientists. These theories provide insights into the relationship between employer-provided rewards and employee-demonstrated workplace behavior that are valuable to those persons involved in the design and the management of compensation systems.

GOALS

Upon concluding this chapter, you should recognize some of the major contributions that assist in providing a better understanding of the motives that stimulate and shape human behavior. You should also begin to appreciate the fact that money and in-kind payments made available through employer-provided compensation can have a significant influence on directing employee workplace behavior.

F or as long as a small select group of individuals has had the opportunity to direct the efforts of others, interest has focused on how to influence people to act in certain ways. One of the oldest of the theories developed to describe how to direct and stimulate human effort is called the carrot-and-stick approach. Its underlying principle is that people strive for rewards—the carrots—and seek to avoid punishment—the stick. (The carrot-and-stick approach relates to the directing of a donkey's efforts by either placing a carrot in front of its nose or hitting its hindquarters with a stick.)

Over the past half century, many behavioral scientists and managers have declared the carrot-and-stick approach to be of minimal value in stimulating human effort. To replace and supplement this approach, a wide variety of motivational theories has been developed and offered as more useful in understanding and directing the efforts of people. The compensation specialist is one person in the organization who has a direct opportunity to design reward systems (or parts of them) that recognize and make use of motivational theories. The test of any theory is in its application—that is, does it work in a real-world setting? No matter how elegant or appealing a motivational theory, it is useful only if it assists an organization in attracting and retaining workers who perform in a competent or possibly superior manner.

A review of some of the more widely-acclaimed motivational theories and their relationship to reward system components will assist in determining their usefulness for directing and modifying employee workplace behavior. This review and analysis may also demonstrate that the carrot-and-stick approach is still "alive and kicking." It may also demonstrate that each of the compensation and noncompensation components can be useful as both carrots and sticks in modifying employee behavior. Obtaining a kind and a quantity of a reward can be a positive incentive for modifying behavior, whereas removal of or failure to provide a reward can act as a strong stick. The issue is truly not whether compensation and noncompensation work or do not work as carrot and stick. Rather, the issue is how to use compensation (1) as an incentive for modifying behavior so that it will be valuable to organizational survival and growth and (2) as a tool for disciplining those who exhibit behaviors that impede organizational success.

THE BLACK BOX ENIGMA

The design, the implementation, and the administration of any reward component, or for that matter the entire compensation or noncompensation system, require a sensitivity to and an understanding of human perceptions, needs, and drives. Given the current state of technology and the framework existing in most organizations, designing and operating of reward systems sensitive to human needs and psyches may be at the best difficult and frustrating and at the worst a mission impossible. The problem centers around an issue that may be called the black box enigma.

The term *black box* as used here refers to the human brain. Because of the wide range of variables that influence the organization and the operation of this mechanism, it is impossible to recognize, much less analyze, how one element relates to another, to truly understand its operation, and then to be able to predict the actions resulting from the internal functions. It is practically impossible for one black box to identify at any particular time what another black box is attempting to satisfy. It is equally unlikely that one black box can select "strokes" that most adequately satisfy identified needs of another black box.

Although the black box concept draws what may appear to be a very bleak picture of the motivational approach to behavior modification, opportunities for modifying or changing employee behavior through compensation rewards may not be as dim as presented here.

Identifying the choice considerations available to employees and the options available to the organization to assist employees in realizing a specific choice may not totally depend on the use of a specific motivational model to predict human behavior. An option available to management is the recognition of cause-and-effect relationships between reward components and performance. Although much of the research focusing on this relationship is of minimal value to the designers and the implementers of compensation systems, it imparts knowledge of the roles of compensation and performance activities as stimuli and responses in the behavior of the employer and employee. This is the black box concept that employers and employees must relate to in performing various activities. In working with the employer black box and the employee black box, it may be almost impossible to understand what is happening internally to either. It is still possible, however, to predict which reward or compensation inputs will stimulate which response activities.

Figure 1-1 depicts the compensation-performance feedback loop in which compensation is a response of the employer to the performance stimuli of the employee and performance is the response of the employee to the stimuli of the rewards received from the employer. There are no assurances that specific stimuli will or will not elicit specific responses, which is typical of the black box concept. In applying the black box concept to motivational theory, it is possible, through the use of observation and experience, to identify reward-performance directions to infer stimulus-response relationships among activities of employers and employees.

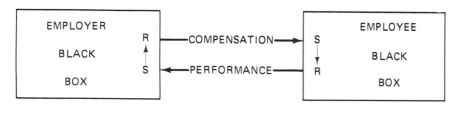

R = response

S = stimuli

FIGURE 1-1   THE DOUBLE BLACK BOX FEEDBACK LOOP

Employee demands, as opposed to employee needs, are firmed or hardened needs expressed as behaviors that are observable and recognizable. They are not those behavior-molding conditions existing within the brain of a specific individual at a particular point in time. All individuals make demands that relate to present and future subsistence, to luxury requirements beyond subsistence, to leisure opportunities and activities, to opportunities for influence, and to saving and investing for future security.

To identify the effect the reward package has on the employees of an organization, it is important to determine which portion of the package provides for subsistence, which portion is available as disposable income, and which portion provides for demands beyond subsistence. Figure 1-2 describes the balancing of employee demands with employer-provided compensation rewards.

When identifying employee demands, certain requirements will appear to be almost universal in nature. At survival or even subsistence level, employee food, housing, and clothing requirements must be satisfied. In addition, the modern worker will almost always expect transportation, some health care, and other benefits that extend beyond subsistence into luxury categories. Although these employee demands are universal, when they are joined together to form a set of requirements for a specific employee, employers may find that they differ significantly.

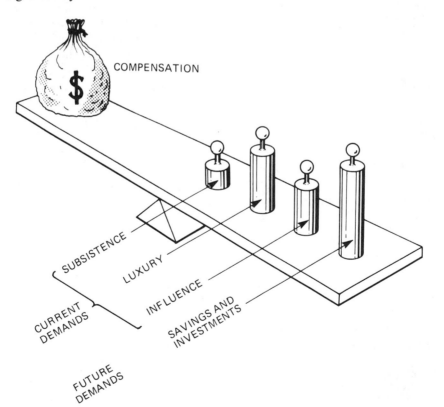

FIGURE 1-2   MEASURES OF COMPENSATION UTILITY

To develop a better understanding of the relationship between employer-provided rewards and demonstrated employee behavior, behavioral scientists have developed theories and models to assist in explaining and predicting this relationship.

Ayn Rand, a leading twentieth century philosopher on human nature, provides some insights into the ability of people to reason that are valuable in explaining the relationship between employee behavior and reward opportunities. Her basic tenet is that the brain provides each person with the opportunity to think. She stated:

> Psychologically, the choice to "think or not" is the choice "to focus or not." Existentially [a free and responsible existence], the choice "to focus or not" is the choice "to be conscious or not." Metaphysically [transcending the natural], the choice "to be conscious or not" is the choice of life or death.
>   Consciousness—for those living organisms which possess it— is the basic means of survival. For man, the basic means of survival is reason.[1]

Returning once again to the employer-employee exchange process, the first demand made on the process by most employees is job security. It is valid and plausible to relate job security directly to survival. With ever-increasing levels of aspirations and expectations, survival does not simply mean a life-style constrained by a subsistence income. Rather, it means a life-style that provides certain amounts of housing, clothing, transportation, education, health, and recreational opportunities that are above subsistence levels today and that improves on these opportunities for tomorrow.

Rand emphasized that humans are able to conceptualize—to organize abstract materials into a meaningful relationship. To survive, they must make choices. The quality of the choice depends on the data and the information available for decision making. Rand further stated that humans cannot survive by making choices strictly for the moment or for physical survival. Total human survival requires action, values, and goals that lead to full and productive lives.[2]

Sigmund Freud once stated that a healthy existence can be achieved only through love and work. Rand enlarged on the work concept by stating: "Everything man needs has to be discovered by his own mind and produced by his own efforts; the two essentials of the method of survival proper to a rational human being are thinking and productive work."[3]

Recognizing the essential contributions work makes to the physical and psychological survival of all workers is the start of designing and managing a practical and useful compensation system. To be practical, workable, and useful, the compensation system must facilitate employee choice opportunities that affect both current and future life-style.

[1]Ayn Rand, *The Virtue of Selfishness: A New Concept of Egoism* (New York: Signet Book, 1961), p. 21.

[2]Ibid., pp. 24–25.

[3]Ibid., p. 23.

If the employee behavior resulting from rationally made decisions is to be of benefit to both the employee and the employer, the compensation system must provide data and information of sufficient quantity and suitable quality.

$$Data + Knowledge = Information[4]$$
$$Information + Judgment = Decision$$

If there is truth in Rand's philosophy that "productive work is the central purpose of a rational man's life,"[5] then the basic requirement of the reward system is not to induce employees to work but, rather, to focus their attention on the fact that workplace behavior acceptable to both the employee and the employer can lead not only to current and continuing survival but to the achievement of life's goals. In addition, Rand's focus on consciousness recognizes the importance of relative considerations. Expectations relating to work and workplace behavior evolve as workers compare the benefits they gain and the contributions they make with those of others.

A MODEL RELATING COMPENSATION TO WORKPLACE BEHAVIOR

From the work of countless behavioral scientists, it may be inferred that four major forces influencing human behavior can be identified: (1) demands for physical survival, (2) development of self, (3) concern for others, and (4) desire for independence. In attempting to satisfy these demands, the conscious, semiconscious, and unconscious components of the human brain institute a process of *thinking*.

Through the thinking process, people *conceptualize* (i.e., develop abstract ideas of the subject under consideration) and then, through the use of their own perceptive skills and abilities, identify and acquire necessary data and information. They then integrate the resulting knowledge gained from processing these data and information into possible courses of action. This is *reasoning*. If these intellectual processes are to result in a conscious activity or behavior, the thinking-conceptualizing-reasoning process must *focus* on a specific course of action or actions. The final choice of action results in identifiable and describable *behavior*. See Figure 1-3.

By relating demonstrated behavior and compensation practices, designers and managers of compensation systems have the greatest opportunity to improve organizational productivity. This does not mean, however, that it is of little value or unnecessary to become involved and attempt to understand the intellectual processes that determine employee workplace behavior. A brief review of the think-conceptualize-reason-focus-behavior model provides insights into the why, what, where, when, and how of the employee intellectual process. Answering

---

[4]Adrian M. McDonough, *Information, Economics, and Management Systems* (New York: McGraw-Hill, 1963), pp. 75–76.

[5]Rand, *The Virtue of Selfishness*, p. 25.

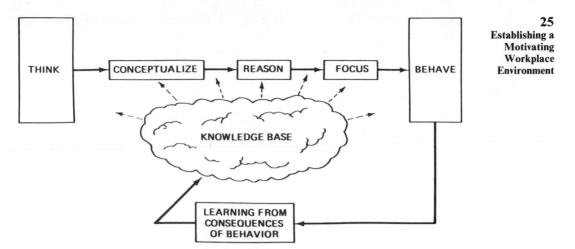

FIGURE 1-3   THE THINKING-BEHAVING PROCESS

these questions posed to the analytical process is extremely valuable to everyone involved in compensation system design and management.

Thinking

To be human, to be alive, is to set goals. Some people set goals that determine their entire life-styles; other set goals that may enable them to exist for the next couple of hours. Whether goals are set through an extensive thinking process or through a process that is barely recognizable to the individual goal setter, goals are set. Once a goal is set, some conscious decision is made as to how best achieve that goal. The decision to do nothing may be the resulting behavior or the decision may include vigorous, innovative activities.

In setting goals, everything that a person knows or possibly has ever known may have the opportunity to influence the thinking and the goal-setting activity. The knowledge that stimulates a certain course of action may come from some recent learning situation, or it may be the result of a learning situation far removed in time and space.

Erich Fromm and Michael Maccoby presented a different approach when they stated, "the contradiction between the theory of instinctively determined vs. learned conditioned behavior could in our opinion be solved if both sides examined minutely the character-passions which are not instinctive, yet not essentially learned, but a dynamic adaptation of the system of psychic energy (character) to given circumstances."[6]

Current research in the area of genetic engineering may add yet another dimension to the thinking and goal-setting activity. This research is attempting to develop a relationship between the human body's production of certain

[6]Erich Fromm and Michael Maccoby, *Social Character in a Mexican Village* (Englewood Cliffs, N.J.: Prentice-Hall, 1970), p. 12.

proteins, the effect these proteins have on DNA-coded molecules, and the resulting intellectual activities.

All knowledge, whether learned or gained through some type of genetic predisposition, is further refined through individualized sets of aspirations and expectations which are defined by each person as goals that identify a desired quality of life with both current and future implications. The time span of the future is limited only by the willingness of the individual to consider future opportunities. An old saying is appropriate here: The future belongs to those who plan for it today.

Conceptualizing

Following the setting of goals, the goal setter then develops abstract ideas of just how these goals can be realized. Now is the time to draw "the big picture" that matches socioeconomic, resource-providing opportunities with the resources required for achieving set life-style goals.

Throughout human history and for the great majority of people, life-style resources become available through work. An argument may now arise that modern legislation for social responsibility makes it unnecessary for people to work. If life-style goals are viewed as being only those of survival, then it does appear that there are limitations on the requirements for people to work. However, if one realizes that most people desire a quality of life beyond survival and, once moving beyond survival that relative considerations are as important, if not more so, than absolute considerations, it becomes apparent that the results of legislation for social responsibility will never supplant the individual's necessity to work. Human aspirations and expectations are not determined by relating and counting some form of absolutes. Aspirations and expectations evolve through comparison activities. The theory of social inequity developed by J. Stacy Adams that is discussed later in this chapter is an excellent example.

Workplace activities afford an opportunity to the great majority of people to achieve the goals of a desired life-style. The workplace provides both compensation and noncompensation rewards, and the workers combine them in some unique manner to satisfy their specific socioeconomic requirements.

Reasoning

Moving from the conceptualization of the big picture (desired quality of life) to its actual painting (specific life-style components), there are many variables that influence individual determination of desired standard of living components. Variables that can be identified and may be useful in relating reward components to differences in kinds and degrees of employee workplace behavior are such employee characteristics as the following:

1. Age
2. Sex
3. Level of education
4. Skills
5. Abilities
6. Traits
7. Health
8. Energy level

9. Family responsibilities
10. Present standard of living
11. Other available income
12. Financial status
13. Years with employer
14. Years on job
15. Type of job
16. Level of job in organizational hierarchy

The reasoning process concerns the way an individual perceives a particular state of existence. Although an individual's perception may fail to recognize a significant part of the issue or state or may even draw an incorrect view of what is existing, unless the perception changes, what the individual perceives is *what exists*.

Focusing

Before the thinking-conceptualizing-reasoning process results in a specific workplace behavior, the employee focuses on a desired goal or some segment of that goal (a subgoal). Both on- and off-the-job situations have a strong impact on the focusing process, in which the employee relates a particular need-want-demand to perceived opportunities for its achievement. The 16 previously described employee characteristics, in addition to all previously gained knowledge, influence employee perceptions. The integration of situational and workplace demands and job requirements and responsibilities as understood and perceived affect the focusing process. It is here that perceptions modify and in turn are modified by expectations. The measurements resulting from this thinking-conceptualizing-reasoning-focusing process determine a behavior that is appropriate in the eyes of the employee.

Feelings of fairness and justice strongly influence individual perceptions. Survival and security requirements have a very low threshold, and any action that influences these two factors will have a direct and probably immediate influence on employee behavior.

Workplace Behavior

What types of behavior do employers expect from employees? What are some acceptable workplace behaviors? Contrary to what many employees believe, employers are not "looking for a pound of flesh." They do want employees they can depend on. To perform work assignments, employees must be present at stated times. Once on the job, employees are expected to perform assigned responsibilities and duties according to stated and acceptable standards.

Most employers want employees to exceed stated and accepted levels of performance. They want employees to use every means at their disposal to improve quality and quantity of output, reduce costs, and minimize wasteful use of resources (including a most valuable resource—each employee's available working time). In many cases, employers urge employees to expand their abilities and increase their worth to employers through additional education, training, and development programs. These efforts enhance opportunities for lateral and upward mobility. In this light, the saying, "There is no such thing as a dead-end job, only dead-end people," becomes meaningful.

Although it is possible to observe each of these identified workplace behaviors, they are not always easy to measure. An essential part of this book pertains to methods and procedures available for measuring identifiable, observable, and desirable workplace behaviors. The essence of a quality compensation system, then, is to instigate and stimulate behaviors that may be identified and observed and that are desirable.

The difficulty in relating the design and the management of the compensation system to employee needs and wants is that all other rewards (noncompensation components as well as compensation components) affect individual perception. The emotional forces in most people frequently exclude what is actually seen or heard, and people often see or hear only what they wish, according to preconceived notions or biases. Even with these limitations, employees do make rational decisions. The highest level of human intelligence comes to the fore when people determine what they are willing to provide and what they are willing to sacrifice to achieve a certain standard of living.

The final count, a fundamental measure of the success of a compensation system, is what *employees do*. It would be extremely valuable if compensation system designers and managers could precisely identify and describe employee wants, needs, perceptions, aspirations, and expectations. However, if an individual had this power, an entirely different issue would arise—an issue of ethics. What type of human value system, or possibly more important, what type of society would allow an individual or one select group of persons the opportunity to peer inside the brains of others and identify the knowledge and the emotional biases that control behavior? Recognizing these limits to understanding and relating to human behavior, the abilities and skills required in compensation management are an understanding of what a compensation system consists of, what type of employee behavior employers wish to influence, and then what behavior can be influenced through a well-designed and skillfully managed compensation system.

It is possible for employers to use rewards and particularly compensation rewards for manipulative purposes. However, employees are not unthinking tools to be manipulated by employers. Employers can influence employee behavior through their own behavior demonstrated through the rewards they provide. Employees have the right and the responsibility to do their own thinking, conceptualizing, reasoning, and focusing before implementing a specific behavior. It then becomes the responsibility of the employer to assess the value and the importance of a specific reward component and the way it influences employee behavior.

IMPACT OF BEHAVIORAL SCIENCE THEORIES AND MODELS

In their attempts to understand why things happen when they do or the way they do, researchers first develop hypotheses, which are sets of assumptions that provide a basis for further investigations or experiments. The results obtained from additional analyses expand reasoning and provide a basis for developing more formal hypotheses, which, when substantiated, lead to the establishment of theories. Many times these theories are difficult to explain to those who have not been involved in the entire learning and research process. To improve understanding and facilitate explanation, the researchers develop models that are simplifications of reality to aid in visualizing the complexities involved in the actual process and, given certain inputs, assist in predicting results.

Models consist of variables and constants and a definition of their interactions. Constants are those components that do not vary within the context of the problem. Variables are those that do change. A constant in a model that attempts to relate employer-provided compensation to employee-provided contributions could be, for example, the total amount of money budgeted to pay for labor costs. A variable could be rates of pay for employees performing a specific job.

Because there are limitations to the number of constants and variables a human brain can recognize and conceptualize, model builders first classify materials that have some similarity of fit and then develop models that separate problems into understandable segments to improve their insights as to what actually occurs.

It would be desirable to develop one model that can represent the complex employer-employee relationship and yet be simple enough to (1) improve understanding of the issues involved, (2) assist in describing how the variables interact so that it is possible to develop practical and worthwhile solutions, and (3) predict probable results from the use of a particular action or set of actions. However, because of the many constants and variables that have an impact on the exchange process, it has been impossible to develop such a model.

Content Theories of Motivation

In developing theories and models to explain human behavior, researchers were, by the early 1920s, identifying those variables that in essence are basic to human survival. Stuart Chase, a prolific writer and popularizer of the works of various social science scholars and researchers of the 1920s and 1930s, identified "the bare essentials which all individuals in all countries in all times have required—the lowest common denominator of healthy biological survival."[7] These basic requirements can certainly be considered as variables that initiate, direct, modify, and stop human behavior. Chase identified 10 wants or behavior-directing variables of humans as food, shelter, clothing, language and education, recreation, government and law, health provisions, religion, art forms, and love.[8] Chase also stated that biological needs are basic but that an analysis of them does not complete the picture. As he stated, "man is a social animal" who has "lived in groups and clans and tribes but never, normally, as an isolated individual or family."[9]

[7]Stuart Chase, *The Tragedy of Waste* (New York: Macmillan, 1925), p. 45.

[8]Ibid., pp. 50, 51.

[9]Ibid., pp. 45–46.

In the late 1930s, Henry A. Murray and his colleagues at the Harvard Psychological Clinic performed in-depth research on personality characteristics. They defined a need as a hypothetical process, the occurrence of which is imagined in order to account for certain objective and subjective facts. They classified needs as being either primary or secondary. Primary needs relate to physical satisfaction and secondary needs to mental or emotional satisfaction. They identified 12 primary needs and approximately 20 secondary needs and further stated that secondary needs depend on and derive from primary needs. Through their clinical work and observations on human behavior, they hypothesized that the satisfying of these needs governed human behavior. In addition to the basic biological needs previously identified by Chase, Murray and his associates listed such needs as affiliation, aggression, autonomy, and dominance.[10]

In 1943 Abraham H. Maslow developed a more rigorous and sophisticated approach for classifying human needs.[11] Maslow's hierarchy of needs identified five levels of need satisfactions in order of basic importance—physiological, safety, social, esteem, and self-actualization. Attempting to satisfy these needs acts as a stimulus to human action. The underlying concept presented by Maslow is that a preceding level of need must be satisfied to a significant degree before the next higher level of need becomes dominant in stimulating human action. Until individuals are able to satisfy to some degree their self-actualization needs (making full use of innate and learned capabilities), their life-styles will have a significant void. It is important to notice that the efforts reported on by Chase and the concepts of Murray and Maslow resulted from clinical experience and intuition. There is only limited empirical research available for supporting these theories.

In developing his hierarchy of needs, Maslow made a statement of interest to anyone who would like a better understanding of human behavior: "Motivation theory is not synonymous with behavior theory. The motivations are only one class of the determinants of behavior. While behavior is almost always motivated, it is almost always biologically, culturally, and situationally determined as well."[12]

David C. McClelland is a psychologist who built on the works of behavioral scientists who had developed hypotheses, theories, and models in an attempt to describe factors that influence human behavior. In the early 1940s, McClelland's investigations into human behavior and personality kindled an interest in gaining a better understanding of why certain individuals achieve success in contemporary society. McClelland and his colleagues identified the need for achievement (n Ach), need for affiliation (n Aff), and the need for

---

[10]Henry A. Murray et al., *Explorations in Personality* (New York: Oxford University Press, 1938).

[11]A. H. Maslow, "A Theory of Human Motivation," *Psychological Review,* vol. 50, 1943, pp. 370–396.

[12]Ibid., p. 371.

power (n Pow) as drives that produced essentially the same results. A colleague of McClelland, J. W. Atkinson, described these needs as a disposition or a potential behavior to strive for success. He further described these needs as a pride in accomplishment (achievement), sense of belonging (affiliation), and a feeling of influence (power).[13]

McClelland identified personality characteristics typical of an individual with a high need for achievement and stated that the need for achievement can be learned through establishing an environment in which it is possible to overcome obstacles and accomplish things.[14] He found that a relatively small number of people have this need. In recent years, McClelland has focused attention on why some people do better in influencing the actions of others. McClelland and Burnham stated that managers who have a personal desire to influence others and to develop a sense of responsibility and teamwork among their subordinates are somewhat more effective managers.[15]

Further investigation into the behavior of managers who achieved various degrees of success enabled Douglas McGregor to identify certain assumptions that successful managers make about workers and those that unsuccessful managers make about workers. He labeled the assumptions made by successful managers as Theory Y assumptions and those made by unsuccessful managers as Theory X assumptions.[16]

Theory Y assumptions are the following:

1. The drive of humans for physical and mental effort involved in work is as natural and rewarding as play, sleep, and laughter.

2. External control and the threat of punishment are old-fashioned means of getting people involved in serving the organization so it can attain its objectives. The nature of humans is such that they exercise self-direction and self-control in an integrative way in the service of objectives to which they are committed.

3. Commitment to objectives is a function of rewards and expectations of rewards.

4. The average human being learns, given the right situation, not only to accept but also to seek responsibility.

5. The capacity for exercising a relatively high degree of imagination, ingenuity, and creativity in solving organizational problems is widely, not narrowly, distributed among people.

[13]John W. Atkinson, "Motivational Determinants of Risk-Taking Behavior," *Psychological Review,* vol. 64, 1957, pp. 359–72.

[14]David C. McClelland, "Achievement Motivation Can Be Developed," *Harvard Business Review,* November–December 1965, pp. 6–8, 10, 12, 14, 16, 20, 22, 24, 178.

[15]David C. McClelland and David H. Burnham, "Power Is the Great Motivator," *Harvard Business Review,* March–April 1976, p. 103.

[16]Douglas McGregor, *The Human Side of Enterprise* (New York: McGraw-Hill, 1960).

6. The nature of work in the modern world is such that the intellectual potential of the average human being is only partly utilized.

Theory X assumptions are the following:

1. Human beings are lazy and will avoid work if it is at all possible.

2. People must be directed, controlled, and motivated by fear of punishment to work as the organization requires.

3. The average human being prefers to be closely supervised, wishes to avoid responsibility, has relatively little ambition, and seeks security above all else.

Underlying Theory X and Theory Y is Maslow's hierarchy of needs. What McGregor is saying is that a manager who recognizes only the basic biological needs of the worker will provide a work environment that permits the satisfaction of only these needs. However, if a manager is to be successful, the higher level needs of workers must be recognized, and workplace activities must to some degree lead to the satisfaction of these needs.

Possibly the most controversial of all theories developed to explain employee workplace behavior is the two-factor theory of motivation developed by Frederick Herzberg. The motivation-hygiene or two-factor theory suggests that two separate sets of factors influence the attitudes and behaviors of workers. Herzberg identified those factors that lead to high levels of job satisfaction and goal-oriented behavior as *motivators* and those that prevent job dissatisfaction as *hygiene* factors. Hygiene factors include company policy and administration, supervision, salary, interpersonal relations, and working conditions. The motivators are achievement, recognition, work itself, responsibility, and advancement. The intellectual basis for the two-factor theory is as follows: Hygiene factors relate to the situation in which the worker performs assigned activities. When these factors are provided in sufficient quantity and quality, they prevent job dissatisfaction. Motivators, on the other hand, relate to what the worker does and how the worker gains intrinsic satisfaction from the job. According to Herzberg and associates, motivators are the factors that truly lead to job satisfaction and superior performance.[17]

From an understanding of employee behavior and employer-provided rewards, the relationship between the hygiene factors and the motivator factors is critical. Intrinsic rewards or satisfaction come from the work itself. The motivators provide workers with intrinsic rewards or job satisfaction. Workers gain a sense of accomplishment, a feeling of being important, or of making a contribution from their job performance. The intrinsic reward develops internally and comes from something the worker wants to do.

On the other hand, the hygiene or extrinsic factors provide rewards originating outside the worker. Since these rewards are not internally generated,

---

[17]Frederick Herzberg, Bernard Mausner, and Barbara Snyderman, *The Motivation to Work* (New York: Wiley, 1959).

they have to be replenished more often and do not have the lasting effect of the motivators. The hygiene factors will direct worker behavior in the short run, but, according to Herzberg, long-run behavioral changes require the use of the motivators.

The theories previously discussed have looked at the specific needs an individual wishes to satisfy and how the ability to satisfy these needs influences workplace behavior.

The absolute amount of satisfaction of needs is not the only force or variable that affects the things people do when working. The relative measures people make concerning the relationship between their workplace efforts and the rewards they receive possibly have far greater impact on human behavior.

Psychologists such as Murray, Maslow, and Herzberg provide content models that focus on what motivates people. For the practitioner responsible for reward-compensation activities, this is an excellent base; but information on *how* to motivate is equally important.

Process Theories of Motivation

A group of process-oriented theorists is carrying on from the work of motivational content theorists. These behavioral scientists develop process models that attempt to explain how workers are motivated. Process model builders such as Festinger, Adams, Vroom, Dunnette, Locke, Porter, and Lawler introduce the influence of equity, expectancy, and goal setting on employee workplace behavior and recognize the importance of relative considerations.

Combining the content models and their focus on what motivates behavior with the process models on how to motivate behavior provides compensation managers with a broad theoretical perspective on design requirements for their compensation systems.

Leon A. Festinger provided an additional insight for understanding human behavior with his theory of cognitive dissonance.[18] Very simply, *cognitive dissonance* is an imbalance between what a person knows or learns and what the value system of the individual considers to be acceptable. When an individual learns something or receives a communication that is incompatible with his or her value system, internal conflict develops, which then results in anxiety or some other emotion that can adversely influence the behavior of the individual.

Festinger stated that cognitive dissonance may occur when individuals make social comparisons. Festinger hypothesized that people (1) avoid situations that are likely to increase dissonance (discord or lack of agreement), and (2) take positive action to reduce dissonance and achieve consonance (harmony). They will refuse to listen to or believe inputs that cause dissonance, and they will accept ideas or views that they feel comfortable with, giving little consideration to the logic or reasonableness of the message or view.

The vital contribution made by Festinger is the theory that employee attitudes and values can have a significant impact on the ways they do things.

[18]Leon A. Festinger, *A Theory of Cognitive Dissonance* (Evanston, IL: Row-Peterson, 1957).

From a compensation point of view, it is not only important to know what needs certain compensation components may satisfy, but also what attitudes and value patterns these employees have relative to the pay and benefits being offered.

Using the cognitive dissonance concept developed by Festinger, J. Stacy Adams developed a theory of social inequity with special emphasis on wage inequity, how it arises, and means for reducing or eliminating it.[19] Adams theorized that inequity exists when Individual A perceives that the rewards received for his or her inputs are relatively less than the rewards received by Individual B, with whom he or she identifies, who has provided the same amount of inputs or less.[20]

$$\frac{\text{A's rewards less A's costs}}{\text{A's investments}} = \frac{\text{B's rewards less B's costs}}{\text{B's investments}}$$

By focusing on individual perceptions rather than individual needs, Adams provided an added dimension for those interested in designing and managing a compensation system.

A lengthy list of human needs with precise definitions and useful methods for classifying them have been presented by a number of behavioral scientists. Festinger, however, centered attention on human perception. He described what happens when events occur that are incompatible with human value systems and analyzed the types of behavior people exhibit to overcome these imbalances or conflicts. Building on Festinger's work, Adams developed a relationship between workplace-related rewards and employee work behavior. When employees perceive inequities, they attempt to balance the equation. The balancing can take two principal approaches: one, requesting more, sufficient, or specific kinds of rewards from the employer; or, two, reducing the investment by doing less work and making fewer contributions.

(1) To explain a model that relates employee behavior to perceptions, it is useful to analyze the value of this model in terms of more complex models, (2) to develop the relationships among these more complex models, and (3) to see how they lead to an improved understanding of the ways in which employer-provided rewards are able to channel employee behavior.

Victor H. Vroom added yet another step for improving the understanding of workplace behavior. His instrumentality theory also relates to the motivation to work. The variables included in this theory are expectancies, valences, choices, outcomes, and instrumentalities. Possibly the most significant contribution made by Vroom, however, is his focus on expectancies.

Expectancy theory had its introduction to modern-day behavioral science theories in the 1930s. The work of early investigators resulted in this definition: *Expectancy* represents ideas or thoughts an individual develops about the consequences that may result from a certain action. The human reasoning

---

[19]J. Stacy Adams, "Toward an Understanding of Inequity," *Journal of Abnormal and Social Psychology,* October 1963, pp. 422–436.

[20]J. Stacy Adams, "Inequity in Social Exchange," in *Advances in Experimental Psychology,* ed. L. Berkowitz (New York: Academic Press, 1965), p. 163.

process identifies possible alternative behaviors of courses of action and the results or consequence of each of these behaviors. The individual then selects a desired behavior, depending on the value of and the likelihood of the occurrence of the consequence.

From his studies, Vroom determined that the effects of motivation on performance are dependent on the levels of ability of the worker and that the relationship of ability to performance is dependent on the motivation of the worker. This interactive relationship is indicated in this way:[21]

$$\text{Performance} = f(\text{Ability} \times \text{Motivation})$$

Vroom further developed the proposition that motivation—the force on a person to perform an act—is "the algebraic sum of the products of the valences of all outcomes and the strength of his expectancies that the act will be followed by the attainment of these outcomes."[22] Vroom differentiated the words *valence* and *value* in this manner: The *valence* of an outcome is the *anticipated* satisfaction from an outcome, whereas *value* is the *actual* satisfaction it provides. A mathematical model of this relationship takes this form:

Valence of × Expectancy that = Force to
Outcome *j*   Act *i* will be   Perform Act *i*
              Followed by
              Outcome *j*

The valence of Outcome *j* will depend on the algebraic sum of such values as

1. Communicated desirability of Outcome *j*

2. Degree of individual desire for Outcome *j*

3. Frequency with which Outcome *j* has been associated with particular reward or punishing outcomes

The expectancy that Act *i* will be followed by Outcome *j* depends on:

1. Communicated probability that Act *i* will be followed by Outcome *j*

2. Objective probability that Act *i* will be followed by Outcome *j*

3. Proportion of trials on which Act *i* has been followed by Outcome *j*

Vroom thus postulates in this model that individuals will perform that activity having the strongest positive or weakest negative force.

The expectancy theory adds a vital theoretical dimension for a better understanding of employee behavior, but it returns designers and managers of

[21]Victor H. Vroom, *Work and Motivation* (New York: Wiley, 1964), p. 203.

[22]Ibid., p. 18.

compensation systems to the frustration inherent within the black box. This limits the theory's usefulness to "real world" practitioners.

Marvin D. Dunnette designed a rather simple model that incorporates ideas developed by Maslow, Festinger, Adams, and Vroom. In his model, Dunnette returned to Maslow's concept of action taken to satisfy a particular need. Dunnette combined needs (deficiencies) with behavior oriented toward satisfying the deficiency. Dunnette's model includes the individual's calculations of *perceived* probability of success of various behaviors before choosing one of them and *perceived* value of the reward before determining the degree of satisfaction of the specific need-drive. An important point raised by Dunnette in analyzing the employer-employee exchange process is that "reality can only be estimated by viewing the world through the eyes of the perceiver."[23] This statement also applies to the equity concept developed by Adams.

In the 1960s, based on his research, Edwin A. Locke developed a theory that could be used to tie together many of the theories on human motivation. He proposed that most employee behavior is consciously goal directed. His goal-achievement model states that people work to achieve goals that they recognize as desirable and important. In fact, goal-achievement efforts increase when the individual responsible for achieving the goal has some voice in goal identification and in selecting the activities that must be performed. He further stated that the highly motivated individual performs best when goal difficulty increases and when the goals are specific and accepted by the worker.[24]

Recognizing the basic fact that human behavior is goal directed, Locke states that goal setting is recognized explicitly or implicitly by virtually every major theory of work motivation.[25] The work of Locke helps not only to tie together the content and process theories of human motivation, but also provides a direct link to the scientific management theory developed early in the twentieth century. In the past twenty-five years, scientific management concepts have frequently been viewed as an antiquated carrot-and-stick approach to motivation.

Behavior Modification Concepts

Fred Luthans and Robert Kreitner took a learning approach for explaining how to modify unacceptable employee workplace behavior.[26] This approach

---

[23]Marvin D. Dunnette, "A Behavioral Scientist Looks at Managerial Compensation," in *Managerial Compensation,* ed. Robert Andrews (Ann Arbor, Mich.: Foundation for Research on Human Behavior, April 1965), p. 36.

[24]Edwin A. Locke, "Toward a Theory of Task Motivation and Incentives," *Organization Behavior and Human Performance,* vol. 3, 1968, pp. 157–189.

[25]Edwin A. Locke, "The Ubiquity of the Technique of Goal Setting in Theories of and Approaches to Employee Motivation," *Academy of Management Review,* July 1978, pp. 594–601.

[26]Fred Luthans and Robert Kreitner, *Organizational Behavior Modification* (Glenview, IL: Scott, Foresman, 1975), pp. 7–15.

differs from the motivational approach taken by Maslow, Herzberg, and, to some degree, Vroom and Dunnette. The motivational approach is based on drives activated to satisfy some current need (deficiency) and is basically a stimulus-response approach in which strength of habit determines the relationship. The learning approach of Luthans and Kreitner is based on the operant behavior work of B. F. Skinner. Skinner classified behavior into respondent (unlearned) and operant (learned) categories. He further stated that operant behavior depends on its consequences and also that the environment shapes, changes, and directs behavior. Skinner's approach to behavior modification differs from the traditional stimulus-response approach in that it views behavior as a function of its consequences, thus reversing the orientation to a response-stimulus (consequence) or stimulus–response-stimulus model. In focusing on operant behavior, designers and managers of reward processes must identify environmental limits, desired specific employee behaviors, and consequences of these behaviors. They can then determine which consequences reinforce the desired behavior.[27]

The key word in the operant learning approach is *controls,* not *causes.* Luthans and Kreitner recognized the value of isolating causes of behavior. However, because of the demands placed on current human resource management and the technological limitations in developing an understanding of human behavior, greater immediate value may be obtained through a knowledge of which consequences signal the individual that certain consequences will follow a specific behavior/behavior pattern.[28]

It is possible to improve an understanding of the operant conditioning concept by reviewing reinforcement theory. Reinforcement theory sets forth three views of human behavior.

1. Individuals take no active role in shaping their own behavior; they are merely agents responding to outside forces.

2. The concept of needs, drives, or goal-directed behavior is unacceptable because of the inability to observe, identify, and measure these forces.

3. Permanent change in individual behavior results from reinforcement of a particular behavior.

There are at least four different ways of implementing reinforcement theory. Each of these approaches focuses on the achievement of acceptable behavior. At the worksite, employers seek the continuation of acceptable behavior and the modification of less-than-acceptable behavior.

The four reinforcement approaches used to encourage and achieve desired behavior are (1) positive reinforcement, (2) punishment, (3) negative reinforcement, and (4) extinction.

[27]Ibid., pp. 24–30.

[28]Ibid., p. 13.

Positive Reinforcement—A procedure that maintains or increases the rate of a response by contingently presenting a stimulus (a positive reinforcer) following the response. Thus, when a stimulus, such as an object or event, follows or is presented contingently as a consequence of a response, and the rate of that response increases or is maintained as a result, the stimulus is called a positive reinforcer. Praise, attention, recognition of achievement and effort, special events, and activities serve as positive reinforcers for many people. Nontechnical terms for a positive reinforcer include incentives, rewards, or "strokes."

Step 1: The employer provides a *cue* (notification or assignment to do something).

Step 2: The employee *behavior* is acceptable (successful accomplishment of assignment).

Step 3: The employer provides a suitable reward-*consequence* (leading to repetition of the demonstrated behavior because of the importance of reward to employee. A reward is a positive reinforcer when the desired behavior increases in occurrence following the contingent presentation of the "reward").

Punishment—A procedure in which an aversive stimulus is presented immediately following a response, which results in a reduction in the rate of the response.

Step 1: The employer provides a *cue* (notification or assignment to do something).

Step 2: The employee *behavior* is unacceptable (assignment performed in unacceptable or unsatisfactory manner).

Step 3: The employer reprimands employee-*consequence* (leads to elimination of exhibited behavior because of the strength or severity of the consequence. Punishment differs from withholding of the positive reinforcer both by kind and degree, but withholding positive reinforcers is a mild form of punishment.

Negative Reinforcement—A procedure that involves the removal of an aversive stimulus as a consequence of a response and results in either maintaining or increasing the rate of the behavior. A behavior has been negatively reinforced if it increases or is maintained due to the contingent removal or reduction of a stimulus. This procedure is sometimes referred to as escape conditioning. For example, when the employee does as asked, the employer stops nagging. The employee's behavior, doing as requested, has been negatively reinforced by the removal of the nagging. Thus, when removed or reduced as a consequence of a response, an aversive stimulus results in an increase or maintenance of that response.

Step 1: The employer provides a *cue* (notification or assignment to do something).

Step 2: The employee *behavior* is acceptable (successful accomplishment of assignment).

Step 3: The employer removes an aversive stimulus.

Extinction—A procedure in which the reinforcement of a previously reinforced behavior is discontinued. This can result in the extinction of both desired and undesired behavior. In nontechnical language, extinction is often referred to as the appropriate withholding of rewards or attention or as the nonrecognition of behaviors that interfere with learning or development.

Extinction (A)—Withholding of a valued reward that, over an extended period, will result in the disappearance of the desired behavior. The decline in the rate of response is extinction.

Step 1: The employer provides a cue (notification or assignment to do something).

Step 2: The employee behavior is acceptable (successful accomplishment of assignment).

Step 3: The employer fails to provide a positive reinforcer-*consequence* (the reward becomes too costly and the employer withholds it, recognizing that in time an unacceptable behavior will probably evolve).

Extinction (B)—Withholding of a valued reward that, over an extended period of time, will result in the disappearance of an undesirable behavior.

Step 1: The employer provides a cue (notification or assignment to do something).

Step 2: Employee behavior is unacceptable (unsatisfactory performance of assignment).

Step 3: The employer fails to provide a positive reinforcer-*consequence*. (Because the employer withholds the reward, the employee eventually eliminates undesirable behavior).

It is important to know not only the type of reinforcer to apply but also when and how often to apply it. A reinforcer may be applied either continuously or intermittently. A continuously applied reinforcer follows every behavior, whereas an intermittent reinforcer depends on one of four schedules: (1) fixed interval, (2) fixed ratio, (3) variable interval, and (4) variable ratio.

Interval Schedules of Reinforcement—A schedule in which reinforcement is made contingent upon the passage of time before the response is reinforced. The two types of interval schedules of reinforcement are (a) fixed interval (FI) schedule—when a particular response following the passage of a specific constant amount of time is scheduled for reinforcement (for example, an FI 3 indicates that reinforcement follows the first occurrence of the response after three minutes have passed) and (b) variable interval (VI) schedule—when a variable time interval must occur prior to the reinforced response; the time interval has a specific average and usually varies within a specified range (for example, a VI 6 indicates that an average of six minutes passes before the response receives contingent reinforcement).

Ratio Schedules of Reinforcement—A schedule in which reinforcement is made contingent upon the emission of a number of responses before one response is reinforced. The two types of ratio schedules of reinforcement are (a) fixed ratio (FR) schedule—when a constant number of responses must occur prior to the reinforced response (for example, an FR 3 schedule indicates that each third response is reinforced) and (b) variable ratio (VR) schedule—when a variable number of responses must occur prior to the reinforced response; the number of responses usually varies around a specified average (for example, a VR 6 means that an average of one of six performances is reinforced).

INTEGRATING BEHAVIORAL CONCEPTS

Lyman W. Porter and Edward E. Lawler, III, developed the theoretical model that describes the variables they consider to have a positive influence on employee behavior.[29]

The Porter-Lawler model, like Vroom's, focuses on performance. Porter and Lawler define *performance* as being a broad range of specific workplace behaviors that relate to the nature of the job and the accomplishment of its assigned responsibilities and duties. The variables influencing performance are value of reward (as perceived by the individual receiving the reward) and individual expectations concerning the likelihood that a given amount of rewards depends on a given amount of personal effort. These expectations may be stated as (1) the probability that *reward* depends on *performance* and (2) the probability that *performance* depends on *effort*. The effort expended is further modified by the abilities and the traits of the individual (the individual's currently developed power to perform) and role perception (the activities the individual thinks are necessary to perform the job successfully).[30] An individual then measures the equity of the rewards, which strongly influences satisfaction gained from effort and provides feedback for the employee's determination of the value of employer-provided rewards in the employer-employee exchange process.

The major addition provided by Porter and Lawler over that offered by Vroom is the concept of perceived equitable rewards. They defined *perceived equitable rewards* as "the amount of rewards that a person feels is fair, given his performance in the tasks that he has been asked to undertake."[31] Here Porter

---

[29]Lyman W. Porter and Edward E. Lawler, III, *Managerial Attitudes and Performance* (Homewood, IL: Richard D. Irwin, and Dorsey Press, 1968), p. 165.

[30]Ibid., pp. 16–40.

[31]Ibid., p. 30.

and Lawler returned to the concepts of intrinsic and extrinsic rewards which are a central feature of Herzberg's two-factor theory. In their discussion of intrinsic rewards, they stated that "the extent to which such intrinsic rewards are obtainable in the work situation will depend primarily on the way in which the job and tasks are structured by the organization."[32] This view coincides with the "work itself" concept promoted by Herzberg. Porter and Lawler also say that extrinsic rewards frequently accompany intrinsic rewards.

Neither Herzberg nor Porter and Lawler discussed the imperceptible connection between extrinsic and intrinsic rewards that minimizes the importance of one or the other. Of far greater importance to compensation designers and managers is the recognition of the interrelations between these two classes of rewards. For example, an employee performs an assignment. The employee is unable to assess the quality or the importance of the performance and gains either a minimal or no intrinsic reward from the work effort. The supervisor, however, pats the employee on the back and offers congratulations on a job well done. In fact, the job was so meritorious that the company provided a "presidential" bonus of $1,000 and public recognition of the performance. There is little doubt now how the employer viewed the work behavior. The employee may not have initially generated an intrinsic appreciation for the work performed, but the extrinsic rewards set into motion and reinforced internally generated feelings of a job well done.

The pay, a bonus, and a paid holiday to Disney World for the family that resulted from workplace behavior are extrinsic rewards. Their value in motivating human effort may be short in duration as expressed by Herzberg; but when extrinsic rewards stimulate or reinforce achievement, recognition, and responsibility, when they relate to advancement and come from the work itself, their effect is extremely powerful. The compounding, synergistic effect that results when extrinsic rewards stimulate and support intrinsic rewards is the shaping force of employee behavior that separates the mediocre organization from the one of high performance.

Here is one of the basic issues concerned in reward and workplace behavior. Many of the predecessors of Porter and Lawler in behavioral science, including Herzberg, focused on the "happy" worker. If workers can gain satisfaction from performing their assignments, their performance will improve, and high satisfaction leads to high performance. Herzberg focused on the motivators because he felt they induce motivation that leads to long-run job satisfaction. Porter and Lawler, on the other hand, contended that satisfaction results from high performance. Since performance is a demonstrated workplace behavior, it is essential that management recognize the quality of employee behavior and reward it in a timely and adequate manner, which then results in an employee's receiving satisfaction from the work performed.[33]

The efforts of James G. March and Herbert A. Simon reinforce the Porter-Lawler approach but present a slightly different justification for empha-

---

[32]Ibid., p. 36.

[33]Ibid., pp. 36–40.

sizing the relationship between performance and rewards. March and Simon developed a general model that adds another variable—level of aspiration—that should be considered when attempting to analyze employee behavior. The March and Simon general model of adaptive motivated behavior has five steps:

1. The lower the satisfaction of the organism, the more search for alternative programs it will undertake.

2. The more search, the higher the expected value of the reward.

3. The higher expected value of the reward, the higher the satisfaction.

4. The higher the expected value of the reward, the higher the level of aspiration of the organism.

5. The higher the level of aspiration, the lower the satisfaction.[34]

March and Simon concluded from their extensive research and model building that organizations that relate promotional and monetary rewards to seniority are less productive than those that relate rewards to some index of production. They also concluded that the more intense the individual relationship to the required performance, the greater the effect of the monetary reward system on the perceived consequence of the action.[35] The message here to compensation designers and managers is to emphasize the positive—that is, relate rewards to performance.

March and Simon further hypothesized that when inducements (employer-offered rewards) are greater than contributions (employee inputs), employee willingness to participate increases. They contended that employee willingness to participate directly relates to satisfaction with the job. Job satisfaction, from their viewpoint, depends on the employee's perception of (1) conformity of the job to self-image, (2) the predictability of job relationships, and (3) the compatibility of the job and other roles.[36]

THE DYNAMICS OF BEHAVIOR CHANGE

The ideas and the theories presented here are valuable to compensation system designers and managers because they recognize that people do exert themselves to satisfy particular needs that originate from either a genetic endowment or from something learned. (Learned behavior can be in response either to something that occurred in the not-too-distant past that is easy to recall or to an existing condition that is quickly identifiable as a cue to specific behavior. Learned behavior can also be the result of a learning experience that

[34]James G. March and Herbert A. Simon, *Organizations* (New York: Wiley, 1958), pp. 48–49.

[35]Ibid., pp. 61–62.

[36]Ibid., pp. 93–111.

occurred in the distant past and is most difficult, if not almost impossible, to identify with a particular behavior.) It is possible that the environment can act on an individual to elicit a certain response. It is also possible that the individual can act on the environment to produce a certain consequence.

The determination of the type of behavior and its strength depends on the perceptions an individual holds relative to the probability of achieving a certain reward and the expected value of that reward. The actual reward then closes the feedback loop and becomes an input into each individual's intellectual mechanism that calculates future probability of such an occurrence and determines its expected value estimates (Vroom's valences) that in turn have an impact on future behavior.

To make better use of the works of behavioral scientists, it is helpful to return to some of the efforts of Sigmund Freud at the turn of the twentieth century. Among Freud's great contributions to a better understanding of human nature is the dynamic concept of human behavior. Because behavior, from Freud's point of view, is an adaptation to realistic circumstances, it conforms to changes in circumstances in which different behavior is more advisable or beneficial.

To increase the usefulness of Freud's work on the dynamic qualities of human behavior, Erich Fromm and Michael Maccoby further separated behavior into behavior traits and character traits. They defined behavior traits as adaptive responses to a given situation that are essentially the result of learning.[37] Because behavior traits result from learning in social situations, they can be changed relatively easily with changing conditions.

Character traits are those behaviors resulting from the energy-charged part of the whole system—character. *The system character is the relatively permanent form in which human energy is structuralized in the process of relating to others and of assimilating nature.* It is the result of dynamic interaction of the system-man and the system-society in which he lives. Fromm and Maccoby further identify these character traits as attitudes; and they define *attitudes* as openness to new ideas, willingness to cooperate, and interest and ability in planning and investing for the future. These character traits or attitudes that begin developing at birth are, in a dynamic sense, a substitute for instinct.[38]

Freud, Fromm, and Maccoby present those involved in channeling human behavior with an additional consideration. It is true that people act to satisfy needs, that their perceptions and expectations modify these needs-related actions, and that cued consequences will strongly influence behavior. To further complicate the issue, it is also true that human behavior is a dynamic process with behavior changes occurring because of environmental changes. On the other hand, behavior may not change with changing conditions because system requirements, or well-ingrained attitudes, do not demand or facilitate such changes.

[37]Fromm and Maccoby, *Social Character,* p. 11.

[38]Ibid., pp. 9–12.

The many variables influencing human behavior and their almost limitless numbers of interactions appear to force compensation system designers and managers to return to the black box and its accompanying mysteries. Although it is impossible to observe the thoughts that go on inside the human brain and from these observations to predict particular types of human behavior, every effort possible must be made to identify desirable workplace behaviors and communicate them to all employees. Designers of compensation systems must then identify the compensation components available for rewarding employees and determine the value employees place on each component. The final step in this process is to offer rewards to employees who demonstrate acceptable workplace behavior.

SELECTED READINGS

Adams, J. Stacy, "Toward an Understanding of Inequity," *Journal of Abnormal and Social Psychology,* vol. 67, no. 5, 1963, pp. 422–436. The author develops a theory of social inequity, focusing specifically on wage inequities. He analyzes the exchange process, looking in particular at the individual elements of the inputs and the outcomes in terms of financial and nonfinancial rewards.

Argyris, Chris, *Personality and Organization: The Conflict Between the System and the Individual.* New York: Harper & Row, 1957. The author presents a study of the need for attention to the task of building consistency between individual needs and organizational objectives. Argyris develops a theory that organizations are structured and managed on the assumption that the members are lazy, immature, and irresponsible and require close supervision. Managerial actions based on these assumptions lead in turn to organizational conflict.

Atkinson, John W., "Motivational Determinants of Risk-Taking Behavior," in *A Theory of Achievement Motivation,* ed. John W. Atkinson and Norman T. Feather. New York: John Wiley & Sons, 1966. The course an individual selects to achieve a certain outcome relates to the strength of his motive, the expectancy of goal achievement, and the value of the incentive offered.

Festinger, Leon, *A Theory of Cognitive Dissonance.* Evanston, IL: Row-Peterson, 1957. When an individual cognition—"knowledge, opinion, or belief about the environment, about oneself or about one's behavior"—produces psychological discomfort, the individual is likely to exhibit dissonance or inconsistent behavior. The author develops a theory concerning the concept of dissonance and the actions that may be taken to reduce it.

Herzberg, Frederick, Bernard Mausner, and Barbara Snyderman, *The Motivation to Work.* New York: John Wiley and Sons, Inc., 1959. This book reports on findings from a study of job motivation. It presents hypotheses regarding the nature of job motivation and the strong impact motivation has had on work. The authors developed their hypotheses and theories from experiences, judgment, and observation.

Locke, Edwin A. "Toward a Theory of Task Motivation and Incentives," *Organization Behavior and Human Performance,* vol. 3, 1968, pp. 157–189. From his research, Locke identifies the overriding influence of goal-directed effort on human behavior. Continuing the works of Drucker, McGregor, McClelland, and others, Locke contends that goal setting is the major factor suitable for integrating various theories of motivation.

McClelland, David C., *The Achieving Society*. Princeton, N.J.: D. Van Nostrand Co., Inc., 1961. The author describes the high achiever as well as the means of measuring the high achievement motive, called "n Ach." For the high achiever, there must be a direct link between high performance and immediate recognition through some form of visible reward.

McGeoch, John A., and Arthur L. Irion, *The Psychology of Human Learning*. London: Longmans, Green & Co., Ltd., 1952. The authors develop the point that rewards are most effective when they relate directly to the behavior they intend to reward.

Mcgregor, Douglas, *The Human Side of Enterprise*. New York: McGraw-Hill Book Company, 1960. This excellent book identifies the importance of integrating the goals of the individual with the goals of the organization. It also identifies two opposite sets of assumptions on how managers view their subordinates.

Maslow, Abraham. *Motivation and Personality*. New York: Harper & Row, 1954. In viewing motivation as "needs" seeking satisfaction, the author groups these needs into five basic categories that form a hierarchy. He argues that higher-level needs normally do not emerge until lower-level needs have been relatively satisfied.

Patton, Arch, *Men, Money, and Motivation*. New York: McGraw-Hill Book Company, 1961. This book stresses the importance of pay as a unique reward that not only satifies basic survival needs but is a highly visible reward that indicates the value of a person to the organization.

Rand, Ayn, *The Virtue of Selfishness: A New Concept of Egoism*. New York: The New American Library, 1964. Rand, a leading twentieth century philosopher whose concepts on ethics and human codes of values, presents an alternative viewpoint to those frequently uttered. Her concern with individuality and rational self-interest focuses attention on free, voluntary, unforced, and uncoerced exchange processes. The philosophical concepts underlying these mutually beneficial exchanges should be of special interest to anyone involved in rewarding and compensating employee effort.

Vroom, Victor H., *Work and Motivation*. New York: John Wiley & Sons, Inc., 1964. The author develops a theory of motivation and its relationship to job performance by viewing the determinants of job satisfaction and the impact of job satisfaction on work performance.

Weick, Karl E., "The Concept of Equity in the Perception of Pay," *Administrative Science Quarterly*, December 1966, pp. 414–439. This discussion of the ambiguities in the formulation of equity theory analyzes the many variables related to equity theory and the problems involved in identifying and measuring the effect of these variables in equity perception.

2

Organizations, Jobs, And People

CONTENT

Chapter 2 describes the formation of organizations and the method (division of labor) by which the accomplishment of organizational missions and objectives becomes possible. In the process of dividing labor requirements, various kinds and levels of jobs are established. In turn, rewards provided by the organization differ according to the requirements made upon the jobholder. Rewards usually vary at different organizational levels.

GOALS

Upon concluding this chapter, you should be aware of the impact work specialization has on the organizing and the grouping of employees. You should also recognize that division of labor is not unique to contemporary human effort, and throughout history humans have focused on how to make the best use of the wide diversity of skills and abilities available in any group. By recognizing group differences, you should be better prepared to develop unique compensation systems for each group.

T o acquire an understanding of how an organization develops, it is helpful to view the activities that occur during its growth. From the time the organization is only a seed of an idea until it is actually producing an output, a sequence of activities occurs as described in figure 2-1.

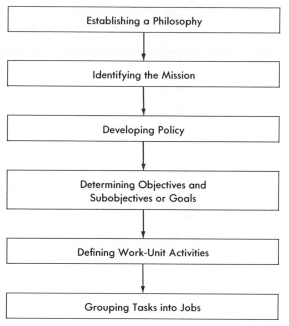

FIGURE 2-1   PRINCIPAL ACTIVITIES IN THE DEVELOPMENT OF AN ORGANIZATION

Underlying any human action is a value system. A value system is a composite of everything an individual understands or has learned. It takes the form of guidelines or limits that direct thinking and behavior. These value-system–based guidelines express both internalized likes and dislikes and rational and irrational judgment.

An idea originates and develops in the brain and through the thinking process of an individual. As the idea begins it journey from the brain to a specific output requiring the efforts of more than one person, a production process starts. When this output of a good or service requires the efforts of more than one person, groups are formed. In some manner and to some degree, direction of effort becomes essential if the group is to be successful in producing its desired output. The value systems of the group leaders and the group members critically influence the direction and the intensity of productive effort. The expression of the value system becomes identifiable through the philosophy of the organization.

Although many organizations do not have written philosophy statements, the oral expressions and the actions of their leaders establish their operating philosophy. The philosophy of the organization, expressed either in written form or through the behavior of its leaders, establishes general guidelines for decision and actions to be taken by all members. The statement of philosophy, whether written or unwritten, thus describes the values of top management or the leaders of the organization. Critical to organizational success is the degree of congruence between the values of all of its members and the philosophy of the organization. A major roadblock to organizational success frequently arises when members fail to recognize a positive relationship between their own values and the philosophy statements or philosophy-based behavior of their leaders.

The next step in moving from ideas and values to concerted action occurs with the identification and the description of the mission of the organization. The mission statement describes in broad or general value-laden terms what the organization wishes to accomplish in the long term. In essence, it details the reasons for the existence of the organization. It provides the linkage between the organization and the environment. The philosophy statement provides standards for guiding employee action; the mission statement identifies desired results that must be translated into action to be taken. Mission statements can be considered as the criteria used for assessing the long-term effectiveness of the organization. The realization of these requirements assists in ensuring the survival of the organization.

To ensure proper and acceptable operations in working toward the accomplishment of its mission-identified end results, an organization develops a policy. Policy statements, like mission statements, are broad guidelines for directing action. Those responsible for formulating policy recognize the influence of human behavior and social demands on the accomplishment of desired organizational output. To be effective in directing employee behavior, policy must support the mission of the organization. It must be sufficiently broad to relate to different actions and behaviors required of the various work units and members of the organization, and it must be understood by all members.

The next step in the idea-to-output process requires the establishment of organizational objectives and goals. The primary objectives are a translation of the broadly developed mission statements into more specific organizational output requirements. These results-oriented statements become further translated into more specific short-term goals for the work units of the organization.

Following the development of organizational and work-unit objectives (subobjectives and goals) each work unit must develop its own function statement. The function statement is, in effect, the charter for the work unit. The function statement identifies the principal activities of the work unit. It further assists in integrating the top-down established organizational objectives and goals with the assignments of each work unit.

From the activities assigned to each work unit come the tasks to be performed by the members of that unit. Work-unit activities become segregated and assigned to specific individuals. These activities become further identified as tasks, duties, and responsibilities of a job. The translation process from the idea to the expenditure of human energy that leads to production of a desired output is now under way. Figure 2-2 describes the evolution of an idea into a product.

To influence and direct this effort, the organization must now consider how it can reward behaviors in a manner that recognizes differences in job requirements. It is through the division-of-labor process that particular tasks are

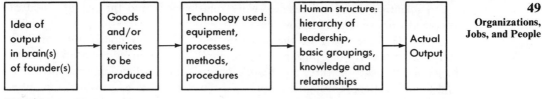

FIGURE 2-2   IDEA TO PRODUCT

assigned to an individual. These tasks, in turn, require specific knowledge and skills of the incumbent and require the performance of the job under a variety of environmental conditions.

DIVISION OF LABOR

Division of labor is common to all creatures. Humans' ability and success in taking the greatest advantage of dividing labor and specializing work requirements among the individuals comprising a social group have helped the human race to dominate all other life forms. The most basic form of such division is reproduction of the species. Responsibilities for reproduction among higher forms of animal life lead to further division of labor and special assignments that directly facilitate the immediate preservation and continuation of the species.

The basis of the employer-employee exchange process is the division of labor, the performance of specialized activities, and the provision of rewards to those who make contributions. The quality and the quantity of rewards normally vary according to the worth of employee contributions as measured by the employer and the value of those contributions as perceived by employees.

Emile Durkheim, the famous French sociologist, recognized the importance of the division of labor when he stated that *what* a person is and *who* a person is depend on and reflect the kind of work a person does. He further stated that the acceptance of a job is the crucial act by which individuals integrate into society and find a definition of self that corresponds to their place in society. Fulfillment and satisfaction from work come from individual achievement and from being a member of a group. However, people do not subordinate themselves unless they view their work relationships as being legal, just, and fair. Organizations require some form of established procedures, specialization of activities, and central direction, which in turn require management to enhance cooperation as it affects collaboration and minimizes the conflict resulting from work requirements.

Late Nineteenth and Early Twentieth Century Contributions

With the significant increase in size and complexity of all kinds of organizations resulting from the changes brought about because of the Industrial Revolution, it became apparent to government and business leaders and to social scientists that the design of work relationships and the management of people at work required improvement.

In the latter part of the nineteenth century and continuing into the twentieth century, work-improvement researchers recognized the advantages to be gained through the three Ss of work design—standardization, specialization, and simplification. Through this process it was possible to provide employees with limited instruction that would enable them to gain a few skills. Then, working in highly repetitive work situations on highly standardized jobs, they could quickly master these skills and become extremely productive. By focusing on this approach, management could reduce costs and, with improved productivity, increase rates of pay for workers having fewer skills and less job knowledge.

Second- and Third-Quarter Twentieth Century Contributions

By the 1920s, work design problems were arising in the more advanced industrial nations. The three-S approach to the design of work began to experience some unexpected and unacceptable consequences. Workers were expressing dissatisfaction with their easily learned jobs—with their highly repetitive tasks.

Concurrent with the increase in financial security gained from performing these repetitive task jobs was an increase in the education and knowledge levels of workers in industrialized nations. The combination of improved education and financial security led to significant changes in worker expectations and aspirations. By the 1950s, workers in the United States were beginning to rebel against their boring work assignments and the managers who frequently used an authoritarian approach for directing work efforts. These workers expressed their dissatisfaction through such workplace behaviors as absenteeism, tardiness, turnover, and unacceptable quality of output. As work dissatisfaction turned to frustration, apathy, and hostility, malicious damage to equipment and materials and theft further reduced organizational productivity.

The managers and the researchers investigating these workplace problems that were causing declines in productivity began identifying various opportunities available to managers that would assist in overcoming these destructive workplace behaviors.

In the 1960s, Frederick Herzberg identified the need for the vertical loading of jobs for overcoming job boredom problems rather than the previously used horizontal loading. Vertical loading required that incumbents have planning and control (measurement) responsibilities for their jobs and not simply be required to do their jobs as directed by their supervisors. Horizontal loading required the enlargement of a job by adding a number of tasks to a job so that it had longer work cycles and would not be so highly repetitive.

Prior to Herzberg's recommendation, a number of behavioral scientists were stating that employees had to have more influence over their work. To achieve this goal, workers should be given the opportunity to make more decisions about how they do their jobs. They should receive adequate and timely feedback on how their supervisors viewed their performance. They should have the opportunity to do a "whole" job and have a sense of accomplishment from performing an important and meaningful assignment. Above all, they must not feel that they are simply an appendage to a machine.

End-of-Twentieth-Century Contributions

With the increasing influence of the computer on the work life of all employees, different approaches and attitudes must be developed relative to the division of labor and employer-provided rewards. The combination of computer-based and -provided information, expanding fragmentation of work and social demands, and increasing scarcity of natural resources will require greater specialization of work efforts. Recognizing the productivity-debilitating issues that evolve when combining specialization with standardization and simplification will require improvement in the way managers and reward system designers do their jobs.

The combination of scarce and high-cost resources with the continuing increase of worker expectations and aspirations will force workers to have greater knowledge and skills in a more highly restricted work area. This ever-expanding requirement to specialize opens the door to the early twentieth century approach to work—"there is a one right way to do something." Even with the increased attention on specialized work effort, employees will be given more opportunity to do their own thing within the confines of identified and understood job requirements and performance standards. The major difference in specialization demands at the end of the twentieth century relates to the changing knowledge and skill requirements for the worker. Although working in highly specialized areas requires in-depth understanding, flexible thinking will negate the need for standardization and simplification.

To be effective, reward system design must recognize the "total" person. It must relate compensation and noncompensation rewards in a manner that is truly synergistic (the combination of all parts results in a final output that is greater than that produced by summing the independent output of each part). As mentioned in the Introduction, the compensation rewards must be adequate to satisfy the subsistence, luxury, and influence life-style demands of the employee. The noncompensation rewards must recognize the psychological and emotional satisfaction that employees demand from their jobs. The reward system that will assist managers in coordinating and directing the efforts of individuals who perform highly specialized work assignments and who will be making extremely unique reward demands from their employers.

Recognizing Worker Contributions

Relating the division of labor to the division of rewards is the cornerstone for establishing equality and equity in the modern organization. All types of organizations operating under all types of governments recognize that the people who make the greatest contributions, whether they are business leaders, innovators of successful change, or excellent performers, receive a significantly larger share of the rewards than the followers or the people who simply meet production standards.

In contemporary history, no industrial state has been able to create an egalitarian society and function effectively. Even in societies that promote equality, there are those citizens who are "more equal" than others and who lay claim to greater shares of the rewards. The citizens who make such claims and receive the benefit of special treatment are, in one way or another, implementing equity within an equality-based society. In an equity-oriented system, those who make the greater contributions enjoy additional rewards—those that do, get.

The reward issue facing modern organizations is not implementation of an equality-based reward process but, rather, the design and the management of a reward system that has its roots firmly grounded in a structure based on equality *and* equity.

The leader, the risk taker, the innovator, the change agent, and the high performer make the contributions so necessary for the survival and the growth of the modern organization.

Organizational Structure

A basic approach for distributing rewards focuses on the level of the job in the organizational structure. The higher the level of the job, the greater the responsibility for the successful operation of the organization. Once an organization employs 100 or more people, it develops a line structure that is common to organizations hiring tens, even hundreds of thousands of people. This common line structure consists of a board of directors and three primary groups of employees—senior management, operating management, and operative employees. This structural arrangement excludes staff personnel who provide advice and support for these groups.

Board of Directors—A typical structure has at its very highest level a board of directors elected by the stockholders or owners. A chairperson directs the activities of the board as its members oversee and guide the operations of the organization. A board of directors normally consists of inside members (those having full-time positions within the organization) and outside members (those elected from the community at large).

Senior Management—the first and smallest group of employees consists of those in senior management. In a small organization, senior management may consist of only the owner or the president. In a larger organization, it will consist of executives and senior managers—those who have responsibility for setting the objectives of the organization, establishing its operating policies, and defining courses of action through the strategies they develop and approve.

In 1976 Arch Patton, a recognized expert on executive compensation, stated that there were approximately 135,000 employees in American businesses who could be truly identified as policy-making executives.[1] Given a work force at

---

[1]Arch Patton, "The boom in executive self-interest," *Business Week,* May 24, 1976, pp. 16, 20.

that time of approximately 85,000,000, this executive group consisted of approximately one-sixth of 1 percent of the total work force. In this text, the group identified as executives is slightly broader. The highest ranking officer of this group, who may be the chief executive officer (CEO) or the president, is responsible for all operations. Normally, an organization will use only one of the two titles. There are times, however, when an organization will have a CEO as well as a president.

Immediately subordinate to a CEO are the chief operations officer (COO) and a number of executive vice presidents. The titles of the individuals holding these jobs may vary. Defined in this manner, executives consist of approximately one-sixth to one-half of 1 percent of the work force.

The next group of officials who closely interact with and support these executives are the senior managers. Depending on the size, kind, and organizational design preferences of the organization, this group will occupy another 2 to 3 percent of all positions. Together with the executives, they make up approximately 3 to 4 percent of any organization.

EXECUTIVES
(⅙ to ½ of 1%)

SENIOR MANAGEMENT
(3 to 4%)

SENIOR MANAGERS
(2 to 3%)

The senior management group is fairly easy to identify. These objective setters, policy makers, and strategy formulators are primarily responsible for improving the effectiveness of the organization. Effectiveness criteria become the measures of their successful performance. In setting objectives, they direct the long-run efforts of all members of the organization. Resource utilization that leads not only to present prosperity but also to future growth is the time-consuming responsibility of senior management.

```
EFFECTIVENESS
The
Primary Measure of Senior
Management Performance
```

Operating Management—The second primary group of managers in an organization is that of operating management. This group spans a wide range of activities and responsibilities, but the one thing all operating managers have in common is an intense concern over immediate results. Operating managers do not have the luxury of concern for the future. The successful operating manager must produce *today*. Areas of involvement that do not produce immediate results are of little meaning or value to the operating manager. Nowhere is Lord Keynes' statement that "in the future we are all dead" more meaningful than at this level of management. If the results of today do not stand on their own, there is no tomorrow for the operating manager. This may be an overstatement, but it is not too far from reality.

GROUP OR DIVISION MANAGERS	
PLANT MANAGERS, STORE PRESIDENTS	OPERATING MANAGEMENT
FIRST-LINE FOREMEN[2]	(Approx. 15% of the total work force)

An operating manager can be a first-line foreman responsible for 12 unskilled to semiskilled workers who daily produce an output valued at approximately $500, or he or she may be a plant manager of a huge automobile assembly plant with a work force of 3,000 employees who produce hundreds of millions of dollars of output per year. No matter what the scope of their jobs is, all operating managers recognize the importance of recruiting, hiring, training, and promoting personnel for the duties of tomorrow and for designing processes and systems for future opportunity and growth. Their basic loyalty and responsibility, however, lie in the *efficient* use of resources—maximizing the output of today at the lowest possible cost. Efficiency is the name of the game played by the operating managers at every level, and efficiency criteria measure their performance. (It must be recognized that efficiency is, in reality, a subset of effectiveness. It is possible to be efficient without being effective. It is not possible to be effective without being efficient.)

```
┌─────────────────────────┐
│        EFFICIENCY        │
│           The            │
│      Primary Measure of  │
│    Operating Management  │
│        Performance       │
└─────────────────────────┘
```

Operative Employees—The remaining 80 percent of the work force are the operative employees—the people in the trenches who make it all happen. Both senior and operating management attempt to convince this group that there is a relationship between the rewards offered by the organization to its members and the results produced by this group. This book focuses principally on the design and the implementation of a compensation system for operative employees.

BASIC GROUPS

Traditionally, the two major groupings with which compensation managers work are (1) managers and (2) operative employees; but as the nation moves toward a service economy, the professional, paraprofessional, and technician groups will require more of their attention. In fact, if the concept of "every

---

[2]The appropriate terminology here depends on how the terms are operationally defined by the particular organization.

employee a manager" becomes more prevalent in the coming decade, managers and operatives, as well as professionals, will require new and/or improved definitions.[3]

Exempt-Nonexempt

Because of exemption from certain requirements of the Fair Labor Standards Act of 1938, as amended, it is necessary to take into consideration the requirements detailed by the U.S. Department of Labor, Employment Standards Administration, Wage and Hour Division as to what is meant by bona fide executive, administrative, professional, and sales personnel. Employees in these categories are *exempt* from the minimum wage and overtime requirements of the act if they meet the test for each category.[4] Employee exemption depends on (1) responsibilities and duties and (2) salary. This organization dichotomy, which separates the exempt (exempt from certain wage and hour regulations) from the nonexempt, relates to almost every organization.

Management

Once the compensation administrator separates the exempt employees from the nonexempt, the two major groups that compose the managerial hierarchy of most organizations should be examined. It is fairly easy to define the top and bottom segments of a group. However, the boundaries or specifications that differentiate these two management groups are frequently vague and defy precise definition.

Senior Management—Senior managers are normally responsible for establishing organization-wide policy. They analyze the broad objectives of the organization and lay the groundwork for the strategic operations that enable the organization to achieve its objectives. They are the ultimate authority group, and the buck stops with them. They not only coordinate major functional operations, but also relate organizational activities to those external forces that have an impact on operations.

Operating Management—Operating managers, on the other hand, are those persons at the scene of the action, those who are responsible for day-to-day operations. They are responsible for implementing operating decisions that enforce established policy and for providing broadly based data and information that either integrate the activities or enable them to improve the operations of those units for which they are responsible. In this light, they interpret strategic requirements into short-range, tactical activities. Not only do they act as interpreters of senior management concepts, they also filter operational prob-

[3]M. Scott Myers, *Every Employee a Manager* (New York: McGraw-Hill, 1970).

[4]A complete description of exemption requirements is found in U.S. Department of Labor, *Executive, Administrative, Professional, and Outside Salesmen Exemptions Under the Fair Labor Standards Act*, WH Publication 1363 (rev.) (Washington, D.C.: Government Printing Office, 1973).

lems, passing on to senior management those needing review. Additionally, they coordinate the activities of departmental and functional units. They are responsible for the goods and/or services produced by their subordinate managers or by the operative employees who report to them. They either have the authority to hire and fire or can recommend the hiring and firing of their immediate subordinates. They are responsible for developing the work schedule as well as for maintaining the quality and quantity standards of their work groups.

The term *executive* as used in this text has a meaning directly related to senior management. However, an executive is defined by the Wage and Hour Division as follows:

1. One whose primary duty is management of the enterprise, or of a customarily recognized department or subdivision.

2. One who customarily and regularly directs the work of at least two or more other employees therein.

3. One who has the authority to hire and fire, or recommend hiring and firing, or whose recommendation on these and other actions affecting employees is given particular weight.

4. One who must customarily and regularly exercise discretionary powers.

5. One who devotes no more than 20 percent (less than 40 percent if he is employed by a retail or service establishment) of his hours of work to activities not directly and closely related to his managerial duties.

6. One who must be paid on a salary basis of at least $155 per week.

7. One who receives at least $250 per week and must meet the "short-cut" test requirements.[5]

The exception in item 7 is called an upset or high salary proviso. A review of these seven recommendations indicates that the term *executive* as defined by the U.S. Department of Labor (DOL) is far broader than that developed in this chapter. By DOL definition, practically all managers are executives, although it is possible that some lower-level managers (supervisors, foremen) may not meet these seven tests. A survey performed by DOL in February 1975 identified 5,585,000 executives in the nonfarm establishments in the private sector. These executives had median weekly earnings of $312.[6] In some organizations, supervisors or working foremen spend a considerable portion of their time performing nonmanagerial activities, and although this is not a sole criterion, it requires close scrutiny on the part of the compensation manager to determine whether

[5]U.S. Department of Labor, *Executive, Administrative, Professional*, pp. 1–2.

[6]U.S. Department of Labor, Employment Standards Administration, *Executive, Administrative, and Professional Employees: A Study of Salaries and Hours of Work* (Washington, D.C.: Government Printing Office, May 1977), p. 1.

such lower-level managers meet the requirements set forth for an executive under DOL regulations.[7]

Administrators

The Wage and Hour Division and the Bureau of Labor Statistics interpret the term *administrator* similarly. The Wage and Hour Division defines an administrator as follows:

(a) The employee's duty must be either:
  (1) Responsible office or nonmanual work directly related to the management policies or general business operations of his employer or his employer's customers; or
  (2) Responsible work that is directly related to academic instruction or training carried on in the administration of a school system or educational establishment.
(b) The employee must customarily and regularly exercise discretion and independent judgment, as distinguished from using skills and following procedures, and must have the authority to make important decisions; and
(c) The employee must:
  (1) Regularly assist a proprietor or a bona fide executive or administrative employee;
  (2) Perform work under only general supervision along specialized or technical lines requiring special training, experience, or knowledge; or
  (3) Execute special assignments only under general supervision; and
(d) The employee must not spend more than 20 percent of the time worked in the work week (less than 40 percent if employed by a retail or service establishment) on nonexempt work—that is, work not directly and closely related to the administrative duties; and
(e) The employee must be paid on a salary or fee basis at a rate of not less than $155 per week. In the case of academic administrative personnel, the salary requirement for exemption must be at least $155 or alternately, a salary which is at least equal to the entrance salary for teachers in the school system or educational establishment or institution by which he or she is employed;
(f) If the employee receives a salary of $250 per week, the "short-cut" test applies.[8]

The exception in item (f) is called an upset or high salary proviso.

The Bureau of Labor Statistics views the administrator as being more of a staff specialist. Administrators normally function in such areas as personnel, accounting, finance, law, medicine, research and development, and planning. The February 1975 survey conducted by DOL identified 1,198,000 administrative employees in nonfarm establishments in the private sector. Their median weekly earnings were $231.[9]

---

[7]U.S. Department of Labor, Employment Standards Administration, *Defining the Terms "Executive," "Administrative," "Professional," and "Outside Salesman"* (W.H. Publication 1281, Regulation 541.115 Washington, D.C.: Government Printing Office, 1975).

[8]U.S. Department of Labor, *Executive, Administrative, Professional*, pp. 3–4.

[9]U.S. Department of Labor, *A Study of Salaries and Hours of Work*, p. 1.

Sales Personnel

An important group of employees that requires the special attention of the reward and compensation specialist is the one involved in the marketing and the sales of the products of the organization. Without customers or clients who desire and are willing to pay for the product, there is little reason for an organization to exist. The design of a reward package that attracts and retains individuals who can perform sales activities in an acceptable manner is a complex and specialized skill. Wide varieties of reward and compensation packages have been and are continuing to be designed to establish a motivating environment for these individuals.

The U.S. Department of Labor has its own special definition for sales personnel who are exempt from overtime requirements. An "outside salesman" is defined by DOL as an employee who is:

(a) employed for the purpose of and who is customarily and regularly engaged away from his employer's place of business;

(b) selling tangible or intangible items such as goods, insurance, stocks, bonds, real estate, or

(c) obtaining orders or contracts for services or use of facilities such as advertising, repairs, etc. (sales of these services are performed away from the employer's establishment);

(d) not working in activities other than those described above; does not exceed 20 percent of the hours worked in the workweek by nonexempt employees of the employer.

There is no salary test for outside salespersons.[10]

Line-Staff

The line-staff division separates those responsible for direct profit-producing output (line) from those responsible for providing advice or service in technically oriented areas (staff). This is a gray area that is difficult to define because functions that in the past were considered to be staff work are gaining recognition as being more directly related to the output of the organization and are now considered to be line activities. One approach that may be useful in separating line and staff is to define *line* as those engaged in the main work of the organization. All others are *staff*.

Pro-Tecs

The pro-tec group consists of professionals, paraprofessionals, and technicians. Traditionally, there has been a wide gap between the contributions, responsibilities, and compensation of the professionals and those of the technicians. As the paraprofessionals achieve maturity and recognition, this gap will diminish. Restructuring the responsibilities and the duties of the entire group will require close observation by all those involved with the human resources of the business.

[10]U.S. Department of Labor, *Executive, Administrative, Professional,* p. 9.

Professionals—Professionals are those employees whose work requires advanced knowledge in a field of science or learning. Although at times there are no specific academic requirements, professionals normally have advanced degrees and the ability to apply their knowledge in a creative and conceptual manner.

There are fairly specific standards for professionals, and normally they must have some form of license or certification. In addition, professionals meeting Fair Labor Standard Act exemption requirements must be paid at least $170 a week and meet four other tests. Those who meet the high salary provisions of $250 a week must meet fewer tests.[11] In the coming years, licensing requirements will spread over a large number of specialized areas, and educational requirements will continue to intensify for this group. A February 1975 DOL survey of nonfarm establishments in the private sector identified 1,613,000 professional employees who met the criteria for exemption. They had median weekly earnings of $276.[12]

At times professionals as well as paraprofessionals and technicians may have managerial duties in addition to their technical assignments. In this case, they frequently command up to 20 percent higher salaries than their peers who perform comparable professional activities with no managerial responsibilities. When making salary reviews for this group, it is wise to remember that their most significant managerial responsibility is their span of control, that is, the number of subordinates directly supervised by a manager.

Technicians—Technicians are those employees who provide semi-professional technical support in their specialized areas. They perform a variety of activities ranging in scope from something that is simple and routine to activities that are quite complex. Their activities may involve responsibility for planning and conducting a complete project of relatively limited scope or a portion of a more diverse project in accordance with objectives, requirements, and methods as outlined by a supervisory paraprofessional or professional.[13]

There are limited licensing and academic requirements for technicians. Knowledge acquired on the job or academic programs such as those offered in the two-year community college associate degree courses are usually sufficient for entry-level technicians. There is an overlap between the advanced technician and the lower levels of the paraprofessional ranks.

Paraprofessionals—Paraprofessionals are the most recent and probably the most dynamic grouping of talent in many organizations. This group currently has rather vague limits. However, the changing nature of technology is providing the demand for paraprofessionals, and they span the gap between the

[11]U.S. Department of Labor, *Executive, Administrative, Professional,* p. 5–8.

[12]U.S. Department of Labor, *A Study of Salaries and Hours of Work,* p. 1.

[13]U.S. Department of Labor, *National Survey of Professional, Administrative, Technical, and Clerical Pay,* March 1980 (Washington, D.C.: Government Printing Office, 1980), p. 6. (This is an annual publication.)

technician and the professional. They do not require the broad, extensive educational background of the professionals, but they are assuming more of the responsibilities that were once the sole prerogatives of the professionals. Many of these responsibility shifts are slow in coming, but they must take place. Poor use of the talents of the professionals and the costs connected with their productive efforts ensures the growth and the future of the paraprofessional. This group is in a stage of rapid transition, and undoubtedly there will be rigid licensing and certification requirements as its members assume roles of increased responsibility and gain commensurate increases in compensation.

Operatives

The employees who do not fall into the managerial, administrative, professional, paraprofessional, and technical groups are the operatives. They perform assignments that range from those given by a few specific and easily understood oral instructions to those requiring in-depth knowledge of specific trades or skills. Representatives of this group are discussed in the following paragraphs.

Skilled Craftworkers—The identifying characteristics of the skilled craftworkers are their training and education programs. In this group, the novice traditionally moves from apprentice to journeyman to master. This education program has a strong on-the-job orientation, but it is possible to acquire portions of it in an academic environment.

To interface with the technology of their trades, the skilled craftworkers have a rather large stock of skills. Their efforts frequently require originality and ingenuity in performing a wide variety of planning, operating, and control functions with regard to their jobs or those of their helpers. In addition, they know the inherent characteristics of the raw materials common to their work and are capable of training the less skilled workers to operate equipment and to use basic raw materials. They frequently interact with the pro-tec group on the best use of technology and the determination of methods and procedures with regard to the material used and the results desired. They also have a high degree of manual dexterity and an ability to work within extremely fine tolerances and precise finishes. This group includes members of the building trades and a wide variety of machinists, mechanics, makers of instruments and models, as well as those responsible for operating and repairing high-technology equipment.

Semiskilled Workers—Semiskilled workers include those moving through the various education and training programs that are necessary to achieve skilled status and those who are becoming more skilled on a particular job but are not adding different skills to their skill inventory. Semiskilled workers perform jobs that range from fairly simple assembly operations to those that require operation of complex equipment within limits set by specific or detailed operating instructions. The members of this group receive brief instructions about their specific assignments. The semiskilled group includes most assemblers, truck drivers, equipment and machinery operators; persons who repair standard office and industrial equipment; and material handlers responsible for verifying, stocking, transferring, and recording a variety of materials.

Unskilled Workers—Unskilled employees must be able to follow simple but relatively few verbal (written and/or oral) instructions. Their jobs usually involve substantial physical effort and require minimum education and only basic communication abilities. Supervisors frequently review their work while work is in progress to ensure conformance with standards, and they almost always review it upon its completion. The unskilled group consists of manual laborers, janitors, and custodians and those who handle simple, routine, material, and processing assignments.

Secretarial-Clerical—In the operative group is a subgroup of employees who primarily fit into the semiskilled area but who actually have characteristics of both the unskilled and skilled employees. With the increasing expansion of both automation and the service-oriented industries, this large, widespread group of workers requires special recognition. Because secretarial-clerical jobs have similar performance requirements in a wide range of organizational settings, these jobs provide compensation managers with a common and valuable base for comparison purposes.

The secretarial-clerical group performs a variety of office practices and procedures that range from simple, manual filing assignments to the preparation of complex reports using automated systems, to secretarial support for high-ranking executives. This group forms the white–pink collar base of organizations.

White Collar – Blue Collar – Pink Collar

In recent years, the classification of workers as being white collar or blue collar has attracted much attention. Such terms as "white-collar woes" and "blue-collar blues" are common. The basis of these woes and blues is the continuing specialization and refinement of the work of these groups, which frequently has gone so far that the jobs provide no intrinsic rewards or opportunities to gain job satisfaction.

In the 1970s, a third color was added to the white- and blue-collar grouping; this new color was pink. The pink-collar description has been developed to focus attention on the kinds of work in which women are the predominant jobholders and where, in many cases, it is said that their pay is unfairly depressed because women predominate in these jobs.

In the last part of the decade of the '70s, women and women's rights organizations have claimed that, in the past, women have been forced into segregated occupations. The pay for jobs in these segregated or traditional women's occupations has been adversely impacted—the pay is lower than that granted to men performing comparable kinds of work. With greater numbers of women entering the work force and an increasingly larger percentage of women in the total work force, equity between job rates of pay in female-dominated work and in male-dominated work will become a critical human resource issue.

The white-collar segment of the work force has historically included the professional, administrative, technical, and secretarial-clerical groups, and the blue-collar segment has been comprised of the skilled and semiskilled craftworkers, the unskilled laborers, and their first-level supervisors. The pink-collar classification includes nurses, medical technicians, noncollege teachers, retail sales personnel, secretaries and clerks, apparel-industry workers, food-service workers, and domestics.

Historically, white- and pink-collar workers have been unorganized. In recent years, however, they have exhibited increased unrest over the pay practices of their employers. To aid in keeping this large, important segment of the work force free of union involvement, managers must improve their understanding of the responsibilities and the duties performed by these workers, develop better standards for measuring performance, and establish compensation systems that provide equitable pay treatment.

Union-Nonunion

Another consideration is whether employees exercise their right to organize and bargain collectively with management. Those members of the organization who select a union to negotiate for wages, hours, and other benefits and working conditions normally become distinctly separate from those who do not delegate this activity to an intervening third party.

In the past, the division was normally between the management group and the operative employees, but in recent years there has been widespread unionization among various pro-tec groups. Even higher levels of operating management have indicated interest in unionization, but the Supreme Court recently upheld existing legislation that exempted management from government protection when involved in collective bargaining activities.

Chapter 4 discusses the effects of unionization on compensation managers and the function they must perform in working effectively with union officials.

Permanent and Temporary Employees

Another approach for grouping employees that is especially important for compensation purposes is the identification of permanent and temporary employees and, within these groups, the further subclassification of full-time and part-time employees. A major way of separating permanent and temporary employees is on the basis of hours worked per week and weeks worked per year.

Permanent Employees—Any person hired for a specific job who is expected to work on a continuing basis and meet certain minimum performance and time-on-job requirements is a permanent employee.

Temporary Employees—Any person hired for a special project or an as-need basis, or for seasonal work, or for any kind of work of a transitory nature is considered a temporary employee. (Although a temporary employee may typically be one who works six months or less in a year, it is not unusual to find employees who have a temporary status in an organization but have been employed for a number of years.

Hours Worked—Typically, permanent employees are expected to work between 35 to 40 hours per week. Although most employees are expected to work a 40-hour work week, it is not uncommon to find office workers and second-shift (4:00 P.M. to 12:00 midnight) and third-shift (12:00 midnight to 8:00 A.M.) workers working 35 to 37½ hours and being paid for 40 hours.

Full-time Employees—A full-time worker is an employee who works the number of hours per week and the number of weeks per year typically required of jobholders in the specific work unit. A typical full-time employee works between 35 to 40 hours per week, 52 weeks per year.

Part-time Employees—A part-time employee is typically any person working on a continuing basis who works less than a full-time employee but performs similar or identical work assignments. In some organizations, there may be a specific hour cutoff that differentiates the full- and part-time employees. A part-time employee may be anyone working less than 35 hours, 30 hours, or 20 hours per week.

Temporary Employment Agencies—Many organizations use an intermediary organization to hire their temporary workers. Those agencies hire workers and then, upon request, send them to the clients. The clients are responsible for assigning the temporary specific work and determining the actual amount of time on the job. Temporary employees are frequently found performing clerical and manual labor kinds of work. There has been increased usage of temporary workers in the security guard, nursing, and computer-related fields.

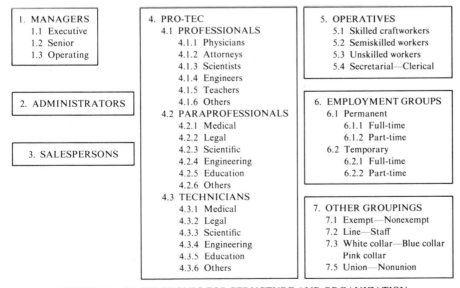

FIGURE 2-3   BASIC GROUPS FOR STRUCTURE AND ORGANIZATION

Compensation systems are designed to meet the demands of permanent full-time employees. The plans normally vary for part-time and temporary employees.

Chart of Basic Organizational Groups

Figure 2-3 identifies the major groups of workers found in the modern organization.

SELECTED READINGS

Elder, James T., "Salary Comparison Method for Experienced Technical Personnel," *Personnel Journal,* July 1968, pp. 467–474. Open-minded collaboration between compensation specialists and technical managers is necessary in order to achieve proper compensation of scientists, engineers, and other personnel oriented toward high technology.

"Move to Organize Professionals Accelerates," *Chemical and Engineering News,* December 9, 1968, pp. 24–27. The inability to define professionals properly is a problem when attempting to unionize them. Among many, there is still a strong feeling that unionism is not consistent with professionalism.

Raimon, Robert L., and Vladimir Stoikov, "The Effect of Blue-Collar Unionism on White-Collar Earnings," *Industrial and Labor Relations Review,* April 1969, pp. 358–374. The authors contend that there is a minimum spillover effect on nonproduction workers' earnings in manufacturing industries from their unionized comrades, and they suggest reasons why this is so.

Sbarra, Robert A., "How to Meet the Compensation Needs of Middle Management," *Business Management,* January 1969, pp. 35, 40–42. Middle management, a heterogeneous group in terms of people, functions, responsibilities, and assignments, has a wide variety of goals, and its effectiveness can seldom be measured through the profit figure. Organizations should develop special incentive plans that fit the needs of each group within this conglomerate of groups.

U.S. Department of Labor, *National Survey of Professional, Administrative, Technical, and Clerical Pay,* March 1980. Washington, D.C.: Government Printing Office, 1978 (annual publication). These bulletins summarize the results of the Bureau of Labor Statistics annual salary survey of selected professional, administrative, technical, and clerical occupations in private industry. In addition, these bulletins provide a basis for categorizing positions by occupations.

———, *Executive, Administrative, Professional, and Outside Salesmen Exemptions Under the Fair Labor Standards Act,* WH publication 1363 (rev.) Washington, D.C.: Government Printing Office, 1973. This bulletin provides a complete description of government requirements that a jobholder must fulfill in order to be exempted from the statutes of the Fair Labor Standards Act.

3

Government Influences

CONTENT

Chapter 3 is a review of major government legislation in the area of social responsibility that has a direct impact on compensation managers in performing their duties.

GOALS

Upon concluding this chapter, you should be aware of the major laws affecting the design of the wage structure and the work opportunities and the economic security of employees. You should be able to recognize the roles of these laws in implementing action necessary for full compliance while meeting the effectiveness and efficiency objectives of both the organization and its employees.

With the arrival of agriculture and widespread domestication of animals, the production of specialized tools and utensils, and the rise of commerce between cities came the enactment of laws, regulations, and injunctions to control the working hours and rewards available for effort exerted on the job. These laws came from custom and tradition and from government and religious jurisdictions. Although religious and government leaders occasionally were rivals for ultimate authority, they normally worked together to regulate the activities of the members of their society.

The earnings of most workers provided few luxuries and basically permitted mere survival. Agricultural workers were entitled to some share of the food they produced and access to fuel and shelter materials. Any earnings available after taking care of food, clothing, and shelter were effectively removed through some form of government taxation or through levies and tithes imposed by religious leaders.

Similar to their scavenging, hunting, and gathering forebears, the farmers and most craftworkers from the dawn of written history until relatively recent times had their work hours controlled by hours of daylight, variations in weather, and climatic changes. As more workers became involved in craft activities and the production of buildings, goods, and services, government and religious leaders recognized the need to regulate working hours. Regulated time off from work allowed for both the replenishment of physical energy and the nourishment of social and spiritual needs. Sustaining these needs led to the establishment of sacred or holy days as well as a weekly day of rest.

Except for possible death during wars or for the occasional periods of famine when large numbers of people perished because of lack of food, agricultural society was a society of certainty, conformity, and uniformity.

By the fourteenth century, however, the rising commercial revolution and the final disintegration of the medieval society introduced change and disorder into the world of work. No longer were earnings set by custom and tradition. By the fourteenth and fifteenth centuries, European workers were negotiating wages, and the early craft guilds (forerunners of the modern unions) were major forces in setting wage rates. As socially controlled "just price" wage rates began to crumble, rulers began to assign specific wage rates for specific occupations to block escalation of wage demands.[1]

A combination of dramatic events was responsible for these changes. Concurrent with a move toward commercial endeavors and increased production of luxury items, the Black Death struck western Europe in 1348. By the time the plague had subsided, the population of Europe had been reduced by one-third. This tremendous loss of population, coupled with increased demands for goods, caused many of the remaining farm laborers to migrate to the cities to seek jobs in the trades and crafts. This movement led to a shortage of farm workers. The need for workers both in the city and on the farm gave workers an opportunity to demand higher wages.[2]

[1]Barbara Nachtrieb Armstrong, *Insuring the Essentials* (New York: Macmillan, 1932), pp. 17–19.

[2]C. Harold King, *A History of Civilization* (New York: Scribner's, 1956), pp. 504–533.

By the sixteenth century, widespread trade and competition for the consumer's money provided an impetus for the rise of the cottage industry. Working in their own homes, families produced goods required by commercial traders at prices lower than those demanded by the urban guilds. Competition for supplying the goods and services resulted in a decline in the prices paid to nonfarm workers of this period.

With the decline in the price of labor and increases in the cost of food and shelter, sixteenth-century workers in England experienced a decline in their standard of living. Commercial workers who had given up their share of the food and the shelter available in the agricultural community for the wages available in a commercial society were unemployed and destitute in many cases. In attempting to improve the plight of the nonfarm worker, Parliament passed a minimum wage act in 1562.[3]

The seventeenth and eighteenth centuries saw the cottage industry that was centered in homes in rural areas move into the homes of the workers in the towns and cities. The individuals responsible for meting out work to these home-workers set rates of pay for pieces produced. Because of the decentralization of work activities and the lack of any mechanism for wage standardization, the piece rates set for cottage industry work were extremely low.

With the invention of the steam engine and other technology that allowed the development of factories for spinning and weaving fabrics, a major change occurred in the way masses of people earned their livelihood through work. Within a hundred years after the beginning of the Industrial Revolution, working conditions had become so bad that, by the latter part of the nineteenth century, the term "sweated" was applied to conditions under which many English workers toiled. "Sweating" applied to "(1) a rate of wage inadequate to the necessities of the workers or disproportionate to the work done; (2) excessive hours of labor; and (3) unsanitary state of houses in which work is carried on."[4]

Demands for improvement in working conditions, fewer hours of work a week and shorter working weeks, and improved pay had already been proposed early in the nineteenth century. A major breakthrough occurred in the United States in 1840 when President Martin Van Buren issued an executive order that established the 10-hour day for workers on government contracts.[5] At this time, a 13-hour day was the norm for most industrial workers. From 1840 until 1866, the 12-hour work day was accepted practice for industrial workers.

Ira Steward, a Boston machinist, provided a philosophical base for an eight-hour day when he stated that wages were determined by worker habits and that because wages depended on wants, the surplus provided by the advancing technology through the establishment of an eight-hour day should result in increased wages for workers.[6]

[3]Armstrong, *Insuring the Essentials,* p. 14.

[4]Ibid., pp. 34–35.

[5]Ray Marshall, "The Influence of Legislation on Hours," in Clyde E. Dankert, Floyd C. Mann, and Herbert R. Northrop, eds, *Hours of Work* (New York: Harper & Row, 1965), pp. 36–53.

[6]Ibid, p. 43.

Following the Civil War, eight-hour leagues were established throughout the United States extrolling the benefits of the eight-hour day. Some states passed eight-hour laws, and the federal government passed an eight-hour law for federal employees. However, all these statutes were weak and provided for only minimal enforcement.[7]

Although many groups continued to champion an eight-hour day, the 12-hour day was still an integral part of the life pattern of many workers in the United States into the 1920s. Efforts toward shortening the work week did, however, result in a reduction of the length of an average work day to 9.5 hours by 1890.

The first major reduction in hours worked weekly by industrial workers resulted from state laws passed to protect women and children.[8] From the 1890s until the 1920s, practically every state had laws limiting the number of hours worked by women or children. See table 3-1.

TABLE 3-1

AVERAGE WEEKLY HOURS FOR AMERICAN NONAGRICULTURAL WORKERS[9]

1850	1860	1870	1880	1890	1900	1910	1920	1930	1940	1980
65.7	63.3	60.0	58.8	57.1	55.9	50.3	45.5	43.2	41.1	35.3

The strong efforts to reduce working hours in the United States that followed the Civil War were accompanied by pressures to increase hourly earnings. The Iron Law of Wages theory formulated by the economist David Ricardo in 1817 stated that "the *natural price* of labour is that price which is necessary to enable the labourers, one with another, to subsist and to perpetuate their race without increase or diminuation."[10] This theory stated in clear terms the wage payment practices followed by most employers from earliest times until fairly recent years.

As early as the fifteenth century, however, urban laborers in England were enjoying a substantial improvement in their standard of living. Food was abundant and cheap, and most laborers were able to pay for their weekly board and lodging with the pay from two days of work a week or less. This opportunity for a better life ended by the 1550s and did not occur again for the working masses until late in the nineteenth century.

With the movement to improve working conditions and reduce hours worked, considerable attention was focused on the establishment of minimum

[7]Ibid., pp. 44–45.

[8]Ibid.

[9]J. Frederic Dewhurst et al., *America's Needs and Resources* (New York: Twentieth Century Fund, 1955) p. 1073; 1980 statistics in U.S. Department of Labor, Bureau of Labor Statistics, *Employment and Earnings, April 1981* (Washington, DC: Government Printing Office, 1981), p. 117.

[10]David Ricardo, *On the Principles of Political Economy and Taxation,* 3rd ed. (London: John Murray, 1821), p. 93.

wage rates and an increase in hourly wages. Initial efforts were focused on the pay provided women and children. Although the earnings received by the male industrial worker were extremely low, payments received by women and children were even lower.

In 1896 the province of Victoria in Australia enacted the first minimum wage law in a modern industrial state. New Zealand and England followed soon afterward with minimum wage legislation covering workers in certain industries. In 1912 Massachusetts passed the first minimum wage legislation in the United States. The Massachusetts law was enacted to protect women and children. By 1923 14 more states had passed minimum wage laws aimed at protecting women and children.[11] In 1923 in the case of *Adkins* v. *Children's Hospital,* the Supreme Court threw out a District of Columbia statute, stating that it was unconstitutional to deprive individuals of their freedom to take whatever job they chose on such conditions as were acceptable to them. This Supreme Court ruling gave judicial sanction to minimum wage legislation.

The first national legislation on minimum wages came with the Davis-Bacon Act of 1931, which required construction contractors and their subcontractors receiving federal funds in excess of $2,000 to pay at least the prevailing wages in their area. The Secretary of Labor was granted the authority to determine the prevailing wages. Amendments to the act provided for employee benefits and required contractors or subcontractors to make necessary payments for these benefits.

The next step by the federal government to enact a national minimum wage law was the passing of the National Industrial Recovery Act (NIRA) of 1933. This attempt to establish a national minimum wage, as had been the case with previous state efforts, was foiled by the U.S. Supreme Court in 1935 when it found the law to be unconstitutional.

The federal government again moved into minimum wage regulations with the passing of the Walsh-Healy Public Contracts Act of 1936. This act requires the payment of the prevailing wage as established by the Secretary of Labor in all government-let contract work exceeding $10,000. This act also requires that time and a half be paid for work over eight hours a day and 40 hours a week.

In 1938 the Fair Labor Standards Act (FLSA) was signed into law, and with this legislation the federal government became deeply involved in regulating minimum wages for the majority of American workers. From the initial rate of 25¢ an hour, the rate reached $3.35 an hour by 1981.

The changes in the minimum wage over the years are listed in table 3-2.

This act and its amendments also contain regulations concerning maximum hours, overtime pay, equal pay, record keeping, and child labor provisions for the majority of American workers.

LEGISLATION INFLUENCING COMPENSATION

Since the 1930s, the enactment of a broad spectrum of federal laws has had a significant impact on the compensation practices of organizations. With

[11]Armstrong, *Insuring the Essentials,* pp. 42–65.

TABLE 3-2

1938	1939	1945	1950	1956	1962	1964	1967
0.25	0.30	0.40	0.75	1.00	1.15	1.25	1.40

1968	1974	1975	1976	1978	1979	1980	1981
1.60	2.00	2.10	2.30	2.65	2.90	3.10	3.35

each new government intervention, opportunities for individual initiative and management activities become more restrictive.

Today, senior management is aware that to survive and grow in a government-regulated environment, an organization must have competent staff members who are able to hire, train, develop, and reward employees within the limits set by government regulations, labor budgets, and employee demands. These ever-increasing pressures shed new light on the value of compensation managers and the requirements they must meet. For these human resource managers and staff officials to do their jobs, they must know not only the wording but also the intent of these many pieces of legislation that direct their daily activities in so many ways. The combination of overly restrictive government codes, unwise enforcement, and ineffective management can adversely affect both the organization in particular and society in general.

The design and the management of a workable compensation system require a solid understanding of the federal, state, and local laws that either directly or indirectly influence how much employees are to be paid, how they are paid, the type and quantity of benefits they receive, and the incentives to be offered. In addition, these laws affect the recruitment, selection, and hiring of new employees; the classification of jobs; the appraisal of performance; and the training, transfer, promotion, termination, and retirement of all employees.

To appreciate the breadth and the depth of the impact of these laws, it is useful to classify the laws under three major categories:

1. Wages, hours, and benefits legislation
2. Wage control legislation
3. Tax treatment legislation

A review of these laws within each major category and a brief description of each of the major compensation-related features assist in providing a valuable perspective of this area (see figure 3-1).

Fair Labor Standards Act (Wage-Hour Law)

The enactment of the Fair Labor Standards Act (FLSA) of 1938 established minimum hourly wages for all employees engaged in interstate or foreign commerce or in the production of goods for such commerce, and for all employees in certain enterprises. In addition, this act established overtime wage requirements and defined specific exempt occupations. Chapter 2 discusses these exempt occupations. From 1938 until the present time, amendments to the act have enlarged the number of work groups covered by the law and have steadily increased the minimum wage. By 1978 approximately 52 million American workers were covered by the FLSA. The minimum wage established by this act, as amended, not only sets a floor or base wage for most employees, but it also acts as an index that leads to an increase in wages received by practically all workers. The act requires employers in covered enterprises to pay time-and-a-half the regular rate received by employees for all hours worked in excess of 40 hours a week. (The employer has some discretion in defining a work week, but it must be fixed and be within a regularly recurring period of 168 hours, e.g., from midnight Tuesday until midnight of the following Tuesday).

Information on the Fair Labor Standards Act and its amendments and the maintenance of records necessary to comply with the act are available from the U.S. Department of Labor, Employment Standards Administration, Wage and Hour Division, Washington, D.C., or its nearest regional office. This department is responsible for the administration and enforcement of the act. Prentice-Hall, Inc., and the Bureau of National Affairs, Inc., both provide looseleaf services that describes in detail the law, its interpretation, and the impact various court rulings have had on enforcement of the act.

Equal Pay Act of 1963

The Equal Pay Act amendment to the Fair Labor Standards Act is the first federal antidiscrimination law relating directly to females. It applies to all employees and employers covered by the Fair Labor Standards Act, including executives, administrators, professionals, and outside salespersons. The act requires equal pay for equal work for men and women and defines equal work as work requiring equal skill, effort, and responsibility under similar working conditions.

When applying various tests of equality, the Wage and Hour Division reviews the whole job. It is possible to see if jobs are the same or closely related in character only by analyzing job content and the kinds of activities required in the performance of the job and the amount of time devoted to these activities. Jobs requiring equal skill, effort, and responsibility are seldom identical in every respect. In determining job comparability, it is necessary to consider degrees of difference in skill, effort, and responsibility involved in job performance.

The U.S. Supreme Court ruled that substantially different or dissimilar working conditions relate primarily to two subfactors—*surroundings* and *hazards*. *Surroundings* measure such conditions as the frequency of exposure to and intensity of toxic chemicals or fumes encountered on the job. *Hazards* take into account the physical environment and its impact on the increased chance of an accident and the possible severity of an injury from such an accident (e.g., falling off of a high platform or working near moving parts).

Under the Equal Pay Act, employers can establish different wage rates based on (1) a seniority system, (2) a merit system, (3) a system that measures

WAGES, HOURS AND BENEFITS LEGISLATION

1931   *Davis-Bacon Act of 1931.* Requires construction contractors receiving federal funds in excess of $2,000 to pay at least prevailing wages in their area.

1935   *Social Security Act of 1935.* Protects workers from total economic destitution by providing retirement, disability, and health insurance protection. Also established federal and state unemployment insurance.

1935   *National Labor Relations Act of 1935.* Provides employees with the right to bargain collectively for wages, benefits, and working conditions.

1936   *Walsh-Healy Public Contracts Act.* Requires payment of prevailing wages in all government-let contract work exceeding $10,000 and time-and-a-half pay for all hours worked over eight hours a day and 40 hours a week.

1938   *Fair Labor Standards Act.* Regulates minimum wages, overtime pay, maximum hours, recordkeeping, and child labor provisions for most American workers.

1959   *Welfare and Pension Plan Disclosure Act of 1959.* Grants U.S. Department of Labor review and regulatory influence over private pension plans.

1963   *Equal Pay Act of 1963.* Requires equal pay for men and women performing equal work.

1964   *Title VII of the Civil Rights Act of 1964.* Forbids discrimination in employment practices such as hiring, training, compensation, promotion, and termination.

1967   *Age Discrimination in Employment Act (ADEA) of 1967.* Prohibits discrimination against workers between the ages of 40 to 65 on account of age in hiring, job retention, compensation, and other conditions of employment.

1973   *Health Maintenance Organization Act (HMO) of 1973.* Requires employers who are subject to the Fair Labor Standards act, who have 25 or more employees, and are currently providing health insurance to offer an HMO option if available.

1974   *Employee Retirement Income Security Act (ERISA) of 1974.* Establishes requirements for fiduciary responsibilities, reporting and disclosure, employee participation and coverage, vesting, funding, and other pension plan features.

1978   *Age Discrimination in Employment Act Amendments of 1978.* Prohibits forced retirement of any employee under 70 years of age unless health or performance of employee necessitates such action.

1978   *Pregnancy Discrimination Act.* Requires that women affected by pregnancy, childbirth, or related medical conditions be treated the same as other employees not so affected for all employment-related purposes, such as receipt of benefits.

WAGE CONTROL LEGISLATION

1942   *Wage Stabilization Act.* Froze wages during remainder of World War II. (It stimulated use of benefits such as paid holidays and vacations in the compensation package.)

1950   *Defense Priorities.* Restricted wage increases during the Korean conflict.

1970   *Economic Stabilization Act of 1970.* Granted the President the authority to impose wage and price control.

FIGURE 3-1   FEDERAL LAWS THAT INFLUENCE COMPENSATION PRACTICES.

1861   *Tax Revenue Act of 1861*. First income tax legislation passed to assist in financing the Civil War. Imposed tax at the rate of 3 percent on income in excess of $800.

1872   *Income tax act repealed.*

1894   Imposed tax on personal income derived from various services. Ruled unconstitutional by the Supreme Court.

1913   Sixteenth Amendment to the Constitution passed granting Congress the right to levy and collect taxes on income from whatever sources.

1913   *Income Tax Law of 1913*. Imposed 1 percent tax on personal income over $20,000 and rose to 6 percent on income over $2 million.

1939   *Internal Revenue Code of 1939*. Codified existing tax laws, making it possible to amend existing laws, and eliminated the requirement to rewrite them.

1950   *Tax Revenue Act of 1950*. Established rules for the favorable tax treatment of what were termed "Restricted Stock Options."

1954   *Internal Revenue Code of 1954*. Repealed the Internal Revenue Code of 1939 and established present tax laws. Modified requirement for restricted stock options.

1964   *Revenue Act of 1964*. Replaced restricted stock options with qualified stock options. Lowered maximum marginal tax rates to 70 percent.

1969   *Tax Reform Act of 1969*. Reduced maximum income tax rate on earned income to 50 percent, raised maximum tax rate on capital gains to 35 percent, introduced 10 percent minimum tax on preference income, established provisions for taxing income set aside for retirement purposes.

1975   *Tax Reduction Act of 1975*. Introduced the Tax Reduction Act Employee Stock Ownership Plan. Allows corporations to claim 11 percent investment tax credit if extra 1 percent contributed to employee stock ownership plan.

1976   *Tax Reform Act of 1976*. Eliminated qualified stock option plans as of May 20, 1981. Sanctioned group legal plans, liberalized tax treatment of deferred payments, increased minimum tax on preference income to 15 percent, increased holding period for capital gains.

1978   *Revenue Act of 1978*. Lowered capital gains maximum tax to 28 percent, continued favored treatment of deferred income, reduced impact of minimum tax, introduced second alternative maximum tax, prohibited discrimination in favor of highly-compensated employee relative to certain benefits.

1981   *Tax Reform Act of 1981*. Reduced individual tax rates by 5 percent on October 1, 1981; 10 percent on July 1, 1982; and 10 percent on July 1, 1983. Reduced maximum tax rates on all income to 50 percent, which in turn reduced the maximum capital gains tax rate to 20 percent from 28 percent as of June 10, 1981. Will "index" individual tax rates which will automatically adjust personal income tax brackets to changes in the Consumer Price Index starting in 1984. Excluded from taxation the first $75,000 of income for Americans employed abroad; also excluded housing expenses in excess of $6,059, a threshold based on a formula tied to the salaries of federal workers. Extended current prohibition against IRS regulations on taxation of fringe benefits to Dec. 31, 1983. Included a provision for recipients of stock options to pay tax at capital gains rate on difference between option price and the actual price of the stock at the time of the sale; options must be exercised in the sequence in which they were made available; the employer is not permitted to deduct the option cost as a business expense.

FIGURE 3-1   Cont.

earnings by quantity or quality of production, and (4) a differential based on any factor other than sex. (These conditions are often referred to as the four affirmative defenses of the Equal Pay Act.) Shift differentials are also permissible under the Equal Pay Act. All these exemptions must apply equally to men and women.

Because of merit system exemptions from equal pay, there have been a number of court rulings defining what are or are not acceptable performance appraisal programs. Chapter 13 discusses in detail methods and procedures useful in designing a performance appraisal plan that discriminates according to employee performance but not according to such criteria as the race, sex, national origin, or religion of the employee.

Civil Rights Act of 1964 – Title VII

Title VII of the Civil Rights Act of 1964, also known as the Equal Employment Opportunity Act of 1964, as amended, is having increasing impact on the hiring, training, compensation, promotion, and termination practices of organizations. The act requires the Equal Employment Opportunity Commission (EEOC) to investigate charges by an employee that the employer has been guilty of unlawful employment practices. Such practices include failure to hire, provide employment opportunities, or promote any individual because of the individual's race, color, religion, sex, or national origin. The immediate effect is that organizations must develop records and procedures that define employment standards based on job requirements. They must also identify working conditions and the manner in which a job is performed. (As of July 1, 1979, administration of the Equal Pay Act and the Age Discrimination in Employment Act were transferred from the DOL to the EEOC.)

Employers have the right to insist that a prospective applicant meet job qualifications, but the qualifications must be well defined and relate directly to success in job performance. Only bona fide occupation qualifications (BFOQ) can be used to discriminate among job applicants. This also holds true for promotional opportunities, but organizations must permit freedom of movement or access to higher rated jobs to all employees.

Organizations found guilty of race, sex and age discrimination in their past hiring or promotional practices have been subject to attorney's fees and court costs in addition to extensive award payments to parties whose rights have been violated. The awards have covered a broad gamut of activities—from back pay for as much as seven years, to immediate promotional opportunities, to adjustments in profit sharing and pension plans. Normally, the award is calculated on what the claimant would have received, based on seniority with the company, had the discriminatory practices not existed.

In addition to these punitive actions, organizations are agreeing to remedial action to remove vestiges of past discrimination. These actions often result in the setting of numerical goals and timetables to remedy present effects of past discriminatory practices. To achieve these goals and timetables, organizations are implementing Affirmative Action programs—results-oriented programs that specifically spell out hiring and promotion goals designed to increase minority and female employment in job classifications in which members of these groups are currently underutilized. Job classifications identified for Affirmative Action programs are (1) officials and administrators, (2) professionals, (3) technicians, (4) protective service workers, (5) paraprofessionals, (6) office and clerical workers, (7) skilled craftworkers, and (8) service maintenance workers.

Comparable Worth Issue

During the latter part of the 1970s and into the 1980s, federal court decisions[12] involving the Equal Pay Act ruled in favor of the defendants and against individuals claiming that the defendants were discriminating against women jobholders in pay practices. These decisions and other pressures brought about by women and minority groups stimulated interest on the part of the EEOC and the Office of Federal Contract Compliance Programs (OFCCP) in investigating the actions they could take through their authority relative to Title VII of the Civil Rights Act and Executive Order 11246, respectively, to eliminate pay discrimination in jobs segregated by sex or race.

The major thesis underlying the comparable worth issue is that where 70 to 80 percent of the incumbents in a job or occupation are women or minorities, there is considerable likelihood that the rates of pay for these jobholders will be adversely impacted.

Because of the strict limitations set in the Equal Pay Act, successful EEOC efforts involving pay discrimination cases rest with Title VII. The course EEOC is developing follows this approach: When jobs are of comparable worth (this topic is covered in detail in chapter 7) and employers pay incumbents in comparable jobs differently and the higher-paid incumbents are men and the lower-paid incumbents are women or minorities, pay discrimination and Title VII violations take place. A key point in the comparable worth issue relates to the Bennett Amendment,[13] which ties Title VII of the Civil Rights Act to the Equal Pay Act. Future decisions regarding comparable worth will focus on two areas: (1) the courts' interpretation of the Bennett Amendment, and (2) the acceptance or rejection of technology (job evaluation is a prime technology in this case) that is capable of identifying and measuring differences in worth among dissimilar jobs.

Affirmative Action Programs

Opportunities for advancement—for greater use of the potential available within each individual—have been the focal point of much of the effort of the Affirmative Action programs. Any such program committed to eliminating

[12]In chapter 7, there is an extensive discussion of the comparable worth issue including an analysis of many of the important court decisions involving the Equal Pay Act.

[13]The argument over the Bennett Amendment [Section 703(h) of the Civil Rights Act] is whether or not Title VII incorporates both the equal pay for equal work and the four affirmative defenses of the Equal Pay Act into Title VII of the Civil Rights Act. If it does, how then should especially the fourth affirmative defense, "a differential based on any factor other than sex," be interpreted?

discriminatory promotional practices must have current and valid job requirements, including up-to-date job descriptions and specifications as well as work standards and procedures. Concurrent with the development of this type of job information program, an inventory of the education, the experience, and the skills (EES) of each employee must be developed.

The manpower EES inventory must then be divided into race, sex, and possibly age groups. The manpower inventories can then be related to each job or classification category, indicating available EES qualifications and potential areas of discriminatory practices where there are indications of significant underutilization or a concentration of minorities and females. (*Underutilization* refers to having fewer minority members or women in a particular job category than would reasonably be expected by their presence in the relevant labor market, job categories, classifications, or grade levels.)

By matching available EES with the EES necessary for advanced jobs or classes, the business is able to identify training and development requirements. By laying such an Affirmative Action foundation, it then becomes possible to develop goals and timetables that will improve the use of minorities and females.

Training and development programs that focus on improving upward mobility for employees must not only have well-designed job description, classification, and grading programs but also well-ordered job progressions that relate to lateral transfers as well as to vertical promotions.

Other Antidiscrimination Laws Affecting Compensation Managers

Civil Rights Act of 1866—Section 1 of the Civil Rights Act of 1866 and the provisions of the Civil Rights Act of 1870 and 1871 have been codified as Title 42, Chapter 21, sections 1981–1983 of the United States Code.

Section 1981, Title 42, U.S. Code precludes job discrimination on the basis of race. A discrimination suit filed under section 1981 does not require that administrative remedies be exhausted, as does Title VII of the Civil Rights Act of 1964. Section 1981 also provides for recovery of compensatory or punitive damages, and the only existing statute of limitations to filing a claim is the statute in the state in which the action is brought. This section does not require an employer to be engaged in interstate commerce.

Executive Order 11246—Executive Order 11246 (9-24-65) as amended by Executive Order 11375 (10-13-67), bans discrimination because of race, color, religion, sex, or national origin by any employer with a government contract of more than $10,000. The orders are enforced by the Labor Department's Office of Federal Contract Compliance Programs (OFCCP). OFCCP regulations require Affirmative Action programs of all employers with 50 or more employees and government contracts of $50,000.

Age Discrimination in Employment Act of 1967—The Age Discrimination Act prohibits discrimination in hiring individuals between 40 and 65 years of age. This act covers employers with 25 or more employees and labor organizations with 25 or more members in an industry invoved in interstate commerce.

Equal Employment Opportunity Act of 1972—The Equal Employment Opportunity Act empowered the Equal Employment Opportunity Commission to prevent any person from engaging in any unlawful employment practice as described in Title VII of the Civil Rights Act of 1964. It also empowered the commission to investigate unlawful employment practices on the part of state government, government agencies, and political subdivisions.

Rehabilitation Act of 1973—The Rehabilitation Act prohibits employers performing under a federal contract or subcontracts exceeding $2,500 from discriminating against handicapped persons. Handicapped persons are those having physical or mental impairments that substantially limit one or more major life activities. This act further requires private contractors with federal contracts of $50,000 or more or hiring 50 or more employees to develop a written Affirmative Action plan. The goal of such a plan is take affirmative action to employ and advance qualified handicapped individuals.

Vietnam Era Veterans Readjustment Act of 1974—The Vietnam Era Veterans Act protects the rights of employees to return to their former jobs after engaging in military service. The employee must make application for reemployment within 90 days after discharge or not more than one year if hospitalization continues after discharge.

An employee qualified to perform the duties of a previously held position must be returned to that position or to a position of like seniority, status, and pay and must be entitled to participate in all benefits offered by the employer that would have been gained by the employee if the employee had been on furlough or leave of absence.

Age Discrimination in Employment Act Amendments of 1978—The Mandatory Retirement Age amendment to the Age Discrimination in Employment Act covers most employees. Beginning January 1, 1979, it prohibits forced retirement of any employee under 70 years of age. College professors and top business executives are exempt from this law, as are employees who have certain bona fide occupational qualifications. The law does not preclude the discharge or layoff of older employees because of unsatisfactory performance. However, an organization must be able to substantiate such actions as being based on job performance. The law also requires certain revisions in pension and profit sharing plans and in medical and life insurance plans.

Pregnancy Discrimination Act—Unwilling to accept the ruling of the Supreme Court in the case of *Gilbert* v. *General Electric*,[14] Congress enacted the Pregnancy Discrimination Act in October 1978. This act is an amendment to the Civil Rights Act of 1964. The act prohibits employers from excluding from employment opportunities (disability insurance, medical benefits, leave, accrual of seniority, etc.) any applicant or employee because of pregnancy or related conditions. Disability by, or contributed to, any of these conditions shall be treated the same as disabilities caused by or contributed to by any other medical condition.

Occupational Safety and Health Act of 1970 (OSHA)—Although OSHA is not directly related to employee compensation, this controversial piece of legislation was passed to ensure as far as possible safe and healthful working conditions for all workers. A safe and healthy working environment must be considered as being an element of the quality of work life for employees. From the perspective of the basic reward model presented in the Introduction of this text, however, these benefits would be part of the noncompensation rewards employers provide to employees.

Governmental Impact on Income Protection

Throughout the twentieth century, federal and state governments have been increasingly involved in providing economic protection for workers who suffer an earning loss due to circumstances beyond their control. Such efforts have resulted in the establishment of programs that provide workers' compensation, Social Security, unemployment security, pension control, and, looming on the horizon, government-sponsored health care.

Workers' Compensation—As the United States moved into an industrial economy at the close of the nineteenth century, the increase of industrial accidents and personal injury suits caused by rapid industrialization underscored the inadequate protection provided to disabled workers. In 1911 this resulted in the enactment of the first enduring workers' compensation laws. Today, workers' compensation covers over 85 million American workers.

Each of the 50 states currently has its own workers' compensation laws and administrative agencies. Although the provisions of the laws vary among the states, they do have six common objectives as follows:

1. To provide sure, prompt, and reasonable income and medical benefits to victims of work-related accidents, or income benefits to their dependents, regardless of fault.

---

[14]*Gilbert* v. *General Electric*, 13 FEP Cases 1657. General Electric had an insurance disability plan which excluded pregnancy-related disabilities. EEOC and Gilbert contended that this was a violation of the Civil Rights Act. The Supreme Court ruling stated that discrimination on the basis of pregnancy was not sex discrimination. It was discrimination based on the person's condition, and no law existed that prohibited discrimination against someone on the basis of the condition of the individual.

2. To provide a single remedy and reduce court delays, costs, and work loads arising out of personal injury litigation.

3. To relieve public and private charities of financial drains incident to uncompensated industrial accidents.

4. To eliminate payment of fees to lawyers and witnesses as well as time-consuming trials and appeals.

5. To encourage maximum employer interest in safety and rehabilitation through an appropriate experience-rating mechanism.

6. To promote frank study of causes of accidents (rather than concealment of fault), reducing preventable accidents and human suffering.[15]

Since the early 1970s, most of the states have enacted massive reforms in their workers' compensation laws. Continuing congressional interest in setting up for the first time minimum national standards for state compensation laws has been the primary impetus for improving job-related accident and illness benefits. Improvements have covered such areas as increased weekly benefits and expanded medical coverage. New rehabilitation provisions provide additional maintenance benefits while a disabled employee participates in a retraining program. Improved liability litigation systems, broader definition and expanded coverage with regard to occupational diseases, and subsequent injuries programs (those that provide liability protection to employers who hire workers who have suffered a prior injury) further protect workers.

Most states require all employers to carry workers' compensation insurance with private, state-approved insurance companies. Normally, each state has some form of minimum provision regarding the size of the business before insurance coverage is compulsory. In states in which coverage is not compulsory, employers may elect not to carry such insurance, but they are then liable to employee lawsuits under punitive conditions.

Some states have their own insurance programs. When this is the case, employers may have to insure with the state or they may have the option of using the programs of private insurance companies. Most states also permit self-insurance. Usually, only large companies take advantage of this option because they can spread the risk over a large number of employees. These self-insurers will normally develop a protective service similar to that established by an insurance company.

Social Security—The Social Security Act of 1935 was established to provide American workers with protection from total economic destitution in the event of termination of employment beyond their control. Employers and employees contribute equally for the benefits provided by this act, as amended. Self-employed persons must pay out of their own pockets an established amount to gain Social Security protection. This government-imposed tax has escalated in

---

[15]*Analysis of Workers' Compensation Laws,* 1980 edition (Washington, DC: U.S. Chamber of Commerce, January 1980), p. vii.

TABLE 3-3

EXISTING AND PROPOSED SOCIAL SECURITY TAX RATES, WAGE BASES,
AND MAXIMUM PAYMENTS FOR EMPLOYERS AND EMPLOYEES

Year	Tax Rate	Wage Base	Maximum Tax
1979	6.13	$22,900	$1,403.77
1980	6.13	$25,900	$1,587.67
1981	6.65	$29,700	$1,975.05
1982	6.70	$31,800	$2,130.60
1983	6.70	$33,900	$2,271.30
1984	6.70	$36,000	$2,412.00
1985	7.05	$38,100	$2,686.05
1986	7.15	$40,200	$2,874.30
1987	7.15	$42,600	$3,045.90

recent years and will increase rapidly in the coming decade with the maximum tax scheduled to be $3,045.90 by 1987. Table 3-3 lists existing and proposed Social Security tax rates, wage bases, and maximum payments. Two avenues are open to employers for minimizing this tax burden: First, they may reduce the total size of the work force; and second, they may reduce the amount of employee turnover. Under present regulations, employers must pay for each employee up to the established total contribution. This payment is mandatory even if an earlier employer had already made contributions toward this amount.

Although Social Security is basically a retirement program, it also established the Federal Old-Age, Survivors, Disability, and Health Insurance System. Social Security provides benefits to over 30 million retired or disabled workers and their dependents. In addition, the original law established the federal and state unemployment compensation system. Amendments to this act also provide for Medicaid and Medicare programs. Concern over the economic stability of the Social Security system may cause Congress to enact significant changes in the Social Security program during the early 1980s.

Unemployment Compensation—The Social Security Act of 1935 created jobless benefit payments up to 26 weeks in duration. When workers become unemployed through no fault of their own, the state provides them with certain weekly benefits. Each state has its own unemployment insurance law that defines the terms and benefits of its unemployment program. Although these programs are legislated and administered by the states, they follow federal guidelines prepared by the Employment and Training Administration, Unemployment Insurance Service, U.S. Department of Labor.

Each state establishes minimum and maximum amounts of weekly benefits, the total number of weeks that an unemployed person may receive such benefits, the qualifying relationship between past earnings and benefits received, and the waiting time after termination of employment before receipt of the first benefit payment. Because of the economic crisis of the 1970s, Congress enacted the Employment Security Amendment of 1970, which made available an extended 13 weeks of benefits during periods of "high" unemployment. Then, on

December 31, 1974 the Federal Supplemental Benefits program was created. This program provides an additional 26 weeks of benefits to those who have exhausted both their regular and extended benefits. These laws provide for special unemployment benefits programs relating to local as well as national conditions. Among some of the benefits are extending jobless benefits beyond the normal 16-week period to as much as 65 weeks and including those individuals who in the past had not been covered by unemployment benefits.

The federal government requires each employer to pay a federal unemployment tax (FUTA) of 3.28 percent on the first $4,200 earned by each employee. The employer actually pays 2.7 percent of the tax directly to the state employment security agency or to some other designated state agency when the state is in compliance with federal mandates. This 2.7 percent rate may be adjusted up or down by the state, depending on its past unemployment insurance payment experience with the particular employer.

A short-time compensation program has recently been introduced into the United States by California. This kind of program has been widely used in Europe for many years. During times of high unemployment, employees share reduced work opportunities by working fewer hours, thus requiring fewer employees to be on layoff. The weeks when employees work a three or four-day work week instead of a normal five-day week, they receive a proportional share of their unemployment insurance for the full days of work lost.

Pension—At the present time, about 50 percent of the nonfarm American work force receive some form of retirement protection from employers through either private pension, deferred profit-sharing plans or thrift/savings plans. In recent years, these private retirement protection programs have increasingly been placed under federal regulations.

The main federal agencies that have review and regulatory influence over private retirement programs are the Labor Department's Office of Welfare and Pension Plans and the Internal Revenue Service (IRS) of the Treasury Department. Some of their authority stemmed initially from the Welfare and Pension Plans Disclosure Act of 1959, as amended, which applied to welfare and pension plans covering more than 25 participants in industries affecting commerce. Welfare plans are those providing medical, surgery, or hospital benefits or care and benefits in the event of sickness, accident, disability, death, or unemployment (not including benefits provided under workers' compensation). The term *pension plan* includes profit-sharing plans providing benefits upon retirement.

In addition to these laws, various tax laws and court rulings over the years have restricted the right of management in the operation and control of their pension programs. The Tax Reform Act of 1969 contained various provisions concerning the taxing of income set aside for the future for retirement purposes. This act, in addition to various IRS policies and regulations, restricts the types of pension plans a business can develop, the benefits involved, and the manner of funding and operating the plans. These IRS policies and regulations cover a range of activites, from pension financing procedures to pension policies that discriminate in favor of highly compensated employees with respect to both coverage and benefits. (A plan is discriminatory unless the contributions for the benefit of lower paid groups covered by the plan are comparable to contributions for the benefit of higher paid employees.)

Pension Reform—During the late 1960s and 1970s, a number of pension plans of American businesses became insolvent. Many workers employed by those businesses at that time and those already retired found their pension plans to be in jeopardy or, at times, worthless. In addition, Senator Jacob Javits of New York stated that there were "three dangerously obsolete assumptions" underlying private U.S. pension plans, as follows:

1. An employee will stay with one company most of his working career.

2. The company can and should use the plan as a "club" to keep the employees.

3. The company will stay in business forever in substantially the same form as when it installed the plan.[16]

To protect pension plans from such failures and obsolete assumptions, leading political figures and government officials initiated plans for reforming private pension plans. Their efforts resulted in the Employee Retirement Income Security Act of 1974 (commonly known as ERISA or the Pension Reform Law). This law establishes fiduciary responsibilities, reporting and disclosure, employee participation and coverage, vesting, funding, limitations on benefits, lump sum distributions, plan termination insurance, and other requirements. There is additional discussion of ERISA requirements in chapter 11. In addition, this law establishes a task force to study the three vesting alternatives of the bill further and to determine the extent of discrimination, if any, among employees in various age groups. The task force will also study means of providing portability of pension rights and other problems resulting from the law. Through 1976, over 10,000 corporate pension plans covering more than 350,000 employees had been terminated because of the additional demands placed on employers by ERISA.[17]

Combining Private Programs with Social Security—Many companies attempt to integrate the benefits provided by their pension plans with those available through Social Security. In 1975, over 7 million retirees received over $14.8 billion from private pension plans; by 1979, almost 19 million retired workers received over $60 billion in Social Security benefits.[18] Because of the dramatic increases in the Social Security premiums paid by employees and employers; the escalator clauses for retirement benefits; and the increased availability of Medicare, Medicaid, and other supplementary benefits, the need

[16]"Compensation Currents: Pension Debate Under Way," *Compensation Review,* Third Quarter 1971, pp. 2–3.

[17]Eugene J. Keogh, "Why Does the Corporation Need to Know About Private Retirement Plans?" 1977 Regional Conference Proceedings, Scottsdale, Ariz.: American Compensation Association; and Charles N. Stabler, "A Closer Look: The New Pension Law May Cut Profits Less Than First Thought," *The Wall Street Journal,* October 1, 1974, pp. 1, 18.

[18]U.S. Department of Commerce, Bureau of the Census, *Statistical Abstract of the United States* (Washington; DC: Government Printing Office, 1981), p. 340, 344.

for coordinating the benefits of private pension plans with Social Security increases.

Some businesses are now providing early retirement programs that offer enlarged pension payments until the retiree reaches the age of 65, at which time, with the start of Social Security payments, the pension payments are reduced. This is but one example of the opportunities available for combining the benefits derived from these two different retirement programs.

With increased government supervision over funding requirements and over the types and security of benefits, some employers may even be forced to abandon private pension plans and look for other forms of benefits with fewer governmental restrictions. When looking for other means of funding employee pensions, employers must recognize that more and more employees view pensions as a right and not as a special benefit.

National Health Insurance—Most American businesses provide some form of health and welfare benefits, including some combination of the following:

1. Life insurance and death benefits.

2. Sickness and accident benefits.

3. Hospitalization and surgical benefits.

4. Medical care, excluding surgery and hospitalization.

The employer, the employee, and the private insurance companies collaborate in providing these benefits. In some cases the employee makes a contribution, and in other cases the business pays the total cost of the premium. (Chapter 11, Employee Benefits and Services, covers this in greater detail.)

The Health Maintenance Organization (IIMO) Act of 1973 requires employers who are subject to the Fair Labor Standards Act and who have 25 or more employees to whom they are now providing health insurance to offer an HMO option if it is available in the area in which the employees reside. HMOs are health-care organizations that provide medical care at a fixed monthly fee. Chapter 11 discusses HMOs in more detail.

At the present time, Congress is working on various forms of national health insurance legislation. It appears that whatever the form, the federal government will continue to play a larger role in financing health care services. Federal intervention in this area will further extend government control of programs that in the past have been primarily controlled by management.

Garnishment of Wages—Another government law that protects the income of the worker is the Federal Wage Garnishment Law, which limits the amount of an employee's disposable earnings that may be garnisheed in any one week and protects the worker from discharge because of garnishment for any one indebtedness. A *garnishment* is a court action or equitable procedure by which earnings of an individual are required to be withheld for the payment of a debt.

The garnishment law identifies *earnings* as compensation paid or payable for personal services, including wages, salary, commission, bonus, and pension or retirement program payments. *Disposable earnings* consist of that part of the earnings remaining after the deduction of any amount required by law, such as the withholdings of federal, state, and local income taxes and federal Social Security tax.

Impact of Wage and Price Controls—The federal government has instituted wage and price controls for use under emergency conditions (e.g., the wage freeze of the Economic Stabilization Act of 1971). Wage controls further restrict an organization in designing its own unique compensation system. Although wage controls have restrictive elements, they need not be strait jackets. Operating within a wage control system, compensation managers must know the legal requirements thoroughly. With this knowledge, it is almost always possible to develop procedures that will stimulate performance by providing special payments to those who make unusual or exceptional contributions.

By providing identical pay increases to all employees (i.e., the 5.5 percent guidelines of the wage and price controls of the early 1970s that became a commonly accepted standard for annual increases for large numbers of American workers), compensation specialists abdicate their responsibilities to recognize contributions of the high-performing employee. Blanket increases of 5.5 percent had a harmful impact on employee performance and in many cases resulted in pay being a "demotivator" rather than a motivator. The standard 5.5 percent increase became, in effect, a normally expected pay increase by all workers with no relationship to improvement in performance or increased productivity of the business. This in fact led to increase in inflation, which wage and price control was designed to limit. However, innovative compensation managers operating within the legal requirements of the controls found ways of distributing pay increases to the most deserving employees, thereby enhancing the motivational value of compensation. For example, one opportunity afforded to a business under the 5.5 percent guidelines was that the business was not required to give a specific raise to an individual employee. Instead, the total raises for all employees could not exceed 5.5 percent of the total wage package of the prior year. Dividing pay increases by a method other than an equal proportion among all employees requires some form of objective performance standards and methods for measuring employee performance against these standards. The division of a lump sum among individual employees requires the innovative talents of skilled compensation designers and wise operating managers.

Tax Treatment Legislation—In the past, most of the statutes of tax reform legislation have had minimal impact on the majority of workers. Most tax legislation has related to sheltering income from current income tax payments and has focused principally on stock options and other estate-building benefits for executives.

Congressional concern mounts each year over which components of the compensation package should be exempted from tax payments on earned income. The Tax Reform Act of 1976 redefined legal, tax-exempt benefits received by employees. The changes in tax exemptions relate to the (1) elimination of sick pay as a tax-deductible, employer-sponsored disability benefit; (2) elimination of tax-deductible, employer-paid attendance to more than two foreign conventions in one taxable year and limitations on travel and subsistence rates to these conventions; and (3) ability to offer prepaid legal services that are tax-deductible to the employer and nontaxable to the employee.

The Revenue Act of 1978 further affects the compensation practices and plans of employers. This act substantially reduces taxes on long-term capital gains for individual taxpayers. Provisions of the act also affect various types of benefits employers provide to their employees.

In the coming years, Congress will scrutinize even more closely the wide range of nontaxable benefits offered by employers to their employees. Many of these current benefits will be considered to be earned income and will add to the tax burden of each worker. As these changes take place, employers and employees will take a much closer look at their benefits programs and make changes that will increase the effectiveness of the benefits while reducing tax burdens to both employers and employees.

Government Welfare Legislation—Current welfare programs and contemplated guaranteed income programs directly influence the wage structure of American businesses. Any government program that provides a person with the option of accepting some form of financial benefit other than that gained from employment indirectly and subtly establishes a minimum wage for any business offering a job to that individual.

The present welfare system began during the depression years of 1929 to 1939. Since its inception, the public welfare system has focused attention on such government-sponsored programs as (1) aid to families with dependent children, (2) aid to the permanently and totally disabled, (3) old-age assistance, (4) medical assistance programs, (5) food programs, (6) rent subsidies, and (7) training programs for persons with low incomes. These programs have frequently been accused of fostering idleness and laziness, but, conversely, proponents just as emphatically state that it is the responsibility of society to be receptive to and to satisfy the basic needs of all its citizens.

In recent years, some states have made major improvements in their welfare programs by findings jobs for those who can work.[19] These states have taken the position that any job is acceptable as long as it meets state and federal standards for wages and working conditions. In addition, these states have improved the provision of welfare services to those who cannot work.

In the past two decades, there have been various state and federal experiments with some form of guaranteed annual income to replace the various welfare programs. Guaranteed annual income would provide cash grants to families having incomes below certain prescribed minimums. Such unresolved issues as benefit levels, the rate of reducing benefit payments relative to outside

---

[19]"How a State with Lots of Poor Is Getting People Off Welfare," *U.S. News and World Report,* October 1, 1973, pp. 33–35.

earnings, and work requirements have blocked the replacement of the current welfare system by the guaranteed annual income plans.

GOVERNMENT INTERVENTION: A POSITIVE EFFECT

The changing nature of work combined with the increasing aspirations and expectations of American workers requires employers to take a second look at social legislation. With the urgent need for improving productivity, organizations must design compensation systems that reward performance and at the same time provide acceptable levels of security for all their members. Security has both absolute and relative components. Organizations frequently fail to recognize the impact that security deprivation has on an employee.

To some degree, federal and state legislation forces organizations to recognize and meet the minimal financial security standards of their employees. By providing a wide variety of programs that meet almost every security-related contingency affecting employees' physiological and psychological basic needs, the organization gives its employees the freedom to develop a cooperative attitude. Otherwise, only under managerial pressures and various types of threats, either explicit or implicit, will most workers provide the services necessary to achieve objectives and goals. Under such conditions, close supervision is mandatory. However, most jobs in American organizations require the employee to take responsible action within relatively broad areas of independent problem solving and decision making. Under such conditions, workers will perform well when there is basic trust between themselves and their managers, and vice versa. A basic cornerstone for such trust is economic security, a continuing reason for government intervention in methods of compensating employees.

Once organizations provide reasonable (to the worker) guarantees for economic security, they can then engage in other programs that improve and heighten the level of employee performance. Some of these programs might be better working conditions, opportunities for advancement through employee training, development leading to promotional opportunities (lateral as well as vertical), and productivity bargaining (in which the worker's mental as well as physical efforts provide valuable contributions for improving performance).

SELECTED READINGS

Analysis of Workers' Compensation Laws: 1980 Edition. Washington, DC: U.S. Chamber of Commerce, 1980. This is an annual publication that provides general information on workers' compensation and an in-depth, state-by-state analysis of the coverage of laws, the benefits provided, the administration of laws, and other special reports.

Asher, Robert, "Business and Workers' Welfare in the Progressive Era: Workmen's Compensation Reform in Massachusetts, 1880–1911," *Business History Review,* Winter 1969, pp. 452–475. An interesting history of the joint efforts of labor and management that resulted in social reforms and the passage of the workmen's compensation law in 1911—often called the "first victory for the idea of the modern welfare state in the United States."

Beirn, Barnet N., "Pension Funding: A Nontechnical Explanation," *Compensation Review,* Third Quarter 1972, pp. 17–24. Although pension funding is a highly complicated process requiring the knowledge of experts, managers with less expertise must have at least a working acquaintance with the procedures and processes. This article uses a hypothetical case to illustrate the fact that various funding methods can produce the same results. It is the actuarial assumptions adopted by the company that determine its funding cost.

Feldstein, Martin S., "Unemployment Insurance: Time for Reform," *Harvard Business Review,* March–April 1975, pp. 51–61. The author contends that it is time to restructure unemployment insurance programs that have not kept up with the times. He suggests structural changes that will eliminate the disincentive elements in the current programs while substantially improving the protection of the unemployed.

Higgins, Robert C., "Income Maintenance and the Welfare Dilemma," *University of Washington Business Review,* Summer 1970, pp. 14–23. A review of current criticisms of public assistance programs and proposed alternatives that analyzes the benefits and costs of some of some of these alternatives.

Highlights of the New Pension Reform Law. Washington, DC: Bureau of National Affairs, September 5, 1974. A text of the Employee Retirement Income Security Act of 1974 with a summary and explanatory statements. It covers the pension reform law that sets minimum standards for protecting employee pension rights. The law ensures that employees who are covered by private pension plans receive benefits from those plans in accordance with their credited years of service with their employer.

Keating, Richard C., "Employee Expectations in Private Pension Plans," *Pension and Welfare News,* November 1971, pp. 45–48, 51. A report on the results of a survey that investigated the pension expectations of participants in private pension plans.

1974 Guidebook to Fair Employment Practices. Chicago, IL: Commerce Clearing House, Inc., February 1974. A brief, practical guide to equal rights laws in the field of employment. This guidebook provides a comprehensive and practical look at what the fair employment law requires and the way those affected by the law can comply with it.

"The Minimum Wage, or How Not to Help the Poor," *Monthly Economic Letter: First National City Bank,* New York: December 1971, pp. 8–10. This article discusses the way the net effect of previous minimum wage legislation has increased unemployment among unskilled workers, especially among nonwhite teenagers among whom the rate has risen to unacceptably high levels.

U.S. Department of Labor, *Comparison of State Unemployment Insurance Laws.* Washington, DC: Government Printing Office, January 1974. Although unemployment insurance was established under the Social Security Act, each state is free (while meeting certain federal standards) to develop its own program. This report, developed by the Manpower Administration, Unemployment Insurance Service, surveys state by state the types of workers and employers that are covered under the state laws, the methods of financing the program, the benefits that are payable, the conditions to be met for payment, and the administrative organizations established to do the job.

4

Union Influences

CONTENT

Chapter 4 reviews past, current, and future union activities and the ways they influence the operations of the organization. This chapter particularly focuses on the impact union activities have on the design of the compensation system and on the job of its manager.

GOALS

Upon concluding the chapter, you should have a basic understanding of union attitudes, the direct influence unions wield over the compensation system of any unionized organization, and the indirect influence they have on the similar systems of nonunionized organizations. In addition, you should have developed an appreciation of the necessity for involving union members (remember, they are *employees*) in designing and implementing the compensation program for a unionized organization.

In 1935 the United States Congress passed legislation that has had far-reaching impact on the operation of American organizations. The National Labor Relations Act of 1935, or the Wagner Act as it is often known, legitimized the labor movement and gave it legal protection. It gave employees the right to self-organization, to bargain collectively through representatives of their own choosing, and to engage in concerted activities for the purpose of collective bargaining or other mutual aid or protection. This act also created the National Labor Relations Board (NLRB) to oversee employer practices and to ensure that employees receive the rights granted under this act.

The union movement in the United States, like its counterparts in Europe, grew from the uniting of journeymen craftworkers who were seeking protection from the arbitrary decisions and harsh treatment meted out by the masters in their respective trades. A union movement worthy of recognition arose in the United States as early as the 1790s. The first unions were located in the major East Coast cities of Boston, New York, Philadelphia, and Baltimore and involved journeymen craftworkers in such trades as carpentry, shoemaking, tailoring, and printing.[1] Their first efforts focused on establishing the minimum wages to be paid journeymen and the amount of hours they were to work and on regulating the supply of apprentices entering a trade. From this start in the early history of the United States, the labor movement has been marked by many peaks and valleys and hard-fought battles on the way to gaining legal recognition and national acceptance.

A group of Philadelphia journeymen carpenters gave the following reason for the existence of early unions: "All men have a just right, derived from their creator to have sufficient time each day for the cultivation of their mind and self improvement; therefore, resolved that we think ten hours industriously imployed are sufficient for a day's labor."[2] The union movement in the major Eastern seaboard cities was strong enough by the mid-1800s to secure a 10-hour day for many trade workers.

In 1866 the National Labor Union was organized with its major goal being the establishment of an eight-hour day. The general public and the major union of this period, the Knights of Labor, failed to give full support to this movement. In fact, the lack of public support also led to the decline and final demise of the Knights of Labor. A new, more powerful union movement arose in 1886 when a number of craft unions formed the American Federation of Labor (AFL). The first president of the AFL, Samuel Gompers, said in 1890, "We want eight hours, we are determined to have eight hours. . . ."

Common law, court rulings, and, eventually, the Sherman Antitrust Act of 1896 effectively blocked union efforts to organize a large mass of American workers. Even with these barriers, the union movement made great inroads into some of the major areas of commerce and industry. Because of their strength in

---

[1] Richard L. Rowan, "The Influence of Collective Bargaining on Hours," In Clyde E. Dankert, Floyd C. Mann, and Herbert R. Northrup (eds.), *Hours of Work* (New York: Harper & Row, 1965), p. 19.

[2] Ibid., p. 18.

these areas of business and their ability to call strikes, unions posed a threat to the country's economy.

From the early 1900s until 1933, union membership varied from a peak of over 5 million members in the early 1920s to slightly over 2 million in 1933. With the passing of the National Industrial Recovery Act (NIRA) in 1933, a form of unionization developed that was not normally found in the AFL—the industrial union. Whereas the craftworkers' union covered only members of specific crafts, the industrial union sought to organize all workers in a plant, a company, or an industry, regardless of occupation.

In 1938 the AFL expelled member unions that joined the Committee for Industrial Organization (CIO), and this split lasted until 1955 when these two major confederations of unions rejoined forces to become the AFL-CIO. Today, however, some of the largest and most powerful unions are not members of the AFL-CIO, including the largest union in the United States—the International Brotherhood of Teamsters. Other nonmembers include the United Mineworkers of America, the United Electrical Workers Union, and the International Longshoremen's and Warehousemen's Union.

The union movement in 1978 consisted of 174 organizations classified as labor unions and 37 organizations classified as professional and state employee associations. Of these organized bodies, 108 are members of the AFL-CIO. In 1978 the labor unions had approximately 21.7 million members, and the associations had approximately 2.6 million. In 1978 the AFL-CIO had an approximate membership of 17.0 million in a work force that totaled more than 100 million members.[3] Figure 4-1 describes union membership as a percentage of the total labor force and table 4-1 lists numbers of union members and union memberships as a percentage of the total labor force.

A September 18, 1981, U.S. Department of Labor Release, noted an actual decline in membership in labor organizations headquartered in the United States between 1978 and 1980. While the total labor force increased from 102.5 million in 1978 to 106.8 million in 1980, the U.S. membership in labor unions during this period declined from 22.8 million to 22.4 million. This small decline in union membership is not as significant as the decline in percent of union members in the total labor force from 1970 to 1980.

Although the union movement derives its strength and influence from its members, the workers' ability to organize and to bargain collectively with their employers stems from the National Labor Relations Act (NLRA) and its two major amendments—the Labor Management Relations Act of 1947 (the Taft-Hartley Act) and the Labor-Management Reporting and Disclosure Act of 1959 (the Landrum-Griffin Act). The Taft-Hartley Act, an amendment to the Wagner Act, principally related to extending government intervention into labor relations. It recognized the right to refrain from or engage in concerted union activities, thus outlawing closed-shop agreements, although it did permit union shops except where prohibited by state laws. The "right to work" laws of a number of states resulted from this act. It also defined certain union unfair labor practices as well as further definitions of employer rights. Furthermore, it

[3]U.S. Department of Labor, Bureau of Labor Statistics, *Directory of National Unions and Employee Associations,* 1979 (Washington, DC: Government Printing Office, 1977), pp. 55–57.

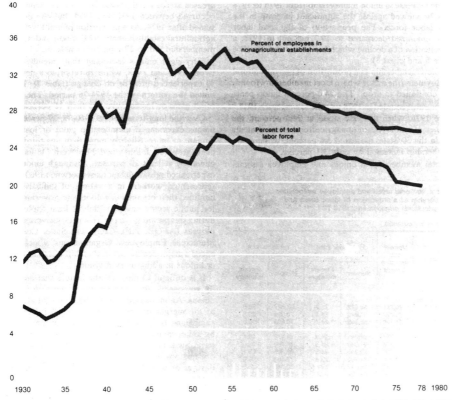

FIGURE 4-1   UNION MEMBERSHIP AS A PERCENTAGE OF TOTAL LABOR FORCE AND
OF EMPLOYEES IN NONAGRICULTURAL ESTABLISHMENTS, 1930–78
Source: U.S. Department of Labor, Bureau of Labor Statistics Bulletin 2079, Directory of National
Unions and Employee Associations, 1979 (Washington, DC: U.S. Government Printing Office,
1980), p. 60.

established the Federal Mediation and Conciliation Services (FMCS) as an
independent government agency. The Landrum-Griffin Act was intended to
protect the rights of union members and was considered to be "the Bill of
Rights" of members of labor organizations. In order to enhance these rights, the
act declared as essential that labor organizations and their officials adhere to the
highest standards of responsibilities and ethical conduct in administering the
affairs of their organizations, particularly as these affected labor-management
relations. It defined in specific terms these ethical standards and procedures for
guaranteeing the safeguard of the rights of union members.

Although the NLRA initially had five titles, the one that most affects
compensation management is Title I. Title I established the National Labor
Relations Board (NLRB), the procedures for determining the exclusive bargaining agent of employees in the bargaining unit, and the conduct of employers,
unions, and their agents that constitutes unfair labor practices.

The purpose of the National Labor Relations Act was to reduce the
number of labor disputes by recognizing the legitimate rights of both employers
and employees involved in negotiations relating to wages, working time, time off

TABLE 4-1

UNION MEMBERSHIP AND ITS NUMBER IN THE TOTAL LABOR FORCE[a]
(NUMBERS IN THOUSANDS)

Year	Membership Excluding Canada	Total Labor Force		Employees in Nonagricultural Establishments	
		Number	Percentage of Members	Number	Percentage of Members
Unions and associations:					
1968	20,721[b]	82,272	25.2	67,897	30.5
1969	20,776	84,240	24.7	70,384	29.5
1970	21,248	85,903	24.7	70,880	30.0
1971	21,327	86,929	24.5	71,214	29.9
1972	21,657	88,991	24.3	73,675	29.4
1973	22,276	91,040	24.5	76,790	29.0
1974	22,809	93,240	24.5	78,265	29.1
1975	22,361	94,793	23.6	77,364	28.9
1976	22,662	96,917	23.4	80,048	28.3
1977	22,456	99,534	22.6	82,423	27.2
1978	22,880	102,537	22.3	84,446	27.1
Unions:					
1958	17,029	70,275	24.2	51,324	33.2
1959	17,117	70,921	24.1	53,268	32.1
1960	17,049	72,142	23.6	54,189	31.5
1961	16,303	73,031	22.3	53,999	30.2
1962	16,586	73,442	22.6	55,549	29.9
1963	16,524	74,571	22.2	56,653	29.2
1964	16,841	75,830	22.2	58,283	28.9
1965	17,299	77,178	22.4	60,765	28.5
1966	17,940	78,893	22.7	63,901	28.1
1967	18,367	80,793	22.7	65,803	27.9
1968	18,916	82,272	23.0	67,897	27.9
1969	19,036	84,240	22.6	70,384	27.0
1970	19,381	85,903	22.6	70,880	27.3
1971	19,211	86,929	22.1	71,214	27.0
1972	19,435	88,991	21.8	73,675	26.4
1973	19,851	91,040	21.8	76,790	25.9
1974	20,199	93,240	21.7	78,265	25.8
1975	19,553	94,793	20.6	77,364	25.3
1976	19,634	96,917	20.3	80,048	24.5
1977	19,902	99,534	20.0	82,423	24.1
1978	20,246	102,537	19.7	84,446	24.0

[a]Source: U.S. Department of Labor Statistics, *Directory of National Unions and Employee Associations,* 1979 (Washington, D.C.: Government Printing Office, 1980), p. 59.
[b]Totals include reported membership and directly affiliated local union members. Total reported Canadian membership and members of single-firm unions are excluded.

with pay, job and income security, working conditions, and quality of work life. The act defines and protects the rights of employees and employers, encourages collective bargaining, and eliminates certain practices on the part of labor and management that are harmful to the general welfare.

The NLRB administers and enforces the act and has two major responsibilities:

1. To conduct representation elections and certify the results.

2. To prevent employers and unions from engaging in unfair labor practices.

Some employers are exempted from the jurisdiction of the NLRB by statute, and others are exempted through testing procedures based on a dollar volume of business for a 12-month period.

MAJOR INFLUENCES IN COMPENSATION PRACTICES

Over the years, various unions have been leaders in improving compensation components related to wages, time off with pay, income security, and conditions affecting the quality of work life. During collective bargaining negotiations, certain unions have made demands that have enabled their members to be front-runners among American workers with regard to some of the compensation components they receive.[4]

Wages

Historically, the number one issue in collective bargaining has been the determination of the wage rate. Since the 1930s, the more powerful unions, typically those having large memberships and representing workers in large, usually profitable organizations (auto, tires, cans, petroleum refining, trucking, steel, aluminum, rail, and coal) have been able to demand and obtain larger than average wage and benefit settlements for their members. Beginning in the 1960s, the hourly wages negotiated between the large manufacturers and their representative unions began to increase significantly over the average rates of pay earned by all manufacturing workers. In 1967, the previously identified workers employed in nine major industries with large union membership received hourly wages that were 19 percent above the all-manufacturing average. By January 1981, the hourly wage differential rose to 46 percent.[5] Among the highest-paid industrial workers are those in the steel industry. In January 1981, the average hourly earnings of a steel mill worker was $12.40.

---

[4]Characteristics and terms of major collective bargaining agreements are obtainable from the U.S. Department of Labor, Bureau of Labor Statistics, and from such major business publication firms as Bureau of National Affairs, Rockville, MD, Commerce Clearing House, Chicago, IL, and Prentice-Hall, Inc., Englewood Cliffs, NJ.

[5]U.S. Department of Labor, Bureau of Labor Statistics. Employment and Earnings April 1981 (Washington, DC: Goverment Printing Office, 1981), pp. 117–133.

In the 1960s, most manufacturers were able quickly and easily to pass on these increased labor costs to the consumer by increasing the sales price of their products. However, by the early 1970s, the steel industry was already having trouble passing on increased prices because Japanese and European steel manufacturers were actively competing with United States steel companies for available business. Then, in the late 1970s and early 1980s, Japanese auto manufacturers became a threat, not only to the profitability but to the survival of the American auto manufacturers as they produced more fuel-efficient cars and sold them at lower prices than those produced by American manufacturers.

In response to their inability to compete with foreign competitors, large American organizations in a variety of industries have requested wage concessions from their unions.

Voluntary constraint by major unions in demanding higher wages or even reducing current wages and thereby reducing the prices of the product of the company—although not revolutionary—is not granted with enthusiasm. Sufficient evidence is available, however, to support the fact that when unions and their representative companies are having survival problems, both sides are making concessions.

When union members in the building and construction trade found their contractors having trouble with nonunionized contractors, agreements were reached to lower union contractor costs without seriously reducing the income of the unionized workers. Concessions have taken such forms as (1) a freeze on the hourly rate for a specified period of time or for the life of a particular contract, (2) a reduction in overtime rates of pay, and (3) an elimination or a reduction of pay increases based on cost-of-living adjustments.

With ever-increasing world competition in the area of available resources and in the sales of goods and services, unions will be forced into being more careful regarding their wage demands. Management will have to be just as careful concerning the demands they accept.

Time Off with Pay

Over the past 30 years, the drive to reduce working hours and total time spent at work has focused on providing workers with more paid holidays and longer vacations. In negotiations with the automobile industry in 1947, the United Automobile Workers (UAW) made a major breakthrough when it gained six paid holidays for its members in that industry.

The UAW-General Motors contract agreement for the period September 14, 1979 to September 14, 1982 granted employees with 20 years of seniority 20 days of paid vacation, 14 paid holidays (1981–1982), including an unbroken Christmas-New Year break, and nine paid personal holidays.

Since the early 1960s, the UAW has had as a long-range objective the achievement of an eight-hour, four-day work week for its members. Securing 43 days off with pay for many of its members has been considered by UAW officials to be a strong step in this direction.

Improvement in vacation opportunities has been pioneered by the United Steel Workers of America (USWA). A significant change in vacation patterns was established in the extended vacation program developed between the United States Steel Corporation and the USWA. In this program, each mill divides its force into two equal components, using seniority as an index. The junior group receives a six-week vacation once each five years, and the senior group receives a 13-week vacation once each five years. Twenty percent of each group take their extended vacation each year. This program is now in its second five-year cycle. In USWA contracts with aluminum producers, this extended vacation benefit has been slightly modified to give workers with 15 years' seniority a 10-week vacation, but these workers still receive pay for 13 weeks of work.

American workers not only enjoy more vacation time off but are now able to take their vacations in months other than the traditional July and August.

Decreasing levels of productivity and increasing prices for goods and services are results of these additional paid holidays and vacations. The major way for employers to counteract these increased labor costs is to invest more capital equipment (i.e., improved technology) that reduces labor requirements. This solution, however, may result in higher rates of unemployment, at least on a temporary basis, which then causes social problems. To alleviate these problems, public programs must be initiated, causing heavier tax burdens on employers and workers to subsidize the unemployed. That, in turn, results in higher costs for goods and services.

Income Security

A promise each union makes to its members is to provide them with the greatest possible income security. Union officials have negotiated a number of different types of agreements to achieve this plank in their platforms. Among them, none has provided more security than the Guaranteed Annual Income (GAI) plan. An agreement reached in 1950 between the National Sugar Refining Company and the union representing its employees at the Long Island refinery was an early development in this area. This contract required that an employee working on Monday be assured wages for at least four days in that week. The next year at its Philadelphia refinery, the first guaranteed annual wage program went into operation. This program guaranteed each member of the bargaining unit 1,936 hours or 242 days of work a year. On an average, workers work between 230 and 245 days a year, depending on their vacations and paid holiday programs.[6]

In the mid-1960s, the International Longshoremen's Association (ILA) negotiated a Guaranteed Annual Income (GAI) plan to provide income security for workers displaced by the change to containerization. Under a collective bargaining agreement that commenced October 1, 1980 and ends September 30, 1983, New York dockworkers receive 2,080 guaranteed hours of pay at the rate of $11.60 per hour for the 1980–1981 period. The rate of pay increases to $14 per hour for the 1982–1983 period.

[6]Harvey A. Young and Michael F. Dougherty, "Influence of the Guaranteed Annual Wage upon Labor Relations and Productivity: National Sugar Refinery's Experience," *Management of Personnel Quarterly,* Winter 1971, pp. 27–32.

Those dockworkers not having been notified of a job for the next day must appear at the union hiring hall by 7:00 A.M. and insert a plastic badge into a computerized system. If they do not receive a call for work, they can check out by 9:00 A.M. and still receive eight hours of pay for that day. Employees who fail to badge-in or to report for their daily assignments receive a debit. The accumulation of a certain number of debits can result in total loss of GAI for the year in which it occurs.

The hours of guaranteed work for dockworkers varies by seaport cities. In Baltimore and Philadelphia, it is 1,900 hours; Hampton Roads, 1,800; Boston, 1,800. Port cities along the western Gulf of Mexico guarantee an average of about 900 hours of pay a year, although the 1980 contract establishes a scale for New Orleans that ranges from 700 to 2,080 hours. The actual GAI received by a specific individual depends on the number of hours worked on an average of the three preceding contract years. Houston dockworkers' scale ranges from 1,000 to 2,080 hours depending on the hours worked in the immediate preceding contract year.[7] The GAI benefit of 2,080 hours provided by New York port employers is estimated to cost them between $40 and $47 million annually.[8] This benefit provides a competitive cost advantage to southern ports and may account for these ports having a faster freight tonnage growth than northern ports during the late 1960s and 1970s.

Another major breakthrough in the area of income security was a Guaranteed Annual Income plan developed between the Ford Motor Company and the UAW in 1955.[9] This plan became known as a Supplemental Unemployment Benefits (SUB) plan because it supplemented unemployment benefits instead of providing a guaranteed annual income. Unions representing workers in the manufacture of steel, rubber, flat glass, and farm equipment added SUB programs to their union contracts in the mid-1950s. The SUB program adopted by Ford and the UAW has been accepted as standard by the UAW and has been copied by other businesses interested in such a program.

The initial 1955 program guaranteed qualified workers (qualified relates strictly to seniority) 62 percent of their annual pay plus $1.50 a week per dependent (up to four) in addition to their regular state unemployment

[7]"Dockworker Loses License as New York Investigates Improper Use of Pay Benefit," *The Wall Street Journal,* Sept. 7, 1977, p. 7; John D. Williams, "Talks on New Dockworkers Pact Slated to Resume, Ending Three-Week Impasse," *The Wall Street Journal,* September 8, 1977, p. 4; personal correspondence from Thomas W. Gleason, International President, International Longshoremen's Association, July 21, 1981.

[8]John D. Williams, "Dock Workers Slated to Vote Tomorrow On New 3-Year Contracts, May End Strike," *The Wall Street Journal,* November 28, 1977, p. 26; John D. Williams, "Dock Union Says Workers Voted End to Walkout," *The Wall Street Journal,* November 30, 1977, p. 30. Personal correspondence from Thomas W. Gleason, International President, International Longshoremen's Association, July 21, 1981.

[9]Norma Pope and Paul A. Brinker, "Recent Developments with the Guaranteed Annual Wage: The Ford Settlement," *Labor Law Journal,* September 1968, pp. 555–562.

insurance. This program was modified in 1965, and those modifications are still in effect.

97
Union Influences

The 1965 program allows each worker to receive half of a Guaranteed Annual Income (GAI) unit for each week worked from the date of hire to a maximum of 52 units. Normally, for each unit given up, a worker receives one week of SUB payment. A worker with less than one year of employment is not eligible for SUB payment. The guarantee period increases until the worker has seven years of employment, at which time all the benefits of the plan accrue. Although the program basically permits a worker to receive one week of SUB payments for each earned GAI unit, it also requires that the SUB fund be at a prescribed level before this happens. The 1974 General Motors SUB fund requires that it have $382.50 per employee in reserve before any worker with 52 GAI units can receive a full year of benefits. In September 1974 the fund had been reduced to $291 per employee. This reduction below the $382.50 minimum requires employees with less than 5 years of service to give up 1.43 units per benefit week, thus allowing them only 36.4 weeks of SUB benefits. It requires workers with five to ten years of service to give up 1.25 credits and receive 41.6 weeks of SUB benefits. Workers receive 95 percent of their after-tax weekly pay less $7.50 for nonincurred, work-related expenses, such as their lunch and transportation to and from work. The unexpected huge layoffs in the automobile industry in 1974–1975 resulted in the depletion of both the Chrysler and General Motors SUB fund accounts in 1975, causing the auto workers to depend completely on state unemployment benefits.[10]

The 1976 contract between General Motors (GM) and the UAW called for changes in the SUB agreement to overcome weaknesses in the system that appeared during the major 1974–1975 layoffs in the automobile industry. GM agreed to increase company payments into the SUB fund from a range of 9¢ to 14¢ to a range of 14¢ to 24¢ an hour for each union employee. The 1979–1982 agreement between UAW and General Motors further increased SUB financing to 17¢ to 29¢. Employees with 10 or more years of service gained additional protection by the establishment of a backup SUB fund that will pay benefits to those employees with high seniority if the regular fund for all workers drops below the level required for payments to continue.

The 1980 SUB agreement between USWA and the steel industry granted steel workers $180 a week plus $1.50 for each of up to four dependents for those workers receiving state unemployment insurance and $235 for those not receiving state unemployment insurance.

A major addition in the SUB program came with the 1977 contract negotiated between USWA and the three big aluminum producers (Alcoa, Kaiser, and Reynolds). This pact established a three-tier inflation security plan. In this plan, all employees receive a guaranteed short-week (i.e., less than 40 hours of work in a specific week) benefit regardless of the condition of the SUB fund. This pact calls for an increase in the SUB allowance. In addition to the

---

[10]"GM Fund Runs Dry This Week," *The Atlanta Constitution,* May 5, 1975, p. 9A.

SUB fund, which guarantees a certain level of earnings to an unemployed worker, an Income Maintenance Program was established to provide a minimum level of income for employees who are downgraded or demoted to a lower level job.

In case of downgrading, Tier I employees—those with two to ten years of service—will receive at least 85 percent of their former pay. Tier II employees—those with 10 to 20 years of service—will receive at least 90 percent of their former pay. Tier III employees—those with over 20 years of service—will receive 95 percent of their pay. The 1980 contract increased the income protection for Tier I employees to 90 percent and for Tier II employees to 95 percent, the same as already being received by Tier III employees.

The SUB plan promoted by USWA was further improved in the 1977 contract negotiated between USWA and the four major can companies (American Can, Continental Can, National Can, and Crown Cork & Seal). This plan guarantees all laidoff workers with 10 years of service 104 weeks (2 years) of SUB payments regardless of the condition of the SUB fund and an additional 156 weeks (three years) of SUB payments if SUB funds permit.[11]

Severance Pay

When workers are permanently displaced as a result of plant closings, technological advances, or economic depressions, they may receive a payment to assist in maintaining a standard of living until new employment is found. Unions have been active in obtaining severance pay protection for their members. The actual amount and timing of receipt of such payment vary significantly. A severance payment may be equal to two or three days of work or as much as the pay for six months or one year of work. Small severance payments are usually made the last day of work, while large severance payments may be made at two or three different times. With the combination of rapid and extensive technological changes and extreme worldwide competition in the sales of goods and services, severance pay protection will become an increasingly more important issue.

Cost-of-Living Adjustments (COLAs)

In recent years, a major thrust of union activities in the field of compensation has been to protect the "real wages" of union members by placing escalator clauses in union contracts.[12] An escalator clause, which is a cost-of-living adjustment (COLA), normally permits at least one wage review each year and a pay raise if it is warranted by an increase in the cost of living. The escalator clause has been an expensive addition (from the perspective of employers) to practically every major union-management contract. Most escalator clauses use

---

[11] " 'Lifetime Security,' " *Business Week,* November 14, 1977, p. 56.

[12] "Real wages" represents the actual purchasing power of pay. In times of high inflation when the rate of inflation is greater than the pay increases of the worker, the real wages have actually diminished even though the actual wages may have increased.

the Consumer Price Index (CPI), which was developed and is maintained by the Bureau of Labor Statistics (BLS) of the U.S. Department of Labor as a standard for measuring change in real income.[13]

In February 1978 the BLS introduced two new CPIs to replace the existing one. The replaced CPI, as updated, had been in existence for over 50 years. The two new indexes are the Consumer Price Index for All Urban Families (Urban Family Index or CPI-U) and the Consumer Price Index for Urban Wage Earners and Clerical Workers (Urban Wage Earner Index or CPI-W). The CPI-U covers approximately 80 percent of the population of the United States, and the CPI-W covers approximately 50 percent of the population of the United States. The CPI-W relates more closely to the replaced CPI. The two new indexes incorporate changes made in the pricing techniques and the methodological changes made in market basket samples, the collection and pricing of goods in the sample, and the ways of analyzing the data. The indexes cover daily life-style out-of-pocket expenses incurred by urban families and urban wage earners. As many as 4,000 individual items may be reviewed every month for determining changes in cost patterns. The items are grouped within such major item classes as food and beverages, housing, apparel and upkeep, transportation, medical care, entertainment, and other goods and services.

Many union officials expressed a fear that a new single, enlarged CPI would smooth out differences in the consumption pattern of different income groups, especially for such items as foods and services. They stated that any index covering 80 percent or more of the population would actually understate the cost of living for urban wage earners and clerical workers. Because this type of worker comprises a large percentage of union membership and with over 7.5 million workers covered by escalator clauses normally tied to the CPI, it is easy to see why union leaders voiced concern over the enlarged urban family index and were responsible for pressuring the BLS to produce two CPIs. This type of pressure is typical of union opposition to any issue or program that may jeopardize or lessen the income security of their members.

In the early 1980s, another problem arose concerning COLAs. With the economy suffering through two years of double-digit inflation, a number of experts accused the CPI of exaggerating the inflation rate.[14] With the COLA doing exactly what it was designed to do—protecting the real wages of employees by granting automatic adjustments to the wages based on cost-of-living changes—it was not only protecting those workers but fueling the flames of inflation by adding to product costs, which, in turn, increased product prices for everyone.

A major problem related to the use of a COLA, especially when only certain groups of employees have their income protected, is that a rate-

---

[13]U.S. Department of Labor, *The Consumer Price Index: A Short Description* (Washington, DC: Government Printing Office, 1971), along with annual updates and changes, provides a basic understanding of the CPI.

[14]"Agency Defends Consumer Price Index But Will Study Other Inflation Measures," *The Wall Street Journal,* January 22, 1980, p. 6.

of-inflation indicator like the CPI does not apply equally to all people. Because of the design of the CPI, those owning their own homes and paying interest on their mortgages at rates below the current rate, those not having to bear the costs of raising children, or those not having high food or clothing expenses may suffer inflationary costs considerably less than people who are living in rental units or who have recently bought homes, and are raising children.

Although CPI-based escalator clauses use a variety of formulae, the one most commonly found is the one that grants a 1¢-per-hour change in the rate of pay for each 0.3 point movement in the CPI. A number of 1980 negotiated contracts call for a 1¢ increase with a point movement of 0.26 in the CPI. This kind of an increase has the problem of "compressing" (making smaller) rates of pay for jobs requiring different skills, efforts, and responsibilities.

Some negotiated escalator clauses have a maximum annual limit or a limit related to the life of the contract (i.e., 8¢ an hour annually or 9 percent of agreed-to base wages over the life of the contract). Much union effort has recently been devoted to gaining acceptance of "topless" or "uncapped" escalator clauses that have no maximum limit.

Another device for relating change in wages to cost-of-living changes is through the use of the "corridor" COLA plan. Under a COLA corridor, wages rise automatically with prices to a certain agreed-on point. Wages then remain unchanged until prices increase to another predetermined point (the corridor). Then when prices go beyond the top level in the corridor, the escalator again takes effect.

A COLA plan agreed to between General Electric and 12 unions called for an increase of 1¢ an hour for each 0.3 percent increase in the CPI. The formula does not function between 7 to 9 percent (the corridor), but if the CPI goes above 9 percent, the COLA once again goes into operation. The COLA corridor is a compromise between a capped or uncapped (topless) COLA.

A major change for improving existing pension plans by adding a partial cost-of-living allowance has been negotiated between the USWA and the three major aluminum companies—Alcoa, Kaiser, and Reynolds. Retired employees receive 65 percent of the average increases payable to production and maintenance employees under their COLA guidelines.

One specialist in the pension field estimates that every one percent increase in COLA will add from 8 to 10 percent to an employer's total pension costs. Another study indicated that from 1967 to 1972 pension costs increased from 4.7 percent to 5.5 percent of payroll cost and from 1.5 percent to 1.7 percent of total expenses. A company that provides full retirement benefits for employees at age 60 instead of 65 could increase pension costs by 50 percent if substantial numbers of employees were to choose to retire at that age.

A second major change contributing to increased pension costs is the 30-year-and-out retirement plan. A 1974 UAW agreement with General Motors permits those employees with at least 30 years of service to receive a $625 monthly pension. This agreement currently has a retirement age limit of 56. There is also a limit to outside earnings. For each $1 retirees earn outside, they

$2 of pension if they earn between $1,680 and $2,880. For earnings over $2,880, there is a $1 reduction in benefits for each $1 earned.

The 1977 agreement between USWA and the steel companies approved the "rule of 65" for determining early retirement. This rule allows workers with at least 20 years of service and whose ages and years of service equal 65 to be granted early retirement if they are affected by extended layoffs, plant shutdowns, or disabilities, and if management does not offer "suitable long-term" employment.

Quality of Work Life

Unions have taken a leading role in upgrading the standard of living of their members by negotiating for improvements in the benefits employers offer to their employees. Many of these benefits strongly influence the quality of work life for all those affected. Some of the major areas of union activity for improving the employees benefits package are discussed in the following paragraphs.

Dental Insurance—Group dental insurance is a major breakthrough. It has been estimated that by 1980 approximately 50 million union and nonunion members and their families participated in group dental insurance benefits. A plan negotiated between the International Harvester Company and the UAW pays 100 percent of the cost for semiannual teeth cleaning; 75 percent of the cost of dental x-rays every three years, as well as of fillings, inlays, and labor in putting on crowns; 50 percent of the cost of false teeth; and up to $500 for orthodontic work.

Group Auto Insurance—One of the more recent additions to the bargaining process has been group auto insurance. Pioneers in this field have been Traveler's Insurance Company, the American Postal Workers Union, and the National Association of Letter Carriers.

Prepaid Legal Insurance—Unions have been a key stimulus in gaining legal insurance for their members. An amendment to the Taft-Hartley Act in 1973 permitted private companies to join with unions to offer legal insurance. After amending the law, prepaid legal insurance became a primary collective bargaining issue.

By the mid-1970s, over 25 labor unions had persuaded employers to help organize and contribute to legal insurance. It has been estimated that by the mid 1980s over 70 percent of all Americans and 50 percent of all lawyers will be involved in group legal insurance plans. These plans currently take a wide variety of forms. One involving members of a Laborer's International Local in Shreveport, Louisiana, requires the member to pay $40 annually. In return, the member receives $100 worth of legal consultation, $250 for office work and research, and up to $325 for court cases. The major uses have been for auto claims, divorce cases, and child custody contests.

Paternity Benefits—A contract between *Newsweek* and the New York Newspaper Guild grants male employees with at least one year of service one week of paternity leave at the birth of a child. This new benefit will probably be offered to more employees in the future.

Vision-care Plan—The UAW-General Motors contract of 1977 provides for eye examinations and free prescription glasses every 12 months and frames once every 24 months for workers and their families.

NLRB RULINGS AND COMPENSATION PRACTICES

Over the past two decades, the National Labor Relations Board (NLRB) and its trial examiners have made a series of rulings that stress the need to involve union officials in the basic elements of the compensation program.[15] A review of a few of these rulings provides a broader appreciation for this need.

Pay Structure—*Shell Development Co.* v. *Association of Industrial Scientists.* Professional Employees.

In order for the union to bargain effectively, the company must provide the union with a written explanation of both salary curves and the merit system, copies of current and past salary curve guides, merit ratings for the bargaining unit employees, and detailed but unidentified lists of individual work assignments, ratings, and salaries.

Salary Disclosure—*Time, Inc.* v. *Newspaper Guild.*
The Newspaper Guild is entitled to know the salary of each employee in the Time, Incorporated bargaining unit. The examiner could find no basis for the company's assumption that employees did not want their salaries disclosed and that the unions had no right to the data.

Wage Discussion—*Jeannette Corp.* v. *NLRB*

A secretary not represented by a union, working for a unionized company that prohibited clerical employees from discussing wages among themselves, discussed her wages with another employee. She was fired for violating the no-wage discussion rule of the company. The NLRB and a U.S. Court of Appeals ruled that the rule and the discharge were illegal. The NLRB and the Court stated that an employer may adopt and enforce a rule prohibiting employee wage discussions during working time, but employees have a legal right to engage in concerted activities for mutual aid and protection. A rule barring wage discussion among employees without any limitation as to time or place would deny freedom of discussion among employees at times and places when such activities could not adversely affect job performance.

---

[15]Most of these rulings have been compiled from current compensation reports in *Compensation Review,* a quarterly publication of the American Management Association and an invaluable journal to anyone involved in compensation management.

In the past, the company had provided the union with wage survey information in connection with grievances but had not identified which rates came from which companies. The board required G.E. to furnish the union with such data, but in the future the board does not require that G.E. reveal the identity of the companies furnishing data to a survey if such data have not been disclosed to it, which protects third-party survey organizations.

Merit Increases

A company was held in violation of the Taft-Hartley Act by continuing, after the certification of a union, its established practices of giving "automatic" and "semiautomatic" merit increases and not giving the union advance notice of the raises. The action of the company violated the portion of the law that affected union rights to bargain on "wages and other conditions of employment."

Bonuses—*Elesco Smelting Corp.* v. *United Steelworkers Union (USWA).*

New ownership of Elesco was required to continue providing a $5 cash payment or a turkey at Thanksgiving and Christmas, as had been a custom for 23 years, and this was not predicated on the company's ability to pay.

Benefits

A. In the process of negotiating a pension plan, a union negotiated an exclusionary contract concerning a company's savings and profit-sharing plan for members of the bargaining unit. This, however, did not preclude those already receiving this benefit from receiving it in the future.
B. A company had to reinstate medical insurance benefits and reimburse employees for any benefits lost when the company unilaterally withdrew coverage during the term of a union contract. The company had sought to prevent employees from duplicating benefits by amending the medical provisions of the agreement to reduce the amount employees would receive if they had other health insurance benefits.

ANALYSIS OF UNION ATTITUDES

Protecting the wages and benefits of its members is a primary union responsibility. In the collective bargaining process, a union devotes much effort and concern to analyzing and questioning the elements of a compensation system and its procedures. Although management frequently criticizes unions for interfering in the development and operation of its pay practices, union complaints are frequently legitimate. The problems that stimulate union "interference" often resemble those causing dissatisfaction in a nonunion organization and frequently are the underlying causes leading to its unionization.

Union Views of Compensation Technology

A review and summary by Edward N. Hay of three articles that appeared in the *American Federationist,* the official publication of the American Federation of Labor, provide insight into organized labor's view in 1947 of the basic mechanics of a compensation program.[16] Surveys and a recent union-based review show no significant change in these views, but they do, however, indicate a renewed interest in this area.[17]

Union leaders almost always fear that any technical system used to evaluate the worth of a job can quickly become a tool for management malpractice. To the untrained, analyzing the worth of a job and developing a pay structure appear to be hopelessly complicated and complex. Moreover, any attempt to reduce complex human factors to a mere mathematical formula is an additional cause for concern among rank-and-file union members. Because of its mathematical base, a compensation system has a disquieting aura of "scientific" precision and permanence. Although achieving precision and permanence is an unattainable goal and compensation managers worth their salt realize that no system will provide an eternally sound relationship among jobs, those who work in the field do strive to develop an accurate and stable system. To do so, they must exercise constant vigilance and maintenance.

Basic Fears and Misunderstandings—A number of basic fears and misunderstandings about the evaluation of a job cause concern among many union leaders and members. First, they feel that no one can judge the relative values of jobs better than the workers themselves. Second, they are unable to understand the use of a fixed number of factors for measuring the value of a job and for establishing wage limits. The means and the methods used for identifying and defining compensable factors are an enigma to the untrained. The assignment of points to the factors magnifies the mystery and increases suspicion that it is only another manipulative device to restrict or lower the pay of workers.

In addition, union members feel that the standards set by an outsider simply do not adequately relate to job differences. This fact is the heart of the reason why each organization must be certain that its compensation system meets its own needs. For these reasons, organizations should request the union members themselves to express their judgment and experience about their jobs. This information will provide a sound foundation for a compensation system.

---

[16]Edward N. Hay, "The Attitude of the American Federation of Labor on Job Evaluation," *Personnel Journal,* November 1947, pp. 163–169.

[17]Howard D. Janes, "Issues in Job Evaluation: The Union View," *Personnel Journal,* September 1972, pp. 675–679; "Union Views on Job Evaluation: 1971 vs. 1978" *Personnel Journal,* February 1979, pp. 80–85; John Zalusky, "Job Evaluation: An Uneven World," *AFL-CIO American Federationist,* April 1981, pp. 11–20.

Union members and leaders sometimes feel that they are at a disadvantage because of the technical training required to develop a compensation system. Although many major unions have staff workers who possess such skill and experience, this expertise often does not exist at the local level and even at times at the national level; union officials not familiar with job evaluation techniques frequently express dissatisfaction with such procedures. It is to the advantage of the organization to keep all union members well informed about the major elements of the compensation package and to educate local union leaders on as many of the basics as possible.

Probably the greatest fear any union member has regarding a management-developed compensation system is that it will block, if not destroy, the collective bargaining process. Collective bargaining is the core of the American labor union movement, and anything that even appears to limit its effectiveness is met with hostility.

Another problem inherent in a well-designed and organized compensation system is that it sets standards. Although unions are not against standards, they do suspect any standard that relates to increased output without an accompanying increase in pay.

INFLUENCING UNION ATTITUDES

Although management is responsible for developing and implementing a compensation system that aids in achieving organizational objectives and goals, it does not have unilateral rights in this area. As pointed out in chapter 3, government regulations have a direct impact on a wage structure. It is equally true that in the unionized organization the union also has a direct and powerful influence.

Through oversights, inability, or unwillingness, management frequently fails to communicate to its unions the essential characteristics and operating procedures of its compensation system. A union has the responsibility for protecting the working rights of its members and for bargaining with management over such issues as methods for evaluating jobs, rates of base pay, overtime and premium pay, incentives, and a wide range of employee benefits. Recognizing this responsibility, management must make sure that union representatives are familiar with not only the components of its compensation system but also the philosophy behind the system.

Although it may be slower and may cause extra problems initially for the compensation manager, a wise approach is to include union representation at every step in the process of building the compensation system. A well-organized, wisely conceived compensation system has nothing to hide from the union. If union disagreements are to arise, it is far better to make acceptable changes before implementation of the system. The extra time and cost involved at this stage are far less than at some later stage. If a program is to be truly workable, it must be understood and accepted. In a union shop, this means union approval. Union hostility and opposition can destroy the best system.

Union Involvement

The best way to gain cooperation in any activity requiring the efforts of diverse groups of individuals is to request and use their active involvement and participation in developing solutions to their problems. Because unions do have a responsibility through the collective bargaining process not only to protect their members but to improve on many of the elements that affect the compensation system both directly and indirectly, the unions should be closely involved in the development and the implementation of the system. Such involvement includes the right to voice opinions regarding, among other things, such factors as the following:

1. What are the work activities of the job?

2. What environmental conditions affect the job?

3. What compensable factors universally relate to all the jobs in the organization?

4. How should compensation survey information be interpreted relative to the jobs in the organization?

5. What is a fair rate of pay for each job?

6. How should seniority be recognized in the compensation system?

7. What type of merit system is acceptable to the union and best for this particular organization?

8. What compensation components should be included in the employee benefits program?

Passive Acceptance and Rejection—It is impossible to state with any degree of accuracy just how a union will interact with management on particular compensation problems. However, a common attitude is one of passive acceptance. The union will accept in theory the need for a compensation system. Normally, the union does not oppose the development of job descriptions, occupational pay rates, or orderly pay rate structures, but the problem with these types of standards relates to their use: Are they to be the standards, or are they to be simply guides for judgment in a later decision-making situation? There is a feeling that any system should be only a guide, with final determination being made through judgment exercised in the collective bargaining process. American unions have traditionally stated that they do not wish to assume the responsibilities of management; they prefer to reserve the right to challenge and criticize management efforts they consider unacceptable. A change in this attitude has occurred in recent years, and labor unions are assuming more important roles in the development of procedures and systems that affect the pay of their members.

In the past, management has found at times that even when unions accepted a pay system in principle, they sabotaged it in operation, thus completely nullifying any real support. A major problem with union involvement as far as the rank and file are concerned is that a compensation system is acceptable when it results in pay increases and unacceptable when it does not. Again, *active* union involvement from the beginning stage of development through implementation can only have a positive effect on improving acceptance of a compensation system. The development of a good compensation system requires the use of the best judgment of *all* members of an organization, including union as well as nonunion members.

Providing Job Security

Although employees join unions for many reasons, foremost among them is a desire for security. Many factors affect security. Current pay; anticipated pay; relationships with superiors, peers, and subordinates; and the employee's physical and emotional states are a few of the more important ones. For most employees, the organization can never completely overcome the possibility of insecurity. However, it can go a long way toward minimizing this basic problem by treating employees fairly and by developing a working environment that tells all employees that their contributions are vital to the success of the organization. When an organization does not offer this kind of security to its members, they will frequently demonstrate an interest in a union. Once unionized, these employees expect their unions to maximize their job security.

FUTURE TRENDS

It is likely that the major changes in labor-management bargaining for the next five years have already been initiated. Some of the important issues that will have an effect on the compensation system are the Experimental Negotiating Agreement (ENA), productivity committees, efficiency improvement, and a variety of pay-for-performance improvement programs.

Experimental Negotiating Agreement (ENA)

In March 1973 the USWA and the 10 major steel companies signed an Experimental Negotiating Agreement under which the union relinquished its right to a national strike in August 1974 when its contract expired. In return for this binding arbitration agreement, the USWA received guarantees of substantial wage increases from the steel companies.

Under the initial ENA, any national issues unresolved by April 15, 1974 would be turned over to a five-man arbitration panel for a final decision. This agreement did not preclude any union local from striking over unresolved local issues. As one steel official said, "All we did is take the crisis out of bargaining; there's still going to be tough negotiations to follow."[18]

[18]Jack H. Morris, "USW Leaders Meet Today to Draft Demands for New Three-Year Steel Industry Contract," *The Wall Street Journal,* January 9, 1974, p. 4.

As a result of the success of the initial ENA, the 10 major steel companies and the USWA agreed to use ENA again in the 1977 negotiations, at which time they agreed to a continuation of ENA in the 1980 negotiations. In addition to agreed-on improvements in benefits and working conditions, all employees affected by the 1974 ENA agreement received a $150 no-strike bonus.

If the ENA spreads beyond the USWA and the steel companies, it will have a definite impact on the compensation process. However, to date there has been little enthusiasm for ENA among other industries and their representative unions. By minimizing the need for crisis decisions, there will be more pressure for well-designed and documented programs and proposals. Agreements negotiated at the last minute frequently become dramatic, and subjective decisions overwhelm well-conceived recommendations. The ENA places far more emphasis on good research, homework, and well-organized proposals.

A major test of the ENA occurred in the fall of 1977 when 17 United Steelworkers locals working in 14 ore mines and several processing plants went on strike. They contended that incentive pay plans are local issues and strikeable but that they are not a nationally bargainable issue. The iron ore workers stated that they earned about 65¢ an hour less than the steel mill workers (about 94 percent of mill workers receive incentive compensation in addition to regular hourly wages), and the ore workers felt that their incentive rates were inadequate. After an extended strike, industry and union officials agreed to an improvement in incentive plans covering 75 percent of the striking workers. The improvement in the incentive plan increased the wages of iron ore workers by approximately 55¢ an hour.

The 1980 agreement between the steel industry and the USWA "decoupled" ENA. In mid 1981, representatives of the steel industry and USWA began discussions concerning the use of the ENA in the negotiation of the 1983 contract. Two major compensation-related issues arose that placed the continued existence of the ENA in jeopardy. Steel industry representatives felt that the steelworkers should not receive the usual 3 percent wage boost since that increase was tied to traditional industry productivity gains and, from the perspective of management, improvement in productivity came from the use of better equipment, not from the harder work of the steelworkers. These representatives also wanted to substitute some kind of a profit-sharing arrangement for the expensive COLA, but union representatives were unlikely to give up the certain protection offered by the COLA agreement for the uncertainty related to any steel industry profit-sharing program. Continuing negotiation by the steel industry and USWA representatives will assess the value of ENA and determine if it will be used in the 1982 bargaining.

Productivity Committees

The USWA has also played a major role in establishing labor-management productivity committees. The 1971 contract between USWA and the steel companies provided for productivity committees at most plants. These committees were designed to encourage the highest possible degree of friendly, cooperative relationships between all levels of management and labor. Even with such a lofty goal, this pioneering union effort to improve working relations between management and the operative employees has been met with skepticism by many rank-and-file members, many of whom suspiciously feel that it is just another management tool to force employees to work harder and produce more with no increase in pay. By the end of 1972, there were only 230 functioning productivity committees among the approximately 1,400 locals in the steel industry. The initial productivity committees were plant-wide, had a total membership of eight, and were scheduled for a two-hour monthly meeting. Two of the four union members were the local president and the chairman of the union's grievance committee.

Based on his experience as a member of a productivity committee, Donald T. Dalena recommended that the plant-wide committee be divided into area committees (in his plant, it has been split into six such units) and that the local's two busiest officers act in an ex officio capacity. He also recommended that, once the committees were organized and functioning properly, they meet twice a month for sessions of up to four hours.[19]

In the three years that Dalena reported he had seen the committees operate, his attitude changed from one of hopelessness to hope. He initially felt that they would fail because they were not based on trust. At the time the article appeared, he felt that these committees have the potential for greatness. To achieve this potential, however, they must be part of a system that receives constant input from both workers and managers, with both sides receiving necessary feedback. Dalena stated that it is time management and labor recognize that they need each other and that the productivity committee may be an excellent way to accomplish this goal. He further stated that in the committee the workers should advise while management listens, weighs recommendations, and then implements them.[20]

An organization that has well-functioning productivity committees will be a great resource in assisting compensation managers achieve their goals. The opportunity to communicate directly with representatives who have the ears of the workers can be invaluable in collecting and disseminating the kind of information necessary for the success of compensation managers. (A review of the Scanlon Plan in chapter 12 discusses the productivity committee in much greater detail.)

Efficiency Improvement

The need for improving the productivity of American organizations weighs as much on the minds of union leaders as it does on those of the captains of industry. The sharp decline in output per man-hour of work (i.e., productivity) first noted in 1974 and continuing into the early 1980s has jolted these leaders

---

[19]Donald T. Dalena, "A Steelworker's View of Productivity Committees," *Industry Week,* September 2, 1974, pp. 42–45.

[20]Ibid.

with the serious problems such a decline poses for all Americans. The continuing decline of productivity together with increases in pay and even greater increases in the selling prices of most goods and services throughout the remainder of the 1970s had the direct effect of reducing the standard of living of many workers. For Americans to enjoy better goods and improved services, all members of the labor force must work together to improve the use of resources, the most precious of these being the human resources that have been the backbone of American industrial success.

Many members of the labor movement still hold the same views that Samuel Gompers, the first president of the American Federation of Labor, expressed almost a century ago. When someone asked him what were the aims of the labor unions, he replied, "More, more, more . . . now." A feeling prevails, however, that there is a decline in this view and that more members of the labor unions, especially the newer and younger ones, want to take a broader view of reward opportunities. Apparently, there is increasing interest in relating economic rewards to productivity improvement. In addition, these new workers are looking for more ways to gain satisfaction from their work and for ways to grow through their own efforts without losing job security.

The no-strike approach developed by the USWA and the major steel companies through their ENA and their continued interest in further implementation and the improvement of productivity bargaining committees are steps toward improving the use of the resources of the organization. However, these are not the only moves made in recent years for labor and management to join together in searching for more efficient ways to do things. Others are discussed in the following paragraphs.

Over the past 10 years, pressure has been increased to link wage settlement to improvement in productivity. Although the term *productivity improvement* invokes in the minds of some union members such ideas as speedup, job elimination, reduction in forces, and even unemployment, some dramatic changes in organized labor's acceptance of labor-saving equipment have been noted. An efficiency improvement program developed between *The New York Times* and *The Daily News* and the International Typographical Union, Local No. 6, permitted these two newspapers to fully automate their production systems. The typographical union is one of the oldest unions in America, and its approval of this contract will radically reduce it in size over the coming years. The major management inducement used to gain union acceptance of new job-eliminating equipment was the guarantee of life-time jobs as well as some seductive incentives to older union members to retire.

Normally, when labor has accepted equipment that will eliminate the jobs of many of their members, management agrees not to fire any of the present workers but to reduce their numbers by attrition, retirement, or retraining and relocation. This type of agreement was negotiated between the union representing West Coast dockworkers—the International Longshoremen's and Warehousemen's Union (ILWU)—and West Coast shippers. Labor agreed to the use of labor-saving, cost-reducing, automated equipment in return for annual work guarantees and no reduction in the current work force through layoffs. A contract negotiated between these groups in 1975 guaranteed workers who were called to work at least one day a week a minimum weekly pay of $250 in 1976.[21]

The increasing impact of foreign competition along with a decline in the supply of essential raw materials has further prompted the leaders of labor and management to recognize the folly and the dysfunctional result of their traditional adversary roles. The common course of improved productivity has led in recent years to a reduction in labor's hostility toward merit or pay-for-performance programs.

Most unions have historically favored some form of a daily wage system and have viewed any type of a productivity-oriented (i.e., piecework) system with suspicion. There is a slow but steadily growing movement in the unions to accept certain programs that make bonuses contingent on productivity. The expansion of such programs depends as much on management ingenuity as it does on labor's acceptance. Chapter 12 focuses on a variety of pay-for-performance programs designed to improve productivity.

There have also been a few cases in recent years in which labor unions have accepted reductions in pay as well as limitations on their rights to strike over local issues.[22] Jurisdictional disputes (i.e., a dispute between two different unions that could lead to a walkout), illegal strikes, slowdowns, and featherbedding (i.e., positions required by contract that make no contribution to an operation) are under review by union leadership.[23] Union leaders are measuring the benefits gained by union members against the effect on productivity and the continued survival and growth of organizations.

Growth in Union Movement

Until recent years, most union members and union activities were part of the blue-collar segment of the work force. However, the past few years have witnessed a rapid growth in the unionization of white-collar workers. The fastest growing and largest union in the AFL-CIO is the American Federation of State, County, and Municipal Employees (AFSCME); many of the government employees joining the AFSCME are those typically considered to be white-collar workers.

A commonly held idea is that there is a spillover effect on the pay of nonunionized white-collar workers from the gains achieved through the efforts of unionized blue-collar workers. In the past, white-collar workers frequently received the same benefits gained by union members without having to pay

---

[21]"Dock Workers, West Coast Shippers Agree on Tentative Pact that Bars July 1 Strike," *The Wall Street Journal,* February 11, 1975, p. 4.

[22]Everett Groseclose, "Conciliatory Mood: Increasingly, Workers Give Up Some Benefits so as Not to Lose Jobs," *The Wall Street Journal,* January 26, 1972, pp. 1, 27; and Richard F. Gibson, "Is Labor Playing a New Role?" *Industry Week,* December 24, 1973, pp. 42–46.

[23]A unique approach to worker slowdowns that has had wide acceptance in recent years is the "go-by-the-rules" slowdown. In this case, workers adhere strictly to work and safety rules and procedures. This approach has a dramatic and quick impact on operations. It can bring almost any organization to a standstill.

union dues or become involved in union struggles. Recently, however, white-collar technical and professional members of many organizations have not received the same benefits won by union members.

In the past, such factors as differing levels of eduction, modes of dress and language, working conditions, and occupational prestige as well as the high proportion of women among white-collar workers have discouraged white-collar union activities. The effects of these factors have diminished with each passing year, however, and continuing management failures to solve the problems of white-collar workers can only hasten unionization among them. As labor leaders become more aggressive in the white-collar field and as the difference between factory production work and white-collar service work becomes negligible, opportunities increase for unionization.

In March 1981, the AFL-CIO began a pilot program that joined the Services Employees International Union (650,000 members) and the Working Women (an organization whose 10,000 members are mainly office workers). This coalition will form a national local with local autonomy designated as District 925 for the express purpose of unionizing the predominantly female secretarial and clerical work force (the "pink-collar" workers described in chapter 2).

Traditionally, professional union members have generally been unwilling to join ranks with the blue-collar crafts and trade unions. However, opening of collective bargaining opportunities for government employees has made some recent and dramatic changes in the area. A significant number of schoolteachers and nurses have joined the union ranks, and the union movement has gained a slight foothold among engineers, scientists, technicians, and college professors.

With the government's changed concept of nonsupervisory managerial employees and the conversion of old-line professional associations into collective bargaining units, organizations will be facing unionization pressures throughout their structure.[24]

SELECTED READINGS

Curtin, Edward R., *White-Collar Unionization Studies in Personnel Policy No. 220,* National Industrial Conference Board, Inc., 1970. A research report examining the unionization of office, sales, technical, and professional employees. It analyzes government data on white-collar employment union membership and representative elections.

Dalena, Donald T., "A Steelworker's View of Productivity Committees," *Industry Week,* September 2, 1974, pp. 42–45. An insider's critical view of the operations of the productivity committee. The author provides ideas on how to improve the committee's operation and stresses its importance to the future success of American labor and management.

---

[24]If the duties of employees are such that union membership would not create a genuine conflict of interest, they have the right to organize and cannot be disciplined for union activities. They must be treated as nonmanagerial employees.

Davenport, Russell W., "Enterprise for Everyman," *Fortune,* January 1950, pp. 55–59, 152, 157–159. A review of the Scanlon Plan and its application by union and management to improve productivity, profits, and pay. It describes in some detail the operation of labor-management committees and the way they work toward achieving common goals that benefit everyone. (Chapter 12 describes in detail the operation of the Scanlon Plan.)

Gooding, Judson, "The Fraying White Collar," *Fortune,* December 1970, pp. 78–81, 108–109. Along with the increase in white-collar employment, there has been a steady erosion in status, relative pay, and job security. These factors are leading to large increases in white-collar unionization. More than money, white-collar employees want promotions and meaningful participation in job-related activities.

Hay, Edward N., "The Attitude of the American Federation of Labor on Job Evaluation," *Personnel Journal,* November 1947, pp. 163–169. An analysis of three articles appearing in the July, August, and September 1947 issues of the *American Federationist* that reveal in detail union attitudes toward job evaluation specifically and structured compensation systems generally. The points raised by the labor writers and by Hay's analysis provide extremely valuable insight even today.

Imunde, Louis V., "Why Federal Government Employees Join Unions: A Study of AFGE Local 916," *Public Personnel Management,* January–February 1973, pp. 23–28. A study of the largest local in the American Federation of Government Employees (AFGE) analyzes why blue- and white-collar government employees join the union. It also attempts to determine differences in reasons for joining unions between government employees and those who work in the private sector.

Schaffer, Beverly K., "Experience with Supplementary Unemployment Benefits: A Case Study of the Atlantic Steel Company," *Industrial and Labor Relations Review,* October 1968, pp. 85–94. An analysis of four years' experience of one company with its SUB plan. This article assesses the plan in terms of protection offered, extent of use, adequacy of benefits, cost, and employee stabilization.

Spiers, Joseph N., "Workers on the Board; European Experience Intensifies," *Industry Week,* September 23, 1974, pp. 31–37. A review and analysis of worker participation on boards of directors. This action, called "codetermination," began in Germany in 1951 with the passing of a federal law requiring coal, iron, and steel companies to have an equal number of worker and stockholder appointees on the board. Although American labor unions contend that they are not interested in achieving company ownership or even control but only in controlling job opportunities open to their members and protecting the union as an institution, it will be of interest to American managers to follow the future of these European codetermination programs.

Thompson, Donald B., "Who Will Follow Steel? Arbitration instead of Strikes," *Industry Week,* October 14, 1974, pp. 30–35. A review of the historic Experimental Negotiating Agreement (ENA) with an eye cast toward its future use by other unions and organizations. At this time, it appears there is no solid evidence that other unions or industries are adopting this alternative to the strike.

Young, Harvey A., and Michael F. Dougherty, "Influence of the Guaranteed Annual Wage upon Labor Relations and Productivity: National Sugar Refinery's Experience," *Management of Personnel Quarterly,* Winter 1971, pp. 27–32. A review of the development of a guaranteed annual wage program and some of the outcomes of this pioneering effort.

Part 2

Identifying Job Content and Determining Pay

Part 2 develops a systematic approach for analyzing and evaluating the unique contributions each job makes toward the achievement of organizational goals and objectives. This is the first step in achieving fair and just compensation.

Throughout this part there are discussions that emphasize the value of certain tools and techniques that enable the compensation manager to analyze the job, identify and describe job content, determine job worth, and set pay. These discussions may indicate that a scientific approach leads to a final and correct answer to compensation problems. Nothing could be further from the truth. There are no absolutes in compensation, only honest endeavors to find a better way.

It is important to understand that although practically any *tool* can do the job, the tool's success depends entirely on the skill and the artistry of its user. It is true, however, that, depending on the situation, some tools do provide better and more accurate approaches to solving compensation problems.

Furthermore, even the best analytical tools in the hands of a competent compensation manager require constant attention. Compensation programs are primarily planning and control programs and as such require frequent adjustment. No compensation program is ever perfect. It must adjust to constantly changing internal and external environmental pressures while at the same time maintaining its integrity and basic stability. This means that the initial design must permit a degree of flexibility to adjust to changing conditions, while allowing the basic concepts of the program to move forward in its directed path. No plan works by itself; it requires a certain dedication by all involved parties—compensation specialists, line managers, and concerned employees.

The variety of pressures applied to the compensation system vary in each organization. For this reason, each must develop its own unique compensation program.

Basic Texts for References in Part 2

The following table outlines chapters from current compensation/wage and salary texts as used for references for chapters 5–10 in part 2.

RELEVANT CHAPTERS FROM OTHER REFERENCE SOURCES

Chapters in Part 2	Other References[a]								
	(1)	(2)	(3)	(4)	(5)	(6)	(7)	(8)	(9)
Chap. 5—Job analysis	5	13	8	7	4	5,6	3	3	11
Chap. 6—Job descriptions	5	9,11	9,10	7	7	10,12	—	5	10
Chap. 7–8—Job evaluation and compensable factor-based job evaluation methods	4,5, 6,7, 11,12	8,9, 10,12, 14,17	7,10 17,18	7,8	1,2, 4,5,6, 7,8,10, 11,14	1,2,3 7,8,9, 10,11, 12	3,4, 12	1,2, 3,4, 6,16	6,7,8, 9,10,12
Chap. 9—Compensation survey	10,14, 18	15,16	11	6	12	13,14, 15,16	5	—	13
Chap. 10—Designing a pay structure	10,11, 12	18	6,13	8	13	17,18, 19,20, 21	5	7,17	13

[a]List of other reference sources:
(1) David W. Belcher, *Compensation Administration* (Englewood Cliffs, NJ: Prentice-Hall, 1973).
(2) J. Gary Berg, *Managing Compensation* (New York: AMACOM, 1976).
(3) J. D. Dunn and Frank M. Rachel, *Wage and Salary Administration: Total Compensation Systems* (New York: McGraw-Hill, 1971).
(4) Thomas H. Patten, *Pay: Employee Compensation and Incentive Plans* (New York: Free Press, 1977).
(5) John A. Patton et al., *Job Evaluation: Text and Cases,* 3rd ed. (Homewood, IL: Richard D. Irwin, 1964).
(6) Milton L. Rock, ed., *Handbook of Wage and Salary Administration* (New York: McGraw-Hill, 1972).
(7) Robert E. Sibson, *Compensation: A Complete Revision of "Wages and Salaries."* (New York: AMACOM, 1974).
(8) Harold Suskin, ed., *Job Evaluation and Pay Administration in the Public Sector* (Chicago, IL: International Personnel Management Association, 1977).
(9) Herbert G. Zollitsch and Adolph Langsner, *Wage and Salary Administration,* 2nd ed. (Cincinnati, OH: South-Western, 1970).

5

Job Analysis

CONTENT

Chapter 5 presents methods for developing and implementing a job analysis program. In addition, it describes the reasons for job analysis and gives hints for avoiding traps in this crucial part of a compensation program.

GOALS

Upon concluding this chapter, you should be able to determine job analysis requirements. You should be familiar with the various procedures and methods available for gathering job data and be able to perform a useful and workable job analysis assignment. You should also be able to relate specific organizational characteristics and requirements to the best method for collecting valid and reliable data.

T he words and the terms common to the field of compensation management are often inconsistently used and imperfectly defined, thus leading to much misunderstanding. This is a problem not only for the newcomer trying to gain an insight into compensation management but also for experienced practitioners, consultants, and researchers in their daily communications. To establish a sound basis for understanding the tools and techniques described and developed in this part of the text, some key terms are defined as follows:

Activity. Any effort produced by a worker that results in some kind of an output.

Element. The smallest step into which it is practical to subdivide any work activity without analyzing separate motions and mental processes. Elements are the individual activity units of identifiable and definable physical and intellectual work that produces an output.

Task. A coordinated series of work activity elements used to produce an identifiable and definable output that can be independently consumed or used.

Duties. One or more tasks performed in carrying out a job responsibility.

Responsibility. One or a group of duties that identify and describe a major purpose or reason for the existence of the job.

Behavior. Observable, identifiable, and measurable activity of a worker in the performance of a job.

Position. Work consisting of responsibilities and duties assignable to one employee (i.e., there are as many positions as there are employees).

Job. Work consisting of responsibilities and duties that are sufficiently alike to justify being covered by a single job analysis. A job may be assignable to one or more employees.

Class. A group of jobs sufficiently similar as to kinds of subject matter; education and experience requirements; levels of difficulty, complexity, and responsibility; and qualification requirements of the work. (It is possible to have a single-job class.)

Class-series. A grouping of job classes having similar job content but differing in degree of difficulty, complexity, and responsibility; level of skill; knowledge; and qualification requirements.

Family. Two or more class-series within an organization that have related or common work content.

Occupation. A grouping of jobs or job classes within a number of different organizations that require similar skill, effort, and responsibility.

Grade. A grouping of jobs or classes of jobs that, although different with respect to kind of subject matter, type of knowledge demands, or kind of work, are sufficiently equivalent by level of difficulty, complexity, and responsibility and by qualification requirements to receive similar pay.

Knowledge. The detailed information, facts, concepts, and theories acquired innately or through education and experience that are parts of specific disciplines and subject areas. Job knowledge is the prerequisite for thinking and action that identifies how things function and describes how to use them in performing assignments and producing acceptable output.

Ability. A natural talent or acquired proficiency required in the performance of work.

Skill. An acquirable behavioral attribute or level of proficiency demonstrated by a person in performing an intellectual or a physical activity of a work assignment.

In designing and implementing a compensation system, the first step is to identify the work content of each job and the knowledge and skill requirements—worker characteristics—required of anyone who could successfully perform job assignments. To differentiate the compensation it provides to employees based on job content and job performance, the organization must be able accurately and precisely to identify the required tasks, the knowledge and the skills necessary for performing them, and the conditions under which they must be performed. This type of analysis enables an organization to establish a sound compensation system, using criteria that validly measure and differentiate job and performance requirements so that all employees receive fair and equitable treatment.

Federal legislation of the past two decades against discriminatory practices by race, sex, national origin, or age has placed extreme burdens on most employers. Because they must demonstrate the validity of their recruitment, testing, hiring, compensation, training, transfer, promotion, and disciplinary practices, the need for accurate and valid job-related data becomes critical.

Practically any method or procedure used for making a personnel-related decision is considered a test. In the broadest sense, the compensation system itself is a test. Tests must be valid, that is, there must be a high degree of association or correlation between the information produced by testing procedures and instruments and the behaviors they describe or predict. (Chapter 13, which focuses on employee performance, describes various ways to validate a testing procedure.) The Equal Employment Opportunity Guidelines on Employment Selection Procedures, Section 1604.7(c), further clarifies this point:

> Evidence of a test's validity should consist of empirical data demonstrating that the test is predictive of or significantly correlated with important elements of work behavior which comprise or are relevant to the job or jobs for which candidates are being evaluated.

For compensation purposes, the establishment of valid pay practices that provide both equal and equitable treatment to all employees begins with the collection and the analysis of job content data and information.

Many reasons can prompt an organization to start a job analysis program. The decision can be the result of a demand by employees or union representatives for a change in job descriptions and the assignment of jobs to pay grades or the development of a classification system that reflects more accurately the work they perform. Legislative mandates for developing nondiscriminatory employment standards or the need to restructure jobs to eliminate artificial employment barriers can also prod employers into such action.[1] It is also possible that good management practices dictate a periodic review and revision of existing personnel practices. Whatever the reason, an ideal spot to begin is with a look at what is happening at the workplace through an analysis of job content.

PRELIMINARY CONSIDERATIONS

The activities involved in collecting, analyzing, and recording job content data must not be taken lightly. Before undertaking this costly operation that will consume the time of many employees, it is wise to review some essential preliminary factors.

Senior Management Support

Does senior management understand what is involved in performing a job analysis? Have time and cost considerations been fully explored? Are they understood and approved? Have the implications of the types of changes that may be recommended because of the analysis been considered? To gain increased output, reduced costs, and improved worker satisfaction, will senior management support the restructuring of certain jobs, the eliminating of others, and the upgrading or reclassification of still others? Such questions must be discussed before starting a job analysis program. This approach helps to minimize the impact of the shock these demands cause senior management. In fact, when management faces a deluge of demands, it frequently reacts by doing nothing. If this could possibly be the result of the project, it may be wise *not* to start a job analysis program.

Operating Managers and Operatives

Have past job analysis programs resulted in no action or, possibly worse, actions contrary to the job security or promotion interests of operating managers and workers? Because of past actions, the work force may demonstrate attitudes to a new analysis that range from apathy to hostility. Certainly, this will influence the success of any job analysis program. Means of overcoming such behavior must be considered either before or during the design of the program.

The success of a job analysis program hinges on the quality and the quantity of data collected. Meeting these twin requirements depends to a large degree on the cooperation and the involvement of the jobholders. All members of the organization must support the program and become involved in all its phases—planning, collecting data, analyzing data, and making necessary changes as identified by the program.

---

[1]Artificial employment barriers arise when employment standards and their related job duties, as expressed in some institutionalized process or instrument, are essentially unrelated to the primary content of the job, or when the employment standards of the job call for the employee to have skills to perform duties significantly above the normal level of duties actually required on that job. This results in the screening out of qualified candidates.

Compensation managers normally emphasize job activities. With increasing pressures from government and unions, however, performance standards and desired end results are requiring more of their attention.

An analysis of job activities and behaviors involves compiling a detailed description of tasks, determining the relationship of the job to technology and to other jobs, and examining the knowledge, qualifications, or employment standards, accountabilities, and other incumbent requirements. Job analysis also involves identifying, collecting, and classifying task statements and job behaviors. A list of task statements provides a detailed analysis of what the incumbent does in accomplishing job requirements, whereas the job behaviors provide insight as to what can be considered acceptable or unacceptable behavior.

Procedures for collecting, analyzing, and recording job activity information are (1) interviews with workers or groups of workers performing the job or with the manager supervising them, (2) observation of the work being performed, (3) completion of questionnaires by workers performing the jobs or by the manager supervising them, (4) completion of logs or diaries by employees indicating each activity as it is performed over a period of time, or (5) any combination of these.

Another method for obtaining job analysis data and information is the use of generalized checklists of job functions or tasks previously developed by the organization or by researchers investigating job requirements for many purposes. An example is the Task Analysis Inventory, which is adapted from the Job Information Matrix System (JIMS) developed by Dale Yoder and C. Harold Stone under a contract from the U.S. Department of Labor.[2] Many organizations have developed checklists of functions, activities, or tasks for specific jobs, classes, or class-series.

Whichever method the job analyst uses, the following seven planning steps are helpful in achieving a successful job analysis.

1. Determine the use of the data and the information.

2. Select methods and procedures for securing job data and information.

3. Schedule the necessary and logical work steps.

4. Identify desired job performance requirements.[3]

5. Assess the present situation.

6. Clarify any deviation between actual job behavior and desired results.

7. Review the data and the information with participant(s).

[2]U.S. Department of Labor, Manpower Administration, *Task Analysis Inventories* (Washington, DC: Government Printing Office, 1973).

[3]Performance—behavior measured in terms of its contributions to the goals and the objectives of the organization.

THE SEVEN STEPS TO JOB ANALYSIS

A compensation program that enhances the maximum use of knowledge and the application of that knowledge within a framework of a wide variety of human relationships is the goal of every organization. Careful attention of the seven planning steps of job analysis will assist those persons responsible for compensation administration to formulate, organize, and develop the tools and the techniques necessary for achieving this objective.

Step One — Determine the Use of the Data and the Information

The scope of job analysis depends on its future use. A precise determination of the purpose(s) of job analysis permits the development of a well-designed plan that will achieve its intended goals. A principal use of job analysis is to aid in developing the following:

1. *Job descriptions* provide a word picture of the job, weaving together its principal ingredients and offering a broad and easily read overview. (Chapter 6 provides a lengthy discussion of job descriptions.)

2. *Job specifications* describe in some detail the essential worker characteristics required of the jobholder and the environment in which the job is performed. These job-related factors assist in determining the worth of the job. (Chapter 6 also provides a lengthy discussion of job specifications.)

3. *Compensable factors* objectively identify and define jobs, making distinctions among them possible and establishing the degree of worth of each job. (Chapter 8 discusses the importance, the description, and the universal characteristics of compensable factors.)

4. *Job evaluations* accurately identify and categorize job information so that it is possible to rank and rate each job with regard to its contribution to the achievement of organizational objectives and goals. (Chapters 7 and 8 provide a detailed discussion of job evaluations.)

5. *Job classifications* place jobs with similar or related duties and responsibilities and comparable employment standards into a manageable arrangement. Such an arrangement facilitates the horizontal and vertical structuring of jobs.

A job classification is a first step in developing job families. (Chapter 7 describes the classification process.)

These basic compensation tools and techniques are then used to contribute to the following areas of managerial accountabilities.

1. *The compensation system* ideally determines pay and other benefits fairly and equitably through the use of acceptable, valid, and understandable objective standards.

2. *Personnel functions* range from initial recruiting, hiring, and placement to training and performance appraisal to termination. These functions are highly dependent on job analysis data.

3. *Manning schedules* are linked directly to data developed in job analysis. They provide clear and concise descriptions of individual jobs, identify current incumbents, and provide insights into more efficient allocation of duties, leading at times to the design of a new job or possibly the elimination of an existing job.

4. *Job worth and contribution identification* provides a basis for gaining common understanding by all employees of the value of each job, of its relationship to other jobs, and of the requirements necessary to perform it. Commonly available identification assists all employees in better understanding promotion and transfer requirements and in recognizing career opportunities.

5. *Affirmative Action programs,* by clearly identifying the knowledge, responsibility, and duty requirements of each job, make it possible to select, train, and develop job applicants for both entry level and promotional opportunities.

Job analysis also considers the requirements of the Occupational Safety and Health Act of 1970 (OSHA). The location of potential sources of occupational hazards and initial insights into procedures for eliminating them should be an essential part of the job analysis program.

Step Two — Select Methods and Procedures for Securing Job Data and Information

Selecting methods and procedures for securing job information requires a broad understanding of the operations of the organization. Two valuable charting tools available to assist the analyst are the organization chart and the process chart.

Organization Chart—A typical organization chart describes the relationship among the various functions and activities of the organization by showing the individuals, the groups, or the departments responsible for performing these functions. Most charts differentiate pictorially between line functions (getting the work done) and staff functions (furnishing expert advice). Figure 5-1 is a basic organization chart.

This organization chart emphasizes the difference between the line functions (solid-line relationships) and the staff functions (dotted-line relationships). The number of levels following a functional box indicates reporting levels relative to designated areas of authority. This picture of the hierarchy of an organization provides an excellent introduction to the functions and the activities of an organization and their interrelationships. In this way, the operations of each job become understandable and meaningful to the analyst.

A word of warning: Existing organization charts are often obsolete and may inaccurately reflect the operations of the organization. In this case, updating is necessary. The updating process, as well as the actual construction of

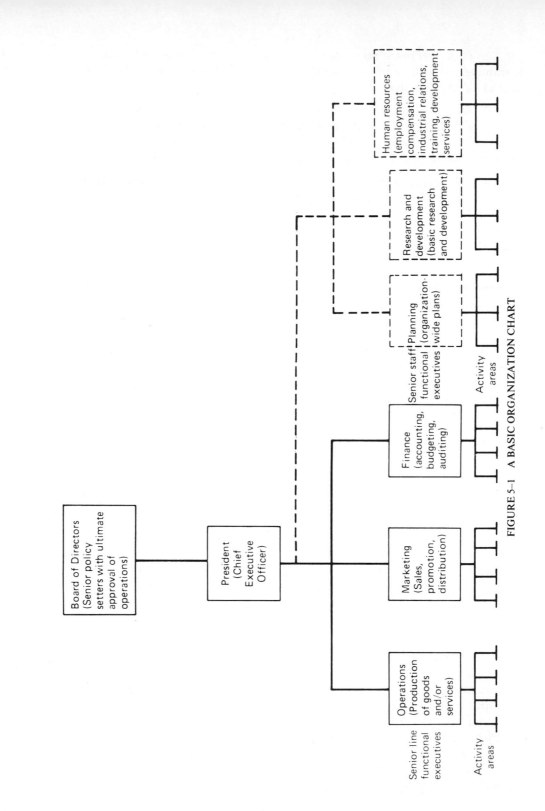

FIGURE 5-1   A BASIC ORGANIZATION CHART

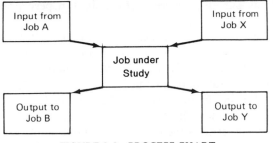

FIGURE 5–2   PROCESS CHART

a chart, is not only a valuable exercise in becoming familiar with the organization, but it is also the first indicator of missing, needed, overlapping, or superfluous jobs. Visualizing the organization makes it easier to understand the characteristics and the value of each job.

Process Chart—A process chart provides the analyst with a more detailed understanding of the job or the flow of work than that obtained from a review of the organization chart. A simple process chart may be one that indicates the flow of inputs and outputs to the job under study, such as that shown in figure 5-2. Or it could take the form of a flow of activities necessary to prepare a particular output, for example, the steps leading to the filling of a customer's order. See figure 5-3.

Once there is an understanding of the basic reasons for the existence of the job, it is necessary to learn more about the specific tasks or duties of the job itself.

Although job analysis focuses on fundamental requirements and activities, no job exists in a vacuum. Its existence means that there is a requirement for a human being to perform some activity(ies). Jobholders bring to jobs their own unique personalities, which means that they perform not only according to

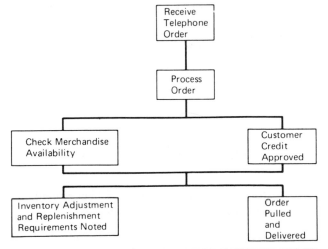

FIGURE 5–3   SAMPLE FLOW CHART OF CUSTOMER ORDER

specific instructions but also according to their own perceptions of how they should be performing.

Why the job exists is an underlying and implicit issue that requires attention when performing job analysis. Is this job necessary? Do the activities performed support the reasons for its existence? Should it be modified? What tasks should be deleted, added, or modified?

Major emphasis in job analysis is on the *what* of the job. What is the job content? What must the incumbent do in the successful performance of the job? The task statements describe principally the *what* of the job.

Basically, *how* is a secondary issue in job analysis. It is not up to the job analyst to prescribe *how* the job is done. The way an activity is performed is the responsibility of the industrial engineer, the training department, or the immediate supervisor. Or it could be determined by the preference of the incumbent. The job analyst has little or no responsibility for reporting how well a job or activity is performed. However, to provide a more complete description or to illustrate the *what* of the job, a *how* explanation is acceptable.

Job analysis must reveal what behaviors a satisfactory or successful worker engages in when on the job. Job analysis identifies the work activities required of a worker performing in a fully proficient manner.

In job analysis, every effort is made to remove the human factor. Although this is difficult, success requires as sterile an analysis as possible (i.e., removal of the jobholder's personal influences). The important thing to focus on here is what the worker is doing, not how it is being done. In later chapters, there are in-depth discussions relating to employee performance, and the unique contributions of the jobholder are discussed at length.

A number of basic considerations influence the selection of the best way to collect job information. Some of the more important are the following:

1. *Geography.* Because of the job's physical location, will a particular method or procedure be prohibitive? Will it be hazardous or too costly for personal observation, thus necessitating a questionnaire, diary, or log?

2. *Environment.* Do noise, heat, rain, wind, or physically dangerous conditions impair data collection?

3. *Technology.* Does the technology favor or disfavor any particular method or procedure?

4. *Routine or nonroutine.* Does work performance or work flow occur in a manner that favors or disfavors a particular method or procedure?

5. *Knowledge.* Does the complexity of the job favor any particular method or procedure?

6. *Personal factors.* Does the basic cultural background of the jobholder preclude or favor a particular method or procedure?

7. *Social factors.* Does social interaction among individuals working together on a job influence the method or procedure?

Other important considerations are the knowledge and the interpersonal qualifications of the job analyst. How well does the analyst understand the goals and the basic outputs of the organization? How well does the analyst relate to those doing the work? How enthusiastic, aggressive, or innovative is the analyst? Will the analyst be able to improvise or make data collection changes when required? Will the analyst be able to distinguish those contributions to the job that are unique to the jobholder from those required by the job itself?

The expectations and the philosophy that the organization imparts to jobholders are also important considerations. The type of encouragement jobholders receive from the organization affects both their job performance and their interactions with any type of data-collecting mechanism. An awareness of these frequently invisible but powerful forces aids in the selection of a data-collecting method.

Step Three — Schedule the Necessary and Logical Work Steps

A time and cost schedule of necessary and logical work steps assists in obtaining job data in conformity with desired results. The development of a job-analysis budget is an ideal approach. Forecasting financial requirements for such a project is not easy initially, but it is especially valuable in preparing a coordinated program that achieves desired results. The fundamentals earlier discussed in Steps One and Two provide some of the basic information necessary for development of such a schedule.

With knowledge of the intended use of the job analysis and a review of the criteria for the selection of particular data-collecting instruments, it is possible to consider the human resources necessary to implement the program. The number of involved individuals; their skill, education, and experience; and the time necessary to perform the job analysis assignment are the primary cost factors.

The development of a budget requires identifying and forecasting the significant events in a job analysis program, as follows:

1. Determining the intended uses of the job analysis. Will it be used for a wide variety of personnel-related functions (i.e., recruiting, selection, performance appraisal, etc.) or only for compensation purposes?

2. Deciding on the type(s) of instrument(s) that will be used to obtain relevant data and information.

3. Identifying the jobs to be studied.

4. Appraising the knowledge of employees and their trust and willingness to assist in

(a) designing and developing data-collecting instruments;
(b) collecting data; and
(c) presenting data in a form valuable for future use.

Step Four — Identify Desired Job Performance Requirements

All data-collecting steps may be potentially weak if they describe only what *is* happening, not what *should be* happening. To overcome this weakness and to discover what should be happening at a particular job requires that the analyst review the job with the jobholder's immediate supervisor, or possibly with a supervisor who is two or more levels above the jobholder. In any case, this review should be done with a supervisor who fully understands the requirements and the outputs of the job.

The identification of what should be happening gives the analyst advance insights into the job. In this way, the analyst can become aware of whether or not the job is being performed in harmony with desired standards. Knowing what should be done allows the analyst to recognize when an incumbent is "puffing up" the job and even to identify cases when an employee is understating job requirements.

Although the manner of job performance and the output may vary with what the analyst understands the job goals to be, these factors must not prejudice the recording of the job information at that particular time. When a job analyst can direct a supervisor's attention to a deviation between what is and what should be, a valuable service has been performed.

Step Five — Assess the Present Situation

The assessment step provides clear, concise, accurate statements that describe the work performed by the jobholder. These work activity description statements are job tasks. Taken together, the job tasks describe the job, which, in turn, produces an identifiable and significant result or organizationally required output. An in-depth analysis of job tasks provides information regarding the knowledge, skills, and abilities (KSAs) required of a worker performing a job.

Step Six — Clarify Any Deviation between Actual Job Behavior and Desired Results

When a deviation occurs between the desired results and the actual behavior, the analyst must verify the analysis with someone—normally the jobholder's supervisor—to get a more accurate picture. A job analysis requiring verification should be so noted. One procedure is to place a "V" at the top of the completed analysis, indicating the need to review and verify that particular job.

It is not unusual to find employees who have had insufficient instruction or training and who are thus unable to obtain the results desired for their jobs. However, deviations between actual job behavior and desired results do not necessarily arise from faulty work effort or work knowledge. There may be valid reasons for deviations. For example, the employee may have developed unique improvements and found a better way of doing the job, or some of the tasks may have been assigned permanently or temporarily to another employee. Other reasons may involve different production requirements, the availability of machinery, revised or new technology, or the array of knowledge among members of the work group. Thus, a complete analysis may require more detailed information.

These deviations may arise because past job descriptions include obsolete duties or duties of minimal importance. Maintaining such inaccuracies may ensure an unwarranted high pay rate for the incumbent or assist managers in building unacceptable "empires" by making jobs appear to be more important than they actually are. Unwarranted or unimportant duties also assist in the development of artificial employment barriers.

Step Seven — Review the Data and the Information with Participant(s)

Because the job analysis touches so many areas fundamental to effective and efficient working relationships, both the worker performing the job and the immediate supervisor must have the opportunity to review the final analysis. This review provides an excellent opportunity to determine if the report is (1) factually correct, (2) easily understood through clear presentation of material, and (3) complete, including everything necessary to describe the job. The report may also require a review by others performing the same job.

This review procedure not only aids in developing accuracy and clarity, but it is also a major step in gaining employee acceptance of the entire compensation program. Involvement at this stage provides employees with the opportunity to gain some insight into the way the organization views their jobs and vice versa. It also enables the employees to take a deep look at themselves in their jobs and to inform the organization about their contributions and the work they actually perform.

Through the seven steps of job analysis, the work station becomes a learning station for both management and employee. This effort frequently results in the determination of many elements of company policy. Furthermore, providing the employee with an opportunity to participate in an exercise that has such important and widespread implications sends a message that every job and every employee are important. Because job analysis contributes to the success of the organization, both management and the incumbent must agree as to its fundamental activities and requirements.

COLLECTING JOB CONTENT, WORKER REQUIREMENTS, AND JOB ENVIRONMENT INFORMATION

Because the end results should be the same, a core of requirements is common to each of the five procedures (observation, interview, questionnaire, diary/log, combination) used for collecting, analyzing, and recording job information. Answers to the following questions provide needed job data:

1. Why is the job being performed?

2. What is actually happening? What tasks are being performed?

3. Which tasks are most critical to overall successful job performance?

4. What are the knowledge and skill requirements and, where applicable, certification and licensure requirements?

5. What are the basic accountabilities or expectations of results that typify the work of an incumbent?

6. What are the physical demands?

7. What are the emotional and intellectual demands?

8. What are the health and safety considerations? What risks or hazards are encountered?

Identifying Job Tasks

The most difficult, most time-consuming, and certainly the most important output of job analysis is the accurate and complete description of all tasks performed by the incumbent. Many procedures have been developed for obtaining job task information, but the following approach has been used with success for identifying and describing job content:

> *Step 1.* Ask the respondee to describe the major activities or things done in performing the job. These major activities are broad categories that, in total, define the scope of the work assignment. Practically all jobs can be described in terms of these overall categories through three to 10 major activity statements.
> *Optional Step 1 or Step 2.* (The following step can either follow Step 1 or be used in place of Step 1. If used as Step 2, the respondee would be asked to think about the first major work activity identified in step 1 and then to complete the following task analysis process. This process would be used for a task description of each major work activity.)
>
> Ask the respondee to describe in detail the work he or she does. The instructions may take this form: Think of the things you do in performing your job. One approach for analyzing your job is to list the first thing you do each day. Then list the various activities you perform in completing your daily work assignments. List also the things you do that are not done on a daily basis, but are performed possibly a couple of times each week, once every two weeks, once a month, etc. In thinking about the work you do, select a verb (for example, writes, files, completes, monitors, carries, transfers, instructs, repairs, assembles, etc.) that best describes the kind of action taken. After selecting the verb, select a common name (noun) that identifies the kind of object that this work activity most directly affects (for example, letters, forms, small motors, etc.). You may further describe the results of the action on the object by identifying the reason(s) you perform the action and the equipment, tools, or work aids you use in performing the action. An example of a Task List Questionnaire follows:

Task Number	WHAT IS DONE? Action Verb	TO WHAT IS IT DONE? Object	WHY IS IT DONE? Effect of the Action	HOW IS IT DONE? Tools, Equipment, Work Aids, Guides Used in the Action

It is not unusual for incumbents to identify 50 to 75 tasks performed in accomplishing job assignments. If Step 1 is used, anywhere from 3 to 12 tasks may be required to further describe each major or broad work activity.

Setting Priorities in Task Statements

To gain a complete picture of the relationship between individual tasks and overall job requirements, task dimensions are used for measuring tasks with regard to various criteria. Through the use of these task dimensions and their related scales, it is possible to infer the order of importance of the tasks and the impact a task has on the overall performance of the job. Some of the more commonly used task rating dimensions are (1) importance, (2) complexity, (3) difficulty, (4) criticality or consequence of error, (5) frequency of occurrence, (6) time spent in performing the task, and (7) relationship to successful overall job performance.

Like other parts of the job analysis process, the measurement of job activities appears to be simple, but this is not so. The task measurement by each scale is open to extreme individual bias. What may be *difficult* for one individual may not be so for another. This also holds true for *complexity*. *Importance* may relate more to a specific situation than to a general statement that is overall job related. *Criticality* is certainly environmentally related. Everything done in performing a job is important or critical. It is not easy to differentiate among activities as to whether *a* is more important or complex than *b*. Remember the old adage, "For the loss of a nail, the battle was lost," or the fact that a "billion dollar space project was scrubbed because of the failure of a 10-cent device." An underlying concept here is that all jobs are important or they should not exist. Conversely, all job tasks are critical or they should be eliminated. A commonly requested bit of information is the percentage of *time* spent on a task. This again appears to be a rational, simple request. However, many similar or identical tasks that employees perform require various amounts of time to complete. Many conditions external to the control of the incumbent determine how much time a specific task requires of an employee. In addition, a task requiring, on the average, far less time than another may be much more critical to the overall successful performance of a position/job.

This brief list of the negative aspects of task measurement does not mean that ordering or measurement is unnecessary. It simply means that measurement is a difficult and complex chore. Here again, the analyst's artistry comes into play. It may be that the ordering of tasks requires the use of all seven measurement dimensions and that ratings be completed by all individuals who perform or are intimately knowledgeable of the position/job.

The following scales may be useful for each of the previously identified task dimensions:

1. *Importance* (as compared to other tasks)
   a. Relatively unimportant
   b. Relatively important
   c. Very important

2. *Complexity* (as compared to other tasks)
   a. Relatively simple
   b. Moderately complex
   c. Complex
   d. Extremely complex

3. *Difficulty* (Relative amount of knowledge and skills needed to perform tasks as compared to other tasks)
   a. Easy
   b. Moderately difficult
   c. Difficult
   d. Extremely difficult

4. *Criticality or Consequence of Error* (If task is not performed or is performed poorly, how damaging will be the consequences to the organization or company?)
   a. Virtually no damage
   b. Very little damage
   c. Moderate damage
   d. Sufficient damage
   e. Considerable damage

5. *Frequency of Occurrence (Either of the two scales may be used)*
   a. Less than once a month   a. Seldom (quarterly, annually)
   b. At least once a month   b. Occasionally (monthly)
   c. At least once every two weeks   c. Periodically (bimonthly)
   d. At least once a week   d. Frequently (weekly)
   e. At least once a day   e. Continuously (daily)
   f. Five times or less a day
   g. More than five times a day

6. *Time Spent In Performing Task*
   a. Considerably less than for other tasks
   b. Somewhat less than for other tasks
   c. About the same as for other tasks
   d. Somewhat more than for other tasks
   e. Considerably more than for other tasks

7. *Relationship to Successful Overall Performance*
   a. The quality of performance of this task has little to no relationship to overall job performance.
   b. The quality of performance of this task may eventually affect job performance, but its impact is relatively minor.
   c. If task is performed consistently below standard, job performance tends to be low. Performance above standard has little influence on overall job performance.
   d. The performance of this task must be at the acceptable level necessary to achieve at least adequate job performance.
   e. The performance of this task must be above an acceptable level necessary to achieve from adequate to superior performance.

To ascertain task importance to *overall successful job performance,* inferences must be made relative to the total pictures presented by the task measurement regarding all dimensions. This task analysis imposes a critical test on the job analyst's knowledge and skills.

Identifying Worker Requirements

Following the description of job tasks, the next step is to identify the knowledge and the skills required of an incumbent who is capable of successfully performing the job. Like job content information, the best source of job-required knowledge and skills is the incumbent. Just as job content information collected from incumbents may be inaccurate, there is a possibility that knowledge and skill information provided by incumbents may be inaccurate or incomplete. To be confident that a complete and accurate listing of knowlege and skills has been obtained, the incumbent's list should be compared with some kind of information provided by other incumbents, higher levels of management, and other specialists involved in job requirements (such as job test design and selection professionals).

An optional approach for obtaining knowledge and skill information is to follow the request for task information with this kind of question:

Please list the knowledge and the skills required in the performance of the tasks you just listed.
(1) Knowledge and Skills
   Example:
   (a) Knowledge of basic accounting principles.
   (b) Skill in operating a typewriter.

(2) How Used
   Example:
   (a) To maintain accounting records.
   (b) To type letters and reports in time allotted, meeting standards required.

Knowledge identification may include such areas as (1) knowledge of organization operating practices, (2) knowledge of basic filing procedures, (3) knowledge of gasoline engine ·mechanics, and (4) knowledge of complex electronic systems. Typical skills required of incumbents are skill in (1) communicating with others, (2) operating a typewriter, (3) setting work priorities, and (4) meeting deadlines under pressure. It must be noted that practically any skill can be described as an ability and vice versa. When doing job analysis for test design and selection, ability identification is of paramount interest. Tests are designed primarily to identify acquired abilities. At this stage in the personnel process, it is possible to identify what an employee *can* do, but not necessarily what that person *will* do when performing a job assignment. Those involved in defining job requirements for determining job worth, however, begin making the transition from abilities to skills (skills being demonstrated abilities). The final step in transition from abilities to skills occurs with performance appraisal. Here, the abilities possessed are not of significance; all that is important is what the individual did while performing the job assignment—the skills the incumbent demonstrated.

Identifying Job Environment Conditions

The third kind of job information normally requested of an incumbent is an identification of workplace conditions. In the past, much attention has been placed on physical conditions and safety factors related to the job environment. In addition to these conditions, interest now is focusing on emotional demands and hazards that affect the health of the worker.

Most of the information related to job environment conditions can be acquired through the use of a checklist. A checklist allows a respondee to make a selection(s) among a number of alternative responses. A properly designed set of checklist statements provides a broad spectrum of possible responses, which enhances the probability that the respondee will find the right descriptions of features that relate to the job under study.

There are also disadvantages in using checklist questions. Employees are unlikely to formulate responses that do not appear as alternative responses for a specific job feature. What may be more harmful is that employees may interpret the alternative responses in a context other than that intended. And, of course, there are employees who will select responses that they feel will place their jobs in the most favorable light, not necessarily ones that most closely relate to their particular jobs.

Examples found in a checklist are:

Physical Conditions. Please check the objectionable conditions under which you must perform your job and check whether the condition exists rarely, occasionally, or frequently.

	Rarely	Occasionally	Frequently
(a)_____ Dust	_____	_____	_____
(b)_____ Dirt	_____	_____	_____
(c)_____ Heat	_____	_____	_____
(d)_____ Cold	_____	_____	_____
(e)_____ Fumes	_____	_____	_____
(f)_____ Odors	_____	_____	_____
(g)_____ Noise	_____	_____	_____
(h)_____ Vibration	_____	_____	_____
(i)_____ Wetness	_____	_____	_____
(j)_____ Humidity	_____	_____	_____
(k)_____ Others	_____	_____	_____

Personal Contacts. Please check items that best describe the nature of the people with whom you have contact:

(a)_____ Skeptical   (e)_____ Emotionally Unstable
(b)_____ Uncooperative   (f)_____ Frightened
(c)_____ Hostile   (g)_____ Confused
(d)_____ Normally courteous (h)_____ Mentally Retarded

ANALYSIS OF FIVE PROCEDURES FOR COLLECTING, ANALYZING, AND RECORDING JOB ACTIVITY INFORMATION

Before the start of any job analysis, those persons responsible for the jobs should know what the goals of the analysis are, who is involved, and what will happen. A wide variety of media is available to communicate this information, including meetings, bulletin boards, company newspapers, or special memos. The following brief memo exemplifies a useful introduction to the program:

COMPENSATION AND YOUR JOB

We at Olympia realize that all employees have a vital interest in and concern with their pay and the policies and procedures used by the company in determining pay practices. To develop a fair compensation program, we have set forth these three objectives:

(1) All employees must understand the responsibilities and duties of their jobs.
(2) There must be complete agreement between employees and their supervisors as to these responsibilities and duties.
(3) All employees must receive fair rewards for the knowledge necessary to solve work-related problems, to make decisions, and to accept other responsibilities required for the successful performance of their jobs.

To reach these objectives, it is necessary to analyze a variety of jobs throughout Olympia. You can help to improve our knowledge of your job by cooperating fully with the individual assigned to analyze it. If your job is selected, you will receive complete information on your role in this project at the time of analysis.

Thank you.

All analysts should do their homework before a job analysis session by learning something about the jobs under review. They may review organization charts or other documents. To gain additional insight, they may wish to interview people throughout the organization who have particular knowledge about the jobs under review.

For the analyst to be accepted at the workplace, the manager in the particular job area should introduce the analyst to the workplace supervisor and the incumbent and request one of them to take the analyst on a tour of the work area. Positive acceptance depends on the worker's trust in the motives of the analyst. A major factor in determining trust is the past treatment the worker has received from the organization. An analyst may have to overcome distrust and bitterness directed against the organization because of past real or imagined betrayals. When jobs are being analyzed in a union shop, it is also necessary to explain the study completely to appropriate union officials.

In the following section, methods of collecting and analyzing job content data and information are discussed.

Interview

The interview method involves analyzing the job by interviewing either the worker performing the job or the immediate supervisor or both. The interview is a face-to-face situation. Depending on such conditions as noise, weather, safety, accessibility, secrecy, privacy, or management desires, the workplace is the first choice for the interview site. If any of these factors interferes, then a different location may become necessary.

The interview is especially dependent on the interviewee's willingness and ability to provide the necessary information. When both the interviewer (the analyst) and the interviewee have enough interest to prepare ahead for the interview, the likelihood of success is enhanced. There is always the possibility that the authority vested in the interviewer may frighten the interviewee, leading to overcooperation in which the interviewee hides the truth about a job by exaggerating its importance. This situation is as dangerous as attempting to learn the truth from a stubborn, uninterested employee who is unwilling to provide relevant and valid job data.

After good background preparation and a proper introduction to the interviewee, the interview begins. Empathy is an important attribute of any analyst.[4] The analyst must recognize each jobholder as an important person. This attitude will assist in establishing an atmosphere of mutual respect and trust. Interviewing should not be taken lightly, for this intrusion into the territory of the jobholder provides a basis for the development of mistrust and hostility. The analyst must always assume that the job is vital to the organization and that the performance of each jobholder is a necessary and valuable contribution. Any other attitude conveys negative thoughts to the interviewee and blocks success.

---

[4]Empathy—the ability to see something through another's eyes. It requires understanding, not sympathy.

A personal interview often assists or allows an incumbent to express views and ideas that would never be stated in writing or that are not recognizable from a limited observation. Granting an employee an opportunity to state some deeply felt views or opinions concerning the job is important, not only for gaining job information but also for allowing the employee to vent feelings that may cause considerable anxiety and hostility. At times, these views should be revealed to those persons who have appropriate decision-making authority. At other times, it may be necessary only to listen and give the incumbent "a day in court."

A number of suggestions for accomplishing a successful interview follow:

1. Request the supervisor responsible for the job to select as an interviewee the individual who knows most about the job. (The supervisor should be careful not to select a self-serving flatterer. In this process, there is also the danger that the worker singled out by the manager may feel that social interactions with the work group are jeopardized. In that case, why not let the work group make the selection?)

2. Establish immediate rapport with the interviewee, introduce yourself, know the incumbent's name, speak in easily understood language, briefly review the purpose of the interview, and explain how the selection was made and what opportunity the incumbent will have to review the final job analysis report for accuracy and validity. Do not exhibit impatience if the interviewee is nervous or ill at ease.

3. When possible, use structured outlines to obtain job information. A form that may be of great help when requesting task information is one similar to that described on page 131. A single page of this form could have room for 8 to 10 task statements and the interviewer would use as many pages as necessary to identify all tasks. Give the interviewee an incompleted form and explain what is meant by a task and how you would like to have the task information presented. In most cases, the employee will soon recognize what is desired and will provide the information by using a verb and an object and stating the effect of the action and the work aids used. In using this approach, follow steps 1 and 2 under Identifying Job Tasks on page 130.

4. When possible, confine questions to one area at a time when asking more than one question. Always focus the discussion on what the incumbent does and the processes, work aids, materials, devices, tools, machines, and so on required in the work activities. Differentiate between what the incumbent does and what the machinery produces. If the interviewee begins to stray from the subject, summarize the data collected to that point and then return to the subject.

Give the incumbent sufficient time to ask additional questions to stimulate thought about infrequently occurring assignments. At this point, it may be a good idea to give the interviewee an opportunity to complain about dissatisfactions. In this manner, the interviewer may discover hidden job issues. Always close the interview on a friendly note and express appreciation for the time and the effort required in the interview.

5. After completing the interview, verify the job data. Normally, the interviewee's immediate supervisor is the best person with whom to check for accuracy. The supervisor will probably be able to interpret the interviewee's comments or clarify certain hazy terms or phrases.

There may be times when it is appropriate to interview a group of incumbents. This situation normally arises when a significant number of employees are performing similar, if not identical, work, or work that closely relates in complexity from one level to the next. Group interviewing requires the interviewer to have an ability to interact with a group of people in situations in which diverse and conflicting views may arise. A well-conducted group interview session should spark different points of view, leading to an accurate and complete description of job activities.

The normal approach for conducting a group interview is to include the immediate supervisor(s) of those involved. There may be times, however, when the workers prefer to speak to the interviewer privately. When this occurs, the analyst is wise to review the situation with the supervisor(s) before conducting the interview. There is nothing wrong in conducting an interview without the presence of the supervisor(s), but they must also be assured that they will be kept informed of everything that transpires.

Questionnaire

The questionnaire is usually the least costly method for collecting data. A well-designed questionnaire is the most efficient way to collect a wide array of job data and information in a short period. However, there is the danger that a respondee will either not complete the questionnaire, complete it inaccurately, or take an excessively long time to return it. A questionnaire may be inappropriate for groups that have minimal reading or writing skills.

The development of a good questionnaire should follow these two suggestions:

1. Insert only those response requests that are absolutely necessary.

2. Require as brief an answer as possible to each request.

Hint: Most people detest completing forms; they consider them to be an invasion of privacy and an absolute waste of time and effort. The factor of trust becomes important when using the questionnaire to develop job data. If the incumbents view the motives of the questionnaire as being vital to their well-being, they will not consider it to be an invasion of privacy.

In addition, a good questionnaire must be neat, with topical areas grouped in a logical order or sequence of activities that relates to the natural flow of work. This type of format assists the respondees in analyzing their jobs so that they are able to identify and clarify significant activities and describe the qualifications and conditions related to job performance.

A pressing issue that faces each designer of a job analysis questionnaire, and one that no text can settle, is the degree of structure used in the questionnaire. To what degree should the questions be open-ended (i.e., in narrative form) and to what degree should the questionnaire consist of a highly structured checklist? Each approach has good and bad points and, as in most cases when such issues arise, the answer is that a mixture of both is best.

A narrative approach permits the incumbent to fully describe the job as it is currently being performed. The questionnaire designer may not take into consideration things that happen on the job and may inadvertently omit items that would be valuable data if they were identified. The open-ended questionnaire requires incumbents to think about their jobs and, from this intellectual exercise, more fully appreciate and understand the whys and whats of the job.

On the other hand, an open-ended questionnaire takes a lot of time to complete and audit. Open-ended questionnaires require a certain amount of writing skill to be completed successfully, and many workers do not have these necessary writing skills. In fact, those with good writing skills can verbally upgrade a job by describing it in terms that make it appear to be more important and complex than it actually is. Individuals with minimal or no basic writing skills may describe the job in insufficient detail, leading to an underestimation of the value of the job.

The structured checklist questionnaire requires more initial development time in identifying all the vital areas in which questions should be asked. A checklist approach often requires a set of questions that determines a magnitude of difference among particular activities under study. It is often difficult to compose a checklist that reflects important differences in a work activity or work requirement. In turn, it is easy for an incumbent to check a response that, in reality, is inappropriate for the level of the job.

A checklist approach requires closer auditing on the part of the analyst. When auditing checklist items, a first step is to compare the checked items with the task statements. Does the level of work activities support the item checked? If the answer is negative or doubtful, the analyst must return to the incumbent to find out why the specific item was checked.

Many job analysis questionnaires contain the following parts:

Introductory Page. Explanation to respondee of the reason why information is being requested and the importance of accurate, complete, and timely response.

Job Demographic Information. List of such items as date questionnaire was completed, job title, job code (if any), respondee's name, name of respondee's supervisor, department, etc.

Job Activity Information. In addition to requested task information previously described, the following two questions may be used:

1. What tasks are you now performing that you think you should not be doing?
2. What tasks are you not now doing that you think you should be doing?

Knowledge and Skills Required. As described earlier in this chapter.
Certificates and Licenses. Any certificates or licenses required by law.

Frequency and Intensity of Work Reviews. Closeness of supervision. Quality control procedures.

Opportunity for Self-design of Work. Rules, procedures, and guidelines available for defining work routines.

Interpersonal Contacts, Purpose of Contacts, and Conditions That Influence Contacts. Who are the people? What are their positions, and why are these contacts made when performing job assignments?

Physical and Emotional Conditions That Influence Incumbent Performance. List of all kinds of environmental conditions that have an impact on the health, safety, and performance of the incumbent.

Respondee Demographics. Previous jobs held by respondee. Years of service with organization. Years on present job.

Supervisor Review. Section that allows supervisor to review respondee's responses, make additions or corrections, and sign questionnaire. *Important:* Even though the supervisor is asked to review a questionnaire, he or she never crosses out or erases a comment made by the respondee.

Observation

In the observation method, the analyst actually observes the jobholder performing the job and records what is seen during this firsthand observation. To analyze the job fully, however, the analyst must observe the complete work cycle. This may be difficult in many jobs because some activities in the job cycle occur at infrequent or irregular intervals. When observation is the only method used to acquire job information, it may be necessary to observe at various periods during the entire work cycle. This may be beyond the ability of the analyst. Observation also may require the analyst to take excessive notes of all data pertinent to the job and to its environment to develop a complete narrative of the job.

Diary/Log

The diary/log normally is a less structured approach than that using the basic job analysis format, although it can contain specific topical questions. Normally, the diary/log requires the employee to record daily activities or tasks and requires considerable effort and diligence. Most people are not sufficiently self-disciplined to detail such activities, and it is sometimes difficult for them to outline accomplishments in clear, concise, and simple language.

At the end of the day, it is necessary to review the diary/log and, from memory, compare it with the activities of the day. The diary/log should also contain sections for recording activities performed at infrequent or irregular intervals (i.e., weekly, monthly, quarterly, etc.). Actually, a diary/log is ideal for this particular purpose. It is also especially useful when working with professionals or on jobs that require a high degree of technical or scientific knowledge.

The lightweight portable tape recorder is a valuable aid in this method. It permits the jobholder to describe work activities vocally and almost at the time of occurrence. The analyst can then transcribe the tape later.

Any combination of the preceding four methods may provide better results than one used by itself. Sometimes the questionnaire, interview, and observation can be combined. This approach requires the incumbent to complete the questionnaire. After reviewing it, the analyst returns to the work site, interviews the employee, and observes the job being performed. The analyst now has a very good working knowledge of the job and is able to ask a variety of questions to obtain in-depth data and information about the job, thus leading to an accurate description of the work required and performed. In fact, observation combines well with any of the methods. One view is worth a thousand words, and the on-site observation of the job is immensely valuable to any analyst. The questionnaire, interview, or diary/log, however, greatly facilitates the identification of particular points that the analyst may have missed earlier because they were hidden from normal view. The analyst must recognize that it is impossible to be a specialist on every job and that it is always possible to miss a significant point.

Structured Task List Questionnaires

Two structured task list questionnaires available for analyzing job content and improving an understanding of the job use comprehensive, detailed, and quantitatively oriented job analysis studies. These two methods are the Job Analysis Questionnaire (JAQ) and the Position Analysis Questionnaire (PAQ).

Both the JAQ and PAQ provide systematic approaches for identifying job similarities and differences within and between organizations. Although these two procedures differ in the methods used for collecting and identifying job tasks or task items, both develop profiles of jobs.

The JAQ requires the identification of specific job task, job environment, and job knowledge items that are descriptive of the sample of jobs to be analyzed. Based on responses of job incumbents to these items, underlying dimensions of job duties are identified. For example, in a JAQ project for Northern States Power, Jerry Newman and Frank Krzystofiak identified 598 task items, 30 job environment items, and 130 job knowledge items that were relevant to the 1,700 exempt positions included in the job analysis. Analysis of the responses to the 598 task items yielded 60 underlying factors that were used to develop profiles of job content for the 1,700 jobs.[5]

The PAQ is the result of over 10 years of research by psychologists at Purdue University involving the study of thousands of jobs.[6] The PAQ is a

---

[5]Jerry Newman and Frank Krzystofiak, "Quantified Job Analysis: A Tool for Improving Human Resource Management Decision-making," a paper presented at the Academy of Management Meeting, Orlando, FL, August 15, 1977.

[6]Ernest J. McCormick, Paul R. Jeanneret, and Robert C. Mecham, "A Study of Job Characteristics and Job Dimensions as Based on the Position Analysis Questionnaire (PAQ)," *Journal of Applied Psychology,* August 1972, pp. 347–368.

structured job analysis questionnaire that uses a checklist format to identify 194 job elements. The checklist provides information about whether the element relates to the job under study and, if it does, to what degree. These 194 job elements relate to behavior required of incumbents and other job characteristics. This approach provides universality of application for the PAQ, making it useful for analyzing almost any job.

The PAQ groups 194 elements within 27 division job dimensions and five overall job dimensions. These 32 dimensions are further grouped within six major divisions. These divisions are (1) information input, (2) mental processes, (3) work output, (4) relationship with other persons, (5) job context, and (6) other job characteristics. From their research, the designers of the PAQ have identified those job elements within the job dimensions that are able to describe job families (i.e., groupings of jobs having comparable responsibility and duty assignments and similar knowledge demands but varying in magnitude of scope, intensity, importance, or skill levels).

The basic assumptions made by the designers of the PAQ are as follows:

1. Job requirements are the same for a given kind of work activity.

2. Job elements that are useful for describing job activities may be reliably identified and rated as they exist within the job under study.

3. Human work has an order or structure, and work-ordered job elements make it possible to determine statistically the nature of that structure.

Computer-based programs score each job under study relative to the 32 job dimensions. This score represents a profile for the job and is compared with standard profiles of known job families. This quantitatively oriented, computer-based analysis also identifies the significant job behaviors and classifies the job. The quantitative characteristics of the PAQ and its ability to group jobs by common characteristics and reflect differences in relative value permit the PAQ also to be useful in establishing rates of pay for jobs.

Both the JAQ and the PAQ are completed by employees familiar with the particular job under study. These employees are normally experienced incumbents or the immediate supervisor of the job. They estimate the various human characteristics or behaviors required in the performance of the job, and they indicate the particular level of the task items (in the case of the JAQ) or job elements (in the case of the PAQ) required for the job under study.

Because of design differences, the PAQ does not provide actual job behaviors as they are but, rather, as they should be. The JAQ, on the other hand, includes a detailed investigation of the technical aspects of the jobs and, by investigating this dimension, comes closer to describing the jobs as they exist in the organization under study.

A method for identifying actual job behavior is available through the use of the Critical Incident Technique (CIT). The CIT requires the random selection of a sufficient number of incumbents who must write short narratives that describe at least one incident about the behavior of a successful incumbent or good job performance of an incumbent and one narrative of an incident involving poor performance or unacceptable job behavior. After they have been written, these critical incident narratives are analyzed to determine whether they could be judged reliable (e.g., stability of data resulting from some measurement process) and to establish agreement for placing the incidents in major categories for classification purposes. By collecting hundreds of such incidents, it is possible to develop a checklist consisting of desirable or undesirable job behaviors based on the past actual performance of incumbents.

The CIT is extremely valuable for identifying and classifying job accountabilities. Accountabilities are statements describing final output(s) of the job or end-result measures. Because it describes job behaviors, the CIT is useful for developing dimensions of job performance. Accountabilities are broad statements of expected job performance.

Compensation specialists must be aware, however, that the CIT identifies job behaviors as they are, not as they should be. A responsibility of the personnel/compensation specialist is to reconcile the variation between the *what is* and the *what should be.*

Methods for Improving Job Content Analysis

Two methods available to assist in analyzing job content data and information are the U.S. Department of Labor (DOL) Methodology and Functional Job Analysis (FJA).

DOL Methodology—Since the 1930s, the U.S. Department of Labor has been involved in developing a methodology for analyzing and classifying job content. Through the research implemented and the training efforts sponsored by the DOL, many government agencies (federal, state, and local) and private sector businesses have received training in the DOL methodology or a variation of it.

The DOL methodology centers on five categories of information that relate to the satisfactory performance of workers on the job. These categories are (1) worker functions, (2) work fields, (3) machines, tools, equipment, and work aids, (4) materials, products, subject matter, and services, and (5) worker traits.

1. The *worker functions* describe what the worker does in relation to *data, people,* and *things.* To describe the varying complexities of data, people, and things, the DOL has developed a scale of values for each category. The highest combination of activities that describes the three areas of worker functions identifies the relative importance of the job. The 24 identifying activities of the worker function areas are shown in table 5-1. Normally, each successive function reading down each column in table 5-1 includes or involves all functions that follow.

2. The *work fields* are the specific methods used to carry out technological or socioeconomic requirements of the job. The DOL identifies 99 categories for further classifying these fields.

TABLE 5-1

DOL WORKER FUNCTIONS

Data	People	Things
0 Synthesizing	0 Mentoring	0 Setting-up
1 Coordinating	1 Negotiating	1 Precision Working
2 Analyzing	2 Instructing	2 Operating-Controlling
3 Compiling	3 Supervising	3 Driving-Operating
4 Computing	4 Diverting	4 Manipulating
5 Copying	5 Persuading	5 Tending
6 Comparing	6 Speaking-Signaling	6 Feeding-Offbearing
	7 Serving	7 Handling
	8 Taking Instruction & Helping	

3. The *machines, tools, equipment, and work aids* are examples of the instruments and the devices that are used to carry out the specific methods.

4. The *materials, products, subject matter, and services* include material worked on, final product produced, knowledge dealt with, and services rendered.

5. The *worker traits* are the factors that describe the requirements made on the worker. They include the following five components: (1) training time, (2) aptitude, (3) temperament, (4) interests, and (5) physical demands.[7]

Functional Job Analysis (FJA)—Sidney A. Fine, a long-time professional in the Employment Service of the U.S. Department of Labor and later a private consultant, has added to the DOL methodology through his Functional Job Analysis (FJA).[8] This spinoff of the DOL methodology stresses the area of worker functions (duties, people, and things) and makes some modifications to the 24 DOL activities used to scale the three major worker functions. The changes are descriptive of work performed in the human services field. In addition, Fine has reversed the numerical coding so that Level One now represents the least complex relationship (more in line with typical classification numbering systems).

The FJA method also uses a number of additional scales to identify job requirements further. These scales include (1) Scale of Worker Instructions that

[7]U.S. Department of Labor, Manpower Administration, *Handbook for Analyzing Jobs* (Washington, DC: Government Printing Office, 1972). This book includes a complete description of the DOL methodology. It is a valuable reference for anyone involved in compensation management and is essential for anyone involved in the use of DOL methodology.

[8]Sidney A. Fine and Wretha W. Wiley, *An Introduction to Functional Job Analysis: A Scaling of Selected Tasks from the Social Welfare Field, Methods for Manpower Analysis No. 4* (Kalamazoo, MI.: W. E. Upjohn Institute for Employment Research, 1971).

identifies levels of discretion available and exercised by employees, and (2) Scales of Educational Development (also used in the DOL methodology) that include a Reasoning Development Scale, a Mathematical Development Scale, and a Language Development Scale.[9]

Fine also claimed that the FJA overcomes one of the major failings inherent in the DOL methodology—failure to relate work performed to the purposes, goals, and objectives of the organization. Fine stated that the FJA incorporates the goals and objectives of the organization into the task statements structured around worker functions and through a "systems approach" to the full articulation of goals and objectives.[10]

The FJA not only is useful for analyzing job requirements but also for providing criteria for evaluating the worth of a job because it distinguishes between functional, adaptive, and specific content skill requirements of each job. Finally, by specifying and defining expected functional performance, it develops criteria useful for appraising the performance of a particular worker.

A MULTIMETHOD, MULTIPROCEDURE APPROACH FOR COLLECTING JOB DATA AND INFORMATION

Complexity is a common aspect of managing the human, capital, and technical resources of an organization. Complexity results from the large number and the wide variety of organization-related variables that interact dynamically. Because of complexity, it is seldom possible to find one method or one procedure that provides data of sufficient quality and quantity to facilitate making sound decisions. Job analysis is no exception. Any one method or procedure has technical limits that minimize its usefulness and stress the need for a multimethod, multiprocedure approach to job analysis.

Job activity/task analysis, which uses such procedures as the interview, observation, the questionnaire, and the diary/log, provides data for identifying and describing responsibility and duty requirements, qualifications, and working conditions. When describing responsibility and duty requirements, analysts attempt to limit the number of statements. It is important to describe job content fully, but a lengthy list of activities or tasks limits identification and understanding of what the job is all about. A skilled analyst must know how to condense and combine job information into broad categories that fully describe the functional activities of the job. The transaction of job tasks into duty and responsibility statements is discussed in detail in chapter 6, Job Descriptions.

On the other hand, quantitative job analysis methods (i.e., the JAQ and the PAQ) take an in-depth view of the job by analyzing it task item by task item. These methods provide a conceptual framework for understanding what job

[9]Sidney A. Fine, *Functional Job Analysis Scales: A Desk Aid, Methods for Manpower Analysis, No. 7* (Kalamazoo, MI.: W. E. Upjohn Institute for Employment Research, 1973).

[10]Sidney A. Fine, Ann M. Holt, and Maret F. Hutchinson, *Functional Job Analysis: How to Standardize Task Statements, Methods for Manpower Analysis, No. 9* (Kalamazoo, MI.: W. E. Upjohn Institute for Employment Research, 1974).

content analysis should provide and they establish cutoff points that differentiate one job from another. The JAQ and especially the PAQ describe *what should be*. Job activity analysis describes *what is*. The CIT study supplies additional job information by identifying acceptable job behavior.

The scope of any job analysis program depends on the intended purpose and use of the collected data. A detailed job analysis study may benefit from combining the more common job activity/task procedures with the quantitative methods and the CIT.

INFLUENCING JOB ANALYSIS DESIGN

It is difficult to identify the beginning of the development of a compensation program. It is almost, if not totally, a "chicken or the egg" situation. Although it may seem logical or realistic to begin with the job analysis,

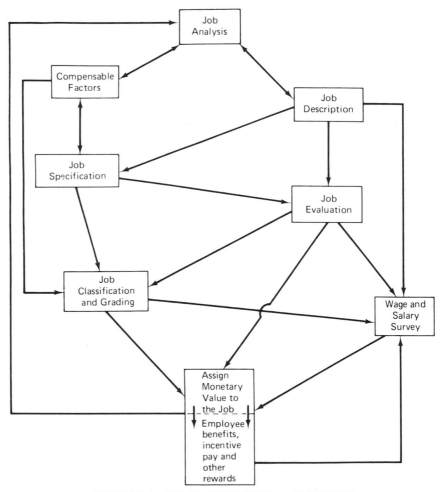

FIGURE 5–4   JOB ANALYSIS INFORMATION FLOW

compensation is truly an open system that requires changes at every step. Figure 5-4 indicates how the steps that follow job analysis provide feedback that may influence and change the original job analysis design.

One of the most important elements of a job analysis is identifying those factors that to some degree are required to perform the variety of jobs in the organization and that contribute to its ultimate success. A new organization or one going through a dramatic growth stage may never have identified those compensable or goal-contributing factors. In this case, the job analysis procedure may have to be fairly broad and rather vague to develop this wide scope necessary to identify the factors contributing to successful performance.

Once these factors have been identified, it is then possible to redesign the job analysis program. In this stage, job analysis procedures become more sophisticated, using improved (i.e., quicker, easier, more concise) data-collecting instruments that permit everyone involved to develop a better understanding of the value and importance of each job and the relationship of one job to another. Job analysis is part of an on-going planning system, and as such it must reflect and report the changes that occur in the organization. It not only identifies crucial organizational problems but also provides the opportunity for forthright and constructive action.

Job analysis provides a direct approach to the daily activities of the organization as well as a view to the future. It enables adjustments to be made to meet the changes as they occur. It also identifies situations in which adjustment cannot be made or that must be postponed because of forces beyond the control of the organization (e.g., legislation or environmental or social pressure). With the elimination or reduction of these barriers, however, a job analysis program assists in altering compensation plans to meet new conditions or trends.

An old saying states that "chance favors the prepared mind." Organizations prepare for their opportunities by constantly trying to improve their compensation systems.

SELECTED READINGS

Benge, Eugene J., "By-products of Job Evaluation," *Personnel Journal,* July–August 1950, pp. 94–99. The author analyzes the many uses of the job description and tells why it must be sufficiently detailed in order to serve the many purposes it is capable of serving.

Berenson, Conrad, and Henry O. Ruhnke, "Job Descriptions: Guidelines for Personnel Management," *Personnel Journal,* January 1966, pp. 14–19. The authors review the basic techniques used in the collection of job data and the preparation of job descriptions.

Burk, Samuel L. H., "Salary and Wage Administration," *Personnel Journal,* September 1936, pp. 105–115. This article provides an excellent introduction to the tools and the techniques available for developing an equitable and workable compensation system by one of the pioneers in compensation administration.

Purves, Dale, "How to Write and Use Management Job Descriptions," *The Office,* January 1966, pp. 144–145, 248, 250, 253. The author provides insight into the need for an analyst to be able to distinguish between why a job exists and how it operates. In addition, the analyst must be able to write with clarity and technical precision in order that the finished document be an important and frequently used instrument.

Suskin, Harold, "Job Evaluation—It's More than a Tool for Setting Pay Rates," *Public Personnel Review,* October 1970, pp. 283–289. The author states that the goal of job evaluation should be more than determining pay rates; rather it is a valuable management tool for position management, job engineering, manpower planning, performance appraisal, and career development.

U.S. Civil Service Commission, *Job Analysis: Key to Better Management.* Washington, DC: Government Printing Office, 1973. This is an excellent, inexpensive, and broad guide to job analysis.

6

Job Descriptions

CONTENT

Chapter 6 discusses the purpose and the use of job descriptions and ways to structure, write, and update them.

GOALS

Upon concluding this chapter, you should be able to develop a job description that accurately, uniformly, and fairly describes a job. In addition you should be able to make it a working part of the human resource system.

A job description is like a blueprint of one of the parts of the organization. Although common to most personnel record systems, the value of job descriptions has been debated repeatedly. Even so, more organizations continue to spend valuable time and money developing this tool of personnel structuring and planning.

Is the job description necessary? Is it vital to the functioning of a well-managed organization? Is it worth what it costs to prepare and maintain?

Answers to these questions require a review of the reasons for the existence and the use of the job description as well as a review of the reasons managers tend to underrate and underuse it.

PURPOSE AND USE OF THE JOB DESCRIPTION

The job description is one of the primary tools for coordinating the human and nonhuman resources of the organization to achieve individual, group, and organizational goals. The job description provides services in a number of vital areas. Among the more important are (1) personnel and compensation management, (2) legal compliance, and (3) industrial relations and collective bargaining. It is recognized that few, if any, organizations use the job description for all areas described in this chapter. However, it is a valuable tool, and anyone involved in the management of human resources should try to make greater use of it.

Personnel and Compensation Management

Practically all organizations seek better ways to plan for their human resource requirements. There is probably no better general-purpose planning tool than the job description, as a brief analysis of its value in the major personnel areas emphasizes.

Personnel Requirements—Together with other tools such as manning charts and work-unit function statements, the job description enlivens the staid organization chart. A job description must always tell it "like it is." For this reason, it must not describe the way the job was performed in the past or how it will be performed in the future. It must describe it as it actually is now. If it does, the job description becomes an integral part of the planning process because any worthwhile analysis of future human resource requirements must relate to the current situation.

The job description is extremely helpful in pinpointing vital personnel requirement gaps as well as in identifying unneeded positions or employees. Thus, it restricts the power of the type of manager who does not like to be tied down by specifics. In a broader sense, it assists in structuring or restructuring the organization. In this connection, it is valuable when decisions must be made as to centralization or decentralization, or with regard to some form of functional, geographic, or product dispersion.

Because current and valid job descriptions enable the organization to make rational decisions in such critical areas, they can help to limit the ego-centered power moves of manipulative executives. The job description helps to reveal obvious, irrelevant, and manipulative schemes. Its value cannot be overestimated in properly recognizing and using human resources.

Recruiting and Screening—The individual who recruits and screens for the vacant job is seldom the one responsible for supervising its performance. Therefore, it is vital that the recruiting and screening personnel have as clear a picture as possible of what the job is all about. To increase their success rate, they should also know something about the behavioral characteristics of the supervisor of the job and the members of the work group. A job description does *not* include this type of information. One way to gain it, however, is through a visit to the work site that includes a review of the job description with the supervisor. Such information as the skills and talents considered to be critical for the success of a new work candidate should be requested. An open mind and keen observation are helpful.

Hiring and Placement—Final selection and placement are normally the joint responsibilities of personnel specialists and the immediate supervisor. When the personnel specialist has total responsibility, however, there is significant reliance on the knowledge, responsibility, and physical working requirements spelled out in the job description to match the candidate's qualifications with the job requirements.

Orientation—Possibly the most important predictor of job success is the first impression gained by the new employee of the job. A supervisor renders an important service when providing a job description to prospective employees for their review and analysis. This initial introduction to the job sets forth its requirements, and it helps the candidate to understand more fully what the organization expects. It also tells new members how their new jobs fit into current pictures of themselves and how these perceptions will conform to their future expectations and aspirations. Incumbents, however, should never consider the job description as a top limit to what can be done by them. They should understand that only their own abilities and interests—not the job description—limit their performance.

Training and Development—It is seldom possible for an organization to fill a vacancy without providing some degree of training to new jobholders so that they can perform the job as outlined in the job description. Possibly even more important, however, is the fact that as the job and its description change, training and development must keep pace. Rapidly changing demands on the output of the organization and on its jobs require that substantial attention be given to developing the human potential of all its members. They not only must be properly trained for the jobs of today, but they must also be prepared for those of tomorrow. Furthermore, training in functional skills and in the use of technology must relate to ever-advancing levels of worker aspirations and expectations.

An organizational environment that breeds trust, security, and recognition of performance acts as a springboard to the development of its employees' abilities and skills in meeting changing job demands. The job description must implicitly convey such qualities. It does this by honestly and accurately describing the job and providing a base for teaching an employee as much as possible about it and its relationship to other jobs and to the organization in general. Thus, the job description not only carries a message indicating the importance of the job itself and of the contributions made by each employee, it also describes how the growth of the organization depends on the growth of its members.

Job Evaluation and Wage Grades—The description and the specification of each job enable the analyst to properly evaluate one job in relation to others. A logical progression is the development of an equitable wage structure, which requires internal equity and a fair comparison with jobs in other organizations requiring similar effort, skills and responsibilities, under comparable working conditions. Evaluating the worth of a job is not only important for an equitable wage structure, it is valuable in providing a base from which to determine employee benefits and merit payments that relate individual performance to the performance of the organization.

Classification and Job Families—The job description makes it possible to identify common job activities and requirements. With the description of enough common activities and requirements, it is possible to identify examples of significant responsibilities, duties, and employment standards for the development of classes and families of jobs.

Compensation Surveys—For surveys to be useful and valid, there must be some understandable method for developing comparability. Here again, the job description provides the word picture that enables organizations producing widely varied outputs in scattered locations to compare jobs they have in common. The value of any survey depends on the quality of the comparability.

Pay Structure—A fair day's pay is as much a relative consideration as an absolute one. The pay structure must permit accurate compensation of workers according to the value of their jobs and the contributions they make toward achieving organizational goals. One of the first steps in developing an equitable pay structure occurs in the accurate description of the job.

Performance Appraisal—Almost all employees want to know how well they are performing. The performance appraisal is a prime mechanism for providing such feedback. To have any degree of credibility, it must relate to actual results. Most effective appraisal processes compare actual with expected or desired results, and the job content and accountabilities sections of the job description provide a base for establishing standards of performance.

Legal Requirements

Changes in legislation, as well as changing emphasis in enforcement patterns, have placed new stress on the importance of the job description.

The Fair Labor Standards Act requires most organizations to support their determinations of exempt and nonexempt employees. Job descriptions provide primary support for such decisions. The Equal Pay Act requires equal pay for employees performing work in similar occupations requiring equal skill, equal effort, and equal responibility under similar working conditions. The job description relates jobs to proper occupational groups and identifies the skills, the effort, and the responsibilities needed to perform the job. A quality job description provides a sound base for determining the comparable worth of jobs and for establishing employment and performance standards for each job. It assists an organization to eliminate artificial employment barriers and meet standards required by Title VII of the Civil Rights Act. The job description should identify working conditions that endanger the health of the incumbent. The specification of safety and health considerations is a vital part of a job description and assists in compliance with the Occupational Safety and Health Act. Chapter 3 covers these and other laws in greater detail.

Industrial Relations — Collective Bargaining

A key labor principle is "equal pay for equal work." Many union demands focus on the elimination of varied pay rates for similar work or the distortion or imbalance of the wage structure among comparable organizations. The job description provides a starting point for standardization in pay rates. Although unions urge uniform rates, organizations must defend themselves by recognizing and identifying which jobs are similar and protecting those pay levels that truly discriminate among jobs that require different levels of knowledge and responsibilities and among employees who provide different contributions.

A Tool for Planning, Operations, and Control

The previous section, which discussed the general areas of use of the job description, showed the importance of job descriptions with regard to improving the effectiveness and efficiency of an organization. The job description is also one of the few tools available to managers that assist them in performing the three basic functions of management—planning, operations, and control.

The job description is basic to operational planning (i.e., the planning of day-to-day activities), and it also serves as a direct link to the area of strategic or long-range planning. Good short- and long-range planning lead to the development and the description of jobs that meet current requirements and into new jobs that ensure the survival and the growth of both the individual and the organization. The job description assists in identifying current training requirements and in acquiring and developing adequate human resources to meet future demands.

From an operations point of view, the most important single part of a job description is that which describes the elements and the requirements of the job as it exists today. There is no doubt that the job description has future orientation, but its roots are in the here and now. Job requirements, whether they are standards related to output, or to recruiting, training, and development to produce the output, are operational considerations.

Although seldom mentioned, the control elements of job descriptions are vital. A major failure of many organizations is the inability to identify, measure, and reward performance. Employees who are rewarded for below-standard performance hold their managers and the organization in low esteem and will do little to improve their skills or contribute to the success of the organization. Conversely, those employees who provide better-than-average performance and receive little or no recognition will either leave or will reduce their efforts until they are on the same level with those making a much smaller contribution. In either case, such individuals will normally be dissatisfied and hostile. Thus, it is apparent that the job description, when used as one of the basic elements for setting performance standards—expected results—becomes a valuable tool of control, an instrument of immense feedback value.

ELEMENTS OF THE JOB DESCRIPTION

Although there is no universal form, most job descriptions contain at least five sections: (1) identification; (2) summary; (3) responsibilities and duties; (4) accountabilities; and (5) specifications. A common format followed in developing a job description is for the identification, summary, responsibility and duty, and accountabilities sections to be on one side of the page with the specifications on the opposite side (see figure 6-1). When a job specification section is not included in the job description, or when the specification section does not adequately describe the minimum education and experience qualifications required by the job, there must be an employment standards section (which normally follows the accountabilities section). Compensable factors, as described through the substantiating data in the sample job specification (figure 6-2), are discussed in detail in chapter 8.

All job descriptions of an organization should follow the same format, and those persons responsible for writing them should receive similar instructions and follow identical guidelines so that in total the job descriptions provide a balanced and fair picture of the organization.

Job Identification

The identification section of the job description takes the following form:

Job Title	Status Job Code
Date	Plant/Division
Written by	Department/Section
Approved by	Grade Points
Title of Immediate Supervisor	Pay Range

IDENTIFICATION

Computer Programmer	*Nonexempt*	*007.167*
Job Title	Status	Job Code
April 10, 1981		*Olympia, Inc.—Main Office*
Date		Plant/Division
Arthur Allen		Data Processing—Information Systems
Written By		Department/Section

FIGURE 6–1   SAMPLE JOB DESCRIPTION

Juanita Montgomery
Approved By

_21_ _2,480_
Grade   Points

Programming Supervisor
Title of Immediate Supervisor

_22,500–25,850–29,200_
Pay Range

SUMMARY

Performs studies, develops and maintains program concerned with employee benefits, focusing specifically on life, medical and hospitalization, accident and disability, and retirement insurance for all divisions of Olympia.

RESPONSIBILITIES AND DUTIES

1. Serves as a member of the employee benefits team of programmers.
   1. Updates, modifies, and designs new applications in such areas as enrollment, premium costs, premium collections.
   2. Maintains existing programs that constitute employee health and retirement benefits program for employees of Olympia.
   3. Develops reports on the status of existing program for which responsible.
2. Recommends needed redesign studies.
   1. Reviews proposed changes in legislation.
   2. Consults with user representatives on proposed changes in existing benefits programs, constraints, and potentially relevant developments.
   3. Discusses with other programmers and software specialists use of most suitable application programming technology.
   4. Identifies impact of program changes on existing computer programs.
   5. Recommends to immediate supervisor changes that should be made in applicable software.
3. Carries out study projects.
   1. Investigates feasibility of alternate design approaches with view of determining best solution within constraints set by available resources and future demands.
   2. Explores desirability of various possible outputs, considering both EDP and non-EDP costs, benefits, and trade-offs.
   3. Identifies types and designation of inputs needed, system interrelationships, processing logic involved.
   4. Develops programming specifications.
   5. Informs supervisor of progress, unusual problems encountered, and resources required.
4. Designs internal program structure of files and records and reviews its operation.
   1. Determines detailed sequences of actions in program logic.
   2. Codes, tests, debugs, and documents programs.
   3. Writes and maintains computer operator instructions for assigned programs.
   4. Monitors existing programs to ensure operation as required.
   5. Responds to problems by diagnosing and correcting errors of logic and coding.

ACCOUNTABILITIES

1. Completion of projects on assigned schedule.
2. Development of programs that best use resources of organization.
3. Prompt recognition of program defects or shortcomings.

FIGURE 6–1   CONTINUED

SPECIFICATION

Factor	Substantiating Data	Level	Points
Knowledge Required	Knowledge of operation and capabilities of computers of Olympia. Detailed knowledge of processes and rules governing programming to carry out assignments. Knowledge of relevant employer and employee benefits program of Olympia.	7	1,250
Supervisory Controls	Assigned responsibility for development and operation of several programs. Consults with supervisor on target dates, unanticipated problems and conflict that arise with other work units of Olympia. Projects reviewed in terms of effectiveness in meeting requirements.	4	450
Guidelines	Published subject-matter procedures, programming standards; modification of existing documentation frequently required. Judgment required in gathering information and developing programs that meet system and client demands.	3	275
Complexity	Wide variety of programs requiring changes to meet exceptions and new technology, changes in benefit designs; must anticipate future changes.	4	225
Scope and Effect	Formulate project recommendations; analyze technical problems; establish specifications.	4	225
Personal Contacts	Representatives of users in other work units, other programmers, and computer operations personnel.	2	25
Purpose of Contacts	Determine program and system requirements; monitor production to correct errors; answer questions; relay instructions; assist other programmers solve their problems.	1	20
Physical Demands	Work is sedentary. Some travel to office of clients.	1	5
Work Environment	Work is performed in typical office setting.	1	5
	Total Points		2,480

FIGURE 6–1   CONTINUED

Job Title—The most important element in the identification section is the job title. A title that correctly and precisely identifies the job is of value (1) for the jobholder's information, and self-esteem, (2) for purposes of job relationships, and (3) for comparison purposes with similar jobs in other organizations.

The title indicates to anyone reviewing the description, and specifically to the jobholder, the particular field of activity of the job, its relationship to that field, and its professional standing. The title should lend some prestige to the job and should contribute to the personal satisfaction of the jobholder. The title should not allude to sex or age requirements. Any implication as to age or sex requirements in the job title or the body of a job description should be eliminated (e.g., fireman to firefighter, busboy to dining room attendant, draftsman to drafter, and waiter or waitress to waiter-waitress). The title is the first step in defining the job and establishing a ranking order with other jobs. It is valuable as an outline to department, division, or functional groupings, a guide for promotions or transfers, and an indicator of training and development requirements.

The job title is especially important when one is attempting to compare the job with similar jobs in other organizations, a process that is critical when developing pay surveys and for recruiting purposes.

Like the job description, it is important to keep job titles current. Jobs with similar duties and similar requirements should have the same title. The *Dictionary of Occupational Titles* is extremely valuable for this purpose.[1] The next section discusses this dictionary at length.

Job Status—The job status section of a job description permits quick and easy identification of the exempt or nonexempt status of the job relative to its compliance with the Fair Labor Standards Act.

Job Code—The job code permits easy and rapid referencing of all jobs. It may consist of letters or numbers in any combination. Each code must have sufficient characters to identify all the jobs in the organization. The code can be a four-character alphanumeric code (e.g., B 735) or even a six-digit numeric code (e.g., 007.167) as used by the U.S. Department of Labor, Employment, and Training Administration in its *Dictionary of Occupational Titles* (DOT).[2] Any other suitable combination of numbers or letters will serve, but brevity is vital.

The DOT is a valuable guide for developing job descriptions. It not only provides job titles and an excellent method for coding jobs; but it describes work performed, worker requirements, clues for relating applicants and requirements,

---

[1]U.S. Department of Labor, Employment & Training Administration, *Dictionary of Occupational Titles,* 4th ed. (Washington, DC: Government Printing Office, 1977).

[2]The *Dictionary of Occupational Titles* actually supplies a nine-digit code, but the final three-digit suffix is seldom used. The complete DOT code takes this appearance: 007.167.018. The 018 suffix identifies additional specialty job titles when the DOT provides only one principal title and job description. In the example, Computer Programmer, if programming activities were specialized by types of data such as machine programming data, business data, scientific research data, and so on, the suffix code could be used to identify business data programming.

and training and methods of entry for specific types of work. The two volumes of the DOT provide a fundamental guide for job comparison purposes.

A brief review of the manner in which the DOT uses its six-character code will aid any organization that develops its own code or that uses the DOT code. An example follows:

007.167

007 —The first three digits signify occupational group arrangement.

0 —Professional, technical, and managerial occupations.

00 —Occupations in architecture and engineering.

007 —Industrial engineering.

.167—The second three digits represent worker trait arrangement: respectively, data, people, and things; .167 specifically relates to engineering, scientific, and technical operations.

.1 —Coordinating data.

.16 —Speaking–signaling to people.

.167—Handling things. (The final three digits relate to worker functions. The section on the DOL methodology in chapter 5 describes in detail these worker functions and what these numbers relate to.)

Date—The date on the job description refers to the date that it was actually written. (Next to the title, the date is the most important job identification datum. It is frequently critical to know when the description was written.)

Written by—This is the person who writes the job description.

Approved by—This space is for the signature and the title of the person who approves the job description.

Plant/Division and Department/Section—This space provides for the precise location of the job.

Grade—This space is for the grade of the job if there is such a category.

Points—If a point system is used, this space provides for the number of points assigned a job.

Title of Immediate Supervisor—This space is self-explanatory.

Pay Range—This space provides for the specific pay or pay range of a job.

Many organizations do not use the plant/division and department/section, grade/level, points, and pay range elements because they consider them to be unnecessary or because rapid changes or variations would require frequent revisions of the job description. It must be remembered that the benefits gained from a current, valid job description are worth the updating costs.

Like most planning tools, job descriptions require constant review and reevaluation, which is a costly process. In a world of rapid change, updating is an absolute necessity; but there never seems to be enough time available to do it.

Furthermore, an obsolete job description may not only be worthless, it also may be harmful because it inaccurately describes a job. This inaccuracy can become an organizational liability or manipulative technique that will give an unfair advantage to the jobholder.

Job Summary

The job summary is normally a word picture of the job that narrates its general characteristics listing only major functions or activities (see figure 6–1). Through the precise ordering and careful selection of words, it indicates clearly and specifically what the jobholder must do. This section of the job description provides enough information to identify and differentiate the major functions and activities of the job from those of others. It is especially valuable to the individual who wants a very quick overview of the job.

Because a primary aim of the job description is to describe the job objectively, correctly, and fully while using as few words as possible, some excellent guides are available to help in writing a job description phrase or sentence, whether in a narrative or an outline form. The section, "Writing Activity Statements," that comes later in the chapter explains how to write brief but clear activity statements useful for writing job summaries.

When selecting words, be consistent in their use. Many words have a variety of meanings. Establish a meaning for a word and stick to it. Also try to avoid ambiguous words. Use quantitative words when possible (e.g., "makes 20 customer contacts daily," not, "makes *many* customer contacts daily"). Avoid making conclusions (e.g., "performs work requiring the lifting of 94-pound bags of concrete," instead of, "performs strenuous work"). It is unnecessary to use stilted $20 words; commonly used, simple English words and terms are always preferable.

Care should be taken in the use of code words when writing job descriptions (e.g., "under close supervision," "general supervision," "considerable," "unusual," etc.). As organizations enlarge and more and different employees are responsible for collecting and analyzing job data and writing job descriptions, it becomes difficult, if not impossible, to achieve total understanding of the meaning of such code words, especially among employees who have some of their job activities defined by code words. Additionally, using code words to describe jobs gives supervisors and even incumbents an opportunity to try to gain unwarranted higher ratings of jobs under review. Using behavioral examples to anchor or further describe code words minimizes misinterpretation.

When code words are used, however, these words should be defined as precisely as possible and their definitions made available to all employees. The following code words for *Frequency of Direction Received in the Performance of a Job* are frequently found in the summary section of a job description. In fact, these terms are the first words used in the summary section.

Under Immediate Direction—Within this job, the incumbent normally performs the duty assignment after receiving detailed instructions as to methods, procedures, and desired end results. The immediate supervisor provides close and constant review while work is underway and at completion of assignment.

Under General Direction—Within this job, the incumbent normally performs the duty assignment after receiving general instructions as to methods, procedures, and desired end results. The assignment is reviewed upon completion.

Under Direction—Within this job, the incumbent normally performs the duty assignment according to his or her own judgment, requesting supervisory assistance only when necessary. The assignment is reviewed upon completion.

Under Administrative Direction—Within this job, the incumbent normally performs the duty assignment within broad parameters defined by general organizational regulations and procedures. Total end results determine effectiveness of job performance.

Under Guidelines Set by Policy—Within this job, the incumbent normally performs the duty assignment using methods and procedures at his or her discretion and limited only by policies set by administrative or legislative authority. Total end results determine effectiveness of job performance.

Responsibilities and Duties

The responsibilities and duties section is the heart of the job description. Responsibilities identify the primary reasons for the existence of the job. These are the major or broad categories of work activities that, in total, define the scope of the work assignments of the job. A responsibility is of sufficient importance that *not* carrying it out or performing it below a minimally established standard will critically impact on required results and demand remedial actions by higher levels of management. Unacceptable performance of a responsibility will result in one or more of the following:

1. Removal from current job that could include lateral transfer, demotion, or even termination.

2. Prohibition of receipt of performance-based rewards.

3. Provision of training and other developmental services.

Duties further describe the responsibilities and could just as easily be called subresponsibilities.

The information used in writing responsibilities and duties statements comes directly from the task statements developed in job analysis (see chapter 5). In making the transition from the task statements to responsibilities and duties statements, the analyst/job description writer must develop a broad understanding of reasons for the job's existence and the demands and the requirements placed on the jobholder.

After gaining this understanding of the job, the analyst reviews the task statements and either (1) selects from 3 to 10 statements that describe the major activities of the job or (2) writes relatively broad activity statements that can be used as umbrella statements that describe major functional areas of work requirements. Knowledge and skill requirements are usually quite valuable in identifying a major activity area. Normally, different functional areas will require different kinds or levels of knowledge and skills and may also be performed in different geographic or physical locations. The time of performance may also aid in establishing major job activities. As already mentioned, a review of the task statements may identify certain tasks that can be used directly as major job activity statements. Sometimes, the combination of two or more tasks may be required to identify a major activity and, at other times, a responsibilities statement must be synthesized to act as an umbrella statement for a number of directly related task statements.

Following the development of the responsibilities statements, the analyst then returns to the task statements in the job analysis and selects those statements that further describe or amplify the responsibilities statement. The responsibilities and duties statement list is complete when the analyst can review the task list developed in the job analysis and identify the presence of each task within the responsibilities and duties statements. This does not require the use of every task statement. Quite often, one task statement can be used to represent a number of tasks identified by the jobholder or one statement can be synthesized to represent a number of task statements. For example, a clerk-typist in a finance department may have identified job tasks as "(1) records expenses incurred by the marketing department; (2) records expenses incurred by the research and development department; (3) records expenses incurred by the warehouse department; (4) records expenses incurred by the manufacturing department, etc." One statement such as "records expenses as incurred by all departments" may be sufficient for this job.

For most jobs, three to seven responsibilities statements are sufficient to describe major work activities adequately. In turn, three to seven duties are usually sufficient to further describe a responsibility.

After identifying the responsibilities and the duties of a job, the next step is to place them in some kind of order so that the reader can obtain a clear and concise picture of the content of the job. Two possible ways of structuring responsibilities and duties statements are (1) to list and sequence by occurrence, and (2) to list by order of importance relative to the overall successful performance of the job.

For jobs that have a routine order of occurrence of work activities, the best way to structure the responsibilities and duties statements is to list that responsibility that normally occurs first, then to follow it with the second responsibility, and so forth, with the final responsibility possibly occurring only at a random or irregular interval. The same procedure can be used for listing the duties within each responsibility.

Jobs having no natural order of occurrence of activities but which must meet specific demands as they arise may follow the "importance" approach for structuring.

In the job analysis chapter, various task measurement dimensions and scales were identified that are useful for making inferences concerning the relative importance of job tasks. The information available from such scaling and measurement procedures can be used to identify the most important to the least important responsibility and also the relative importance of the duties that further describe each responsibility. Using the same approach as described in ordering responsibilities, duties can be listed by importance. When reviewing the responsibilities and duties of a job description written in this manner, the reader immediately recognizes the key or crucial activities of the job.

At the conclusion of the list of responsibilities and duties statements it may be useful to include the sentence, "Performs other assignments as required." This builds into the job an area of flexibility. This sentence is however, a potential area for entrapment. It is specifically included to give supervisors flexibility in detailing work assignments. If an assignment is being performed consistently over an extended period of time however, it must no longer be considered temporary in nature. It should be added to the regular assignments of the job so that the employee receives full recognition for work performed and is compensated accordingly.

Writing Activity Statements (Tasks, Duties, Responsibilities)—The key to a useful and valuable job description is the clear, concise description of the required work activities of the job. This, like many other compensation-related efforts, appears to be a fairly simple assignment. It is far from simple, however; it is a demanding and difficult challenge that faces all involved in describing work content.

First and foremost, those responsible for writing job activity statements must describe precisely what they mean. Because of the many crucial organizational- and employee-related programs that are rooted in the job description, extreme effort and discipline are required in the production of job descriptions.

The job analysis phase obtains information that details what the job is all about. Translating this information into activity statements requires the writer first to think, "What do I want to say?" and, second, "How do I say what I want to say?" Because of the need for brevity and clarity, the suggested syntax of *action verb + object + why and how descriptive information* becomes the "control tower" syntax that establishes a measure of conciseness for those writing activity statements. The "control tower" approach exerts a degree of discipline in the writing style. By starting the sentence with the action verb, third person, present tense, the resulting direct and vigorous writing style permits the verb to pull the rest of the words in the statement and make it truly an action-oriented statement. In reality, the subject of the sentence is the job title. For example, in the job description of a *payroll clerk,* an activity statement reads, "Records daily hours worked." The statement truly reads "*Payroll clerk* records daily hours worked."

Selecting the most appropriate/applicable verb to describe the action taken is the secret in writing an accurate activity statement. In most cases, more than one verb can be used for starting the sentence. Many verbs have more than one meaning, and it is here in the selection of the most suitable verb that care and attention should be given. For example, in clerical assignments related to working with forms, the verb "handles" frequently appears in the activity statement. Does "handle" mean review the data on the form for accuracy, enter data on the form, transcribe data to other forms, transfer the form to other individuals, etc.? Verb selection requires a search-and-think effort to identify the word that best describes the activity. This kind of effort will be invaluable in reducing vagueness or ambiguity when reviewing a job description. Selecting the right verb tells the reader exactly what is happening on the job. The right verb—the most appropriate verb—must be a verb the person performing the job and those reviewing the job description recognize and understand. In other words, a commonly used word will, in most cases, be the best word. Beware of jargon—in-house words used by specific occupational groups—because those outside the specific occupational field may be unable to recognize the true meaning of the verb, leading to an inaccurate interpretation of what is happening on the job.

The action word glossary located in the back of this text is designed to assist those writing job descriptions to have an ample supply of effective verbs. Once an organization has developed a useful set of job descriptions, it would be most useful to review their activity statements and develop an action word glossary for the specific organization.

It is unnecessary to start an activity statement with the words "Responsible for." The activity statements in a job description are responsibilities statements and the term "responsible for" is superfluous. Although the format of activity statements may take either an outline or paragraph form, the approach presented in this text uses an outline presentation. The outline form requires that each statement stand on its own merit and facilitates a reader's quick review. The paragraph form too often permits a statement to hide behind a series of commas, semicolons, or periods in the paragraph and remain unrecognized.

Accountabilities

The accountabilities section of a job description briefly describes the major results achieved in the satisfactory performance of the job responsibilities and duties. It acts as a guide for the goal-setting process that integrates job requirements with jobholder contributions.

Job Specifications

The section on job specifications provides information to determine the worth of a job. This section identifies the knowledge and responsibility demands made on the incumbent and the physical and emotional conditions under which the incumbent must work. The design of the job specification section and the information it provides relate to the kind of job evaluation plan used by the organization. Normally, job specifications are part of the job descriptions when an organization uses a compensable factor–based job evaluation plan (see chapter 8). In this case, the job specification provides substantiating data that assist in identifying the level or degree of the compensable factor as it relates to the job being described. The sample job specification section described in figure 6–1 relates to the compensable factors used in the Factor Evaluation System (FES) (see chapter 8).

Employment Standards

When a job description does not include a specification section, or if the specification section does not adequately identify *employment standards* or *job qualifications*, then an *employment standards* section should follow the Accountabilities section. Employment standards relate to (1) levels of education, which may include actual description of language and mathematical skills required and reasoning skills needed to comply with job performance; (2) levels of experience, which may be further divided into general and specialized categories; (3) abilities and skills; (4) physical standards, which may include actual lifting or pressure exerted (by pounds) in the performance of the job; and (5) certification or licensure requirements. If any of these standards is not applicable, it is unnecessary to include it. Even when a specification section is part of a job description, it may be worthwhile to include an employment standards section to spell out minimum qualification requirements for the job for selection procedures.

Writing a brief but accurate job description that is useful for a variety of management functions is an art. Success in writing it depends primarily on the availability of sufficient job data. The various tools and techniques of a properly performed job analysis can provide such data. Success also depends on the knowledge of the writer. A combination of the job analysis data and the writer's own knowledge can produce a job description that becomes a valuable job information tool.

Many of the guides and the outlines presented in this chapter can assist writers of job descriptions to develop their own procedures and skills. However, the approaches given here need not be considered inflexible. They are meant to be an outline from which each individual can develop the procedures that best satisfy the requirements of a particular organization, assignment, or individual aptitude.

CLASS SPECIFICATIONS

Class specifications are the written descriptions of the major activities and features of jobs included within a class (see figure 6–2). (A class is a group of jobs that have sufficiently similar responsibilities and duties, have the same entrance requirements, receive the same amount of pay, and can be referred to by the same class title although they may have different job titles (e.g., class title—Senior Clerk; job titles—Chief Payroll Clerk, Market Analyst Clerk, Senior Production Control Clerk, etc.).

A typical format for a class specification consists of:

1. Encompassing class title,

2. Brief description of basic purpose of class,

3. Sample of duties performed by jobs in the class, and

4. Minimum qualifications in terms of education, experience, skill, or ability.

Purpose of Class:

Performs advanced and complex clerical duties. Requires some skill in typing. Operates all kinds of standard office duplication equipment. Trains new hires and lower-level clerks on work procedures and may provide direction as to the timing and the correct performance of assignments to lower-level employees. Must be thoroughly familiar with department operating procedures and be skilled in reviewing, analyzing, and reconciling data of a complex nature from a variety of sources.

Examples of Duties:

1. Maintains various records and files.
2. Compiles data periodically and prepares reports, informative fact sheets, etc.
3. Operates various office machines such as calculator, keypunch, duplicating equipment.
4. May type letters and reports.
5. May post and maintain various records and program data.
6. May handle payroll, purchase orders, and payment of bills.
7. May perform high volume of detailed work.
8. May make arrangements for travel, meetings, conferences, or other miscellaneous office functions.
9. May make detailed counts for inventory purposes.
10. Acts as receptionist; answers telephone and personal inquiries either first hand or through referral; refers visitors and secures and transmits routine information.
11. Assists the public by checking routine records and files for requested information. Performs related duties as required.

Minimum Qualifications:

Knowledge of grammar, spelling, and arithmetic.
Knowledge of office information and data, processing, storing and retrieving practices, and procedures and use of standard office equipment.
Skill in typing reports and memoranda.
Skill in directing work of other clerks.
Skill in communicating to employees in other work units and to other people outside the organization.
Ability to understand and carry out oral and written instructions.
Ability to work with minimal supervision and little verification.

FIGURE 6-2   SAMPLE CLASS SPECIFICATION

SELECTED READINGS

Cleavelin, Clifford C., "What's in a Job Title?" *The Management Review,* January 1959, pp. 56–57. Developing a good job title system is a vital step in establishing clear-cut organizational guides and structures. A correct title is restrictive enough to identify the function involved, yet broad enough to avoid a cluttering of nonuseable distinctions.

Gehm, John W., "Job Descriptions—A New Handle on an Old Tool," *Personnel Journal,* December 1970, pp. 983–985, 993. Failure to spell out the results expected on a job has permitted the employee and management alike to emphasize "how to play the game" instead of focusing on acceptable performance.

"Is Your Ablest Assistant Locked in Your Desk?" *Business Management,* November 1967, pp. 57–58. The job description may be unglamorous, underrated, and underused; but it is one of the most valuable tools management has for setting up an organization or for reorganizing and updating an existing structure. It points out how a job he'ps meet the objectives of a business.

"Job Description: Key to Hiring Right Man," *Industry Week,* April 10, 1972, pp. 61–62. One reason that companies sometimes hire the wrong person is the failure to start the search with an adequate description of the job and the person they want to fill it.

Mescon, Michael H., and Donald O. Jewell, "The Position Description as a Communication Link," *Atlanta Economic Review,* January–February 1975, pp. 31–33. The authors contend that the traditional position description can be transformed into a vital, working vehicle useful for accomplishing both the objectives of the organization and the individual; achieving this requires continuous study, implementation, and evaluation.

Russell, Richard S., "How Do You Describe a Job?" *Supervisory Management,* December 1959, pp. 15–19. A thoughtful job description, avoiding bias or prejudice, may even improve the performance of an employee; and it may aid the supervisor in managing his department more effectively.

Walsh, William J., "Writing Job Descriptions: How and Why," *Supervisory Management,* February 1972, pp. 2–8. Another in the series of "how to" articles presented by *Supervisory Management.* This article provides those interested in this subject with yet another view of the mechanics one must be aware of in writing a job description.

7

Job Evaluation

CONTENT

Chapter 7 discusses in detail the processes and the procedures available for evaluating the jobs of an organization and also the issues that must be resolved when implementing a job evaluation plan.

GOALS

Upon concluding this chapter, you should have a basic understanding of the reasons for job evaluation, some of the available methods for performing such evaluation, and the strengths and the weaknesses of these methods. In addition, you should be aware of the importance of developing and training a job evaluation committee. You should also be aware of the procedures available for overcoming barriers that frequently block the development, the implementation, and the administration of a sound evaluation system.

In the early 1880s, Frederick W. Taylor's search for ways to improve the productivity of the Midvale Steel Company led to a formal and systematic study of assigning pay to jobs. This study became known as *job evaluation,* and it was a major breakthrough in further eroding the influence of the pre-Industrial Revolution work methods of the guilds.

From this start, job evaluation slowly became part of the administrative function of many businesses. However, it was not until the 1920s that job evaluation began to achieve fairly widespread acceptance in business, industry, and government.

Historically, job evaluation encompasses all the tools and techniques described in chapters 5 through 10, but in an attempt to give a more precise meaning to job evaluation, this text views it as that part of the process in which the organization finally decides the relative importance of one job as compared to another.

The combination of the dynamic nature of work in a high-technology society and the unceasing demands of employees on the reward systems of organizations establishes the need for job evaluation. The following are among the more important reasons for implementing a job evaluation program:

1. To establish an orderly, rational, systematic structure of jobs based on their worth to the organization (worth normally relates to the importance of the job or its contribution to the overall attainment of the goals and objectives of the organization).

2. To justify an existing pay rate structure or to develop one that provides for internal equity.

3. To assist in setting pay rates that are comparable with similar jobs in other organizations. This enables the organization to compete in the marketplace for the best available talent and also allows employees to favorably compare the pay they receive with that received by employees doing similar work in other organizations.

4. To provide a rational basis for negotiating pay rates when bargaining collectively with a recognized union.

5. To identify a ladder of progression or direction for future movement to all employees interested in improving their compensation opportunities.

6. To comply with equal pay legislation and regulations determining pay differences according to job content.

7. To develop a base for a merit or pay-for-performance program.

COMPARABLE WORTH

Discussions relating to the difference in pay received by males and females started as early as 1919 when the major industrial nations of Europe recognized the problem and began developing legal procedures for overcoming this social issue. Efforts in this area seldom went beyond the discussion stage and, even after laws were enacted in Western Europe following World War II, little effective action ever occurred.[1]

A major reason for the lack of effective action relates to the meanings of such words as *equal, comparable, similar, like,* and *same.* In fact, prior to passage of the Equal Pay Act, the U. S. Congress discussed the use of the word *comparable* as a substitute for the word *equal.* After considerable debate, it was decided that the word *comparable* would result in too broad an interpretation of the Act and the word *equal* remained the official direction the Act was to take.

The issue underlying *comparable worth* is how can valid and accurate comparisons be made between unlike jobs? This issue, in reality, is the entire purpose of job evaluation and underlies the problem job evaluation experts have faced since becoming involved in this area in the nineteenth century. Whether or not an organization uses some kind of a systematic, orderly, and rational process to measure the worth of unlike jobs for pay practices, *jobholders are paid differently and different jobs are recognized as being worth different amounts to the organization.*

In the late 1970s, this issue that had been smouldering for over half a century began attracting public interest. This issue relates principally to the fact that when women dominate an occupational field, the rate of pay for jobs within those occupations appears to be unfairly depressed when compared to the pay men receive when working in jobs where they are the dominant incumbents within the occupational field.[2]

This problem gave birth to the cries of "job segregation" and "pay discrimination." Women's rights groups and government agencies responsible for eliminating employment discrimination practices—principally, the Equal Employment Opportunity Commission (EEOC) and the Office of Federal Contract Compliance Programs (OFCCP)—began taking an extremely active role in resolving the apparent disparity between rates of pay for men and women in segregated occupations. (Segregated occupations are those occupations in which at least 70 and possibly 80 percent of the incumbents are of one sex.)

In the late 1960s and throughout the 1970s, these organizations focused their attention primarily on employment practices that led to "systemic discrimination" and its resulting "disparate impact." The early EEOC and OFCCP actions in the area of systemic discrimination centered on selection criteria for initial hiring decisions and for use in making promotion decisions.

[1]For a detailed analysis of the development of the comparable worth issue outside the United States, read the Janice R. Bellace paper, "A Foreign Perspective," in the book *Comparable Worth: Issues and Alternatives* (Washington, DC: Equal Employment Advisory Council, 1980).

[2]Those interested in obtaining an in-depth overview of the comparable-worth issue may wish to read these two articles in the *University of Michigan Journal of Law Reform:* Ruth C. Blumrosen, "Wage Discrimination, Job Segregation and Title VII of the Civil Rights Act of 1964" (Spring 1978), and Bruce A. Nelson et al., "Wage Discrimination and the 'Comparable Worth' Theory in Perspective" (Winter 1980).

Efforts in these areas have resulted in women and minorities moving into a wider range of jobs and better-paying jobs. With each passing year, however, women working in what are considered traditional female kinds of work have witnessed little improvement in their wage rates when compared with the pay men receive for doing traditional male kinds of work. In fact, government pay statistics indicate that the disparity between pay for women and men, rather than shrinking, increased in the decades of the '60s and '70s.

With more attention being placed on compensation practices, women's groups who felt that women were the victims of discriminatory practices began taking their concerns to court. They requested judicial relief under the Equal Pay Act and the Civil Rights Act from such unfair practices.

Within months after the passage of the Equal Pay Act of 1963, Congress passed the Civil Rights Act of 1964. Just prior to the passage of the Civil Rights Act, the Bennett Amendment was added to the Civil Rights Act to ensure that the Equal Pay Act would continue to provide the basic laws regarding pay practices. The Bennett Amendment simply states that an employer cannot be charged with violation of Title VII with regard to discrimination in pay unless that employer is also violating the Equal Pay Act.

By the late 1970s, it became apparent both to women's rights groups and government civil rights enforcement agencies that if they were to make any headway in the area of pay discrimination, the courts would have to take a different or looser interpretation of the Bennett Amendment and of the requirements set forth in the Equal Pay Act.

It became further apparent to those groups advocating better pay treatment for women in female-dominated occupations that if they were to achieve success under the Civil Rights Act, particular attention would have to be placed on the four affirmative defenses established in the Equal Pay Act: (1) seniority, (2) merit, (3) quality or quantity of work, and (4) any condition other than sex. (See chapter 3 for further discussion of the Equal Pay Act.) A major strategy developed was that if a defendant could not demonstrate that pay differences were the result of any one of the first three defenses, the defendant then must be discriminating because of sex (the fourth affirmative defense) and thus violating the Civil Rights Act which bars discrimination because of sex.

An analysis of some of the more important court cases of the 1970s identifies areas of success in promoting women's rights, but these court cases also underscore the limits to court action.

Angelo v. *Bacharach Instr. Co.* 14 FEP Cases 1778.
This case arose because the defendant company was paying male and female bench assemblers different rates of pay. The court ruled that before equal pay standards—equal skill, effort, and responsibility under similar working conditions—apply, it must be shown that jobs done by men and women have substantially the same content (i.e., terms and conditions of work).

Bourque v. *Powell Electrical Manufacturing Co.* 19 FEP Cases 1524.
A female buyer established that she was discriminated against when she showed that she performed work substantially equal to that of male buyers but for less

compensation. A male buyer eventually performed other duties but these were never assigned to the female buyer although she had the qualifications to perform them.

Christensen v. *State of Iowa.* 16 FEP Cases 222.
The court found for the defendant although it was paying its female clerical force less pay than its male maintenance workers and even though the results of a point factor job evaluation plan determined the jobs to be essentially equal by assigned points. The court ruled that the market must be taken into consideration when making final pay determinations and that jobs are considered equal only when assignments are similar.

DiSalvo v. *Chamber of Commerce of Greater Kansas City.* 13 FEP Cases 636.
In this case, the defendant was found guilty of unfair employment practices because it paid a female associate editor considerably less than it did the male communications specialist hired to replace her. They performed substantially the same duties and the additional duties assigned to the male replacement, such as photography, were considered inconsequential. The female received $8,200 a year, and the male received $12,000 a year.

County of Washington v. *Gunther,* 25 FEP Cases 1521.
Plaintiffs claimed that their wages were depressed because of intentional sex discrimination, since the county had paid them less than their own job evaluation survey indicated their jobs were worth. The U.S. Supreme Court stated that the women were not claiming that they were entitled to increased pay based on a comparison of the intrinsic worth of their jobs with that of other jobs in the same organization or community. The jobs in question were female matrons and male jailers. The jailers guarded over ten times as many inmates while the matrons spent considerably more time performing clerical assignments. These differences in assignments, in turn, required different effort and responsibilities and thus did not meet Equal Pay Act standards. However, the matrons claimed some of the difference in pay was due to sex bias. The high court ruled that Title VII bars sex bias in pay.

Howard v. *Ward County No. Dak.* 14 FEP Cases 548.
A female deputy sheriff performing work substantially equal to higher-paid deputies in skill, effort, and responsibility was unlawfully discriminated against. The award for back pay was predicated on the pay received by a major in the sheriff's office as uncontroverted evidence that the female deputy did work equal to that performed by the major.

IUE v. *Westinghouse Electric Corp.,* 23 FEP Cases 588.
This ruling held that in the absence of explicit statutory language or a U.S. Supreme Court ruling, it will not be concluded that Title VII allows discriminatory behavior on the basis of sex when it comes to compensation practices when the same behavior would be prohibited if based on race, religion, or national origin. The compensation practices in this case involved the setting of lower wage rates for job classifications that were predominantly filled by females although these jobs did not necessarily involve equal or substantially equal work.

Lemons v. *City & County of Denver.* 22 FEP Cases 959.
The court found the defendant not guilty of violating Title VII despite the contention that it pays nurses (a female-dominated occupation) less than it pays

persons doing comparable work in male-dominated occupations. The defendant used the market to set wage rates of nurses.

Marshall v. *Hodag Chemical Corp.* (N.D. Ill., 1978) 16 EPD #8323.
The court found against a chemical manufacturing company that was paying higher wages to a male analytical chemist than to a female analytical chemist even though they had equal job duties. Although the male had performed some supervisory duties and had more academic credentials, the Equal Pay Act does not require jobs to be identical, only substantially equal.

Marshall v. *Farmers Ins. Co.,* (N.D. Kan. 1978) 17 EPD #8581.
A female promoted to policywriter supervisor began at a lower pay level than males similarly promoted and was never granted salary parity with her male peers. Although on several occasions the female received raises equal to or greater than her male peers, her lower starting salary kept her at a pay disadvantage, which was considered a discriminatory practice.

Peltler v. *City of Fargo.* 12 FEP Cases 945.
This ruling held that although male police officers were more skilled than their female counterparts, the job content for issuing tickets for parking and other nonmoving violations did not justify higher pay for the males.

Taylor v. *Weaver Oil & Gas Corp.* 18 FEP Cases 23.
Female draftspersons received lower starting salaries and lower pay increases than their male counterparts. The pay differentials were justified by the extra duties of some employees and by differences in experience and job performance.

From these court rulings, it is evident that the courts, when involved in pay discrimination cases, place considerable importance on (1) job content, (2) ordering of jobs by such compensable factors as skill, effort, and responsibility or their equivalent, (3) actual duties performed and quality of job performance, (4) relating of actual pay received by incumbents to preset limits of the jobs, (5) education and skills actually required in the performance of current assignments, and (6) influence of the market on the actual pay assigned to a particular job.

To further clarify how pay decisions are to be made and what technologies are to be used in making these decisions, the EEOC in 1976 commissioned the National Academy of Sciences (NAS), an independent research institute, to investigate whether appropriate job measurement procedures exist or can be developed. The results of the findings of NAS were documented in *Job Evaluation: An Analytic Review,* and unofficial guidelines were published in 1979. Of particular interest to those involved in job evaluation and comparable worth were the five unofficial guidelines established by NAS. These unofficial guidelines are:

1. Each enterprise that uses job evaluation procedures should use a single job evaluation system for all its employees.
2. The employer should make explicit the criteria of worth for jobs in the enterprise—that is, there should be an explicit and open policy about what attributes of jobs are regarded by the enterprise as deserving compensation.

3. When factor-based job evaluation procedures are used, the choice of measured factors should adequately present the criteria of job worth enunciated in conformity to point 2.

    a. The employer should make explicit the basis for the choice of factors and the relationship of the measured factors to the concept of job worth held by the enterprise. The employer should take care to ensure that the factors identified thoroughly account for all of the compensable features of jobs.

    b. Specifically, the employer should ensure that the choice of measured factors is equally appropriate for the evaluation of all jobs and is not biased in favor of or against jobs held mainly by particular race or sex groups.

    c. If use of a job evaluation system results in jobs held mainly by women or minorities scoring lower on the average than jobs held mainly by white males, it is the obligation of the employer to demonstrate that the choice of measured factors is justified by business necessity—specifically, that the measured factors validly measure the criteria of job worth held by the enterprise and that no other measurable factors are available that would be equally valid but less discriminatory.

4. In point factor systems, the range of scores for each factor should represent the full range of variability of the job feature being measured and the division of the full range into levels should be accurately specified.

    a. Factor scores should be chosen to represent the full range of variability of the feature of the job being evaluated.

    b. The specification of the available levels of a factor must be justified in terms of the firm's definition of job worth (point 2) and must be accurately described. In particular, factor level descriptions should be written as concretely as possible, with careful specification of equivalences for different types of jobs.

5. In point factor systems the factor weights must be chosen in a bias-free way.

    a. Because jobs held mainly by women tend on the average to pay less than jobs held mainly by men, the use of existing wages to derive factor weights in unacceptable unless the employer can show that such weights are unbiased with respect to sex.

    b. The specification of factor weights by the employer to reflect the relative importance of job factors to the enterprise imposes an obligation on the employer to ensure that the chosen weights do not have an adverse impact on women or minority workers or, if they do, that they are justified by business necessity.

This chapter and the one that follows focus on the different methods available for evaluating job worth. Because of the increased attention being placed on job evaluation and because of national and international interest arising from the claims of job segregation and pay discrimination, the strengths, the weaknesses, and the opportunities of the more widely-used job evaluation methods are discussed in detail.

CLASSIFYING JOB EVALUATION METHODS

Over the years, professionals interested in improving the quality of job evaluation and increasing understanding of evaluation methods and procedures have established a number of ways to classify the methods and to group the tools and the techniques of job evaluation. The classification process should improve perception and understanding of what job evaluation can do. The process should also identify the necessary criteria for establishing meaningful relationships that promote the highest possible degree of objectivity when determining job similarities and differences. A quality classification of job evaluation methods should assist managers in selecting the method that best fits their requirements.

Traditionally, job evaluation methods have been classified as *nonquantitative* and *quantitative*. Nonquantitative methods include the *ranking* method and the *classification* method. Quantitative methods include the *factor-comparison* method and the *point* method. This text uses a different approach. Job evaluation methods are classified here into whole job methods and methods using *compensable factors* (see table 7-1). Whole job methods include (1) the whole job ranking method, (2) the market-pricing method, (3) the market-pricing guideline method, and (4) some position classification methods. Compensable factor–based methods are discussed in chapter 8.

TABLE 7-1

JOB EVALUATION METHODS[a]

Whole Job Methods	*Compensable Factor-Based Methods*
Whole Job Ranking Method	Narrative Factor Methods
Market-pricing Method	Position Classification Methods
Market-pricing Guide Line Methods	(USCSC "GS" Method)
(Smyth-Murphy, Evalucomp)	Time Span of Discretion Method
Position Classification Methods (Predetermined Grading, Intraoccupational and Interoccupational Approach)	(Jaques)
	Problem-solving Method (Charles)
	Broadbanding Method (Paterson-Husband)
	Broad Classification Methods
	Maturity Curve Methods
	Frequency Distribution Methods (Global)
	Numerically Scored Factor Methods
	Point Methods (Lott, Bass)
	Factor Comparison Method (Benge)
	Point–Factor Comparison Methods
	General Point–Factor Comparison Methods (NMTA, NEMA)
	Occupational Point–Factor Comparison Method (FES)
	Factor-Guide Chart Profile Methods
	General Factor Guide Chart Method (Hay)
	Occupational Factor Guide Chart Method (USCSC–Oliver Committee)
	Some Statistical Analysis Methods (PAQ) (Foster-TPF&C Method)

[a]Names and items listed in parentheses are major examples of that specific evaluation method.

Job-to-job evaluation methods require the evaluator to consider the whole job and to establish an order by determining the overall worth of jobs as they compare with one another. A number of these methods are discussed in the following sections.

Ranking Method

The simplest job evaluation method is that of ranking each job relative to all other jobs. In this method, the evaluator compares all jobs with every other job and arrives at a list of jobs ranked from most to least valuable.

In an organization in which the evaluators are intimately familiar with the job being evaluated, they may have to direct their decision-making processes only to a job title. In other cases in which there is less familiarity with job content and requirements, the documentation may range from a brief summary of activities to a job analysis or job description. These documents describe in depth the responsibilities, duties, and accountabilities of the job, minimum qualifications for selection, standards of performance, and normal or typical environmental conditions within which an incumbent performs job activities.

This method is the quickest and least costly of all job evaluation methods. When evaluators know the jobs they are working with, the whole job ranking method can produce accurate results. The problem with this method is the lack of substantiating data to justify the final result. There is nothing for the jobholders to discuss with the evaluators except the final results, and it is difficult for anyone simply to accept "This is the way it is because I said so."

Another major disadvantage of the ranking system, and probably the most important, is that it provides no yardstick for measuring the relative value of one job to another. Therefore, it is not too helpful in developing a scale of pay rates based on the relative value of all jobs. It also provides little assistance in comparing jobs in different or geographically dispersed units when there is no basis for equating jobs that differ by kind of subject matter or kind of work but that have similar levels of difficulty, responsibility, and qualification requirements.

In addition, the ranking method is quite inflexible. It does not readily identify changes in job content, which could lead to internal equity inconsistencies; nor does it recognize shifts in labor market demands. Finally, there is always the danger that when evaluators are familiar with both the job and the jobholder, the behavior and the personality of the worker unduly influence the evaluators' estimate of job worth. An existing pay rate may cause a similar type of bias. Ranking, however, is always valuable as a first step in job evaluation or for teaching anyone the basic concepts of evaluation. It certainly fosters a basic understanding of the evaluation process.

Paired-comparison Procedures—Paired-comparison procedures are invaluable for job ranking purposes. Two of these are the deck-of-cards procedure and the stub selection procedure. A description of each of these procedures follows with an adaptation of the stub-selection procedure described in table 7-2.

TABLE 7-2

PAIRED-COMPARISON RANKING TABLE

Columns Rows	Messenger	Data Proc. Mgr.	Data Entry Opr.	Exec. Sec.	Computer Opr.	Sys. Anal.	Control Clk.	Programmer	File Clk.	Asst. Dir.	TOTAL
Messenger	—										0
Data Processing Manager	X	—	X	X	X	X	X	X	X	X	9
Data Entry Operator	X		—						X		2
Executive Secretary	X		X	—	X		X	X	X		6
Computer Operator	X		X		—		X		X		4
Systems Analyst	X		X	X	X	—	X	X	X		7
Control Clerk	X		X				—		X		3
Programmer	X		X		X		X	—	X		5
File Clerk	X								—		1
Assistant Director	X		X	X	X	X	X	X	X	—	8

Place X in box where item in row is more important than item in column.

One of the simplest yet most effective of the paired-comparison procedures used for ranking a group of items is the deck-of-cards procedure in which the rater uses the following steps:

1. Place each name (job title) or item to be compared on a separate card and into a pile.

2. Choose two cards from the pile, compare them, and select the best.

3. Hold the best in your hand and discard the loser into a new pile.

4. Select another card from the first pile, compare with card in hand, choose the best, and discard the loser in the new pile.

5. Continue with this step until the original pile has been depleted.

6. Place the card in your hand in a second new pile. This is your top selection.

7. Repeat all steps using the first new pile as the replacement for the original pile for your eventual second choice.

8. Continue the above steps until all remaining names have been placed in the pile with your first choice. This then will give you your ranking for the group.

An additional step that may be included in this process to exclude rating bias is to perform the entire process a second time. Beginning in step 2, however, identify the lowest or least important item and then build to the highest by always returning to the pile that item rated higher. This reversal process should provide the same order of rank. Any discrepancy uncovered then be comes an area for further investigation.

Stub Selection Procedure

Another paired-comparison procedure used for ranking attempts to overcome two basic weaknesses of other procedures: (1) the inability of the brain to store and compare a large variety of items (in fact, it is difficult for most brains to compare more than five items at one time), and (2) the halo effect (i.e., once an item is judged to be superior to a number of items, it begins to carry an inborn superiority over items that follow.) In the following example, each number represents a name or term of items (job title) to be compared. In this case, the largest number circled represents a specific choice.

1. Cut out the stubs.

2. Circle the largest number of each stub (the circled item is considered a vote).

3. Make a pile for each circled item.

4. Upon the completion of all comparisons, count the stubs in each pile.

5. The pile with the largest number of stubs is the highest ranking item, the next largest number is second, and so on. The lowest ranking item receives the fewest votes.

1	2						
1	3	2	3				
1	4	2	4	3	4		
1	5	2	5	3	5	4	5

An adaptation of the stub selection procedure is to develop a matrix in which all the items to be compared are listed in both the rows and the columns. In the boxes formed by the intersection of the rows and columns, the rater places an "X" where the item in the row is more important, valuable, or some other characteristic than the item in the column. The item receiving the highest score (i.e., number of "X"s) is most important, valuable.

Paired comparison is unwieldy when one is comparing large numbers of items, as shown by the following formula. This formula determines the number of comparisons to be made for a given number of comparison items:

$$\frac{N(N-1)}{2} \text{ where } N = \text{the number of comparison items}$$

For example:

$$\text{Comparing 7 factors } \frac{7(7-1)}{2} = 21 \text{ comparisons}$$

$$\text{Comparing 15 jobs } \frac{15(15-1)}{2} = 105 \text{ comparisons}$$

Slotting—After the initial ranking, it is possible to put or "slot" additional jobs among those already ranked and to assign an appropriate pay rate. The slotting process is in essence another paired-comparison procedure in which the job to be slotted is compared with an existing scale and placed in the appropriate slot. This method seems to be most appropriate for the small organization in which the expenses involved in developing a more sophisticated method are not worth the derived benefits. It is also valuable for ranking senior management jobs in larger organizations or as a first step in validating more sophisticated evaluation plans. Slotting is an essential feature of the market-pricing guide line method discussed later in this chapter.

Market-Pricing Method

The market-pricing approach uses the labor market to set the worth of jobs. In this method, the organization first develops narratives that describe job activities and jobholder requirements. These narratives (ranging from a title to an extensive job description) are communicated (by phone, in person, through the mail) to other organizations hiring individuals who perform similar work assignments in the same labor markets. Requests are made to provide data about what the other organizations are currently paying workers performing similar work. (Chapter 9, Compensation Survey, covers the collection, the analysis, and the dissemination of compensation data in detail.) When using a pure market-pricing method, an organization allows the market to dictate the pay of the job and thus its relative worth.

A number of important issues are involved in market pricing. Among them are the following:

1. It is difficult to establish the true identity and meaning of a job through narratives used to describe that job to representatives of other organizations without understanding the environmental context of the job in the organization that is requesting pay pricing data.

2. Total reward and compensation practices vary dramatically among organizations; and although it is a significant compensation component, pay is still only one component. Using market pay data may lead as easily to overpayments as to underpayments. (External competitiveness replaces requirements for assessing internal equity.)

3. Pay survey data are susceptible to a wide variety of errors.

4. An organization may relate to more than one labor market in filling the various jobs of its work force, and it must collect data from organizations in the appropriate markets.

5. Many competitors in the labor market will not provide pay data, or they may provide it in a form that is of minimal value for decision-making purposes. There is always the possibility that the pay data provided are not accurate and do not validly describe the pay practices of the organization.

Market-Pricing Guide Line Methods

Richard C. Smyth and Matthew J. Murphy developed a guide line method to overcome the inherent weaknesses of the pure market-pricing approach. Their method permits the influences of internal equity to interact with existing market rates when an evaluator is determining the rate of pay for the jobs of an organization.

The Smyth-Murphy guide line method consists of the following key elements: (1) a guide line scale, (2) a job description containing scope data (data that identify and define job importance), (3) market pricing, and (4) a horizontal guide line display.[3]

The *guide line scale* is a standard scale of salary ranges, including a series of salary grades and a minimum, midpoint, and maximum rate of pay for each. (Chapter 10 provides a detailed discussion of the development of all elements of

---

[3]Richard C. Smyth and Matthew J. Murphy, *The Guide Line Method of Job Evaluation* (Rhinebeck, NY: Smyth & Murphy Associates, Inc.).

a pay structure.) Smyth and Murphy contend that a 5 percent difference in midpoints between grades is ideal. This difference permits the development of a larger number of grades that in turn provide the compensation manager with the flexibility of moving a job up or down one or two grades without creating major feelings of inequity. It also permits increased opportunity for more precise distinctions between jobs. Depending on the variety and the number of jobs to be allocated within the pay structure, the number of grades could range from the 30s to the 70s.

Preparing realistic job descriptions includes *scope data*. This type of job description helps to identify key or benchmark jobs—those for which it is possible to determine what other comparable employers are paying for directly comparable jobs.

The third step is to conduct a compensation survey (see chapter 9) to accomplish *market pricing*. Smyth and Murphy state that in their experience it is normally possible to identify 40 to 60 percent of the jobs of an organization as being key jobs. By relating the midpoint of the pay grade that is closest to the average salary paid by other employers, it is possible to assign each key job to a pay grade that relates the key job to the amount other employers pay for a comparable job. At this point, the members of the organization who are responsible for evaluating the job can exercise their own judgment if there is a difference in views about the placement of the job on the wage scale. When differences arise over the actual payment to be allocated to a key job, evaluators normally are permitted to adjust that job up or down one pay grade. An adjustment of two grades is sometimes permitted. After completing the ranking process, it is then possible to slot all the nonkey jobs among those already identified and located on the vertical guide line scale.

The fourth step is to develop *horizontal guide line displays* that relate jobs in various departments or plants where each job evaluation group conducted the third step independently of the others. This process relates two or more vertical guide line displays, thereby ensuring internal equity within the pay structure. For further discussion of vertical and horizontal comparisons, see "Position-job Classification—Intraoccupational and Interoccupational Approach" later in this chapter.

The American Management Associations (AMA) also provides a market-pricing guideline method called Evalucomp. Evalucomp consists of eight unique components: (1) standard position description, (2) predetermined salary structure, (3) executive compensation service market rate data, (4) Evalucomp job evaluation manual, (5) implementation workbook, (6) Evalucomp installation kit, (7) salary administration policies and procedures model, and (8) employee salary administration handbook model. The AMA states that it is possible to install Evalucomp without in-depth salary administration expertise. Evalucomp is similar to the guide line method of Smyth and Murphy. A major variation between Evalucomp and the Smyth-Murphy guide line method is that Evalucomp uses a 6 percent difference between midpoints in its pay structure design, whereas the guideline uses 5 percent.

The Market and the Comparable Worth Issue—A major point made by advocates of women's rights is that the market discriminates against women.

They support their thesis by using pay data that show, from a macro analysis, that women have historically earned and continue to earn approximately 60 percent of what men earn. In organizations where large numbers of men work in traditionally male jobs and large numbers of women work in traditionally female jobs, the differences in pay frequently do not accurately reflect the differences in job requirements.

The market advocates state in opposition that the market is still the best, most accurate, and least discriminatory identifier of job rates of pay. In attacking the macro pay statistic presented by the women's rights advocates, the market advocates state that macro data have not improved for several reasons. First, in the past 20 years, the percentage of women in the work force has almost doubled and, second, many women entering the workforce have minimal or no job-related knowledge and skills and are occupying entry-level jobs. Finally, large numbers of women continue to leave the work force and take a number of years off to raise a family. In this crucial period, their male peers stay in the work force and build the experience and seniority necessary for promotion to more advanced and higher-paying jobs. Undoubtedly, both the women who attack the market as discriminatory and the market proponents who support the market as the best indicator of job worth have valid points to make and use statistics in a light that best supports their particular view.

In using the market for determining job worth, some problems with the collection and the analysis of pay data have already been discussed. It may be worthwhile also to review basic economic concepts underlying the use and the value of market data for determining job rates of pay. The macro-economic concept of supply and demand states that, in the long run, in a free and open market where both the suppliers of human resources (workers) and the providers of wages (employers) have access to all necessary information, the market (meeting place of employers and workers) will allocate workers to jobs. Underlying this concept is the thought that all workers will attempt to maximize the "monetary" worth of their work efforts. Many workers, however, find that there are only so many jobs available, that there is a limit to their mobility, and that they have a constant demand for money to meet life-style expectations. Even when jobs are available, skill requirements are difficult to meet and are not easily acquired. In fact, rapid changes in technology are making job acquisition even more difficult for the unemployed worker or the worker seeking new employment.

Anyone who recruits, selects, and hires personnel knows that there are all kinds of markets for all kinds of jobs. In many cases, these markets are extremely difficult to identify and define with any degree of precision. For decision-making purposes, most job-seekers have limited information about available reward or pay opportunities. Furthermore, most of them have a limited conception of the employer-provided rewards that are offered to them in exchange for their availability, capabilities, and performance. In turn, few of even the most sophisticated of selection devices predict with high degrees of precision which applicants will be the best performers.

In reality, large employers in most communities establish their own market and small employers who are either unable or unwilling to meet job rates of pay established by the dominant employer do not pay the market rate. Even the largest of employers has only so many job opportunities. Workers looking for jobs usually have little choice between working and not working. Only when job rates of pay approximate what an unemployed person can receive from some welfare or unemployment program does the job seeker have the chance to select no work (with government-provided income) rather than work for a wage in order to have sufficient income to maintain a specific standard of living.

The idea of the market being the best allocator of resources may be fairly strong when it comes to the purchase of foods, housing, transportation, and luxuries. It is highly questionable, however, that the market is as free, unbiased, and open to individual choice when it comes to individuals making decisions regarding where they work and what they will work for. These issues all place a considerable shadow on the value of the market as a determinant of job worth and job pay.

Position (Job) Classification — Predetermined Grading Approach

Since the 1920s, there have been numerous approaches developed for evaluating jobs through the use of the position-job classification method. One approach to job classification that closely approximates the whole job ranking and slotting approach is the use of the predetermined pay grade method. Chapter 10 discusses in detail the design and the use of pay grades and the part they play in the development of a pay structure. Simply, a pay grade is a defined area that establishes a specific rate of pay or a range of pay for all jobs that meet certain specifications.

The first step in developing a predetermined pay grade approach is to identify and describe key or benchmark jobs that would normally be paid at the highest and lowest levels of pay and sufficient jobs between these two points to establish an orderly scale of pay relationships. Job content requirements and features common to key or benchmark jobs receiving approximately the same rate of pay are identified. Using this job content and common features, narrative classification standards are written that describe the kind of work found at each pay grade with examples from jobs assigned to the pay grade. The pay grade narrative must have sufficient detail so that (1) nonbenchmark job descriptions can be compared with the grade narratives and (2) these jobs can then be placed in the appropriate pay grades.

Pay grade classification standards contain a broad description of required knowledge, representative tasks, and basic qualifications of jobs included within the predetermined pay grade. Standards may also include a description of compensable factors in terms applicable to the work performed by the jobs in the classification and describe the level or levels of difficulty and limits of these factors. (Job classification plans using compensable factors are further described in chapter 8.) These narratives of class standards can become quite long and complex when they provide enough detail to differentiate among the many jobs included in some predetermined pay grade.

A particular weakness of the job classification-predetermined pay grade approach is that when comparing nonbenchmark jobs to the grade description, the nonbenchmark job may contain activities that relate to activities that are in more than one pay grade. Among the various activities of the job being evaluated, a specific activity may relate to an activity that is comparable to an activity in a lower pay grade, while another activity relates to an activity similar to the one described in the pay grade, and yet another activity relates to an activity that is higher than the one described in the pay grade. The same is true when a pay grade uses compensable factors, except that among the various job activities, one may relate to one level of a compensable factor, another to another level of a compensable factor, and so on. The question then arises as to which pay grade the job under review should be assigned.

Position (Job) Classification — Intraoccupational and Interoccupational Approach

Job classification frequently uses an approach for evaluating jobs that closely resembles the whole job ranking method. This method first requires that all classes of jobs be ranked within an occupation or family. The identification and the measurement of magnitudes of differences among classes having similar requirements permits the establishment of a hierarchical ordering among the classses, thus providing for an intraoccupational or vertical ranking.

Following the intraoccupational ranking, the next step is to establish an interoccupational or horizontal ranking to permit comparability among classes in widely differing occupations. It is possible to relate classes within various occupational groups in the same horizontal plane by using key classes, which are classes in which responsibilities, duties, and qualifications are clearly recognized and understood. In this way, those making comparisons can identify classes having equal, greater, or lesser requirements. This step is similar to the development of the horizontal guideline display in the market-pricing guide line method. Developing horizontal relationships is especially useful when an organization has a number of families that vary widely because of their respective responsibilities and duties or when an organization has traditionally viewed the families as differing significantly.

The development of horizontal comparability is difficult. There are few persons wise and impartial enough and with the understanding and the knowledge to sift through the (1) objectives of the organization, (2) activities and goals of various classes, (3) measure of contributions these dissimilar classes make to the achievement of the objectives of the organization, (4) various responsibilities and duties of the jobs within these groups as compared to jobs in other classes, and (5) value of the jobs in achieving both group and organizational objectives.

Developing comparability among key classes at the highest, the center, and the lowest end of the hierarchy of value provides a framework of adjoining ladders within which to slot other classes. (The paired-comparison procedure is again useful here.)

Table 7-3 is a chart used by Olympia city government for slotting classes in three dissimilar work units. This simple example of relating unlike classes in dissimilar occupations is not in any way meant to be an exact or operational comparison of a real-world situation. It is valuable only in describing a method for relating comparability. Making comparisons among classes in various occupations is a difficult and dangerous assignment; but it is possible through analysis of work performed and through determination of difficulty, responsibili-

TABLE 7-3

AN INTRAOCCUPATIONAL AND INTEROCCUPATIONAL COMPARISON CHART

Clerical—classes of jobs concerned with making, classifying, and filing records, including a wide variety of verbal communications. (DOT Codes 201., 209.)	*Nursing*—jobs concerned with administering nursing care to the ill or aged. (DOT Codes 075., 079.)	*Public safety*—classes of jobs concerned with protecting the public, maintaining law and order, detecting and preventing crime, directing and controlling motor traffic, and investigating and apprehending suspects in criminal cases. (DOT Code 375.)
		Police Chief
	Director Nursing Service	Desk Officer
Executive Secretary[a]	Head Nurse[a]	
Special Occupation Secretary[a]	Special Duty Nurse[a]	Commanding Officer[a]
Stenographer		Detective
Secretary[a]	General Duty Nurses[a]	
	Licensed Practical Nurse	
Clerk-Typist		
File Clerk[a]	Nurse's Aide[a]	
Miscellaneous Machine Operator		

[a]Key classes.

ty, education, experience, and skill requirements. After ranking the key classes horizontally, the paired-comparison procedures again provide a useful method for comparing classes in different occupational groups.

COMPENSABLE FACTOR-BASED METHODS

Although initially developed in the 1920s and 1930s, compensable factor job evaluation plans did not receive wide-scale acceptance in the world of work until the end of World War II. In the past 30 years, however, compensable factor–based job evaluation methods—especially those using some kind of a numerical scoring—have had wide acceptance. Because of their use, the lack of understanding of their core—compensable factors, and the current attention focusing on comparable worth, detailed discussion will be devoted to compensable factors and compensable factor–based job evaluation methods in chapter 8.

DATA AND INFORMATION REQUIREMENTS

One thing common to all job evaluation processes is the need for expert judgment. The success of any job evaluation program relates directly to the quality of the decisions made by those responsible for designing the program and making it work. In turn, the quality of the decision relates directly to the quality and the quantity of available data and information. To grasp the meaning of this process, a basic understanding of the concepts involved in the terms *data, knowledge, information,* and *judgment* is necessary.

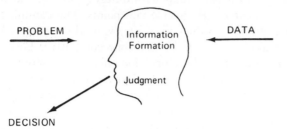

FIGURE 7–1   DIAGRAM OF THE DECISION EQUATION

Data denotes unevaluated facts. They are presumed to be valid.

Knowledge combines data and evaluation for anticipated future use.

Information is the measure of the net value obtained from the process of matching the elements of a present problem with appropriate elements of data. In this sense, information is a process that occurs within a human brain when a problem and the data for its solution are brought into productive union.[4]

Judgment is the process of forming an opinion by comparing or evaluating bits of information.

Decision equations take the following form (see also figure 7-1):

$$\text{Data} + \text{Knowledge} = \text{Information}$$
$$\text{Information} + \text{Judgment} = \text{Decision}$$
$$(\text{Decision} + \text{Luck} = \text{Success})$$

A primary duty of the compensation department is to gather, process, and distribute job data and information. Part 2 of this text provides insight and approaches for the development of such data and information. Basic data for the job evaluation process are (1) the job description, together with any necessary supporting documents (e.g., the job analysis questionnaire) and (2) work performed in the development of the evaluation method (such as the study that goes into the identification, the definition, and the weighting of compensable factors).

JOB EVALUATION COMMITTEE

Job evaluation is neither simple nor precise. It is a problem-solving, decision-making process that requires the subjective judgment of the best minds in the organization. Because of varying interests and dissimilar backgrounds, views will quite often be different, thus contributing to the complexity of the activities of the job evaluation committee. At times there will be excessive

---

[4]Adrian M. McDonough, *Information, Economics, and Management Systems* (New York: McGraw-Hill, 1963), pp. 75–76.

discussion and debate. Shortcuts are impossible, however; and the process of discussion and debate adds to the success of a well-organized, functioning committee.

By establishing a job evaluation committee, the organization makes possible analysis of jobs by individuals with differing organizational, technical, and social backgrounds and with diverse viewpoints. The committee should be involved from the beginning to the end of the evaluation process. An organization may find it valuable to use more than one committee. For example, one composed of senior managers and senior union officials (if there is a union) may be best qualified to select an evaluation plan, whereas one composed of operating managers and lower level union officials may be best for selecting key jobs and evaluating all nonmanagement jobs in the organization. The number of committees is unimportant; guidelines for their effective operation are identical.

Size and Composition

A committee should preferably consist of from 5 to 12 members. The members should have a broad knowledge of organizational activities and goals and a basic familiarity with job relationships and job contributions. Additionally, members should be familiar with the theories, the concepts, and the technologies included in compensation management.

Training

All committee members should receive necessary data and information to heighten and sharpen their knowledge and judgment in evaluation. Examples of practical application or exercises should relate directly to any type of theoretical, abstract information. However, committee members should receive no more training than is absolutely necessary.

Training and Use of Key Concepts—Each committee member should receive a job evaluation manual developed by those responsible for the design of the job evaluation program. This manual is useful both as an orientation to the process and as a guide in the problem-solving, decision-making activities required in (1) selecting an evaluation plan, (2) identifying key jobs, (3) evaluating all remaining jobs, and (4) assisting in the development of fair and equitable wage scales.

The manual should contain a brief description of the compensation policies of the organization. For example:

> The management of Olympia, Inc. wishes to provide equitable pay to every member. For this reason, it must recognize the contributions made by all jobs and their relationships to other jobs in order to develop a fair division of the funds available for pay purposes among all its members.

If one of the tasks of the committee is to select an evaluation plan, then the manual should contain a brief description of each plan with a list of the advantages and the disadvantages of each. Members should review the plans before a joint training and discussion session. The actual selection meeting follows the training session, and at this time the compensation specialist can still answer any questions or unanswered doubts about any of the plans.

Role of Training in Job Evaluation—The ranking of jobs as to their difficulty and their importance relative to one another is the crucial element of job evaluation. At this stage, some specific and detailed training is essential. A well-designed training program should have at least the following two behavioral or learning objectives for each committee member.

1. Skill in looking for and seeing the same things when analyzing a job description.

2. An understanding and an acceptance of the procedures used in the job evaluation plan in order to reach agreement on the relative value of all jobs.

A variety of training techniques and aids is available for achieving these twin goals. A first step could be to provide all members of the committee with a completed job analysis information format of a well-known, simple job and have them develop a job description. After writing the job description, they could then analyze each step, its meaning and use. A review and a critique of their work help all members to gain a better understanding of the process. The next step could be to take a set of jobs in one department and analyze them as if establishing a scale of key jobs. These jobs must be ranked in an absolute scale of importance. Then, using the appropriate evaluation technique, they must be assigned a relative importance.

The training program has one fundamental goal—development of the judgment of all committee members to enable them to understand what is important in a job, its relative difficulty, the importance of its responsibilities and duties, and its minimum performance qualifications.

The job evaluation committee may be called on either to provide opinions or to make decisions with regard to a wide range of issues or problems related to compensation. Three major reasons for the existence of such a committee, however, are for (1) selecting a job evaluation method, (2) identifying key or benchmark jobs, and (3) evaluating job worth.

Selecting a Job Evaluation Method

Although job evaluation committees normally operate within a previously selected job evaluation method, there are times when the first assignment of a committee is the selection of the job evaluation methodology. When the committee has this responsibility, it is not only their first assignment, it is also the one that is most important and difficult.

When the committee is responsible for this decision, its members must become knowledgeable about the various kinds of job evaluation plans, their features, and their strengths and weaknesses, as well as how the plans best meet the requirements set forth by the organization. It is not only acceptable but highly recommended that the compensation staff specialists develop a completed staff work presentation in which the pros and cons of each evaluation method and its specific features are offered to the committee. The compensation department staff may even make recommendations after presenting the benefits and the costs connected with each. It is then the responsibility of the committee to evaluate the staff work and make a final recommendation. The committee may become involved in the actual evaluation process, but normally this is too time-consuming and such details are left to the staff work of the compensation department.

Identifying Key or Benchmark Jobs

A careful selection of a limited number of jobs that adequately describe a wide span of activities, duties, and work requirements enhances the success of any job evaluation program. These well-known jobs, called *key* or *benchmark* jobs, represent large numbers of workers and are common throughout the industry or in the general locale under study. Because of the restricted number of these key jobs, they furnish only a limited amount of data, but their commonality and acceptance provide a basis for sound understanding and agreement of the tasks and human requirements necessary for the achievement of organizational goals. Job evaluation based on selected key jobs provides a more valuable data base than one using masses of data obtained from hundreds of jobs. Normally, 15 key jobs are enough. If at some stage it is necessary to drop two or three, it will not be critical. The number of jobs to be identified as key jobs, however, depends on how many are being evaluated.

Before selecting key jobs, the compensation department must screen all jobs and select those that meet key job requirements. The potential key jobs presented to the evaluation committee should require a wide variety of technological and interpersonal skills, as well as rates of pay ranging from lowest to highest. A full, detailed job description is necessary for each job.

Evaluating Job Worth

Finally, the crucial stage of determining the relative worth of jobs arrives. Individual biases, self-preservation, and the defense and promotion of the worth of specific jobs are problem areas that constantly arise at this stage. Committee members recognize that decisions made at this step have a direct impact on the base pay of the job, and the psychological pressures are evident in all discussions leading to a final rating. The quality of previous work efforts in providing job content data and developing a skill in relating levels of factors to job requirements directly affect the results achieved.

Chairing a Job Evaluation Committee

Although there is much truth in the old adage, "two heads are better than one," trying to obtain *one* wise decision from two or more heads can often be exasperating. A job evaluation committee that achieves its goals must maintain independence of thought and must encourage each member to develop ideas and present them, recognizing that any idea requires critical analysis and review.

Good judgment is not a universal trait. The ability to harmonize differences is an individual skill, and the committee member selected to be the chairperson should be adept in facilitating agreement. As is true in any area of leadership, there are many guides to help an individual be a successful committee chairperson. Probably none is more important than to focus on the problem at hand, making sure that the idea, rather than the individual presenting it, becomes the center of attention. It is unlikely that any idea is the brainchild of just one person. In all probability, it is the accumulation of masses of data and information gathered and developed by many individuals.

Seven guidelines for assisting a committee chairperson develop a smoothly functioning, self-respecting group follow:

1. A good leader *does everything possible to help members preserve their own images.* All people are vitally concerned with their images because self-images represent a level of need achievement. Most people cease to cooperate when their motivators cannot operate, when they cannot satisfy their needs by doing something.

2. A good leader *directs aggression where it belongs—against the problem, not the people trying to solve it.* This is important because it encourages a free flow of ideas. Time is put to innovative use rather than being used to attack the ideas of others.

3. A good leader *demonstrates to the members of the group that no one should lose and that all should win.* The leader honors every idea, no matter how small or wild.

4. A good leader *provides every member with the opportunity of chairing a meeting.* This gives each one practice in this activity, which is one of the fundamental skills that every leader must acquire. The essence of the teacher-leader-counselor function is to enable each member to grow and learn about the responsibilities of leadership by practicing them.

5. A good leader *develops a unique style and permits every other member to do the same.* Productivity can be increased and workmanship improved only by enlisting the genius of the group (i.e., the collective knowledge and abilities of all the members of the group in its service). It is just as important to learn to be a willing participant as it is to be a good leader.

6. A good leader *serves the group.* The communication process in the problem-solving group is based on the concept of *synergism,* the process by which the cooperative efforts of two or more people taken together are greater than the sum of the efforts taken separately.

7. A good leader *always sees to it that the problem-solving group has an expert in it.* The expert is that member of the problem-solving group who best understands the factual aspects of the problem under discussion. Therefore, the

expert is the one who can make the best decisions about the relative strengths and weaknesses of proposed solutions. Because this person is also a group member and a participant, the expert must think in a truly flexible manner. When needed expertise is not available in the group, a person skilled in the particular area under consideration may be requested to join the group. The expert helps to identify and analyze the problems; the leader then takes over for the problem-solving phase. To preserve the unstructured environment of the group, there should be no attempt to make other members as knowledgeable as the expert. The expert is there to serve as the resource person. The leader must determine when to shift into the problem solution phase.[5]

Operating a Job Evaluation Committee

Once the committee has received the necessary training and is on its own, guidelines are available to improve the likelihood of its success. In an evaluation process, it is best if members perform their own ratings of the jobs assigned by the compensation staff before the meeting of the whole committee. There is always the possibility that in an open meeting certain individuals will take a dominant role and other members will accept their views or become apathetic or hostile. It is unlikely that such actions will provide the quality of effort or contribution necessary for the committee to succeed.

A method developed in the 1960s for using committees—the Delphi Technique—may be extremely valuable for use in job evaluation.[6] In this technique, much of the committee member's work is done independently. Through the use of a communication medium—ranging from an in-house mail service, to a telephone, to the postal service, to a sophisticated computer-based terminal—each member performs an evaluation assignment and sends it to a central location where the views of all committee members are compiled, analyzed, and returned to them. The report states the evaluation of each member, the average evaluation of all, and the range of ratings. The evaluators then review the analysis and, after viewing the ratings of other members, may change their evaluations or may stay with their original selection. At this time they may also wish to comment on the reasons for their particular ratings. After receiving this additional and/or revised information, the central processing unit then analyzes all the evaluations again and presents its findings. At this stage, it may be best to bring the committee together to review the decisions and comments; or another rating may be necessary. In any case, the Delphi Technique can provide the following advantages to an organization:

1. It saves the time of the committee members by permitting them to do much of the initial evaluation in their own offices.

[5]Richard I. Henderson and Waino W. Suojanen, *The Operating Manager: An Integrative Approach* (Englewood Cliffs, (NJ, 1974), pp. 135–136.

[6]Olaf Helmer, "The Use of the Delphi Technique in Problems of Educational Innovations" (Santa Monica, CA: RAND Corporation, 3499, December 1966).

2. It limits the influence that recognized or so-called "experts" may have on the group (in the Delphi communication process, no attempt is made to identify a score with a particular individual).

3. It requires each member to present individual views and develop individual ideas.

In analyzing the evaluations of the committee members, various methods are available for identifying the quality of agreements. Furthermore, the degree of disagreement is more important than the amount of agreement in selecting key jobs or evaluating their worth. If one or more members has a wide range of disagreement with the view of the majority, it may be necessary to eliminate a job when developing key job groups or to redefine or develop evaluation procedures.

In the final discussions, a summary sheet showing the individual evaluations is helpful. When evaluating the worth of a key job, you may rule that if the evaluation has a greater divergency than three consecutive levels or degrees it may be necessary to reevaluate the job or to eliminate it.

A wide variety of techniques is available to secure an evaluation method that is both valid and reliable. Any evaluation process must recognize the need for validity and reliability. *Validity* is the extent to which a measuring instrument measures what it is supposed to measure. *Reliability* is a measure of internal dependability of a testing or evaluation mechanism to assure that it measures consistently.

The methods for measuring the quality of validity and reliability can become very sophisticated and are beyond the scope of this text. This fact does not imply in any way that these tests are unimportant. It does mean that, normally, fairly simple, straightforward procedures are useful in determining such qualities. When these procedures are unacceptable, it may be necessary to call on experts in testing and evaluation to develop methods for obtaining valid and reliable committee measurements.

Typical Rating or Evaluation Errors—Any time people measure or perform evaluations or appraisals of any type certain errors are almost inevitable. Among the more common pitfalls are the following:

1. *Central Tendency*. The evaluator rates all jobs the same way. It is very difficult for the evaluator to discriminate among jobs of varying levels of difficulty, skill, importance, and the like.

2. *Loose Rating*. The evaluator consistently rates jobs higher than other raters do.

3. *Tight Ratings*. The evaluator consistently rates jobs lower than other raters do.

4. *Halo Effect*. The rater holds a high opinion of one element or feature of the job and rates other elements or features of the job at this same elevated level.

5. *Horn Effect.* The rater holds a low opinion of one element or feature of a job and rates other elements or features of the job at the same depressed level.

6. *Jobholder Effect.* The rater knows the jobholder and rates the person, not the requirements of the job.

THE COMMITTEE AND THE COMPENSATION STAFF

The compensation manager and his or her staff have a unique relationship with the job evaluation committee because the committee acts as both a problem-solving and a decision-making unit. These roles are different, and the relationship between the compensation staff and the committee varies accordingly.

Problem-Solving Role

The job evaluation process is one of continuous identification and analysis of problems and the development of various solutions to them. Compensation affects every member and every part of the organization, and for this reason the problems confronting the compensation department and the job evaluation committee are as broad as the organization.

As problem solvers, the committee assists the compensation staff in the following functions:

1. *Identifying* the problems as to the who, what, when, where, how, and why of observed differences or misunderstandings.

2. *Classifying* the problems by separating symptoms from problems and by describing the cause, type, and nature of the problems.

3. *Searching for and gathering* data to provide sufficient information to understand better the relationships under study.

4. *Evaluating* data by relating facts to symptoms and causes for initial development of solutions.

5. *Developing* alternative solutions through the structure of various combinations of procedures and plans.[7]

When the job evaluation committee works as a problem-solving team, its members act as advisors to the compensation manager. They provide expert eyes and ears to aid the manager in identifying compensation needs that exist throughout the organization. The compensation manager in the team approach is the senior member of the group and has the final responsibility to act. This can

---

[7]Chapters 10 and 16 of *The Operating Manager: An Integrative Approach* by Richard I. Henderson and Waino W. Suojanen, contain detailed analyses of the problem-solving and decision-making processes. (Englewood Cliffs, NJ: Prentice Hall, 1974).

at times be difficult because these same committee members may also act as decision makers, and in that role they can either accept or reject many of the concepts or plans developed by the compensation staff.

Decision-Making Role

The final role played by the job evaluation committee occurs when it makes the judgment that approves or disapproves a vital element of the job evaluation process. Although in many cases the committee provides only wisdom and knowledge, with final judgment left in the hands of the compensation manager or a higher level manager, its influence often extends beyond these boundaries. In certain situations, the committee may actually have final approval rights on the method of job evaluation and its design features, the designation of key jobs, and the basic structure of the pay system.

When the committee has the power to commit the resources of the organization to a particular course of action, it acts in a senior role to the subordinate compensation manager.

The challenge confronting both the job evaluation committee and the compensation staff—be it problem solving or decision making—is not for amateurs. It requires knowledge and patience from both. A job well done in problem solving can lighten the load of decision making, and, in reverse, a poor job of problem solving can condemn any job evaluation program to certain failure.

It is not easy for a junior member of an organization (the compensation manager or staff member may frequently be junior in an organizational sense to the committee members) to supply direction and counsel to senior members. In many problem-solving meetings, however, this is necessary because the compensation staff member may frequently be the expert in the group and, as such, is the leader in the problem-solving phase. The establishment of proper rapport between the compensation staff and the job evaluation committee requires mutual trust and confidence.

THE COMPENSATION CONSULTANT AND THE JOB EVALUATION COMMITTEE

Organizations often call upon consultants to assist in developing their compensation programs. Because compensation management is highly specialized, organizations often do not have members who are knowledgeable enough to perform the duties associated with it. In this case, if a consultant or consulting group is retained, the consultant can best serve the organization by acting as an appendage to the compensation staff. Consultants serve the same role as staff officials when working with the job evaluation committee and should receive the same consideration from the committee as would be given to staff members. In fact, the committee may wish to consider the compensation staff members as internal consultants. Thus, whether or not the committee works with internal or external consultants, the relationship should be identical.

Job evaluation is a team problem. It is impossible for one individual to possess the broad knowledge or in-depth understanding of all jobs that is necessary to bring about a successful job evaluation program. The secret to developing a successful job evaluation program is to supply sufficient data and information and then to have the whole committee arrive at the wisest decisions possible.

SELECTED READINGS

American Management Associations, *Salary Determination.* New York: AMACOM, 1972. This American Management Associations publication is an excellent reference source for some of the topical areas covered in part 2 of this text, but it is particularly valuable for gaining additional insight into a variety of compensable factors.

Baum, Bernard H., and Peter F. Sorenson, Jr., "A 'Total' Approach to Job Classification," *Personnel Journal,* January 1969, pp. 31–32. The authors advocate the abolition of time and motion studies as well as the elimination of traditional job descriptions and classifications. They advocate, instead, the study of jobs from a behavioral and results standpoint.

Hay, Edward N., "Job Evaluation Discussion," *Personnel Journal,* September 1948, pp. 149–154. This article is an interesting dialogue between Hay (the editor) and the readers who sent letters to the editor about the use of job evaluation. It provides an easy-to-read, understandable overview of the compensable factors. (Other discussions of interest appear in *Personnel Journal,* December 1949, pp. 262–264; January 1950, pp. 302–307; October 1950, pp. 180–182.)

O'Conner, Richard W., "A Connecticut Yankee's Clerk," *Journal of Systems Management,* January 1969, pp. 12–16. A review of the way 17 organizations analyze the importance of their clerical jobs, describing various compensable factor systems and the weights applied to their individual compensable factors.

Treiman, Donald J., ed., *Job Evaluation: An Analytic Review,* Interim Report to the Equal Employment Opportunity Commission, Staff paper prepared for the Committee on Occupational Classification and Analysis Assembly of Behavioral and Social Sciences, National Research Council, Washington, DC: National Academy of Sciences, 1979. The report concludes that there are three weaknesses in existing job evaluation procedures in evaluating low-paying jobs held primarily by women: The relative ranking of jobs tends to be highly dependent upon which factors are used in the evaluation and how heavy each factor is weighted; job evaluation is inherently subjective, making it possible that well-known processes of sex-role stereotyping will be operative, resulting in an underevaluation of jobs held predominantly by women; many employers use several job evaluation plans, which makes it impossible to compare the worth of jobs in different sectors of a firm.

U.S. Civil Service Commission, *Classification Principles and Policies,* Personnel Management Series, no. 16, Washington, DC: Government Printing Office, 1963. Designed for use and guidance of federal classification and personnel officers, this publication provides a summary of classification principles, policies, techniques, and procedures, and it also touches on the goals and importance of classification.

————, *Supervisory Grade-Evaluation Guide and Qualification Standard,* Personnel Management Series, no. 22 Washington, DC: Government Printing Office, 1970.

This manual provides guidance in determining the grade value of a supervisory position as well as being an additional analytical tool for use in reviewing organizational structure for position management and control purposes.

Warner, Kenneth O., and J. J. Donovan, eds., *Practical Guidelines to Public Pay Administration,* vol. 1, Chicago, IL: Public Personnel Administration, 1963. This series of 15 papers provides a topical framework for anyone involved in developing and installing pay plans in the public area specifically or in the field of compensation generally.

———, eds., *Practical Guidelines to Public Pay Administration,* vol. 2, Chicago, IL: Public Personnel Administration, 1965. A further discussion of the subject areas developed in vol. 1, with additional topics in such areas as benefits, incentives, and longevity.

8

Compensable Factor–Based Job Evaluation Methods

CONTENT

Chapter 8 discusses procedures used for identifying, defining, and weighting compensable factors and various job evaluation methods that use them. Compensable factors are paid-for, measurable qualities, features, or requirements that are common to many different kinds of jobs. These factors differentiate jobs by the knowledge and the skills required, the levels of difficulty and responsibility, the nature and qualification requirements of the work, and the conditions under which jobholders perform their work. They are described in such a way that it is possible to differentiate among jobs according to their worth to the organization. In turn, compensable factor–based job evaluation plans use one or more of these factors to measure the worth of jobs to an organization.

GOALS

Upon concluding this chapter, you should have a basic knowledge of compensable factors and the more commonly used compensable factor-based job evaluation methods. You should also have an understanding and an appreciation of how to use these job evaluation methods, as well as of their value in relating to comparable worth issues.

A major issue facing compensation managers is the development of a procedure that permits a systematic, precise analysis of all jobs. There are many procedures for identifying and ranking the importance of unlike jobs with regard to the overall scheme of organizational objectives and goals; but those that are based on properly identified, defined, and weighted compensable factors may be the most valuable and useful.

In this chapter and the remaining chapters of part 2, there are lengthy discussions that identify quantitatively oriented components used in developing a workable compensation program. However, this in no way implies that these procedures are scientifically pure with regard to exactness of measurement. The entire area of compensation is and always will be subjective. The more sophisticated the organization, its work-units, and its technology, the more stressful and important are relative issues.

To understand the relative value of each job and to use the collective knowledge and judgment of every member of the organization, it is the responsibility of compensation specialists to develop procedures that limit confusion, are as simple as possible, and build understanding. One approach for reaching such goals is through the use of compensable factors. Compensable factors objectively identify and define jobs, making distinction among them possible and establishing degrees of difficulty or contributions of each.

Without an in-depth analysis of the jobs of the organization, it is impossible to identify, define, and weight compensable factors. This is one of the reasons the well-designed and successfully implemented job analysis program forms the backbone of any compensation system. Through job analysis, it is possible to identify those common qualities or features that to some degree are required in the performance of all the jobs in the organization.

Before beginning this study, it is important to realize that hundreds of compensable factors have been identified and defined. The federal government and a wide variety of associations and consulting organizations have developed specific groupings of compensable factors that apply to many organizations and require little or no modification. There are discussions of a number of these throughout this chapter.

A major issue developed in this text is that every organization responds uniquely to a variety of external and internal influences. Because of its uniqueness, each organization must use a job evaluation method that best fits its own particular needs. This does not imply, however, that an organization cannot use a previously developed, commonly accepted program and set of compensable factors. However, one must be warned that even though a program has had wide acceptance, it may not fit the needs and requirements of every organization.

DEFINITION

Compensable factors are paid-for, measurable qualities, features, or requirements that are common to many different kinds of jobs. Since these factors represent neither identifiable job activities, specific observable behaviors, nor measurable outputs, they are synthetic features. Synthetic in this context means that these factors are a composition or combination of qualities, features, or requirements of a job that, taken together, form a coherent whole. Compensable factors are features or qualities intrinsic to the job and are considered essential in the successful performance of work assignments.

DESCRIPTION OF COMPENSABLE FACTORS

To be useful, a compensable factor must be common to a wide variety of jobs. This characteristic, in turn, requires that the compensable factor be abstract. The broader the job universe covered by a compensable factor, the more abstract it must be. The more abstract the factor, the more difficult it is to describe it with words and terms that provide similar meaning to those having a vested interest in job evaluation.

Because most compensable factor–based job evaluation methods are designed to cover many different kinds and levels of jobs, the factor description and classification scheme normally consists of two or more further redefinitions of the primary compensable factor. This redefinition-classification process moves from the general or most abstract to the specific.

To facilitate the use of compensable factors within a job evaluation method, it is common practice to classify the factors into three major categories: (1) universal factors, (2) subfactors, and (3) degrees or levels.

Universal compensable factors are the general, relatively abstract, and complex qualities and features that relate to all kinds of jobs. To make these abstract universal factors more understandable and easier to relate to relative to the kinds of work employees do while performing their job assignments, a subset of factors is used to further describe each universal factor. These are frequently called *subfactors*. Subfactors are statements that more precisely define the specific attributes of a particular job. (Many compensable factor–based job evaluation methods, however, do not use subfactors.) The second subset of factor definition involves the development of *degrees* or *levels*. These degrees or levels provide a "yardstick," or measurement scale, that assists in identifying the specific amount of the factor required in the performance of the job.

Through the division of compensable factors into universal factors, subfactors, and degrees, it is possible to simplify comparison, enabling all interested parties to meet on common ground for discussion. The division also provides a basis for relating job value to a wide range of rewards.

The three categories of compensable factors are discussed in the following.

Universal Factors

In the early 1900s, most work-related compensation research focused on the development of incentive wage payments, but already a few efforts were being made to institutionalize systematic job evaluation. By the 1920s and 1930s, fair and acceptable base wages had become a critical organizational requirement.

In the early 1930s, A. W. Bass, Jr., a pioneer in job evaluation, identified skill, responsibility, and working conditions as the primary work identification factors requiring segregation and measurement for developing base wage differentials.[1] During this same period, another of the pioneers, Eugene J. Benge, identified mental requirements, skill requirements, physical requirements, responsibility, and working conditions as the five most often used factors.[2] From these efforts and from those of other early compensation specialists, representatives of major electrical equipment manufacturers—Western Electric, General Electric, and Westinghouse—developed a job evaluation plan for their own use and for the use of members of their trade association, the National Electrical Manufacturers Association (NEMA). This plan had a job rating scale that used four universal factors—*skill, effort, responsibility,* and *job conditions.* In the late 1930s, the National Metal Trades Association (NMTA), now known as NMTA Associates, accepted the NEMA plan for use by its members. This plan, with minor modifications, is still one of the most commonly used job evaluation methods and is probably responsible for more "spin-offs" than any other plan.[3]

A major refinement in universal factors occurred when Edward N. Hay and Dale Purves developed the Guide Chart–Profile Method for establishing salary standards.[4] This method used *know-how, problem solving,* and *accountability* as factors. Hay did much of his initial work in a service-oriented business—a major bank—rather than in a factory environment.

Possibly the most significant use of universal factors developed with the Equal Pay Act of 1963, which identifies four tests for measuring substantially equal work, the performance of which requires *equal skill, equal effort,* and *equal responsibility* when performed under similar working conditions (these are very similar to the NEMA-NMTA factors). With the enactment of this law, it has become increasingly important for an organization to develop and use pay practices that can be not only substantiated and justified to its work force but also defended in court.

In January 1977 the U.S. Civil Service Commission (CSC), currently known as the Office of Personnel Management, began implementation of a point-factor plan called the Factor Evaluation System (FES). The FES is the result of seven years of study and research to improve the methods and procedures used for classifying General Schedule (GS) nonsupervisory jobs.

From this research involving approximately 4,000 jobs, 26 federal agencies, and 256 field installations, nine factors were identified as having universal

[1]A. W. Bass, Jr., "Evaluating Shop Jobs by the Point System," *Iron Age,* September 10, 1936, pp. 42–44, 47, 123.

[2]Eugene J. Benge, *Job Evaluation and Merit Rating* (New York: National Foremen's Institute, 1946).

[3]American Association of Industrial Management, *Job Rating Manual (Shop).* (1969 edition) (Melrose Park, PA: AAIM, 1969).

[4]Edward N. Hay and Dale Purves, "The Profile Method of High-level Job Evaluation," *Personnel,* September 1951, pp. 162–170, and "A New Method of Job Evaluation: The Guide Chart–Profile Method," *Personnel,* July 1954, pp. 72–80.

applicability to approximately 1,500,000 nonsupervisory GS positions. These are as follows:

1. Knowledge required by the position
2. Supervisory controls
3. Guidelines
4. Complexity
5. Scope and effect
6. Personal contacts
7. Purpose of contacts
8. Physical demands
9. Work environment

Table 8-1 shows the similarities and differences among a number of groups of universal factors developed over the past four decades.

A compensation manager will seldom work with more than five to nine universal factors. The major consideration in defining the factors is to make sure that they cover all common job elements. The omission of any one element could greatly undervalue certain jobs relative to others, thus destroying the legitimacy of the entire evaluation program.

As stated previously, *knowledge, skill, know-how,* or whatever term(s) a particular system uses, relate to one universal factor. The following list gives the definition of several systems for this particular universal factor:

Skill (Bass). The knowledge of a subject combined with mastery of its techniques. Such skill, however, must presuppose a certain inherent intelligence.

TABLE 8-1

GROUPS OF COMMONLY USED UNIVERSAL FACTORS

Bass	*Benge*	*NEMA-NMTA*	*FES*
Skill	Mental requirements	Skill	Knowledge required by the position
Responsibility	Skill requirements	Effort	Supervisory controls
Working conditions	Physical requirements	Responsibility	Guidelines
	Responsibility	Job conditions	Complexity
	Working conditions		Scope and effect
			Personal contacts
			Purpose of contacts
			Physical demands
			Work environment

Hay and Purves	*Equal Pay Act*
Know-how	Skill
Problem solving	Effort
Accountability	Responsibility
	Working condition

Mental requirements (Benge). Either the possession of and/or the active application of inherent mental traits, plus acquired general education and/or acquired specialized knowledge.

Skill (Benge). Acquired facility in muscular coordination and/or acquired specific job knowledge (experience).

Skill (NMTA-AAIM). Defined only by listing its subfactors: *education, experience, initiative,* and *ingenuity.*

Know-how (Hay and Purves). Includes every kind of knowledge or skill required for satisfactory performance of the job. Specifically, it includes every skill gained through experience and all kinds of required education or special training.

Knowledge (FES). The nature and the extent of information or facts that the worker must understand to do acceptable work and the nature and the extent of the skills needed to apply these knowledges.

This variety of definitions, which all say more or less the same thing, makes the semantics issue apparent. The only solution to this problem is (1) an understanding of the various jobs of the organization and (2) a careful choice of words to describe the relevant factors.

The Argument Against Using Working Conditions and Physical Requirements as Universal Factors—When a job requires excessive physical effort or performance under unsatisfactory or stressful conditions, technology and automation usually can minimize, if not eliminate, the majority of problem areas. With over 50 percent of the work force employed in service industries, only 25 percent in manufacturing, and probably less than half of that group working under distressing and/or dangerous (D & D) conditions, it is inaccurate to apply the term *universal* to such factors. Although 10 percent of the work force may still be working for varying periods of from less than 10 percent to 100 percent of the time under D & D conditions, there is a solution to the problem other than including them with the compensable factor segment of the program.

Possibly a more equitable solution would be first to identify and define what an organization considers to be D & D conditions and then to assign a flat premium to be paid to anyone involved. The fee could vary according to the percentage of time an individual worked under those conditions, but it would have no relationship to the type of work performed. In other words, an unskilled laborer would receive the same D & D premium as a senior manager when the working conditions were the same. Individuals who must perform work assignments that are highly repetitive and routine or who perform within very strict scheduling requirements may suffer emotional stress that could also be considered a D & D condition.

D & D premium pay could also be based on the amount of time a person was involved under such conditions, that is, those working more than 75 percent of the time would receive 100 percent of the premium; from 25 to 75 percent, 50 percent; less than 25 percent, none. Such programs would be similar to the hazardous duty pay used extensively by the armed forces. The job analysis

TABLE 8-2

UNIVERSAL FACTORS AND THEIR RESPECTIVE SUBFACTORS

Bass	*NMTA (AAIM)*	*Hay and Purves*	*FES*
SKILL 1. Intelligence or mental requirements 2. Knowledge required 3. Motor or manual requirements 4. Learning time	**SKILL** 1. Education (5)[a] 2. Experience (5) 3. Initiative and ingenuity (5)	**KNOW-HOW** 1. Practical procedures, specialized knowledge, and scientific disciplines (8) 2. Managerial (4) 3. Human relations (3)	**KNOWLEDGE REQUIRED BY THE POSITION (9)[b]** 1. Nature or kind of knowledge and skills needed 2. How these knowledges and skills are used in doing the work
WORKING CONDITIONS 1. Physical application 2. Nervous application 3. Occupational working conditions	**EFFORT** 1. Physical demands (5) 2. Mental or visual demands (5)	**PROBLEM-SOLVING** 1. Thinking environment (8) 2. Thinking challenge (5)	**SUPERVISORY CONTROLS (5)** 1. How the work is assigned 2. The employee's responsibility for carrying out the work 3. How the work is reviewed
RESPONSIBILITY 1. Relate directly to type of work performed in a machine shop business	**RESPONSIBILITY** 1. Equipment or process (5) 2. Material or product (5) 3. Safety of others (5) 4. Work of others (5)	**ACCOUNTABILITY** 1. Freedom to act (7) 2. Job impact on end results (4) 3. Magnitude (4)	**GUIDELINES (5)** 1. The nature of guidelines for performing the work 2. The judgment needed to apply the guidelines or develop new guides
	JOB CONDITIONS 1. Working conditions (5) 2. Unavoidable hazards (5)		**COMPLEXITY (6)** 1. The nature of the assignment 2. The difficulty in identifying what needs to be done 3. The difficulty and originality involved in performing the work
			SCOPE AND EFFECT (6) 1. The purpose of the work 2. The impact of the work product or service
			PERSONAL CONTACTS (4)[c]
			PURPOSE OF CONTACTS (4)[c]
			PHYSICAL DEMANDS (3)[c]
			WORK ENVIRONMENT (3)[c]

[a]All numbers in parentheses refer to the number of degrees or profile statements which further define or measure the subfactors.

[b]The unique design features of FES incorporate the subfactor descriptions directly into the description of the respective universal factor and the degrees (or levels as termed in FES) apply directly to the factors.

[c]There are no subfactors for this factor.

should provide enough information to identify those jobs requiring effort under distressing and/or dangerous conditions.

Subfactors

Although there are five to ten widely accepted and used universal compensable factors, the number of subfactors that provides for a more precise description of jobs ranges into the hundreds. Table 8-2 identifies the subfactors of some of the universal factors used by four of the previously mentioned systems. This is only a small sample of subfactors available to describe common features of a job. A review of table 8-2 emphasizes the semantics problem that constantly confronts the compensation manager. Until a term has been carefully defined, there is a great likelihood that a wide variety of words or groups of words say the same, or nearly the same, thing. Because subjectivity and relativity issues are important in compensation management, concerned parties must have a similar and clear understanding of the issues, and this requires careful use of words and terms. Minimizing and eliminating verbal misunderstandings are a vital part of the job of any compensation specialist.

Although there can be a problem of semantics in any area that must be defined, the major problem related to subfactors is not one of definition but of overlap. Just as failure to identify and define a universal factor can lead to serious *underevaluation,* the use of more than one factor to identify identical or even fairly similar elements of a job can lead to *overevaluation.* It is easy for the compensation manager to fall into the overlap or overevaluation trap.

The first step in eliminating the danger of overlap is to keep the universal factors fundamental and to be as general as possible in defining them. Then, as the subfactors develop that further define the universal factors, it is important to keep to specifics and be as precise as possible. Finally, after completely identifying all subfactors, each one must be reviewed with all the others (including those that identify other universal factors) to be sure they are not stating the same thing.

Table 8-3 reviews some of the systems using the universal factor, subfactor, and degree approach. It further illustrates a variety of ways to define subfactors.

A review of the subfactors in table 8-3 demonstrates various ways to define rather similar universal factors.

Degrees (Levels)

Degrees provide the most precise and specific description of a job. Through their use it is possible to develop an orderly approach for measuring each job relative to every other job in the organization. The grouping of the specific degrees from the available subfactors furnishes a unique profile for each job. For this reason, degrees are frequently called *profile statements.* Because they are unique, it is normally required to use more than one word or even a small group of words to define them. A pragmatic approach available to the specialist

TABLE 8-3

FACTOR AND SUBFACTOR DEFINITIONS

Skill (Bass). Subfactors described through the use of the following terms:
1. Intelligence or mental requirements
2. Knowledge required
3. Motor or manual skill
4. Learning time

Skill (NMTA-AAIM)
1. *Education.* The basic trades training of knowledge or "scholastic contact" essential as background or training preliminary to learning the job duties. The job knowledge or background may have been acquired either by formal education or by training on jobs of lesser degree or by any combination of these approaches.
2. *Experience.* The time it would take a "normal" person working under "normal" supervision to learn to apply the assigned education effectively in the performance of the job, assuming that each element was supplied about as rapidly as the individual could absorb it.
3. *Initiative and ingenuity.* The independent action, the use of judgment, the making of decisions, and the amount of resourcefulness and planning the job requires as determined by the complexity of duties performed.

Know-how (Hay-Purves)
1. *Practical procedures, specialized knowledge, and scientific disciplines.* Practical specialized, technical, professional, or administrative knowledge.
2. *Managerial.* Human skills in evaluating, motivating, organizing, or developing people, singly or in groups.
3. *Human relations.* Degree of human relations.

Knowledge Required by the Position (Factor Evaluation System)
Nature and extent of information or facts which the workers must understand to do acceptable work (e.g., steps, procedures, practices, rules, policies, theories, principles, and concepts) and the nature and the extent of the skills needed to apply these types of knowledges. To be used as a basis for selecting a level under this factor, a given type of knowledge must be required and applied.

responsible for defining degrees consists of describing the simplest requirement or the minimum acceptable standard for that factor, moving to the most complex or highest possible requirement, and then, in succeeding stages, working up and down the ladder of importance. At this definition stage, such nebulous modifying terms as *minimal, slight, moderate, average, considerable, broad,* or *extensive* often become part of the profile statement and part of the semantics problem. These terms are most valuable in developing a series of profile statements that provide an orderly scale of importance or levels of magnitude. To overcome some of the semantic or definitional problems, however, it is important to clarify these nebulous modifiers by combining them with concrete examples of activities, specific operations, compensable qualities or features or behavioral terms applicable to the activities being performed in the jobs. Joining the commonly used modifier with a specific activity phrase promotes common understanding and blocks wide and varied interpretation. For example, instead of saying, "Job requires considerable physical demands," say "Job requires considerable stooping, bending, lifting, and walking in filling order trays."

When using degrees or levels to define a subfactor, the two major areas to consider are (1) the number of degrees necessary and (2) the methods necessary to describe differences adequately. The series of degrees or profile statements must develop an observable scale of differences or levels of magnitude that define the subfactor in terms of increasing importance, complexity, or difficulty. It is important that there be no more degrees, or profile statements, than absolutely necessary, but enough should be used to describe adequately the complete range of differences.

Investigations into observable differences were conducted in the early nineteenth century by Ernst H. Weber (1795–1878).[5] His efforts became known as Weber's law, which states, "The increase of stimulus necessary to produce an increase of sensation in any sense is not an absolute quantity but depends on the proportion which the increase bears to the immediate preceding stimulus." Or, more simply stated, the small perceptible difference in two objects is not absolutely the same, but it remains relatively the same. That is, it remains the same fraction (percentage) of the preceding stimulus. For example, if one can distinguish between 16 and 17 ounces, he or she should be able to distinguish between 32 and 34 ounces but not necessarily between 32 and 33.

$$\frac{17-16}{16} = \frac{1}{16} = C_1 \qquad \frac{34-32}{32} = \frac{2}{32} = C_1 \qquad \frac{33-32}{32} = \frac{1}{32} \neq C_1$$

The addition in only the first two cases is one-sixteenth of the preceding stimulus.

In the 1940s, Edward N. Hay conducted a series of studies based on Weber's law of just observable differences and noted that a 15 percent or approximately one-seventh difference in the importance of one factor as compared with the preceding factor was discernible by trained raters at least 75 percent of the time.[6] This 15 percent difference provided a valuable criterion, index, or rule of thumb for a variety of uses when developing a scale or a grouping in which just observable magnitudes of difference are an important issue. In review, it appears that there must be at least a 15 percent difference between any two factors in the compensation area before there is any workable recognition value.

Using the 15 percent index, it appears that seven degrees should be adequate for defining the magnitudes of difference of a subfactor. Although in

[5]*Encyclopaedia Britannica:* Micropaedia, vol. 10, 15th ed. (Chicago, IL: Encyclopaedia Britannica, 1974), p. 593.

[6]Edward N. Hay, "The Application of Weber's Law to Job Evaluation Estimates," *Journal of Applied Psychology,* 34, 1950, pp. 102–104.

the study of degrees the number seven may not be an absolute, it can probably be used as a good midpoint, with a range of five to nine degrees providing adequate descriptions for any subfactor. That is:

$$1/5 = 20\% \qquad 1/7 = 14.3\% \qquad 1/9 = 11.1\%$$

Hay's research and Weber's law once again stress the importance of relativity to the compensation manager. Many issues are governed by the general principle of relativity in which changes are estimated in terms of the thing that has been changed, not in terms of the absolute change effected.

Since job evaluation involves concept identification, research into specific spans of attention and short-term memory may also be of value when attempting to solve magnitudes of difference problems. Possibly some of the most interesting research in this area has been done by George A. Miller of Harvard.[7]

Miller's research on concept identification and short-term memory investigated how individuals learn to identify specific dimensions and to select the correct dimension when facing a specific stimulus. Many of the decisions job evaluation personnel must make relate to their involvement in complex situations in which they must make observations within a short time. To be effective under such conditions, these individuals must learn to classify stimuli. Most people can learn to respond almost perfectly to a reasonable number of previously learned and classified stimuli. In his research, Miller recognized that there are severe limits to the capacity of short-term memory. He concluded that short-term memory is used primarily for identifying lists of unconnected events. (In the world of the job evaluator, these unconnected events are the activities—job requirements—related to the establishment of job worth.) Short-term memory not only uses few items for measurement, but also operates on a "push-down" principle for retrieving information stored in the brain (last-in, first-out is an example of the push-down principle).

Miller theorized that most people can work concurrently with five to nine items of information (e.g., criteria, dimensions, factors, variables) when making decisions. The more different items with which an individual works concurrently and the more input information required for analysis and discrimination purposes, the greater the likelihood of making errors. When evaluating job worth relative to one variable—for example, knowledge required or decision making—it is possible to misidentify or inconsistently evaluate that specific feature. On the other hand, too many variables overly complicate the recognition and evaluation process, leading to ineffective or risky uses of evaluation.

Over the years, Miller and other researchers have noted that individual short-term perceptual and memory abilities normally permit discrimination of about seven variables. The great majority of people can work with five variables. Using less than five may unduly restrict an individual's ability to discriminate, and the result will not be as consistent as it should be. On the other hand, few

[7]George A. Miller, "The Magical Number Seven Plus or Minus Two: Some Limits On Our Capacity For Processing Information," *The Psychological Review,* March 1956, pp. 81–97.

people can use more than nine variables. Using more than nine variables may result in an individual making discriminations or demands that are too fine relative to that person's memory.

The writings of both Hay and Miller indicate that a fairly restricted number of distinctive job features or qualities should be used when involved in the identification, the observation, and the measurement of job worth.

WEIGHTING AND SCORING

Sooner or later anyone involved in the evaluation process must come to grips with its primary purpose: the establishment of an internally equitable base pay for each job. It is for this reason that the entire compensable factor process has been described in such detail. By identifying and defining each factor, it is easier to evaluate each one relative to all the others. Thus it is easier to rank and rate each job.

When reviewing the objectives of the organization, it often is apparent that some factors are more important than others. When this occurs, weighting each factor as to its importance in the scheme of organizational objectives and goals is necessary. The weighting or comparison process must be as exact as possible, while recognizing that the process consists of subjective judgments made by experts in the field. Extremely sophisticated statistical procedures are used to analyze large numbers of individual decisions and then to identify differences in the value or in the weights of compensable factors. The weighting of the previously discussed nine FES factors required the use of more than 60 rater panels involving hundreds of job specialists. These rater panels rank-ordered hundreds of jobs relative to the FES compensable factors. The rank-order data were transformed into arc sine scale values which eventually were transformed into point scores for each factor.

The FES method has 4,480 points; the three basic factors in the Hay Associates method, successor to the Hay-Purvis methodology, normally require the use of 6,480 points; and the NMTAAssociates plan, successor to the NEMA-NMTA plan, has 825 points. The total number of points used is a matter of individual choice. The method must provide a sufficient number of points so that a significant difference in points can be awarded to jobs that are of different worth and so that the points can be further translated into a money value that accurately indicates the difference in worth of the jobs of the organization.

One pragmatic approach available for determining the number of points required in the job evaluation method is to inspect the range of pay from the lowest-paid to the highest-paid member. If the base salary of all members is to be determined through the use of a single scale or pay structure and a single job evaluation plan, a sufficient number of points to differentiate among all jobs from the lowest to the highest must be designed into the system. If there is more than one scale or structure, that is, one for exempt (managerial, administrative, and professional) employees and one for nonexempt (operative) employees, then this problem becomes less important. Chapter 10 discusses in detail the entire process of assigning a rate of pay to a job.

For example, if an organization decided to use one method to evaluate all its jobs, the following thinking process would be helpful in determining the number of points required: The president currently receives an annual salary of $105,000, and the lowest-paid workers earn $3.50 an hour or $7,000 based on a 40-hour, 50-week work year. A rough measure of the total points necessary is obtained by dividing the highest salary by the lowest. In this case, $105,000/ $7,000 = 15. There must be a sufficient point spread within the degrees to permit the most important job to receive an evaluation 15 times greater than the least important job. This is true only if all jobs are related on a single linear pay scale (see chapter 10).

When using a linear relationship and a single pay scale and when the difference in pay or expected pay between the highest and lowest jobs is a factor of 15, the point spread from the minimum to the maximum among the degrees should be at least a factor of between 18 to 20. The reason for this is that it is unlikely that the very lowest job would receive the minimum rating in every factor. It is equally unlikely that the highest-paid job would receive the maximum number of degree points for every rating factor.

When using a point factor job evaluation method, the number of points assigned to the factor indicate the weight of the factor. In turn, when developing degrees to profile the factor or subfactor, the number of points assigned to the factor is also the number of points assigned to the highest degree of the factor. In most cases, the lowest degree is assigned a certain number of points.

In the Factor Evaluation System example in table 8-4, the maximum total number of points assignable to a job is 4,480, while the minimum total number of points assignable to a job is 190. The difference is a factor of $4,480/190 = 23^+$. The difference in pay earned in 1981 by the lowest-paid GS-1 and the highest paid GS-15 is

$$\frac{\$50,112}{\$7,960} = 6.3$$

or approximately a factor of 7. The point spread developed within FES should be more than sufficient to differentiate jobs into the 15 GS pay grades.

When assigning points to degrees, the use of Weber's law may once again be helpful. If it is felt that there is a just observable difference between each degree, the highest number of points for the factor can be assigned to the highest degree. Dividing this value by 1.15 (1 for the initial value and 0.15 for the Weber-Hay 15 percent difference) will give the next value of the next highest degree. Succeeding values should continue to be divided by 1.15 until a value is obtained for all degrees.

Because of the way of describing a degree, it is, at times, possible to determine a just observable difference above and below a degree statement. In this case, each degree could have a +, 0, − scoring process. If this were the case and the 15 percent difference approach were used, a score would be assigned to

TABLE 8-4

FACTOR DESCRIPTION TABLE

Factor	Points for Factor	Value of Factor as Percentage of Total (Weight of Factor)	Number of Levels	Points for Each Level
Knowledge required by the position	1,850	41.3%	9	50,200,350,550,750,950,1250,1550,1850
Supervisory control	650	14.5%	5	25,125,275,450,650
Guidelines	650	14.5%	5	25,125,275,450,650
Complexity	450	10.0%	6	25,75,150,225,325,450
Scope and effect	450	10.0%	6	25,75,150,225,325,450
Personal contact	110	2.5%	4	10,25,60,110
Purpose of contact	220	4.9%	4	20,50,120,220
Physical demand	50	1.1%	3	5,20,50
Work environment	50	1.1%	3	5,20,50
Total	4,480	99.9%		

each step in the degree scoring process. A third approach would be to simply have a half step between each verbally identified degree (i.e., 1, 1½, 2, 2½ . . .). This approach permits the evaluators to make a selection midway between two identified and defined degrees.

Other Weighting and Scoring Methods

Using Weber's law as a basis for developing a 15 percent increase in each step of the degree rating scale is an example of a geometric progression. A geometric progression is one in which a base value increases or decreases as a function of multiplication or division by a constant.

The arithmetic and random progression methods are also suitable for developing a rating scale. In an *arithmetic* progression, a base value increases or decreases by adding a constant value to the base or subtracting one from it. Many organizations use this equal interval method because they feel it is easier to explain and justify. For example:

Base value 20   Constant increase 5
Step 1   20
Step 2   25
Step 3   30
Step 4   35

A *random* progression uses no set value to increase or decrease the base. For example:

Base value 20
Step 1   20
Step 2   25
Step 3   40
Step 4   75

The process of identifying, defining, and weighting compensable factors is an arduous task; and it requires the cooperation of every member of the organization. But if it is possible to gain understanding and agreement at this stage, the organization has made a giant step toward the development of a workable and acceptable compensation program. Although building such a solid base may at times appear to be hardly worth the effort, it is important to remember that this foundation supports many of the primary operations of the organization.

A NONSTATISTICIAN'S APPROACH TO WEIGHTING COMPENSABLE FACTORS

A mathematical procedure called *normalizing* provides a simple approach to weighting a set of compensable factors. In this approach, a group of job experts or a job evaluation committee first reviews the compensable factors and then establishes a rank order for the factors. (The paired-comparison procedure is extremely useful for this purpose).

After ranking the factors, the highest-rated factor is assigned a value of 100 percent. Then a value is assigned the next highest factor as a percentage of its importance as compared to the 100 percent factor. This relative comparison process is repeated for each remaining factor. In this procedure, each factor is always compared with the highest-rated factor.

For example, Olympia Service Center rank-ordered the four compensable factors in its job evaluation plan as follows:

Column 1	*Column 2*		*Column 3*
	Percentage of		
	Highest		*Weight of*
Order of Rating	*Rated Factor*		*Each Factor*
(1) Knowledge and its Application	100	$\dfrac{100}{290} =$	34.5
(2) Problem solving	70	$\dfrac{70}{290} =$	24.1
(3) Communication	60	$\dfrac{60}{290} =$	20.7
(4) Work environment	60	$\dfrac{60}{290} =$	20.7
	290		100.0

In the next step, all values in column 2 are added, totaling 290. Then the values in column 2 are divided by the total of column 2. This value is the normalized weight of each factor. The same procedure can be used for weighting the subfactors within a factor.

COMPENSABLE FACTOR METHODS

The compensable factor approach to job evaluation split into several different methods in the 1920s. Most job evaluation methods currently in use are quite similar to those developed approximately 50 years ago. The two basic compensable factor methods are those using a narrative approach and those using some kind of numerical scoring.

The person given credit for the development of the narrative approach is Ismar Baruch.[8] Baruch was responsible for developing and implementing the position classification method of job evaluation for the federal government. The classification method has been widely used by public sector organizations.

[8]Committee on Position-Classification and Pay Plans in the Public Service, *Position-Classification in the Public Service* (Chicago, IL: Civil Service Assembly of the United States and Canada, 1941). This report is frequently referred to as the Baruch Report.

At about the same time Baruch was identifying and defining the compensable factors useful in allocating jobs in the federal government, Merrill R. Lott was introducing a 15-factor point method for evaluating jobs in an industrial setting.[9] Eugene J. Benge and his associates followed shortly thereafter in 1926 with their factor comparison method of job evaluation, which was intended to be an improvement over the Lott point method.

The two basic compensable factor methods mentioned above, as well as other methods, are discussed in the material that follows.

Narrative Factor Methods

Narrative factor methods involve identifying and defining compensable factors. The definition process requires clear and forthright descriptions of the factors so that those involved in matching relative job content with factors will be able to interpret precisely and relate the compensable factor standards to the job. This same requirement is made even when assigning weights and points to a factor. However, because no numerical scale is used in the narrative approach, the word descriptions assume greater importance and extend throughout the entire process. The descriptions of the factors or their relative levels of difficulty or importance must be defined within the job. The factors and the factor levels must again be defined within the standard that describes the class to which jobs will be assigned and to the specific pay level or pay grade in order finally to establish the worth or pay rate of the job. This approach is similar to the development of predetermined grade standards described in chapter 7.

Position Classification Method—Position classification is the term applied to the method of job evaluation used widely by a variety of public agencies and jurisdictions.[10] As developed by Baruch, position classification includes the identification and the description of a number of universal compensable factors, the writing of detailed specifications for a class of positions (class standards), the writing of a detailed position description, and the allocation of a position to a class. This method requires the use of in-depth job analysis. The job analysis provides a listing of the tasks and qualifications required in job performance.

Construction of a position classification plan normally involves the establishment of broad functional areas of work activities (professional, administrative, technical, clerical, etc.), which are frequently called occupations or families. These broad groups are then further divided into class-series that group jobs that have common content and require similar but varying levels of knowledge and skills.

Compensable factors used in various position classification plans in the federal government can vary like their counterparts in private sector plans. Factors used in the position classification system of the General Schedule Guidelines of the federal government are (1) qualifications required, (2) nature

[9]Merrill R. Lott, *Wage Scales and Job Evaluation: Scientific Determination of Wage Rates on the Basis of Services Rendered* (New York: Ronald Press, 1926), pp. 46–59.

of supervision received, (3) guidelines, (4) originality required, (5) nature and variety of work, (6) recommendations, (7) decisions, and (8) purpose and nature of person-to-person work relationships. The federal Wage Grade Guidelines include the following factors: (1) skill and knowledge, (2) responsibility, (3) physical effort, and (4) working conditions.

Position classification as used in the federal government does not relate all eight factors to all occupations. The narrative formats are not consistent. Furthermore, because of both the length of the narrative and the inconsistency in format, employees and supervisors frequently have difficulty in relating the narrative standard to their positions when reviewing the results of evaluation. Another difficulty with the narrative approach is that the standards may require rewriting when there are changes in the responsibilities and the requirements of the position or occupation.

Time-span of Discretion (TSD) Method—Elliott Jaques initially proposed a different way to evaluate job worth in the 1950s, contending that the differences in responsibility required in the performance of jobs establish the differences in job worth. He further contends that the responsibility in a work role can be measured by determining "the longest period of time which can elapse in a role before the manager can be sure that his subordinate has not been exercising marginally sub-standard discretion continuously in balancing the pace and the quality of his work."[11]

Jaques maintains that the time-span of discretion a jobholder has in the performance of his work is the basic factor in determining pay, stating that commonly held social norms provide an "unconscious awareness" among all employees that differences in pay should relate directly to differences in time-span of discretion.[12] He further states that to define this span it is necessary to determine the following:

1. Whether it is a single- or multiple-task job (the time-span of a multiple-task job is that time required to perform the longest task).

2. The quality and quantity standards used as a basis for determining substandard performances of discretion.

3. The normal length of time between the time a subordinate starts a task and the time his superior checks his performance.

---

[10]The terms *position* and *job* usually have identical meanings when discussing the administration of pay and classification in the public sector. An important exception to this rule, however, is in the federal government where, by regulation and tradition, a *position* relates to the work activities of a person performing within General Schedule (GS) Guidelines and a *job* relates to work activities of a person performing within guidelines established for Wage Grade (WG) employees.

[11]Elliot Jaques, *Time-span Handbook* (London: Heinemann Educational Books, 1964), p. 10.

[12]Elliot Jaques, *Equitable Payment* (New York: Wiley, 1961), p. 17.

Although Jaques maintains that the use of this one universal factor makes it possible to reduce conflict over wage inequities, the results of a series of studies conducted in the 1960s and 1970s fail to support his position.[13] Time-span, however, may be one additional technique available to compensation managers to assist them in developing equitable levels of pay in their organizations.

Problem-solving Compensable Factor Method—A. W. Charles proposes problem solving as a single universal factor useful in evaluating all jobs in an organization, from the lowest to the highest.[14]

The Charles approach uses ordinal rather than cardinal relationships in performing job-to-job comparisons based on problem-solving complexity. Ordinal numbers (first, second, third, etc.) provide a specific or absolute position in a series; cardinal numbers (1, 2, 3, etc.) permit numerical scoring and the establishment of percentage differences in comparing job worth. The Charles method results in a ranking of jobs through the use of a factor rather than the use of the whole job.

The first step in the problem-solving compensable factor method is to develop a two-dimensional matrix that lists all the jobs to be compared in both the rows and columns. In the squares formed by the intersection of the row and column, if the job in the row has greater problem-solving responsibilities than the job in the column, a plus sign is placed in the square. The job accumulating the most plus signs has the largest amount of problem-solving responsibility and is thus the most important job in the matrix.

The following steps involve joining together the matrices that describe the problem-solving responsibilities of the various departments of the organization. An analysis of the multidepartment matrix then establishes the order of importance of all jobs in the organization.

Charles contends that multicompensable factor plans are not truly universal in scope and that the use of cardinal point values establishes a scale of values that further compound the error by assuming that the quantities to be measured are meaningful. Charles's method claims to correct these basic job evaluation errors.

Broadbanding Method—T. T. Paterson and T. M. Husband proposed yet another plan for evaluating jobs that claims to overcome the purely subjective

---

[13]A few of the studies conducted analyzing Jaques' time-span theory are discussed in: Thomas Atchison and Wendell French, "Pay Systems for Scientists and Engineers," *Industrial Relations,* October 1967, pp. 44–56; Paul S. Goodman, "An Empirical Examination of Elliot Jaques' Concept of Time Span," *Human Relations,* May 1967, pp. 155–170; Michael E. Gordon, "An Evaluation of Jaques' Studies of Pay in the Light of Current Compensation Research," *Personal Psychology,* Winter 1969, pp. 369–389; Jerry L. Gray (ed.), *The Glacier Project: Concepts and Critiques* (New York: Crane and Russek, 1976); Don Hellriegel and Wendell French, "A Critique of Jaques' Equitable Payment System," *Industrial Relations,'* May 1969, pp. 269–279; George T. Milkovich and Keith Campbell, "A Study of Jaques' Norms of Equitable Payment," *Industrial Relations,* October 1972, pp. 267–271.

[14]A. W. Charles, "Installing Single-Factor Job Evaluation," *Compensation Review,* First Quarter, 1971, pp. 9–17.

TABLE 8-5

THE BROADBANDING METHOD

Band	Type of Decision	Decision
1. Band O	Defined	Decisions permitting very limited discretion.
2. Band A	Automatic	Decisions permitted within restricted process of operation.
3. Band B	Routine	Decisions based on broad skills implementing a process.
4. Band C	Interpreting	Decisions made within limits of operating programs.
5. Band D	Programming	Decisions made within limits set by organizational policy.
6. Band E	Policy Making	Decisions made within broad interpretation of the law.

measure of essentially personal factors that are an inherent weakness in previously developed methods of job evaluation.[15] Paterson and Husband stated that this weakness is especially apparent when organizations try to compare unlike jobs. From their research, they find that all jobs differ according to the kinds of decisions made in performing them.

Paterson identified six levels or bands of decision that make it possible to differentiate among all jobs. They are shown in table 8-5. Paterson and Husband stated that the advantages of using the decision bands are the ease with which they can be installed and the basic fairness in relating job worth to decision-making requirements.

The Civil Service Commission for the Province of Ontario has developed a classification plan that makes an even more intensive use of the broadbanding approach. Their approach uses four compensable factors: (1) knowledge, (2) judgment, (3) accountability, and (4) level of contact. This method requires the construction and the use of benchmark job descriptions that identify a specific degree of difficulty, skill, and worth in each of the four factors in an occupational group.

Broad Classification Methods

Broad classification methods do not depend on matching comparable jobs or classes. They do depend, however, on matching broad groups of relatively homogeneous jobs (homogeneous by industry, by specific profession, by geographic area, etc.). The two basic broad classification methods are the

[15]T. T. Paterson and T. M. Husband, "Decision-Making Responsibility: Yardstick for Job Evaluation," *Compensation Review,* Second Quarter, 1970, pp. 21–31.

maturity curve method, which classifies pay by years since the jobholder obtained his or her degree or by age of employee, or by years on the job, and the *frequency distribution method,* which analyzes pay data from the viewpoint of a frequency distribution of the rates of pay of relatively homogeneous professions.

Maturity Curve Method—The maturity curve method has been used principally in the professional field where jobs defy precise description. In fact, these professional jobs depend to a great degree on what the jobholders themselves decide to do at a particular time. The jobs have both broad and loose limits, and the pay of individual workers depends on how well they perform the broad range of job assignments.

The maturity curve, whether it examines the age of the employee, the years since the employee received an undergraduate or graduate degree, or the employee's years of experience in a specific professional position, provides data concerning general levels of pay for different jobs. The theory behind the use of these factors is that professional employees normally must have certain qualifications before they are hired and a certain amount of experience before becoming proficient in their professions. Thus, maturity best reflects the market worth of these points. When using a maturity curve method based on age alone, evaluators must be aware that they could be in violation of the Age Discrimination in Employment Act.

Maturity curves frequently show the 10th, 25th, median, 75th, and 90th percentiles of pay for each level by age, years since degree, or experience. These percentiles then provide a salary range for each designated level. Some organizations have found it possible to relate performance to the percentile curves by having the pay amounts of the top-ranked 10 percent of their professionals near the 90th percentile, whereas the bottom-ranked 10 percent of their professionals receive that pay indicated for the 10th percentile.[16]

In testing the maturity curve method, one group found that age or years since degree explained only a comparatively small amount of the variance in salaries.[17] Not only does elapsed time fail to explain pay differences adequately, but it is likely that this method will fall into the correlation-causation fallacy trap of assuming that a relationship between A and B is caused by either A or B, whereas in fact it may be caused by C or some other factor or factors.

On the other hand, no method fully explains any relationship. If a method is to be helpful in describing pay differentials, it is important to know the techniques and their strengths and weaknesses and how to use them.

Another issue related to the correlation-causation fallacy trap involves the

---

[16]The following three articles provide an in-depth review of the maturity curve method, its strengths, weaknesses, and uses: George W. Torrence, "Maturity Curves and Salary Administration," *Management Record,* January 1962, pp. 14–17; Edward A. Shaw, "The Maturity Factor as an Aid in Administering Professional Salaries," *Personnel,* September–October 1962, pp. 37–42; Ralph Kulberg, "Relating Maturity Curve Data to Job Level and Performance," *Personnel,* March–April 1964, pp. 45–50.

[17]Orval R. Grigsby and William C. Burns, "Salary Surveys—The Deluge," *Personnel Journal,* June 1962, pp. 274–280, 297.

use of market data or external environmental data to establish internal relationships.

Frequency Distribution Method—The frequency distribution method, which is also known as the Global Plan, is useful in analyzing pay differentials among managerial and professional jobs that have a broad range of duties and are difficult to describe precisely.[18] The Global Plan, as in any frequency distribution method, requires some form of homogeneity—the more homogeneous the data, the more valid and reliable they are.

In the Global Plan, the first step in achieving homogeneity is to survey firms producing similar output. The next step is to separate jobs with similar responsibilities and duties into the following broad categories.

1. Scientific—professional, supervisory
2. Scientific—professional, nonsupervisory
3. Administrative—supervisory
4. Administrative—nonsupervisory

The respondee to an instrument such as that shown in table 8-6 then provides pay data on a frequency distribution for each category. From such data collection instruments, it is possible to display graphically a variety of relationships. The display may compare one organization with another or the initiating organization with an industry average.

As in the maturity curve method, the frequency distribution method provides a guide for group pay levels and is of little or no value as a basis for the pay of an individual. As mentioned previously, averages (i.e., measures of central tendency) may not describe an individual, a particular job, or a specific situation. They are extremely useful, however, in providing guidelines or assisting in setting limits. They assist decisionmakers in knowing what to expect and what is acceptable.

Numerically Scored Factor Models

Over the past 60 years, various quantitatively oriented compensable factor evaluation methods have been designed to improve precision and orderliness and to minimize the subjectivity inherent in job evaluations. As these numerically scored evaluation plans have acquired greater acceptance, the term *scientific* has been used further to establish their value and objectivity.

Assigning numerical scores through the use of weighted and scored compensable factors to jobs being evaluated helps to provide structure and orderliness, but there are definite limits to the objectivity and the scientific purity of these scores. Advocates of job evaluation methods that do not use weighted and scored compensable factors often state that such methods are

---

[18]Kenneth E. Foster, Gerald F. Wajda, and Theodore R. Lawson, "Global Plan for Salary Administration," *Harvard Business Review,* September–October 1961, pp. 62–66.

	TABLE 8-6						
	SCIENTIFIC—PROFESSIONAL[a]						
	Supervisory				*Nonsupervisory*		
Monthly Salary Interval	*(A) No. of Persons*	*Percentage of Column (A) Total*	*Average Age*	*(B) No. of Persons*	*Percentage of Column (B) Total*	*Average Age*	
Under $900							
$900–$999							
$1,000–$1,099							
$1,100–$1,199							
$2,900–$2,999							
$3,000 and over							

[a]This same type of instrument with minor modifications may be used for data collection in the maturity curve method by adding columns such as "Years since Undergraduate Degree," "Years since Master's Degree," or "Years in that Position."

pseudoscientific, arbitrary, self-deceiving, and illusory and that the very act of weighting makes the entire process even more subjective and questionable. However, pragmatic and empirical studies over the past 50 years have provided compensation personnel with compensable factors that are logically and philosophically sound and valuable in defining job differences and evaluating job worth.

Numerically scored compensable factor job evaluation methods provide a rational framework for justifying evaluation determinations. They allow for a number of individuals to use subjective judgment in a systematic manner in making evaluation decisions. This opportunity for many individuals to make decisions based on common criteria normally produces more valid results than those made by one individual, even when the person is an "expert" in the field. Increased participation in job evaluation also brings about increased acceptance of the entire job analysis and job evaluation process. *Once again, a warning:* The use of a numerical value or point scores does not mean that the method produces scientifically objective results. Scores permit the quantification of judgments rendered on the relationship between preset standards and the requirements of the job under review. All job evaluation processes are subjective. They require the greatest care in all stages of design, implementation, and administration. An analysis of some of the various approaches to job evaluation that use numerically rated compensable factors will aid in understanding the issues involved and in deciding which method is most suitable for a specific application.

Point Method—The point system evolved from the works of such job evaluation pioneers as Lott, Benge, Bass, and Burk. The early point factor plans had from 12 to 24 factors. The critical issue in determining the actual number of factors in a job evaluation plan relates to the ever-present problems of over-evaluation and underevaluation when rating jobs. If critical compensable factors are omitted, there is a serious likelihood that the job can be *underevaluated*. When using more than one factor that describes the same value of a job, *overevaluation* can result.

The point method uses the following procedure:

Step 1. Identify and define the factors useful in describing the fundamental elements of the general nature of all jobs under study.

Step 2. Weight the factors and assign a specific value to each factor. (In the Lott method, the total value of all weighted factors equals 100 and the value of each of his 15 factors is some percentage of 100—see nonstatistical approach to weighting described earlier in this chapter.)

Step 3. Identify a sufficient number of key or benchmark jobs to cover the entire range of difficulty or importance of all factors.

Step 4. Using each factor, assign a value of from one to ten to each key job. The job demanding the greatest possible degree of a factor receives a 10 and the job demanding little or no amount of a factor receives a one. Values between one and ten are assigned to other jobs using the same procedure.

Step 5. Multiply weighted factor value (step 2) by the key job value (step 4). This provides a point score for each factor for each job.

Step 6. Add scores for all factors for each job.

Step 7. Order jobs relative to total points earned.

The ordering of jobs relative to each factor provides a yardstick or scale of values for assigning a value to other jobs through the use of slotting or the paired-comparison procedure.

Factor Comparison Method—Following in the footsteps of Lott, Eugene J. Benge and his associates developed the factor comparison method for the Philadelphia Rapid Transit Company in 1926. This method uses a series of rankings and slottings to determine both the relative value and absolute worth of a job.

Benge's factor comparison method was another step in the development of universal compensable factors. It also made use of key jobs for developing factor scales that adequately represent the level of requirements basic to each other.

Instead of using a point scale like Lott's, Benge's plan develops a wage rate scale for each factor. After assigning a wage rate to each key job and defining the universal compensable factors, it is possible to develop a wage rate or monetary scale for each factor. By establishing a monetary scale for each universal factor, all other jobs in the organization can be evaluated. (This scaling method gave rise to the other name for this evaluation process—the weighted-in-money method.) Summing the monetary value of all factors for a particular job establishes its pay rate.

Benge's factor comparison method of job evaluation can be performed in eight steps. These steps are:

Step	Activity
1	Jobs to be evaluated are ranked. This step assists in developing a better understanding of the values and contributions of each job.
2	From information provided through a market survey, a going rate of pay is assigned to each key job.
3	Using the five compensable factors identified by Benge (skill, mental demands, physical demands, responsibility, and working conditions), each rater privately ranks each key job by each factor with the lowest number—one—indicating the job receiving the highest level of value for that factor.
4	The job evaluation committee as a whole reviews ratings of each member and comes to a final, agreed-upon ranking. If members cannot agree to the ranking of a particular job—if consensus cannot be reached, it may be necessary to eliminate that job as a key job.
5	Each committee member now assigns a monetary value to each factor with the sum of the monetary values for factors equal to the market or going rate of pay for the job.
6	In a step similar to step 4, the job evaluation committee members reach an agreement on the monetary value of each factor for each job. The final value is not a mathematically derived average value but rather a "meeting of the minds" average.
7	Using the money values for each factor, the committee develops a monetary scale for each factor. All of the remaining jobs of the organization are compared with the factor scale and, through a slotting process, assigned a specific value for each factor. The sum of the monetary values assigned to each job for all factors then becomes the pay for the job.
8	As a final check, the committee develops a final key job ranking schedule that compares job ranking, money ranking, and monetary value by each factor for each key job.

The weakness in Benge's method is similar to that in Lott's—that is, the establishment of a scale of values. In the factor comparison method, the evaluators must know the existing rate of pay for a key or benchmark job. The dynamic work environment that exerts so much influence on work content and job requirements reduces the stability of pay relationships among jobs. In addition, the pervasiveness of the marketplace and inflationary conditions result in market variations and constantly changing rates of pay. These two conditions are sufficient in themselves to question the value of any plan that uses the market as the primary measuring scale for determining relative job worth.

In addition to these problems, it is extremely difficult to allocate a specific pay rate based on money among five or more factors of a specific benchmark job. The determination of the weight of a factor and its scoring is the most crucial and difficult part in developing any numerically scored factor evaluation method. Problems related to the use of market pay information for establishing internal worth relationships are discussed in detail in the section, "The Market and the Comparable Worth Issue," in chapter 7.

Point-Factor Comparison Methods

In the 1930s, the Western Electric Company adopted a point-factor comparison method that used universal factors, subfactors, and degrees as standards for measuring job worth. The major difference between this method and the ones developed by Lott and Benge was the use of point-scored degrees to describe the magnitude of differences or levels of difficulty existing within a compensable factor.

General Point-Factor Comparison Methods—Spinoffs of the Western Electric plan were general point-factor comparison methods introduced by the National Electrical Manufacturers Association (NEMA) and the National Metal Trades Association (NMTA), now known as the American Association of Industrial Management (AAIM) or NMTA Associates. These plans or variations of them have been adopted and used by thousands of organizations. The major differences among the wide variety of general point-factor comparison plans are the number of factors and subfactors used and the description and the value assigned to the degrees of each. The similarity among general point-factor comparison plans is the use of universal factors, subfactors, and degrees as the standards for determining job worth. (Some plans do omit the use of the subfactor and go directly from universal factors to degrees.) These plans normally can relate to a wide variety of jobs in diverse businesses and industries.

The use of the universal factor–subfactor–degree approach provides a standard scale of values that permits an understandable and precise approach for comparing and evaluating unlike jobs.

Occupational Point-Factor Comparison Method—In 1977 the U.S. Civil Service Commission (CSC) developed a point-factor method that differs from the previously developed point-factor methods such as those of the NMTA and the NEMA and their many offshoots. When the CSC developed its Factor

Evaluation System (FES), it slightly modified the compensable factor approach as presented in chapter.[19] In the FES, the CSC first developed primary standards or standard-of-standards. This set of standards consists of the nine factors defined in universal terms that are applicable to all nonsupervisory General Schedule (GS) jobs.

After establishing the primary standards, the next step in the FES is the development of factor-level descriptions for the series. (This is the application of the primary standard to a specific occupation or to groups of closely related occupations.) By further defining the factors in terms of the work/job content of a specific occupation, the system is applicable to a wide variety of jobs and provides a significant amount of flexibility to the system.

The third step in the FES is the development of benchmarks. Benchmarks describe an actual job situation that typically represents a significant number of jobs in an occupation. With the benchmark descriptions, the FES provides three sets of standards for evaluating the worth of jobs. Moving from the broad, universal definition in the primary standards to the more specific definition in the series standards to the very precise definition in the benchmarks furnishes evaluators with a wide range of information that facilitates quick and accurate evaluation of a job and a wide degree of flexibility in matching a job under study with an appropriate standard.

Because the FES factors are defined in terms of class-series work content or actual benchmark job content, it is unnecessary to use the subfactor stage as developed in this chapter. This, in turn, allows for the FES levels (identical to degrees as developed in this chapter) to describe directly the magnitude of differences within a factor.

Very few organizations require the amount of detail necessary for a compensable factor program similar to that of the CSC. It will probably be the late 1980s before all 400-plus GS occupations have been described by factor-level descriptions for the series and their relevant benchmarks. The efforts of CSC to date, however, indicate that this may be a landmark approach for the design of a job evaluation plan using point-rated compensable factors.

Factor Guide Chart–Profile Method—In the 1940s, Edward N. Hay and Dale Purves developed a profile method for evaluating jobs that is one of the more popular methods used today. More than two thousand businesses throughout the world now use the Hay Plan.

The Hay Guide Chart–Profile Method uses three universal factors: (1) know-how, (2) problem solving, and (3) accountability. When applicable to the needs of a specific organization a fourth factor–working conditions–is used. Each of the three primary (universal) factors is more precisely identified by dimensions (or subfactors). A guide chart is used to identify, define, and score the worth of each factor. Each guide chart is a two-dimensional matrix. The

---

[19]U.S. Civil Service Commission, *Instructions for the Factor Evaluation System* (Washington, DC: Government Printing Office, May 1977).

levels of importance or difficulty of a subfactor determine the actual number of rows and columns in the matrix. When a guide chart is used, the job being measured is evaluated against the standards set in the chart. A point score is obtained where factor degrees intersect.

The know-how guide chart includes three dimensions: (1) the requirement for specialized, technical, or practical know-how, which forms the rows of the know-how chart; (2) the requirement for breadth of know-how to integrate different kinds of managerial activities, which forms the columns of the guide chart; and (3) the requirement for human relations skills in selecting, motivating, and developing people, which is a dimension inside each level of the breadth dimension.

The second factor, problem solving, includes two dimensions: (1) the environment in which the problem solving takes place, which forms the rows of the problem-solving chart, and (2) the limits and the controls over original thinking (i.e., the nature of thinking required), which form the columns of the problem-solving chart.

The third factor, accountability, also has three dimensions or subfactors. The row dimension is freedom to act. The column dimension is the job's impact on end results. Inside each level of the column dimension is the third dimension—the magnitude of the end result that the job most clearly affects.

The fourth factor, working conditions, has three dimensions. Physical effort has four levels and forms the rows of the matrix; environment, with five levels, forms the columns. The third dimension, hazards, is described by columns within each of the five levels of environment that identify the amount of hazards present on the job.

The descriptions that form the rows and the columns of the guide chart provide a measure of the level of difficulty, or importance, of each factor. When matching the factor requirements of a specific job to the guide chart standards, the intersection of the most appropriate row and column descriptor provides a point value.

The know-how, accountability, and working conditions guide charts provide actual point scores. The problem-solving guide chart, however, provides a percentage score. The percentage value identifies the amount of know-how used in solving problems. The problem-solving point score is determined by multiplying the problem-solving percentage against the point score previously determined for the know-how factor.

A major advantage of the Hay Plan is that by having a large number of businesses using a similar evaluation plan, it is easier to compare jobs for determining external competitiveness. Hay Associates provides its clients with pay surveys that are easy to use and quite valuable for a business that wishes to determine its pay posture in comparison with other businesses in its region or with those that provide similar services or products.

Benchmark Guide Chart Method—The Benchmark Guide Chart Method of job evaluation attracted attention when the U.S. Civil Service Commission's

Job Evaluation and Pay Review Task Force introduced the Factor Ranking/
Benchmark Method in the mid-1970s.[20]

This method is a composite of a number of previously discussed factor
methods. It requires (1) identifying and describing the relevant compensable
factors, (2) weighting and assigning points to factors, and (3) placing of two or
more factors on one guide chart (similar to the Hay Profile Charts) for use in the
point rating of jobs being evaluated.

Similar to any compensable factor job evaluation method, the key to
successful implementation and administration of the Benchmark Guide Chart
Method is the collection of enough valid job content and job requirement data
and information to write descriptions that are current and understandable, and
have an orderly format. The next step is the development of benchmark job or
class descriptions that identify areas of work content and requirements, including information that permits accurate comparisons with identified, defined, and
weighted factors.

There are two approaches available for those interested in using a
Benchmark Guide Chart Method. One involves the use of *general factor* guide
charts, and the second uses *occupational factor* guide charts.

Factor guide charts are similar to the profile charts used in the Hay Plan.
The factors, subfactors, and degrees are defined in terms broad enough to cover
a wide range of jobs and can be used by organizations that vary widely in size
and geographic location and that provide diverse outputs.

Occupational guide charts are similar to factor guide charts, but the
factors relate to a specific occupation. The job content and the requirements of
the jobs that make up a specific occupation provide the information for
preparing an occupational guide chart. Occupational guide charts are, in reality,
a refinement or added step of the factor guide chart method.

The Benchmark Guide Chart method developed by the U.S. Civil Service
Commission includes the following occupational guide charts:

1. Professional, Administrative, and Technological occupations (PAT)

2. Supervisory and Management occupations (SAM)

3. Clerical Personnel, Office Machine Operators, and Technicians
(COMOT)

4. Protective Occupations/Law Enforcement (POLE)

5. Trades and Crafts occupations (TAC)

6. Executive, Scientific, and Medical Occupations (ESM)

The guide charts for each of these six broad groups use different sets of
factors to evaluate jobs in each occupational group, and the weights of the

---

[20]Philip M. Oliver, "Modernizing a State Job Evaluation and Pay Plan," *Public Personnel
Management*, May–June 1976, pp. 168–173.

factors differ from one occupation and group to another. To ensure consistent and fair relationships among jobs in these diverse occupations, factor guide charts must be developed before preparing occupational guide charts. The factor guide charts provide general definitions of the compensable factors and set limits for degree definitions and assignment of point values to ensure acceptable interoccupational alignments.

Multiple Regression Methods

In the past decade, a number of organizations involved in compensation consulting activities have developed various regression models for determining the worth of executive, managerial, and professional jobs. Multiple regression analysis is a statistical technique that investigates the relationship between a dependent variable (the money worth of a job) and two or more independent variables (various compensable factors). By using multiple regression, it is possible to predict the compensation of a job by considering two or more compensable factors simultaneously. Compensable factors used in regression models may include managerial rank, reporting level, number of exempt employees supervised, sales, and return on investment. Kenneth E. Foster, Director, Compensation Planning, Towers, Perrin, Forster & Crosby, has been a leading advocate of this approach.

The Position Analysis Questionnaire (PAQ) methodology developed by industrial psychologists at Purdue University has also been used to accurately predict existing wage rates for all jobs in an organization or, basically, how employers value the jobs in their organizations. By using (1) the 187 PAQ job elements that provide information input, mental processes, work output, relationships with other persons, and job-context related information, and (2) the 7 PAQ job elements that provide pay/income information, and by processing this information through the use of a step-wise regression model, PAQ is able to capture an employer's pay policy.[21]

Although at first glance, the PAQ methodology may appear to differ significantly from the previously described numerically scored compensable factor methods, the difference may not be as great as first appearances seem to indicate. The PAQ is described as a worker-oriented structural job analysis procedure to distinguish it from the more traditional job-oriented job analysis procedures. The job-oriented approach identifies the activities the incumbent performs, whereas the worker-oriented approach (that used by PAQ) tends to identify the human behaviors involved in job activities. On close investigation, it becomes apparent that it is extremely difficult to describe the differences between job-oriented tasks (activities) and worker-oriented behaviors (activities). In fact, PAQ experts state that it is possible to use only a small number of the 187 PAQ job elements—approximately nine—to predict wage rates.

[21]David D. Robinson, Owen W. Wahlstrom, and Robert C. Mecham, "Comparison of Job Evaluation Methods: A 'Policy-Capturing' Approach Using the Position Analysis Questionnaire," *Journal of Applied Psychology,* vol. 59, no. 5, 1974, pp. 633–37.

A number of these predictive job elements are (1) education, (2) job-related experience, (3) control devices (from turning an off-on switch to operating a keyboard), (4) arranging/positioning (placing objects, people, etc., in a specific position or arrangement), (5) body positions/postures (position employee takes when working, e.g., sitting, standing, walking, climbing, kneeling), (6) kinds of oral communication, (7) supervision or direction given, and (8) amount of job structure (degree to which job activities are predetermined).[22] The eight PAQ job elements do not appear to be very different from the more common traditional compensable factors described earlier in this chapter.

SELECTED READINGS

American Association of Industrial Management, *Job Rating Manual (Clerical, Technical, Supervisory)*. Melrose Park, PA: AAIM, 1969. This manual contains definitions of factors and respective degrees used in rating office, clerical, engineering, administrative, sales, and supervisory jobs.

————, *Job Rating Manual (Shop)*. Melrose Park, PA: AAIM, 1969. This manual contains definitions of factors and respective degrees used in rating production, maintenance, and service jobs.

Bass, A. W., Jr., "Applying the Point Method of Evaluation," *Iron Age,* October 8, 1936, pp. 58–60. This article contains a description of the compensable factors used in the point method and an outline for their application when establishing a rating scale.

Bass, A. W., Jr., "Evaluating Shop Jobs by the Point System," *Iron Age,* September 10, 1936, pp. 42–44, 47, 123. Another of the pioneers describes the theory and the advantages of the point method for setting up and justifying rate differentials.

Benge, Eugene J., *Job Evaluation and Merit Rating*. New York: National Foreman's Institute, Inc., 1946. This manual of job evaluation procedures by one of the pioneers in the field is still an outstanding reference for anyone wishing to gain a better understanding of this area.

Charles, A. W., "Installing Single-factor Job Evaluation," *Compensation Review,* First Quarter 1971, pp. 9–20. Using problem solving as the key measuring factor, all jobs can be equitably evaluated and arranged in a company-wide matrix.

Gill, Earle F., "Management Positions Can Be Evaluated Successfully," *Personnel Journal,* April 1949, pp. 407–413. This is one of the first articles to describe a three-factor compensation system. It defines the three factors, *know-how, decisions,* and *responsibilities,* and describes the method for applying them by General Foods and its consultant.

Hay, Edward N., "Characteristics of Factor Comparison Job Evaluation," *Personnel,* May 1946, pp. 370–375. The author, one of three members of the original Philadelphia group (Benge, Burk, and Hay), argues that the factor comparison method is superior to the point method and states his case as to its advantages and

[22]Committee on Occupational Classification and Analysis, Assembly of Behavioral and Social Sciences, *Job Evaluation: An Analytic Review*. Washington, DC: National Academy of Sciences, 1979, pp. 168–170.

how to develop and use it. (This is the first of a series of articles in *Personnel* that are invaluable to students of compensation management.) See also *Personnel,* July 1946, pp. 46–56 and September 1946, pp. 115–124.

Hay, Edward N. and Dale Purves, "The Profile Method of High-level Job Evaluation," *Personnel,* September 1951, pp. 162–170. The authors introduce the profile method of job evaluation, successfully developed by them and used by General Foods in 1946. The profile method evolved into the system currently used by Hay Associates, a premier consulting firm in compensation management. Further descriptions of this method may be found in *Personnel,* January 1953, pp. 344–354; July 1954, pp. 72–80; and *Personnel Journal,* April 1958, pp. 403–406.

Kulberg, Ralph A., "Relating Maturity Curve Data to Job Level and Performance," *Personnel,* March–April 1964, pp. 45–50. This article discusses a relatively simple method of job evaluation that assists compensation managers to verify the soundness of pay ranges without losing sight of the fundamental principles of salary administration.

Pasquale, Anthony M., *A New Dimension to Job Evaluation.* New York: American Management Association, Inc., 1969. A brief analysis of some of the traditional methods of job evaluation as well as a review of the Smyth-Murphy guideline method for job evaluation.

Paterson, T. T., and T. M. Husband, "Decision-Making Responsibility: Yardstick for Job Evaluation," *Compensation Review,* Second Quarter, 1970, pp. 21–31. The authors contend that decision-making is common to all jobs and that the kinds of decisions made will differentiate jobs. They identify six basic kinds of decisions that define a whole range of jobs.

Shaw, Edward A., "The Maturity Factor as an Aid in Administering Professional Salaries," *Personnel,* September–October 1962, pp. 37–42. A discussion of the maturity curve method for evaluating jobs. This method is especially useful with scientific and engineering types of position. The article reviews the scope and the limitations of this approach to job evaluation.

9

Compensation Survey

CONTENT

Chapter 9 provides information that enables an organization to collect data which allow it to compare its total compensation and pay practices with those of other organizations participating in the same labor market.

GOALS

Upon concluding this chapter, you should be able to design and conduct a compensation survey that will generate desired compensation data and information. You should be able to use this market-related data as an additional guide for designing a pay structure that helps establish a motivating work environment.

The compensation survey is one of the most helpful tools available to the compensation manager. The data it provides enable an organization to compete in relevant labor markets. It is primarily a planning tool. As do all such tools, it demands valuable time both from within the organization and from those outside who contribute their own organizational data inputs. Compensation surveys provide data that identify competitive pay rates set by the market, whereas job evaluation identifies internally equitable relationships.

Units and interested individuals within the organization often conduct their own surveys to compare their pay with that of similar jobs in other organizations. This practice often results in piecemeal, inaccurate data, leading to job dissatisfaction and declining productivity. If for no other reasons, an organization should formalize the process to ensure that compensation data and information are as correct and valid as possible in order to overcome the inaccuracies resulting from informal surveys and to provide a sound basis for developing a pay structure that is competitive with external markets.

A survey enables the organization to learn what other organizations pay their employees in general as well as their rate of pay or range of rates of pay for specific classes of jobs. Although the pay of an individual job is in many ways an internal matter relating to individual requirements and contributions, the going rate—or market rate—that is paid by other organizations in a specified area for a comparable job influences the pay structure of practically every other organization in that area.

The very term *going rate* implies that there is a standard rate for a job in a community. Normally, this is not so. It is more likely that a variety of rates exists, and the survey process makes it possible to identify this range and a central tendency figure—a mean, median, or mode—for each job.

"Going wage" rates in a certain labor market also reflect type of organization, supply and demand of labor, ability to pay, union demands, and cost of living or other related standard of living factors, as well as unique requirements and reward features of the particular organization.

Chapters 5 through 8 stress the evaluation of the worth of one job as compared to that of all other jobs for a wide variety of organizations. These chapters provide compensation managers with the information necessary to assist them in designing and disseminating surveys in order to collect and analyze data that will enable their organizations to have a pay structure competitive with other organizations drawing from similar labor markets. The survey can also aid in developing an externally competitive wage structure that makes recruiting easier and provides a cornerstone for retaining employees and maintaining their goodwill and job satisfaction.

REASONS FOR CONDUCTING A SURVEY

A good place to start in developing a survey is to answer these two questions: (1) Is it necessary to conduct a survey? (2) If so, why? A look at some of the factors discussed in the following paragraphs will help provide the answers.

Factor 1: Hiring and Retaining Competent Employees

The success of an organization depends on skilled employees who see in their jobs the opportunity to promote their own self-interest as well as the interests of the organization. Contributing employees are those who help solve organizational problems, which leads to improved output and reduced waste. Motivated, well-trained people are required. Turnover, absenteeism, and uncaring, uninvolved attitudes destroy the efficiency of any organization. To survive, let alone grow, an organization must constantly search for the best applicants possible and strive to keep those it has already hired and trained.

The survey enables the organization to know what rates of pay the labor market demands and to direct its efforts toward maintaining and even improving upon these market participation rates of pay.

Factor 2: Promoting Worker Productivity

People work for rewards—that is, the carrots. Some rewards come from the job itself (e.g., the satisfaction and achievement derived from expending innovative effort), whereas others satisfy off-the-job needs. A reward package that tells workers their jobs are important and that they have done a good job goes a long way toward promoting positive, productive efforts.

Practically all workers measure their pay in both absolute and relative terms. The absolutes concern the ability of earned income to buy desired goods and services. In relative terms, workers compare their pay with that of coworkers, close friends, associates, and relatives from their geographical community or community of interests. If workers are to see their pay as being fair and equitable, it must satisfy their absolute requirements and it also must appear to be fair in comparison to the pay of their associates.

A primary means for an organization to maintain pay credibility and promote a feeling of fairness and equity among employees is through using surveys and making changes when unacceptable variances arise.

Factor 3: Developing an Adequate and Acceptable Pay Structure

Equal pay for equal work, equal pay for comparable worth, and pay that rewards individual contributions are more than intraorganizational principles. In developing a pay structure, an organization must recognize equivalent levels of knowledge and application of that knowledge in the responsibilities and the duties of the job. The organization must also provide incentives for effort and must encourage development of each employee. It must (1) review rates of pay of those competing in the labor market, (2) have a good idea of how other organizations provide for lateral as well as vertical promotions, and (3) recognize total compensation opportunities and their relationship to the pay structure. By focusing on these three areas of concern, an organization can first determine if it actually needs survey data and information. Recognizing that the collection and the analysis of survey data are costly, this judgment must always be made before conducting a survey: Do the benefits outweigh the cost? At this stage, it may be possible to identify and use a third-party survey developed by some public or private organizations that will supply enough data for decision-making purposes. (A discussion of some of these surveys follows later in this chapter.)

No matter whether the decision is made to implement a new compensation survey, to cooperate with an existing one, or to use one or more predeveloped surveys, compensation managers should be aware of the factors relating to the scope, the method, and the procedure involved. The development of such knowledge permits compensation managers to determine not only whether there is a need for a survey but also to determine the type to be used; when, where, and how it will be used; who will use it; and who will be involved.

SCOPE OF SURVEY

Once a decision has been made about the need for a survey, the next step is to determine its scope. The answers to a series of questions provide a start. Such questions as the following are helpful:

1. Where is the organization having its greatest trouble hiring and retaining employees?

2. Where is worker dissatisfaction centered?

3. Where do quality and productivity problems appear to be most serious?

4. Where does it appear that market rates outweigh internal rate relationships?

5. Where is market competition for particular skills or exotic talents most fierce?[1]

Recognizing that compensation factors influence every group, a wise procedure for developing answers is to begin with a broad overview of the organizational structure. Through a series of refinements, it is possible to pinpoint those areas requiring survey data. A review could take the following form:

1. Do the problem areas include only exempt (managerial/administrative or professional) categories, or are they in the nonexempt area?

---

[1] Exotic jobs are relatively new or different jobs in which demand far exceeds the supply of qualified applicants. This creates a special situation in which pay offerings are considerably higher than those normally justified through conventional evaluation or pay structuring processes. These jobs may have a temporary or short-term worth.

2. Within these exempt or nonexempt categories, do the problems center among middle-management jobs, particular professional jobs, certain clerical jobs, and so on?

3. Is it possible to define these jobs further by responsibility areas or by particular knowledge requirements (such as environmental planners), or by particular job classifications (such as computer operators)?

Having determined internal requirements, the compensation analyst's next step in determining the scope of the survey is to decide where to look for the needed data. Direction is provided by the following questions:

1. Is the local labor market the dominant source of supply for the jobs requiring survey data?

2. Are these managerial or professional jobs in which the labor market encompasses specific regions or the entire nation? Or possibly are they international in scope?

3. Are these jobs found only in specific industries?

After reviewing these questions, the next step is to identify organizations that hire from the specified labor markets. One must decide if it is important to include only those organizations in comparable industries, or, if the survey is to be made for a public sector organization, if it is necessary also to survey private employers. The issue is to obtain a true picture of the compensation offered by *all* organizations competing in the labor market. A survey that limits respondents to a type or a size of industry or to a sector of the economy (public or private), or to only a portion of the actual labor market will result in biased data that may provide invalid or unrealistic results.

As the variety of organizations responding to a survey broadens, the need for different types of compensation data, as well as for statistical methods for analyzing these data, increases. A major problem arising in any survey is comparability. It is highly unlikely that any two jobs in two different organizations are identical. The forces existing in each organization influence each job, imparting certain unique characteristics. This uniqueness results in different compensation patterns. Even when jobs have the same job titles or when their responsibilities, duties, or specifications are described in the same way, they probably are not identical. These comparison problems again stress the fact that compensation management is an inexact science; it is an art best performed by those who understand its fine differences and use all available tools and techniques to identify them, structuring the process accordingly. The survey is a tool of the artist. There are certain quasi-scientific procedures that will assist in developing a valid and useful picture of the compensation labor market, but ultimately the success of the survey depends on the skill of the surveyor.

After identifying the labor market and the potential suppliers of compensation data, the next problem is to determine the best method for collecting the data.

Key Job Matching

Key job matching, the most commonly used survey method, requires respondees to match key or benchmark jobs with similar jobs in their organizations through comparison with identification data supplied by the survey. Key jobs used for compensation surveys are highly visible jobs that are common to a variety of organizations and normally employ many workers.

The identification data may simply take the form of a job title, and the survey may request respondees to identify similar jobs in their organization, listing rates of pay, pay range, and number of employees in those jobs. It is logical to assume that the more identification data made available to the respondees, the better the match, but then the quality-quantity data problem arises. What is meant by *sufficient* data? What should the data provide? What are the benefits and costs? It is expensive to provide data because of the initial research and preparation costs and the printing and mailing costs. If the respondees are overwhelmed by the physical size of the survey, there is a good chance they will cast it aside and not respond. Too much data are often more damaging than too little. One of the best solutions is the *thumbnail sketch,* which is a brief recap of a job description that provides information concerning general and specific responsibilities or duties and other remarks or notations that will assist in differentiating the job under review from others that may to some degree have similar requirements or titles.[2]

Success with a key job matching survey requires careful selection and definition of jobs to be used for comparison purposes. The guidelines in the list below are helpful here. The job should:

1. Have widespread and common usage.

2. Be precisely defined and have a title that has a fairly uniform meaning and is not easily misconstrued.

3. Be performed in a rather similar manner by most organizations.

---

[2] The bulletins of the Bureau of Labor Statistics that describe their Area Wage Surveys normally have Occupational Descriptions in their appendixes that are typical examples of these thumbnails sketches. The Bureau of Labor Statistics is an invaluable source of compensation data. Anyone involved in this area should first check the wide variety of bulletins, reports, and so on that it makes available to the public, usually free or at a minimal cost. A basic guide for anyone involved in surveys is U.S. Department of Labor, *BLS Handbook of Methods for Surveys and Studies* (bulletin 1711) (Washington, DC: Government Printing Office, 1971).

4. Be an elementary job of a class when it is part of an class-series. When possible, however, all skill levels within a class-series should be used. This limits the tendency to identify several different jobs as one and minimizes development of a bimodal or even trimodal distribution.

5. Be commonly used in a collective bargaining situation.

Following these guidelines carefully, however, will not ensure receipt of valid and reliable compensation data. Certain problems can form a barrier to the success of any key job matching survey. For example, the job defined in the survey may have unique responsibilities and duties, thus providing poor matching prospects. Or, the manner of defining jobs for constructing a job or class-series may vary to such a degree among the respondees' organizations that it is almost impossible to arrange pay rates for a series from one or even two jobs within the series.

In most cases, the key job method requires from 10 to 30 key or benchmark jobs, with 15 as a good average. The survey situation is the final determinant; a large organization may require a larger number. Rates of pay and pay ranges from 15 jobs covering the spectrum of the pay structure normally provide sufficient reference points to check or assist in developing a valid and workable pay structure.

The ideal condition for conducting a key job survey exists when each organization uses the same compensable factors and evaluation plan to identify and weight each job. This is seldom the case, but it is helpful to know the standards or procedures used by the respondees for evaluating their jobs. The key job survey method is illustrated later in this chapter.

Key Class Matching

The identical procedures and problems used for key job matching apply to matching classes of jobs because a class of jobs is nothing more than a grouping of comparable jobs. The area and industry wage surveys of the Bureau of Labor Statistics are of the key class matching nature. In these procedures, letters of the alphabet identify the class-series hierarchy, with an A class being most advanced, followed by B, C, and so on, for less senior classes within a series.

Occupational Survey Method

The occupational survey method has been developed to overcome many of the inadequacies and the weaknesses of the key job or key class comparison methods.[3] This method begins by identifying certain basic occupational groups—accounting, manufacturing, personnel, purchasing, and so forth—and then identifying certain class-series within the occupational groups. For example, purchasing should include procurement, procurement expediting, and the

[3]Morton Adelby, "Wage and Salary Surveys: The Occupational Approach," *Personnel,* November–December 1960, pp. 36–44.

like. A thumbnail sketch and a code number are used to describe and identify each occupation. Each organization responding to the survey is requested to list by class title and hierarchy (A, B, C, etc., or I, II, III, etc.) those classes it has within each specific occupation. The respondee is also requested to list for each class the minimum and the maximum as well as the average rate of pay and the number of employees in that class.

Proponents of the occupational method state that some of the advantages are as follows:

1. It does not require the respondee to match specific jobs.

2. It is easier for the respondee to report objective data.

3. It provides pay data on a greater number of jobs.

4. It simplifies summarization and analysis of raw data.[4]

There is no doubt that this method, when properly used, results in broader samplings of occupational hierarchies than those achieved through key job matching. It is debatable, however, as to how much easier it is for an organization to respond to it and whether or not it provides a more stable base for updating and revision. Like any survey method, its true strength depends on its design, execution, and analysis.

Job Evaluation Method

The job evaluation method requires that all parties participating in the survey use the same general method for evaluating jobs. This method compares job content (as measured by points or grades) with pay in dollars. The comparison produces a series of curves that identify minimum, midpoint, and maximum pay for jobs of comparable content, as measured by points or grade level.

The job evaluation method minimizes job comparability error, but the surveyor must recognize the possibility that some organizations may use different point systems for evaluating similar jobs and that the importance of job content may be interpreted differently even when identical compensable factor information is used. If the survey is to produce valid and relevant data, the unit making the survey must be aware of any differences in the manner or the method used by the respondees for identifying and evaluating the worth of their jobs.

Hay Associates, an international compensation consulting firm, produces this type of survey annually for its more than 2,000 clients.[5] In 1977 approximately 400 clients provided survey data to the Hay organization.

---

[4]Ibid., pp. 43–44.

[5]Milton L. Rock, ed., *Handbook of Wage and Salary Administration* (New York: McGraw-Hill, 1972), chapter 3, pp. 60–66.

A variation of the job evaluation method is to request the responding organization to provide pay data and job descriptions for selected jobs. The surveying organization then evaluates the jobs using its own evaluation system. This procedure provides the surveying organization with two job point figures derived in an identical manner and one pay amount. All that remains is to solve for the other pay figure–that is, the appropriate pay the surveying company should provide given the quality of respondee data.

Broad Classification Method

Two major broad classification methods, the maturity curve method and the frequency distribution method (previously discussed in chapter 8), are also useful in collecting pay rate data for relatively homogeneous professions. The various broad classification methods provide easily understood guides for grouping pay levels. These methods help the surveyee to respond with desired and accurate data and the surveyor to develop useful summaries.

SURVEYS CONDUCTED BY THIRD PARTIES

Many organizations conduct compensation surveys each year using ready-made or "canned" surveys. Some of the better known of such packaged surveys are discussed in the next several paragraphs.

Bureau of Labor Statistics (BLS) Surveys

The Bureau of Labor Statistics annually conducts three basic types of surveys: (1) area wage surveys, (2) industry wage surveys, and (3) professional, administrative, technical, and clerical (PATC) surveys.

Area Wage Surveys—In 1980 the BLS performed 180 area wage surveys, including 30 in Standard Metropolitan Statistical Areas (SMSAs), and the remainder for other government agencies. These surveys focus on clerical and manual occupations in a wide variety of manufacturing and nonmanufacturing industries. They provide pay data for classes of jobs through such pay measures as mean, median, and the middle or interquartile range (the second and third quartiles or the middle 50 percent) (see figure 9-1).

The area wage surveys also provide data on weekly work schedules, paid holidays and vacation practices, and health insurance and pension plans, as well as on shift operations and differentials. Other related compensation data such as profit-sharing plans, sick leave plans, and wage payment systems are obtained through these surveys.

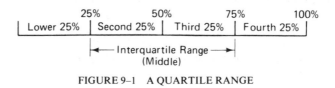

FIGURE 9–1   A QUARTILE RANGE

Industry Wage Surveys—The industry wage surveys cover 50 manufacturing and 20 nonmanufacturing industries that provide work for over 22 million employees. These surveys are conducted on a regularly recurring five-year and three-year cycle for a number of comparatively low-wage industries. (Publication may not be until as much as a year after the survey is conducted.) The surveys provide pay data for straight-time, first-shift workers in selected jobs as well as wage frequency distributions for broad employment groups, that is, production and related workers or nonsupervisory workers. Similar to the area wage survey, they also provide data on weekly work schedules, shift operations, and the like. Additionally, they provide pay data on labor-management agreements for employees in the building, trucking, printing, grocery store, and local transit industries. These pay data include rate per hour, hours per week, and employer contributions to insurance and pension funds.

On a national basis, the BLS covers nearly all manufacturing, utilities, and mining industries, and provides estimates for regions and major areas of concentration. Surveys in the trade, finance, and service industries are limited to approximately 20 metropolitan areas.

Professional, Administrative, Technical, and Clerical (PATC) Surveys— The PATC surveys cover 80 occupation levels in the fields of accounting, legal services, personnel management, engineering, chemistry, buying, clerical supervisory, drafting, and clerical. Definitions of jobs in these fields provide for classification according to appropriate work levels. The classifications relate to specific pay grades in the General Schedule (GS) of the Federal Classification Act and facilitate comparison with jobs in private industry.

The pay earnings in this survey include straight-time earnings as well as production bonuses, commissions, and cost-of-living increases. This survey is conducted in businesses with 2,500 or more employees located in metropolitan areas.

Limitations—The BLS surveys do have some limitations. Some users may find the geographic areas covered unsuited to their organizations. In addition, the surveys may not relate to their labor market. The timing of the BLS surveys minimizes their usefulness. There is a wide diversity in data, and the possible change of participants from one survey to the next may unduly influence or change the mean or median.

Administrative Management Society (AMS)

The Administrative Management Society of Willow Grove, Pennsylvania, conducts an annual survey of 13 clerical jobs, 7 data-processing jobs, and a number of middle-management jobs. The AMS collects data on more than 550,000 employees' salaries from a wide variety of industries throughout the United States, Canada, and the West Indies. These data are provided on a local, regional, and national basis. Pay data include such measurements as average, median, and first and third quartile pay. In addition to pay data by job and region, the survey includes data on hours worked per week, daily overtime, weekly overtime, number of paid holidays, length of vacations, and union membership.

American Management Associations (AMA)

The American Management Associations of New York furnish a broad range of executive, managerial, and professional compensation data. The data include jobs from that of the chief executive officer through middle management to supervisors. The surveys also cover staff, administrative, professional, and sales personnel. They separate pay data not only by a wide range of industries but also by sales volume of business and by functional responsibilities.

Federal Reserve System

Each of the 12 Federal Reserve Banks (FRB) conducts compensation surveys semiannually, annually, or biannually, depending on the compensation requirements of their districts. It is the policy of the Federal Reserve Board that the pay of their employees be competitive with the pay of other employees in their district. To achieve this policy objective, each FRB compares the pay of its most common jobs with similar jobs in other organizations. Pay data collected from the FRB survey are available to all participants in the survey and, at times, to nonparticipants upon request.

Professional, Trade, and Industrial Associations

Most professionals belong to national associations that represent their particular career fields. These associations provide a variety of services to their members. One highly desired and commonly provided service is the conducting of an annual compensation survey of their members and providing the summarial data in some association publication. Over the years, the quality of these surveys has improved, and the interest in the results has steadily increased. Similar to the professional associations are trade and industrial associations. They represent organizations providing comparable types of goods and services. These trade and industrial associations also perform compensation surveys for their members and provide them with the results. The members of these associations read the results of the surveys, and these results may have a significant influence on them.

Others

A large number of other organizations also perform wage surveys. Among these are many national consulting firms, and, in each metropolitan area, a variety of local organizations. National publication firms such as the Bureau of National Affairs (BNA) and Prentice-Hall, Inc., report findings of surveys in their trade bulletins. The American Management Associations' quarterly publication, *Compensation Review,* contains a wide range of valuable articles in the field of compensation, including a review of current survey activities.

The following lists identify business and professional journals and magazines and organizations that perform or provide some form of a compensation survey. The item in parentheses describes the particular type of survey the identified unit performs or reports.

BUSINESS AND PROFESSIONAL JOURNALS AND MAGAZINES

Administrative Management (reports AMS surveys)
Business Automation (EDP personnel salaries)
Business Management (boards of directors)
Business Week (annual survey of executive compensation)
Chemical and Engineering News (chemists)
Chemical Engineering (chemical engineers)
Chemical Week (computer systems specialists)
Datamation (data processing positions)
Dun's (executive compensation)
Engineer (engineers)
Financial Executive (financial and accounting management)
Forbes (senior management)
Fortune (senior management of Fortune 500 organizations)
Hospital Administration (nurses)
Industrial Engineering (industrial engineers)
Industrial Research Development (scientists, engineers working in R&D, quality control)
Industry Week (executive compensation)
Infosystems (data processing personnel)
Medical World News (reports on survey by American Academy of General Practice)
Modern Office Procedures (white-collar workers pay and benefits)
Monthly Labor Review (reports on BLS surveys)
Nation's Business (AMS white-collar surveys)
Professional Pilot Magazine (professional pilots)
Profit Sharing (profit sharing distributions)
Public Relations Journal (public relations personnel)
Sales Management (sales and marketing executives)
U.S. News & World Report (employee benefits, management compensation)

U.S. GOVERNMENT

Civil Service Commission, Bureau of Intergovernmental Personnel Programs (100 state government job classes)
Department of Labor, Bureau of Labor Statistics (described in text)
Department of Commerce, Bureau of the Census (study of income)

Administrative Management Society (AMS)—Maryland Rd., Willow Grove, PA 19090 (as described in text)

American Association of Engineering Societies—345 E. 47th St, New York, NY 10017 (engineers' salaries)

American Association of University Professors (AAUP)—Suite 500, One DuPont Circle, NW, Washington, DC 20036 (college and university faculty)

American Chemical Society—1155 16th St. NW, Washington, DC 20036 (professionals in chemistry)

American Compensation Association (ACA)—P.O. Box 1176, Scottsdale, AZ 85252 (compensation management positions, payroll budgets for salaried employees)

American Federation of Information Processing Societies—2100 L St. NW, Suite 420, Washington, DC 20037 (information processing personnel)

American Hotel and Motel Association—888 7th Ave., New York, NY 10019 (17 hotel and motel unionized job classifications; management jobs)

American Management Associations (AMA)—135 W. 50th St., New York, NY 10020 (as described in text)

American Society for Personnel Administrators (ASPA)—19 Church St., Berea, OH 44017 (personnel and industrial relations executives)

American Society of Association Executives—1 Las Olas Circle, Apt. 20, Fort Lauderdale, FL 33316 (association executives)

American Society of Corporate Secretaries—One Rockefeller Plaza, New York, NY 10020 (corporate directors' fees and other reimbursements)

Association of Consulting Management Engineers (ACME)—347 Madison Ave., New York, NY 10017 (consultants)

Bank Administration Institute—P.O. Box 500, Park Ridge, IL 60068 (bank officers)

Battelle Institute—505 King Ave., Columbus, OH 43201 (R & D scientists and engineers)

Business International Corp.—One Dag Hammerskjold Plaza, New York, NY 10017 (expatriate allowances and fringe benefits)

Chamber of Commerce of the United States—1615 H St. NW, Washington, DC 20062 (employee benefits and workers' compensation by stock)

Child Welfare League of America, Inc.—1346 Connecticut Ave. NW, Washington, DC 20036 (13 administrative and professional child welfare staff jobs)

College and University Personnel Association—11 Dupont Circle, Suite 120, Washington, DC 20036 (administrative positions in higher education)

The College Placement Council, Inc.—65 East Elizabeth Ave., Bethlehem, PA 18018 (job offers for college graduates)

Committee on Corporate Law Department of the Association of the Bar of the City of New York—42 West 44th St., New York, NY 10036 (law department attorneys)

The Conference Board, Inc.—845 Third Ave., New York, NY 10022 (total top executives compensation package)

The Dartnell Corp.—4660 Ravenswood Avenue, Chicago, IL 60640 (executive , compensation, sales personnel)

Educational Research Services, Inc.—1815 N. Fort Myer Dr., Arlington, VA 22209 (salaries paid professional personnel in public schools)

The Endicott Report—Northwestern University, Evanston, IL 60201 (job offers for college graduates)

Engineers Joint Council—345 E. 47th St, New York, NY 10017 (engineers)

Financial Executives Institute—633 Third Ave, New York, NY 10017 (financial and accounting managers)

Health Insurance Institute, 277 Park Ave., New York, NY 10017 (health insurance plans)

International Foundation of Employee Benefits Plans—P.O. Box 69, Brookfield, WI 53005 (employee benefits)

International Information/Word Processing Association—1015 North York Rd., Willow Grove, PA 19090 (14 job titles in information/word processing)

International Personnel Management Association—1313 E. 60th St., Chicago, IL 60637 (62 job classes in governmental jurisdictions)

Life Office Management Association—100 Colony Sq., Atlanta, GA 30361 (mid-management, top 7 officers, actuarial personnel, and area differentials for life insurance industry)

Midwest Industrial Management Association—9845 W. Roosevelt Rd., Westchester, IL 60153 (managers of manufacturing, distribution, and warehousing firms)

Mortgage Bankers Association of America—1125 15th St. NW, Washington, DC 20005 (mortgage bankers compensation)

National Association of Mutual Insurance Companies—7931 Castleway Drive, Indianapolis, IN 46250 (executives in the insurance industry)

National Education Association—1601 16th St. NW, Washington, DC 20036 (classroom teachers)

National Society of Professional Engineers—2924 Stuart Drive, Falls Church, VA 22042 (all branches of engineering)

National Telephone Cooperative Association—2626 Pennsylvania Ave. NW, Washington, DC 20037 (31 job classifications in the telephone industry)

New York Chamber of Commerce and Industry—200 Madison Ave., New York, NY 10016 (6 different surveys on office salaries, personnel practices and benefits)

New York Port Authority—1 World Trade Ctr., New York, NY (wage & salary survey)

Scientific Manpower Commission—1776 Massachusetts Ave., NW, Washington, DC 20036 (biennial survey of engineers)

Tool and Die Institute—77 Busse Hwy., Park Ridge, IL 60068 (tool and die industry)

PRIVATE CONSULTING ORGANIZATIONS

A. S. Hansen, Inc.—1080 Green Bay Rd., Lake Bluff, IL 60044 (annual Weber survey of data processing jobs)

A. T. Kearney Inc.—100 South Wacker Drive, Chicago, IL 60608 (hospital administrators)

Abbott, Langer & Associates—Box 275, Park Forest, IL 60466 (A three-volume publication, containing annotated bibliographies of over 1,000 wage & salary surveys; *Inter-City Wage & Salary Differentials; Compensation in various professional fields*)

Arthur Young & Co.—277 Park Ave, New York, NY 10017 (top management, CEOs, senior financial management, and middle management of jobs in accounting and finance)

Associates for International Research, Inc. (AIRINC)—8 Eliot St., Cambridge, MA 02138 (executive living costs)

Cole & Associates—10 Post Office Square, Boston, MA 02109 (banking personnel)

Compensation Institute—869 Via de la Paz, Pacific Palisades, CA 90272 (geographic salary and cost of living differentials; *Encyclopedia of Competitive Pay & Comparable Worth; Sales Compensation and Executive Compensation for Small and Medium-sized Companies*)

Dietrich Associates, Inc.—P.O. Box 511, Phoenixville, PA 19460 (engineering salaries and benefits)

Educational Research Services, Inc.—1800 N. Kent St., #1020, Arlington, VA 22209 (professionals in teaching)

Frederic W. Cook & Co.—90 Park Ave., New York, NY 10016 (executive compensation)

George B. Buck Consulting Actuaries—2 Pennsylvania Plaza, New York, NY 10001 (pension programs)

Hay Associates—1845 Walnut St, Philadelphia, PA 19103 (Hay Associates clients and biennial noncash compensation survey)

Heidrick and Struggles, 245 Park Ave., New York, NY 10017 (boards of directors, senior corporate officers)

Hewitt Associates—102 Wilmot Road, Deerfield, IL 60015 (top and middle management)

Hospital Compensation Services—115 Watchung Drive, Hawthorne, NJ 07506 (hospital and nursing home employees)

International Compensation, Inc.—Two Center Plaza, Boston, MA 02108 (international compensation)

Lee and Paulin Associates—120 S. LaSalle St., Suite 1051, Chicago, IL 60603 (long-term incentive compensation)

Management Compensation Services (MCS)—7579 East Main Street, Scottsdale, AZ 85251 (subsidiary of Hewitt Associates, biennial executive perquisite study, executive compensation in companies with a minimum sales volume of $200 million and in companies with sales less than $150 million, executive compensation in foreign countries, compensation of managers below the executive level, and study of five nonsupervisory sales positions and four sales management positions)

McKinsey & Co.—611 West Sixth St., Los Angeles, CA 90017 (all levels of management)

Olanie, Hurst & Hemrich—3250 Wilshire, Suite 1700, Los Angeles, CA 90010 (executive compensation in California)

Patton Consultants—Des Plaines, IL (top management)

Reggio and Associates, Inc.—125 South Wacker Dr., Chicago, IL 60606 (area salary differentials)

Robert Half Personnel Agencies—522 Fifth Ave., New York, NY 10036 (financial and data processing prevailing starting salaries)

Runzheimer & Co., Inc.—Runzheimer Park, Rochester, WI 53167 (living cost comparative services)

Segal Associates—730 Fifth Ave., New York, NY 10019 (executive compensation)

Sibson & Co.—Research Park, 1101 State Rd., Princeton, NJ 08540 (executives)

Smyth & Murphy Associates—577 Little Silver Point Rd., Little Silver, NJ 07739 (financial incentives and fringe benefits for management)

Thomas R. Conlon & Associates, 93 Pine Street, Deer Park, Long Island, NY 11729 (executive perquisites)

Towers, Perrin, Forster and Crosby—600 Third Ave, New York, NY 10016 (top and middle management)

Wytmar & Co.—10 South Riverside Plaza, Chicago, IL 60606 (chief executive officers and other executive compensation)

Benefits and Weaknesses of Third-party Surveys

Surveys conducted by third parties provide certain benefits to their users, but they also have some weaknesses. Among the benefits are the following:

1. They are relatively inexpensive and require little of the user's time.

2. The participant supplies the data, and the data are already summarized for user's interpretation.

3. Third-party surveys usually have large numbers of respondees and thus are more likely to provide a statistically sound sample size.

Among the weaknesses of ready-made, third-party surveys are the following:

1. The user is unable to select the jobs being surveyed and to identify respondents.

2. The user is unable to weight data by the importance of the responding organization to the user.

3. The user is unable to control what data are collected. Some data included in the survey report may be irrelevant while other important data collected could be omitted.

4. The survey may require resummarizing to meet user requirements.

COLLECTING SURVEY DATA

After making the decision to perform a survey and having determined the general method, the next step is to decide on the techniques for collecting the survey data. The most simple is the telephone. Other increasingly complex techniques include the personal interview, the questionnaire, and group conferences.

Telephone

Telephone surveys are useful for collecting data on a relatively small number of easily identified and quickly recognized jobs. Telephone contact can be made quickly with compensation specialists in comparable organizations throughout a particular region or even on a nationwide basis. These answers provide data for immediate or emergency use. This technique is also useful for clarifying issues, checking discrepancies, or obtaining data overlooked when using other collection methods. One drawback of this technique is that it places a great burden on respondees because it requires their immediate time and attention, which may be in demand elsewhere. Because of this type of imposition, the telephone survey should be as concise as possible.

Mailed Questionnaire

The mailed questionnaire is the most common technique for collecting survey data. It not only permits respondees to complete it at their discretion, but it allows time for careful thought and deliberation in job matching. The questionnaire is useful for collecting data on 100 jobs or on only ten jobs. However, time is money, and time as well as the costs incurred in preparing, producing, distributing, completing, and analyzing questionnaires requires that no more data be requested than absolutely necessary.

When using a mailed questionnaire, do not expect more than a 50 percent response before the third or fourth week. A telephone follow-up after the second and fourth weeks may speed up the process and may also stimulate some responses that otherwise would never occur.

Personal Interview

Probably the best technique for collecting data is the completion of a questionnaire during a personal interview. A well-trained interviewer who knows every aspect of the survey intimately and is especially conversant with the functions and the factors of the jobs is invaluable for collecting valid and reliable data.

In the job matching process, the interviewer may review relevant organizational records (job descriptions, wage structures, organizational charts, etc.) and possibly even observe a job in action. The interviewer may personally record pay data from payroll or other records provided by the selected respondee. This process relieves the respondee of much of the clerical work and the necessity for making subjective judgments from limited descriptive data.

As in any successful interview, the interviewer must have the confidence and the cooperation of the interviewee. Once an interviewer has developed such interpersonal relations, it is always easier to return for a follow-up assignment or to obtain additional or special data over the telephone or through the mail.

Conference

Although the conference is one of the least used techniques for collecting compensation data, it has certain strengths. If a group of specialists has common data requirements and if the location is not a problem, this technique may be ideal.

Prior to the meeting, one individual must prepare an agenda detailing its purpose, the types of compensation data to be reviewed, and the jobs (with their descriptions) to be matched. When conference attendees have done their homework and come well prepared, the quality and the quantity of data developed in a fairly short period of time can be remarkably good.

The conference technique also promotes closer understanding among those responsible for compensation management, a greater awareness of business similarities and differences, and an increased willingness to cooperate when interaction and data flow are vital.

Improving Data Collection

Successful data collection depends on the quality of human interaction among those involved in the survey process. Cooperation may be difficult to attain. Responding to a survey is a costly, time-consuming affair, and before becoming involved, a respondee will often ask, "What's in it for me?" The promise of a well-developed summary of the survey after it has been completed often encourages the respondee to participate.

A respondee should recognize that goodwill and cooperation in completing a survey are just plain good business. Although there may not be a current need for such compensation data, it is entirely possible that in only a short period of time a situation may arise that demands the services or assistance of others for this very purpose. Mutual need is an extremely strong motivational factor for gaining cooperation. Introductions from an association, a friend, or even a superior in the respondee's organization may be helpful in opening what otherwise would be a closed door.

Selecting Respondents

Which organizations should be requested to participate in the survey? The following questions may help you to make a choice:

1. Which organizations appear to have significant influence on applicants seeking employment?

2. Which organizations have lost their employees to the organization conducting the survey?

3. Which organizations require incumbents to perform jobs having similar job content?

4. Which organizations have enough jobs similar to those identified in the survey to make their responses valuable?

In addition to identifying respondents, the organization conducting the survey should also attempt to identify and send the survey to the individual having either approval authority or responsibility for providing survey data. The respondent should receive a duplicate of the survey for company records and for comparison of the final results with the data generated there. A file copy is also helpful in completing future surveys.

STATISTICAL PROCEDURES AND TOOLS

The entire survey process is subject to statistical validation. However, it is seldom possible or even necessary to survey the entire labor market. Instead, the sampling method can be used for obtaining pay data.

Statistical Sampling

Statistical sampling is a study of relationships that exist among selected items that form a specific group and are representative of the entire group. The group from which the sample is drawn is called the *universe* or *population,* and the sample itself is known as the *sample universe* or *sample population.* The objective of statistical sampling is to provide data that accurately describe the parent population or universe.

Those involved in pay surveys will find that, among the various sampling techniques, either the *random sampling* or, *stratified random sampling* technique will be adequate for their purpose.

Random Sampling—The random sampling technique uses a variety of statistical methods that may include the development of an array of data and the use of a table of random numbers. A random sample is selected from the universe, without regard for any type of preselection (i.e., each unit of the universe has an equal and independent chance for selection).

Stratified Random Sampling—In stratified random sampling, the universe is first divided into various strata or segments. Segmentation may be by type of business, by size of organization (number of employees, dollar volume, etc.), by geographic area, or some other characteristic. Then, after stratification has been completed, stratified random sampling follows the same selection procedures as those used in random sampling. That is, a random sample is conducted within the strata.

Both of these sampling techniques make it possible to collect valid pay data that provide an adequate basis for comparing entire pay structures or the rates of pay of specific jobs, classes, or occupational groups.

Weighting—An integral part of the stratified random sampling technique is the *weighting* of collected data. It is possible that the data from one organization are more important than the data from another. If this is the case, weighting is important. For example, in stratifying the universe, one organization is selected from each of two strata. Then, if one stratum contains 60 percent of all jobs and the second stratum contains only 40 percent of the jobs, when the total universe is analyzed, the data received from the organization representing the first sample receives 50 percent more weight than the other and the development of any measurement statistic from the data is influenced proportionally.

$$60\% - 40\% = 20\%; \quad \frac{20}{40} = 50\%$$

A major weighting issue that often faces the compensation manager revolves around the location of the labor market. As a rule of thumb, data from outside the labor market as well as that representing a limited part of the local labor market (approximately 15 to 20 percent) are not weighted. Normally, weighting occurs only when the data represent a deep and broad cross section of the local labor market.

Another factor to be aware of when weighting data relative to specific jobs is that employers hiring the largest number of employees are not necessarily the ones hiring the largest number of employees for a specific job. It may also be necessary to eliminate data from organizations that report only one or two incumbents. These jobholders may perform assignments not normally required or detailed in the job description. This holds especially true when using a nonweighted approach to data manipulation.

The entire purpose of sampling and weighting is to minimize the effect of developing a biased sample—one that does not accurately represent its universe or parent population. A review of a statistics or sampling text may be necessary if these mathematical issues arise. Chapter 13, pages 131–133, *BLS Handbook of Methods* (BLS Bulletin 1711), contains a brief but precise discussion of the sampling and weighting procedures used by the Bureau of Labor Statistics.

No doubt, the more closely one adheres to proper sampling methods, the better the quality of survey data, but this does not preclude the old standby— *trial and error*. Furthermore, it is not always easy to define the labor market. Its definition may be one of individual or organizational perception. Even if one accurately defines the market and identifies those organizations that make up the market universe, there is nothing to guarantee that faithful following of proper sampling methods will produce desired results. For these and other reasons, sampling frequently results in a trial and error operation. In itself, this is not bad. If each trial is objective, it becomes possible to reduce the margin of error successively and to improve the value of the survey.

MEASURING STATISTICS

A wide variety of yardsticks enables compensation managers to compare the various elements of the pay structures in their organizations with those in others. Mention has been made of the more commonly used measuring statistics. The two most used measures of central tendency are the *mean* (average) and the *median* (the middle value in an array of all values received). In addition to some measure of central tendency, a range of values is important. The range values may be the average low and average high value of all data received, or they may simply be the lowest and highest value received. The range is frequently divided into tenths (deciles), quarters (quartiles), or thirds.

For pay comparison purposes, many feel the interquartile (the middle 50 percent) range to be the best indicator of the span of the range. Using the interquartile range eliminates the effect of widely divergent values at either end of the pay spectrum.

In compiling pay data, most surveys allow for differences when a standard work week is less than 40 hours. For example, a conversion factor is normally applied to the pay of employees who work only a 35-hour week and receive time and a half (or some other premium) for hours worked in excess of 35. If the employee receives an additional straight-time pay for hours worked between 35 and 40, no conversion factor is normally applied.

When requesting pay rate data, the surveyor should try to identify the time period that most frequently applies to the pay of the jobs in the survey or the practices of responding organizations. The most often used pay rate time periods are hourly, weekly, monthly, and annually. Table 9-1 is helpful in converting pay rates from one time period to another.

Finally, an analysis for accuracy assists in improving the quality of the survey. Recording errors are not only possible but probable, but most of them can be eliminated by careful checking.

TABLE 9-1

CONVERTING PAY RATES FROM ONE TIME PERIOD TO ANOTHER

	Hourly	*Weekly*	*Monthly*	*Annually*
Hourly		× by 40	× by 174	× by 2,088[a]
Weekly	÷ by 40		× by 4.35	× by 52.2[a]
Monthly	÷ by 174	÷ by 4.35		× by 12
Annually	÷ by 2,088[a]	÷ by 52.2	÷ by 12	

[a]Most years include one extra working day, and for that reason work hours in one year are 2,088 and the number of work weeks in a year are 52.2 (a leap year may include two extra working days).

The survey is a potential source of valuable problem-solving data. It can provide data regarding every aspect of the compensation area, including data on the pay of specific jobs as well as more general data on the pay of broad occupational groups. It also is a valuable source of employee benefit data and policy data that affect the entire pay structure.

Figure 9-2 is a survey package developed by the compensation manager of Olympia, Inc. It includes the following:

1. Letter of transmittal
2. The survey
3. Summary sheet

Letter of Transmittal

The letter of transmittal is an official letter explaining the survey and requesting the addressee to participate. It should be brief, informative, and interesting enough to attract attention and achieve intended results. The letter should contain information about the purpose of the survey, its value to the addressee, the classes of jobs to be covered, the manner in which the survey will be conducted, assurances of confidentiality, and methods or procedures for completing it. This letter of transmittal is often preceded by a short, simple letter or phone call requesting participation in the survey.

The Survey

The survey instrument should be clear and precise with the questions stated in such a way that they will not be misunderstood. The respondee should be able to answer with a check, one or two words, or a number. The survey should require minimum research effort on the part of the respondee. The format as well as the questions should make sense and should project a sense of importance to the respondee. If the questionnaire is fairly extensive and goes to a wide variety of participants, it may be worthwhile to eliminate sections that are not applicable to certain participants on their particular surveys.

The survey in figure 9-2 consists of three sections: Organizational Policy, Employee Benefits, and Job and Pay Data. Each section serves a useful and different purpose, but together they provide an in-depth picture of the compensation system of that organization.

Organizational Policy—The first section on organizational policy provides an insight into the framework that sets the limits of the compensation structure of the organization. This permits the surveyor, or those responsible for compiling and analyzing data, to allow for differences that affect the pay scale.

Employee Benefits—With employee benefits consuming, at a minimum, 25 percent of the employer's compensation dollars and now rising toward 50

COMPENSATION SURVEY PACKAGE
1. Letter of Transmittal

Dear _____ :

    In accordance with our telephone conversation, I am enclosing a survey questionnaire with a self-addressed, stamped envelope. Thank you for agreeing to participate.

    The survey has three sections: Organizational Policy, Employee Benefits, and Job Data. Answers to the *policy* section will assist us in relating compensation differences among the participating organizations. Because of their ever-expanding importance and cost, *employee benefits* have become increasingly important to many organizations. The *job data* section is the heart of the survey. If you have any doubt about the similarity of the job you match with the one we describe, please feel free to comment in the margin beside the matching job. Or, if you wish, send us a copy of your parallel job description and we will do the matching.

    To ensure anonymity of your response, we will not list organizations by name or make any grouping where it is possible to combine such data as number of organization, size of organization, or number of employees so that identification of a specific organization is possible. *We have coded each survey only to allow us to check with you concerning any missing data or where it appears that the data may have been incorrectly transcribed by transposing numbers or placing a number in the wrong column.

    After compilation and analysis of the surveys, each participating organization will receive a summary. If you need further information or clarification of summary data, please call me.

                    Sincerely yours,

                    Compensation Manager
                    OLYMPIA, INC.

. . . .

*A Bit of Information for the Surveyor:

    A National Labor Relations Board ruling required a company to provide the following information to its bargaining union:
        (1) Area wage rates,
        (2) Companies surveyed,
        (3) Identification of which rates came from a particular company.
However, the NLRB does not require an organization to disclose the identity of the companies if it is not furnished such information. In essence, this protects companies using survey data provided by outside parties. ("Total Disclosure of Wage Data," *Compensation Review*, Third Quarter 1971, pp. 5-6.)

FIGURE 9–2   COMPENSATION SURVEY PACKAGE

COMPENSATION SURVEY PACKAGE (Cont.)

2. The Survey

Organizational Policy

Staff and Hours

Number of employees? _____

How many hours per week do your employees normally work? _____
How much time allotted for lunch? _____
How many breaks? _____ How much time allotted for them? _____

Do you have a 4-day workweek? YES _____ NO _____

Do any of your employees work on shifts? YES _____ NO _____
If YES, answer below:

Shift	*Shift Hours*	*% Premium Pay*
Evening (2nd)	_____	_____
Late Night (3rd)	_____	_____
Other	_____	_____

Do you have any form of Flexitime (allowing employees to choose working hours)?
YES _____ NO _____

Salary Payment Policies

If your standard number of hours worked per week is less than 40, do you pay overtime for hours in excess of the normal workweek but less than 40? YES _____ NO _____

If certain groups within the organization have less than a 40-hour workweek, please list them.

Group	*Hours*
_____	_____
_____	_____
_____	_____

What is overtime rate for individuals required to work on regularly scheduled holidays?
1¼ times normal pay _____ 2 times normal pay _____ Other _____

Have you paid a bonus or made a supplemental salary payment at any time within the past 12 months? YES _____ NO _____ If YES: Date of last one _____
Approximate % of Salary _____

Have you granted any general across-the-board adjustments in salary within the past 24 months? YES _____ NO _____ If YES:

	Date	*Approximate % Adjustment*
1.	_____	_____
2.	_____	_____

Are they linked to the Bureau of Labor Statistics Consumer Price Index?
YES _____ NO _____ If linked to any other price index, please indicate. _____

Starting Salaries – High School Graduates

What is your average starting salary for a high school graduate with *no* work experience who cannot type or take shorthand? $ _____

What is your average starting salary for a high school graduate with *no* work experience who can type 50-60 words per minute accurately? $ _____

What is your average starting salary for a high school graduate with *no* work experience who can type 50-60 words per minute and take shorthand 80-90 wpm? $ _____

FIGURE 9–2   COMPENSATION SURVEY PACKAGE (CONT.)

COMPENSATION SURVEY PACKAGE (Cont.)

Starting Salaries — Community College-Technical School Graduates

What is your average starting salary for a technical school graduate who has a usable technical skill? $ _____

What is your average starting salary for a community college graduate with an Associate Degree pursuing a *non-technical* occupation in your firm? $ _____

Starting Salaries — College Graduates

What is your average starting salary for a college graduate with a Bachelor's degree in Business Administration, Accounting, Finance, Economics, Management, etc., pursuing a *non-technical* occupation in your firm? $ _____

What is your average starting salary for a college graduate with a Bachelor's degree in Engineering, Mathematics, Statistics, etc., pursuing a *technical* occupation in your firm? $ _____

Employment Policies

Do you pay employment agency fees for non-college graduates? YES _____ No _____
If YES: Do you pay fee at time of employment? YES _____ NO _____
If NO: When? _____

Do you require that aptitude tests be passed prior to employment? YES _____ NO _____

Employee Benefits

Paid Vacations

What paid vacations are allowed?

Years Service (inclusive)	Weeks of Vacations Allowed		
	Nonexempt	Exempt	Executive
0–1	_____	_____	_____
1–4	_____	_____	_____
5–9	_____	_____	_____
10–15	_____	_____	_____
Others	_____	_____	_____

Can unused vacation be carried over the following year? YES _____ NO _____
If YES, how many days? _____

Paid Holidays

How many paid holidays do you grant? _____

Christmas Day	_____	Independence Day	_____
New Year's Day	_____	Labor Day	_____
Washington's Birthday	_____	Veteran's Day	_____
Good Friday	_____	Thanksgiving Day	_____
Memorial Day	_____	Employee's Birthday	_____

Sick Leave

Do you have an official sick leave plan? YES _____ NO _____

How many days of sick leave do you grant per year? _____

Do you have a waiting period before an employee is eligible for sick leave? YES _____ NO _____

FIGURE 9–2   COMPENSATION SURVEY PACKAGE (CONT.)

COMPENSATION SURVEY PACKAGE (Cont.)

Do you have a lifetime maximum number of sick leave days an
employee can take?   YES _____ NO _____

Do you have a plan that permits the employee to convert
sick leave to other uses?   YES _____ NO _____

If YES, check the applicable conversion:

Cash _____   Carryover to future years _____
Vacation _____   Credit at retirement _____

Other Leaves

Do you grant leave with pay for any of the following reasons?

Reason	Number of Days	Reason	Number of Days
Jury Duty	_____	Death in Family	_____
Marriage	_____	Dental Appointment	_____
Graduation Exercises	_____	Other	_____
Family Illness	_____		

Thrift Plan

Do you have a thrift plan? YES _____ NO _____

How much does the employer contribute per $1.00 of employee contribution?
(Please circle appropriate amount)
$0.25, $0.50, $0.75, $1.00, other (if other list amount) _____

Credit Union

Do you offer a credit union? YES _____ NO _____

What interest do you pay on savings? _____

What interest do you charge on loans? _____

Insurance Benefits

Do you have a group hospitalization and/or surgical plan? YES _____ NO _____

If YES: What per cent is paid by employer? _____ %

What is monthly cost to employee? Single Plan $ _____
Family Plan $ _____

Is there a major medical addition to the regular insurance plan? YES _____ NO _____

If YES, what is the one-time illness maximum? $ _____

What is the lifetime illness maximum? $ _____

At what amount of "out-of-pocket" employer cost per illness does the major medical plan
assume full responsibility? $ _____

FIGURE 9–2   COMPENSATION SURVEY PACKAGE (CONT.)

COMPENSATION SURVEY PACKAGE (Cont.)

Do you have a group dental plan? YES _____ NO _____ If YES: What per cent is paid by employer? _____ %

Do you have a group life insurance plan? YES _____ NO _____

If YES, is it contributory? YES _____ NO _____

If YES, what percentage does the employer pay? _____ %

Is amount of insurance made available a percentage of annual salary? YES _____ NO ___

If YES, what amount of insurance is made available as a multiple of annual salary? (please circle appropriate figure)
1.5, 2.5, 3.5, other (if other, list) _____

Is there a base to your insurance plan? YES _____ NO _____

If YES, what is the base? $ _____

Is there a cap to your insurance plan? YES _____ NO _____

If YES, what is the cap? $ _____

Pension Plan

Do you have a pension plan? YES _____ NO _____

Does it include all employees? YES _____ NO _____

   If NO: Which groups are excluded? _____

_____   _____

Is it integrated with Social Security? YES _____ NO _____

How do you determine average salary for pension purposes? (Please circle your method)
   Salary of final 3 yrs., 5 yrs., 10 yrs., career average, other (if other, please describe)
_____

Is it a defined benefit plan? YES _____ NO _____

If YES, what formula do you use for determining final pension benefits?

_____

Is it a defined contribution plan? YES _____ NO _____

If YES, how do you determine contributions?

_____

Which ERISA vesting plan are you using?

_____

What is your normal retirement age? (Please circle appropriate number)
   55, 60, 62, 65, other (if other, please state) _____

FIGURE 9–2   COMPENSATION SURVEY PACKAGE (CONT.)

COMPENSATION SURVEY PACKAGE (Cont.)

Do you have an early retirement eligibility?   YES _____ NO _____

If YES, how do you determine (please circle appropriate method)
Age,   Service,   Age and service,   other (if other, please describe) _____

_____   _____

Have you provided a pension plan supplement for retirees in the
past five years?   YES _____ NO _____

Do you provide death benefits for retirees?   YES _____ NO _____

Do the retirees contribute to the death benefit premiums?   YES _____ NO _____

General

Do you provide a cafeterial service for your employees?   YES _____ NO _____

If YES, do you subsidize the operation?   YES _____ NO _____

If YES, % subsidization _____ %

Do you provide parking for all employees or subsidize parking fees?
YES _____ NO _____

If subsidized, approximate cost per employee: $ _____

Do you have a labor union among your non-clerical employees?   YES _____ NO _____

Do you have a labor union among your clerical employees?   YES _____ NO _____

Do you have an educational reimbursement plan?   YES _____ NO _____

If YES, for what programs (circle appropriate programs)
High School,   Undergraduate,   Graduate,   Vocational

If YES, what percentage of tuition do you reimburse? (circle appropriate amount)
50%,   75%,   100%,   other (if other please list) _____ %

Merit Review Plan

Do you have a merit rating plan for executives?   YES _____ NO _____

Briefly describe: _____

_____

Do you have a merit rating for non-executives?   YES _____ NO _____

Briefly describe: _____

_____

FIGURE 9–2   COMPENSATION SURVEY PACKAGE (CONT.)

COMPENSATION SURVEY PACKAGE (Cont.)

Job Data

Our Job Title _____   Other Possible Titles _____
Job Code   _____   _____

Thumb-Nail Job Description:

Special Notes: This section of the form must be completed by the surveying organization
                   prior to the printing of the form. (See text material on *Job Data* for example)

· ·

PLEASE COMPLETE THIS FORM FOR YOUR COMPARABLE JOB:

Job Title: _____

Job Code: _____

Minimum Pay: _____ (or entry-level hiring rate)

Maximum Pay: _____ (or maximum longevity rate)

Please indicate on each line the number of employees receiving the particular rate of pay and
indicate the rate under the applicable column.

NUMBER OF EMPLOYEES	DOLLARS				AVERAGE YEARS ON THIS JOB
	PER HOUR	PER WEEK	PER MONTH	PER YEAR	

FIGURE 9–2   COMPENSATION SURVEY PACKAGE (CONT.)

COMPENSATION SURVEY PACKAGE

PAY SUMMARY SHEET FOR EACH JOB IN THE SURVEY

Job Title _____   Job Code _____

Job Summary:

Reporting Data

   Number of firms   _____

   Number of employees   _____

   Average pay reported   _____

Actual Pay Data

   Number of firms reporting   _____

   Lowest reported pay rate   _____

   First quartile pay rate   _____

   Median pay rate   _____

   Third quartile pay rate   _____

   Highest reported pay rate   _____

Range Data Reported

   Number of firms reporting   _____

   Lowest reported pay range   _____

   Median reported minimum range   _____

   Median reported of the median
    of the ranges   _____

   Median reported maximum range   _____

   Highest reported pay range   _____

Ranking of Reported Pay

   Pay shown below is rank-ordered from low to high. If the first value begins at "0," the list is in deciles. If the first value begins at "1," the figures are actual pay. (Deciles were used when more than 25 individual pay rates were reported.)

0 _____				
1 _____	6 _____	11 _____	16 _____	21 _____
2 _____	7 _____	12 _____	17 _____	22 _____
3 _____	8 _____	13 _____	18 _____	23 _____
4 _____	9 _____	14 _____	19 _____	24 _____
5 _____	10 _____	15 _____	20 _____	25 _____

FIGURE 9–2   COMPENSATION SURVEY PACKAGE

percent, it is vital for those analyzing compensation data to have a grasp on the benefits package.

Job Data—The job data section may be expanded to include as many jobs or classes as necessary to accomplish the mission of the survey. A typical job description in the matching process may take this form:

Title—Stock Clerk   Other Titles—Counterman
Code—233.387   Stock attendant
                                                             Supply clerk
                                                             Stockroom clerk

Thumbnail sketch:

Assists in the operation of the stockroom by filling all stock requisitions; receives and inspects incoming supplies and notes defects and shortages. Replenishes shelves or bins with needed items. Wraps supplies and makes all necessary preparation for mailing.
Note: Has no supervisory responsibility; along with senior clerk, accountable for stock.

Actual Pay Data—In the past, many surveys collected average pay data. Such data included number of employees; their average pay; and the minimum, midpoint, and maximum pay of the pay range for the particular job. This procedure is basically unacceptable for current compensation decision-making purposes. The survey should collect *actual* pay data for each person in each surveyed job. This type of data makes it possible to identify *actual* pay practices and develop a true picture of what the array of pay data for a job actually looks like.

Compensation managers now recognize that pay for a job is not normally distributed and that a mean value may be inadequate or may not provide an accurate statistic for making decisions. Pay data for most jobs relate to a nonparametric distribution, not to a normal one. A nonparametric distribution is one in which the mean, the mode, and the median are not the same. Because such distribution is usually the case, median, percentile, decile, and quartile data are more valuable than average data. The only way a survey can generate the more valuable data is for the initial collection instrument to capture actual, individual pay rates.

In the past, it was difficult for many respondees to provide such data because of the type of payroll systems in use. Today, however, with well-designed computerized payroll systems and excellent printouts of the current pay for each employee, actual pay data for each employee are available.

A major hurdle the surveyor still must overcome is to demonstrate to the respondees why it is to their advantage to spend the time to provide pay data for each incumbent on each job in the survey. A first and most important step in overcoming this barrier is to explain to the respondee why survey data based on individual pay rates will be critical for making good compensation decisions.

Job Summaries

The compensation survey summary should include a complete schedule of all pay data for each job in the survey. The pay summary sheet should include the job title, job code, job summary, and pay data. Providing actual pay data or pay data by deciles is valuable for determining externally equitable pay relationships.

Date Data Was Collected

In times of rapid inflation, users must know when data were collected so that they are able to reconcile survey-provided data. This is highly important when users of third party surveys compare data from a number of different surveys. Users should age data. One approach is to age data to January 1 of the coming year.

A simple adjustment/aging procedure may take this form:

Job	Survey Pay Data	Date of Survey	Adjustment to Desired Date	Adjusted Market Value
___	___	___	___	___
___	___	___	___	___
___	___	___	___	___

Summary Sheet

When completing the summary sheet, you should record data by job classes. It is also preferable to keep broad occupational groups together and to separate the exempt categories from the nonexempt. At the discretion of the surveyor, a recap of employee benefits may be included.

Permission to Include Name of Company

To ensure maximum value of the survey to all respondees, the survey summary and analysis should include a list of all participating organizations. At the outset, the surveyor must request permission from participants to include the names of their organizations. It is vital for those persons using or reviewing the compensation data for decision purposes to know the names of the organizations that provided the data. Without written permission, however, the use of a participant's name may lead to legal action. All the surveyor must do is to include with the survey a brief form letter stating that the participating organization permits its name to be included in a list of participants and that the list will not in any way reveal confidential data and information. A member of the participating organization signs the letter and returns it with the completed survey.

Checklist

A careful review of the survey documents shown in figure 9-2 reveals the extensive amount of time that must be spent in the development of the survey, the completion by respondee (i.e., the participating organization), and the final analysis. Such a review reemphasizes the need to request no more data than absolutely necessary and to lighten the burden on the participant by designing a survey format that is easily understood and simple to follow.

Answering the following questions concerning major areas is helpful in determining the extent of the survey requirements:

Classification of Job or Occupation—

1. Is the pay problem unique to a small number of jobs or to one occupational group?

2. Is the job unique or exotic?

3. Which jobs are key or benchmark jobs?

Pay Structure—

1. Are data required for structuring the entire pay plan or for only one group (i.e., nonexempt, clerical, professional)?

2. Is the pay structure of our organization so unique that pay data from other organizations will be of little value?

3. Do other organizations face similar pay issues?

Labor Market—

1. Has the labor market been properly identified?

2. Does the organization compete in a variety of labor markets (i.e., local or regional for lower-level jobs and interregional or national for more specialized occupations or professions)?

3. Are demographic variables important considerations (i.e., rural or urban, population of community)?

Influence of Competing Organizations—

1. Do those organizations hiring the largest number of employees or the largest number of employees for a specific job or occupational group dominate the labor market?

2. Is there a relationship between the dollar volume of business and the leadership roles in the setting of pay rates?

3. Is there a relationship between similarity of output (product or service) or type of organization (public or private, profit or nonprofit)?

Providers of Survey Data—

1. Is it possible to use survey data developed by national organizations (BLS, AMA, AMS, etc.)?

2. Are local surveys conducted? If so, are they worthwhile? Is it possible to co-op with one?

Development, Implementation, and Analysis of Survey—

1. Is skilled talent available to develop and implement the survey?

2. Is skilled talent available to compile and analyze data output?

3. If not, where is talent available or how can unskilled employees be trained and developed to perform this activity?

4. What types of individuals should be selected for these activities?

5. What technical and interpersonal skills are necessary?

6. When was survey data collected?

Secrecy—

1. Will secrecy either prohibit participants from responding to the survey or possibly provide invalid or meaningless data?

2. What procedures will best assure confidentiality of respondee's data?

SELECTED READINGS

Burns, John E. and Daniel P. Dutchak, "Report Program Generator in Compensation Surveys," *Industrial Management,* December 1972, pp. 11–13. A description of the way one computer programming language—Report Program Generator (RPG)—makes it possible to expand the scope and to increase the accuracy and the currency of compensation surveys.

Cassidy, Edward W., and James H. Kelly, "Rewarding Professional Growth," *Compensation Review,* First Quarter, 1971, pp. 34–38. The addition of career-area descriptions proves a valuable adjunct to maturity curves in defining the worth of scientists and engineers.

Foster, Kenneth E., "Job Worth and the Computer," *Personnel Journal,* September 1968, pp. 619–627. By using a computer-based salary survey retrieval information system, the author shows that it is possible to develop a compensation data base that meets the five critical tests of economy, reliability, validity, flexibility, and timeliness. He describes a system that combined the salary information from a number of companies. The system was valuable in assisting these companies expand their capability of direct job pricing at a reasonable cost..

———, "The Plus Side of Salary Surveys," *Personnel,* January–February 1963, pp. 35–43. This article discusses the development and the maintenance of a sound compensation structure that requires accurate, up-to-date information. The survey is a tested and trustworthy source of such information if appropriately designed and implemented.

———, "Accounting for Management Pay Differentials," *Industrial Relations,* October 1969, pp. 80–87. A report on a survey of 2,500 programming, engineering/scientific, and marketing managers in 19 companies suggests that a combination of such factors as size of organization, number of personnel managed, and experience and education level of the managers are highly predictive of current wage levels.

Patton, Arch, "Pay Surveys: Inflation's Forcing Edge," *Business Week,* January 13, 1975, p. 14. A valuable insight into the worth, the meaning, and the impact of pay surveys by the person who designed and directed the first industry-wide survey of executive compensation in 1950. The author underlines the importance of designing and executing surveys but stresses that even more important is the need to interpret them with common sense.

Samuels, Norman J., "Developing a General Wage Index," *Monthly Labor Review,* March 1971, pp. 3–8. This author points out that the failure to develop a single measure that describes wages makes it very difficult for anyone truly to answer the question, "How much have wages increased?" This limits the value of any tool used to measure wage rates among various organizations, industries, markets, and so on.

10

Designing A Pay Structure

CONTENT

Chapter 10 describes the blending of senior management philosophy, external influences, and technical considerations in the design of a pay structure.

GOALS

Upon concluding this chapter, you should be able to design a pay structure that recognizes the differences in internal relationships among the jobs of the organization. In addition to recognizing internal contributions, your pay structure should take into consideration market demands that permit the organization to compete with other employers for available and desirable human resources.

Decisions that provide guidelines for the compensation manager to follow in developing a pay structure are made at the higher levels of the organization. These policy decisions include guidelines concerning

1. minimum and maximum levels of pay (taking into consideration ability to pay, government regulations, union influences, and market pressures);

2. the general relationships among levels of pay (between nonexempt and exempt senior management and operating management, operatives and supervisors); and

3. the division of the total compensation dollar (i.e., what portion goes into base pay, what portion into benefits, what portion into merit pay or pay-for-performance programs).

Additionally, senior management decides how much money to allot for the total compensation package, that is, how much will go into pay increases for the next year, who will recommend them, and generally, how they will be determined. In other words, will they be based on seniority, on merit, or on cost-of-living adjustments? If they are based on merit, who will make the determination? Last, but not least, decisions made at this level determine the extent to which compensation policies are detailed and communicated throughout the organization. At this point, the issue of open or secret compensation policy becomes one of the most important issues facing this level of management.

Although decisions made at the top seldom determine specific employee pay rates, they do set guidelines for compensation managers. From guidelines, these managers must consider the issues and make acceptable and workable determinations concerning the following:

1. What is the lowest rate of pay that can be offered for a job that will entice the quality of employees the organization desires to have as its members?

2. What is the rate of pay that must be offered to incumbents to ensure that they remain with the organization?

3. Does the organization desire to recognize seniority and meritorious performance through the base pay schedule?

4. Is it wise or necessary to offer more than one rate of pay to employees performing either identical or similar work?

5. What is considered to be a sufficient difference in base rates of pay among jobs requiring varying levels of knowledge and skills and responsibilities and duties?

6. Does the organization wish to recognize dangerous and distressing working conditions within the base pay schedule?

7. Should there be a difference in changes in base pay progression opportunities among jobs of varying worth?

8. Do employees have a significant opportunity to progress to higher-level jobs? If so, what should be the relationship between promotion to a higher job and changes in base pay?

9. Will policies and regulations permit incumbents to earn rates of pay higher than established maximums and lower than established minimums? What would be the reasons for allowing such deviations?

10. How will the pay structure accommodate across-the-board, cost-of-living, or other adjustments not related to employee tenure, performance, or responsibility and duty changes?

PAY STRUCTURE MECHANICS

Chapters 5 though 8 provide information on how to develop data to facilitate the fair and equitable ordering of jobs into natural groups based on comparable responsibility, knowledge, and skill requirements. The establishment of an internally fair relationship among jobs is as important to each jobholder as it is to management. Management must be able to substantiate its reasons for the placement of jobs into a specific order. Because of this, strong recommendations have been made in this text to provide in-depth job analysis, develop useful job descriptions that are current, and implement an evaluation plan that provides a basis for establishing a systematic ordering of jobs.

Chapter 9 discusses the use of the compensation survey to generate data and information regarding the pay that comparable jobs are receiving in relevant labor markets. Valid data, interpreted properly, enable compensation decision-makers to relate the pay received by their employees to that provided by other competing organizations. Acquiring external data assists in establishing a competitive pay posture that permits the organization to hire and retain reliable, highly competent employees.

With the generation of internal and external pay data and information, managers are now ready to design a pay structure. Its development requires (1) determining a trend or pay policy line, (2) deciding on the need for one or more pay structures, (3) displaying job data, (4) establishing the characteristics of the pay structure (number, width, and height of pay grades and the overlap among them), and (5) locking overlapping pay structures (when using more than one).

These five technical features determine to a large degree the unique compensation characteristics of the organization. Above all, they inform employees how the organization values their jobs, what job and compensation advancement opportunities are available, and how competitive the pay practices are with other organizations.

Determining a Pay Policy Line

Each organization must develop its own pay policy line which is a trend line or line of best fit that best represents the middle pay value of jobs that have been evaluated or classified to have particular worth. A line of best fit produces a trend line by minimizing the sum of the squares of the vertical deviations around the line. A line of best fit can be either a straight or curved line. In either case, it is one that best represents the middle pay value (i.e., the center tendency) of all jobs or the benchmark or key jobs used to establish a pay policy line.

A useful or practical first step in developing a pay policy line is to establish the lowest and highest rates of pay for the organization. With the identification of these two rates of pay, the next step is to draw a line connecting them (see figure 10-1a).

The line connecting the lowest-offered to highest-offered rates of pay could be the pay policy line for the organization, or it could be at least a first approximation of a pay policy line. Pay structure designers normally find that even for entry-level jobs a higher rate of pay is provided once an employee demonstrates acceptable performance and remains on the job for some probationary period. The same process works in an opposite manner relative to the highest rate of pay to be offered to an incumbent in the most highly paid job. Here, the employee receives a rate of pay lower than the maximum rate and, through tenure and demonstrated performance, works to gain the maximum attainable pay. Another simple procedure for establishing a pay policy line is to obtain the market rate or going rate of pay for the lowest-paid and highest-paid jobs. Connecting these two points can also provide a first approximation for a pay policy line (see figure 10-1b).

The procedure most organizations normally follow in establishing a pay policy or trend line is to identify the market rates for various key or benchmark jobs that cover the entire pay spectrum from lowest to highest rates of pay. By plotting the pay-rate information obtained through surveys on a chart, a scatter diagram can be developed (see figure 10-1c).

(a) Lowest to Highest Rate of Pay

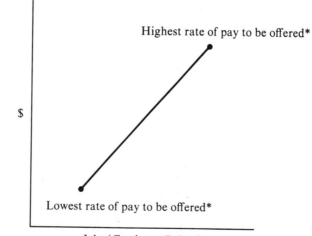

*Rates set by individual(s) with compensation decision authority

FIGURE 10–1   PROCEDURES FOR ESTABLISHING A PAY POLICY LINE

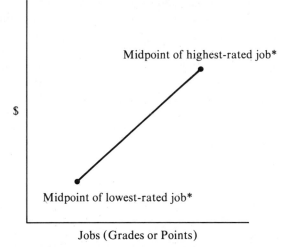

*Midpoint value obtainable through a survey of relevant labor markets. A competitive midpoint is the "going rate" or average or median rate of pay for a surveyed job.

(c) Scatter Diagram and Least-Squares Line

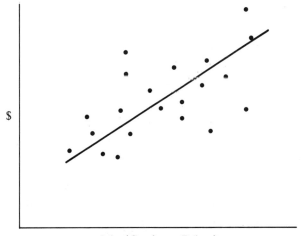

Scatter Diagram—A compensation scatter diagram plots the points on a chart where each point represents a job. Plotted job data provide a convenient way to see an entire array of relationships and identify natural groupings of jobs. The paired coordinates for locating each point are the evaluated score for the job and its actual pay.

A scatter diagram uses the job points as a scale for the horizontal axis (the x axis or abscissa) and the dollar value of the job as the scale for the vertical axis (the y axis or ordinate). (In plotting pay survey data, the x coordinate will normally be the points assigned to the job used for matching purposes. The y coordinate will be the dollar value surveyed organizations indicated they pay for the job.)

Different procedures are available for developing a trend line from a scatter diagram that range from the very simple line-of-sight of freehand procedure to the two-point straight-line method to the fairly complex least-squares procedure, which uses statistical analysis.

The *line-of-sight (freehand) procedure* is a simple way to determine the trend line. In most cases, this procedure provides an acceptable first approach to what the trend line will look like. Using this approach requires the data analyst to perceive visually (to "eyeball") a line that cuts through the center of the points on the scatter diagram and that minimizes the vertical differences among points in the same vertical plane.

The *two-point procedure* is also very simple involving drawing a line that connects the lowest and highest values. When this procedure is used, it is possible that the lowest and highest points are truly aberrations—illogical or unacceptable pay data—and should have been eliminated from consideration. An arithmetic procedure that minimizes the likelihood of such an error is to array the pay data and divide them into two groups having the same number of values, selecting the median (middle) value of the lower group as one point and the median value of the top group for the other point. Both the line-of-sight and the two-point procedures require nothing more than a pencil and straight-edge (i.e., ruler) for drawing the line. If a curved line is more suitable for providing a line of best fit, a piece of string can be used in drawing it.

The *least-squares method* is a statistical procedure that produces a trend line by minimizing the sum of the squares of the vertical deviations around the line.

With the accessibility of modern calculators and computer programs, mathematical calculation problems are of secondary importance. Because of these technological advancements, the least-squares method is a practical alternative for developing a line of minimum deviations. A five-step process describing the least-squares methods appears on pp. 269-271.

There are computer programs using multivariate analysis that will permit the computer terminal operator to input x (job evaluation score) and y (pay rate) variable data. The computer, through a stored algorithm, analyzes the data and develops a visual display of a line of best fit.[1]

In using any procedure, it is essential to analyze visually the line and the location of the points above and below it before accepting it as a line of best fit. After setting an initial pay policy line, it may be possible to eliminate some of these outlying points (i.e., outliers). They may not be eliminated, however,

---

[1]An algorithm is a prescribed set of well-defined rules or procedures for the solution of a problem in a finite number of steps.

THE LEAST-SQUARES METHOD FOR
DETERMINING LINE OF BEST FIT (TREND LINE)

The following steps comprise the least-squares method for determining the line of best fit or trend line.

Step 1

The equation for a straight line will be used, since most pay distributions approximate a straight line. This equation is $Y = a + bX$, where

Y = actual pay rate (or job rate of pay from survey data)
X = evaluated points for organizational job
a = constant—where line of best fit intercepts (crosses) Y axis
b = constant—slope of line of best fit

$$\left(\frac{\Delta Y}{\Delta X} \text{ or } \frac{Y_2 - Y_1}{X_2 - X_1} \right)$$

(The larger the value of the slope, the faster the rate of change. The impact of the slope on the pay structure is that the greater the slope of the pay policy line, the greater the difference in pay between jobs of similar worth.)

Step 2

The formula for the straight line must be developed by solving for the constants a and b for a particular distribution of actual pay and evaluated points or points of organizational job used for matching purposes and pay rate of comparable jobs. This is accomplished by solving two simultaneous equations.

(1) $\quad\quad\quad\quad\quad\quad\quad \Sigma Y = Na + b\Sigma X$
(2) $\quad\quad\quad\quad\quad\quad\quad \Sigma XY = a\Sigma X + b\Sigma X^2$

where

ΣY = sum of the pay rate column
ΣX = sum of the point cross column
ΣXY = sum of the cross products of pay rates and point values
ΣX^2 = sum of the squares of the point values
N = number of jobs evaluated

For example, the Least Squares table (10-1) lists nine jobs and their respective points. The mathematical manipulation of the evaluated points and the respective rates of pay provide the data necessary to solve these two simultaneous equations.

TABLE 10-1

LEAST-SQUARES

Jobs	X points	Y rate	XY	X²
A	50	2.00	100.00	2500
B	75	2.30	172.50	5625
C	100	2.65	265.00	10000
D	125	3.05	381.25	15625
E	150	3.50	525.00	22500
F	175	4.00	700.00	30625
G	200	4.60	920.00	40000
H	225	5.29	1190.25	50625
I	250	6.08	1520.00	62500
Σ	1350	33.47	5774.00	240000

Step 3

Solve the simultaneous equations by substituting the values from the Least Squares Table.

(1) $\qquad \Sigma Y = Na + b\Sigma X$

(2) $\qquad \Sigma XY = a\Sigma X + b\Sigma X^2$

(1) $\qquad 33.47 = 9a + 1350b$

(2) $\qquad 5774.0 = 5774.0 = 1350a + 240,000b$

Multiply (1) by $1350/9 = 150$:

(1) $\qquad 33.47 (150) = 9a (150) + 1350b (150)$

(1) $\qquad 5020.5 = 1350a + 202,500b$

Subtract (1) from (2) and solve for b:

(2) $\qquad 5774.0 = 1350a + 240,000b$
(1) $\qquad \underline{5020.5 = 1350a + 202,500b}$
$\qquad\qquad 753.5 = \qquad\quad + 37,500b$

$$b = \frac{756.5}{37,500} = \frac{753.5}{37,500}$$

$$b = .02$$

Substitute value of b in equation (1) and solve for a:

$$33.47 = 9a = 1350 (.02)$$
$$9a = 33.47 - 27$$

$$a = \frac{6.47}{9} = .718 \text{ or } .72 \text{ (rounding off)}$$

The equation for the line of best fit for this distribution is

$$Y = .72 + .02(X)$$

Step 5

To determine points for plotting the line, substitute X values for the highest-rated job, the lowest-rated job, and one intermediate point as a check point (see Line of Best Fit, figure 10-2).

$$Y_L = .72 + .02(50)$$
$$Y_L = 1.72$$
$$Y_I = .72 + .02(150)$$
$$Y_I = 3.72$$
$$Y_H = .72 + .02(250)$$
$$Y_H = 5.72$$

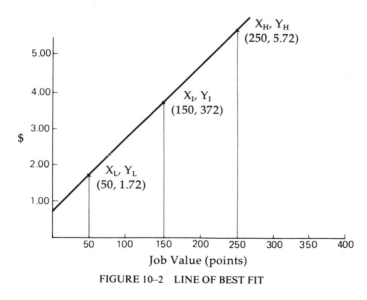

FIGURE 10–2   LINE OF BEST FIT

A curve may be plotted using these three sets of paired coordinates:

$$(X_L, Y_L) = (50, 1.72)$$
$$(X_I, Y_I) = (150, 3.72)$$
$$(X_H, Y_H) = (250, 5.72)$$

without an analysis of why they developed and whether it is permissible to eliminate them.

For example, when technological changes have simplified the job but the job has never been reevaluated and the jobholders' rates of pay have not been reduced in line with the job requirements, it is possible, even necessary, to disregard these data points when developing a pay policy line. This principle also applies in cases in which, strictly because of seniority increases, individuals are receiving rates of pay out of line with job requirements.

Many organizations use the pay policy line to set midpoint values for all their jobs. Pay policy lines are useful when plotting pay survey data and comparing them with the internal pay structure. From the pay policy line, organizations establish the minimum and maximum pay levels, the relationship between pay grades, and the range of a pay grade.

Deciding on the Need for More Than One Pay Structure

Whether there is a need for more than one pay structure is an early decision that must be made by those responsible for structure design. There are a number of logical and rational considerations for having multiple pay structures that focus on the forces that influence the actual pay of the various occupational groups comprising most organizations. A review of occupational groups as identified in chapter 2 assists in forming an understanding of how various forces influence the pay of different groups. It is not unusual for large organizations to have at least three pay structure lines—one for blue-collar manual labor, craft, and trade workers; another for nonexempt white-collar salaried workers; and a third for managerial, administrative, and professional exempt employees.

In relating the actual pay provided to a specific job or class, a number of issues must be resolved. These issues are as follows:

1. What does the organization consider to be the appropriate value of each job as it relates to all others?

2. What historical influences alter internally fair relationships?

3. How will the organization relate its pay policy to labor markets or externally competitive demands?

4. To what degree do negotiated collective bargaining contracts influence pay considerations (directly for the unionized organization, indirectly for many that are not unionized)?

Chapter 2 identified such occupational groups as clerical workers; unskilled, semiskilled, and skilled craft and trade workers; technicians; paraprofessionals; professionals; administrators; and managers. To some degree, each of these occupational groups requires different pay treatment. The establishment of different treatment may require different pay structure design. A brief review of the forces that influence the pay of each of these groups assists in clarifying some of the related issues.

Clerical Workers. In the past, unions have had little impact on the pay of this occupation. Pay received normally relates to local labor market rates.

Unskilled and Semiskilled Workers. This group is also related to local labor markets, but it is also a highly unionized labor force. Local, regional, and even national labor contracts strongly influence the rates of pay of jobs in these occupational groups.

Skilled Craft and Trade Workers. These are highly mobile and highly unionized groups influenced by regional and national pay schedules and differentials.

Technicians and Paraprofessionals. These are normally nonunionized groups influenced principally by local and regional pay practices.

Professionals and Administrators. These are highly mobile groups whose rates of pay relate to their disciplines or functional areas of responsibility. The widespread use of pay surveys for these groups influences regional and national pay scales to such an extent that the data become the major force in setting their pay.

Managers. The pay of this occupational group varies dramatically among its levels. The pay of lower-level operating managers is closely related to the pay received by the upper levels of operative employees. The pay of executives is related to such business and industry factors as sales volume, profit, return on investment, number of employees in the organization, and so on. The pay of top and upper level operating managers is influenced directly by the pay received by the executives of their respective organizations and certain individual and organizational-related performance criteria. The availability and the extensive use of surveys have a strong influence on the pay of managers at all levels and in all organizational settings.

A quick analysis of the pay scatter diagram (in figure 10-1c) provides a first indicator of the need for more than one pay structure. If there appear to be disjointed groupings or distinct breaks in the rates of pay of various jobs, as shown by the scatter diagram, the pay structure designer may decide that more than one trend line will be required for setting up a workable pay system.

Displaying Job Data

The use of multiple pay structures may at first glance appear to be the answer to meeting the pay demands of various occupational groups. However, it may only open a Pandora's box to the issues concerning inequity, unfairness, and unacceptability.

Even when there is an apparent need for more than one trend line or pay policy line that would then lead to more than one pay structure, there is a

(a) Three disconnected linear pay structures where $Y = a + bX$.

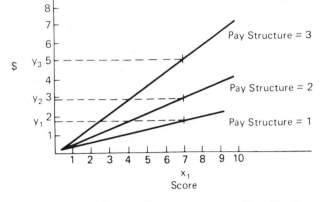

Same point score x_1 with different slope for each line—"b" resulting in 3 different pay structures that in turn results in three different rates of pay—y_1, y_2, and y_3

(b) A curvilinear pay structure where $Y = ab^x$.

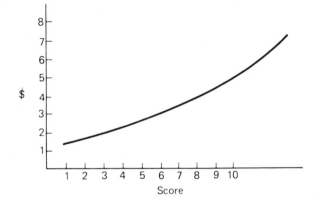

Curvilinear relationship turning upward to the right results in higher rates of pay at upper grades for comparable absolute increases in point score

(c) Curvilinear pay structure on semilogarithmic plotting paper.

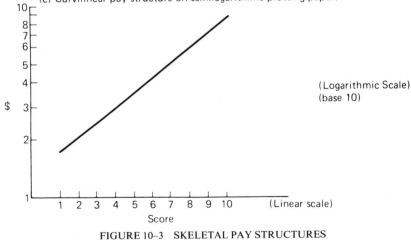

(Logarithmic Scale)
(base 10)

FIGURE 10–3   SKELETAL PAY STRUCTURES

statistical procedure available for avoiding multiple structures. This procedure permits the presentation of pay data through some form of curvilinear relationship rather than a relationship that must relate to a straight line. Figure 10-3 describes various mathematical procedures for developing trend or pay policy lines.

When the pay of the jobs in an organization uses an arithmetic progression and takes the form of a straight line, the pay policy line can be described by the equation $Y = a + bX$. Figure 10-3a describes three trend or pay policy lines. However, when pay rates vary by some constant rate of increase—a geometric progression—it is then possible to use an exponential curve for the trend line, which can be described by the formula $Y = ab^x$ (see figure 10-3b). The use of a geometric progression develops a pay scale that turns upward on the right-hand side, providing higher levels of pay for the higher levels or grades within one continuous pay structure. The rate of pay received proportionate to the scored value of the job is greater for those receiving higher point scores than it is for those receiving lower point scores. This helps to avoid the disruptive effects of a multiple structure pay system.

Both the straight and curved line approaches for displaying job data normally use a grid that has an arithmetic (linear) scale for both the horizontal (x) axis and the vertical (y) axis. An arithmetic scale is one in which equal distances represent equal *amounts* of whatever value is being displayed.

Another approach for displaying job data uses a logarithmic scale or grid for one or both axes. Many job data displays use a logarithmic scale on the vertical axis and a linear scale on the horizontal axis. This type of grid is called a *semilog display*. Some job data displays require the use of logarithmic scales on both the horizontal and vertical axes, a type of display called a *log-log grid*. Equal distances on logarithmic scales represent equal *ratios*. Figure 10-3c describes a *semilog grid*.

Logarithmic scales must begin with a positive value (any value). In using a scale for a pay structure, it is preferable to select an initial value that relates closely to the minimum pay value of the structure. This could be an hourly figure or a weekly, monthly, or annual rate. For example, when using the pay scale to identify hourly wage rates, if no rate is below $4 an hour, it is ideal to use $4 as the initial value.

A single logarithmic cycle accommodates a 10-fold increase; two cycles, a 100-fold increase. It is unlikely that a need would ever arise for more than three cycles when constructing a semilogarithmic (semilog) presentation of a pay structure. A complete description of logarithms can be found in an applied statistics text.

Figure 10-4 provides logarithmic equivalents for a linear scale. The logarithmic values are used to identify the linear scale values on the vertical axis when developing a semilog presentation of a pay structure. A semilog grid is useful when there is an extreme variation in the data to be displayed on one of the axes. If the data of the variables to be displayed on both axes vary widely, then a log-log grid is useful.

First cycle linear scale value Initial value 1	First cycle logarithmic value equivalents	Second cycle linear scale value Initial value 10	Second cycle logarithmic value equivalents
1	0	10	1.000000
2	0.301030	20	1.301030
3	0.477121	30	1.477121
4	0.602060	40	1.602060
5	0.698970	50	1.698970
6	0.778151	60	1.778151
7	0.845098	70	1.845098
8	0.903090	80	1.903090
9	0.954243	90	1.954243
10	1.000000	100	2.000000

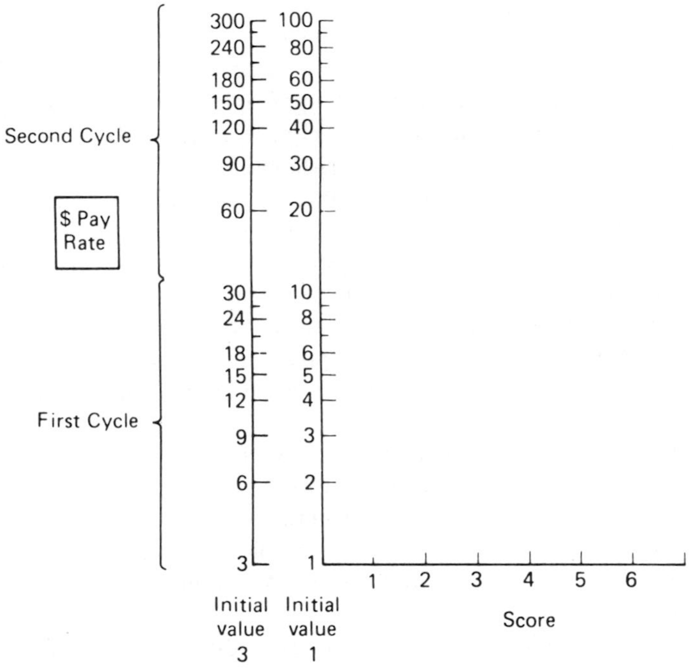

FIGURE 10–4   TWO-CYCLE SEMILOG GRID

Data that have a geometric relationship and appear as a curved line on a linear grid appear as a straight line on semilog or log-log grids because logarithmic scales represent geometric relationships—that is, equal ratios, not equal amounts as described with arithmetic or linear scales.

Care in the Use of Numbers—Compensation managers have to be very careful how they interpret and use pay data. Although the old adage says "Figures don't lie," the misuse and misinterpretation of figures can result in poor or inappropriate decisions. A major interpretation issue is the use of average or central tendency values and the way these should be calculated.

Two values of central tendency used in analyzing pay relationships are the *mean* and the *median*. When determining the market value or going rate of a job, the average value or mean is frequently the value selected. Should it be selected? The first thing to consider is that the pay for a particular job is hardly ever normally distributed—that is, it is rare that the mean, the median, and the mode are identical values. In fact, the median is normally 3 to 4 percent less than the mean.[2] This occurs because the lower values of the pay for most jobs have fairly precise lower limits, and the rates of pay advance rapidly to the value having the highest frequency, then tail off for some distance until reaching the highest value. This type of distribution is called a *nonparametric distribution* (see figure 10-5). The rates of pay for most jobs form a nonparametric distribution.

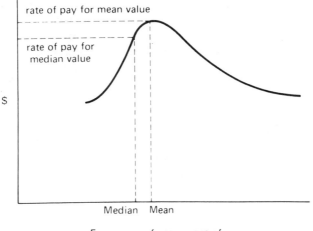

FIGURE 10–5   A NONPARAMETRIC PAY DISTRIBUTION

There are times, however, when the mean rather than the median is a better statistic to use as a value of central tendency and vice versa. The mean is superior when (1) using small samples and (2) computing year-to-year changes. The median is superior when (1) a sample has widely varying values and does not approximate a normal distribution and (2) the compensation manager wishes to identify a "typical" pay rate. On the one hand, the mean provides the rate of average pay; on the other, the median provides the rate of pay for the jobholder in the middle of the pay distribution. In most cases, the median value is what the decision maker is looking for. If an organization wishes to set its pay policy line around the rate of pay received by the middle jobholder and then uses the mean as the value for setting pay practices, it may be overpaying by 3 to 4

[2]In an analysis of 80,000 pay rates, Robert J. Greene, director of the A. S. Hansen, Inc. *Annual Weber Survey on Data Processing Positions,* found that in 68 out of the 70 data processing jobs the median value was 3 to 4 percent lower than the mean value. An analysis of Bureau of Labor Statistics data produces similar results.

percent. For example, if Olympia's pay policy states that the rate of pay for employees should be 5 percent higher than the market and that the market is to be a middle rate of pay, and if it then uses mean values to determine a pay policy or trend line, it could be paying almost 10 percent over what the middle jobholder is receiving in the labor market. Managers using pay information in this manner are thus responsible for furthering the inflation of wage payments.

In working with average pay information, compensation specialists may at times wish to use weighted averages or modified weighted averages rather than raw or unweighted averages. Although not too useful a statistic, the data that many surveys provide result in a *raw or unweighted average*. When organizations provide only average pay data for jobs and then these data are summed and divided by the number of averages included within the sum, the result is an unweighted average. A *weighted pay average* recognizes the number of employees receiving a specific rate of pay from each unit (i.e., organization) providing pay data. An example of developing unweighted and weighted average data occurred when RICH Compensation Consultants collected and summarized pay data for the job of senior clerk-typist (see table 10-2).

TABLE 10-2

UNWEIGHTED AND WEIGHTED AVERAGE PAY DATA

Business	Senior Clerk-Typists	Annual Pay Rate	Total Annual Pay
Olympia	14	$ 9,700	$135,800
Alpha	3	10,200	30,600
Omega	5	10,900	54,500
Delta	8	9,400	75,200
	30	$40,200	$296,100

Raw or Unweighted Average $\dfrac{40,200}{4} = \$10,050$

Weighted Average $\dfrac{296,100}{30} = \$ 9,870$

Because Olympia employs almost 50 percent of the senior clerk-typists in this survey and those organizations with higher rates of pay are not that much higher than Olympia, the weighted average ($9,870) is somewhat less than the unweighted average ($10,050).

A *modified weighted average* reduces the influence of an unusual population. RICH Compensation Consultants conducted a pay survey and collected the pay data shown in table 10-3 on data entry operators. When using modified weighted averages for pay data, the influence of an employer with an extremely

TABLE 10-3

MODIFIED WEIGHTED AVERAGE PAY DATA

Business	Data Entry Operators	Hourly Rate of Pay	Total Hourly Pay
Omega	14	$3.20	$ 44.80
Alpha	9	3.50	31.50
Olympia	50	4.00	200.00
Delta	16	3.65	58.40
Gamma	6	3.85	23.10
	95		$357.80

large number of employees in a particular job is reduced as shown in the following steps:

Step 1. Determine average number of employees per company.

$$\frac{95}{5} = 19$$

Step 2: Identify the excess or difference in population between the population of the highly influencing organization and the average population.

In this example, Olympia is the employer with the highly influencing population:

$$50 - 19 = 31$$

Step 3: Reduce the influence of the organization having the large population to some arbitrary figure. A frequently used arbitrary value is 10 percent of the excess population plus the average population:

$$10\% \times 31 = 3 + 19 = 22$$

Step 4: Develop a modified weighted average:

Omega	14 × 3.20 =	$ 44.80
Alpha	9 × 3.50 =	31.50
Olympia*	22 × 4.00 =	88.00
Delta	16 × 3.65 =	58.40
Gamma	6 × 3.85 =	23.10
	67	$245.80

*Olympia as the influencing organization is the only organization to have its population modified.

$$\text{Modified Weighted Average} = \frac{245.80}{67} = \$3.67$$

$$\text{Weighted Average} = \frac{357.80}{95} = \$3.77$$

By reducing the influence of Olympia in the survey, the modified average value is approximately 3 percent less than the weighted average.

Identifying Lowest and Highest Rates of Pay

In identifying the lowest and hghest rates of pay, the most influential consideration for many organizations is the legal issue. What are the minimum standards prescribed by the federal government through regulations set under the Fair Labor Standards Act of 1938 as amended (Wage and Hour Law)? In some cases, the Davis-Bacon Act (1931) and the Walsh-Healey Public Contracts Act (1936) may also influence the lower end of the pay scale or set a floor for base pay. Some states set even more rigorous minimum requirements than those set by the federal government, and when this is the case, state laws preempt federal regulations. Organizations that must collectively bargain will normally have their lowest rates of pay set through negotiations with their representative unions. Even when an organization is nonunion, collectively bargained wage rates have a significant influence on practices to be followed by nonunionized organizations. Another major consideration beyond union impact on the labor market is the general influence a particular labor market has on wage rates. Where employment is high and insufficient numbers of people are seeking entry-level jobs or specific kinds of jobs, minimum wage rates must be high enough to attract a sufficient number of job seekers who are able and willing to adequately perform job assignments. A floor set too high, however, may force all following rates also to be set overly high, causing excessive labor costs, which may in turn limit competitiveness and profitability.[3] On the other hand, too low a level may result in an inadequate number of suitable applicants and may result in a pay structure that is disproportionately lower than necessary to meet hiring, retention, and performance requirements. A main reason for the wage survey is to assist in solving this basic pay structure problem.

The upper limit or highest rates of pay are a more subjective consideration where senior policymakers determine what they believe to be an acceptable rate of pay for jobs considered to be of highest worth to the organization. Some of the factors that normally influence policy makers when making decisions that relate to the pay provided for their most critical jobs are:

1. Traditional or past practices.

2. Ability of the organization to pay.

3. Pay provided by other organizations for comparable jobs.

4. Need to attract sufficient personnel or individuals with specific talents and skills.

5. Other compensation components provided to high-level personnel.

---

[3]The increase of the base minimum or floor pay of an organization will normally have a "ripple" effect on all or a significant number of its jobs. The ripple effect occurs when the increase at the bottom end of a pay structure in turn increases the rates of pay of the higher-paid jobs.

The chief executive of the organization usually earns the highest rate of pay, which establishes the maximum or ceiling rate. At the chief executive level, it is more difficult to relate the contributions the job makes to the success of the organization than it is at lower levels. For this reason, the performance of the chief executive officer significantly influences the pay of the job. The higher the job level, the more difficult it is to set reasonable pay with mathematical precision.

Although not always the case, there is frequently a reverse progression through the managerial ranks in which pay for a less senior job bears a direct relationship to that of the job directly above it. In effect, what happens is that the government, the union, or the labor market sets the minimum level, and the organization, its performance, and chief executive pay set maximum levels. Or, in other words, labor markets set minimum pay levels and product markets determine maximum levels of pay. In the public sector and in nonprofit organizations, however, maximum pay may be that set by legislation for the most senior elected or appointed official.

Identifying the lowest and highest rate of pay is a basic step in establishing a pay policy line. After identification, the next step is to establish what management expects to be the average or central tendency value paid to the lowest rated job and the average pay rate of the highest rated job. These highest and lowest average values should be the midpoint of the pay for those jobs assigned this rate when there is a range of pay available for each category. When there is only one rate of pay assigned to a job or group of jobs, then normally the average or midpoint value is that single rate. The midpoint value is normally the market or "going rate" of pay for that job or a very close approximation.

One of the first statistics of value in pay structure design is the r_{h-l} ratio. This statistic identifies the ratio between the highest and lowest midpoint pay rates expected.

After reviewing pay data information, the compensation management team at Olympia decided that the lowest midpoint pay range expected for the nonsupervisory clerical trades and crafts structure would be $7,600 a year and the highest midpoint would be $22,800 a year.

$$r_{h-l} = \frac{\text{highest expected midpoint pay rate}}{\text{lowest expected midpoint pay rate}} = \frac{\$22,800}{\$\ 7,600} = 3.0000$$

Determining Progression from Lowest to Highest Pay Rate

In chapter 7, there was a brief discussion of applicable differences between midpoints when describing the procedures used in the application of the Smyth-Murphy Guide Line Method and the Evalucomp of the AMA. The Smyth-Murphy method stresses the value of a 5 percent difference between midpoints; Evalucomp uses a 6 percent difference. Opinions and methods actually used vary far more than the 1 percent difference between these two methods. Midpoint-to-midpoint pay progressions range from as low as 2.75

percent to as high as 20 to 25 percent (normally low midpoint-to-midpoint differences are found in pay structures of lower paid, unskilled, semiskilled, and clerical employees, whereas high midpoint-to-midpoint differences are found in the pay structures of the executives and the senior managers of an organization).

When determining applicable or appropriate midpoint-to-midpoint differences, the following issues should be recognized and considered:

1. The smaller the difference between midpoints, the more pay rates available to assign to a specific job because there will be many more grades available within the pay structure. That is, a 3 percent midpoint-to-midpoint difference may result in 50 or more pay grades, whereas a 20 percent difference may result in five or six pay grades.

2. The more pay rates available, the greater the opportunity of assigning jobs with similar responsibilities and duties and comparable knowledge and skill requirements to equivalent rates of pay.

3. The greater the difference between pay rates, the easier it is for jobholders to perceive differences in worth between jobs. (Refer to Weber's law on just perceptible differences.)

4. A large difference between midpoints may require having more than one pay structure.

Rates of differences between midpoints are not the only consideration in this phase of the design of the pay structure. Designers must also consider the uniformity of change between midpoints. Should all midpoints increase at the same rate of differences, or should they vary as jobs move toward the higher end of the pay structure? A uniform approach is always easier to justify and substantiate, but in using a single pay structure, it may be necessary to increase the difference between midpoints in moving from the low to the high end of the structure. For those jobs at the lower end of the pay structure, a 5 to 7.5 percent difference between midpoints may be appropriate; at the top end, the distance between midpoints may vary from 15 to 20 percent.

The compensation manager must be aware by this time that there are no firm rules for setting specific quantitative guidelines for developing a pay structure—only acceptable indicators. When determining the difference between midpoints, all the previously mentioned issues once again come into play. The possibility of having a constant percentage throughout the structure or the need to change midpoint differences depends on organizational requirements. Those organizations using a standard difference between midpoints will normally use a value ranging between 5 and 15 percent.

There are those who feel that a 5 percent difference between midpoints is ideal because it allows for a greater number of grades within a set pay structure. The greater number of grades then permits greater opportunity for placement of jobs in different grades. These same proponents of the 5 percent difference also state that there can be a 5 percent judgmental error made in any job evaluation. The opportunity to move a job up or down a pay grade permits adjustment for such errors.[4]

Setting the Midpoint—The factor most influencing the midpoint value is probably the going rate or market value of the job. The midpoint may also come from internal data of what has normally been considered a standard rate for the job. Once the midpoint rate is set for an entry level job (or one near entry level), the adjoining midpoint rates may be set by multiplying (if above) or dividing (if below) by the particular rate. For example, Olympia decides that there should be a 15 percent difference between midpoints. An identified lower grade midpoint is $4.00 an hour; the next highest midpoint is $4.00 an hour × 1.15, or $4.60 an hour.

Developing Pay Grades

After identifying midpoint or market rates for the jobs of an organization and determining acceptable percentage progression between midpoints, the compensation designer is now ready to develop pay grades. Pay grades are nothing more than convenient groupings of a wide variety of jobs or classes similar in work difficulty and responsibility requirements but possibly having nothing else in common. Grades provide a connecting link between the evaluation and classification processes and the assignment of pay to a particular job or class. A pay grade may provide for a single rate, or it may allow for a range of pay within a certain grade.

Pay grades are an integral part of the pay structure. Most pay grade systems have certain common or general characteristics. Some of these are as follows:

1. Each grade provides for a range of pay, although there are single rate pay grade structures that, as the title implies, provide for only one rate of pay within the grade.

2. Within a pay grade range there is a minimum, a midpoint (this normally is the pay within a single rate structure), and a maximum pay.

3. The range from the minimum to the maximum within a single pay grade may vary from 20 to 100 percent. The most common range is from 30 to 35 percent.

4. The number of steps within a grade may also vary. Grades having steps will normally have from three to ten steps, with six to seven in-grade steps being most common.

5. There is a direct relationship between the rate of increase per step and the number of steps within a grade. The federal government General Schedule

---

[4]Richard C. Smyth and Matthew J. Murphy, *The Guide Line Method of Job Evaluation* (Rhinebeck, NY: Smyth & Murphy Associates, Inc.).

(GS) has ten steps for most grades with a percentage increase between steps of approximately 3.33 percent or 30 percent within the grade—the spread from minimum to maximum rate of pay.

6. The midpoint of each pay grade is normally a constant percentage greater than the one preceding it. This percentage normally varies from 5 to 15 percent.

7. Adjoining pay grades normally overlap. If there is a 30 percent range within a pay grade and there is a 10 percent difference between midpoints, there will be a 67 percent overlap.

8. The requirements of the organization will provide answers to the correct number of grades, the number of steps within grades, and the rates of progression within and between grades. The four principal considerations that have strong impact in this area are as follows:

a. Identifying the number of different kinds of jobs in the organization.

b. Determining the number of pay structures used by the organization. If the organization uses only one structure for both exempt and nonexempt employees, it will probably have more grades than if it uses more than one.

c. Using steps within grades to recognize seniority or longevity. Many organizations use the steps between the minimum and midpoint to recognize seniority pay increases.

d. Using steps to recognize merit increases. Some organizations use steps between midpoint and maximum to recognize merit increases.

The General Schedule (GS) grade system of the federal government has the following general characteristics:

1. Grades: 18

2. Steps within grades: 10

3. Percentage increase from minimum to maximum within each grade: 30 percent

4. Differences between the fifth steps of adjoining pay grades range from a low of 9.9 percent to a high of 19.8 percent. (There is a 9.9 percent difference between steps 5 of grades 10 and 11; there is a 19.8 percent difference between steps 5 of grades 11 and 12.)

The number of pay grades to be included within a pay structure varies with the circumstances—there is no right number. Therefore, compensation system designers and managers all face the same answer—it all depends. It all depends on demands of the organization: What is acceptable to top management? What do employees perceive as fair? What is administratively practical? What best recognizes differences in job worth, employee behavior, and the opportunity to maintain a logical and rational control over wage payments? Too many grades require a very fine evaluation among jobs. Referring to the work of Weber and Hay, it is unlikely that truly fine differentiations between jobs or classes are possible. On the other hand, too few grades can result in the failure or inability to recognize significant differences in difficulty, responsibility, or knowledge requirements among jobs and classes.

There are organizations that use market surveys and guidecharts for establishing job rates of pay that have 70 to 80 and possibly more pay grades. Some behavioral scientists today are promoting the idea of using as few as four to six pay grades.

The issues to be considered and the results of using a large number of pay grades versus the use of a very small number are as follows:

1. Is there to be only one pay structure that will include all jobs from the lowest entry-level job requiring minimum education, experience, and skill to that of the chief executive officer demanding a large amount of knowledge and skills to cope with the responsibilities of the job? If this is the case, it is likely that even a small organization with, say, 500 employees would require 18 to 30 pay grades.

2. Is it desirable to have a small variation between pay grades—somewhere between 4 to 6 percent? If this is the case and the organization is using only one pay structure, then it would not be unusual to find 50 to 75 pay grades being used. By having a small variation in pay grades, a mistake made in assigning a job to a pay grade that is one or even two grades too high or too low relative to job worth would hardly be noted (remember Weber's law). More grades also allow for the assignment of jobs with different evaluations to different pay grades. When having a large number of pay grades, the overlap (this will be discussed later in the chapter) between pay grades will be large—in the vicinity of 70 to 85 percent.

3. A small number of pay grades will normally result in less overlap between them. It will also require the assignment of more jobs to the same pay grade. Having fewer pay grades permits a greater spread, allowing increased recognition of growth of job knowledge through seniority and merit in-grade pay increases. The larger the range in a pay grade, the greater the opportunity to pay employees differently who perform the same job or equivalent kinds of work.

Single Rate Pay Grade—It is possible for a pay grade to be one point in the pay structure. In the case of a single rate pay grade, the rate is usually the "average" rate in the market place (i.e., the competitive midpoint or the amount a competent, fully trained employee would expect to receive for that job). Depending on its pay policy and competitive posture, an organization with a single rate pay structure can certainly raise or lower the rate it pays for a job in comparison with the "going" or market rate.

Organizations with only single rate pay grades frequently use the terms *flat rate* or *standard rate* to describe their pay structures. A flat rate structure appears most often in organizations in which pay rate negotiations between management and unions are common practice, or in small organizations, or in industries using skilled craftworkers. The single rate structure provides no opportunity for progression within the grade, although this weakness is partly overcome by having closely related classes of jobs with closely associated pay grades.

Pay Grade Dimension—A midpoint-to-midpoint progression provides the width dimension to a pay grade. The height of a pay grade is its spread. When establishing a spread within a pay grade, the first question is what the spread or height of the pay grade should be. Like most other compensation questions of this nature, there is no right or wrong answer.

The *range* or *spread of the range* of a pay grade is the difference between the upper and lower limits of the pay grade. The range may be expressed in absolute dollar amounts or as a percentage. When expressed as a percentage, the range is the

$$\frac{\text{maximum dollar } - \text{ minimum dollar}}{\text{minimum dollar}}$$

Pay grade spread, like midpoint progression, can vary widely depending on pay policy and business practices. In many cases, the spread from the midpoint to the maximum pay rate of a grade and the spread from the midpoint to the minimum pay rate of a grade are uniform throughout the structure. The major reason for uniformity is ease in explaining and justifying a basic fairness in the structure design.

However, many compensation professionals believe that the spread of the grades should increase in progressing through a pay structure. At entry levels, a typical spread is ±10 percent on either side of the midpoint. At the upper levels of management, the spread may reach ±30 percent. The reasons for a narrow pay spread at entry level and a broader spread at the professional and managerial levels are based on several philosophical considerations. Management frequently considers entry-level jobholders as "transients" and, in a relatively short period of time, these jobholders will have the opportunity to progress to higher-level jobs. There is also the feeling that lower-level jobs can be mastered quickly, that they make a limited contribution to the success of the organization, and that holders of lower-level jobs have relatively little influence in changing the nature of the job. For these reasons, movement below or above the "going rate" should be relatively restricted.

The philosophy related to upper-level jobs is that they require extended periods for jobholders to become fairly competent. Those persons holding these jobs are, in most cases, career personnel; and these jobs are extremely critical to the success of the organization. Upper-level jobholders have a greater influence over the success of job activities, and they can stretch their jobs by making them more important through their individual contributions. For these reasons, the spread of the pay grade is much higher than at lower levels.

Determining Minimum and Maximum Rates of Pay—Most organizations set the minimum and maximum rates of pay for their grades relative to demands they wish to make upon their pay systems. The spread of the pay range provides an opportunity to differentiate the pay received by the newly hired person, the probationary employee, the competent employee, and the excellent performer. The pay grade range also provides an opportunity to recognize extended and faithful service.

The most practical method of establishing lower and upper limits for a pay grade is first to establish a midpoint line at a competitive level and then to determine what percentage of spread is required on either side of the midpoint to accomplish objectives that may be attained through a well-designed pay grade.

Internal Pay Grade Design Considerations—With the establishment of minimum, midpoint, and maximum rates of pay, the next step is to determine if the grade itself is to have a more detailed internal structure. Many pay grades have steps within each grade. Organizations use in-grade step pay increases for a number of reasons.

The design of a pay range frequently permits the initial steps (often to midpoint) to relate specific growth periods to time on the job. Normally, as jobholders reach these time milestones, they have attained additional job knowledge and receive an automatic pay increase to the next step. The automatic progression is common where the new jobholders receive training in the operation of certain types of equipment or in working within well-defined procedures so that they reach acceptable degrees of competency within certain periods of time.

A relatively simple pay structure suitable to these conditions is one with three steps. The first step is the pay provided to the newly hired person or to an incumbent who has just been placed on the job. The time required to move from the first to the second step is normally called the *probationary period,* which may range from 30 days to one year. It is within this period that the incumbent demonstrates an ability to perform the job. At the successful completion of the probationary period, the incumbent receives the second step in the pay range. The third step is achieved when job performance indicates competency (see figure 10-6).

Step progression related to merit is not nearly so cut and dried as the growth process. Theoretically, increases through these steps relate directly to the performance and contributions made by the jobholder. Many organizations use the steps beyond the midpoint for merit pay increases. If, for example, there are three steps beyond the midpoint, an ideal situation is one with 10 to 15 percent of those qualified in the first step beyond midpoint, 70 to 80 percent in the second

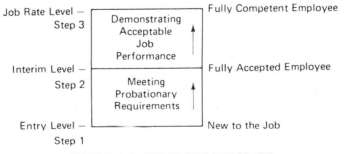

FIGURE 10–6   THREE-STEP PAY GRADE

step, and 10 to 15 percent in the highest step in the pay range. In many mature organizations with long-standing pay structure plans, it is not uncommon to find 70 to 80 percent of all employees at the maximum step in the pay range. This is a prime indicator that something may be wrong with the pay structure and that it requires some review and analysis. Chapter 14 discusses in detail the use of merit increases and the impact of these increases on the pay structure.

The major problem in any progressive step procedure is the overwhelming influence of seniority (time in service). In real-world situations, growth and merit criteria frequently become subverted into a seniority system. This condition develops because of the difficulty organizations face in recognizing growth or merit. The use of seniority measurements in lieu of understandable growth standards and acceptable merit standards is a trap every compensation manager must avoid at all costs. A possible first step toward avoiding this problem is to recognize seniority outside the pay range by allowing fixed pay rewards for time in service and then developing workable standards for growth and merit.

In the 1970s, another major issue emerged relating to the improper use of in-step increases within a pay range—the use of in-step increases in lieu of cost-of-living adjustments. When organizations did not provide adequate across-the-board increases or changes in the overall pay structure to maintain the real income or current living standards of employees, piecemeal changes were made by granting employees, when possible, in-step pay increases. These increases came about because of general inflationary trends in the economy and had nothing to do with either seniority or merit. The answer to this problem is for organizations in some way to relate pay structure design and changes to variations in cost of living. Chapter 14 discusses this issue in detail.

Spread of Range and Steps—The spread of a range within a pay grade may vary anywhere from 10 percent to 50 percent on either side of the midpoint of a pay scale. Normally, a range of 10 to 20 percent on either side of the midpoint is common. With pressures to decrease the number of pay grades and to improve recognition of performance, pay ranges of 15 to 50 percent on either side of the midpoint will become prevalent.

The size of each pay step within a grade may increase arithmetically (absolutely), geometrically (by a constant percentage), or randomly. In most cases, geometric increases are preferable. There may be a deviation in the percentage of increase between steps at certain points in the structure (i.e., the lower half of the structure may have a 30 percent spread within the pay grades and the upper half a 50 percent spread). In this case, the structure may be termed a *split structure,* or in reality it may become two structures or substructures making up the major structure.

Identifying Pay Grade Dimensions—If the midpoint and the desired percentage spread of the range to the maximum and minimum limits is known, it is a matter of simple mathematics to identify the upper and lower limits of the pay grade. If the midpoint is $5.00 and the spread of the range to the maximum rate of the grade is 14.0 percent and the spread to the minimum rate is also 14.0 percent, the maximum is then equal to $5.00 times (100 percent + 14.0 percent) or $5.00 × 1.14 or $5.70. The minimum limit is $5.00 times (100 percent − 14.0

percent) or $5.00 × .86 or $4.30. The actual total percentage spread of the range is

$$\frac{5.70 - 4.30}{4.30} = \frac{1.40}{4.30} = 32.6\%$$

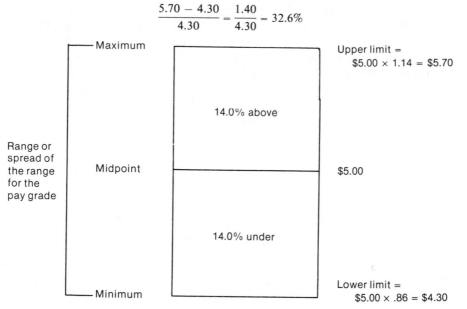

When the midpoint and the percentage spread of the range are known, the following mathematical procedure can be used to obtain the maximum and the minimum of the pay grade. The first step is to determine the minimum of the pay grade. The minimum is obtained by first adding half of the percentage spread of the range to 100 percent and then dividing the midpoint by this amount. For example, the midpoint is $5.00 and the range is 33 percent. To obtain the minimum:

$$\frac{\$5.00}{(100\% + 16.5\%)}$$

or

$$\frac{\$5.00}{1.165} = \$4.29.$$

The maximum is then obtained by multiplying the minimum by 100 percent plus the percentage spread of the range. Continuing with the above example with $4.29 being the minimum and the spread of the range being 33 percent:

$$\$4.29 × (100\% + 33\%) \text{ or } \$4.29 × 1.33 = \$5.71.$$

After determining the minimum, midpoint, and maximum pay rates, the number of steps in the range is the center of focus. A fundamental concept here is that each step has true recognition value and makes some impact on the recipient. The smaller the incremental step, the less the recognition and the smaller the motivational force on the recipient. Pay steps have had incremental increases beginning with 2 percent, but again, recognition factors are resulting in greater increases between steps. Increases of 5.0 to 7.5 percent between the steps in this grade produces a seven-step pay scale (begin by multiplying $4.29 by 100 percent plus 5 percent or 1.05 and then each subsequent value by 1.05) (see figure 10-7). Using this approach, the midpoint (step 4) is not quite $5.00 and the maximum is $5.75, which exceeds the actual maximum of $5.71. Slight adjustments to the step rates can be made to make the fourth step equal to the midpoint and the seventh step equal to the maximum of the pay grade.

		5% difference between steps	5% difference adjusted to meet grade requirements
$5.71 maximum	Step 7	$5.75	$5.71
	Step 6	$5.48	$5.45
	Step 5	$5.21	$5.21
$5.00 midpoint	Step 4	$4.97	$5.00
	Step 3	$4.73	$4.74
	Step 2	$4.50	$4.50
$4.29 minimum	Step 1	$4.29	$4.29

FIGURE 10–7   A SEVEN-STEP PAY SCALE

The actual range of a pay grade is frequently an amount arbitrarily selected by an individual or individuals with compensation policy decision-making responsibilities. There are, however, some issues that could affect the final value selected. If the range is small and the minimum or lower limit relates closely to the market, the entry rate of pay is more attractive to those looking for employment. There is also an unsatisfactory side to this story. When entry and maximum limits are too close, long-term employees feel that the organization does not recognize their services and loyalty, and there is an unsatisfactory compression of pay rates within the pay grade.

Pay Grade Overlap—Following the identification of the midpoint, upper limit, and lower limit of the pay grade, the next step is to establish the relationship between adjacent pay grades. The pay structure may have no overlap between pay grades and look like this:

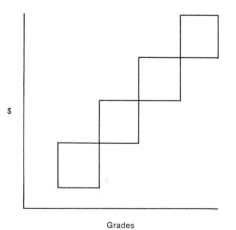

$

Grades

or the pay structure may have overlapping pay grades and look like this:

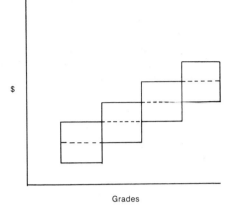

The overlaps between pay grades are those pay opportunities that are identical in adjacent pay grades:

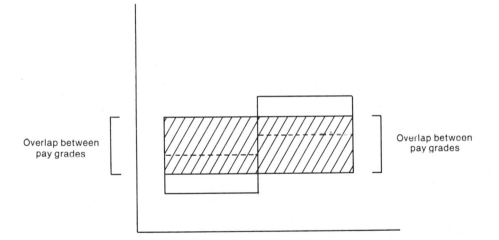

The difference in midpoints and the spread of the pay range then determine the amount of overlap between adjoining grades. An overlap of approximately 70 percent is not unusual between adjoining pay grades. A theory underlying overlap between pay grades is that the amount of overlap should equal the similarity of responsibilities, duties, knowledge, and skills that exist among jobs in the adjacent pay grades (i.e., 80 percent overlap equates to an 80 percent comparability in responsibilities and duties, knowledge, and skills in jobs assigned to these pay grades).

For example, the pay structure of the Olympia Nursing Home has a difference between midpoints of 15 percent and a pay range within each grade of 33 percent. Grade level 5 has a midpoint of $5 an hour (see figure 10-8).

$7.55

$6.57 $6.61

$5.71 $5.75 $5.67

$4.96 $5.00 $4.94   Grade Level 7*

$4.35 $4.29   Grade Level 6

$3.73   Grade Level 5

Grade Level 4

*With overlap of approximately 54% no overlap exists
between pay grades 4 and 7.

Overlap between GL 4 and GL 5

$4.96
− $4.29

$ .67 − overlap between GL 4 and GL 5

$4.96
− $3.73

$1.23 − range of GL 4

$$\frac{.67}{1.23} = 54.5\% \text{ 5 percent of the range}$$

Overlap between GL 5 and GL 6

$5.71
− $4.94

$ .77 − overlap between GL 5 and GL 6

$5.71
− $4.29

$1.42 − range of GL 5

$$\frac{.77}{1.42} = 54.2^* \text{ spread of the range}$$

FIGURE 10–8   PAY STRUCTURE OVERLAP

An overlap between pay grades provides an opportunity for the excellent performer in the lower pay grade who has long tenure (i.e., high seniority) to earn more than the new, less experienced person in a more senior pay grade. The philosophy here is that the skilled, high performer in a lower graded job can be making a greater contribution than the less experienced incumbent in the next higher grade. When there is minimal distance between midpoints (less than 7.5 percent) and the grades have limited spread (15 to 25 percent), overlap will extend for a number of grades. Some experts in pay structure design feel that overlap beyond three adjacent grades—four grades in total—should be avoided.

A major problem with pay grades that have a large overlap is that an employee already in the upper end of a pay grade who receives a promotion to a job in the next pay grade—even a promotion that results in an advancement two or three pay grades up the pay structure—may not receive much of a pay increase nor have an opportunity to increase the amount of future pay. Many compensation policy decision makers feel that in order for a promotion to have a true incentive value, it should carry with it at least a 10 percent increase in pay. This is one of the major reasons for the warning that in a well-designed pay structure there should be no overlap between pay grades that are four grades apart.

Pay Rates Below Minimum and Above Maximum—Some organizations pay newly hired employees with no experience rates 10 to 20 percent below the established minimum. Some organizations have a cap (i.e., limit) on any pay increase an employee can receive at one time. It is possible for an employee to be promoted to a new job in a pay grade considerably higher than the one presently occupied and have the cap on the pay increase prohibit the promoted employee from immediately receiving the minimum level of pay for the new job. The term *"green circle"* applies to any incumbent receiving a rate of pay below the minimum of the pay grade.

Some organizations provide superseniority pay increases to their employees with long tenure. These superseniority pay increases may place the employee in a pay step that extends beyond the maximum of the pay range. The term *"silver circle"* identifies the incumbent in a superseniority pay step. Some organizations also allow for merit increases that could extend the pay of the incumbent beyond the established maximum. The term *"gold circle"* identifies incumbents receiving this in-step pay increase.

Mature organizations with many high seniority employees frequently encounter a problem called "running out of range." In this case, an organization finds that a large number of its employees are at the top of the pay range, and morale suffers as they realize there is little to no opportunity for further pay increases. There is no easy answer to this problem. One solution may be some type of 10-year, 15-year, or 20-year seniority cash bonus. Another solution is to ensure real income maintenance by some type of living cost adjustments.

Number of Pay Grades—When determining the number of grades in a pay structure, it is not necessary or even advisable that every grade have a job or class assigned to it. This is especially true in a young, fast-growing business in which initially there may be unfilled grades that will be filled later.

Table 10-4 is useful for (1) determining the approximate number of pay grades when the ratio of the midpoints of the highest and lowest pay to be included within the pay structure (r_{h-l}) and the percentage difference between midpoints have been identified, or (2) when the number of grades to be used have been selected, r_{h-l} has been calculated, and the midpoint-to-midpoint percentage increase must be determined. The approximate number of pay grades is found on the table by referring to the column with the desired percentage of progression (midpoint to midpoint) and looking down through the column to the value that most closely approximates the calculated r_{h-l} value. Reading across the row to the "No. of Grades" column gives the number of grades the progression will yield.

After the number of grades and r_{h-l} value have been determined, the value that most closely approximates the calculated r_{h-l} value is found by referring to the appropriate "No. of Grades" row and moving across. Reading up that column to the top will identify the midpoint-to-midpoint percentage necessary to yield the number of grades.

Although this table includes data for only 25 pay grades and a midpoint-to-midpoint difference from 2.75 percent to 9.5 percent, the table can provide additional values. For example, to use a 15 percent midpoint-to-midpoint progression and an r_{h-l} of 2.9593, a compensation designer should divide 15 percent by 2, enter the 7.50 percent column, and continue down the column until the value of 2.9593 has been reached. By reading across the row with that value to the "No. of Grades" column, the value "16" is found. Dividing 16 by 2 provides the answer: eight grades.

Table 10-4

RATIO TABLE FOR PAY STRUCTURE CALCULATIONS

No. of Grades	% Progression (Mid to Mid)													
	2.75%	3.00%	3.25%	3.50%	3.75%	4.00%	4.25%	4.50%	4.75%	5.00%	5.25%	5.50%	5.75%	6.00%
1	1.0000	1.0000	1.0000	1.0000	1.0000	1.0000	1.0000	1.0000	1.0000	1.0000	1.0000	1.0000	1.0000	1.0000
2	1.0275	1.0300	1.0325	1.0350	1.0375	1.0400	1.0425	1.0450	1.0475	1.0500	1.0525	1.0550	1.0575	1.0600
3	1.0558	1.0609	1.0660	1.0712	1.0764	1.0816	1.0868	1.0920	1.0973	1.1025	1.1078	1.1130	1.1183	1.1236
4	1.0848	1.0927	1.1006	1.1087	1.1168	1.1249	1.1330	1.1411	1.1494	1.1576	1.1660	1.1742	1.1826	1.1910
5	1.1146	1.1255	1.1364	1.1476	1.1587	1.1699	1.1811	1.1924	1.2040	1.2154	1.2272	1.2388	1.2506	1.2624
6	1.1453	1.1593	1.1733	1.1878	1.2021	1.2167	1.2313	1.2461	1.2612	1.2762	1.2916	1.3069	1.3225	1.3381
7	1.1768	1.1941	1.2114	1.2293	1.2471	1.2654	1.2836	1.3022	1.3211	1.3400	1.3594	1.3788	1.3985	1.4184
8	1.2092	1.2299	1.2508	1.2723	1.2939	1.3160	1.3382	1.3608	1.3839	1.4070	1.4308	1.4547	1.4789	1.5035
9	1.2425	1.2668	1.2915	1.3168	1.3424	1.3687	1.3951	1.4220	1.4496	1.4773	1.5060	1.5347	1.5639	1.5937
10	1.2767	1.3048	1.3335	1.3629	1.3927	1.4234	1.4544	1.4860	1.5185	1.5512	1.5851	1.6191	1.6538	1.6893
11	1.3118	1.3439	1.3768	1.4106	1.4449	1.4803	1.5162	1.5529	1.5906	1.6288	1.6683	1.7082	1.7489	1.7907
12	1.3479	1.3842	1.4215	1.4600	1.4991	1.5395	1.5806	1.6228	1.6661	1.7102	1.7559	1.8021	1.8494	1.8981
13	1.3850	1.4257	1.4677	1.5111	1.5553	1.6011	1.6478	1.6958	1.7452	1.7957	1.8481	1.9012	1.9557	2.0120
14	1.4231	1.4685	1.5154	1.5640	1.6136	1.6651	1.7178	1.7721	1.8281	1.8855	1.9451	2.0058	2.0681	2.1327
15	1.4622	1.5126	1.5646	1.6187	1.6741	1.7317	1.7908	1.8518	1.9150	1.9798	2.0472	2.1161	2.1870	2.2607
16	1.5024	1.5580	1.6154	1.6754	1.7369	1.8010	1.8669	1.9351	2.0060	2.0788	2.1547	2.2325	2.3128	2.3963
17	1.5437	1.6047	1.6679	1.7340	1.8020	1.8730	1.9462	2.0222	2.1013	2.1827	2.2679	2.3553	2.4458	2.5401
18	1.5862	1.6529	1.7221	1.7947	1.8696	1.9479	2.0289	2.1132	2.2011	2.2918	2.3870	2.4848	2.5864	2.6925
19	1.6298	1.7024	1.7781	1.8575	1.9398	2.0258	2.1151	2.2083	2.3057	2.4064	2.5123	2.6215	2.7351	2.8541
20	1.6746	1.7534	1.8359	1.9225	2.0125	2.1068	2.2050	2.3077	2.4152	2.5267	2.6442	2.7656	2.8924	3.0253
21	1.7207	1.8060	1.8956	1.9898	2.0880	2.1911	2.2987	2.4115	2.5300	2.6530	2.7830	2.9178	3.0571	3.2068
22	1.7680	1.8601	1.9572	2.0594	2.1663	2.2787	2.3964	2.5200	2.6502	2.7857	2.9291	3.0782	3.2329	3.3992
23	1.8166	1.9159	2.0209	2.1315	2.2475	2.3698	2.4982	2.6334	2.7761	2.9250	3.0829	3.2475	3.4188	3.6032
24	1.8666	1.9734	2.0866	2.2061	2.3318	2.4646	2.6044	2.7519	2.9080	3.0713	3.2447	3.4261	3.6154	3.8194
25	1.9179	2.0326	2.1555	2.2833	2.4192	2.5632	2.7151	2.8757	3.0461	3.2249	3.4150	3.6146	3.8239	4.0486

TABLE 10-4 (cont'd)

No. of Grades	6.25%	6.50%	6.75%	7.00%	7.25%	7.50%	7.75%	No. of Grades	8.00%	8.25%	8.50%	8.75%	9.00%	9.25%	9.50%	No. of Grades
				% Progression (Mid to Mid)								% Progression (Mid to Mid)				
1	1.0000	1.0000	1.0000	1.0000	1.0000	1.0000	1.0000	1	1.0000	1.0000	1.0000	1.0000	1.0000	1.0000	1.0000	1
2	1.0625	1.0650	1.0675	1.0700	1.0725	1.0750	1.0775	2	1.0800	1.0825	1.0850	1.0875	1.0900	1.0925	1.0950	2
3	1.1290	1.1342	1.1396	1.1450	1.1503	1.1556	1.1610	3	1.1664	1.1718	1.1772	1.1826	1.1881	1.1936	1.1990	3
4	1.1996	1.2080	1.2165	1.2252	1.2337	1.2423	1.2510	4	1.2597	1.2685	1.2773	1.2861	1.2950	1.3040	1.3129	4
5	1.2746	1.2866	1.2986	1.3110	1.3231	1.3355	1.3480	5	1.3605	1.3734	1.3859	1.3986	1.4115	1.4246	1.4376	5
6	1.3543	1.3702	1.3862	1.4028	1.4190	1.4357	1.4525	6	1.4693	1.4867	1.5037	1.5210	1.5386	1.5564	1.5742	6
7	1.4390	1.4593	1.4798	1.5010	1.5219	1.5434	1.5651	7	1.5868	1.6093	1.6315	1.6541	1.6771	1.7004	1.7237	7
8	1.5290	1.5542	1.5797	1.6061	1.6322	1.6592	1.6864	8	1.7137	1.7421	1.7702	1.7988	1.8280	1.8577	1.8875	8
9	1.6246	1.6552	1.6863	1.7185	1.7505	1.7836	1.8171	9	1.8508	1.8858	1.9207	1.9562	1.9925	2.0295	2.0668	9
10	1.7261	1.7628	1.8001	1.8388	1.8774	1.9174	1.9570	10	1.9989	2.0414	2.0839	2.1274	2.1718	2.2172	2.2631	10
11	1.8340	1.8774	1.9216	1.9675	2.0135	2.0612	2.1087	11	2.1588	2.2098	2.2610	2.3135	2.3673	2.4223	2.4781	11
12	1.9487	1.9994	2.0513	2.1052	2.1595	2.2158	2.2721	12	2.3315	2.3921	2.4532	2.5160	2.5803	2.6464	2.7135	12
13	2.0705	2.1294	2.1898	2.2526	2.3160	2.3820	2.4482	13	2.5180	2.5894	2.6617	2.7362	2.8125	2.8912	2.9713	13
14	2.1999	2.2678	2.3376	2.4103	2.4840	2.5607	2.6379	14	2.7194	2.8030	2.8879	2.9756	3.0656	3.1586	3.2536	14
15	2.3374	2.4152	2.4954	2.5790	2.6641	2.7528	2.8423	15	2.9370	3.0342	3.1334	3.2360	3.3415	3.4508	3.5627	15
16	2.4835	2.5722	2.6638	2.7595	2.8572	2.9593	3.0626	16	3.1720	3.2845	3.3997	3.5192	3.6422	3.7700	3.9011	16
17	2.6388	2.7394	2.8436	2.9527	3.0643	3.1312	3.2999	17	3.4258	3.5554	3.6887	3.8271	3.9700	4.1187	4.2717	17
18	2.8037	2.9175	3.0355	3.1594	3.2865	3.4198	3.5556	18	3.6999	3.8487	4.0022	4.1620	4.3273	4.4997	4.6775	18
19	2.9790	3.1071	3.2404	3.3806	3.5248	3.6763	3.8311	19	3.9959	4.1662	4.3424	4.5262	4.7168	4.9160	5.1219	19
20	3.1652	3.3091	3.4913	3.6172	3.7803	3.9520	4.1280	20	4.3156	4.5099	4.7115	4.9222	5.1413	5.3707	5.6085	20
21	3.3630	3.5242	3.7270	3.8704	4.0544	4.2484	4.4479	21	4.6608	4.8820	5.1120	5.3529	5.6040	5.8675	6.1413	21
22	3.5732	3.7556	3.9786	4.1413	4.3483	4.5670	4.7926	22	5.0337	5.2848	5.5465	5.8213	6.1084	6.4102	6.7247	22
23	3.7966	3.9997	4.2472	4.4312	4.6636	4.9095	5.1640	23	5.4364	5.7208	6.0180	6.3307	6.6582	7.0031	7.3635	23
24	4.0339	4.2597	4.5339	4.7414	5.0017	5.2777	5.5642	24	5.8713	6.1928	6.5295	6.8846	7.2574	7.6509	8.0630	24
25	4.2861	4.5366	4.8399	5.0733	5.3643	5.6735	5.9954	25	6.3410	6.7037	7.0845	7.4870	7.9106	8.3583	8.8290	25

The process can be reversed when grades and r_{h-l} are known and a midpoint value not in the table is desired. *Warning:* The ratio should never be divided by 2. Ratios do not progress arithmetically.

EXPANDING OR FAN-TYPE PAY STRUCTURE

Pay policy and job demands may require designers to develop a pay structure that varies the difference between midpoints and fans the spread within a pay grade in moving from the lower-level jobs to the higher-level jobs.

A single-structure pay plan that covers a wide number of jobs in an organization can start with entry-level jobs or the lower end of the nonexempt group with a 5.0 percent difference between midpoints and a ±5.0 to 7.5 percent grade spread. A second step in the structure can include skilled clerical workers and experienced production, crafts, and trades workers; and it can involve work requiring greater amounts of responsibility and increasing levels of knowledge and skill. In such a case, the structure design has a 7.5 to 10.0 percent difference between midpoints and a spread of from ±7.5 to 12.5 percent. The third step can include technicians, paraprofessionals, and first- and second-level operating managers. At this stage, the midpoint differences vary from 10.0 to 12.5 percent and the grade spread increases to ±15.0 percent around the midpoint. The fourth step includes administrative, professional, and upper-level operating management personnel; and the midpoint differences vary from 15.0 to 20.0 percent with the grade spread around the midpoint ranging from 20.0 to 25.0 percent (differences in spread relate to other compensation opportunities such as bonuses and the various types of incentive plans frequently made available to this group). A fifth step includes executives and other senior management personnel. Here again, depending on other compensation opportunities, the pay structure may have a 20.0 to 25.0 percent difference between the midpoints and a grade spread as great as ±50 percent on either side of the midpoint. Figure 10-9 describes such an expanding or fan-type pay structure.

Many organizations prefer to use market information for determining both midpoint-to-midpoint pay differences and the spread of pay from midpoint to maximum and midpoint to minimum. There is no doubt that survey data are extremely valuable for establishing a competitive or midpoint pay rate and, from these competitive or midpoint pay rates, appropriate midpoint-to-midpoint pay differences are self-revealing for most.

Many specialists who make extensive use of survey data consider that first and third quartile values from surveys provide valuable information for establishing minimum and maximum pay values for a job or a grade. From examination of many surveys, it does appear that the first and third quartile values generally range from 10 to 13 percent below and above midpoint (mean or median) values. If an organization considers this amount of spread to be practical, then first and third quartile data are valuable. The major issue involved in setting competitive midpoints and ranges from survey data is whether the data are accurate and appropriate.

Proponents of the expanding pay structure have a number of reasons for

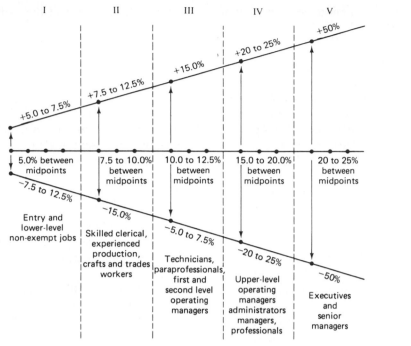

FIGURE 10–9 EXPANDING OR FAN-TYPE PAY STRUCTURE

promoting it. Among these are such points as (1) entry level jobs make minimum demands on the incumbents, (2) incumbents in these entry-level jobs can do little to change the nature of the job, and (3) these incumbents usually move to higher-level jobs. At the other end of the job spectrum, additional arguments concern the need for senior managers and executives to have greater opportunities for pay progression in the senior level jobs and the fact that it takes much more time for a senior level manager to reach a midpoint level of competency.

These considerations are open to review with pay compression daily increasing in importance and the attendant relative pay differences between lower- and middle-level jobs becoming less. Pay compression occurs when pay decreases between jobs having different levels of responsibility, duty, knowledge, and skill requirements. With the reorganization of organizations leading to fewer levels of management and more specialists and with the demand for fewer pay grades and more opportunity for pay increases within the grades, designers of pay structures may not use an expanding or fan-type approach. Rather, they may find it more valuable to use a structure that has a wider spread at the lower pay grades.

There is an additional justification for the narrowing approach. This is that, at the top levels, very few workers are hired or will accept jobs at the lower end of a pay range, but the newly hired employee or the individual who is promoted frequently starts at least at the competitive pay rate and moves up from there. This means that at the upper end of the structure the spread goes only from midpoint to maximum and there is little to no use of the midpoint to minimum range.

INTERLOCKING MULTIPLE PAY STRUCTURES

Organizations often use one evaluation method for determining the worth of lower-paid jobs (crafts and trades, clerical, nonsupervisory workers) and another for higher-paid jobs (technical, professional, administrative, and managerial). The use of more than one method will usually result in a different scatter diagram that may in turn result in a pay policy line with a different slope and y intercept.

The designers and the managers of a multiple-structure pay system must have confidence in their structures and be able to justify the reasonableness and fairness of using more than one. The first step in developing a defense for such a system is to evaluate the higher-level, nonmanagement jobs using the managerial evaluation method and evaluate lower-level nonmanagement jobs using the nonmanagerial evaluation method.

The second step in this process is to determine what the monetary worth of these upper- and lower-level jobs would be in the opposite pay structure. This cross-evaluation identifies the differences in pay received by the jobs in each structure. Answering the following questions will identify the strengths and the weaknesses or differences in the design of the multiple pay structure:

1. How does each job fare under each structure? Does it appear that under one structure a certain job receives a "windfall" or an undeserved higher rate of pay than in the other structure? Which jobs receive unduly harsh pay treatment?

2. Can these differences in pay be justified?

3. Can one structure be used in place of the two structures?

4. Are the jobs being placed in the proper pay structure?

After performing a cross-evaluation, it is possible to develop a scatter diagram from the cross-evaluated jobs to establish a separate pay policy or trend line. The x and y paired coordinate points for each job are the evaluation points received under the evaluation methods used for developing the two pay structures. The lower-level pay structure evaluation method can be used to provide the y axis data points, and the upper-level pay structure evaluation method can be used to provide the x axis data points. Analyzing the data points may reveal a distribution that will produce a trend line that will "kink" or curve dramatically upward or downward, or it may identify a specific break area. The points of the scatter diagram may spread over such a wide area that it prohibits the development of a meaningful regression line.

An analysis of the trend line will assist designers of pay structures in testing the validity of their multiple-structure systems. An inability to relate adjoining or overlapping ends of a pay structure may be a strong indication that there are some weaknesses in the design of one or both structures. These weaknesses should be identified and corrected.

REVIEW OF THE BASIC ELEMENTS OF THE PAY STRUCTURE

This chapter has described the elements of a pay structure that permit rewarding those members who have accepted additional responsibilities for expanding their own competencies and for providing increased and in-depth services to the organization. Thus, the differentials of the pay structure provide the incentive for the extra effort and the essential contributions. Figure 10-10 shows the basic elements of such a structure.

In building a pay structure, the first step is to set midpoint, minimum, and maximum rates, including minimum and maximum rates for each pay grade and for the organization as a whole. Then one must determine the number of grades,

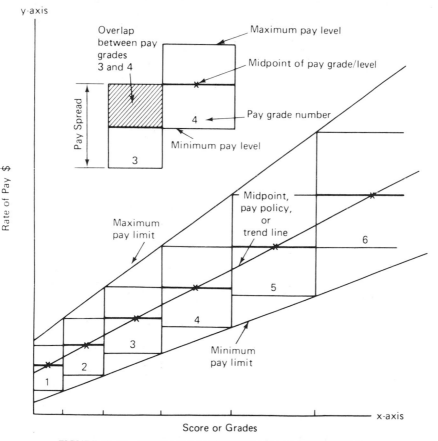

FIGURE 10–10   THE BASIC ELEMENTS OF A PAY STRUCTURE

the range of pay within each grade, the amount of overlap between adjoining pay grades, and the difference between grade midpoints.

Much of the thinking in this area is now in a stage of transition. Where in the past it was not uncommon for a large organization to have three different pay structures with 30 to 40 grades within each, today there is a tendency to simplify the process.

Pressures exerted from both within and without the organization are forcing the redesign of the organizational structure. Such pressures as increased efficiency, equal pay for equal work, and recognition of performance are sparking a reduction in the number of levels within the organizational structure. These factors have the direct effect of reducing the number of grades. With such reduction, it is possible and even necessary to increase both the number and the size of steps within each grade. This, combined with improved performance appraisal techniques, provides the organization with a greater opportunity to recognize performance, to differentiate between the inexperienced and the proven, between those willing to provide the extra effort and those just willing to get by. Survival of the organization depends on its ability to identify the equality of contributions made by its jobholders and to properly compensate them.

As an organization reduces the number of levels in its structure, it reduces the opportunity for its members to gain vertical promotion (grade to grade), but by increasing the spread of the range for a pay grade and the pay importance of each incremental step within the range, it provides an opportunity for horizontal promotion (within a grade). In this manner, the attention of the organization focuses in the proper direction—on the job itself.

Not only does the pay structure weave together internal requirements, but it also enables the organization to compare itself with its external competitors in the human resources marketplace. The ability to make market comparisons, as well as an ability to relate to economic changes, permits the organization to raise the entire level of the pay structure when necessary, making it competitive with its environment without changing internal relationships.

After the pay structure has been completed, it faces the difficult test of workability, understandability, and acceptability. Success requires constant maintenance, which is often monotonous and, in many ways, drudgery. Without maintenance, however, the best-designed and best-built compensation structure will deteriorate and fail in its primary mission—the development of an organizational atmosphere that stimulates employee motivation, resulting in superior performance.

SELECTED READINGS

Burk, Samuel L. H., "A Case History in Salary and Wage Administration," *Personnel*, February 1939, pp. 93–129. This article is a review of the way one company developed a practical application of its job evaluation program and the pitfalls and obstacles it encountered along the way. It reconciles theory with application.

Hay, Edward N., "The Characteristics of Salary Grades," *Personnel*, November 1946, pp. 189–198. An excellent review for developing a sound, symmetrical salary structure. It describes procedures employed in setting up an equitable structure of rate ranges and salary grades. (An additional article by Hay on this subject appeared in *Personnel,* March 1947, pp. 339–352.)

Schuster, Jay R., "Job Evaluation at Xerox: A Single Scale Replaces Four," *Personnel,* May–June 1966, pp. 15–19. This article describes a change in the nonexempt wage structure at Xerox Corporation. The change from four wage structures to one included a review of all compensable factors, resulting in the identification and the weighting of 10 compensable factors. All the nonexempt jobs were then reviewed followed by a reevaluation of all jobs using the revised evaluation system.

Thomsen, David J., and Robert A. Smith, "What Are 'Average' and 'Above Average' Salaries?" *Compensation Review,* Second Quarter, 1974, pp. 18–26. An excellent discussion on the use of logarithmic data, regression lines, and central tendency statistics.

Torrence, George R., "Correcting Out-of-Line Rates of Pay," *Management Record,* September 1960, pp. 10–13. A discussion of the way some companies bring their outsize salaries into line without impairing employee morale.

Part **3**

Completing the Compensation Package

P art 2 presented an in-depth approach for evaluating job worth. Its goal was to furnish compensation managers with sufficient information to allow them to design a compensation structure—one, it is hoped, that would provide equality of compensation for those jobs requiring equal skills, efforts, and responsibility under similar working conditions and that would provide equity of pay for jobs requiring differing levels of those factors. Additionally part 2 recognized forces external to the organization and their influence over pay practices. Part 3 now analyzes the other compensation practices necessary to attract and retain employees and stimulate superior performance.

In the beginning of the twentieth century there was a boom in the movement from a rural, agricultural economy to an urban, industrial economy in many nations. As more workers moved away from the security of farming, hunting, and fishing, money became necessary not only for advancement but also as an increasingly important factor of survival.

The managers of organizations and the designers of pay systems in the expanding industrial empires of the late nineteenth and early twentieth centuries recognized the importance of money as a basis for stimulating hard work. The pay earned in the industrial complexes offered security and survival and the inherent promise of a better life for the workers and their families. The workers' expectations of an improved life-style was an exceedingly strong stimulus that caused them to expend the efforts necessary for organizations to succeed. With the opportunity to earn more money and the ever-increasing array of available goods and services to spend it on, hard work and effort had a positive, motivational meaning to most workers.

Under these conditions, managers and engineers began designing work methods that made it easier for workers to produce larger outputs on their jobs. These experts focused on standardization, specialization, and simplification of job activities and on setting performance standards. Employees focused *their* attention on purchasing goods and services with the money earned in meeting or exceeding work standards.

Less than 25 years after identifying money as a prime motivator of worker effort and after developing procedures and methods for improving and expanding worker productivity, managers began to question the value of money as a motivator. Managers and experts in work design realized that "man does not live by bread alone." By the 1920s, behavioral scientists began identifying factors other than money that strongly influence employee behavior in the workplace.

Studies conducted at the Hawthorne Plant of Western Electric in Cicero, Illinois, became a landmark for recognizing the importance of the individual and the various ways in which a worker can either facilitate or block the achievement of organizational goals and objectives. Elton Mayo and Fritz J. Roethlisberger, the principal investigators in this study, thus began a long line of behavioral research that has provided important insights into people and their jobs.

From the 1940s through the 1960s, "need" theories were introduced and accepted in the world of work. Motivational psychologists attempted to order human needs and relate workplace behaviors to them. Studies by behavioral scientists investigating human needs often stressed the relative *unimportance* of money or pay as a stimulus for improving workplace performance.

Whether employees of the 1960s were basically any different from those of the early 1900s is difficult to determine, but the conditions under which they worked were certainly different. In the 1900s, economic security was a long-dreamed-of goal and an individual responsibility. A better life for themselves and their children was, for the first time for most members of the working class, an achievable expectation. Then, from 1914 through 1945, two world wars, a number of regionalized economic recessions, and a major worldwide depression instilled a sense of insecurity and a fear that a better life might not be possible through hard work and effort in the industrial complexes.

Following World War II, the industrial nations implemented sociopolitical programs aimed at guaranteeing worker security. It was in this environment that behavioral scientists began questioning the value of money as a motivator of human effort.

In the late 1960s and early 1970s new concerns for the economic security of workers were voiced. Many people questioned the ability of the state to guarantee a good life "from womb to tomb." Worker effort once again was thought to be the key ingredient for maintaining and improving the standard of living. Economic security once again depended, it was thought, on improved worker performance and expanded productivity.

By the mid-1970s, with expanding rates of inflation, scarcity of resources, and worldwide concern about the way to allocate these scarce resources, disposable income once again attained the importance to the worker that it had in the first quarter of the twentieth century. The theories have traveled full circle.

Managers in all types of organizations once again recognize that in the compensation offered to employees lies the opportunity to attract and retain quality personnel who are able and willing to provide superior performance.

Chapter 11 of part 3 examines the employee benefits and services component of the compensation package. Over the past 20 years, employee benefits and services have become such an important part of compensation that it is difficult to attract and retain quality personnel unless this package meets certain established and recognized minimum standards.

Chapter 12 analyzes a number of individual and group pay-for-performance plans that provide extra income to encourage employees to improve their output. Linking the amount of pay to work output is a vital part of many effective pay policies. There is no reason to doubt that performance-related payments will continue to be a crucial link in transforming employee, technological, and raw material resources into outputs of sufficient quality and quantity to provide the capital and the profit necessary for the continued existence and growth of organizations.

Chapter 13 centers on performance appraisal. If there is an ambiguous area in the entire compensation process, it is in the assessment of worker performance. Many jobs in the service and technological economy of today do not lend themselves to counting output as a means of identifying acceptable performance. Performance appraisal has become a "damned if you do, damned if you don't" process. Appraising performance is one of management's most important responsibilities. All too often, it is done poorly and reduces workers' performance instead of being a factor leading to performance improvement. Differences in performance must be recognized, but they must be measured in a manner that discriminates according to performance, not to other criteria.

Finally, compensation managers must administer the compensation program. Labor and merit budgets must be developed and implemented. Capital available for compensation payments must be allocated among the many options available for rewarding service and contribution. The maintenance of systematic records, and the management of the compensation program are issues that daily confront managers. Chapter 14 discusses these issues.

Employee acceptance of the compensation package is a vital goal. Imparting to each member of an organization an awareness that the design and the administration of the compensation package is inherently fair and just requires deliberate, thoughtful effort. It is vital to communicate the what, why, how, when, where, and who of compensation. Chapter 14 also provides insights into methods and procedures for improving the communication of such information.

11

Employee Benefits
And Services

CONTENT

Chapter 11 presents and discusses major classes or kinds of benefits and services and the methods used to cost them. In addition, it discusses the flexible or cafeteria benefits plan as an involvement procedure that permits employees to participate in decisions affecting their welfare, leading to a better understanding and appreciation of the benefits made available to them. In turn, employees tend to develop a more positive attitude toward employers, which leads to improved contributions and increased productivity.

GOALS

Upon concluding this chapter, you should be familiar with available benefits and services and have a working knowledge of how to classify and cost them. In addition, you should understand the implications of the flexible or cafeteria benefits plan and be aware of its strengths and some of the difficulties that block its development.

The very expensive but often forgotten stepchild of the total compensation package is that segment frequently called *fringe benefits*. These benefits are primarily the in-kind payments employees receive in addition to the payments they receive in the form of money. At one time, fringe benefits were of marginal importance, but this is no longer true. In many organizations today, they account for at least 35 percent of the total compensation cost for each employee, and possibly in the next decade they will reach 50 percent. (Some organizations have already exceeded this point.) When an element of the compensation package reaches this proportion, it is no longer marginal. The fringe benefits of yesterday have evolved into the employee benefits and services of today.

The rapid expansion of the benefits program over the past three decades has been attributed to four causes:

1. The imposition of wage ceilings during World War II forced organizations to offer more and greater benefits in place of wage increases to attract new employees and to keep current workers.

2. With the increasing unacceptability of autocratic management and the decline of paternalism, instead of using threats or a variety of protective procedures, organizations have used benefits to gain employee compliance and loyalty, which has resulted in a more acceptable form of paternalism.

3. Possibly the most important reason has been the rise of union influence and the steady increase of wages to the point where they now satisfy the basic needs of the employees they represent. In turn, this has led to increased interest and bargaining for more and greater benefits.

4. In recent years, inflation, rising wage levels, and heavier income tax burdens have aroused increased interest in tax shelters at lower levels in the organizational structure. Many employers are now providing an even greater array of benefits that employees consider valuable. This approach reduces the tax burden of the employer and, at the same time, increases the disposable income available to employees by providing benefits and services they would otherwise have to purchase with after-tax dollars.

Although the emphasis on benefits is of rather recent vintage, progressive benefit plans had their origins prior to the twentieth century. The Wallpaper Craftsmen and the National Wallpaper Company negotiated a guaranteed annual wage in 1894, and by the early 1900s, many companies had instituted insurance programs.

The depression of the 1930s caused the federal government to institute a variety of programs to provide workers with some form of economic security when they were faced with an inability to work due to lack of employment opportunities, health problems, or old age (discussed in chapter 3).

Today, the number of different benefits and services offered by employers ranges into the hundreds. In addition to paying employees fairly and adequately for their contributions in the performance of their jobs, organizations also assume a social obligation for the welfare of employees and their dependents. Although these social benefits are not directly related to product or service output, employers expect that they will improve productivity—first, through increased job satisfaction leading to improved quality and reduction in turnover and absenteeism, and, second, by instilling in each employee a sense of security leading to improved loyalty and morale. Although many compensation and motivation experts question that employee benefits and services stimulate improved worker performance, there is little doubt that an unacceptable or limited package may deter high-quality workers from seeking employment with a particular employer or may cause a worker to move to an employer who offers a better package of benefits and services. A good program assists in developing a motivational atmosphere that will stimulate an individual to join an organization and stay with it.

Benefits and services become complicated very quickly because of the number of available components, the variety of optional features within a component, and their legal and financial interactions, thus requiring the full-time efforts of specialists. It is, however, the responsibility of the compensation manager to call on these specialists, to be able to communicate with them, and to use their talents for the benefit of all members of the organization. To communicate effectively, the compensation specialist must know the compensation components that comprise employee benefits and services, their distinguishing features, and what they provide to employees.

Employee benefits are those compensation components made available to employees that provide (1) protection in case of health-related problems and (2) income at some future date or occasion (e.g., upon retirement, termination of employment, or meeting of certain objective criteria). *Employee services* are compensation components that may or may not be included within an employee benefits program. These service components further contribute to the welfare of the employee by filling some kind of a demand. These services usually enable the employee to enjoy a better life-style or to meet social or personal obligations while minimizing employment-related costs.

EMPLOYEE BENEFITS

Most compensation components included within employee benefits are made available through some kind of an insurance plan. A very important group of benefit components, however, are frequently non-insurance based and provide income to the employee at some future date.

Employee benefits can be further classified under these six major groups: (1) disability income continuation, (2) loss-of-job income continuation, (3) deferred income, (4) spouse or family income continuation, (5) health and accident protection, and (6) property and liability protection. Each of these groups contains a number of compensation components. Each of these components may have a variety of features that may be made available only to certain employees or certain groups of employees. An identification of the major compensation components within each of the six groups and a brief description of some of the more significant features follows.

Disability Income Continuation

When employees are unable to work because of an accident or some health-related problem, disability income continuation payments assist them in maintaining their existing life-style without major modification. Various disability income continuation components provide weekly or monthly payments in lieu of the regular earned income paycheck. The following 11 components are among the more commonly available disability income continuation plans. Although all components will seldom be available to employees, components can be packaged to maximize employee protection while maintaining costs within reasonable limits for the employer. The major components are:

1. Short-term disability
2. Long-term disability (LTD)
3. Workers' Compensation
4. Nonoccupational disability
5. Social Security
6. Travel accident insurance
7. Sick leave
8. Supplemental disability insurance
9. Accidental death and dismemberment
10. Group life insurance: Total permanent disability (TPD)
11. Retirement plans

Short-term Disability or Accident and Sickness Plans (A&S)—This component provides payment while the insured is absent from work due to an accident or illness. The benefits provided by these plans usually range from 50 to 75 percent of the employee's base pay. Most plans have a waiting period before payment begins. For example, many contracts require a seven-day waiting period with regard to sickness. In other words, the employee does not collect any benefits until the eighth day of absence due to an illness. On the other hand, there frequently is no waiting period for an accident claim, and when there is one, it seldom exceeds three days. Often, there is a limit to the number of weeks of payment per disability; 26 weeks is a commonly used period for this short-term income maintenance program.

Long-term disability (LTD)—Long-term disability insurance is an alternative method for providing incapacitated employees with long-term security. These employees are probably those most in need of assistance because they have the burden of added medical expenses with reduced or no income.

Many LTD plans are funded in conjunction with the pension plan of the organization, although some LTD plans use self-insurance funding procedures, and many more use the normal insurance approach with specific premiums and reserves to cover all claims. The LTD claims for a large group averages slightly less than five years.[1] LTD plans usually replace between 50 to 75 percent of base

---

[1]James H. Brennan, Jr., "What Makes LTD a Special Benefits Problem?" *Compensation Review,* First Quarter, 1974, pp. 26–34.

pay. Payments usually graduate in size with the largest payments in the first two years and then a leveling of payment for the remaining years.

Workers' Compensation—State laws now require almost every employer to provide employees with occupational disability insurance. Although income benefits vary among the 50 states for permanent total disability, most states will pay lifetime benefits, although a few limit payment periods from 330 to 650 weeks. The payments range from a minimum of $87.50 to a maximum of $608.00 a week, depending on the wages of the disabled employee and the state laws. Some states also have a maximum limit for payments. Most states use a formula of two-thirds of the average weekly wage to calculate disability payments. The benefits for a temporary disability are, in most cases, similar to those for permanent total disability, except that the period of payment is limited to the time of disability.

Each state has its own schedule of income benefits for types of injuries, dismemberments, or loss of use. Funds are also available for rehabilitation and for maintenance expenses while the worker is undergoing retraining. (An additional discussion of Workers' Compensation laws is in chapter 3.)

Nonoccupational Disability—Workers in Puerto Rico and in five states— California, Hawaii, New Jersey, New York, and Rhode Island—who incur temporary disability arising from nonoccupational illness or injury receive partial income maintenance through these disability laws. The duration of these payments is normally 26 weeks. The actual amount of payment depends on the wage of the employee before being disabled. Employee contributions provide a major funding source for these plans.

Social Security—The Social Security Act of 1935 established the federal Old-Age, Survivors, Disability, and Health Insurance System (OASDHI). Under this system, totally and permanently disabled employees may be eligible for cash disability payments and Social Security. To qualify for Social Security- OASDHI Act benefits, workers must have spent a sufficient period of time in covered employment or self-employment and must be disabled as defined by the law. Payments begin after a worker has waited five full calendar months and continue to age 65. At that time, the worker is transferred to the retirement rolls.

Travel Accident Insurance—Organizations that require employees to travel frequently carry travel accident insurance. This plan provides additional protection in cases where employees are disabled or killed on a work assignment. Payments usually start the first day of the disability and are usually either a fixed schedule that varies disability payment by base earnings or a flat percentage of the regular rate of pay.

Sick Leave—Sick leave assures employees of pay when they are unable to work because of illness. Many organizations allow a specific number of days of leave each year, with 12 days (or one day a month) being a fairly common figure. Some limit is usually set on the number of days an employee can accumulate. Many organizations limit the time to a one- or two-year accumulation to provide protection in case of an illness of two to four weeks or more. Short-term health and accident disability insurance then takes over and, for even longer periods of illness, long-term insurance and Social Security come into effect. Some organizations now pay employees for the accumulation of sick days up to a set number, for example, up to six months' base pay upon retirement.

A recent trend has been for organizations to "buy back" unused sick leave time by paying their employees a daily equivalent pay for each day of sick leave not used. When organizations feel that sick leave is encouraging absenteeism, policy is tightened by such measures as requiring a doctor's written explanation of the illness, not paying for the first day, and, in some cases, reducing the number of days allotted. One organization has what it calls a "well pay" benefit. An employee with perfect attendance during the month receives an extra day's pay for that month.

Other organizations, however, object to providing double payment simply to make sure their employees report to work. They feel that they are already paying for employees to be there and that those who come to work get a "presenteeism" bonus. The view regarding double payment may be legitimate, but absenteeism and abuse of sick leave are also legitimate concerns. There is no doubt that sick leave pay does encourage unjustified absenteeism.

Supplemental Disability Insurance—Some organizations provide a small and select group of their top management employees with supplemental disability income plans. These plans are designed to bring the disability income available to top executives more closely in line with what they receive as regular pay and are designed to minimize reverse discrimination. (Reverse discrimination in this case means that, although lower-paid employees may receive disability payments that equal anywhere from 50 percent to over 100 percent of their base pay, top executives will receive only from 10 percent to 50 percent of their base pay.)

Accidental Death and Dismemberment—This plan provides a range of benefits in case of accidental loss of limbs or sight. The actual amount of benefits varies according to the extent of the injury or dismemberment. Most employees required to travel in the performance of company business receive a full range of life and accident insurance while away from their home base.

Group Life Insurance: Total Permanent Disability (TPD)—Many group life insurance plans have a total permanent disability feature. This feature grants an employee equal monthly payments over a period ranging from 60 to 120 payments. When the face value of the policy is small, the number of payments may be below 60.

Retirement Plans—Many retirement plans have some form of disability retirement benefits. These plans often have some service and age requirements. A commonly used service requirement is 10 years, and the age limit may be 50.

To limit the undesirable possibility of the disability benefit reducing the average retirement benefits, many organizations have added a long-term disability option to their benefit programs.

Loss-of-Job Income Continuation

Loss-of-job income continuation plans are designed to assist workers during short-term periods of unemployment due to layoffs and termination. The seven major compensation components that comprise this group of compensation benefits are:

1. Unemployment insurance
2. Trade Adjustment Assistance (TAA)
3. Supplemental Unemployment Benefit Insurance (SUB)
4. Guaranteed Annual Income (GAI)
5. Individual account plan
6. Severance pay
7. Job contract

Unemployment Insurance—The major loss-of-job income continuation component is the unemployment insurance services provided through state-sponsored actions under the Social Security Act of 1935. Depending on the laws of each state, there are minimums and maximums to unemployment coverage with the formulae used to calculate actual unemployment payments using two variables—amount of weekly base pay and time employed. A typical computation of unemployment payment is 50 percent of base pay up to 66.7 percent of the weekly wage for employees in the state.

Initially, the Social Security Act of 1935 provided up to 26 weeks of coverage under state laws. "Extended" benefits were established under the Employment Security Administration Act of 1970, granting additional coverage up to 13 weeks during periods of high unemployment. In December 1974 the federal Supplemental Unemployment Benefits Program was initiated in response to high unemployment, providing an additional 26 weeks of coverage to workers who had exhausted both regular and extended benefits.

Employers pay federal and state employment insurance tax. Employees usually pay nothing. The federal tax is on the first $6,000 of earnings at a rate of 3.4 percent, which is split into 2.7 percent for the state and 0.7 percent for the federal government. It is possible for a particular organization to earn a credit for the full 2.7 percent based on its unemployment experience rating and the unemployment tax regulations of a specific state. Some states have a maximum rate that goes higher than 2.7 percent and a taxable wage base that is in excess of $6,000.

Trade Adjustment Assistance (TAA)—Workers who have been laid off or have had their working hours cut by 20 percent or more because of increased imports are eligible for special benefits under the Trade Act of 1974. These benefits include cash payments of up to 70 percent of a worker's weekly wage for up to one year while the worker is looking for a new job.

Supplemental Unemployment Benefit Insurance (SUB)—Chapter 4 describes in detail this kind of plan. Basically, SUB plans have been developed through collective bargaining. Within limits set by the amount available in the SUB fund, eligible employees who are out of work through no fault of their own may receive up to 95 percent of their base pay. These SUB payments are usually coordinated with unemployment insurance payments.

Guaranteed Annual Income (GAI)—Chapter 4 also describes in detail this kind of plan. GAI plans are normally found within a collective bargaining situation and employees who receive such protection are guaranteed pay for a specific number of hours worked per year (e.g.: 1,500; 1,800; 2,080).

Individual Account Plan—This plan requires the employer to make certain predetermined and negotiated contributions to the account of each covered employee. The fund provides payments to the employee when there are work suspensions other than disciplinarian layoffs or labor disputes.

Severance Pay—Although not as common as those previously mentioned, a one-time payment upon severing a worker's employment is paid by some organizations. These payments may range from two to three days' pay to as much as one year's pay, to a certain fixed amount. The payment frequently depends on the total length of service before separation.

Job Contract—This kind of plan is usually made available to senior-level management employees and to highly skilled and desired professionals. Individuals receiving such a contract are guaranteed a certain income for a specific period of time with certain obligations normally required of the recipient. If, for any reason, the employer terminates employment, the employee receives the payments due on the unfinished terms of the contract.

Deferred Income

The opportunity to retire with economic security after completing a useful work life is a basic goal of almost all employees. This goal increases in importance as workers age. In the past, retirement did not appear to become an important issue until the employee passed the age of the mid 40s or early 50s. Currently, however, even much younger employees have become increasingly concerned about what the future holds and the income security and the life-style they may expect on reaching normal retirement age.

The compensation components identified within this dimension of the compensation system provide financial assistance for workers after they retire and also increase the size of their future estates. Over the years, employers have established the following kinds of compensation components to assist employees accumulate capital and meet future financial goals. The components are:

1. Social Security
2. Pension plans
3. Profit sharing
4. Savings and thrift plans
5. Keogh plans
6. Individual retirement accounts (IRAs)
7. Simplified employee pension plans (SEP)
8. Stock purchase plans
9. Stock option plans
10. Stock grants
11. Tax-sheltered annuities
12. Tax-sheltered purchases
13. Investment trusts

Social Security—Today, millions of Americans are the beneficiaries of the federal Social Security program, while many more millions are paying premiums to qualify for Social Security benefits. Social Security now provides retirement income to those electing to retire at the age of 62. Maximum benefits become available after a worker reaches 65, although it is possible for an employee to increase benefits slightly by working until the age of 72. The actual amount of retirement benefits depends on the age at start of retirement, the recipient's years of work, average earnings during that period, and number of eligible dependents at the time benefits start.

Beginning in June 1975, Social Security benefits were linked to the Consumer Price Index (CPI). Each year that the CPI increases by 3 percent or more, benefits will be adjusted upward in the same way. If, however, Congress increases benefits in a given year, there will be no cost-of-living adjustment for the following year.

Pension Plans—Possibly the most costly and complicated part of the deferred income benefits program is the pension plan. Employer-provided retirement programs, including Social Security costs, in many cases, account for approximately 35 percent of the cost of all benefits. In this area, the compensation manager will require the counsel of a pension specialist. The pension plan must not only provide adequate retirement benefits, it must also meet the approval of a number of federal agencies and, in many states, comply with a variety of state laws.

Each pension plan must qualify under certain Internal Revenue tax codes if the employer wishes to deduct pension costs as a business expense for income tax purposes, and if the benefits accrued to the employees are not to be considered as taxable income until benefits are distributed to them.

In addition to the Internal Revenue tax codes, most pension plans must now comply with the Employee Retirement Income Security Act of 1974 (ERISA), which places strict requirements on privately operated pension plans. The Taft-Hartley Act also requires the unionized company to permit its unions to participate in the administration of its pension plan.

Most pension plans take the form of either group pensions, deferred profit sharing, or savings plans. To provide the employee with the best set of retirement benefits, each organization must design its own plan, taking into consideration the type of organization; the range in type of benefits offered; and the basic needs, characteristics, and demands of its employees.

The *group pension plan* is the basic approach, although organizations often combine it with some form of deferred profit-sharing or savings plan to enhance its value. Usually, these extra monies are placed in a trust fund and prudently invested for further gains. Supplemental retirement funds accrued in this manner provide many employees with their only opportunity for creating an estate. (Unfortunately, trust fund management has not always performed according to expectations.)

Some organizations provide for the total funding of their group pension plans, whereas others require some share of employee contributions. By requiring employee contributions, it is possible to provide more liberal retirement benefits.

All pension plans are concerned with the following four basic issues:

1. *Standard retirement age.* In most cases, 65 has been considered the standard retirement age. Pressures have been brought to bear to reduce this to 62, 60, and even 55. Some unions have demanded the 30-and-out option (retirement after 30 years of service) that permits retirement of some employees in their late 40s. The federal government enacted legislation in 1978 that raised the age of forced retirement to 70. Amendments to the Age Discrimination in Employment Act are discussed in chapter 3.

2. *Size of benefits.* The size of benefits has been steadily increasing, and the influence of inflation has resulted in some pension plans being tied to cost-of-living indexes.

Various methods are available for determining retirement income. One of these is the percentage formula method that includes a certain base pay and a base rate. Procedures for determining these two values include the average pay earned by employees during their total employment, or the pay of the last five years or even of the highest five years of pay. The base rate may be as low as 20 percent and as high as 75 percent. Some methods are related directly to length of employment, whereas others are simply a flat rate after reaching a required number of years of employment.

Many pension plans are providing from $600 to over $1,500 a month to those employees retiring at the age of 65 with 30 years of service.

3. *Early retirement.* Any retirement before age 60 has been considered early retirement. The 30-and-out program resulting in retirement opportunities for many in their 50s would warrant this designation. Some organizations permit employees to retire, with reduced pensions, as early as 10 to 15 years before the normal retirement date. A major reason for early retirement is to open more jobs for younger employees. In times of escalating prices, however, early retirement is not as desirable as during periods of a stable economy, and many older employees hold on to their jobs to earn that extra increment of pay to cover added costs of living.

4. *Vesting.* Vesting refers to earned pension rights that are not forfeitable for any reason. (The employees' rights to benefits attributable to their own

contributions can never be forfeited.) With respect to employer contributions, there are three alternative formulas for achieving vested pension rights under the Pension Reform Act of 1974 (ERISA). They are as follows:

1. 100 percent vesting after 10 years of service.

2. 25 percent vesting after five years of service, increasing 5 percent a year to 50 percent vesting after ten years, and by 10 percent a year to 100 percent vesting after 15 years.

3. 50 percent vesting after five years of service if the employee's age and years of service total 45 (or after ten years of service, if less), and increasing by 10 percent a year thereafter.

The Pension Benefit Guaranty Corporation (PBGC), part of the Department of Labor, administers pension plan termination insurance programs. The corporation provides insurance protection for employer liability upon termination of a pension plan.

A voluntary portability program permits the tax-free transfer of vested pension benefits. The PBGC also administers this program. Employees may place their benefits in this clearinghouse. If the former employer releases the vested rights when the employee leaves the business, the right may then be transferable to the next employer's qualified plan without tax consequences. It is also possible to maintain the funds in PBGC until the employee retires, at which time the funds are either paid out to the retiree or used to purchase an annuity from an insurance company.

Many pension plans permit an employee upon retirement to elect to receive a reduced pension so that the pension continues in force after death, granting the spouse continued income. Other plans allow the spouse to receive from 20 to 50 percent of the normal retirement income. This is more costly than the first option and has been thought of as being unfair to those who have no spouse.

Profit Sharing—Although profit-sharing plans are discussed in some detail in chapter 12, the *deferred profit-sharing plan* merits attention here. In this program, a certain amount of company profits is credited to the account of each employee. Employees or their beneficiaries receive these benefits upon retirement or death or under specifically stated circumstances such as disability, severance, or emergencies.

Savings and Thrift Plans—Many organizations have developed employee *savings plans* that encourage employees to set aside certain amounts of their earnings in order to have a more secure and happier retirement. The organization stimulates such a program by matching a certain percentage of the employee's savings—usually ranging from 50 to 100 percent. Most programs specify a limit to the amount an employee can place in such a plan. This limit usually ranges from 5 to 10 percent of the employee's pay. The total savings are then placed in a trust fund and invested for distribution on retirement. There are two types of savings plans: (1) a long-range program that focuses on retirement, and (2) the short-range type. The thrift or short-term savings plans are popular and rapidly growing benefits. When they meet certain qualifications, they provide tax breaks to both employee and employer. A primary requirement is that both employer and employee contribute and that the allocation of company funds among participants be proportionate to contributions. Most plans now include all employees. (In a union shop, however, the plan requires the acceptance of the bargaining group.) Frequently, eligibility requires one year of service and/or that the employee be at least 21 years old.

Although there is a tendency to permit employees to contribute beyond certain preset requirements, most plans allow them to contribute 6 percent of their pay. Most companies match this with a contribution of from 50 to 100 percent.

The vesting consideration is the principal difference between the thrift/short-term savings plan and the long-term savings plan. The short-term plans usually grant the employee full vesting rights to employer contributions from two to four years after the contribution is made, whereas in the long-term plan it may require 15 years.

Keogh Plans, Individual Retirement Accounts or Annuities (IRAs), and Simplified Employee Pension Plans (SEP)—Special acts of Congress established these three plans to enable employees meeting certain conditions to supplement their existing pension plans or to enable those not covered by a tax-qualified pension or profit-sharing plan to contribute to their own retirement accounts.

The SEP plan merges the normal employer-provided pension plan with an IRA. It permits employers to establish a simple pension plan that is easy to administer and explain and that stipulates how much the employer can contribute to their employees' IRAs.

Stock Purchase Plans—Another way to promote employee savings and assist employees develop an estate is to establish a stock ownership plan for employees. Such a plan not only encourages thrift but stimulates increased employee identification with the company through ownership. Two different purchasing procedures may be used, as follows:

1. *Payroll Deduction—Open Market.* Each payday, a designated broker receives the authorized payroll deduction of each employee for purchasing shares of the company stock on the open market. The broker purchases shares of stock equivalent to the payroll deduction for each employee.

2. *Payroll Deduction—Mass Purchasing.* The company itself accumulates funds from employee deductions and purchases stock on the open market in a bulk order. It then distributes full shares equivalent to employee contributions at certain specified times.

Recent changes in federal law have stimulated renewed interest in employee retirement programs and encouraged employee ownership of stock in the company. Employee Stock-Ownership Plans (ESOPs) permit employers to take advantage of certain tax privileges when granting stock to employees. Past variations of the ESOP have been the retirement plan used by Sears, Roebuck and the plan known as the Kelso Plan (used by companies to raise capital).

In the ESOP, a company borrows money from a financial institution, using its stock as security. Over a prescribed period of time, the company repays the loan. With each loan repayment, a certain amount of the stock that was used as security for the loan is placed into an Employee Stock-Ownership Trust (ESOT) for distribution at *no cost* to all employees. This stock then becomes part of an employee profit-sharing or retirement program. Not only do employees receive the stock upon retirement, but they also receive special tax credits for the value of the stock that the company bought for them. The ESOP plans qualifying for tax benefits under the Tax Reform Act of 1976 are called TRASOPS.

Additional benefits of the plan to the company are as follows:

1. The company can sell its stock and redeem it without reducing the true value of the stock (because it is held by the financial institution as security for the loan).

2. The company can increase its working capital, cash flow, and net worth.

3. The company can pay off the loan and redeem the stock through the use of pretax dollars and, at the same time, receive special tax credits.

Stock Option Plans—Some businesses provide designated employees with the opportunity to purchase set amounts of company stock at a specific price within a prescribed time period. Stock options are normally made available to key officials whose actions have measurable effect on the end results of the business. There are a wide variety of stock option plans; a number of them are further described in chapter 15, Board of Directors and Senior Manager Compensation.

Stock Grants—Stock grant plans assist select groups of employees to acquire stock in the business without any cost to them. Normally, certain specified criteria must be met in order for the official to receive the grant. These plans are described in detail in chapter 15.

Tax-sheltered Annuities, Tax-sheltered Purchases, and Investment Trusts—These plans are deferred income plans provided by organizations to assist employees in developing sizeable estates and sheltering their income from income tax levies.

Spouse and Family Income Protection

Most employees have dependents and, from their work-related efforts, they attempt to ensure the future welfare of their dependents in case of their death. One component, life insurance, and a number of other compensation components previously identified and described have specific features to assist a worker's dependents in the event of such a calamity. The major components available to protect workers' dependents are:

1. Pension plans
2. Social Security
3. Life insurance
4. Workers' compensation
5. Accidental death and dismemberment
6. Travel accident insurance

Pension Plans—Many pension plans have a joint and survivor life income features that normally grant the spouse and, at times, children, until reaching the age of 18, with certain postretirement monthly income payments. When an employee selects such an option, the monthly pension payments to the employee are actuarially reduced. Preretirement spouse and family death benefits are an included feature in most pension plans. Eligibility requirements for such benefits are usually age and service.

Social Security—Social Security also provides beneficiaries of deceased workers covered by Social Security with certain payments. These survivors can be the spouse, dependent children, dependent parents, and, under certain conditions, the divorced spouse. The amount of the payments depends on the (1) earnings of the worker, (2) length of time in the Social Security program, (3) age when benefit payments started, (4) age and number of recipients other than worker, and (5) state of health of recipients other than worker.

Life Insurance—This component provides financial assistance to the family upon the death of the insured. Normally, the life insurance program is part of a group plan. The group plan permits the organization and the employee to benefit from lower rates based on the total value of the group policy.

The policies usually have some fixed limit of coverage with a dollar maximum frequently ranging between $150,000 to $200,000. A rule of thumb quite often used in determining the amount of coverage is to have it equal two years' wages or salaries. Some organizations also tend to increase life insurance coverage with increasing years of service. Some policies permit employees to increase their coverage at a nominal amount and to purchase life insurance for dependents. If many employees request such options, they can usually take advantage of some group feature that permits reduced rate.

Most companies pay 100 percent of the base premium, with employees paying for any additional available options. When employees contribute to the plan, the split ranges from 50–50 between employer and employee to 80–20, with the employer paying the 80 percent.

Most life insurance plans have such standard features as the following:

1. Including all employees regardless of health or physical condition.

2. Permitting an employee to convert to an individual life insurance policy without a physical examination upon leaving the organization (within a prescribed time limit).

3. Insuring employee and dependents for 30 days after separation.

4. Continuing coverage for retired employees.

Workers' Compensation—Workers' Compensation insurance also provides burial expenses and income benefits for widows and children.

Accidental Death and Dismemberment—This component provides a fixed lump-sum benefit to a beneficiary when the death of an employee is accidental.

Travel Accident Insurance—This previously described plan provides beneficiaries of an employee killed while on a work assignment with a lump-sum payment.

Health and Accident Protection

Organizations provide their employees with a wide variety of insurance services to assist them and their families maintain a normal standard of living when unusual or unexpected health-related adversities occur. Health care insurance plans cover medical, surgical, and hospital bills resulting from an accident or illness. Among the more commonly provided health-related compensation components are:

1. Basic medical, hospital, and surgical insurance
2. Major medical
3. Comprehensive physical
4. In-house medical services
5. Post-retirement medical
6. Comprehensive health plan
7. HMOs
8. Workers' Compensation
9. Dental
10. Vision
11. Hearing-aid
12. Social Security (Medicare)

Basic Medical, Hospital, and Surgical Insurance—These basic health care plans take two major forms—commercial insurance or hospital service plans—for protecting employees against expenses resulting from such care.

Hospitalization plans offered by commercial insurance companies usually provide fixed cash benefits for hospital room and board as well as for certain other hospital charges. This plan pays directly to the insured who, in turn, pays the hospital.

The hospital service plan provides service rather than direct cash payments, paying for room, board, and other necessary hospital services. The major national provider of these services is the Blue Cross system.

The *surgical expense benefits* are similar to the hospitalization plans. Both the commercial insurance companies and the service plans follow a similar procedure of listing a schedule of payments for different types of operations. Some plans allow for doctors' charges to relate to the patient's income. Patients having an income below a certain level pay nothing more than that listed on the schedule of payments, whereas patients having an income above the prescribed level may be charged a higher fee and may be responsible for the difference between the charged fee and the scheduled payment. Currently, most plans reimburse surgical fees on a 100-percent-of-reasonable-and-customary-charge basis. Blue Shield is the surgical counterpart of the Blue Cross hospital service plan.

Other medical coverage included in *medical insurance plans* continues to expand every year. Some of the more important additions are payments for *diagnostic visits* to the doctor's office or *home visits* by the doctor. Although still rare among medical benefits, the *annual physical* is beginning to appear in more health insurance programs.

Another recent addition to health care insurance plans is the extension of comprehensive health care benefits to include some of the survivors of deceased company employees and retirees.

A relatively new provision in medical insurance programs is for outpatient and nonhospital *psychiatric care*. These programs frequently have some form of a coinsurance requirement ranging from 10 to 15 percent. Usually, provisions limit the number of visits permitted in a fixed period of time as well as the charges accrued in one year.

Opening the door to emotional health benefits also includes *alcohol and drug rehabilitation services*. Employees suffering from alcohol and drug abuse problems are receiving medical treatment under these recently developed psychiatric outpatient benefits programs.

Major Medical—This is a group insurance plan designed to assist employees pay medical bills incurred because of serious or prolonged illnesses. Major medical plans will usually have the following features:

1. Deductible charge—usually the first $100.

2. Lifetime dollar maximum—usually $250,000.

3. Stop-loss feature—usually employee pays maximum of $1,000 out-of-pocket costs in any one year and plan covers all additional costs.

Comprehensive Physical—Some organizations now provide all employees with an annual comprehensive physical. This has been a long-standing benefit for senior management officials in many organizations.

In-house Medical Services—Some large organizations have their own medical staff. When such a staff is available, employees may receive not only free medical care, but also pharmacy services at little to no cost.

Post-retirement Medical—To provide health care protection for retired employees, many organizations have, in recent years, extended their health-care plans to these retired workers. The loss of health care insurance 30 days after retirement has been a serious concern to employees ready to take retirement. This additional benefit has been offered to reduce this concern.

Comprehensive Health Plan—Some organizations provide health care coverage through the use of a comprehensive plan rather than a basic and major medical plan. Most comprehensive plans establish a maximum coverage. The dollar maximums are set on treatment charge per year, per illness, or lifetime. The most common overall comprehensive maximums are $100,000 and $250,000.

HMOs—The Health Maintenance Organization (HMO) Act of 1973 is a federal initiative for stimulating the development of a nationwide, prepaid health care system. This act furnishes a meaningful alternative to providing health care services to their employees. The HMO focuses its attention on providing health care with emphasis on preventive medicine at a fixed, monthly fee.

An HMO may be independently or federally funded. It provides routine medical services 24 hours a day, 365 days a year at a specific site. The establishment of an HMO is a very expensive undertaking and requires a minimum of from 3,000 to 5,000 subscribers to open. Employers who are members of an HMO make prospective reimbursements or prepayments so that their employees can receive guaranteed health care services on demand.

Workers' Compensation—These previously described state laws also provide medical benefits and hospital care for insured and disabled employees.

Dental—A major added medical coverage is that of comprehensive *dental care benefits* (described briefly in chapter 4). A number of systems have been developed for providing both the protection against the cost of basic types of dental protection plans: (1) schedule plans, (2) comprehensive plans, and (3) combination plans.[2]

The *schedule plan* lists payments for each dental procedure performed. There is no deductible in this plan.

The *comprehensive plan* provides a percentage reimbursement of 50 to 80 percent on covered expenses after an initial deductible (the insured pays the first $25 to $50). The plan may contain an annual (a few hundred dollars) and lifetime ($5,000 or more) limit to benefits.

The *combination plan* provides a fixed fee schedule for some dental expenses and a deductible on some or all types of dental expenses with a possible limiting coinsurance clause in which the insured pays some percentage of the fee up to 15 to 25 percent.

A number of different methods have been developed for organizing dentists. In some cases, the insurance carrier enlists a panel of dentists to provide services. In other cases, the labor union or employer may do the organizing. In still other cases, a group of dentists may form their own private corporation and provide services to the employer or union on some contractual agreement.

Vision—Recently, *vision care* has been added to some plans. Vision care provides employees with one eye examination and one set of prescription glasses each year. This benefit may be of limited value, however, as most vision care claims are under $50.

---

[2]J. F. Follman, Jr., "Dental Insurance," *Pension & Welfare News,* August 1973, pp. 20, 22, 24, 72.

Hearing Aid—Although it affects a smaller number of employees than does the vision aid plan, a benefit that may be of greater value is the hearing-aid plan, because the cost for a hearing aid ranges from $200 to $300.

Social Security—Through its *Medicare* program, Social Security provides significant benefits for a wide range of health care services to almost everyone aged 65 or older. This program protects those individuals against costs of extended hospitalization, convalescent care, and major doctor bills. The Medicare program enables employers to reduce their cost of extending health care insurance to retirees or active employees 65 or older. There is, however, no age limit to Medicare benefits to people with kidney disease who require dialysis or to individuals who have received Social Security disability benefits for two years.

Limiting the Rise of Health Care and Other Benefit Component Costs

Health care cost containment options have been developed by employers seeking alternative approaches for limiting or containing rapidly escalating costs of health care benefits. The most direct approaches are to (1) require employees to make a contribution (share in the premium cost) to the benefit or to increase the contribution if already doing so; (2) increase the amount of the deductible or require a deductible payment where none exists; (3) increase the coinsurance percentage or establish coinsurance where none exists (share in cost for a medical treatment); and (4) add no new features to a benefit plan unless others are removed or reduced in cost.

In addition, the stressing of health maintenance and the introduction of utilization reviews have been initiated to reduce ever-increasing health care costs.

Utilization reviews require employers or their designated agents to check the health care services received by their employees and the quality of these services. They identify the health benefits employees are actually using and what it is costing employers to provide them. This review process must be ongoing because it should analyze what happens to employees after they receive health care services.

Health maintenance, that is, preventing illness, is far less costly than curing illness. Encouraging employees to invest in staying well provides immediate and long-term benefits to both employees and the employer. Employees must realize that they are primarily responsible for their own health. Stress reduction, exercise, proper diet, and minimization of substance abuse (reducing dependence on alcohol, narcotics, and other drugs) all have a payoff in increasing the energy level of healthy employees. A payoff of the organization may be less costly insurance premiums.

Another approach some organizations have used is to institute self-insurance plans.

Self-insurance as an alternative is being used by more employers as they assume responsibility for certain health-related risks. Health-related risks now being covered by employers themselves through self-insurance are short-term disability benefits, basic group health insurance, long-term disability, survivor income, and group term insurance. Commercial insurance supplements self-insurance programs for risks that seldom occur or that could result in substantial financial loss. Self-insuring employers may use a third party to pay claims under an administrative service contract.[3]

Property and Liability Protection

Of rather recent vintage is the addition of compensation components that provide personal property and liability protection for employees. These property and liability protection components include:

1. Group auto
2. Group home
3. Group legal
4. Group umbrella liability
5. Employee liability
6. Fidelity bond insurance

Group Auto.—Within the next ten years, auto insurance will probably become a common benefit. The current pattern is for an employer and an insurance company to develop a group plan through which the employee saves approximately 15 percent of the premium cost because of the group rate reduction. Payments are normally made through a payroll deduction. As group auto insurance develops, it is quite likely that employers will make some contribution.

Group Home—A new benefit is for the employer and an insurance company to develop a plan to provide homeowners with insurance. The employer makes a savings in the premium cost through some kind of mass purchase and the payment of premiums through a payroll deduction.

Group Legal—Although some organizations with legal departments have always provided employees with legal advice concerning tax problems and garnishments, a full range of legal counseling through legal insurance plans is relatively new. (This new benefit was discussed briefly in chapter 4.)

Two types of prepaid legal insurance plans now exist. One is the "open panel," which permits an employee to seek an attorney who will perform the legal service for the fee scheduled in the policy. The other is the "closed panel," which requires use of one of a number of specified attorneys.

Most plans developed to date require some amount of employee contribution, having annual fees that range from $10 to $25, with total policy costs that range from $100 to $150 annually.

Group Umbrella Liability—With law suits granting ever-higher settlements, liability coverage beyond that found in the normal auto and homeowners' policies becomes more important to many employees. Commercial insurance companies are now offering employers group umbrella liability plans that provide increased liability coverage for employees at minimal cost.

[3]Carlton Harker, "Self-Insurance—An Employer's Option," *Personnel Journal,* May 1977, pp. 251–252.

Employee Liability—Because of the greater likelihood of lawsuits and the increased liability of employees for actions they take when performing their jobs, organizations now provide their top decision makers with liability insurance. These insurance plans provide coverage in the millions of dollars. Employees in such sensitive positions as top executives and members of the board of directors are those now receiving such protection.

Fidelity Bond Insurance—Organizations may make the premium payments for the fidelity bond insurance required of employees who must be bonded in order to perform certain job assignments.

EMPLOYEE SERVICES

Employers provide employees with a wide array of services that assist them have a better life-style. In some cases, these services grant employees time off with pay. In other cases, the services include in-kind benefits that most employees value and which, if employees purchased themselves, would require the expenditure of their after-tax dollars. By providing these services for employees, the employer usually receives a tax deduction and, in most cases, the good or service received by the employee is not considered an earned income item. Even in cases where employees may be charged with additional earned income for the receipt of the good or service, the charge to income is considerably less than the cost that would have been incurred by the recipient. The two major sets of components that comprise the employee services group are (1) pay for time not worked and (2) income equivalent payments and reimbursements for incurred expenses.

Pay for Time Not Worked

From an employees' perspective, possibly the most desired but frequently unrecognized benefit is time off with pay. There are numerous time-off-with-pay components and employees usually receive their daily base pay rate as the rate paid for these time-off opportunities. The more common time-off-with-pay components are:

1. Holidays
2. Vacations
3. Jury duty
4. Election official
5. Witness in court
6. Civic duty
7. Military duty
8. Funeral leave
9. Illness in family leave
10. Marriage leave
11. Paternity leave
12. Maternity leave
13. Sick leave
14. Wellness leave
15. Time off to vote
16. Blood donation
17. Grievance and contract negotiations
18. Lunch, rest, and wash-up periods
19. Personal leave
20. Sabbatical leave

TABLE 11-1

COMMON HOLIDAYS

Most Commonly Offered	*Other*
New Year's Day	President's Day (third Monday in February)[a]
Good Friday	
Memorial Day (last Monday in May)[a]	Columbus Day (second Monday in October)[a]
July 4th	Presidential Election Day
Labor Day	Veterans Day
Thanksgiving Day (fourth Thursday in November)	Friday after Thanksgiving
	Day before Christmas
Christmas Day	Day before New Year's

[a]These are the Monday holidays observed by federal employees and by some state and private enterprise employees.

Holidays—Most organizations now provide employees with 9 to 12 paid holidays a year (see table 11-1). Some organizations also offer from one to three floating holidays a year in which the selection is left to the discretion of the employee or is mutually agreed on between the employer and the employees. Some organizations allow employees to observe a holiday on their birthdays.

Most employers determine holiday pay in the same way they determine vacation pay. Those employees who are required to work on holidays because of the nature of the business are usually given compensatory time off (alternative time off with pay at the discretion of the employee with the approval of the organization) and/or premium pay for the day worked. Most organizations observe a holiday on Friday if in reality is falls on a Saturday and on Monday if in reality it falls on a Sunday.

Vacations—Although vacations vary widely, some plans have been liberalized in recent years; and many organizations provide a vacation package similar to the following:

1. One week after six months to one year of service.

2. Two weeks after one to three years of service.

3. Three weeks after five to ten years of service.

4. Four weeks after 15 to 20 years of service.

The extended vacation program developed between the United Steel Workers (USWA) and U.S. Steel described in chapter 4 is an innovative change in the traditional package. To minimize the disruptive effect of the mass of employees taking a summer vacation, U.S. Steel also pays its employees a $50 bonus for each week of regular vacation starting in a payroll week beginning in April, May, September, or October, and $75 for each week of regular vacation starting in a payroll week beginning in February, March, November, or December.

The method of computing vacation pay often depends on the type of work and the manner of compensating an employee. Those receiving a regular weekly salary usually receive their base salary rate. Some organizations pay two percent of the employee's annual earnings for each week of vacation. Those employees paid on an incentive basis may have their vacation pay based on some average weekly earnings for a specified period before the vacation. Some organizations are now providing their employees with a *vacation banking plan,* which enables employees to trade off all or part of the value of unused vacation, which is in turn collected upon termination or retirement.

Jury Duty—Many employers pay their employees who serve on juries. The employees usually receive the difference between their regular eight-hour pay and the amount they receive for each day of jury duty. Some employers permit employees to receive jury duty pay in addition to their regular pay.

Election Official—Some employers grant employees who work as election officials time off with pay at the difference between their base rate of pay and the amount received as an election official.

Witness in Court—When employees are required to appear as a witness in court, some employers grant these employees time off with pay during their courtroom appearance.

Civic Duty—Some organizations provide a specified number of days off with pay to employees providing services to civic organizations.

Military Duty—Many employers provide from one to two weeks off with pay, depending on the military obligation of the employee and the length of service with the organization.

Funeral Leave—Many employers grant employees one to five days off to attend the funeral of a member of the immediate family.

Illness in Family Leave—Many employers grant one to five days off to employees to allow them to assist in caring for members of the immediate family.

Marriage Leave—Some employers grant up to five days of paid absence for those planning to continue employment after marriage.

Paternity Leave—Some employers grant up to five days of paid absence for the father to assist his wife after the birth of a child.

Maternity Leave—Few organizations provide specific paid days off for maternity leave, but most organizations permit pregnant employees to use sick leave and annual leave for paid time off while on maternity leave.

Sick Leave—Previously discussed under Disability Income Continuation section.

Wellness Leave—A recent addition to this classification is a feature aimed at combating absenteeism. Each employee receives a half-hour of paid leave for each week of perfect attendance during all regularly scheduled work hours.

Time Off to Vote—Some employers grant employees a paid hour or two of time off to vote in local, state, and national elections.

Blood Donations—Some employers grant employees paid time off to donate blood. The time may vary from that sufficient to go to a mobile unit to up to four hours to go to a blood bank.

Grievance and Contract Negotiations—Most unionized organizations permit time off with pay to employees who are involved in a grievance procedure or in certain union activities, specified by contract.

Lunch, Rest, and Wash-up Periods—Some organizations grant employees wash-up time (organizations may allow employees involved in extremely dirty work up to 30 minutes to clean up prior to leaving their jobs for the day), rest periods and/or coffee breaks (usually a 10 to 15 minute break twice a day), and lunch periods (usually 30 minutes).

Personal Leave—A variety of special personal excused absences are permitted for time off with pay.

Sabbatical Leave—A few organizations now permit certain employees to have up to one year of sabbatical leave for performing work that has value to society or enhances the professional qualifications of the employee.

Income Equivalent Payments and Reimbursements for Incurred Expenses

This group of compensation components includes some of the most diverse and most desirable kinds of goods and services employees receive from their employers. Many of these components and new ones that appear almost daily are in response to changes in the economic situation and to tax demands. This broad group of services provides employees with the opportunity for an improved and more enjoyable life-style. Some of the more common components are:

Tax-free Benefits or Services

1. Charitable contributions
2. Counseling
   Financial
   Legal
   Psychiatric/
   Psychological
3. Tax preparation
4. Educational subsidies
5. Child adoption
6. Child care
7. Subsidized food service
8. Discounts on merchandise
9. Physical awareness and fitness programs
10. Social and recreational opportunities

11. Parking
12. Transportation to and
    from work
13. Travel expenses
    Car reimbursement
    Tolls and parking
    Food and entertainment
        reimbursement

14. Clothing reimbursement/
    allowance
15. Tool reimbursement/
    allowance
16. Relocation expenses
17. Emergency loans
18. Credit union
19. Housing

Charitable Contributions—Many employers now match, either totally or by some percentage, contributions made by employees to their favorite charities or educational institutions. There may be a limit to the contribution the organization makes to a specific charity of any employee.

Counseling—Organizations often ask to what extent they should counsel employees. Some experts feel that counseling is acceptable only when employees are unable to function on their jobs because of a problem that impairs their work activity, or when they specifically request it.

Counseling activities include attentive listening by a supervisor to an employee's problem in an attempt to identify and understand what is blocking acceptable performance. Often, the problems identified by the employee only camouflage more serious, hidden items. When a supervisor is unable to assist an employee resolve a conflict, the next step is referral to an in-house specialist who is able to provide additional counseling skills. When more serious psychological problems arise, the employer may refer the employee to a private practitioner. (See previously mentioned health-related benefits in this chapter.)

Some of the counseling benefits now provided, in addition to *medical* and *psychological* services, include *financial* counseling (suggesting how to make up a family budget and live within it to overcome existing indebtedness problems, and how to maximize use of current income in developing a future estate), *family* counseling (covering a wide range of family activities, including marital, child, financial, and other personal problems), *career* development (encouraging and assisting employees to look toward the future and to where their best opportunities lie), *out-placement* (assisting those who lose their jobs involuntarily and those disenchanted with their present jobs to find new ones), and *legal* counseling (how to protect oneself when having legal problems).

Tax Preparation.—This service assists employees in meeting tax requirements and may include the identification of legal methods for reducing or deferring tax liabilities.

Educational Subsidies—Educational opportunity provisions are appearing in more benefit plans. In the past, large organizations have provided tuition aid plans for employees who have completed their second year of college or who wish to continue in a graduate program. Traditionally, these programs have ranged from the total payment of all tuition and benefits to the payment of some percentage (50 to 75 percent), to a flat fee per year ($250 to $350). New programs provide educational benefits to (1) those employees who wish to complete their high school education, (2) those who would like to start their college programs, and (3) those who are interested in enrolling in a vocational-technical program.

In addition to these external education and training programs, many firms are implementing a wide variety of in-house educational programs ranging from remedial work on basic literacy to training aimed at improving job opportunities.

Some companies also provide college tuition, textbooks, and training material support for dependents of employees. A broad range of scholarships is also available for children of employees.

The intended purpose of these programs is to provide each employee with as many educational opportunities as possible, with the goal of minimizing frustration over the lack of future opportunitites because of educational deficiencies.

Child Adoption—Recently, a few firms have been providing employees with financial assistance for legal and other service costs incurred in adopting a child. One employer reimburses its employees as much as 80 percent of the adoption cost up to $800; another provides total reimbursement up to $500.

Child Care—Child care as an employee benefit is just beginning. Some of the programs started over the past five years have had poor employee participation because of high cost, transportation problems, or competition from other more convenient child care centers. The successful programs are close to the employee's workplace (frequently in the same building), and the employer provides 50 to 75 percent of the operating costs.

Subsidized Food Services—Many companies provide employee dining facilities. Furnishings and equipment range from benches and vending machines to elaborate cafeteria services. Most food operations are nonprofit, and vending machine profits usually go into some type of additional employee benefits fund. Some firms provide food services below cost and absorb these costs because they consider that well-fed employees are healthier and thus able to work more effectively. This is one of the most sought-after company-provided services.

A common feature in smaller companies, offices, and the service type of business is free coffee, soft drinks, and snacks. Some firms have set up free coffee and soft drink stands and eliminated the traditional coffee break in an attempt to minimize some of its adverse effects. For example, the normal scheduling of coffee breaks frequently occurs when the work efficiency cycle of the employee is at its highest peak, and the break destroys this cycle.

Discounts on Merchandise—Many firms, on their own or in conjunction with merchandising businesses, provide discounts for employees on a large range of products. In addition, businesses that produce desirable products frequently make them available to employees at a liberal discount. Some organizations have equipment that some employees find extremely useful. When replacing it, instead of selling to companies involved in the resale of such equipment, the organization offers it to employees. The price is usually about what the organization would receive for it on the used equipment or used machinery market.

Physical Awareness and Fitness Programs—More organizations are now providing educational and training programs to assist participants improve their understanding of what they must do to improve their physical and emotional health. In addition, some organizations provide facilities and even grant time off to participate in physical fitness activities.

Social and Recreational Opportunities—Social and recreational opportunities are probably the oldest of the benefits and the ones that cause the greatest concern over whether benefits are worth the costs. These programs include the annual summer picnic, company-sponsored athletic events, dancing clubs, card and game parties, craft activities, and social service activities that provide a valuable community need. The major considerations an employer faces here are the following:

1. Do employees really want them?

2. How many will benefit?

3. Are activities sufficiently varied to cover the diversity of employee desires and wants?

With extended amounts of time off and greater employee interest in travel, many organizations work with travel agencies to acquire flight and tour services at reduced costs in order that employees may have additional leisure-time services.

Parking—Over the years, many companies have provided parking facilities; those in downtown areas frequently pay for employee parking. Because parking has become an ever-increasing and irritating problem, employees give this benefit high priority. Employees involved in carpooling frequently receive preferential parking treatment.

Transportation to and from Work—As transportation costs increase, employers are becoming involved in various benefits to help reduce employee transportation costs. In some areas, large employers have supported commuter bus services that operate between the company facility and selected stops close to the residences of many employees. Other employers provide mileage allowances for employees who car pool.

Travel Expenses—Employees who use their own automobiles while performing work assignments may receive a specified allowance or a mileage reimbursement. These employees normally receive reimbursement for all toll and parking expenses. Many employees who travel on company business may also receive either a food and entertainment allowance or reimbursement for all such incurred expenses.

Clothing Reimbursement/Allowance—When dangers are inherent in the job, some companies require employees to wear safety clothing, which they provide at either no cost or a discount or grant an allowance for purchase by the employee. This minimizes the costs related to accidents and also saves on the wear and tear on personal clothing. In addition, employers grant an allowance for or provide work clothing (coveralls) to employees in many types of rough and/or dirty work. In recent years, many service-related organizations have provided employees with well-styled career clothing. There is often a choice among a number of daily apparel options. Employees sometimes participate in the original design and selection of the items. The management of airlines, restaurants, banks, hotels, automobile rental agencies, and the like, feel that career clothing permits the public to identify more easily with their employees. Well-styled, free clothing in which the employees have selection opportunities overcomes some of the dissatisfactions they may have about wearing uniforms.

Tool Reimbursement/Allowance—Organizations hiring employees to do specific kinds of work that requires the use of small or hand tools frequently reimburse employees who must purchase these tools to do their work assignments or grant an allowance for tool purchases.

Relocation Expenses—Many organizations are attempting to reduce the number of transfers of their employees, but it is still necessary occasionally to move employees from one location to another. Moving is frequently a traumatic experience for a family. To ease the burden, employers not only pay the cost of moving the household goods and the family but also frequently provide financial assistance in selling the previous residence and buying the new one. Companies use many different procedures. In some cases, they purchase the old home, and in others they provide a fixed fee for any differences incurred in mortgage costs. Another procedure involves the development of an "eligibility schedule," which lists the reimbursement a transferred employee receives. The amount depends on the length of residence at the previous location and any cost-of-living differential between previous and new locations. These payments are made over a number of years.[4]

Emergency Loans—A service some employees find very useful is the opportunity to obtain emergency loans at little or no interest. To minimize the abuse of such a privilege, limits are set on the size and the number of times an employee can obtain such loans.

Credit Unions—Normally, credit unions are separate businesses made up of members of a particular company or group of companies to provide benefits for the members. Credit unions are organized in a number of ways, but one of the more common ways is that each employee of a company who wishes to become a member must purchase a share of stock for $5 to $10. This stock and additional savings deposits accrue interest at a rate determined by the board of directors. Quite often, members can make savings deposits through payroll deduction plans (in most cases, interest begins on the first day of the month of the deposit) as well as through direct deposits (if made by the tenth of the month, direct deposits draw interest from the first, otherwise from date of deposit).

Any employee who is a member of the credit union can apply for loans at a rate determined by the board of directors. Loan eligibility terms and loan rate of

---

[4]Raymond W. Speck, Jr., "Tailoring the 'Extras' That Go with Transfers," *Compensation Review,* First Quarter, 1970, pp. 29–35.

interest are much more favorable than those found in normal commercial institutions.

Housing—With the high cost of housing, some organizations (frequently those with available and choice property) are building homes, condominiums and rental units for a select group of their employees. Rental costs or purchase prices are normally below existing market prices. Employers use this service to attract individuals who might otherwise be reluctant to join or remain with the organization.

The following list of desirable tax-free and tax-favored services, when provided, are usually offered only to a select group of employees:

Tax-free Services	*Tax-favored Services*
1. Professional memberships	1. Medical expense
2. Professional meetings	reimbursement
3. Professional journals	2. Chauffeur-driven car
and newspapers	3. Company car, plane, yacht
4. Special moving and	4. Company-provided facilities
relocation allowances	and diversions
5. Pay for spouse on	5. Personal use of company
business trip	credit cards
6. Home utility allowance	6. Vacation accommodations
7. Home entertainment allowance	7. Special loan arrangements
8. Home servants allowance	
9. Season tickets to	
entertainment events	
10. Use of assistant for	
personal services	

COSTING BENEFITS

Although in many cases benefit costs now exceed 35 percent of total payroll costs, employees frequently place minimal value on these benefits, take them for granted, and fail to consider them as an incentive for improving work performance. A major trouble spot in this area is the inability of employees to understand the range and the depth, and to appreciate the value of the benefits they receive, mainly because employers have failed to communicate the value of their benefits programs to them. A central issue is that many organizations have never performed an in-depth cost analysis of their benefits programs and so have never developed accurate and valid figures to describe them. Costing is an absolutely essential prerequisite to any worthwhile benefits communication program.

Costing Methods

Four methods have been developed for costing benefits and services. Although each has a particular value, it is frequently more effective to combine two or more. The four commonly used costing methods are the following:

1. Annual cost of benefits and services for all employees.

2. Cost per employee per year.

3. Percentage of payroll (annual cost divided by annual payroll).

4. Cents per hour (cost per employee per hour).[5]

Annual Cost—The annual cost method provides total annual cost figures for each benefit. An organization should develop accounting procedures that compute such costs. The continued growth of computerized accounting and bookkeeping procedures will help to capture these costs. This method is especially valuable in developing budgets and for fully describing the total cost of the benefits program.

Cost per Employee per Year—Simple bookkeeping procedures permit the development of annual costs per employee of particular benefits (especially those benefits and services in the category of pay for time not worked and in some of the employee security and health benefits). However, bookkeeping is more complex for other benefits (particularly those involving group insurance, for example, and components provided to special groups of employees, for example, a bowling team). In these cases, firms must maintain accurate records of total costs of each program per year and of those employees who are recipients. It is then possible to divide the total cost of the program by the number of employees receiving the benefit or the service and allocate the costs to each employee.

In addition to determining the cost of each benefit, companies may also wish to know the aggregate cost of benefits per employee. Here, the employer simply accumulates the total cost of all benefits and services and divides that figure by the average number of workers employed during the year.

When an employer tells employees of the amount the organization has paid to obtain the annual benefits offered, this figure probably has some impact. However, to achieve the greatest effect, the information should be given to the employees along with a cents-per-hour total and a cents-per-hour breakdown per benefit.

Percentage of Payroll—Computing the percentage of payroll costs requires a determination of just what the organization includes as payroll costs for work performed. Some firms include only straight-time costs and consider premiums as being part of benefits costs. This problem emphasizes the importance of identifying and defining benefits and services and often requires major policy decisions by senior management.

After identifying and classifying all compensation costs, nothing more is necessary other than a simple mathematical computation to determine the cost of each component and the total cost of benefits and services as a percentage of payroll. This figure is valuable in comparing benefit and service costs with those of other organizations.

---

[5]Harold Stieglitz, *Computing the Cost of Fringe Benefits: Studies in Personnel Policy, No. 128* (New York: National Industrial Conference Board, 1952), pp. 4–19.

Cents per Hour—The cents-per-hour figure also varies among organizations because of the different ways to identify and define the term *hour*. To one organization, hours may mean an arbitrary figure calculated by multiplying the days the organization operated during the year by eight hours (250 days × 8 hours = 2,000 hours); to another company, it may mean the total of actual hours worked by the employee. In the latter case, it is possible to calculate cents per hour by dividing the total benefit costs by the total number of hours worked during the year.

The cents-per-hour method probably is most frequently used in expressing the cost of benefits. It is especially valuable to an organization that must bargain with unions over wages, hours, benefits, and other issues. In discussing the total compensation package, it is then possible to relate direct wage rates to benefit costs and to develop a cost for the total package.

The cents-per-hour method is also valuable in communicating the cost of benefits to employees because they can relate this figure to their hourly pay. The major problem here is that this figure may not have an impact on the employee because it is still a relatively small number. A service worker being paid $5 an hour may not attach much significance to the fact that the company paid $2 in benefit costs for each hour worked. On the other hand, the significance of the benefit may seem greater if the figure is given as $4,000 a year ($2 × 2,000 hours/year).

FLEXIBLE OR CAFETERIA BENEFITS PLAN

The flexible or cafeteria benefits plan was originally designed to enable senior executives, top professionals, and managers to individually choose many of their benefits and services. In the future, more employers will use this plan for all employees as a way to communicate the costs and the value of benefits programs.

The flexible benefits plan permits an employee to select benefits and services within certain limits. These include total benefit dollars available and those benefits that are mandatory for all employees because of legal requirements, security needs, or majority rule. Before involving the employee in the selection process, however, the employer must identify the available alternative benefits and services, and the employer must determine the cost of each benefit and service as well as a total permissible cost for the entire package.

Basically, the flexible benefits plan accomplishes four goals that are fundamental to the development of a successful program. It increases or improves employee:

1. Appreciation of the interest and desire of the employer to improve the quality of life of each employee.

2. Productivity.

3. Understanding of the value and the cost of each benefit and service component.

4. Understanding of the value and the cost of the total benefits program.

Although companies and managers are spending more time and money to improve their benefits programs, little has been done to inform employees of this effort and to explain its impact on their lives. If employers are to realize any motivational value from the large sums spent on their compensation programs, they must recognize that such spending in itself has little or no motivational value. It is one thing for an employer to exchange pay for the efforts of employees; it is another to develop a variety of procedures that enables workers to have some voice in how they perform their work and in the rewards they receive for their contributions. A central theme of this text is the way, through involvement opportunities in well-conceived, well-designed, and well-imple- mented compensation programs, employees can improve their understanding of why and how they receive rewards for their work.

The rapid increase in benefits offered is no mystery because it is in this segment of the compensation system that the organization has the opportunity to provide some stability to the quality of the worker's life and to promote opportunities for improving it.

To provide these advancement opportunities in the employee's work life, as well as to enhance its stability, management must completely understand the value and the cost of each part of the compensation system. Unfortunately, the one area in which minimal value and cost analysis has been performed is that of employee benefits—here the "fringe" mentality lingers. Through classification and costing of benefits, the employee is able to recognize their true importance and value.

To develop a benefit value and cost analysis, organizations must first classify their benefits and services, then identify those available within each classification, and, finally, cost each in terms understood by those involved.

After classifying and costing benefits and services, the next step is to provide employees with this information. Informing employees of their opportu- nities for participating in the selection of available benefits and services increases the motivational value of the benefits program. In taking time to recognize the large amounts of money it spends on benefits, an organization is made more aware of the need to spend some small percentage of these funds in communicating their value and costs to its workers. The flexible benefits plan is ideal for this purpose. It lays the groundwork that enables employees to recognize more fully how important the employer considers them as contributing members and what the employer is attempting to do to improve the quality of their work lives.

Worker Expectations and Preferences

Because of increased employer interest in identifying what employees want in the way of benefits and services, researchers are developing new and better ways to examine employee attitudes, expectations, and preferences.

Even when well-designed, properly implemented, and carefully analyzed, the traditional attitude survey has inherent weaknesses that make its usefulness questionable. A typical, well-designed survey probes for employee views on specific subjects. In the case of employee attitudes on benefits and services, it focuses on such issues as (1) employee expectations concerning prospective benefits, (2) opinions about the way benefits received compare with those offered by other employers, (3) use and understanding of currently available benefits, and (4) employee desires for currently unavailable benefits.

An attitude survey investigating such issues may use open-ended questions or require the employee to select one of a number of responses such as "strongly disagree," "satisfactory," or "strongly agree." Open-ended questions provide the opportunity to submit a wide range of opinions, but they take much time, both for the respondent to complete and the investigator to review. Forced-choice questions are easy to score, but they limit response opportunities.

A better way to determine employee benefit desires is by using preference surveys. The major difference between the traditional attitude survey and the preference survey is that in the attitude survey employees normally identify their positions on a subject, whereas in the preference survey they make selections among alternatives.

John Foley, president of Compac Systems, Inc., has developed a preference survey procedure using a series of matrices that require respondents to order by rank their benefit choices among a number of options.[6] The three underlying considerations identified by Foley are valuable to anyone interested in analyzing employee benefit preferences. These considerations are as follows:

1. What does the employee now have? An addition to a currently available benefit is usually less valuable than an entirely new benefit.

2. What can the employee use? Use depends on current life-style. It is difficult to identify any long-term utility.

3. What is the employer prepared to provide? This is the primary issue. It relates to what an employer can afford and is willing to offer.

A preference survey requires that more information be provided than that usually offered in an attitude survey. Preference survey design assumes that employees do not have information available at their fingertips. To make choices, they must be able to identify clearly what they must sacrifice in order to gain something else.

Foley states that to obtain high-quality preference information, employees must be treated as intelligent adults. A well-designed survey (1) informs the respondent what the procedure is all about, (2) states how the information will be analyzed, (3) maintains confidentiality, (4) furnishes feedback, and (5) tells respondents what they can expect from the survey.

Because a benefits preference survey relates so closely to employees' current life-styles, demographic data profiles on respondents are critical (i.e., age, sex, marital status, job level in organizational structure, etc.). The "here and now" consideration also limits the life expectancy of preference information.

[6]Presentation by John Foley at the American Compensation Association Eastern Regional Meeting, Atlanta, GA, May 12, 1977.

Foley states that it is good for about two years. To have any degree of confidence in pay preference data, a sample should include at least 100 respondents.

Benefits preference information reveals that there is no direct relationship between what a benefit costs an employer and the value an employee places on it.[7] In fact, the amount an employer spends on a specific benefit is of little importance to an employee.

Although employee demographic data do reveal some interesting general patterns concerning benefits preferences, the number of variables having an impact on a group of workers in a given situation makes it difficult, if not impossible, to identify any fixed pattern of responses or to assume that the responses of one group would be those of another group. A major difficulty about benefits preferences is that employee values are conditioned by the opportunities available to a specific employee at a point in time.

Micro Approach

By allowing employees to select their level of benefits as well as the composition of these benefits, both management and specialists can gain a better understanding of what employees want in their package and how benefits can satisfy some of their needs.

It is highly unlikely that one program will satisfy all or even a majority of employees. Young married workers may highly value some type of maternity or paternity benefit, whereas older employees look for a pension plan that will, in a few years, provide reasonable security. A single female may be interested in a travel club, but an older bachelor may place far more value on a stock option. Is it possible to develop a benefits program that reflects the needs and the values of each employee?

The Mix—Any such plan must include *nonoptional* items, including the government-required benefits of Social Security, Workers' Compensation, and unemployment insurance, as well as certain group life, health, medical, accident, and pension plans that require full participation before an insurance company will provide them.

Most likely, there will be a set of *semioptional* items, including benefits provided principally by insurance companies (or other companies in certain areas) in which they charge a flat rate after analyzing certain organizational features. For example, if an insurance company offers a flat fee for life insurance but more of the older employees select this option, the skewed distribution may require a change in the rate. An answer is either to change the rate relative to the age of the applicants or to make the benefit nonoptional if it is desired by many employees.

Optional items include many of the components previously listed in the Pay for Time Not Worked and Income Equivalent Payments classifications. Whether the components are nonoptional, semioptional, or optional, each must carry a price tag. Employees can choose the component they desire within total

---

[7]Wilbur G. Lewellen and Howard P. Lanser, "Executive Pay Preferences," *Harvard Business Review,* September–October, 1973, pp. 115–122.

cost limits set by the organization. This microanalysis approach permits employees to weigh the cost and value of each component against every other component.

Macro Approach

The flexible or cafeteria benefits plan does not give management the right to abdicate its responsibility to develop and present a benefits and services program that provides each employee with a certain degree of security and opportunity for growth. No doubt, the flexible benefits plan will emphasize for many employees its micro aspects, but it will also understate its overall impact. A number of procedures are open to organizations for minimizing this negative effect. First, administrative costs will prevent employees from changing benefits at will. Employers must establish time schedules for stopping or exchanging benefits.

Second, organizations will probably have to expand their benefits counseling program to advise employees about the value of benefits and to assist them in making selections that are in their own best interests. This service could be the beginning of a broader and more valuable full-service counseling program that could bring employer and employee closer together.

Establishing a Flexible or Cafeteria Benefits Plan

Much planning and deliberation are necessary before starting a flexible benefits plan. A number of groups must have a voice in its initial design. Three major groups that must participate are (1) senior management (for setting objectives and determining policy), (2) compensation and human resource specialists (for guiding the development of and assisting in constructing a program that meets organizational objectives and the perceptions and demands of the employees), and (3) the employees (for providing initial inputs about what should be included in a benefits program, ranking by value, and, finally, making choices).

Senior Management—Senior managers must first decide what they would like their benefits program to accomplish. If it is to provide essential security needs, they must define what these needs represent to employees at a point in time. Should the program provide security for today? Or should it include tomorrow and many tomorrows? Should it cover only the employees or also their immediate families? Should it cover practically all health-related problems? Should it cover legal and financial problems? Should it include social and leisure activities?

After considering these issues, policymakers can outline the types and the depth of benefits they wish to provide. With increasing interest in employee participation in the benefit selection process (e.g., the flexible benefits plan), policymakers now must decide whether to permit such employee selection. They then must determine the limits of the benefits package (nonoptional versus optional and total cost of package).

Another policy decision relates to whether the employer and employee share the costs. What contribution, if any, will the employee make for each benefit? How much can the employer afford to pay?

Many benefits have eligibility requirements built into their initial design; others have government restrictions; still others have organizational requirements. Determining who qualifies, the length of service requirements, and the quality and the quantity of benefits are all policy decisions.

Compensation Specialists—Compensation specialists form the functional group that spearheads the task force. The task force, consisting of members from throughout the organization, is responsible for developing data and information that assist senior management in making correct decisions. These decisions in turn, provide the groundwork for developing a workable and acceptable benefits program.

The task force includes many specialists. Some are expert in project management with experience in directing the planning, operations, and control efforts of a variety of individuals with a variety of interests and skills toward the accomplishment of predetermined objectives and goals. Others are systems and computer specialists who have expertise in developing systems and providing mechanisms for collecting, analyzing, and disseminating a wide variety and masses of data. Also included are financial and accounting specialists who have expertise in the financial and accounting areas of the organization. There are legal specialists who understand the legal implications of specific benefits that must comply with certain state or federal statutes. And there are external benefits specialists who have specialized knowledge of the particular benefits under review.

Employees—Through a variety of mechanisms, (i.e., counseling, attitude and preference surveys), the employees provide operating management (including the task force) and senior management with their thoughts on the types and the variety of benefits and services needed and their priorities.

Collecting Data—Data may be collected in a number of ways. If the organization is not too large and has a relatively homogeneous work force in one general location, it is possible to begin with an attitude or preference questionnaire developed initially by the task force. The form can secure and rank data on the benefits desired by the work force. If the organization is large, it may be necessary first to study the work group through an analysis of such characteristics as the following:

Age	Number of dependents
Base salary	and their ages
Step or location in	Amount and sources of
pay grade	other income
Geographic location	Sex
Marital status	Years of service
	Years on present job

By using a number of these characteristics, it is possible to develop a stratified random sample of the entire work group that can provide the task force with a good idea of employee expectations, perceptions, and demands.

Depending on convenience as well as on time and cost considerations, the sample group can meet with members of the task force or provide benefit needs and priority data through a questionnaire. From data collected through the stratified random sample, it is then possible to develop a questionnaire for use by 100 percent of the work force.

Changes in Legislation.—The Revenue Act of 1978 and the Miscellaneous Revenue Act of 1980 provide additional options to flexible benefits plans. The 1978 legislative changes make it possible for eligible employees to select between cash or other currently taxable compensation components or one or more nontaxable components (medical expense insurance, group life insurance plans, disability insurance, etc.) and only those components subject to taxes are taxable. (Prior to 1978, having the option to select taxable items could make the entire benefits program taxable.)

The 1980 act further broadened flexible benefits opportunities by granting with this kind of plan the option of having cash or deferred profit-sharing arrangements. This enables companies to offer employees a choice under qualified stock bonus or profit-sharing plans between currently taxable cash payments or tax-free deferrals that become taxable when actually paid.

Basic Issues

Senior management has the responsibility of determining the total value of benefits and approving the percentage breakdown of this total into optional and nonoptional items. Senior management also must determine the number of optional components and their monetary value that an employee may select (in this case, such criteria as a percentage of base income or a fixed amount per year by length of service and base income are useful).[8]

Other issues common to most flexible benefits plans that require resolution are the following:

1. Will the flexible benefits plan comply with Internal Revenue Service standards by not discriminating in favor of highly compensated employees?

2. Will overloading the plan with nonoptional items to guarantee employee security negate the intent and the value of the plan, leaving few opportunities for individual choice?

---

[8]Those interested in implementing a flexible or cafeteria benefits plan would gain from a review of "Flexible Benefits From Concept to Implementation—the *TRW Story*," presented at the 1975 American Compensation Association National Conference and described in the proceedings of this conference. This presentation provides an in-depth review and analysis of the problems and the complexity of implementing a flexible benefits program that includes options within hospital/medical/accident insurance and life insurance programs. The address of the American Compensation Association is P. O. Box 1176, Scottsdale, AZ 85252.

3. Will the plan recognize change in employee basic levels of pay during the benefit year?

4. Will the plan recognize change in employee dependents or marital status?

5. Will the plan recognize changes in premium or benefit cost?

6. When, during the year, will an employee be permitted to make changes in a benefit?

SELECTED READINGS

Baytos, L. M., "The Employee Benefit Smorgasbord: Its Potential and Limitations," *Compensation Review,* First Quarter, 1970, pp. 16–28. A focus on the smorgasbord (cafeteria) approach to benefits, especially as it applies to salaried employees. These same procedures and analyses are useful in developing such a plan for all members of the organization.

Ellig, Bruce R., "Determining Competitiveness of Employee Benefits Systems," *Compensation Review,* First Quarter, 1974, pp. 8–34. An excellent discussion of benefits systems regarding cost to the company, cost to the employee, and value to the employee. This article is especially useful in assisting anyone interested in developing a benefits system make effective use of the biennial employee benefits survey made by the Chamber of Commerce of the United States.

Employee Benefits 1977. Washington, DC: Chamber of Commerce of the United States, 1977. A biennial analysis of employee benefits, this publication is the most prominent and widely quoted source of benefit cost data. An ability to understand and use this excellent survey is a must for anyone involved in the development and the operation of an employee benefits program.

Gordon, T. J., and R. E. LeBleu, "Employee Benefits, 1970–1985," *Harvard Business Review,* January–February 1970, pp. 93–107. An in-depth analysis of benefits now on the scene and those that will emerge by 1985. It describes changes in those benefits presently in effect and some vital information concerning the emergence of new benefits.

Herzig, Howard Z., "How Much Are Your Benefits Worth?" *The Personnel Administrator,* May–June 1972, pp. 16–17. A review of benefit costs and a description of various methods for communicating employee benefits as well as ways of personalizing individual employee benefits. This article explains how reports of dollar value of benefits can be made more effective.

Nielson, Niels H., "Organizing Benefits Like a Business," *Pension & Welfare News,* December 1971, pp. 85–89. A discussion of the way an organization should design, administer, finance, and manage its benefits program so it is run like a business rather than a "fringe." The author advocates a proactive approach to benefits instead of one that is reactive.

Paine, Thomas H., "Flexible Compensation Can Work!" *Financial Executive,* February 1974, pp. 56–58, 60, 62, 64, 66, 68. A hard look at flexible (cafeteria) benefits plans, identifying the potential dangers and weaknesses as well as the basic strengths. This review focuses on Internal Revenue Service guidelines and the legal difficulties encountered in designing and implementing such a benefits plan.

Schuster, Jay R., "Adding New Components to a Compensation Package," *Pension & Welfare News,* October 1969, pp. 35–38. A review and an analysis of a survey that collected data on compensation and benefits preferences of employees of two organizations.

Stieglitz, Harold, *Computing the Cost of Fringe Benefits: Studies in Personnel Policy,* no. 128. New York: National Industrial Conference Board, Inc., 1952. A review of the why, what, and how of costing fringe benefits with an in-depth analysis of the benefits programs of nine major organizations, including their comments and viewpoints on why to include or exclude particular benefits.

Yount, H. Hoover, "Total Compensation—Cost, Comparison, and Control," *Compensation Review,* Fourth Quarter, 1971, pp. 9–19. A total audit of compensation costs of a midwestern bank indicates the value of an audit for discovering areas of excessive internal compensation expenditures as well as a means for establishing industrywide measures of compensation.

12

Work Premiums and Performance-based Rewards

CONTENT

Chapter 12 describes work premiums, pay-for-performance, and merit pay components of a total compensation system. It discusses various examples of each, with particular emphasis on performance-based rewards.

GOALS

Upon concluding this chapter, you should have an understanding of various components of a compensation system that stimulate contributions above and beyond normal standards and how such components interact and interrelate. These components are work premiums and performance-based rewards. You should understand the importance of dignity in work and should have at least an acquaintance with the mechanics of a program that can assist in creating a work environment that stimulates quality employee performance.

Although work premiums and performance-based rewards cover distinctly different segments of the compensation program, they have a common thread in that they stimulate contributions above and beyond commonly held standards or expectations.

Work premiums provide extra compensation for work effort that is normally considered burdensome, distasteful, hazardous, or inconvenient. These premiums cover such areas as pay for overtime work, shift work, weekend or holiday work, work that is offensive to any of the senses, or work that is potentially hazardous.

Performance-based rewards assist in developing a productive work environment by rewarding those employees who contribute toward improving organizational output beyond certain predetermined standards. Performance-based rewards include a variety of piecework, merit pay plans, cost-reduction, and short-term profit-sharing programs, short-term contests, suggestion plans, and special awards. In all cases, organizations offer these rewards to attract and hold motivated employees.

WORK PREMIUMS

A major characteristic of work premiums is that in certain cases they must comply with federal Wage and Hour Law requirements. Most organizations must pay a time-and-a-half premium after 40 hours of work in a week. Practically all other premium considerations involve individual organizational decisions (and union acceptance if the organization is unionized).

Overtime

Almost every firm, at one time or another, runs into a situation that requires its employees to work more than 40 hours in a week. Overtime is a useful device for cutting payroll costs, even though those working overtime receive work premiums. In fact, a good rule of thumb to follow is that an organization that never pays overtime is overstaffed. Most organizations that pay time-and-a-half or even double-time premiums for overtime find these charges to be less than the cost of having a full-time employee hired for the purpose of eliminating the need for overtime. In addition, when overtime is not excessive, most employees appreciate the opportunity to earn more money.

Beyond excessive overtime work requirements, the major overtime problem encountered by most organizations is scheduling. Because of the potential problems lurking in this area, many organizations take special care in determining overtime policy. The policy may include such elements as (1) who must work overtime, (2) what kind of notice an employee should receive, (3) the way overtime is distributed, and (4) what premium rates are offered.

Because many jobs require specialized knowledge, certain employees may be obligated to work overtime. In some cases, managers are responsible for giving due notice, but a sudden emergency may require the manager to have a certain latitude concerning overtime scheduling. The problem is to differentiate between the true emergency and managerial laxities.

Because many employees like to receive pay premiums from overtime work, the scheduling process, in addition to recognizing knowledge requirements and seniority, must also take into account those persons last receiving overtime work and those who *do not* desire overtime. One way to solve the scheduling problem is to make two lists: (1) the "green" list for those who voluntarily wish to work overtime, and (2) the "orange" list for those who do not. As long as possible, only those on the green list should receive overtime work. Those on the orange list should work overtime only after the green list has been exhausted. Workers may change from one list to the other at their request. To prevent scheduling chaos, however, it may be worthwhile to allow changes only at three-month intervals.

In addition to federal time-and-a-half requirements, overtime rates may vary according to the time of day or the day of the week (weekday, Saturday, Sunday, or holiday). Some organizations also vary in their definition of a regular workweek. Although most follow federal 40-hour workweek guidelines, a few have 35- and 37½-hour workweeks.

Shift, Weekend, and Holiday Work

Practically every company that requires a second (4:00 P.M. to midnight) or third (midnight to 8:00 A.M.) shift pays some form of shift differential. The third shift usually receives a higher premium than does the second shift. This pay is normally considered as part of the employee's base pay. The shift premium may be either a flat amount added to the normal first shift (day) rate or a percentage increment such as an additional 10 percent of that rate. Salaried employees doing shift work usually receive an additional monthly increment to their base rate.

Employees who work a Monday-to-Friday schedule usually receive premium pay for work performed on weekends or holidays. Saturday pay is usually at the time-and-a-half rate; Sunday and holiday premiums are sometimes computed at a double rate. An employee seldom receives weekend or holiday pay in addition to overtime. When the premium rates vary, however, the employee will receive the highest rate for the day.

Reporting, Call-Back, Standby, and Cleanup Time

Another group of premiums businesses provide to employees for their availability, knowledge, and job skills includes special payments for reporting, call-back, standby, and cleanup time.

A reporting premium guarantees a certain amount of pay to a worker who reports and finds no work available. When a worker has not been given adequate notice of the unavailability of work because of weather conditions, lack of materials, or other such reasons, some organizations provide reporting premiums. A normal reporting premium is four hours of pay for being sent home without work. Many organizations state in their compensation policy that they are under no obligation to pay a reporting premium when the lack of work is due to conditions beyond their control. Some organizations have the following reporting time policy:

1. The worker receives a full day's pay if work has begun and is stopped through no fault of the employee.

2. The worker receives a full week's pay for working a full day on the first working day of the week.

3. The worker receives pay for a minimum of four hours if scheduled or notified to report for work but no work is available.

Employees who have a certain skill that may be critically needed at any hour receive a call-back or call-in premium. In essence, this worker is on standby and must be available for a work assignment at any time outside of normal working hours. Workers normally receive a call-back premium any time they are on a standby alert. Whether they work or not is unimportant. Once called in to work, they receive their regular pay and any other earned premiums or differentials.

Standby or idle time payments provide an employee with a guaranteed amount of pay even when there is no work to perform. The most common reasons for lack of work are a machine breakdown or a stop in the flow of work because of a shortage of materials. These conditions are usually temporary in nature, and the employer prefers to pay the employee to stand by until the problems are corrected. At that time, the employee returns to the normal assigned duties. The standby guarantee is usually equal to the employee's normally earned hourly rate of pay.

Workers who perform assignments that require them to change clothing, shower, or perform other such activities receive their regular rate of pay for a certain amount of cleanup time. The cleanup requirement may come from dirty working conditions, strenuous work activities, or conditions dangerous to health (e.g., working in radioactive areas requiring special clothing and cleaning activities).

Burdensome, Distasteful, Hazardous Work

Offensive working conditions are those in which the environment of the work activities require effort in excessively dirty or filthy conditions. Also included are conditions where radiation, dust, fumes, or other noxious odors, or excessive cold, heat, or dampness affect breathing, vision, hearing, taste, or the employee's general health. Also, employees who must work in what are normally considered unsafe areas such as extreme heights (i.e., 60 feet above a certain base), or where moving machinery or other physical conditions make the workplace hazardous, may receive work premiums. These premiums vary proportionally with the degree of unsatisfactory or hazardous conditions involved. Some organizations provide a premium of one and one-half times the normal rate of pay for working under such conditions. In some cases, the premium is double the normal rate.

PERFORMANCE-BASED REWARDS

Performance-based rewards are often the most maligned part of the total compensation package. They are valuable to the employer only when they promote employee contributions above and beyond the normal expected standards of effort. On the other hand, they have meaning to the employee only when they are used to recognize the individuals, work groups, or organizations that provide such contributions.

The major source of contention concerning performance-based rewards is that they are ineffective in lowering costs, improving quality, and increasing productivity. All too often, they are so mechanical and inflexible that they fail to meet changing conditions. To overcome these deficiencies, the review of performance-based rewards must be continuous. The entire process must provide meaningful standards as well as accurate and valid identification of the quantity and the quality of contributions. Only those organizations that have developed methods and procedures that not only identify standards and contributions accurately and validly but also gain worker acceptance with regard to their equity and fairness find their programs working.

Those firms that have developed and successfully operated performance-based reward programs find their efforts rewarded by increased productivity, lowered costs, and profitability that would be only a dream to most managers. The payoff from a good pay-for-performance program is so dramatic that every organization should make a determined effort to design and implement one to fit its needs and operation.

Throughout this text, the idea that there is no cookbook or one special approach to compensation has been emphasized. This is especially true in the area of pay-for-performance or merit pay programs. It is impossible to imitate or duplicate the program of another organization and expect success. When designing and implementing a program, each organization must take into account many variables that are unique to its own situation. Examples of such variables are the following:

1. Type of product or service.

2. Method of producing or delivering it.

3. Ability to specify quality and quantity of product or service.

4. Employee needs, perceptions, and demands; personal background and history.

5. Business requirements, history, and background.

6. External environmental pressures, including consumers of product or services, legal requirements, and society in general.

Each of these factors requires consideration in the design phase of a performance-based reward program and must be monitored constantly to ensure continued viability and validity. These programs must recognize ability, promote achievement and risk taking, and they must reward individual differences. They therefore require the rare combination of technological workability, organizational honor and reliability, and employee trust and acceptance. They promote the willingness of workers to work together as a team.

Developing Performance Standards

Standards related to any aspect of the compensation system must withstand the most intense scrutiny and analysis by those whose compensation they affect. Work- or job-related standards, whether they are used for evaluating jobs, setting equitable rates of pay, or assessing worker performance, must meet two basic criteria.

1. Standards must be consistent; that is, a standard must recognize similar employee inputs by providing similar employer outputs. (If job knowledge, responsibility requirements, and working conditions are similar, base rates should likewise be similar. Similar work effort by employees having similar skills and motivation should result in comparable piecerate earnings or performance appraisal ratings.)

2. Standards must be fair. Whatever the final purpose of the standard, those persons working under its rules must accept it as just and reasonable.

The development and the administration of quality, quantity, and time standards is the responsibility of three distinct groups in many organizations: (1) operating management, (2) compensation management, and (3) industrial engineering.[1] The operating managers have final responsibility for any activity related to compensation of their units because it is they who are held accountable for performance. Their success, however, depends to a large degree on the expertise and the assistance provided by the compensation managers and the industrial engineers who have design responsibilities. Although the purpose of this book is to develop an understanding of and ability to implement the functional responsibility of the compensation manager, it is wise to take a look at the activities and responsibilities of the industrial engineers (IEs).

The IEs begin their work by developing an understanding of the goods and/or service output of the organization. In accordance with the design of the output and to achieve organizational objectives, the IEs assist in the layout of the plant and the facility and are responsible for production design, process planning, job content, and work methods. They determine the preferred procedures for work flow and the methods for performing work activities; they then set quality, quantity, and time standards. Through these efforts they develop a

---

[1]See Richard I. Henderson and Waino W. Suojanen, *The Operating Manager: An Integrative Approach* (Englewood Cliffs, NJ: Prentice-Hall, 1974).

fair distribution of work requirements and clarify individual areas of responsibility. As mentioned previously, the IEs attempt to develop the most efficient procedures and methods, but because of the human element involved, it is difficult to determine a "one right way."

Although the IEs develop preferred solutions, it is possible that the employee actually doing the work may be able to develop a better way. It is the responsibility of operating managers to relate the preferred methods of the IEs to the innovative approaches of the employee. This is one part of the concept of meaningful work.

Much of the work performed by the IEs determines or at least influences, the type of pay-for-performance program. For this reason, compensation managers must understand and integrate the work of the IEs with their own programs.

The compensation manager follows the IE and reviews each job with regard to the human qualities, the responsibilities, and the knowledge required to perform the job. This review allows the compensation manager to set the base pay for the job and to design the pay structure for the organization.

Piecework Programs

Probably the oldest of all pay-for-performance programs are those that tie the workers' earnings directly to the number of units produced. The major differences among piecework programs are the procedures used to determine the rate of pay offered for units produced and the manner in which the extra payments are made.

Piecework programs are most effective in rewarding the performance of an individual or a small group because rewards are determined by units produced per hour or day. It is essential that those responsible for production be easily and clearly identified, and this is practically impossible in large groups. The major focus of these programs is to overcome the weakness of a fixed wage program in which workers receive an hourly, weekly, or monthly rate of pay that remains unaffected by rates of productivity or the amount of work performed.

Setting Standards—Nearly all piecework programs involve operations in which workers have considerable control over their output.[2] In industries in which production operations are largely machine-paced, such as automobile assembly lines, cigarette manufacturing, chemical processing, and pulp and paper production, piecework programs are almost nonexistent. Since piecework programs reward extra effort, the first requirement of any such program is to set fair output standards that define what an average worker under normal conditions should produce in a set period of time (normally on an hourly or daily basis).

Over the past 100 years, various methods have been developed to measure and determine standard output. No system is foolproof, and even the most

[2]George L. Stelluto, "Report on Incentive Pay in Manufacturing Industries," *Monthly Labor Review,* July 1969, pp. 49–53.

scientifically contrived system includes some subjectivity. The major measurement procedures are stopwatch time studies, synthetic time studies, and work sampling. The development of standards is usually the responsibility of industrial engineers.

Because work standards have a direct impact on one of the most important elements of the work cycle—the worker's paycheck—they are a source of worker problems and grievances. Before IEs can set standards, operating conditions at the workplace must have a degree of uniformity. These uniform conditions include methods of doing the work; procedures for delivering, handling, and removing materials; quality of raw materials; types of equipment and their maintenance; and quality standards of output. Workers must have control over work output, and there must be a clear relationship between effort and output. Variations in any of these areas have a direct impact on output, but it is practically impossible not to have them. Additional problems related to setting standards are those involved with (1) making allowances for fatigue and personal needs, (2) recognizing unavoidable delays, (3) determining the representative of persons being timed, and (4) leveling final findings. (Leveling occurs when the analyst reviewing the work rates the worker as being faster or slower than the average worker in doing the job or elements of the job.) Through the leveling process, the time required for the worker to do the work is either increased or lowered, depending on the leveling rate assigned by the analyst.

If piecework programs are to succeed, there must be some "give" on both sides. When variations occur, organizations must honor certain commitments. At the same time, workers must trust management and understand that changes must be made at times if the organization is to be competitive and provide a product that meets consumer demands. This can be accomplished with a bit of communication between management and workers. Assurances made and followed through will produce astonishing results.

Two symptoms of error in setting standards show up in what are called *loose* and *tight* standards or rates. When a standard is loose, management contends that workers' earnings are excessive, taking into account the extra effort involved in producing the output. On the other hand, employees complain of tight standards when, after producing the extra effort, they realize earnings lower than they expected.

Three commonly used techniques for setting performance standards are through the use of (1) time and motion study, (2) micromotion analysis, and (3) work measurement. A brief description of each technique follows.

Time and Motion Study—In the oldest and simplest of the three techniques—time and motion study—an analyst makes a time study by closely watching a worker and using a stopwatch to time performance. Most studies include a detailed analysis of each work element. The analyst then relates each element to the normal time required for the entire work cycle.

Time and motion study provides data on the time required by a "normal" worker to perform a specific operation. A "normal" worker refers to a qualified, experienced employee performing at an average pace while working under conditions that usually prevail at the work station.

Time-study analysts who provide accurate data must have an understanding of the job and be able to develop a harmonious relationship with the employees being studied. Employees tend to be suspicious and distrust anyone who studies their performance, and this distrust may manifest itself in many ways. Workers being appraised may attempt to either inflate their performance (make their contributions appear to be more important) or even deflate their performance (make their contributions appear to be less important). The skilled analyst must be able to "rate" employees. Rating is the establishment of the degree to which the employee being studied performs better or worse than a "normal" worker.

Micromotion Analysis—A more sophisticated approach than time and motion study is micromotion analysis, which requires photographing a worker performing a job. The camera operates at a constant speed—usually 1,000 frames a minute. By analyzing the film, the analyst can determine work patterns for each part of the worker's body. By studying each movement and counting the number of frames necessary to document a complete cycle of work, a methods analyst is able to determine acceptable methods and set standards. Using this approach, Frank and Lillian Gilbreth established basic elements that proved to be most valuable for analyzing physical work relationships.

Work Measurement—Following the work of the Gilbreths, time-study engineers devised methods for combining standard time value with each basic work element or fundamental motion. By assigning time values to these fundamental motions, engineers are able to work in a laboratory and synthesize the motions necessary to perform an assignment and to set a time standard for the work under study. Some of the better known synthetic time systems are Methods-Time Measurement (MTM), Work Measurement, Basic Motion Time-study (BMT), and Dimensional Motion Times (DMT). Each of these methods was developed primarily for industrial application and relates to jobs having observable and measurable manual labor inputs. They all provide work standards that come from an analysis of job content. However, they are not free of subjectivity; and all require personnel skilled in the method being used. Both a strength and weakness of work measurement is that each job standard requires an individual analysis, which is time-consuming and thus costly.

Elements of Standards—Most piecework programs provide each worker with a guaranteed wage rate if standards are not met. Three of the most common methods used to determine the guarantee are (1) to set it equivalent to the federal or state minimum wage, (2) to use some form of a job evaluation process, or (3) to set the standard through collective bargaining if the organization is unionized.

After setting the guarantee, management must determine its base for standards of performance. Two systems are available: (1) setting the base on what an average worker produces, and (2) setting it on what a motivated worker produces. The definition for the *average worker production standard* is the output produced under normal conditions by an average worker with average education, experience, and skill who is physically fit for the job. The definition for the *motivated worker production standard* is the output produced by a motivated worker with sufficient education, experience, and skill who is physically fit for the job and who works at an incentive-induced pace that can be maintained day after day without harmful effect.[3] No matter which base is used, it usually receives a 100 percent value as the standard.

The next step is to decide on an *incentive rate.* Most organizations pay their motivated output rate at 25 to 35 percent above what they would consider to be a fair rate of the output of the average worker. An incentive rate of 30 percent appears not only to be a fair and equitable reward for the extra effort, but it also provides maximum motivational impact on most workers.[4]

Certain types of piecework and pay-for-performance plans call for a sharing of gains achieved from increased productivity. This distribution of savings in direct labor costs between the employee and the employer is frequently called the *participation rate.* This rate is normally expressed as a figure such as 100–0 (100 percent), 75–25, 50–50, and so on. The first figure is the employee's share. In a 100–0 or 100 percent plan, the employee receives credit for all production above normal. Most individual piecework plans are of the 100–0 type. (In fact, the 100–0 plan is known as the *straight piecework plan.*) On the other hand, most group plans have some degree of employer sharing (less than 100 percent plan.)

Another element requiring consideration in the setting of standards is whether to *limit* or *cap incentive earnings.* Occasionally, incentive plans cause conditions that make management question the value of having no limit to possible earnings. By using proper procedures and methods to determine output standards and by ensuring minimal change in the variables controlling the production process, it is unlikely that the average employee will exceed an incentive rate by more than 10 to 20 percent. If the worker does, all the better for the company. That worker has found a better way to do the work. This is one of the pluses of the direct incentive plan that few realize.

On the other hand, as mentioned previously, operational variables can change. Since there is no limit to change brought about by employee ingenuity and creativity, without the knowledge of management, workers may change work methods, create and design tools or other fixtures to improve performance, or even manipulate working conditions to enable them to increase earnings without increasing output. These changes may not only vary output; they may also downgrade quality. Playing the "beat the rate" game usually has a harmful effect on productivity. Those who propose a limit on incentives state that, through the use and acceptance of such limits, management and employees can develop agreements for maintaining programs that will provide fair earnings

---

[3]Paraphrased from a definition developed by Marvin E. Mundel, *Motion and Time Study: Principles and Practice,* 4th ed. (Englewood Cliffs, NJ: Prentice-Hall, 1970), p. 311.

[4]Mitchell Fein, *Wage Incentive Plans* (Norcross, GA: American Institute of Industrial Engineers, 1970), p. 28.

while minimizing actions that permit employees to make excessive earnings without providing comparable effort and output. The other side of the coin, however, is that if there is lack of honor and trust between labor and management, these "beat the rate" games will exist in any incentive plan whether or not it has a limit to earnings. Placing such a limit can minimize employer loss in direct labor payments without adequate output, but it also has the possibility of negating the very heart of any incentive program.

Types of Piecework Programs—By combining various elements of piecework programs, a number of plans have evolved over the past century. The straight piecework plan is the most simple of these. In this plan, the organization determines either an average or a motivated standard of units of output per period of time and sets a base wage rate and an incentive rate. The worker receives full credit for all production above the normal or average base.

The *measured day work plan,* which is a modification of the straight piecework plan, sets rates for an extended period of time. In addition to measuring output, the measured day work plan may use certain characteristics of the merit rating type for setting the guaranteed work rate. The philosophy underlying a day work plan is that for an agreed rate of pay the worker provides a certain output. The worker receives this rate for an extended (or contracted) period. At the end of the period, management reviews the worker's performance, and a new rate is set for the next period. The higher the level of output and performance, the higher the guaranteed rate of payment.

The *differential day rate plan* is a variation of the *basic day rate plan.* The basic day rate plan guarantees workers their earnings, thus promoting their economic security. It is particularly effective when there is a need to emphasize quality or when the operations are machine-paced. It has the shortcoming, however, of failing to stimulate worker interest, motivation, and productivity.

Through slight modifications, the day rate plan becomes the differential day rate plan (an incentive plan). The modifications include the establishment of a base output and an incentive or standard output. If workers produce the base output or less, they receive the day rate guarantee. If they produce the standard output, they receive some incentive increase. Normally, the differential day rate or standard time plan (its other name) uses a 20 percent incentive. To receive the incentive, workers may have to produce the standard output on an hourly or daily basis, or even for an entire pay period. The major factor that differentiates the standard time plan from the straight piecework plan is that in the standard time plan, the standard refers to time per unit of production rather than money per unit of production. A standard hour is the amount of work done by an average worker in one hour at a normal pace to earn the base rate.

Other Piecework Plans—A number of the pioneers in the field of scientific management developed their own piecework plans.

In his *differential piecerate plan,* Frederick W. Taylor established two different rates for the same job. The higher rate per unit was paid when the work was completed in the set time or less and in acceptable condition (this rate was normally 20 percent higher than the lower rate). The worker received the lower rate per unit for taking longer than the established time to complete the job.[5]

Henry L. Gantt developed the *task and bonus plan,* a modification of Taylor's plan that permitted new and inexperienced employees an opportunity to receive certain minimum levels of pay. Whereas under the Taylor plan workers received pay based strictly on units produced, Gantt set a minimum guarantee and then established a bonus for production above certain standards.[6]

Dwight V. Merrick developed the *multiple-wage plan* in which he modified Taylor's plan by replacing the 20 percent bonus with a two-step increment that provided workers with a 10 percent bonus when they reached 83 percent of standard and the additional 10 percent when they achieved standard.[7]

The *efficiency plan* of Harrington Emerson is yet another modification of the Taylor plan. Emerson established a small bonus to be paid when the employee reached 67 percent of standard, with small incremental percentage bonus increases in base wages until standard was reached. For production over standard, the employee received a bonus that increased by 1 percent for each 1 percent increase in efficiency.[8]

Although these plans relied on some form of time study to develop basic work standards, at approximately the same time a group of engineers were developing piecework plans that used past performance or self-developed standards to set basic output requirements.

The first of these plans was the *premium plan for paying labor* developed by the Canadian engineer, Frederick A. Halsey, in the 1880s. In the Halsey premium plan, the worker received a guaranteed hourly wage plus a percentage of the wage for any time saved. The percentage of savings suggested by Halsey was 33 percent. The actual production standards were determined by past performance.[9] Using an example developed in Halsey's time, if a worker is paid 30 cents per hour and the unit of production requires ten hours of work, the worker receives an additional 10 cents for each hour saved over the ten hours required to complete the job.

A variation of the Halsey premium plan was developed by James Rowan of Glasgow, Scotland, in 1898. In the *Rowan plan,* the worker received an increase

[5]Frederick W. Taylor, "A Piece Rate System," *Transactions of the American Society of Mechanical Engineers,* vol. 16, 1895, pp. 856–905.

[6]Henry L. Gantt, "A Bonus System of Rewarding Labor," *Transactions of the American Society of Mechanical Engineers,* vol. 23, 1902, pp. 341–372.

[7]Dwight V. Merrick, *Time Studies as a Basis for Rate Setting* (New York: The Engineering Magazine Co., 1920).

[8]Harrington Emerson, *The Twelve Principles of Efficiency,* 5th ed. (New York: The Engineering Magazine Co., 1917).

[9]Frederick A. Halsey, "The Premium Plan of Paying for Labor," *Transactions of the American Society of Mechanical Engineers,* vol. 12, 1891, pp. 755–780.

in guaranteed wages by a percentage identical to the reduction in the time expected to complete the job.[10]

Around 1910, Charles Bedaux, dissatisfied with inadequacies inherent in the time-study practices used at that time, developed a plan based on his measure of human productivity. Through an analysis of the types and the frequency of human movements necessary to perform a job, Bedaux developed standard units that he felt would measure the relationship between output and physical energy. The basis of the Bedaux plan is a unit of measurement called a *B*. The *B* is a combination of a fraction of a minute of work and a fraction of a minute of rest.[11] Sixty *B*s represent a standard performance per hour.

The effort requirements of a job are identified by a certain number of *B*s per hour, or *B*-hour units. In the initial Bedaux plan, when a worker produced more *B*-hour units than normal (exceeding production standard in the normal piecework system), the sharing of gains achieved through increased production was 75 percent to the worker and 25 percent to the related indirect workers and immediate supervisors. Later variations of the Bedaux plan gave 100 percent of the gain to the worker. For example, if the standard for a job is eight hours, but the worker completes the job in six hours and the hourly rate of pay for the job is $5, the bonus is:

Step 1. Standard points $\quad= 8 \text{ hours} \times 60 \text{ } Bs = 480 \text{ points}$
Points required $\quad= 6 \text{ hours} \times 60 \text{ } Bs = 360 \text{ points}$
Extra bonus points $= \text{standard} - \text{required} = 480 - 360 = 120$

Step 2. Using a 75 percent bonus system, the bonus equals

$$0.75 \times \frac{(\text{bonus points} \times \text{hourly earning})}{60 \text{ } Bs}$$

$$= 0.75 \times \frac{(120 \times 5.00)}{60} = \$7.50 \text{ bonus}$$

There have been a number of variations of the Bedaux plan. One developed by Hasbrouck Haynes used "manits" as the standard for work measurement. *Manits* is an abbreviation for man-minutes as the unit of time measurement. The manit developed by Haynes is defined as four-fifths the amount of work that a normal worker is able to turn out in a minute of time without exertion. Similar to the *B*s in the Bedaux plan, manits in the Haynes plan measure worker output.[12]

---

[10]Sir Wm. Rowan Thomson, *The Rowan Premium Bonus System of Payment by Results,* 2d ed. (Glasgow, Scotland: McCorquedale and Company, 1919). A verbatim discussion of the basic steps of the Rowan plan is included in Charles W. Lytle, *Wage Incentive Methods, Their Selection, Installation,* and *Operation,* rev. ed. (New York: The Ronald Press, 1942), pp. 259–260.

[11]L. C. Morrow, "The Bedaux Principle of Human Power Measurement," *American Machinist,* February 16, 1922, pp. 241–245.

[12]Charles W. Lytle, *Wage Incentive Methods: Their Selection, Installation, and Operation,* rev. ed. (New York: The Ronald Press, 1942). Both the Bedaux and Haynes plans are discussed at length in chapter 11, "Constant Sharing Plans with Minute as Time Unit," pp. 224–255.

Rewarding Indirect Labor—Piecework plans in general were born at the time of the rise of craft trades in the thirteenth and fourteenth centuries. At that time, the master craftsman received full rewards for his labor, while his helpers and apprentices earned little more than subsistence wages. The thorny issue of fair and equitable payment for personnel who support and make possible the productivity improvement of the direct laborer (the person actually performing the measured task) confronts many organizations to this very day.

The Bedaux plan was one of the first of the piecework-type plans that attempted to solve this enigmatic issue. A major consideration that frequently blocks resolution of this problem is the variety of activities and jobs performed by indirect labor. In many cases, these workers assist a number of direct laborers. They may perform functions that include providing, sorting, or preparing raw materials; removing finished materials; inspecting; training; maintaining equipment or records; and general supervising. It is difficult to maintain a high level of performance among the direct laborers without providing those who support them with some type of a reward.

Some pay-for-performance plans for indirect laborers provide that they receive the same percentage increase above normal as that earned by the direct laborer. Other plans develop standards based on hours worked to units of product produced or some variation thereof. When using piecework programs in small group operations, the indirect labor jobs are often scheduled in the activity requirements of the group.

As with other elements of the incentive package, the indirect labor issue must not be set aside because of the difficulty involved in developing acceptable solutions.

Group Use of Piecework Plans—Most of the discussion concerning piecework plans has involved individual effort, but piecework programs can be just as effective for stimulating the performance of small groups.

There are two basic approaches for developing group piecework plans. The first is identical to that described for setting individual piecework standards. It requires setting work standards for each member of the group and maintaining a count of the output of each member. The difference between this group approach and that related to individual piecework arises in the method of payment. The group approach may use one of the following payment methods: (1) all members receive the pay earned by the highest producer, (2) all members receive the pay earned by the lowest producer, and (3) all members receive payment equal to the average pay earned by the group.

The second and far more unique approach is to set a standard based on the group's final output. This approach does not relieve management of the responsibility of performing a detailed analysis of the work performed by each member. Work-flow and work-processing information are still necessary for establishing the initial balancing of work tasks and activities among the members. Once production is underway, the group may vary to meet its own demands any work-balancing system developed by management. This approach is more useful when all members work together to complete a single product.

The first approach would be applicable when members are performing similar or identical assignments.

The advantage of the group approach is not only the simplification of measuring output but the support the individual members provide one another. A well-knit, properly managed work group assists in training new and less experienced members. It also rotates jobs so that it makes the most effective use of its human resources. The members also aid one another in overcoming both on- and off-the-job problems that affect group performance. The piecework incentive plan provides a goal that assists in coordinating and directing group efforts for the benefit of the organization, the group, and its individual members. As mentioned earlier, the membership of an effective work group varies between five and 12 members. An optimum size is probably seven.

In most well-functioning work groups, the total earnings (base pay plus any pay-for-performance earnings) are split equally among the members. It is possible that the group itself may wish to grant a larger percentage to the more senior or experienced members, but this is the exceptional case and is strictly a group decision.

Cost–reduction or Productivity Gainsharing Programs

Over the years, a variety of productivity improvement programs has been developed that focus on reducing costs. These plans provide for the employee to share with the employer any benefits gained from reduction in costs. The philosophy underlying this type of program is that cost reduction is both an opportunity and the responsibility of every member of the organization. If responsibility for cost reduction has organization-wide acceptance and if each member seizes every opportunity to reduce costs, an employer can meet almost any competitive challenge, grant job security to each member, and provide high rewards for work efforts.

In recent years, a new term that has caught the fancy of many authors writing in the area of productivity improvement has been *productivity gainsharing*. Productivity gainsharing is basically a sharing by the organization with their employees of "bottom-line" improvements obtained through increased productivity. Gainsharing in this approach involves all or a significant number of employees in some kind of group sharing and total employee involvement. The purpose is to permit employee involvement and commitment to improving the performance of their organization.

Each member has the opportunity to conserve both human and material resources. In addition, through the constructive use of innovation and creativity, better ways can be found to perform existing operations. By tapping the ingenuity of the entire work force, it is possible not only to reduce costs through elimination of wasted materials and labor but also to develop new or better products or services that strengthen the company and increase job security. Each cost-reduction plan provides a formula through which workers receive a share of the money saved as a result of improvements in work practices.

A first requirement for any cost-reduction or gainsharing plan is the determination of a standard measure of performance. Once management and the work force agree to a standard, it is possible to compare actual performance with the preset standard. The difference between the two is attributed to the efforts of both workers and management. Because both groups have a direct impact on cost reduction, most plans call for a sharing of savings. Some plans provide for a 50–50 split; others, 67–33; and some may require that 75 percent of the total savings go back to the workers and 25 percent remain with the company.

To be successful, a cost-reduction or gainsharing plan must have the complete support of senior management. Beyond mere approval of plan development and implementation, senior management must be certain that the plan is well-conceived and executed. A cost-reduction plan must relate business objectives to the standards identified as improvement targets. It must recognize the need to provide data that may, in the past, have been considered top secret. The plan must consider the variables that affect these standards and the way they will be managed when they change sufficiently to have an impact on the credibility or the viability of the plan. Some of the variables that can have an influence on the operation of a cost-reduction plan follow:

1. New machinery or other technological changes.

2. Changes in methods, procedures, or processes.

3. Product mix.

4. Raw material availability and cost.

5. Labor cost.

6. Customer service requirements.

7. Delivery procedures.

8. Inventory policy.

9. Sales price of product or service.

10. Financing and funding patterns.

To develop a plan that has a chance to survive, let alone succeed, thoughtful and lengthy planning must precede implementation. A review of four well-known cost-reduction plans provides insight into the basic components of such plans.

Scanlon Plan—In the mid-1930s, Joseph N. Scanlon, then president of a local union in a Mansfield, Ohio, steel company, developed his union-management cooperation plan in which it was stated that if management would reopen its doors during a shutdown brought about by the Great Depression, the union would engage with the company in cost reduction through production committees.[13] He further refined the plan in 1944 by developing a ratio of payroll to sales value as a measure of performance at the Adamson Company in East Palestine, Ohio.

The original plan developed by Scanlon required good management, mutual respect, integrity, and trust on the part of both management and labor, and a strong labor force that recognized its responsibilities for making its business stronger and more competitive. An ideal Scanlon plan would include every member of the business, but among its many variations, it may include all production employees, all nonexempt employees, or all employees up to a certain level of management. Normally, once implemented, it is the only pay-for-performance plan operating in the business.

The basic elements of the Scanlon plan are as follows:

1. The ratio.
2. The bonus.
3. The production committee.
4. The screening committee.

The *ratio* or norm is the standard that serves as a measure for judging business performance. The ratio is

$$\frac{\text{Total labor cost}}{\text{Sales value of production}}$$

The ten variables previously listed as having an impact on cost-reduction plans in general have an impact on this ratio as well. Many organizations, however, find that this ratio is fairly stable over an extended period. A common value lies between 37 to 42 percent. Prior to establishing such a ratio, it is wise for management to analyze its labor costs and sales value of production for at least the preceding two years. It is not uncommon, however, for an organization to go back at least seven years. It is helpful if this analysis is done on a month-to-month basis to identify seasonal fluctuations. The ratio may be changed, but the number of changes must be kept to an absolute minimum.[14]

The amount of the *bonus* depends on the reduction in costs below the preset ratio. The normal method of distributing the bonus is for the first 25 percent of the bonus to go into an escrow account to reimburse management when the ratio rises above the predetermined normal base. Any amount remaining in escrow at the end of the year becomes part of the Christmas distribution. Seventy-five percent of the remaining funds, or 56.25 percent of the

---

[13]Frederick G. Lesieur, ed., *The Scanlon Plan . . . A Frontier in Labor Management Cooperation* (Cambridge, MA: MIT Press, 1958).

[14]In a personal letter to this author, dated January 22, 1975, Frederick Lesieur stated that in the inflationary spirals of 1972–1974, as material costs outstripped wage increases, Scanlon ratios had to undergo frequent changes. Those persons involved in managing Scanlon plans found, however, that these changes were made with minimal difficulty.

total bonus, then goes to the workers on a monthly basis. The 18.75 percent remaining in the bonus pool goes to the company. In addition, the company also gains from better use of its assets. The basis for each individual's share of the bonus is his or her monthly earnings as a percentage of the monthly total labor costs.

A *production committee* is formed in each major department and consists of from two to five worker representatives and one representative of management (normally the unit's foreman or supervisor). The purpose of the committee is to use the vast wealth of imagination and ingenuity lying untapped in the workers' brains. The committee develops employee suggestions to increase productivity, improve quality, reduce waste, and improve methods of organizational operations. It also develops an understanding of all production costs and disseminates this information throughout the business. This committee normally meets twice a month.

The *screening committee* consists of top members of the plant management and worker representatives, usually eight to 12 members. It reviews the monthly bonus, discusses current production problems, and considers all suggestions for organizational improvement. It discusses all aspects of business trends relative to the enterprise, from competitors for product and labor, to sales and shipment policies, orders, quality, customer problems, to the general business outlook. This committee normally meets once a month.

Rucker Plan of Group Incentives—Another plant-wide, cost-reduction incentive plan has been developed by the Eddy-Rucker-Nickels Company.[15] This incentive plan has a philosophical base similar to that of the Scanlon plan. The Rucker plan has been most successful in manufacturing companies that are already profitable, that have reasonably good employee-management relations, and that employ between 50 and 800 people. It has been used to add an incentive in "day rate" shops, to replace unsatisfactory piecework plans, or as a supplement to satisfactory piecework plans to provide incentive to those employees it does not cover.

A major difference between the Scanlon plan and the Rucker plan is the norm or base used to establish a measure of productivity. The Rucker plan's measure of productivity is called *economic productivity*. It is the output of value added by manufacture for each dollar of input of payroll costs. Value added by manufacture is the difference between the sales income from goods produced and the cost of the materials, supplies, and outside services consumed in the production and delivery of that output. Payroll costs are all employment costs paid to, because of, or on behalf of the employee group measured. Accounting procedures similar to those used for developing the ratio in the Scanlon plan are used to develop the economic productivity measure of the Rucker plan.

To earn a monthly bonus, there must be an increase in the production value per $1 paid over the predetermined standard. All increases are deposited in a

[15]Carl Heyel, ed., *The Encyclopedia of Management,* 2d ed. (New York: Van Nostrand Reinhold, 1973), pp. 895–900.

bonus pool, with two-thirds of the bonus paid out to the employees monthly and one-third held in reserve until the end of the year. This reserve provides a cushion for accounting adjustments or for periods when the standard is not met. After a final year-end audit, all the reserve is distributed to the employees.

Improshare—The Improshare plan,[16] an industrial engineering–based productivity measurement and sharing plan, was developed in the mid-1970s by Mitchell Fein. This plan uses easy-to-obtain past production records to establish base performance standards. It may include both hourly and salaried employees, incentive and nonincentive employees, or any designated group. The organization and its employees share in a 50/50 division of all productivity gains.

The first step in the Improshare plan is to identify those groups to be included in the plan and the products to be produced. The next step is to establish the *base period,* the *base period product costs,* and the *base productivity factor (BPF).* The base period is the period of time used to establish productivity standards. The base period product costs are those costs used by management during the base period that represent the direct labor hours to produce a product by major operations and by total products being produced. These costs are usually determined through some form of engineered time standards for all operations, totaled to obtain an overall engineered time standard for each product. The BPF represents the relationship in the base period between the actual hours worked by all employees in the plan and the value of work in standard man hours produced by these employees, as determined by the product costs used by management for the base period.

After establishing all required base period performance data, the organization then calculates current performance in hours worked and output produced. By comparing current output and hours worked against base period standards, hours saved (Improshare earned hours) are calculated. Then, using Improshare designed hours gained, the employee share of the improvements is calculated.

There are three controls established in the Improshare plan that permit changes in the measurement standards. They are (1) a ceiling on productivity improvement of 160 percent, (2) cash buy-back of measurement standards, and (3) 80/20 share of improvements created by capital equipment.

The employees receive the productivity monthly gain as a percent increase in their regular pay. By using a 50/50 sharing of productivity gains and setting a 160 percent ceiling on productivity performance, the maximum employee gainsharing is 30 percent of regular wages. When gains of over 160 percent are achieved, that amount over the 160 percent is "banked." If in the next performance calculation period, the productivity gain is less than 160 percent, the "banked gain" is added to the gain for the next pay-out period. When high productivity continues and the productivity calculation remains above 160 percent, management has the right to buy back the gain over 160 percent. If, for example, the gain for the year rests at 180 percent, employees receive 50 percent

---

[16]Mitchell Fein, *An Alternative to Traditional Managing* (Hillsdale, NJ: Mitchell Fein, 1980), pp. 28–41.

of the difference between 180 and 160 in a one time annual bonus payment. If the employee's hourly rate of pay was $5 and the employee worked 2,000 hours in the year, the buy-back bonus for the employee would be calculated in this manner:

$$20\% \text{ (buy back)} \times 50\% \text{ (division of gain)} \times \$5 \text{ (hourly rate)}$$
$$\times 2,000 \text{ (hours worked)} = \$1,000 \text{ (buy-back bonus)}$$

Then, in turn, the base period standard for future calculation would be increased by

$$\frac{1.8}{1.6} \text{ or } 1.125$$

When gains are made because of the introduction of new equipment, new technology, etc., management receives 80 percent of the gain and the worker receives 20 percent.

Kaiser-Steel Union Sharing Plan—In 1963 the United Steelworkers of America (USWA) and the Kaiser Steel Corporation negotiated a cost-reduction incentive plan. Kaiser Steel already had a plantwide piecework plan similar to those in most basic steel plants. One of Kaiser's principal aims was eventually to replace its existing incentive system with this cost-reduction or cost-sharing plan. The plan had many of the elements found in both the Scanlon and Rucker plans, but it also had special features that met the circumstances and problems of the Fontana, California, steelmill of Kaiser. The major difference concerned the standard for determining improvements in performance.

The cost standards developed by Kaiser and the USWA used the costs actually incurred during 1961. Included in the standards were a constant base established at a zero level of production, a labor standard, and a materials and supply standard. The formula developed for distributing the gains saved from cost-reduction efforts was 32.5 percent to the employee with the remaining 67.5 percent split between management and the public (that portion of the savings that resulted in increased taxes). Many other features were incorporated initially into the plan to satisfy already existing problems (the Stieglitz[17] study covers in detail all aspects of the initial plan).

In 1972, nine years after establishing the plan, the USWA Local 1869 at Fontana struck for changes and improvements in their cost-reduction program. Some of the comments on the effectiveness of the plan follow:

1. The workers had a difficult time relating their performance to the monthly bonus. (They identified immediately with the more conventional piecework incentive plan.)

2. Payment under the plan was limited by the economic slowdown of that time.

[17]Harold Stieglitz, *The Kaiser-Steel Union Sharing Plan Personnel Policy Study, No. 187* (New York: National Industrial Conference Board, 1963).

3. The plan was unsuccessful because it did not eliminate the need for the conventional incentive plan.

4. The union was dissatisfied with the statistics provided by management to compute the cost-sharing savings on materials.[18]

During the first nine years of the plan, the man-hours necessary to produce a ton of steel dropped from 8.93 in 1963 to about 7.30 in 1972, with a low of 6.60 man-hours in 1969. (Information is unavailable as to the impact of improved technology in this reduction.) Kaiser employees had been earning approximately 21¢ per hour more than their counterparts throughout the country between 1967 and 1971.

The resolution of the strike resulted in the following changes in the initial plan:

1. Those on incentive base rates were granted certain guarantees in order to overcome the complaint that the cost-sharing plan was not offering as much extra money as the more conventional incentive type of work available at the mill.

2. Renegotiation rights concerning the plan would be at the same time as that for the basic contract.

3. Losses for a particular month would not be offset by the gains in another month.

4. Cost of vacations, including extended vacation and supplemental unemployment benefits (SUB), would not be deducted from the employees' share of the gain.

5. Factory procedures that resulted in different rates of pay to workers on the same job would be eliminated.[19]

The Kaiser plan and its results certainly underscore the concept that the cost-reduction plan in itself is not a panacea for improving management-worker relations or for improving productivity. It is a step along the path toward such goals, but the steps are not achieved without intelligent understanding of the problems and diligent effort on the part of all concerned.

Profit Sharing

Profit sharing has developed hand in glove with the concepts of democracy and the worth and dignity of human labor. An early American sponsor of profit sharing was Albert Gallatin, who introduced it into his glassworks factory in New Geneva, Pennsylvania, in 1794. Maison Le Claire, owner of a house

[18]"Complexity May Undo Kaiser Sharing Plans," *Industry Week,* February 14, 1972, p. 14.

[19]"Kaiser, USWA Agree on Cost-sharing Plan," *Industry Week,* March 27, 1972, p. 19.

painting and decorating business in Paris, France, has been credited with being the "father of profit sharing." He earned this title not because his was the first such plan but because it was one of the most successful. He introduced his plan in 1842.

Today, profit sharing is widely accepted as a fundamental part of the compensation program of over 150,000 American businesses. Profit sharing has been defined by the Council of Profit Sharing Industries as any procedure under which an employer pays or makes available to regular employees, subject to reasonable eligibility rules, in addition to prevailing rates of pay, special current or deferred sums based on the profits of business.

There are essentially three different types of profit-sharing plans in existence today:

1. *Cash or current payment plan,* which provides for the distribution of profits relative to some predetermined division by either cash or company stock, or both, within a short period following the earning of the profit and the determination of the proportionate shares.

2. *Deferred plan,* which provides for placement of earned funds into an escrow account for distribution at a future date (this plan usually provides the financial support for the pension program of the business).

3. *Combined plan,* which has the features of both.

With the enactment in 1974 of the Employee Retirement Income Security Act (ERISA), many additional financial responsibilities and burdensome administrative details have been placed on organizations that use profit sharing to finance pension plans. Because of this law and its associated problems, many firms changed their profit-sharing programs to provide for some form of annual payment, thus requiring their employees to develop their own retirement programs.

A major philosophical issue behind all profit-sharing programs is the need to educate employees on the importance of profit, the employees' effect on profit, and how increased profits benefit them. A major weakness of many profit-sharing plans is that once they have been incorporated into the compensation system, they become institutionalized, accepted as permanent, unchanging fixtures, and have little to no motivational impact on employees for improving their work performance. If a profit-sharing program is to have motivational impact, the rewards offered to the employee must vary with the success of the business. A clear relationship must exist between rewards and performance. For this reason, payment for effort must have as close a time relationship to the performance period as possible. Monthly or bimonthly bonus payments are excellent; quarterly, semiannual, or annual payments are acceptable but certainly less a motivator unless the reward is very large or has worker recognition and acceptance. One of the premier profit-sharing plans that over the past 40 years has provided the type of stimulation desired by every business is the plan developed by James F. Lincoln of the Lincoln Electric Company, Cleveland, Ohio.[20]

Lincoln's Incentive System—Upon being made general manager of the Lincoln Electric Company in 1914, James Lincoln established an incentive compensation plan. After 20 years of effort, the incentive plan evolved substantially into the plan that exists today. Its principal features are as follows:

1. The company guarantees 30 hours of work 50 weeks a year to each employee who has at least two years of service. (It guarantees no specific rate of pay, and the worker must be willing to transfer from one job to another and work overtime during periods of peak demand. The company reserves the right to terminate the agreement providing six months advance notice is given.)

2. Standard job evaluation procedures set the base wage, using the six compensable factors of mentality, skill, responsibility, mental application, physical application, and working conditions to determine the importance of each job. The combination of job evaluation and labor market requirements then sets the actual dollar worth of the job.

3. The majority of employees are on a piecework incentive plan. The factory products—arc welding equipment and electric motors—lend themselves to standardized operation and the setting of rates. Both the workers and management, however, recognize labor's opportunity to improve both the quality and the quantity of output. Every possible job that can be standardized has a piece rate. Rates are set through the use of normal time-study procedures. The jobs that are not on piece rates include clerical work, tool room operations, maintenance and repairs, and experimental work. New employees and employees on new jobs receive a temporary exemption from piecework standards. Employees in a few small assembly operations work on a group piecework plan.

4. All employees may participate in the suggestion program with the exception of department heads and members of the engineering and time-study departments (suggestions for improvements are a fundamental part of their jobs). Any suggestions that lead to organizational progress (e.g., improved manufacturing methods, sales, procedures, waste reduction, or new or improved products) are considered during merit rating.

5. Twice a year, a merit-rating program appraises the actual work performance of each employee. This appraisal program uses four report cards. Each card rates the work performance according to one of the four following work variables: (1) *dependability* (the ability to supervise oneself, including

---

[20]*Lincoln's Incentive System and Approach to Manufacturing* (Cleveland, OH: The Lincoln Electric Company, 1972). (A compilation of various articles describes Lincoln's incentive plan and operation.)

one's work safety performance, orderliness, care of equipment, and effectiveness in the use of one's skills); (2) *quality* (one's success in eliminating errors and reducing scrap and waste); (3) *output* (one's willingness to be productive, not hold back work effort or output, and recognize the importance of attendance); (4) *ideas and cooperation* (initiative and ingenuity in developing new methods to reduce costs, increase output, improve quality, and effect better customer relations). The supervisor doing the rating informs subordinates of their scores. The individual scores for each group are posted by number only. It is possible, through the process of elimination, to identify the score of a specific employee. Many employees openly state their scores. Managers at levels above that of immediate supervisor responsible for appraising performance take an active role in reviewing all merit ratings.

6. Each employee annually has the opportunity to purchase from ten to 25 shares of company stock. Upon the employee's retirement or termination of employment, the company has an option to repurchase the stock. Currently, about 25 percent of the employees own 45 percent of the stock.

7. Employees elect representatives to an "advisory board." This board has the opportunity to suggest changes in policies and operation; however, the final decision on all changes is made by management.

8. Independent work groups or "subcontractor shop" operations, in which employees have the opportunity to earn specified piecework rates, perform their own quality control and develop their own production procedures in completing subassembly operations within given cost, quantity, and quality parameters.

9. All profits of the business are split three ways: (a) the corporation retains a certain share for capital improvement and financial security; (b) shareholders receive approximately 6 percent to 8 percent dividends based on the book value of the two types of company stock; and (c) employees receive all remaining profits.

10. The annual cash bonus earned by the employees closely approximates their annual earnings. The actual distribution an employee earns is a function of the employee's annual earnings as a percentage of the total labor cost, individual performance appraisal merit rating, and total amount of profit earned by Lincoln Electric.

The year-end bonus plan was initiated when James Lincoln turned down a request for a 10 percent increase in wages in 1934 because he felt the profit picture would not warrant such an increase. The workers then responded with the request for a year-end bonus if, through increased productivity and lowered costs, the year-end profits were larger. After some deliberation, Lincoln agreed to this efficiency-oriented proposal. To everyone's surprise (including Lincoln's), the bonus amounted to $350 instead of the $35 to $50 expected by Lincoln. In 1980, over 2,600 employees shared a bonus of $46 million. Over the past several years, the annual bonus has ranged from a low of 88 percent to a high of 115 percent of annual earnings.

By many standards, Lincoln Electric is not an easy place to work. There is no room for the "goof off" or "I don't care" worker. The success of the entire business depends on a high level of contribution by each member. There is a mutual understanding of need and a mutual respect based on democratic principles espoused and lived by James F. Lincoln.

The democratic principles go much deeper than the basic elements of the previously described incentive system. For example, there are no reserved employee parking spaces; there is one cafeteria (with excellent food) and all employees—workers and managers alike—sit wherever spaces are available. In addition, there is a policy of promotion from within that requires all promotional opportunities to be posted (including many senior positions). There are no definite lines of promotion, and promotions are given by qualification only. The benefits program includes a two-week paid vacation for employees with one year of service, three weeks for 13 years of service, four weeks for 19 years of service, and five weeks for 25 years of service. There is a paid medical, surgical, and hospital plan; life insurance; and a retirement plan beginning at age 60 with pension based on years of service and total earnings excluding bonus. Other benefits include an annual picnic, company dinner, and a Quarter-Century Club.

In addition, employees may challenge any time study. If a time study results in a lowering of a rate, the involved employee may request transfer to a job that pays an equal or higher rate. Piece rate is not a tool of speedup but rather a tool of fair and equitable distribution of rewards for the effort of a motivated employee. There is no limit to earnings, and no rate can be changed unless there has been a change in method, design, or tooling. Employees challenge less than one-fifth of 1 percent of all rate changes. There is a periodic review of all rates.

The principles of incentive compensation are a fundamental part of the democratic process. Lincoln Electric has the *highest-paid* factory workers in the world and, measuring in units of work produced, the *lowest-cost* workers in any factory in the world in a similar line of work.[21]

Other Profit-sharing Programs—A program similar in many ways to the Lincoln system is that of the Facom Company, a French mechanical tool manufacturer that has achieved a growth rate and international market position similar to Lincoln's.[22] Its profit-sharing program involves employees of all levels. Its 1,300 employees enjoy salaries in the upper range of their industry and, in addition, earn shares of the profit ranging from 18 to 25 percent of their annual wages.

[21]J. F. Lincoln, "Incentive Compensation: The Way to Industrial Democracy," *Advanced Management,* February 1950, pp. 17–18.

[22]The information on Facom comes from the article by Jean Bedel, "25 Years of Participation," *Management,* Nov. 1972, pp. 66–73.

The business is split into 100 sections, with a maximum of 20 members in each section. These sections operate as responsibility centers, making a wide variety of operational decisions including the development of the budget and the establishment of section wages and all costs. The sections receive viable and meaningful feedback on all operations.

Similar to Lincoln's plan, profit-sharing distributions are a proportion of annual earnings. Because of national legislation, Facom modified its plan to make direct payments of 70 percent of profit sharing, placing the additional 30 percent in a reserve account for the future security of its employees. Just as in the Lincoln plan, Facom employees may acquire stock in the company (approximately 45 percent of the employees own stock).

Although the local union has not actively opposed the plan, it does feel that since the basis of profit sharing is on earned income, managers receive a greater share of the rewards. Workers who become actively involved in the Participation Committee complain that many workers wish only to draw their bonus and take little part in the working sessions of the committee.

When Facom initiated its plan in 1948, it had no profits. In 1972 it earned a profit of 18 percent on sales (the average rate for the 500 largest firms in France for 1972 was about 4 percent). Using a productivity index (1962 figures act as a base of 100) of the main European countries that produce hand tools, Facom had achieved a figure of 337 in 1972 as compared to 194 for German companies and 153 for companies in the United Kingdom.

Eastman Kodak is another American company with an enviable record of employee profit-sharing distribution that extends back to 1912. This plan directly relates to cash dividends declared on Kodak stock. The profit-sharing dividend is paid to all employees and the payment is based on average earnings of the last five years. Last year the rate was 3.175 percent of average earnings times the number of years worked up to five. Thus, someone earning $30,000 who was with Kodak for one year would receive $30,000 \times 3.175\% = \$952.50$. If the employee worked five years or more and earned $30,000 for each of the five years, he or she would receive $30,000 \times 3.175\% \times 5 = \$4,762.50$. In 1981, Kodak distributed about $224,200,000 to 85,700 employees.[23] The wage dividend for the average employee has, in recent years, ranged between 12 to 15 percent of annual earnings.

Short-term Contests and Suggestion Plans

Many organizations develop special contests, games, or promotions to stimulate extra effort to achieve a particular goal. These special goals may focus on productivity or quality improvement; development of a better safety record; or reduction of costs, absenteeism, or tardiness.

---

[23]"Kodak Rochester-area Employees to Receive $146.7 Million Wage Dividend March 20," *NEWS* (Rochester, NY: Eastman Kodak Company, March 18, 1981).

Most contests encourage some type of individual effort and foster a spirit of competition. Quite often, organizations design and implement contests to overcome boredom and lethargy and offer the winners certain "bragging rights." The range of prizes offered to stimulate the special effort includes merchandise, cash premiums, special trips, trading stamps, and even time off. Quite often, the prizes focus on rewards of interest to other family members (particularly the spouse). Recognition of the influence of the spouse assists in gaining greater interest in winning a particular premium.

The major difficulty with such contests is that in the design phase organizations fail to consider the full effect that a contest may have. Quite often, contests have unanticipated results from misdirected efforts that produce unhealthy side effects. It is essential before implementing a contest that organizations attempt to identify and recognize its impact on overall objectives.[24]

Ever since the 1880s when the suggestion box was introduced into American organizations, the employee suggestion has been a major factor for improving operations, products, or services. For example, in 1974 General Electric Company disbursed $3,053,982 to its employees for more than 69,000 adopted suggestions.[25] Practically every incentive plan recognizes the importance of the suggestion and provides rewards for stimulating employee creativity and innovation. The suggestion system has been a major element of any employer plan to encourage greater employee involvement.

Many systems have failed because of the following factors:

1. Management lacks interest and fails to support the system.

2. There has been insufficient time to review and analyze the suggestions.

3. Those developing suggestions fear the impact of the suggestions on fellow workers.

4. Supervisors consider suggestions to be a personal threat.

5. Some creative individuals are unable to describe or articulate their ideas accurately.

To generate more suggestions and improve suggestion programs, organizations should always be specific when informing an employee about the reasons an idea was not adopted. Some organizations help employees prepare suggestions; others permit employees to present suggestions to evaluation committees. In some cases, a suggestion is never removed from the process by anyone other than the individual making it. In this case, it may be restated, modified, or better described to clarify it.

[24]David R. Hampton, "Contests as Misdirected Motivators," *Compensation Review,* Second Quarter, 1970, pp. 32–38.

[25]"The Checkoff," *The Wall Street Journal,* May 20, 1975, p. 1.

Special Awards

To reinforce a desired, demonstrated employee behavior, employers recognize that the particular behavior should receive prompt recognition. Many organizations now offer a variety of one-time incentive awards that focus on the results of a particularly meritorious employee behavior.

An excellent example of this type of program is the awards plan of IBM, which has designed an awards program that recognizes significant performance in the employee's assigned job.[26] These one-time awards are in addition to any incentive or merit increase program that is part of the normal compensation program for IBM employees.

The IBM award plan has three distinct parts. The first recognizes accomplishment at the local level. This award, called the IBM Informal Award Plan, allows the immediate supervisor, with approval from the next highest level of management, to recognize an employee's exceptional diligence or contribution to a higher-level award (when that contribution was not significant enough to allow that employee to participate in the higher-level award). Cash awards are the most common of the informal awards. The informal award has a value limit of $1,500.

One of the favorite awards, however, is what management in some areas calls "Dinner for Two." By making this impromptu award, the immediate supervisor not only has the opportunity to pat an employee on the back with some type of verbal praise but can say, "Thanks a lot for that splendid effort. Would you take your spouse out to dinner and send me the bill?"

The second category is the Outstanding Contribution Plan designed to recognize achievement of outstanding value to IBM. This plan has two parts. One is the Outstanding Innovation Award Plan that rewards innovativeness and creativity resulting in outstanding economic or prestige value to IBM. The second is the IBM Division Award that recognizes achievements having an economic, commercial, or industrial value. It is primarily nontechnical. The awards range from $2,500 to $20,000, with approximately 60 percent ranging from $2,500 to $5,000; 35 percent, from $5,000 to $10,000; and the remaining 5 percent, up to $20,000.

The final category is the Corporate Award by which IBM recognizes a previous outstanding contribution that has been of extraordinary significance to IBM. These awards are almost totally technical and provide at least $10,000 to the recipient. They are made annually at a Corporate Recognition Event banquet. This company spends approximately $8 to $10 million a year on all three categories of award plans.

Few employers have the need or the opportunity to provide an incentive plan like that of IBM, but the basic philosophy is valuable and useful to every employer. An intrinsic reward every worker receives from working is recognition of a job well done. Everyone enjoys the feeling of being wanted, being a member

---

[26]This information was provided by James M. Bridgman at the Eastern Regional Meeting of the American Compensation Association, Atlanta, GA, May 13, 1977.

of a select, successful group, being appreciated, and being able to make a contribution that enhances the opportunity for success of all the group members. There are still those who argue that money has a negative impact on the intrinsic rewards an employee receives in performing a job. However, what better way does an employer have to recognize above-average effort or exceptional contributions than to publicly provide a monetary or in-kind payment (dinner for two) that clearly demonstrates to all employees how much the organization values performance?

Seasonal and Other Awards

For an award to have the greatest impact on employee behavior, it should immediately follow that behavior. This is not always possible or practical. Employee expectations and perceptions also influence timing.

Christmas Bonus—One of the most common times for an organization to provide extra pay or a special bonus is immediately before Christmas. The Christmas bonus can range from a gift such as a ham or a turkey to a gift certificate or to a monetary payment computed in a number of ways. Some of the more common ways to calculate Christmas money bonuses are (1) a thirteenth month paycheck (a cash payment equivalent to one month's earnings); (2) some percentage of annual earnings; (3) an award based on years of service; and (4) distribution of funds from a profit-sharing or cost-reduction plan.

Many employees look forward to their Christmas bonus as a source of money for shopping which magnifies its value. Most employees live from paycheck to paycheck. Their established living patterns consume their total earnings with little to no funds available for savings. The arrival of the Christmas holiday season and the desire to provide gifts for family and friends places a heavy burden on the ability of the employee to pay for these gifts. The Christmas bonus, in essence, becomes a Christmas savings plan that allows the employee to have the opportunity to make additional purchases at this time of year.

Organizations having a vacation period in which all employees receive their vacation at the same time often set their annual bonus payment to precede the vacation to permit employees with minimal cash reserves to make greater use of their time off.

Length-of-Service Awards and Seniority Rewards—Although seniority rewards are normally a direct part of the compensation system, some organizations recognize long-term service—10, 15, 25, 30 years—through some form of special recognition awards (the diamond-studded lapel pin or the gold watch, for example).

The most recent view is that seniority or length-of-service rewards should not be part of the basic compensation system but, rather, an element of the benefits program. Many people (especially those in the union movement) believe that seniority is the one stabilizing factor available to all employees. It enables employees to know where they stand relative to their co-workers, where they have been, and where they are going. It makes the future easier to live with and more acceptable. It is still possible to recognize to some degree the importance of seniority through a separate years-of-service bonus and to achieve some of the other needs satisfied by seniority through improved objective recognition of performance by managers. (Chapter 14 covers bonuses recognizing seniority in greater detail.)

Referral Awards—Employees who refer applicants who subsequently accept employment and become full-time employees receive a small cash award for their efforts.

A well-designed reward scheme should reflect the desire of the organization to recognize individual, group, and company-wide performance. It should assist in coordinating the efforts of all employees and demonstrate the ability of the organization to reward individual performance as well as that of the individual as a group member.

The value of each reward described in this chapter has some finite limit. In reaching that limit, the effectiveness of the incentive decreases or, in some cases, vanishes. Using a combination of incentives, it is possible to recognize the importance of human labor as well as its strengths and weaknesses. The development and the implementation of a dynamic incentive program stimulate human motivation to the point that individual, group, and organizational goal achievement have the greatest chance for success.

SELECTED READINGS

Barkin, Solomon, "Wage Incentive Problems in Arbitration," *Labor Law Journal,* January 1970, pp. 22–27. A discussion of the barriers blocking the development and the implementation of incentive plans. Barkin lists seven problem areas and describes possible solutions to them. He feels that the only solution is to rework and clarify the rationale of wage incentive systems.

Eisenberg, Joseph, "Using Incentives to Control Costs," *Wharton Quarterly,* Fall 1968, pp. 30–35. An analysis of procedures and considerations necessary for developing a wage incentive program with easy-to-follow charts and formulas.

Fein, Mitchell, *Wage Incentive Plans.* Norcross, GA: American Institute of Industrial Engineers, 1970. In addition to describing the basic elements of an incentive plan, the author describes what goes wrong with incentives and points out how the degeneration of incentive plans can be prevented.

Guide to Modern Profit Sharing. Chicago, IL: Profit Sharing Council of America, 1973. A complete and authoritative review of current knowledge and thinking on profit sharing. It serves as a detailed background guide for updating existing plans or creating new ones. It covers such areas as the nature of profit sharing, cash plans, provisions of qualified profit-sharing plans, operating a profit-sharing plan, and trends and developments in profit sharing.

Lesieur, Frederick G., ed., *The Scanlon Plan . . . A Frontier in Labor-Management Cooperation.* Cambridge, MA: MIT Press, 1958. This is required reading for anyone interested in developing an incentive program that will join all the competitive elements of an organization into cooperative, goal-oriented teams. It describes in detail the basic elements of the Scanlon plan.

Lytle, Charles Walter, *Wage Incentive Methods: Their Selection, Installation, and Operation,* rev. ed. New York: Ronald Press, 1942. An in-depth review and analysis of the various piecework, time, and bonus incentive plans briefly discussed in this chapter and procedures for installing them. It also discusses the use of incentive plans for indirect work and incentives for office employees, supervisors, and executives.

Mundel, Marvin E., *Motion and Time Study: Principles and Practices,* 4th ed. Englewood Cliffs, NJ: Prentice-Hall, 1974. A valuable resource book for those wishing to know more about the principles, the concepts, and the techniques of a motion and time study. Although largely a how-to-do-it text, it does pay attention to the why, when, and where of such practices.

Rachel, Frank M., and Donald L. Caruth, "Work Measurement: A Valuable Tool for Management," *Management Services,* January–February 1969, pp. 23–34. Despite difficulties, more than 75 percent of all office work can be measured and standardized. This article includes a review of various types of work measurement and their value in determining manpower needs, scheduling and distributing workloads, determining costs, comparing performance, and paying incentive wages.

Stelluto, George L., "Report on Incentive Pay in Manufacturing Industries," *Monthly Labor Review,* July 1969, pp. 49–53. A report on piecerate or production bonus plans and the industries that use them, as well as the number of employees covered by such plans. It also discusses future trends and prospects for such plans.

Stieglitz, Harold, *The Kaiser-Steel Union Sharing Plan, Personnel Policy Study No. 187.* New York: National Industrial Conference Board, 1963. This in-depth report places into perspective the key features of the plan and the motives and factors contributing to their development. It also provides a detailed explanation of the major provisions of the plan, including employment security, gainsharing, and handling of incentive pay.

Wolf, William B., *Wage Incentives as a Management Tool.* New York: Columbia University Press, 1957. A discussion of the value and the use of various types of wage incentive systems and their impact on productivity. Through the use of different wage incentives, it is possible to achieve varying levels of productivity. The author shows that it is possible that incentive programs may result in lowered levels of output instead of increased levels.

13

Performance Appraisal

CONTENT

Chapter 13 presents an analysis of the many parts of the performance appraisal process. It lists reasons for using performance appraisal and identifies pitfalls inherent within this activity.

GOALS

Upon concluding this chapter, you should be aware that, properly done, performance appraisal makes a valuable contribution to organizational success. If poorly done, however, it can be very harmful. In addition, you should be able to identify the basic parts of the appraisal system and assist in developing a basic program that meets the needs of the organization.

I t is unlikely that any managerial problem has attracted more attention, or has so successfully resisted solution, than arriving at a valid method for appraising performance. The victims of unfair appraisal occupy jobs at all levels. Because of failure in this area, many employees, including most union members, feel that the only solution is to eliminate it and to replace it with the one basic measuring criterion that is relatively free of subjective bias—seniority.

It is normally very difficult for one person to critically appraise the performance of another. Basically, performance has two parts—quantity of output and quality of output. A major issue in measuring each is *time*. In moving up the organizational hierarchy, the period of time increases from work performed or demonstrated behavior to the ability to measure results of that behavior—the quality and the quantity of output.

Even in repetitive, routine, mechanistic activities, counting units produced is often an unsatisfactory measure of performance because quality is also an issue. Quality has a variety of subjective factors. Furthermore, quality problems can at times remain hidden or they can surface at later stages in the product or service process, making it difficult to identify the responsible party(ies). As modern industrial nations move from manufacturing to providing services, the issue of quality becomes more important and also more difficult to resolve because it becomes harder to pinpoint.

To overcome the difficulties of making performance appraisals, many organizations do one of two things: they either do nothing, or they implement meaningless appraisal programs, which provide the appraisee with little constructive assistance in improving workplace behavior. If organizationally provided rewards are ever to stimulate performance, improvement must begin with the correct appraisal of performance.

Unacceptable excuses include the following: (1) employees are never satisfied with the appraisal, (2) employees are unwilling to accept average or below-average ratings, or (3) a below-average appraisal results in a disgruntled, unhappy performer. It is imperative that those whose performance is unsatisfactory should receive additional help through counseling, coaching, and/or training. If these aids are of no avail, the incompetent employee must be removed.

Jacob Bronowski, world-famous scientist and humanist, may have uncovered a basic barrier that blocks success in appraising worker performance. From his research and studies on the ascent of man, Bronowski states that man's biological makeup dictates his view of the world. The nature of the human eye and brain and the capacity to develop symbolic language allow the eye and the brain to provide an *interpretation* of what surrounds mankind as opposed to *absolute reality*.[1]

Recognizing and accepting that what an individual sees is interpretive and not objective lends perspective to the appraisal process. Improvement will result when those responsible for the design and administration of the appraisal process use their skills and efforts to make it easier to identify performance realities.

[1]Jacob Bronowski, *The Origins of Knowledge and Imagination* (New Haven, CT: Yale University Press, 1977.)

This will lead to minimizing the variances resulting from the natural individual tendency to provide a unique interpretation of reality that has deeper roots in imagination than in objective reality.

THE PROCESS

Since World War I, management specialists have developed a number of techniques designed to appraise total performance *fairly, accurately,* and *objectively.* As each new instrument arrived on the management scene, it received much fanfare and publicity. So far, none has achieved these lofty goals. An analysis of the process may shed some light on the barriers that block development of a successful appraisal program.

Government Regulations and Court Rulings

Employees constantly exert pressure on supervisors to learn where they stand and on their compensation managers to provide an equitable relationship between pay and performance. As if these internal pressures were not enough for management to face, federal legislation and court rulings make the entire appraisal process more complex and difficult to manage.

Title VII of the Civil Rights Act of 1964 and Equal Employment Opportunity Commission (EEOC) guidelines state the following:

1. Employers must take affirmative action not to discriminate because of race, color, religion, sex, or national origin when making employment decisions.

2. Employment decisions include those involved in the selection, training, transfer, retention, promotion, and compensation processes.

3. Any paper-and-pencil or performance measure used in making employment decisions is a test.

4. A test must be fairly administered and empirically validated.

Most formal performance appraisal techniques rely on paper-and-pencil methods to identify employee work behavior. The information provided by these techniques assists management in making employment decisions. The EEOC and the courts recognize the impact that the appraisal process has on employment opportunities and the possibility of inherent bias in many parts of the process. The EEOC and the courts have played and will continue to play an important role in developing the process of performance appraisal.

A review of a few of the court rulings that have identified and defined the responsibilities management must accept in designing and managing its appraisal program indicates the direction organizations must take with performance appraisal.

Griggs v. *Duke Power Company,* 3 FEP Cases 175. In this landmark case, the central issue was that an educational restriction on an employment decision is useless unless it can be proved that there exists a bona fide occupational qualification (BFOQ) between the test and actual job performance. The burden of proof is on the employer to show nondiscrimination in any employment decision related to discrimination.

Allen v. *City of Mobile,* 3 FEP Cases 1226. Service ratings of black police officers were discriminatory. Special performance appraisal programs outlined by the court must be implemented.

McDonnell-Douglas Corporation v. *Green,* 5 FEP Cases 915. Simple proof is enough to prove nondiscrimination, but tests must be job related.

Moody v. *Albemarle Paper Co.,* 10 FEP Cases 1181. Supervisors must use some criteria in making employment decisions. Performance ratings that do not have a job content base have a built-in bias, and such tests must be validated statistically.

Wade v. *Mississippi Cooperative Extension Service,* 12 FEP Cases 1041. Trait rating systems can be subjective and biased and are usually not based on job content. There must be a BFOQ between trait and work performed. Data must be provided that show a relationship between appraisal instruments and job analysis and show that the appraisal instrument is a valid predictor of job performance.

Davis v. *Washington, DC,* 12 FEP Cases 1415. Face validity is sufficient for validating police officer selection and training tests.

McDonald v. *Santa Fe Trail Transportation Co. Inc.,* 12 FEP Cases 1577. Reverse discrimination is illegal. The Civil Rights Act covers all employees.

The EEOC guidelines and these court rulings as they influence performance appraisal may be summarized as follows:

1. Performance rating methods must be job related or validated.

2. Content or performance rating methods must be based on thorough job analysis.

3. Raters must have been able consistently to observe ratees perform their assignments.

4. Raters must use the same rating criteria, and ratings must be scored under standardized conditions.

5. Criteria used for appraising performance must not unfairly depress the scores of minority groups.

6. Appraisal forms and instructions to raters are an essential part of the process and require validation.

7. Criteria such as regularity of attendance, tenure, and training time are usually not considered part of actual work proficiency. Because they are

frequently used as performance appraisal criteria, they require validation evidence.

Validity of Performance Appraisal Instruments

For performance predictors to be acceptable to the EEOC (the federal agency responsible for administering most civil rights legislation) and the federal courts, they must be valid and reliable.

Concurrent Validity—For concurrent validity to exist, there must be a statistical correlation between the predictors of performance (the appraisal item on the form) and the actual job performance. Individuals receiving high ratings on the form perform better than those receiving low ratings.

Content Validity—The degree to which scores on a test may be accepted as being a representative sample of all job behaviors required in the performance of a job is called content validity. This is a pragmatic or empirically based validity where there is an easily identifiable relationship between appraisal form items and job-related activites and situations.

Criterion-related Validity—Criterion-related validity is a statistical statement of the existence of a relationship between scores on a predictor and scores on a criterion measure. Measures of job success as identified by various factors on a performance appraisal instrument must relate either positively or negatively to employee job performance (criterion) or some set of performance subfactors (criteria).

Predictive Validity—When predictive validity exists, initial predictions made by the reviewer are confirmed at a later date. An appraiser rates a subordinate as promotable. The employee receives a promotion and does well on the job. This may be an indicator that the appraisal instrument has predictive validity.

Face Validity—The practical, job-directed relationship between the predictor of performance and actual job performance is termed face validity.

Construct Validity—Construct validity is the degree to which scores obtained through a test may be interpreted as measuring a hypothesized or synthesized property (the construct—motivation, intelligence). The issue involved in measuring a psychological quality in performance appraisal is the ability to obtain an objective measure of the quality. The appraisal instrument designer must clearly identify and describe what constitutes the psychological quality or construct. For example, cooperation is a trait or construct on the form and employees rated high on cooperation actually are more cooperative than employees rated low. The measure has construct validity. The problem then is how to get an objective measure of cooperation.

Reliability is a measure of the consistency or stability of a "test" (perform-ance appraisal is a test) over time or with its use by different raters. A reliable test is one that provides similar or comparable results regardless of when it is used or who uses it.

There are basically three different methods used for determining the reliability of a performance appraisal test. They are: (1) test-retest method, (2) subdivided test method, and (3) parallel test method.

Test-Retest Method—The test-retest method requires the administering of the same test at two different times. This method is the easiest to use of the three, but its ability to determine reliability is questionable. The first time an individual takes a test (completes a performance appraisal instrument), a learning effect occurs. When the same individual uses the same test instrument a second time, the responses to certain questions may be influenced by the learning experience from the first time the instrument was used. When the test-retest method is used for determining consistency, it is difficult if not impossible to separate change in job performance that the test is determining from the effect of learning on the appraiser.

Subdivided Test Method—The subdivided test method requires that a test be split into two equal parts (equal in that they both cover the same performance behaviors). The test can be administered as one test. Then the comparable test items are split into equivalent halves for scoring purposes. If the test is reliable, each half will give the same or comparable ratings. The division can be by odd-even numbers, and the actual test items can be randomly placed or placed by any other method. It is only necessary that each part represent all types of test questions asked in the original instrument.

Parallel Test Method—The parallel test method uses two completely comparable or equivalent performance appraisal instruments. The items or appraisal dimensions included in each form do not have to be identical, but they must cover the same performance behaviors and have a measuring scheme that permits a comparison of the behaviors. The parallel tests may be administered consecutively or after a lapse of a period of time. If the tests are reliable, they must provide the same results. The major problem with this method is the difficulty of developing two tests that are truly equivalent.

Intrarater and interrater reliability—Performance appraisal tests must also meet intrarater and interrater reliability standards.

Intrarater reliability means that the same rater using the same instrument at different points produces the same test results. The performance appraisal problems here are: (1) the test subject's behavior may have changed and (2) the rater forces the second result to be the same as the first by remembering the ratings given the first time.

Interrater reliability means that different raters produce the same results using the same instrument over a period of time. The problem of actual changes in employee behavior over time must not be misconstrued as an inadequacy in the design of the instrument.

An additional source of variation in performance appraisal test scores is a change in the appraisee's duties or work assignments from one appraisal period to the next.

What Is Performance Appraisal?

Performance appraisal is the formal process, normally using some written instrument, that identifies a jobholder's contributions and workplace behaviors. The first objective in appraising performance is to encourage employees to put forth their best efforts so that organization can reach its mission and goals. Through the appraisal process, the organization identifies and recognizes these efforts and rewards employees in such a way that it enhances their opportunities to achieve individual goals.

Performance appraisal occurs constantly in every organization. Even when it is not part of a formal system, individuals and groups informally appraise performance. Through the informal process, they identify individual and unit differences. At the same time, they frequently set informal limits or "bogies" on what individuals or units may produce, thereby intentionally limiting productivity.

The appraisal process should permit—in fact, promote—successful goal attainment. Without a formal process, appraisal will take an informal route. While it is true that the organization has certain influences and opportunities within the informal processes, its influence and control (feedback) opportunities are much less in the informal than in the formal system.

Why Perform Appraisals?

Organizations find that the performance appraisal often fails to achieve its mission. When appraisal is done poorly, or even done well under unsatisfactory operating conditions, it may lead to increased employee anxiety and hostility, resulting in poor use of both human and nonhuman resources, increased costs, and declining productivity. The result may even lead to the decay and demise of the organization. On the other hand, if an organization is to grow and prosper, it must identify those outputs, and the units, groups, and individuals responsible for their achievement that will lead to successful operations. It must be able to reward and expand its areas of strength and improve or at least minimize its areas of weakness. Success in these areas requires some form of performance appraisal. Seven major uses of performance appraisal are:

1. Organizational planning

2. Employee performance feedback

3. Compensation decisions

4. Employee movement decisions (lateral transfer, demotion, promotion, layoffs and termination)

5. Training and development opportunities

6. Manpower planning

7. Validation of selection procedures

THE JOB

Almost a century ago, Frederick W. Taylor and his colleagues and contemporaries recognized that, if useful methods were to be developed for improving productivity, work content and the way workers perform their assignments must be the center of research activities. However, with the advent of behavioral scientists in the world of work—particularly those who focused on identifying individual differences through testing "intelligence," "aptitude," and "attitude" and predicting job-related behaviors by identifying specific unsatisfied needs—interest waned in observing the job itself for establishing job competency.

Organizational use of arbitrary standards set by these "intelligence," "aptitude," and "attitude" tests came under direct fire in 1971 with the *Griggs* v. *Duke Power Company* Supreme Court decision. Although it had been known for some time that so-called intelligence tests had limited value in predicting job competency, the tests were easy to administer and relatively inexpensive. Few managers or workers complained about their usefulness or value. The Civil Rights Act of 1964, the EEOC, and court rulings changed these ideas and forced managers to look for other alternatives to predict and identify job competency and performance effectiveness. To find suitable replacements for these tests, personnel specialists returned to the job and to the analysis of job content.

Various techniques have proven to be useful for generating job-related data and information and for establishing criteria that are both valid and useful for identifying job competency and performance effectiveness. Four techniques using direct analysis of job activities provide different sets of measures that have application in performance appraisal: (1) work method analysis, (2) job analysis, (3) critical incident technique, and (4) objective or goal setting.

Work Method Analysis

Industrial engineers study jobs to find, among other things, ways to standardize, simplify, and specialize work procedures. Among the various techniques useful for these purposes are (1) time and motion studies, (2) micromotion analysis, and (3) work measurement. Each technique not only provides engineers with a better understanding of the job and ways to make it easier for a worker, but also increases overall productivity of the worker and the work group. These techniques require a careful, detailed analysis of work requirements and usually have these major goals: (1) finding a best way to do the job, (2) determining what should constitute a fair day's work, and (3) setting performance standards that provide fair pay for work performed. Chapter 12 describes in some detail industrial engineering approaches for establishing performance standards.

Job Analysis

Traditional job analysis studies a job performed by workers currently holding the job. If more than one person works at the job, analysis may include all or a percentage of jobholders. This analysis provides information on job responsibilities, duties, education, experience, and skill requirements, as well as on conditions under which the job is normally performed. Chapter 5 covers this technique in detail; and all of part 2, in one way or another, relates to job analysis. Most new jobs are in the service industry. Because their content varies from day to day and output is often difficult to observe and measure, job analysis becomes an increasingly important tool for analyzing job content and identifying job activities.

Critical Incident Technique (CIT)

In 1949 John C. Flanagan identified an approach to improve the quality of performance appraisal.[2] The approach used the critical incident technique (CIT) as developed by the American Institute for Research. (The critical incident technique is a spin-off from the critical incident method which is discussed in detail later in this chapter.) This approach requires the systematic observation of actual job performance and behavior, which provides information that helps to identify and define *critical* job requirements.

Flanagan defines such a requirement as a duty the jobholder must perform to be considered effective or successful (or ineffective and unsuccessful) in job performance. Individuals observing and reporting these incidents are normally supervisors or associates of the employee involved in the incident. The incident must relate to an important aspect of the work and must describe an *actual* behavior "which is outstandingly effective or ineffective with respect to the specific situation."[3]

Critical incident information may be obtained through personal interviews or in writing. G. P. Latham and R. R. Scott identify three questions that must be answered to establish incident quality as follows:

1. What were the circumstances surrounding this incident? (Background or context)

2. What exactly did this individual do that was so effective or ineffective? (Observable behavior)

3. How is this incident an example of effective or ineffective behavior? (So what?)[4]

---

[2]John C. Flanagan, "A New Approach to Evaluating Personnel," *Personnel,* January–February 1949, pp. 35–42.

[3]Ibid., p. 42.

[4]G. P. Latham and R. R. Scott, *Defining Productivity in Behavioral Terms,* (Tacoma, WA: Weyerhaeuser Company, 1975), p. iv.

In one reported study, Latham and Scott interviewed 28 operators and five supervisors.[5] These 33 individuals were asked to reflect over the past 6 to 12 months and to describe specific incidents they had actually observed. Latham and Scott identified an effective behavior as one that the observer considered as contributing significantly to the accomplishment of the objective. Ineffective behavior, if occurring repeatedly or even once under certain conditions, would cast doubt on the competency of the individual performing the assignment.

Another less rigorous procedure available for identifying critical incidents is to have experienced employees review a list of job activities and then have them identify examples of "good," "average," and "poor" behavior.

Critical incidents relating to a specific job can be collected over time and can be classified under more general categories that relate closely to major job performance requirements. These major categories are often called *performance dimensions*. A performance dimension is a set of related job behaviors necessary for job performance. There should be enough performance dimensions to cover all essential behaviors of the job completely.

Objective or Goal Setting

The previously discussed three techniques for collecting, analyzing, and summarizing job data and information require a detailed analysis of job content. Objective or goal setting, the fourth technique, differs significantly. It requires definition of the purpose of the organization, from which a series of objectives and goals are set that tie together all jobs in the organization. This hierarchy of objectives and goals in turn directs the contributions of each jobholder toward the accomplishment of the organization's central purpose.

Anthony P. Raia describes a cascade approach to objective setting.[6] The cascade approach starts with a clear, concise statement of the central purpose of the organization by the board of directors. This statement provides the guidelines for formulating long-range objectives and the strategic plans to be used to accomplish them. From these long-range objectives, more specific short-range goals are identified and defined. This redefinition of objectives continues throughout the organizational hierarchy, and objectives are restated in terms of the responsibilities or contributions expected of each job.

Organizations must set goals that transcend the employees and their work groups. Only in this manner is it possible to minimize suboptimizing work patterns.[7] By identifying and redefining objectives into a hierarchy of goals that unites the whole work force, an organization sets one of the first conditions necessary to produce an environment in which both management and employees recognize the value and necessity of their contributions. In its most democratic form, the goal-setting process involves the subordinate in the setting of perform-

---

[5]Ibid., p. 2.

[6]Anthony P. Raia, *Managing by Objectives* (Glenview, IL: Scott Foresman, 1974), p. 30.

[7]*Suboptimizing* describes behavior that overemphasizes goal achievement at a lower level, often to the detriment of attaining objectives at a higher level of the business.

ance standards and performance goals and in determining the activities needed to achieve these results. In this way, the process helps to reduce employee fears that are inherent in any system that measures individual behavior. Loyalty and allegiance to broadly based organizational objectives go a long way toward minimizing unsatisfactory behavior at work—behavior that can lead to suboptimizing work patterns.

TECHNIQUES FOR PERFORMANCE APPRAISAL

The constant search for new and better ways to appraise performance has led to the development of many techniques for appraising performance. Among these are the narrative descriptive review techniques for reviewing employee performance. These techniques include the essay, critical incident, and field review methods. Another commonly used approach is the ranking method in which all employees in a particular job or work unit are rank-ordered relative to some single global or universal factor such as overall performance or effectiveness.

A series of more sophisticated techniques uses some form of checklist or rating scales. This approach requires the development of lists of descriptive statements of employee traits or behaviors. Raters then select from these statements those that best describe the workplace performance of the appraisee. The checklist approach includes simple, weighted, and forced-choice checklists. The rating scale technique may use traits, job behaviors, or job responsibilities with associate scales being the basis for rating. Finally, among the large list of techniques available for appraising performance is the management-by-objectives approach.

Narrative Descriptive Review Techniques

A number of appraisal techniques require the appraiser to provide a written description of the employee's performance. Several different approaches are used.

Essay Method—The essay method requires the appraiser to describe the employee in a number of broad categories that may include the (1) appraiser's overall impression of the employee's performance, (2) promotability of the employee, (3) jobs the employee is now able or qualified to perform, (4) strengths and weaknesses of the employee, and (5) training and development assistance required by the employee.

Although this method may be used as an independent appraisal technique, it is most frequently found in combination with others. It is extremely useful in filling information gaps about the employee that often occur in the more highly structured methods.

The strength of the essay method depends on the writing skills and the analytical ability of the appraiser, and many supervisors have writing difficulties. The essay method can consume much time because the appraiser must collect the information necessary to develop the essay and then write it. A problem arising here is that appraisers may be rated on the quality of the appraisals they give. The quality standards for the appraisal may be unduly influenced by appearance and grammar rather than content. Thus a "high-quality" appraisal may provide little information about the performance of the appraisee.

Critical Incident Method—The critical incident method requires the appraiser to maintain a log on each employee containing observations of what the supervisor considers to be successful or unsuccessful work behavior. This method demands continuous and relatively close observation. Time elapsing between the observed behavior and its description has a definite impact on the accurate description of what occurred. An example of a positive critical incident follows:

4/18—Employee demonstrated a broad range of job knowledge in uncovering the cause of a quality problem with product "A" that Quality Assurance had been working with for over a month.

An example of a negative critical incident is:

7/28—Employee responded impulsively and with little tact when employee "Z" refused to work overtime in order to complete a prior assignment.

Like the essay method, the critical incident method is time-consuming and costly, and it requires the appraiser to have good analytical skill and the ability to provide straightforward, honest descriptions. An appraiser who is an extremely competent writer and analyst may provide an impression to those reviewing the description that can bias the review either in favor of or against the appraisee. This is not to imply that competent writing skills are undesirable but simply that good writers have an advantage using these methods.

Although the critical incident method was designed to overcome subjectivity, it has had little effect in reducing rater bias. Raters hesitate to describe an event that they may consider to be detrimental to a particular individual or that possibly casts a doubt on their own managerial skills. They may also tend to be inconsistent—for example, they attack one individual by blowing a situation completely out of proportion, and then they protect another individual by deciding that the demonstrated workplace behavior is not worth the time and effort it takes to describe it.

Workers frequently develop anxiety and hostility when they know their supervisor is keeping a log on them. To protect themselves, they may hide their actions and keep information from their supervisor that, if known, could lead to a poor performance appraisal but also could lead to improvement.

The critical incident method is valuable in that it focuses on actual job behavior, not impressions of ambiguous traits. Although incidents do not lend themselves to quantification, they can be useful when providing employee feedback on performance and when counseling.

Field Review Method—In the field review method, the appraiser, normally a representative of the personnel department or at times a staff member of the specific work unit, interviews the employee's immediate supervisor.

Based on the supervisor's responses to a series of questions, the employee is rated. This method does not use forms or rating factors. Normally, the appraiser or the staff specialist provides a simple "outstanding," "satisfactory," or "unsatisfactory" rating.

Appraisers making field reviews normally receive much training in ways to conduct the interview. As a result, they have developed their writing skills. Being independent at the work scene, they normally will have less bias (for or against the appraisee) than does the immediate supervisor, although the supervisor can still supply biased information. These appraisers may be more able to pinpoint areas requiring training and development assistance. Requiring the use of an additional person in the process increases the cost of the appraisal, but it may focus greater attention on the process by both the immediate supervisor and the unit conducting the interviews.

Ranking Techniques

The simplest, least costly, and possibly one of the more accurate appraisal techniques (especially in working with small groups where the appraiser intimately knows each member) is that which requires the appraiser (normally the immediate supervisor) to rank from best to poorest all members of a work unit or workers performing the same job.

Straight Ranking—Straight ranking normally appraises employees relative to one factor such as performance or effectiveness. When appraisers are familiar with the members of their work unit, have intimate knowledge of the job and employee inputs and outputs, and are able to suppress biases related to personality differences and to focus on work behavior, this appraisal technique will give very good results. The straight ranking technique can provide a high degree of interrater reliability (i.e., different raters give the same results). A major problem, however, is that rankings are difficult to justify to those ranked, especially those who fall in the bottom half of the group rated.

Research indicates that practically *all* employees consider their own performance average or above average. Thus, from an employee's point of view, a below-average ranking is unacceptable and, in most cases, is considered unjustified. Ranking can stimulate intragroup hostility, resulting in lowered productivity and more worker dissatisfaction. Ranking is weak in relating the members of one group to those of another group. A relatively low-ranked employee in a high-performing unit may be superior to a highly ranked employee in an average or moderately performing work unit. In the same unit, there may be considerable difference between a worker ranked as fourth over fifth, whereas workers ranked seventh, eighth, and ninth may be essentially the same in performance.

Categories of Performance	Percentage of Employees to Be Allocated
Superior	5
Above average	15
Average	60
Below average	15
Unacceptable	5
	100 percent

Forced-distribution Ranking—A slight variation of the straight ranking technique is forced distribution. This technique requires the appraiser to allocate a certain percentage of work group members to certain categories that may include superior, above average, average, below average, and unacceptable performance. The percentage of employees to be placed in each category usually approximates the bell-shaped curve or normal distribution. Five percent fall in the top and bottom categories, 15 percent in the next two, and 60 percent in the middle category.

Both the number of categories and the percentage of employees to be allocated to each can vary according to the design considerations of a specific business.

A number of procedures are available for ranking employees. Among these are the deck-of-cards procedure, the stub selection and the paired-comparison ranking table which have been previously described in chapter 7. Two other procedures that are extremely useful when involved in performance appraisal are the card-stacking procedure and alternative ranking.

In the *card-stacking* procedure, the rater receives a deck of cards. Each card contains the name of one employee.

1. The rater is first asked to make three stacks. Stack One contains the cards of all employees who are above-average performers. Stack Two contains the cards of all employees who are average or acceptable performers. Stack Three contains the cards of all employees who are marginal, below average, or unacceptable performers.

2. The rater then counts the number of cards in each stack to see if there are 30 percent in the above average stack and 30 percent in the below average stack. If Stack One (above average) contains more than 30 percent, the rater must identify the least effective performers of this stack and place their cards in Stack Two (average performers) until Stack One contains 30 percent. Then Stack Three must be checked for the 30 percent quota and the same procedure performed. If Stack Three contains more than 30 percent, then the excess is placed in Stack Two. If Stack Three (or Stack One) contains less than 30 percent, then the rater takes the best cards of the performers of Stack Two and places them in Stack One, or takes the poorest performers of Stack Two and places them in Stack Three. Upon the completion of Step Two, there will be 30

percent of the employee cards in the above average stack, 40 percent in the average stack, and 30 percent in the below average stack.

3. The final step is to review Stacks One and Three and place one-third of each stack in the best of the above average performance group and the poorest one-third of the below average stack in a separate stack. There are now five stacks containing the superior 10 percent, the above average 20 percent, the average 40 percent, the below average 20 percent, and the least effective or poorest 10 percent.

Each stack of employee cards could then be rated using the paired-comparison deck-of-cards procedure to give a final ranking of all employees.

Another available approach is *alternative ranking*. In alternative ranking, the appraiser has a list of all employees to be ranked. The first selection is the employee the appraiser considers to be the best performer. The name of this employee is placed on the first line of a sheet of paper that has numbered lines, one for each employee to be ranked. The appraiser then strikes the ranked employee from the list. The second selection is the employee considered to be the lowest rated performer; this employee's name is placed at the bottom of the list and is also crossed out of the original list. The third employee ranked is the highest remaining in the original list; fourth is the lowest rated remaining employee, whose name is placed on the rank-ordered list and stricken from the original list. This process continues until all unit members are ranked.

An alternative ranking list (with 20 employees to be ranked) follows:

1. Highest rated employee

2. Next highest rated employee

3. Next highest rated employee

   .

   .

   .

   .

18. Next lowest rated employee

19. Next lowest rated employee

20. Lowest rated employee

Ranking techniques give little to no assistance to the supervisor when counseling employees or providing feedback about why they received specific rankings. They do, however, minimize such constant errors as the halo and horn effects, strict and lenient ratings, and central tendency (these constant errors are discussed in detail later in the chapter).

Another fairly common technique used to identify and measure employee performance is the checklist. This technique requires the development of a list of trait, behavior, or other job characteristics that are useful for identifying successful or unsuccessful job performance. The three basic variations of the technique are the (1) simple checklist, (2) weighted checklist, and (3) forced-choice checklist.

Simple Checklist—The simple checklist method uses a collection of traits, behaviors, or other job characteristics. These lists may include from 15 to 50 different characterstics. The rater reviews the lists and checks those characteristics that best identify the performance of the individual being rated.

Some typical checklist items are the following:

1. Maintains systematic and orderly records.

2. Instructs new employees in a manner that encourages learning.

3. Provides clear and detailed instructions to subordinates.

4. Uses company property only for organization-related use.

Weighted Checklist—The weighted checklist method adds a degree of sophistication by assigning a weight to each item, thus permitting a numerical score in the rating process. Experts trained in testing and evaluation procedures normally review the items and by using various psychological and statistical procedures weight the items and assign a numerical value to each. The items may include those that identify both positive and negative job performance characteristics. Raters select those that best fit the demonstrated performance of the employee during the appraisal period. Normally, the rater does not know the weight of the numerical value assigned to each item.

Forced-Choice Checklist—An even more sophisticated checklist method is one using forced choice. This method involves combining the checklist items into groups containing from two to five statements. There may be as many as 50 groups from which the rater makes selections. The design of the groups is usually such that each item appears to have equal desirability or to be of equivalent value.

The rater selects the one item that best identifies the workplace behavior of the appraisee. In some cases in which the group may include from three to five characteristics, the rater may be asked to select the item that best describes the performance of the appraisee and the item that is least descriptive.

A simple forced-choice selection may require a rater to choose between the words *energetic* and *trustworthy*. Because both words connote socially acceptable characteristics, it is difficult, if not impossible, for the rater to make a selection that has an intent other than to provide the most accurate description of the appraisee. A more complex example of a forced-choice selection requires a rater to select from a list of statements the one most descriptive of the employee's behavior. For example, a list may be set up in the following way:

Most Descriptive	Least Descriptive	Item
☐	☐	Reviews work of subordinates and provides assistance as needed.
☐	☐	Follows up on all delegated assignments to ensure conformance with operating procedures.
☐	☐	Requests employee opinions and uses them when conditions permit.
☐	☐	Meets deadlines on work assignments.
☐	☐	Praises those whose workplace behavior has earned such recognition.

Upon completion of a forced-choice checklist, the items selected as most and least descriptive (when requested) are grouped together. From these final groupings, index of discrimination and index of desirability scores are developed, which purport to identify the degree of successful job performance.

The major goal of the checklist technique is to minimize bias. In theory, the rater acts as a recorder of observed behavior and not a judge and, in this manner, will not demonstrate typical patterns of rater bias. In reality, however, individual perceptions of actual behavior are still an unresolved issue.

The development of the weighted checklist and, to a far greater degree, the forced-choice checklist requires the effort of skilled professionals. Such checklists are extremely costly to design. Raters are also leery of using any system that is not familiar enough so that they know the final determinations of their efforts and the effect their ratings will have on the future of their subordinates (whether for pay adjustments or future career opportunities). Evidence does not indicate that the forced-choice method provides more accurate measurements of employee performance. This method also provides little opportunity to identify areas of employee improvement or assistance in employee counseling.

Rating Scale Technique

A commonly used and probably the easiest to administer of all performance appraisal techniques is the one using a list of qualities that in some manner relate to job performance. Raters use scales to indicate the degree of the quality of performance as demonstrated by the employee and as observed by the rater. This technique is also often referred to as a *graphic rating scale*.

Rating scales use words or phrases as labels to identify the degree or quality demonstrated. Each point on a rating scale must be meaningfully different. Although identification points on a scale can vary from two to 15 or even more, a scale of values that is applicable to most performance appraisal instruments ranges from 5 to 10. To provide effective distribution of scores, the scale must have an adequate number of intervals.

When identifying too few interval points (fewer than five), there is a good chance that the scale omits valid measures of performance. When the scale contains too many (normally, more than 10), the interval descriptors are repetitious and make it very difficult for a rater to distinguish between interval points. Weber's law of "just perceptible differences" again must be considered when determining the number of interval points on a rating scale. The idea of the 15 percent perceptible difference requirement focuses the efforts of scale designers on using from six to eight points (see Weber's law in chapter 8).

The issue of *odd* and *even* numbers of interval points also arises. When using an odd number, raters have the tendency to use the average or central tendency values. This is not necessarily unacceptable because most employees do behave in an average manner, but all too often the appraiser uses a mid value for rating a quality to avoid making a decision. An *even* number of interval scales does not permit the rater to use an average value but, rather, forces a decision that differentiates among the large group in the middle—slightly above or slightly below average.

Two widely used procedures for labeling scales are (1) those using single words or short adjectival phrases—*simple adjective rating scales* and (2) those using lengthy phrases or sentences that describe a specific observable behavior—*Behavioral Anchored Rating Scales (BARS)*.

A simple adjective rating scale may be one that measures a quality by such descriptors as *poor, below average, average, above average, superior*. Behavioral Anchored Rating Scales (BARS) require extensive time and skilled personnel to develop. This type of scaling device is discussed later in this chapter in the section on job behavior.

The typical appraisal instrument using a rating scale first lists or describes a particular performance-related quality (e.g., trait, job behavior, job duty) and then provides some type of scale for the rater to identify the degree to which the employee demonstrated that quality. For example, one of the qualities selected for appraising performance may be the trait *effort*.

Effort—Considers accuracy, neatness, and attention to detail; is also industrious.

The next step is to develop a scale that measures the degree of the trait that best characterizes the appraisee. The scale may be a continuum with terminal anchors, such as

Unacceptable   Acceptable

with instructions to the appraiser to place a checkmark along the line at the point that most accurately identifies the degree of the trait as demonstrated by the employee.

Another approach to scaling may be to provide a discrete or multiple-step rating scale in which the rater ranks the trait according to its importance in the job's performance and checks the box that most adequately describes the trait characteristics of the appraisee.

	(unimportant)	*(marginal)*	*(average)*	*(very important)*
	(1) ☐	☐	☐	☐

EFFORT

(Considers accuracy, neatness, and attention to detail; is also industrious.)	Provides less than acceptable effort.	Maintains minimum acceptable standards of effort.	Provides reasonable effort.	Consistently provides superior effort.

(2) ☐ ☐   ☐ ☐ ☐ ☐ ☐ ☐   ☐ ☐

In (1) above, the appraiser rates the trait according to its unimportance or importance in the performance of the job. In (2) above, the appraiser then indicates the appropriate degree of the trait for the appraisee. A trait rating scale may list as many as 25 qualities.

Rating scales are useful for measuring three general categories: (1) trait-related qualities, (2) behavior-related qualities on the job, and (3) job duties such as those listed with the responsibilities and duties section of the job description.

Mixed Standard Scale—The mixed standard scale was designed to minimize halo effect and leniency errors. This scale consists of three statements that describe good, average, and poor performance relative to a specific dimension or trait. The three statements describing a number of different performance dimensions or traits—Friedrich Blanz and Edwin E. Ghiselli identified 18 traits—are grouped together in a random order.[8] The Blanz and Ghiselli example has a list of 54 statements (18 traits × 3 statements for each trait). An appraiser then treats each statement independently of all other statements and appraises the employee relative to the statement. A "+" indicates the appraisee is better than the description; a "0" means the appraisee fits the statement and a "−" indicates the appraisee is worse than the statement.

The relatively large number of statements—in the example, 54—and their random order mix minimizes the chance that the appraiser will identify the designed order-of-merit of each set of descriptors. This in turn reduces the opportunity of the appraiser to rate the statements with regard to their designed order rather than honestly relating the statement to the appraisee's demonstrated workplace behavior. This type of scale permits a seven-point score for each dimension or trait being rated, as in the following table.

---

[8]Friedrich Blanz and Edwin E. Ghiselli, "The Mixed Standard Scale: A New Rating System," *Personnel Psychology,* Summer 1972, pp. 185–199.

STATEMENTS FOR A DIMENSION OR TRAIT			
I	*II*	*III*	*Point*
+	+	+	7
0	+	+	6
−			+	5
−	0	+	4
−	−	+	3
−	−	0	2
−	−	−	1

For example, using the performance dimension, ensures Effective Crew Training:

Good Performance Statement: Looks for more efficient training methods and uses them.

Average Performance Statement: Has crew fully trained for normal job functions and adequate backup for all jobs.

Poor Performance Statement: Ignores training procedures and does not have trained backup on key jobs.

The mixed standard scale requires a detailed job analysis to identify the basic or primary activities, functional areas, or responsibilities or performance dimensions of each job. Supervisors of those intimately familiar with the job are then asked to recall critical incidents which provide examples of good and poor job behaviors. Behaviors further identified as critical job behaviors are then related to the previously identified job activities, etc. The behaviors are again scored on a scale, e.g., 1 to 7, or 1 to 9, with 1 representing a very poor performance behavior and the highest value representing a very good behavior. From this list, the three statements for each activity or dimension are identified. From a standpoint of design, the mixed scale procedure is similar to the forced-choice method.

Trait-related Qualities—Performance appraisal instruments using traits were introduced into industry along with the scientific management movement at the turn of the century. The traits used in these instruments are those characteristics firmly anchored in human behavior that show themselves on the job and that influence performance. To minimize differences in interpretation, each trait requires careful definition. Even with such care, human perception will vary significantly among individuals. Another weakness of all trait-rating instruments is that a high rating does not necessarily correlate with good performance.

Traits have traditionally been the most commonly used category of qualities used to appraise employees. An almost limitless number of traits is available. Although trait-rating techniques have traditionally been accepted by management as being worthwhile indicators of performance, federal legislation and court rulings of the past ten years have cast a dark shadow over their credibility. The integrity of trait-rating performance techniques and their ability to reflect actual performance have been questioned. The many different ways people interpret traits and the potential for bias in any trait-rating appraisal technique have caused doubt about the worth and value of all trait-rating techniques.

Although there are literally hundreds of traits available for appraising performance, most techniques include from 10 to 15. The following are some of those commonly used:

Punctuality	Cooperation	Personality	Loyalty
Attendance	Dependability	Judgment	Courtesy
Effort	Initiative	Attitude	Integrity
Conduct	Intelligence	Adaptability	Honesty

Job Behavior—With the advent of the Equal Employment Opportunity Commission (EEOC), concern intensified over developing testing instruments (performance appraisal in most cases must be considered a test) that do not discriminate adversely against any group and that can be validated as being related to the job. In the performance appraisal area, attention focused on the development of instruments with a firm foundation in actual job behavior. Gathering and analyzing data and information necessary for the development of performance appraisal processes based on behavior follows a path similar to that previously discussed in developing job evaluation mechanisms.

The measurement of performance-relevant behavior requires intensive analysis of job requirements and extensive review of potential job behavior of employees. These efforts assist in identifying and describing the array of behaviors employees are able to demonstrate when doing a specific job. A job content and job behavior analysis provides the following:

1. Identification of performance dimensions (factors).

2. Definition of performance elements—subdimensional or subfactor criteria.

3. Determination of behavioral anchors for performance dimensions or performance elements.

4. Development of Behavioral Anchored Rating Scales (BARS).

The identification of *performance dimensions* is derived directly from an analysis of job content and job behavior. An analysis of goals set in the performance of a job may also be a valuable source for identifying performance dimensions. The analysis of job content focuses on identifying the tasks of the job. This analysis also identifies the education, the experience, and the skill necessary to perform the job, and the environmental conditions existing at the workplace. The analysis of job behavior, however, focuses on specific employee behavior that can be observed, defined, and measured while doing the job. These types of analyses identify those behaviors that are critical to effective job performance.

Jobholders and supervisors who are familiar with the job identify these performance incidents and critical behaviors required for performance. From a broad list of such incidents, knowledgeable job performers, supervisors, or skilled staff specialists identify those job behaviors that are similar in content; and they cluster them under specific performance dimensions. An issue that arises when listing any group of either job evaluation or performance appraisal factors is whether they are equal in importance or should be differentially weighted. Resolving the weighting issue is one of the problems facing designers and administrators of the performance appraisal program.

An example of a performance dimension is as follows:

Application of knowledge—Analyzes work and sets initial work priorities before involving others in work process. Identifies critical work issues, information needed, whom to contact, and when to make requests to complete assignments on schedule.

In 1949 J. C. Flanagan identified six performance dimensions.[9] In a study conducted from 1972 through 1976, psychological researchers of Sears, Roebuck identified seven dimensions that relate closely to those established by Flanagan.[10] G. P. Latham and R. R. Scott identified four dimensions in 1975.[11]

Performance dimensions should be independent of every other dimension, but collectively all of them should cover the major behaviors required in successful job performance. This coverage is essential if an appraisal instrument using performance dimensions is to have content validity.

Flanagan (1949)	*Sears (1972–1976)*	*Latham & Scott (1975)*
1. Proficiency in handling administrative detail.	1. Technical knowledge.	1. Work performance.
2. Proficiency in supervising personnel.	2. Application of knowledge.	2. Job commitment.
3. Proficiency in planning and directing action.	3. Administrative effectiveness.	3. Interactions with others.
4. Proficiency in technical job knowledge.	4. Work relations.	4. Planning, organizing, and setting priorities.
5. Acceptance of organizational responsibilities.	5. Response to superiors.	
	6. Directing subordinates.	
	7. Personal commitment.	

A performance dimension that validly relates to a job should be useful in the following four personnel areas: (1) *S*election, (2) *T*raining, (3) *A*ppraisal, and (4) *R*ewarding (STAR). If a performance dimension is not appropriate or useful in any one of the four functional areas, its validity is highly questionable.[12]

[9]Flanagan, "A New Approach," p. 42.

[10]Robert H. Rhode, *Development of the Retail Checklist Performance Evaluation Program* (Chicago, IL: Sears, Roebuck and Co.), pp. 26–37.

[11]Latham and Scott, *Defining Productivity,* pp. 13, 14.

[12]The STAR concept was developed by A. Daniel MacIntosh, Management Consultant, Atlanta, GA.

Through the use of the critical incident technique or a modification of it, employees identify *performance elements*. These are identifiable, observable, and measurable behaviors described in one sentence or a single paragraph. Information for writing these performance elements may be gained through personal interviews, a questionnaire, or both. By analyzing all job responsibilities, employees identify those behaviors leading to job success or failure. From these lists of behaviors, specialists identify those that cover or fully describe a specific performance dimension. Behavioral analysts first collect performance elements. Then, through the use of factor analysis—a statistical procedure—they analyze these elements and group them with those having similar content in the more global performance dimensions.

When supervisors or specialists review performance elements for validation purposes, they answer such questions as the following:

1. How important is this element in your unit of authority?

2. Is it observable to the degree that you can rate an employee on it?

3. Does it contribute to effective job performance?

4. Does each employee have a relatively equal on-the-job probability of demonstrating the described element?

The acceptance or rejection of performance indicators depends on a review by two or more sets of qualified observers who are knowledgeable about the job and who are observing the same job behavior. These raters must have significant agreement as to the importance of the behavior and the frequency of its occurrence.

The identification, validation, and weighting process may take the following approach:

Step 1: A group of jobholders and their supervisors identify performance incidents (job-related behavior) required in the performance of the job under review.

Step 2: A second group of jobholders (performing the same job) and their supervisors review the performance incidents and assess the degree of job relevancy of each identified incident. The resulting relevance rating scale may take this form:

Relevancy Rating Scale (Lowest Number—Highest Relevancy Rating)
1—Extremely Relevant
2—Very Relevant
3—Relevant
4—Somewhat Relevant
5—Irrelevant

Step 3: A third group reviews and analyzes relevant performance incidents, joining those that basically identify the same behavior or behaviors that are so similar as to be difficult for most people to perceive as being different. The performance incidents then become the performance elements.

Step 4: The elements are then weighted as to their worth in the performance of the total job.

Step 5: A final review ensures that each identified, relevancy scored, and weighted performance element ties directly to the responsibilities, the duties, and the accountabilities of the job.

A review by experts of employee-defined behaviors that are critical to both superior and unacceptable job performance leads to the establishment of *behavioral anchors*. The behavior considered most negative or unsatisfactory and that considered most positive or extremely acceptable become the two behavioral anchors for the performance dimension or performance element. An example of behavioral anchors is as follows:

Most Positive—Solves problems affecting job performance no matter how complicated or time-consuming problem resolution may be.

Most Negative—Fails to identify the critical issue when attempting to resolve workplace problems.

The middle-out approach is also valuable for setting behavioral anchors. This approach starts by first identifying and defining standard behavior. The scales are incrementally defined in moving away from standard behavior. This allows for an open-ended setting to the most and least desirable behaviors.

The CIT is again most valuable for identifying and defining these anchor points.

Behavioral Anchored Rating Scales (BARS)—Behavioral Anchored Rating Scales are additional descriptions of various degrees of behavior between the most negative and most positive behavioral positions. These interval descriptions are critical if performance appraisal is to be an essential part of the compensation program. They identify in behavioral terms a complete range of behaviors relative to a performance dimension or performance element of a single job or group of jobs. Each behavior from the most negative to the most acceptable provides intervals for the assignment of specific numbers of points or is useful for setting some rating or ranking order for demonstrated behavior. By having the descriptors represent equal or nearly equal intervals, the behaviorally described performance appraisal can provide a point score for tying performance appraisal to salary administration and for assisting in implementing a pay-for-performance or merit program.

When analyzing the BARS that relate to a particular dimension or performance element, there are at least two methods for identifying employee behavior. First, the rater selects that behavior statement that best identifies employee behavior, or second, the rater identifies a minimum threshold (i.e., no behavior listed below it describes the employee's behavior) and a maximum threshold (i.e., no behavior listed above it describes the employee's behavior). A combination of the two methods is possible.

This entire technique using performance dimensions, performance elements, and BARS is the easiest of all performance appraisal techniques to substantiate and justify. It comes directly from demonstrated workplace behavior. The potential for gaining face, content, and concurrent validity (see discussion on validity earlier in this chapter) is far greater than in a technique based on worker traits. In most cases relevant worker traits can be described in behavioral terms and thus can be converted into identifiable job-related behavior.

Job Responsibilities/Performance Standards—The responsibilities/ performance standards technique directly concerns the responsibilities listed on the job description. The rater appraises employee performance by using performance standards derived from specific responsibilities as basic appraisal criteria. Because the technique uses job responsibilities, a separate appraisal form must be developed for each job. The appraisal form lists the performance standards and the criteria for identifying how well the jobholder performs each responsibility. In addition, these kinds of appraisal forms may include space for the rater to indicate the relative importance of each responsibility. This type of appraisal often fails to recognize employee contributions that are crucial to work group and organizational success. Examples include willingness to accept additional responsibilities, adaptability and creativity in solving problems at the work station, and assisting other members to achieve acceptable performance standards.

Management by Objectives (MBO) Technique

The performance appraisal technique known as management by objectives (MBO) requires the supervisor and the subordinate jointly to discuss and develop goals for some future period. These goals then become standards by which to measure the subordinate's performance. In the review session, both the supervisor and the subordinate assess actual goal accomplishment. This process provides the supervisor with an excellent opportunity to discuss the subordinate's work behavior and provides appropriate feedback on demonstrated performance.

In this goal-setting technique, the supervisor acts as teacher, leader, and counselor. When properly performed, the technique emphasizes the supervisor's role as counselor and minimizes the role of judge. To be a successful counselor in these sessions, the supervisor must be a good listener and observer. The process is basically one of self-appraisal by the subordinate. Performed in any other way, it is of little value.

A goal-setting session may ideally take the following form:

1. In an informal and unstructured environment, the supervisor and the subordinate discuss objectives of the organization and the work group in simple, straightforward language and relate the work activities of the subordinate to these objectives.

2. The subordinate then sets one to three goals for the coming period (which should seldom extend beyond the next two or three months). The subordinate has usually worked on developing these goals before the meeting.

3. The subordinate and the supervisor mutually agree on each goal, then analyze them, and identify as many attainment steps as possible that will lead to reaching the goals successfully.[13] (For operational success, there is a limit to the number of goals set, but there is no limit to the number of attainment steps identified in the problem-solving process—the more the better.)

4. The subordinate and the supervisor then discuss the likelihood of successfully performing each attainment step and the priority one step has over another.

5. The supervisor attempts to provide any information the subordinate needs or wants to know.

6. At all times, the supervisor must convey through demonstrated behavior that the goals are those of the subordinate. The supervisor is a resource person ready and willing to assist the subordinate in every way possible. However, the goals are the subordinate's, and the subordinate has primary responsibility for achieving them.

7. Each goal should be specific, stimulating, achievable, and relevant. Each goal and its attainment steps should be in writing.

In the appraisal follow-up session, the subordinate and the supervisor analyze the subordinate's successes and failures. This session focuses on the attainment steps rather than on the goals. If the subordinate has failed to reach a goal, each attainment step is reviewed in an attempt to find the barriers to success. Together, the subordinate and the supervisor may decide that they have not identified the critical attainment steps, or they may decide that the goal was unattainable considering the existing situation. On the other hand, it is important to recognize those steps that led to success because this information may benefit others pursuing similar goals.

The purpose of the goal-setting session is to improve organizational performance through the individual's growth. It is a cooperative venture in which the subordinate has the opportunity to exercise self-control and self-appraisal of work behavior.

Much recent work on improving organizational performance focuses on the work group. This type of emphasis minimizes the importance of individual appraisal. Goal setting is as effective for appraising group performance as it is for appraising that of individuals. The major problem is that the rater requires even greater skills as a teacher, leader, and counselor.

---

[13]Attainment steps are the heart of the goal-setting process. They are work-behavior activities identified as being fundamental to the successful attainment of a particular goal.

Management by objectives is most valuable when it is used in conjunction with other appraisal techniques. It provides a minimal amount of common ground for comparing the performance of one individual with that of another because the goals of different individuals may vary drastically.

Although goal setting centers on results and allows the employee to have an important part in setting goals as well as achieving these results, an MBO technique usually takes about two years to take hold and function properly.

MINIMIZING BARRIERS TO EFFECTIVE PERFORMANCE APPRAISAL

Although most of this chapter focuses on performance appraisal techniques and the design of various instruments, the barrier to effective appraisal is *human,* not *technical.* The measurement and the appraisal of performance in most situations require analysis that depends on the human eye and brain and, as Bronowski states, the eye and the brain provide an interpretation of reality, not a view of absolute reality. The weak links in the process are those that tie the appraiser, the appraisee, and other review authorities into the process.

A first step in identifying ways to improve the inefficiencies and the ineffectiveness resulting from human limitations is a review of those persons involved in the appraisal process.

Who Are the Appraisers?

Appraisers, raters, superiors, and *supervisors* are names that often identify those who appraise the performance of other individuals. The process may at times involve members of the organization other than the appraisee and the rater. In fact, research indicates that the use of more than one rater is advantageous in reducing bias resulting from differences in rater perception and demonstrated employee behavior. John Miner favors including superiors at levels above the immediate supervisor as long as the raters have adequate knowledge of the performance of the individual being rated.[14] In addition to the immediate and higher level superiors, some organizations promote self-rating and permit peers, co-workers, subordinates, and staff personnel specialists to input data into the rating process. In addition to minimizing bias through the use of more than one rater, involving raters at different levels provides a variety of rating considerations from different points of view.

Immediate Supervisor—The management of most organizations usually believes that because of close contact, immediate supervisors are best able to appraise subordinates. However, there is a distinct possibility that the personal biases of the immediate supervisor can have a detrimental impact if there is not an additional reviewer.

---

[14]John B. Miner, "Management Appraisal: A Capsule Review and Current References," *Business Horizons,* October 1968, p. 86.

Appraiser's Immediate Supervisor—The appraiser's immediate supervisor normally has endorsement or review authority. Through this review, the appraiser's immediate supervisor monitors and controls the appraisal process. (Review authorities may be more than one level above the immediate supervisor.) Although this individual can disagree with the appraiser's rating, the reviewer will not change the original rating. Raters at this vantage point may place more attention on goal attainment, acceptance of responsibilitiy, and job knowledge, whereas the immediate supervisor focuses on the accomplishment of responsibilities and duties. When ratings differ, attempts are made to resolve any differences.

Active involvement and commitment on the part of the review authority can reduce rater bias. In most cases, even when the rater's superior actually appraises the subordinate's performance, little difference is found in the two ratings. The secret of effective review is genuine involvement, not merely bureaucratic "rubber stamping."

Peers and Co-workers—Although seldom used as appraisers, peers and co-workers have possibly the best insight into identifying leadership skills and future potential. Because of the possible combination of peer insights and peer competition, the organization whose environment promotes high levels of individual stress and need for self-protection may find that the costs incurred through added anxiety and hostility far outweigh the benefits gained from the added knowledge of peer insights.

Immediate Subordinates—Other seldom-used but possible additions to the appraiser group are immediate subordinates. Although they may tend to overrate their supervisor, they do identify his or her effectiveness in communicating job knowledge, interest in subordinates as individuals and team members, and skill in coordinating the subordinates' efforts into effective teamwork.

Self—Self-rating has received support in recent years as more organizations become involved in goal setting. A valid program requires the organization to identify and subdivide goals. It then requires involved employees to develop their own goals that assist the group and organization to achieve theirs. Setting goals and then analyzing successes and failures gained in their achievement provides valuable opportunities for self-rating. Self-rating is especially valuable for self-development.

Committee—Using a committee for appraisal permits more than one person to have an immediate input. This approach allows various perspectives to be considered at one time. Committee members are usually managers one level above the employee being appraised and have had contact with the employee during the past appraisal period. The committee may also consist of managers at various levels who are aware of the employee's performance. Just as committee appraisal may result in fair and just treatment, it can also result in a "kangaroo court." A weakness in using committees is excessive use of time.

Staff Personnel Specialists—Well-trained specialists from the personnel department often assist in the employee appraisal. In most cases, when they are part of the appraisal process, they work together with individuals who have had the opportunity to directly observe the appraisee's performance.

A 1977 study by the Conference Board revealed that almost 95 percent of the respondents stated that the *immediate supervisor* was the appraiser. Others identified as appraisers were *self* (about 13 percent of the time), *groups or committees* (about 6 percent), and *representatives of the personnel department* (about 6 percent). Representing less than 1 percent each were consultants (internal and external), peers or co-workers, and subordinates (0 percent in this study).[15] This study also found that the appraiser's immediate superior was a reviewer about 70 percent of the time, with the personnel department performing reviews about 30 percent of the time and the appraiser's immediate supervisor's superior about 20 percent of the time.[16]

Who Are the Appraisees?

A performance appraisal method used in the early stages of the Industrial Revolution was a four-sided piece of wood approximately two inches long and one inch wide that was painted a different color on each side and hung over the work station of each employee. Each day, the supervisor would turn the side to the color that he thought denoted the employee's performance for the preceding day—black for bad, blue for indifferent, yellow for good, and white for excellent.[17]

Performance appraisal in the early part of the twentieth century also focused on operative employees. In the past two decades, however, there has been a notable trend toward eliminating performance appraisal among nonexempt employees and focusing on performance appraisal at the executive, managerial, and professional levels of the organization.

One reason for lack of interest in appraising nonexempt employees is the inability of organizations to develop valid and workable measuring instruments. Another reason is the strong allegiance of the operative levels to seniority. Many organizations consider their nonexempt, operative jobs to be highly procedural and technically oriented, and they think that all that is necessary to appraise performance of the operative is to measure output. If this were the case, the idea of not appraising the performance of lower-level employees might be valid. Often, however, this is not the case. Even when the job requires that the employee follow specific procedures, 100 percent performance goes far beyond the faithful performance of some list of activities.

[15]Robert I. Lazer and Walter S. Wikstrom, *Appraising Managerial Performance: Current Practices and Future Direction,* Conference Board Report No. 723. (New York: The Conference Board, Inc., 1977), p. 26.

[16]Ibid., p. 28.

[17]E. C. Bursk et al., eds., "The Life of Robert Owen," in *The World of Business,* vol. 3 (New York: Simon and Schuster, 1962), pp. 1345, 1350.

Acceptable employee performance at all levels has elements that are difficult to specify. Employee contributions that affect output quality, reduction in costs, and identification and solution of nagging problems are evident at every level. Measurement of these contributions requires some form of appraisal. Acceptance of seniority as the only criterion for rewarding performance is not only unacceptable but wrong. This does not mean that seniority should not be recognized; it does mean that seniority and on-the-job performance are not the same thing and may not have a direct relationship. It is almost impossible to operate an organization that places a high value on human talent and individual differences without having a system for appraising performance.

When Should Appraisals Be Performed?

Traditionally, it has been common practice to perform a formal performance appraisal once a year. The proponents of the annual appraisal state that, if held more frequently, formal appraisals tend to become mechanical, worthless procedures. A semantics problem arises here as to the meaning of the term *formal appraisal.* If it means completion of some special form, then this consideration may have some validity. If it applies to the entire process, however, then it is most likely incorrect.

The appraisal process should be continuous. To identify employee performance and potential strengths and weaknesses successfully, formal elements may require consideration at least bimonthly (every two months) or quarterly.

An intensive study conducted by the General Electric Company into the effectiveness of its appraisal system resulted in a Work Planning and Review (WP&R) report.[18] Among its conclusions were that (1) comprehensive annual performance appraisals are of questionable value, and (2) coaching should be a day-to-day, not a once-a-year, activity.

Some of the appraisal techniques and instruments described in this chapter lend themselves to frequent use and to certain forms (of a fairly simple nature) that require completion on a monthly, bimonthly, or quarterly basis. These forms by themselves or combined with other instruments, promote the ongoing requirement as described in the General Electric WP&R report.

The bimonthly or quarterly appraisal process permits an averaging of a number of reports, thus de-emphasizing the importance of any one appraisal or any one set of activities. Furthermore, the once-a-year appraisal may overemphasize recent activities and thus distort their actual value—another reason for using an appraisal system that has continuous elements.

Minimizing Appraiser Bias

Along with considerable effort being expended to improve the design of appraisal instruments, equally important work has been directed toward improving the skills of the appraiser. Recognizing the perception and interpretation

---

[18]Herbert H. Meyer, Emanuel Kay, and John R. P. French, Jr., "Split Roles in Performance Appraisal," *Harvard Business Review,* January–February 1965, pp. 123–129.

issues that foster unacceptable subjectivity biases, designers and managers of appraisal processes have identified typical appraiser errors and some of the reasons for their continuing existence. They have subsequently developed approaches for minimizing them.

Typical Appraiser Errors—Over the years, appraisers have been found guilty of making the following rating errors:

1. Halo effect.

2. Horn effect.

3. Central tendency.

4. Strict rating.

5. Lenient rating.

6. Bias about recent behavior.

Halo Effect. In the halo effect, a rating of excellent in one quality influences the appraiser to give the appraisee a similar rating or to rate the appraisee higher on other qualities than actually deserved.

Horn Effect. In the horn effect, a rating of unsatisfactory in one quality influences the appraiser to give the appraisee a similar rating, or to rate the appraisee lower in other qualities than actually deserved.

Central Tendency. Central tendency provides a rating of average or around the midpoint for all qualities.

Strict Rating. In strict rating, the appraiser rates the appraisee lower than would the normal or average appraiser. The appraiser is overly harsh in rating appraisee performance qualities.

Lenient Rating. In lenient rating, the appraiser rates the appraisee higher than would the normal or average appraiser. The appraiser is overly loose in rating appraisee performance qualities.

Bias about Recent Behavior. The appraiser rates the appraisee by recent behavior and fails to recognize the most commonly demonstrated behavior during the entire appraisal period.

Underlying Reasons for Appraisal Errors—Like all other employees, appraisers are human. They are subject to the same problems and forces that influence all human behavior.

In addition to weaknesses related to perception, there are other behavior influencing forces such as the following:

1. Desire to be accepted.

2. Concern with job security.

3. Concern with self-protection.

4. Affiliation with those holding similar views or having similar qualities.

5. Limitations because of lack of prior education, previous experience, or developed skills.

Desire to be Accepted—All human beings have both instinctive and learned behavior determinants regarding social processes. The need for social affiliation may be stronger and easier to observe in some individuals than others, but each person requires some type of social interaction and underlying any successful interaction are feelings of concern, comradeship, and respect. When one employee rates the performance of another, the chance that this rating could damage the acceptance of one by another is a distinct possibility.

Concern with Job Security—All competent supervisors know that their success depends on the cooperation, effort, and contributions provided by their subordinates. If in the appraisal process they inappropriately (not necessarily inaccurately) rate certain employees, the performance of the entire group (not only the inappropriately rated employee) may suffer. Most supervisors realize that their own job security and the performance of their work unit usually go hand in hand.

Concern with Self-protection—Anyone who has ever worked with people realizes that the range of behaviors people can demonstrate relative to some incident or issue defies the imagination. Performance appraisal can be crucial to an individual. An individual's response to an unsatisfactory performance appraisal can range from absolute indifference to becoming so distraught that the appraisee murders the appraiser. Very few appraisers like to be in such a position and, although the chance for such a drastic retaliation is unlikely, concern for personal retaliation often influences appraisal ratings.

Affiliation with Those Holding Similar Views or Having Similar Qualities—It is always easier to relate to people who have similar perspectives. Factors that may influence perspective include race, sex, national origin, educational background, work experience, physical characteristics (e.g., height, weight, length of hair), place of birth, or location of residence. Factors that influence perception are innumerable, but it is easier to communicate and be with people who have similar views. It is also easy to see that those who do possess such qualities will probably receive higher appraisal ratings from persons with the same qualities than those who do not. These differences often do not arise because of specific, conscious action. Rather, they may result from a subconscious minimization of unacceptable activities by an individual holding similar views and a subconscious overreaction against those holding dissimilar views.

Limitations because of Lack of Prior Education, Previous Experience, or Developed Skills—Although it is important to recognize the previously discussed four influencing forces, most organizations have fairly strict procedures that minimize the unsatisfactory influences of these forces. Education, experience, and skill limitations, however, are fertile grounds for improvement.

Educational opportunities abound in every aspect of the performance appraisal process. Appraiser educational programs can include instruction on the following:

1. Purpose and use of the appraisal process.

2. Objectives and goals.

3. Standards used for measuring performance.

4. Design of the appraisal instruments. The appraiser must understand each factor (i.e., dimension) and the scales used for measuring its demonstrated degree.

5. Measurement indexes used to identify the demonstrated degree of a performance quality.

6. Meaning of appraisal to employees.

7. Procedures available for *preparing* for performance appraisal.

8. Ways to implement appraisal interviews and to provide feedback to employees on their performance. Of all the aspects of performance appraisal, this is probably the one area that offers the greatest opportunity for improvement. The costs involved in improving an appraiser's skill in implementing face-to-face conversation with subordinates on performance issues are outweighed by the derived benefits.

9. The range of subjective influence on performance appraisal and the types of rating errors made by appraisers and possible ways of minimizing them.

10. Recognition of equity and equality and the impact of appraisal on these two vital areas of concern to all employees.

Educational assistance can also include preappraisal forms to be completed by the appraiser. They require the appraiser to collect and review relevant data and information that, in essence, requires doing the self-instruction "homework" necessary to be ready for the appraisal.

Appraisal experience opportunities can be enhanced in many ways. Through role playing, educational programs, and the use of instant-replay video tape recordings, appraisers can develop their skills. By having experienced appraisers go through the entire process with the student appraisers, the students can increase their familiarity and understanding of the process. They can learn physical movements and even facial expressions that facilitate success. They can also learn to eliminate things that may lead to failure.

Skill improvement starts with identifying the skills necessary for accomplishing an appraisal. The next step is to identify those skills currently possessed that are sufficient to meet appraisal demands and those that must be developed. With recognition of skill strengths and weaknesses, appraisers can then make their choice regarding the interest and effort they wish to expend for these needed improvements.

Enhancing Appraisee Acceptance

Although most employees have some fears about performance measurement, they nevertheless want some form of fair, accurate, and objective appraisal. Almost all employees want to know from their supervisors how they are performing their jobs. They not only want this information in absolute output terms but in terms that relate their performance to that of others doing similar work. In addition, each supervisor must be able to recognize individual differences and their relationship to worker productivity, as well as what is necessary to assist each person grow and prosper.

A fundamental precondition for gaining acceptance of appraisal is the establishment of standards that are understood by the employees and that from their point of view are fair and just.

Performance requirements must be stated in terms that give the appraisee the following information:

1. What criteria will be used to measure performance?

2. How will performance be measured?

3. Who will do the appraisal?

4. When and where will the appraisal be done?

5. What inputs does the employee have during the appraisal process and what type of feedback is to be expected and when will it be received?

6. What assistance can be expected to improve performance?

7. What rewards or opportunities will be made available because of performance that is above standard?

When employees have this type of information, they know what the organization expects of them, what assistance is available, how to request assistance, and what they can expect when providing specific levels of performance. Answering these questions helps employees to know where they are today, where they want to be tomorrow, and what job performance can do to help them move toward their goals. Most important is the fact that employee acceptance of the appraisal process directly influences the trust the employee has in the organization.

Four major factors related to performance appraisal that highly influence the development of a trusting workplace environment are the following:

1. Collecting data that accurately describe the job and allowing and encouraging employees to make inputs into the identification of job-related behaviors and the development of the performance standards for their jobs.

2. Participating in the identification of resources required in the successful performance of work assignments and in the allocation of the limited resources available to the work unit.

3. Designing understandable appraisal instruments and expressing work standards in language that relates to the way employees actually perform their assignments.

4. Developing supervisor-subordinate (appraiser-appraisee) interview sessions that allow for mature interactions—those that are natural and minimize defensiveness. This does not require appraisers to change their normal behavioral patterns. It does require them to realize the impact their behavior has on their subordinate appraisees.

A workplace environment that generates both security and opportunity for future growth while minimizing stressful situations certainly enhances appraisal acceptance. Establishing this type of environment goes far beyond the performance appraisal process. Every aspect of managing people and their work relates to the development of a quality work life. However, performance appraisal is an integral part of a healthy work environment in which trust is an essential ingredient.

SELECTED READINGS

Hayden, Robert J., "Performance Appraisal: A Better Way," *Personnel Journal,* July 1973, pp. 606–617. A recommendation to first analyze the purposes of the appraisal and then develop the techniques necessary to satisfy the diversity of management needs for appraisal. The author presents an approach for satisfying employee development as well as administrative requirements.

Henderson, Richard I., *Performance Appraisal: Theory to Practice.* Reston, VA: Reston Publishing Co., 1980. A practical guide for understanding the many parts of a performance appraisal system and how these parts fit together and interact with one another.

Kellogg, Marion S., *What to Do About Performance Appraisal,* rev. ed. New York: AMACOM, 1975. One of the best recognized books in its area. It summarizes what companies and researchers have learned about performance appraisal. It includes detailed how-to-do-it chapters covering the major elements included in the performance appraisal process.

Lazer, Robert I. and Walter S. Wikstrom, *Appraising Managerial Performance: Current Practices and Future Dirction,* Conference Board Report No. 723. New York: The Conference Board, Inc., 1977. This report is the most current and comprehensive review of appraisal practices in the United States. It is also a good primer for anyone interested in learning the nature of the appraisal process and the problems requiring resolution before appraisals can be a positive force for improving business productivity.

Levinson, Harry, "Management by Whose Objectives?" *Harvard Business Review,* July–August 1970, pp. 125–134. According to this article, management by objectives, combined with performance appraisal, is self-defeating. MBO is truly "one of the greatest management illusions, serving simply to increase pressure on the individual." The author does not completely reject MBO, but he argues for a better understanding of motivational theory to overcome its potential pitfalls.

McGregor, Douglas, "An Uneasy Look at Performance Appraisal," *Harvard Business Review,* May–June 1957, pp. 89–94. After summarizing the major objections to appraisal, including supervisor inadequacies in evaluating and interviewing, emotional stress placed on the person being evaluated, failure of the process to effect any real change in the employee, and irrelevancy to employee career goals or corporate objectives, the author describes goal setting as an approach to appraisal that is much more sound and that avoids the major pitfalls of the traditional approach.

Meyer, Herbert H., Emanuel Kay, and John R. P. French, Jr., "Split Roles in Performance Appraisal," *Harvard Business Review,* January–February 1965, pp. 123–129. Studies conducted at the General Electric Company reveal that attempting to use an appraisal interview session concerned with only one performance for both employee salary action and improvement of work performance invites conflicting results. The authors also recognize that when specific goals and deadlines are mutually established and agreed on by the subordinate and the superior, work performance improves.

Miner, John B., "Management Appraisal: A Capsule Review and Current References," *Business Horizons,* October 1968, pp. 83–96. A broad review of performance appraisal research reveals the merit of using more than one rater in the appraisal process, the importance of feedback, and the strengths and the weaknesses of certain appraisal tools and procedures.

Oberg, Winston, "Make Performance Appraisal Relevant," *Harvard Business Review,* January–February 1972, pp. 61–67. A review of nine of the most commonly used appraisal techniques, describing the strengths and weaknesses of each. The author then shows how each technique can be used singly and in combination with different performance appraisal objectives.

Raia, Anthony P., *Managing by Objectives.* Glenview, IL: Scott Foresman, 1974. One of the pioneers of MBO provides a clear understanding of the fundamental tools required to design and to implement an effective MBO system.

Tosi, Henry L., and Stephen Carroll, "Management by Objectives," *Personnel Administration,* July–August 1970, pp. 44–48. Although management by objectives appears to be effective in linking performance to rewards, it does not appear to serve other appraisal activities as well. Formalizing MBO may reduce its positive value to the organization.

Whisler, Thomas L., and Shirley F. Harper, eds., *Performance Appraisal, Research and Practice.* New York: Holt, Rinehart, & Winston, 1962. A basic review of all the elements that comprise the performance appraisal process. An excellent primer for anyone wishing to know more about how to develop and implement performance appraisal.

Winstanley, Nathan B., ed., *Current Readings in Performance Appraisal.* Scottsdale, AZ: American Compensation Association, 1974. A broad and comprehensive review of what has been taking place in the past 10 years in the performance appraisal of employees. It focuses on the emerging knowledge of the need for feedback in the appraisal process. In addition, it notes the trend away from factor rating scales—particularly when performance appraisal centers on personal development.

14

Compensation Administration

CONTENT

Chapter 14 analyzes many of the parts of compensation administration. It identifies and discusses those individuals and groups with a voice in determining the guidelines to be followed in compensating employees. It also describes some of the practices currently being followed by compensation professionals and discuss the reasons for their actions.

GOALS

Upon concluding this chapter, you should be aware of the relationship between compensation practices and organizational objectives. With an understanding of organizational objectives and policies, the compensation administrator integrates compensation with the behavior employees demonstrate in assisting the organization to survive and grow. In fine tuning compensation practices to organizational objectives, specialists relate it to internal job relationships, external market rates, individual contributions, and local and national economic conditions.

Once hired, and after working for a week or at the most a month, the employee receives a paycheck for work performed. Experience is gained from performing job assignments and with continuing orientation to the organization and its various reward practices. As a result, the employee develops a unique view of the relationship between pay and the assigned job, pay and performance, pay as a part of the total compensation package, and compensation as a part of total membership rewards.

Pay and compensation policy now become real and important considerations. The employee begins to search for answers to such basic questions as the following:

1. When is the next pay day?

2. When is the first increase possible?

3. What are the criteria for raises?

4. What are the eligibility requirements for vacations?

5. How long is the first vacation?

6. How many paid holidays are there? What are they? Are there eligibility requirements?

7. What are the criteria for promotions?

8. Are cost-of-living adjustments provided?

9. How are overtime opportunities determined?

10. Is an employee's pay ever reduced?

Answers to these questions help to acquaint the employee with the organization. After they have been answered, a second group of questions arises that affects worker performance and organizational productivity and profitability even more critically. The employee now recognizes that the job not only dictates a standard of living, but it also defines the social status and economic worth of the individual. Among such questions are these:

1. Is this a permanent job?

2. Will the job and its rewards offer income security?

3. Will the job and its rewards provide a satisfying life-style?

4. Does the job permit extra effort, and will the organization recognize special contributions?

5. Will the job provide opportunity for self-growth and career development?

6. Do the job and its rewards compare favorably with those available in the area or with comparable jobs in other organizations?

Organizational success depends to a significant degree on the assumptions and the expectations employees develop concerning the intellectual, emotional, and physical efforts they exert and the rewards they receive for improving productivity of the organization.

TYING IT ALL TOGETHER

The reasons behind the time and the costs expended in designing and implementing job analysis, job evaluation, compensation surveys, pay structures, benefits packages, pay-for-performance programs, and appraisal of performance now become apparent. The employer must pay the employee for services rendered. A compensation program that develops internal equity, permits the organization to compete in the labor market, and stimulates employees to exert extra effort has a bottom line meaning—fair pay to employees and profit to the organization.

Skilled administrators keep a well-designed compensation program alive and current and improve those parts of it that do not meet employer needs and employee demands.

For most companies, labor costs consume much of the money available for staying in business. For the average company, labor costs consume between 35 and 45 percent of total income. For labor-intensive organizations, labor costs may exceed 60 percent, whereas for some industries that are capital intensive and spend a major share of income on raw material or preassembled products, labor costs may drop to 10 to 15 percent. Whether 15 percent or 60, labor costs have a significant impact on organizational profitability. The proper design and administration of the compensation program is therefore very important.

Employee confidence in the stability and the fairness of the compensation system develops by setting pay levels that ensure each person a rate of pay and total compensation that are internally fair compared with that received by every other member and externally competitive with that received by others performing similar jobs in other organizations in relevant labor markets. Serious differences in pay levels (either internally or externally) often result in the (1) loss of competent employees to other organizations providing better compensation opportunities, (2) inability to attract qualified personnel, and (3) destruction of a work environment that stimulates superior performance.

Because of the many diverse parts of a compensation system, it is inherently complex; yet it must be made as understandable as possible to all employees. Its administration can increase the system's complexity, or it can be a positive force toward increasing understandability. All employees should be aware of what the organization is providing in money and in-kind payments to obtain their services. They should know why they are receiving these payments, how they are determined, who makes the determinations, when payments are available, and what opportunities are available to each employee to influence the amount.

At the topmost levels of the organization, those same individuals who set overall organizational objectives, approve the strategies necessary for achieving these objectives, and establish the policies that act as guidelines for acceptable employee behavior, also determine annual labor budgets. These budgets may consist of a personnel and a merit budget.

The *personnel budget* includes all personnel pay costs in gross figures. It identifies the total number of employees in each unit and the money necessary to pay them for the coming budget year. The *merit budget* is theoretically the money allocated for rewarding superior performance. Normally, merit funds are allocated to each unit relative to its percentage of total labor cost. For example, if Department A of Olympia has a labor cost of $1 million and the total labor budget for Olympia is $30 million, Department A would receive one-thirtieth or 3.33 percent of the merit budget. This allocation procedure does not differentiate between department performances or internal pay structure differences among departments.

Labor budget reviews and recommendations start with decisions made by the *compensation committee* of the board of directors. A small, select group of usually three to five outside (i.e., nonmembers of the organization) directors make up the committee. They have significant influence on the compensation received by the chief executive officer and other members of senior management. They may also review the compensation opportunities made available to all employees. Personnel of the compensation department may provide the committee with information on current market practices, or they may use the services of contracted outside compensation consultants. Chapter 15 contains additional discussion of this committee.

The *chief executive officer* has ultimate responsibility for all decisions made in the operation of the organization. This officer, as final decisionmaker, reviews, makes recommendations for necessary changes, and approves labor budgets and all compensation strategies.

The responsibility for the development of the initial amounts to be described in the labor budget rests in the *finance department* or the *office of the controller*. Financial analysts review projects and programs for the coming year, develop projections of revenue, identify major costs involved in producing outputs that result in revenue, and allocate a certain amount of money to labor budgets.

A *salary administration committee* consisting of from three to seven members, usually including the chief financial officer, the senior personnel officer, and other senior management officials, reviews the budget and makes allocation recommendations and decisions. The committee reviews the total budget and the allocations made to the various major units of the organization. In analyzing the allocations, the committee reviews historical records regarding past outputs and incurred labor costs by department projected outputs for the coming year and economic conditions that may affect projected operations. It reviews recommendations made by department heads and supervisors that fall outside the scope of standing operating procedures and gives required approval or makes necessary adjustments. This committee also functions as a review body on existing compensation policy and makes recommendations for necessary changes.

Decisions made by this committee then go to the personnel and compensation departments. Specialists now transmit labor budget opportunities to the respective division or department heads. With the information on funds available for employee compensation, the personnel department makes available a variety of information that assists major division or department heads and their subordinate managers in making the best decisions possible for allocating funds to specific groups and units and for individual compensation.

The *job evaluation committee* usually consists of the first and middle levels of operating management. Their major responsibility is to ensure internal fairness among nonmanagerial jobs by determining job worth according to some evaluation plan. Chapter 7 discusses the design and the operation of this committee in detail. Figure 14-1 describes the flow of compensation information among the various individuals and groups responsible for compensation decisions.

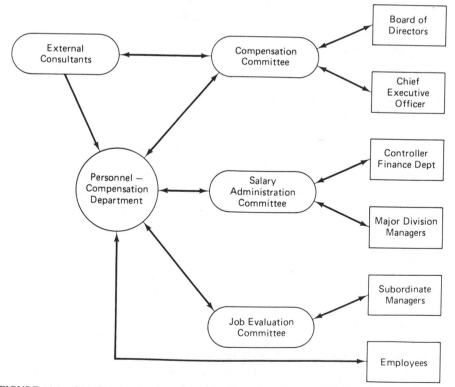

FIGURE 14-1   COMPENSATION INFORMATION FLOW AND COMPENSATION DECISION POINTS

TABLE 14-1

PAY ADJUSTMENT AND PROMOTION RECOMMENDATION RESPONSIBILITIES

Immediate Supervisor	Appraises performance; makes pay adjustment or promotion recommendations.
Department Head	Reviews recommendations of subordinate supervisors; initiates action for pay adjustment and promotion.
Personnel and Compensation Departments	Reviews department head recommendations for compliance with compensation policy and budget and promotion guidelines. Advises department heads on propriety of actions. Processes all necessary record-keeping data and information.
Senior Management	Grants final approval for all compensation adjustments and job changes. Approves or denies requests that extend beyond policies and guidelines. Approves policy changes. Sets annual labor budget and departmental allocations.

The final step in the determination and the allocation of pay to employees rests with the *department manager* and the *immediate supervisor.* These two persons usually have the closest contact with the employee. They review the requirements of their units and the performance of the employee. They analyze the performance of each employee relative to that of others and, within limits set by policy or compensation department guidelines, recommend the allocation of the disposable portions of the budget among their subordinates. Table 14-1 describes pay adjustment and promotion recommendation responsibilities.

COMPENSATION ADMINISTRATION ISSUES

Throughout this text, the complexity of compensation has been mentioned as a problem blocking the design and the management of an effective and efficient compensation system. The first step in unraveling the mysteries of compensation is to identify what determines the actual compensation received by an employee and then to resolve the problems that relate to these compensation issues.

The major issues that influence the pay of each employee are as follows:

1. Internally defined worth of job.

2. Market influences on pay levels.

3. Ability or willingness of the organization to pay.

4. Competitive posture of the organization.

5. Desire of the organization to keep its employees "whole."

6. Guidelines for compensation administration.

7. Allocation of dollars among base pay, benefits, and pay-for-performance programs.

8. Recognition of seniority and merit.

9. Impact of legislation.

10. Recognition of personnel-related actions through pay adjustments.

11. Differences in compensation for permanent, temporary, full-time and part-time employees.

Internally Defined Worth of a Job

Part 2 specifically focuses on the design and development aspects of establishing and defining job worth. With the development of a pay structure, compensation administration faces the task of maintaining the internal equity relationships. It is here that the organization recognizes the abilities of employees and differentiates their pay according to the knowledge, skills, and responsibilities required in job performance and in the conditions under which employees work. Pressures to meet the pay demands of various individuals and groups and policy restrictions placed on pay opportunities make maintenance of the compensation plan extremely difficult.

When compensation opportunities relate to some type of well-defined procedures, some employees will constantly be searching for ways to improve their own welfare. No system has ever been devised that some individuals have not found ways of redesigning it to meet their specific needs. Compensation systems are extremely vulnerable to such actions. The combination of skilled manipulation by self-serving individuals and lack of interest by administrators often results in the gradual breakdown or destruction of the system over time.

Market Influences on Pay Levels

Market rates for some jobs are very stable, whereas others have an extremely erratic market relationship. Supply and demand are basic. Organizations bidding for those individuals who have job skills that are scarce will force pay rates to escalate. Chapter 9 describes market influences and ways of collecting market pay data. The maintenance of the pay structure requires organizations constantly to return to the market, collect data, and review current structure(s) with existing market rates.

Ability and Willingness of the Organization to Pay

Above and beyond all other influences, the amount of money an organization is willing to spend for compensating its employees is the limiting factor. A new organization in a competitive environment may have only limited funds.

One in a monopolistic situation may, however, have fairly substantial amounts for this purpose. Recognizing the relationship between labor costs and profitability, many employers feel that the more they restrict labor costs, the greater will be their opportunity to increase profit.

Some industries have traditionally paid their employees low rates of pay. When employees in some of these low-paying industries demand increases, employers find that the consumer will not pay the resulting additional cost for the product or service. Therefore, the employer goes out of business. Other firms have exceedingly high markup (profit potential) on their output and are able to pay employees at much higher levels than those that operate within very narrow profit constraints.

A small percentage change in labor costs can cause a large change in profitability. Although becoming a more difficult issue, labor costs and their relationship to productivity and profitability still provide greater opportunities for employer influence than almost any other cost of doing business.

Competitive Posture of the Organization

Does senior management wish to use its compensation dollars to attract the highest quality of personnel available? It may not be necessary to have superior performers for the organization's successful operation. Competent or possibly marginal types of employees with average or even below-average education, experience, skill, interest, and attitudes may be sufficient to meet the labor demands of the organization. The critical demand made by these types of employers is for the employee to be present at work and perform assigned duties.

After identifying what the market rate of pay is for a job or job family, an organization may use the pay posture guideline chart in table 14-2 to establish its pay schedule.

Desire of the Organization to Keep Its Employees 'Whole'

To many employers, the very term *cost-of-living adjustment* (COLA) conjures up the image of the devil. Over the past decade, many employers have felt that if they did not think of nor discuss this term, it would go away. Like it or

---

TABLE 14-2

PAY POSTURE GUIDELINE CHART

Quality of Personnel Desired	Pay Rate Offered
Superior	Premium—6 to 10% above market rates
Above Average	Fully Competitive—5% above market rates
Average	Competitive—Meets market rates
Below Average	Marginal—1 to 5% below market rates

not, in one way or another, it has always been present and always will be. The only question is: How will an organization use its compensation system to keep its employees "whole"?

There are a number of ways an organization can keep its employees "whole" (able to maintain real purchasing power). Among these are (1) an equal dollar pay adjustment for all employees, (2) an adjustment to the pay policy (pay structure) line, (3) cost-of-living adjustments, (4) area wage differentials, (5) in-step pay grade or pay grade advancements.

Equal Dollar Pay Adjustment—The term *across-the board pay increase* normally means that all employees are granted a one-time annual pay raise. For example, if an organization provides a $500 annual pay increase, the employees' normal time payment schedule is adjusted relative to this $500 increase. Hourly employees receive $500/2080 hours = $0.24 per hour pay increase. Those on a weekly salary receive $500/52 weeks = $9.62 per week pay increase. An across-the-board pay raise provides an identical raise to employees in all jobs. When this occurs, and since the design of most pay structures uses relative relationships (percent difference from minimum to maximum of a pay grade or percent difference between midpoints), the entire structure becomes distorted and relationships become invalid.

A basic part of the philosophy that underlies across-the-board increases relates to the issue that the increase in the price of bread is the same for everyone. The problem here is that "man does not live by bread alone," and most workers design their life-styles around their job-related earnings. Life-style includes subsistence (food, clothing, shelter, and transportation), luxuries, and savings for the future. Considering all of these complex issues, the argument for across-the-board pay raises becomes much weaker.

The underlying strength of an across-the-board pay increase is that it supposedly is the most democratic action to take because it treats every employee equally. This has a sweet ring to employees in the lower end of the pay scale, but what about the employees who perform jobs requiring more responsibility and greater levels of knowledge and skill? A basic feature of any well-designed compensation system is that it provides compensation on an equitable basis. It offers compensation rewards that relate to the contributions made or offered by the employee.

Pay Structure Adjustment—An organization may increase the entire pay structure by a certain percentage. If, for example, the pay structure adjustment is 6 percent, the value of the minimum, midpoint, and maximum rates and the steps within each pay grade are increased by that amount. (See figure 14-2.) This procedure then grants management room within the structure to upgrade the employee's pay. The employee does not necessarily receive a pay increase of 6 percent. The actual individual increase is a management decision. This approach provides an additional opportunity for an organization to increase pay relative to some type of merit or performance criteria. Organizations using the merit guidechart procedure for determining pay increases can include a factor in the guidechart that would add a pay-structure adjustment to the merit increase.

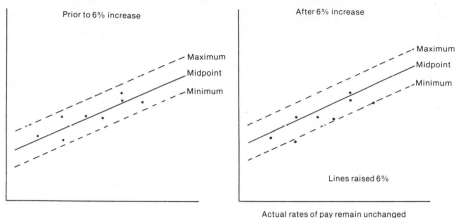

FIGURE 14-2   ADJUSTING THE PAY LINE

Cost-of-living adjustment (COLA)—Most cost-of-living adjustments are related to the Consumer Price Index (CPI), a monthly report issued by the U. S. Department of Labor, Bureau of Labor Statistics. Chapter 4 describes some formulas that unions and organizations use for implementing base pay (and pension rates of pay) adjustments. Some organizations use the actual increases in the CPI and make a monthly adjustment in employees' pay based on the change in the CPI.

The State Farm Mutual Automobile Insurance Company has four separate categories for determining the monthly pay of managerial employees: (1) base pay, (2) merit increase, (3) COLA, and (4) geographic differential. For example, the base pay of an office manager was established at $10,000 when the CPI was 100. The employee received a $2,000 merit increase, and the CPI was 260 at the end of the year. The base pay plus the merit increase equals $12,000—the CPI adjustment is 12,000 × 2.60 or $31,200.

Area Wage Differentials—Some nationwide firms that have employees performing similar jobs in different locations provide an area wage differential based on differences in living costs. The Bureau of Labor Statistics issues an *Urban Family Budget Index* for 40 Standard Metropolitan Statistical Areas (SMSAs). However, these indexes do not cover the entire United States because there are approximately 281 SMSAs in the nation.

In-step Pay Grade or Pay Grade Advance—Although it is a very unsatisfactory approach, many organizations grant their cost-of-living adjustments through in-step advances within the pay grade. This practice corrupts the intended purpose of in-step pay grade advances, which is to recognize merit and seniority.

Attracting Workers Having Knowledge and Skills That Are in Short Supply—Another major reason for structural change occurs when workers with specific kinds of knowledge and skills are in short supply. This is possibly the most difficult problem that pay-structure designers face. If the shortage is temporary, it may be possible to provide some type of bonus to recruit employees with the required knowledge and skills. This, however, opens up the problem of what to do with employees currently performing the jobs. It may be possible to bring the new employees into the job at an advanced step or location in the pay grade, but this also causes conflict with employees currently on the job who are at lower levels of pay. This situation may be a sign of an improperly evaluated job, and it may be that a reevaluation could place the job in a higher pay grade. It may be possible to add some responsibilities and duties to the job, resulting in a higher evaluation and grade assignment.

The final solution may require the establishment of a separate pay structure for exotic or high-demand jobs. Possibly the only design structure that satisfies problems related to these types of jobs is the market-pricing approach to job evaluation and the assignment of pay.

Lump Sum Salary Increase Plans—A recent addition to the compensation administrator's tool kit is the lump sum salary bonus. Mutual insurance companies developed this program and are its primary users.

Lump sum bonuses allow organizations to offer employees salary increases due to economic adjustments, merit increases, or seniority increases in large amounts at one time. Organizations unable to offer employees incentive bonuses can also use this plan. By 1982 more than 100 companies, both insurance and noninsurance, are expected to offer lump sum bonuses. Organizations offering the plans report that 50 to 70 percent of the eligible employees opt for the plans and those who are ineligible expressed an interest in signing up.

Most organizations provide lump sum bonuses to eligible employees automatically, those not wanting the plan must state so.

Employees benefit from the plans by receiving a large amount of money at one time for major purchases, loan repayments or the chance to invest money and draw interest. Employees, however, must be disciplined and control their expenditures.

Employers benefit from a plan with a high degree of visability and employee acceptance. Also the plans are relatively inexpensive to operate. The main cost to employers is a loss of interest on investment funds from paying the bonuses.

Lump sum bonus plans work as follows:

1. Employers set employee standards of eligibility (e.g., organizational officers, exempt or non exempt employees, or employees with years of service ranging from none to five). Part-time employees may also be eligible providing they meet certain income levels.

2. When an employee is eligible for a pay adjustment, the full first year amount of the adjustment is calculated. The employee then receives the total annualized amount of the adjustment minus all involuntary tax adjustments. If the bonus is offered after the first of the year, the bonus may be divided into two payments—one for the adjustment from the initial date of adjustment to the end of the year and the second payment at the first of the year, covering the period from the first of the year until the date ending the full year of the adjustment. Some organizations make no deduction from the lump sum payment, a few others include voluntary deductions from the bonus.

3. At the end of the 12 months for which the bonus was offered, the pay adjustment is then added to the employee's regular earnings and appears as an appropriate increase in the earnings for the pay period. At that time, if new adjustments are made, the employee is then eligible for a new lump-sum bonus for the coming year.

4. Few plans permit renewal of a lump sum bonus into the second year, but, as previously mentioned, new adjustments grant employees the chance for a lump sum bonus for the coming year.

5. Employees who terminate during the period in which a bonus was paid must repay the unearned portion of the bonus. Many plans call for complete recovery by the employer, but exempt recovery in case of death or disability.

Another index number useful for monitoring pay action is the *range index*. The range index is computed by dividing actual rate of pay minus the minimum rate of pay by the spread of the range. Range indexes can be calculated for various groups of employees (e.g., exempt, nonexempt, by pay grade, by specific occupation or classes of jobs, or by employee demographic characteristics such as sex, race, or age). The range index keeps compensation managers informed of employee movement through the pay grade.

Using a pay scale with an $8,000 minimum salary and a $12,000 maximum salary, we can compute a 37.5 percent range index number with the following equation:

$$\text{Range Index} = \frac{\text{Actual Rate of Pay} - \text{Minimum Rate of Pay}}{\text{Maximum Rate of Pay} - \text{Minimum Rate of Pay}}$$

$$= \frac{9,500 - 8,000}{12,000 - 8,000} = \frac{1,500}{4,000} = .375 = 37.5\%$$

Guidelines for Compensation Administration

Various policies, regulations, and rules define limits within which compensation administrators can make changes. The most limiting factor influencing compensation opportunities is the labor budget. As previously described, this budget normally identifies the amount of money available for annual employee compensation. The labor budget of an entire organization is the total of the labor budgets of every unit of the organization. These budgets normally do not state the exact amount of money to be allocated for the pay of a specific employee, but they do state how much is available to a specific unit. Discretion in allocating pay is left to department heads and to supervisors for rewarding those worthy of merit increases or those who are able and willing to supply a specific skill.

An index number that is extremely useful to those involved in reviewing and auditing pay practices is the compa-ratio, which is the total pay received by all employees in a pay grade divided by the midpoint of the pay grade multiplied by the number of employees in the pay grade.

$$\text{Compa-ratio} = \frac{\text{Total actual pay received by all employees in the pay grade}}{\text{Midpoint of the pay grade} \times n}$$
$$(n = \text{number of employees in pay grade})$$

An index number of 1.0 normally indicates that there is an acceptable distribution of employees in the grade. An index that moves toward 0.8 indicates (1) possible underpayment of employees in the pay grade or (2) a significant number of employees in the grade who are new to the jobs within it. An index moving toward 1.2 may indicate (1) a very senior work force in the grade, (2) possible inflation (overly high ratings) of employee performance when merit is being recognized by in-step movement through the grade, (3) cost-of-living adjustments being made through the use of in-step pay increases, and (4) pay rate not in line with the market requirements. The low and high values of the compa-ratio (i.e., 0.8 and 1.2) depend on the spread of the pay range. The values 0.8 and 1.2 occur with a 50 percent spread of the payrange. Compa-ratios can be used not only to identify the level of actual pay for all jobs in a grade but also to identify pay practices of specific jobs within a grade.

The timing of pay adjustments has an impact on compensation administration. Many organizations use anniversary dates for all adjustments. This date may be that of being hired or promoted into the position. The anniversary date allows for individualized pay treatment, but this may not always be the most preferred course of action. Organizations using a merit pay plan may find it best to review the performance and the pay of all employees in a segment of the organization or pay classification at one prescribed time. This practice allows for improved comparisons, as well as the tying of pay adjustments to certain natural breaks in the manner in which business is conducted. An example of a poor time to give a pay increase is at the first of the year. Deductions for Social Security payments stop for some employees at some time during the fourth quarter of the previous year and the increase in their paychecks reflects that the deductions have stopped. The first paycheck of the new year includes a resumption of the Social Security deduction. An employee could possibly receive a 10 percent increase in pay and with increased income tax withholdings, Social Security deductions, and other deductions arising at the start of the year receive less spendable earnings than in the last paycheck of the past year. Pay adjustments should be timed to have the greatest psychological impact on the employee, improve management decisions, and ease administration.

Pressure to provide equality of compensation has been felt by compensation managers for some time. Many employees performing jobs with minimum levels of knowledge, skill, and responsibilities have, through collective bargaining, had their pay rates and total compensation opportunities greatly improved. Their compensation approximates and, at times, is even better than that paid to supervisors or to those performing jobs requiring more knowledge and skills and acceptance of greater responsibilities.

Placing all employees on salary is one of the more recent applications of egalitarianism. Employees being paid by the hour feel they are second-class citizens. They feel that if they themselves are to receive fair treatment, all employees should be on salary.

The basic impetus in this direction is that a salaried employee receives a prescribed amount of money each week that does not depend primarily on the number of hours worked. It is important, however, to recognize that nonexempt salaried employees are still paid by the hour as far as those responsible for enforcing wage and hour requirements of the Fair Labor Standards Act are concerned. Employers must keep a record of hours worked by each employee (this does not require the use of a time clock) and pay time-and-a-half to *all* nonexempt employees who work more than 40 hours in any one week, whether or not they are on a salary. Employees working under some type of pay-for-performance system may find it a disadvantage to be on a salary.

With the rise of egalitarianism, cries of compensation injustices become stronger. Compression occurs when jobs requiring advanced levels of education and experience, more skills, and higher degrees of responsibility receive comparatively smaller increases in compensation opportunities. Compression is related directly to the concept of equity. Those performing jobs requiring more knowledge, greater skills, and increased responsibilities find that rewards are inadequate for these added contributions. To overcome compression problems, compensation policies may state that there must be a 15 percent differential between the pay received by the highest-level nonsupervisory personnel and that of their immediate supervisors. Organizations are now turning to some type of overtime payments for supervisory personnel who are required to work more than 40 hours a week. Most such personnel are exempt under Fair Labor Standards Act requirements, but employers are providing overtime pay for reasons of fairness. Overtime may not start until the exempt employee has worked 45 hours, there may be a cap to overtime hours, or a limit may be set by base pay (e.g., employees receiving base pay greater than $45,000 a year are not eligible for overtime payments). Each organization, depending on its particular requirements, is wise to devise its own standards in this area.

Unionized companies may also find it important to review compensation adjustments to nonunion employees. If an organization almost always adjusts the compensation of its nonunion members to meet changes made during contract negotiations, nonunion members will secretly hope that the unionized members will receive the best settlements. They know that in a short while, their own compensation will reflect these improvements. This, in turn, may lead to an extremely strong pro-union sentiment among nonunion members of the organization that may not be in the best interests of management.

Compensation policy and guidelines specify the time when salary adjustments are to be made, the size of a pay increase an employee can receive at one time, and the distribution of increases based on performance. (A later section on seniority and merit discusses this issue.)

Allocation of Compensation Dollars among Base Pay, Benefits, and Pay–for–Performance Programs

Chapter 11 discusses the ways in which benefits programs are consuming an ever-larger share of the dollars available for employee compensation. Benefits now consume from 30 to 40 percent of each dollar available for compensation. Stated in another way, for every dollar spent on base pay, premiums, and differentials, the employer spends from 40 cents to 67 cents on employee benefits. Most employers recognize that there is a limit to the motivational value of employer-provided benefits. The apparently unending upward spiral of increasing benefit costs is a concern to most employers.

With more money required to purchase food, housing, clothing, and transportation staples, employees are seeking increases in take-home pay. At the same time, most employers have only so much money available for employee compensation. One alternative that benefits both employers and employees is an increase in productivity, which allows employers to generate more income relative to raw material, labor, and capital costs. Increased revenue can be shared with employees without bankrupting the organization. Most organizations provide limited opportunities to nonmanagement employees to increase earnings through improved performance.

In seeking improved performance, compensation specialists must first identify all costs involved in compensating employees. They then must look at the various opportunities available for improving the motivational value of the compensation system. A major goal of this text is to identify various ways to design and develop a total compensation system that can influence or modify employee behavior so that employee performance and organization productivity are improved. A review of the following 10 statements will assist those persons responsible for compensation decisions to achieve this goal:

1. Employees must have enough current, valid, and useful information about the work expected of them and the rewards they are to receive if they are to make decisions that benefit both the organization and themselves.

2. Most employees establish their life-styles by the amount of pay they receive for the work they do.

3. Employees determine the fairness of compensation by comparing their pay and other compensation components with those received by other workers.

4. Employees can make complex mathematical computations to compare the value of one compensation component with others.

5. Employees recognize that differences in knowledge requirements, skills, job responsibilities, working conditions, and performance should command a difference in pay and other benefits.

6. Employees normally prefer to make their own choices of desired goods and services. They do recognize that at times it is preferable for employers to act as their agents because of expertise in purchasing the best goods or services and, through mass buying, providing considerable savings for everyone.

7. Employees realize the importance of tax-sheltered goods and services as earned income becomes subject to higher rates of income tax.

8. Most employees prefer immediate payment to future payment, even if the discounted value of the future payment is considerably more than the value of the present payment.

9. Employees feel that it is the responsibility of the employer to keep them "whole" (able to maintain real purchasing power).

10. Employees realize that their security depends on the stability and the growth of the organization.

The issues of seniority and merit have been discussed from a variety of viewpoints throughout the text. A well-designed compensation system recognizes and addresses these vital issues.

Seniority provides a certain amount of security to all employees. Length of service identifies to some degree loyalty to the organization. Most organizations try through their compensation system to recognize seniority, that is, employee loyalty. The amount of such benefits as vacation time, pensions, insurance, and thrift plans varies directly with increased length of service. In-step pay grade progressions often are tied to time in grade. Many merit plans are misnamed. When 90 to 100 percent of the employees receive a merit increase, the great likelihood is that the merit plan is truly a seniority plan. When a superior performer receives an 8 percent increase; a commendable performer, 7 percent; and the great majority of the remainder, 6 percent; it is probable that merit has had little to do with the pay increases. Organizations would be far better off to call their pay-adjustment programs by more appropriate titles. If the program is truly based on seniority, it should be called a seniority or length-of-service plan.

An alternative to tying pay increases to length of service is using a one-time seniority bonus. This practice is becoming more appealing to employers. Such a plan may call for a 5 percent bonus based on highest annual earnings on the anniversary date of completion of five years of service, with possibly a 7.5 percent bonus after ten years, and a 10 percent bonus after 15 years. A bonus of this size may have a strong incentive impact on the employee. It has the added advantage that the organization is not adding seniority to its base pay plan and making seniority payments a permanent part of the compensation package.

It is much more difficult to develop a merit pay program based on individual performance. A step in the right direction is the design and the development of an appraisal process that recognizes individual effort. However, employers must recognize the problems and costs involved in developing reliable and valid performance appraisal procedures and instruments. Chapter 13 discusses this subject in detail. Employers must also recognize that all employees deserve the right to know where they stand and how well they are doing. Some type of performance appraisal is a necessity for most organizations. Without a formal process, implementation of a merit or pay-for-performance program is almost impossible.

In conjunction with performance appraisal, some organizations are turning to *merit guidecharts* for determining pay adjustments and for ensuring differentiation of pay based on demonstrated employee performance. Merit guidecharts vary among organizations, but they basically have similar characteristics. Guidecharts usually identify the employee's (1) current performance rating and (2) location in a pay grade. The intersection of these two dimensions identifies a percentage of pay increase based on the performance level and location of the employee in grade. See table 14-3. (In some cases, instead of a percentage increase the guidechart identifies a specific dollar adjustment. In these cases a guidechart may be designed for each grade.)

TABLE 14-3

A SIMPLE MERIT GUIDECHART[a]

		Performance Rating			
Location in Pay Grade		*Superior*	*Good*	*Improve-ment Desired*	*Unac-ceptable*
		(Percent Adjustment to Current Pay)			
Maximum—100th Percentile					
	4th Quartile	5%	2%	0	0
75th Percentile					
	3rd Quartile	6	3	0	0
Midpoint— 50th Percentile					
	2nd Quartile	7	4	2%	0
25th Percentile					
	1st Quartile	8	5	3	0
Minimum— 0 Percentile					

[a]The following statement may also be included with the guidechart: In no case will the percentage increase shown multiplied by the current pay of the employee result in an amount of pay that exceeds the maximum of the assigned pay grade for the job of that employee.

The rationale for paying different rates of pay to individuals receiving identical performance ratings is that those in the upper quartiles are already receiving more pay and this permits those in the lower levels of the pay range to improve their situations.

To ensure a complete range of performance ratings, appraisers may be required to distribute their ratings according to some predetermined mix. A typical forced distribution may take the order shown in table 14-4.

Actual percentage values in the performance pay adjustment boxes of the merit guidechart shown in table 14-5 may have two components. One is a value

TABLE 14-4

FORCED DISTRIBUTION OF EMPLOYEE PERFORMANCE RATINGS

Performance Rating Level	*Percentage of Appraisees at Each Level*
Distinguished	5
Superior	10
Commendable	35
Competent	35
Marginal	10
Unacceptable	5[a]

[a]This rating percentage is not mandatory and may be combined with that in the marginal level.

TABLE 14-5

MERIT GUIDECHART COMBINING PERFORMANCE RATINGS AND PAY
STRUCTURE ADJUSTMENTS

		Performance Rating			
	Location in Pay Grade	Superior	Good	Improvement Desired	Unacceptable
Maximum—100th Percentile					
	4th Quartile	$5 + x$	$2 + x$	0	0
75th Percentile					
	3rd Quartile	$6 + x$	$3 + x$	0	0
Midpoint— 50th Percentile					
	2nd Quartile	$7 + x$	$4 + x$	$1 + \dfrac{x}{4}$	0
25th Percentile					
	1st Quartile	$8 + x$	$5 + x$	$2 + \dfrac{x}{2}$	0
Minimum— 0 Percentile					

that is related to a market-required or cost-of-living adjustment to the pay structure, and the second is the performance adjustment.

The x in the guidechart represents the percentage change in the pay structure. If, for example, the structure were increased by 6 percent, then each employee receiving an x increase would receive 6 percent plus the performance rating increase. Those receiving no x increase would be receiving a relative pay cut and would regress within the pay grade. Those receiving a fraction of the x ($x/4$, $x/2$) would also not be receiving the full benefit of the pay structure change.

Combining the structure and merit components in the annual pay increase program has some significant implications. From a perspective of real income, employees receiving less than a 6 percent increase are actually receiving a reduction in pay (taking the view that the organization feels that a 6 percent adjustment is necessary to meet market requirements of cost-of-living changes). Without instituting an actual pay cut, this provides an opportunity to reduce the pay of the overpaid employee, the poor performer, or the one who has retired on the job. It also allows for a rapid increase in pay for the employee in the lower portion of the pay grade who is performing well.

An additional element frequently inserted into this type of process is to vary the performance review dates relative to the location of the employee in the pay grade. Employees in the lower quartiles of the pay grade are reviewed more frequently and thus have the opportunity to receive more frequent pay increases. A schedule of performance review and subsequent pay adjustments may take this form:

Location in Grade	Minimum Period Until Next Review
Above maximum	By exception only
Fourth quartile	15—18 months
Third quartile	12—15 months
Second quartile	9—12 months
First quartile	6 months
Below minimum	6 months

In addition to using a merit guidechart for performance adjustments, some organizations are finding one-time lump-sum performance bonuses to be a better reward. Such a bonus may be paid once or twice a year. It must be re-earned by meeting identified performance criteria. By separating seniority and merit increases from base pay, employees can recognize what they are being paid for.

Impact of Legislation

In the 1930s federal legislation provided American workers with retirement, unemployment, collective bargaining, and minimum wage and hour protection. In the next 40 years, more laws were enacted to protect a large group of American workers against unfair and unjust personnel practices. Various laws influence the compensation administration practices of almost every organization. Chapters 3, 11 and 13 stress some of the major areas in which such practices must be in line with government requirements.

Compensation managers must continue to be alert to any practice that violates Fair Labor Standards Act requirements. Those employees who are exempt from overtime pay must meet the exemption tests established by the Department of Labor. For example, personnel working as computer specialists, programmers, and systems analysts cannot be exempted from overtime pay through the use of a professional exemption, although the executive or administrative exemptions may be appropriate. Clerical personnel (and many others, as well) starting their work day before the established beginning, working during their lunch break, or continuing their work day after the normally defined quitting time could place their employers in jeopardy of violating wage and hour requirements and cause them to be open to large fines.

Personnel and compensation specialists may wish to analyze (before the government requires it) all in-grade pay increase and promotion practices. In line with EEOC requirements and affirmative action planning and other federal legislation, organizations should identify by pay grades the percentage of the work force who are members of protected groups within such categories identified by race, sex, national origin, age, and physical and mental handicaps. Additionally, annual pay increases and promotions should be reviewed by analyzing the impact they also have on these protected groups.

Payroll work force analysis should identify the following factors:

1. Number of members and percentage of each protected group in each pay grade.

2. Number of members and percentage of each protected group in each step of a pay grade.

3. Number of members of protected groups and their percentage in comparison with the applicable total work force receiving in-step pay increases within each grade.

4. Number of members and their percentage in comparison with the total applicable work force receiving promotions.

5. Number of members of the protected groups and their percentage in comparison with the applicable work force receiving specific performance appraisal rating (i.e., number rated superior, number rated proficient, etc.).

The use of the computer-based information system and its applicability in this area are discussed later in this chapter.

Although the elimination of unfair, nonvalidated discriminatory practices has taken a large proportion of the interest and the time of personnel and compensation specialists, other government mandates may be even more important.

With the rapid increase in pay rates, the rule of 72 may be important to note. When multiplying a base value (e.g., 100) by 7.2 percent, the value will double in 10 years. With continuing inflation and escalating wages, an annual wage increase of 7.2 percent would result in a doubling of that wage in 10 years. While wages have been increasing, income tax rates have been static. Income taxes are consuming a higher percentage of employee earnings. Where in the past only senior management personnel had earnings that made them look for loopholes in tax regulations to exempt or defer part of their earned income from taxation, workers at lower levels now share this concern. The 1981 changes in tax regulations do, however, result in the reduction in the tax rates for the years 1981, 1982, and 1983 and provide for the indexing of income tax rates based on changes in the Consumer Price Index beginning in 1985.

The benefit issue now takes on an entirely different meaning to many employees. What services that would ordinarily require purchase with after-tax dollars can an employer provide to employees? It is possible that employers can purchase these services, take them as a tax-deductible part of doing business, and provide them as part of the employee compensation package. Employers have never received appropriate recognition from employees for the in-kind services they have provided. It is now more important than ever for employers to identify employee wants, even segregating those wants by such categories as age, sex, and marital status, and then to identify the various actions available to satisfy various demands. The discussion of flexible benefits in chapter 11 covers this subject in much greater detail.

The rapid escalation of the Social Security tax for both the employer and the employee (discussed in chapters 3 and 11) and the added requirements and costs mandated under ERISA force employers to review their entire pension programs. Integrating Social Security with existing pension plans or even eliminating the pension plans in favor of an Employee Stock Ownership Plan (ESOP) or a Tax Reduction Act Stock Ownership Plan (TRASOP) are actions already being taken. (These plans are discussed in chapter 11.) An ESOP as defined under the Tax Reduction Act of 1975 is a TRASOP, often called a "301" ESOP.

Government wage and price controls to curb unacceptable inflation are specters that haunt employers. Very few organizations benefit from such controls. More intervention by government agencies into operations is undesirable. No one can predict when such actions may occur, but proper maintenance of a sound and effective compensation system is the best protection any organization can develop if wage and price control occurs. Each piece of legislation that affects compensation policies and practices requires greater knowledge and skill on the part of compensation specialists.

Recognition of Personnel-Related Actions Through Pay Adjustments

The many daily activities affecting employee workplace behavior often result in some type of compensation action. Changes in job responsibilities and duties should be recognized. Such changes may not have an immediate impact on an employee's pay, but a number of small changes in individual job activity when reviewed collectively can require a change in the grade or the pay rate of a job.

Compensation policy may require that each employee receiving a promotion should receive at least a 10 percent pay increase. At the same time, compensation policy may state that no employee receive more than a 25 percent increase in one calendar year. A possible conflict arises when an employee hired into a low-level job receives both an in-step length-of-service (LOS) increase and a merit increase at the end of six months that result in a 15 percent pay increase. The employee three months later receives a promotion to a job whose pay grade has a minimum pay level 15 percent higher than that now earned. This may cause some problems for the employee and the compensation department.

The employee may receive the maximum increase available within policy limits, then be *green-circled* (i.e., receive a rate of pay less than the pay grade minimum) and be advanced to minimum as soon as all compensation policy requirements are met. Another alternative is to have the policy requirement waived for this person. The presence of green-circled employees may also indicate that workers have been placed in the wrong jobs and are unable to perform the jobs relative to minimum acceptable standards.

Compensation actions taken in regard to a demoted employee require considerable thought. Is it permissible (under compensation policy) to lower the employee's pay to the scale appropriate to the new job? Is it necessary to *red circle* the employee (i.e., to designate a rate higher than the established maximum for the job and to hold the employee at that level until pay structure adjustment brings the employee within the maximum rate for the job)?

If an employee is transferred to a new assignment, is the assignment temporary or permanent? If temporary, is there to be a pay adjustment if the job has a pay level different from the one from which the employee transferred?

Layoffs and leaves of absence, as well as moving from full-time to part-time employment, all have compensation implications beyond base wages.

Seniority relative to the length of service increases may be an issue. Vacation opportunities, holidays, pension plans, and other benefits may be influenced by such personnel actions.

Various parts of the compensation package are influenced differently by actions ranging from promotion to termination. Supervisors and employees must be made aware of how these actions influence employee compensation. This is basically a communication and administration issue.

Differences in Compensation for Permanent, Temporary, Full-time, and Part-time Employees

The rapid increase in the use of temporary and part-time employees by all kinds of organizations is forcing compensation system designers and administrators to investigate the differences in compensation for these employees. Everything in this book relates primarily to permanent full-time employees. *Permanent full-time employees* are those workers hired and scheduled to work the number of hours per week and weeks per year that are standard for that work unit. A standard work year normally consists of 52 weeks per year (excluding holidays, vacations, and possible layoffs), with a workweek ranging from 32 to 40 hours. An average workweek in the United States today consists of approximately 37 hours.

Part-time employees, on the other hand, work less than a full workweek. Normally, they are scheduled to work from 20 to 32 hours per week, although, in some cases, part-time employees work less than 20 hours per week.

Temporary employees are hired to perform assignments that usually do not extend beyond six months in duration. A temporary worker may work on either a full-time or a part-time basis.

Permanent part-time and temporary full-time and part-time employees frequently receive a compensation package that differs significantly from that provided to permanent full-time employees in the same job classification. Usually, the hourly rate of pay for the job is the same no matter what the employment status of the incumbent. (Paying different rates of pay for the same job because of employment status could possibly lead to Equal Pay Act or Title VII violations.) Permanent part-time and temporary employees usually receive entry-level rates of pay for the job and may receive some kind of pay adjustments (depending on their length of service and performance in the job) similar to that offered new permanent full-time employees.

Permanent part-time employees frequently earn vacation, holiday, and sick pay benefits in direct proportion to their scheduled hours of work (i.e., a 20-hour part-time employee working in a unit that normally schedules full-time employees for a 40-hour workweek would receive one-half the vacation, holiday, time-off-with-pay benefits earned by the full-time worker).

Medical, disability, and life insurance plans vary dramatically among organizations. In some cases, part-time workers receive none of these benefits. It is more common, however, to find some kind of a pro rata receipt of benefits, based on a proportion of hours worked, scheduled for permanent full-time employees. With regard to retirement programs, ERISA requires that employees who work at least 1,000 hours in any calendar year, regardless of classification, be eligible for retirement, thrift, and stock plans.

Temporary employees frequently receive few or no benefits unless they meet ERISA requirements for retirement programs. Many organizations today hire their temporary work staff directly through second-party employers. In this case, those employers who provide the workers on an "as needed basis" pay all labor costs. The temporary employee negotiates a pay rate directly with the second-party employer who then bills the client employer for all temporary help provided.

PROVIDING COMPENSATION DATA THROUGH A COMPUTER-BASED INFORMATION SYSTEM

The various compensation procedures and tools are valuable in organizational planning, operations, and control. The purposes of these procedures and tools are to evaluate the job, to assess employee contributions on the job, and to determine total employee compensation. To be of maximum use, the data and the information generated by these procedures and tools must be timely, complete, and valid. The computer-based information system (CBIS) plays an important role in ensuring that this goal is achieved.

In the past, a primary failure of compensation systems in general was an inability to provide current, relevant data. The CBIS can now provide compensation managers, as well as other organization members, with up-to-date, valid, and useful planning, operations, and control data.

These data help senior management shape organizational policy and make strategic decisions. The compensation data required in both the short and the long run have an impact at the top levels of the organization. Some of these data can be used in the design of organizational and compensation policy, formulation of budgets, and allocation of labor dollars to base pay, benefits, and pay-for-performance plans. Well-designed compensation data files provide more than simple lists. These files also can provide information that reveals patterns and trends. Such information enables managers to recognize potential problem areas when making specific types of decisions or continuing to take certain actions.

If made available in an understandable form, these data can assist members at all levels in analyzing their performance. Because of the complex nature and role of compensation and reward systems, a CBIS in this area interfaces with almost every organizational activity.

One of the first computer applications in most organizations involves payroll procedures. The administrative, accounting, and clerical operations in this area have made good use of the computer ever since its introduction to the world of work.

Future strength will continue to be based in the computer's analytic capability. Three major areas in which a compensation-focused CBIS can assist problem solvers and decision makers are (1) job planning, (2) human resources planning, and (3) compensation recordkeeping and maintenance.

The first of these areas, job planning, is a dynamic process that has its roots in the initial development of the organization and relates directly to changes in organizational procedures, methods, and output. Effective job planning demands a constant analysis of output requirements so that job activities provide the desired quality and quantity of output. Some of the important uses for computerized job planning files are discussed in the following paragraphs.

1. Job description files have in the past seldom been computerized. However, lists of responsibility and duty statements can be developed and placed on some kind of a job description activity file through the use of properly identified and adequately described tasks. The key to such action would be a list of action verbs and objects. The first step in this process would be the development of a glossary of verbs that relates specifically to an occupation or to the kinds of work performed in the organization. These action words, together with a list of objects, would be stored in the computer with additional explanatory information that describes the why, how, etc., of the action to be manually inserted, permitting the establishment of new or revised responsibility and duty statements.

Once an organization has developed a list of action verbs, defined them relative to the specific uses and demands of the organization, and identified the organization-specific objects that relate to these verbs, the most critical barrier to implementing computer-based job description files is overcome.

2. Job evaluation files have been successfully established by those responsible for developing the Position Analysis Questionnaire (PAQ). (See chapter 8). From the 187 worker-oriented elements used in the PAQ, 9 elements have been identified that are useful in capturing the pay policy of an organization or in identifying how an organization values its jobs. Once organizations begin to develop master files of job tasks statements or job responsibility and duty statements and are using some kind of a point-scored compensable factor evaluation plan, the computer can be extremely useful for determining job worth.

3. Job classification and grading files can maintain jobs in their proper classes and grades, making it possible to monitor the number of jobs in each.

4. Compensation survey files are probably too expensive for any one organization, but it is possible that a group of organizations could form a special company to gather, analyze, and disseminate current, reliable and valid compensation data to its members.[1] A special organization of this type would have the ability to recognize individual differences among the members submitting the data. In working with the individual organization, it would develop common compensation definitions and procedures so that the data provided by each member would have greater value when accumulated into indexes or averages.

---

[1] Kenneth E. Foster, "Job Worth and the Computer," *Personnel Journal,* September 1968, pp. 619–626.

5. Pay structure files now provide timely and efficient data in a relatively inexpensive manner. From payroll data, in conjunction with classification and grading files, pay structure files can provide by pay grade or class an average salary, midpoint, pay range, number or percentage of employees in each pay grade or class, and an audit of each pay category by affected group (EEOC categories).[2]

6. Appraisal files can permit more accurate identification of the job performance of each employee and can provide an effective way to audit and monitor the distribution of appraisal ratings. Computerization allows the use of more effective and efficient appraisal tools to transmit accurate and valid information through the upper levels of organizations where promotion and progressive transfer decisions are made. It can also provide feedback to appraisees. It affords them the opportunity to see how management regards their performance and possibly allows them to compare it with that of other employees so that, if necessary, they can try to improve their performance.

With the development of this type of work-related analysis, the amount of data available for monitoring the comparison purposes is limited only by the demands of the organization. The principal inhibiting factor is not cost but rather the possibility of flooding users with so much data that they drown in it.

Human Resources Planning

A second area in which a compensation-focused CBIS can help management is human resources planning. Although the compensation manager is not directly responsible for identifying or developing human resources, much of the compensation data generated are extremely valuable to those who are responsible. On the other hand, the compensation manager often requires human resources data generated in other areas of the organization. Some of the basic data maintained on computerized files are as follows:

1. Employee personal history files obtained data initially from the application form, which provides such data as date of birth, age, birthplace, sex, race, marital status, next of kin, dependents, medical history, home address, and home telephone number.

2. Employee work history files provide data about past jobs, past performance, education, skills inventory, current job title and organization, work location and name and title of immediate superior, vacation and time-off history, absenteeism and tardiness, safety, discipline, and grievance records, and work suggestions. The wide variety and nature of these data require collection sources throughout the organization.

3. Employee career planning data include in-grade pay increases special, recognitions, promotions, transfers, trait inventories, listing of knowledge and skills and, possibly, aspirations and expectations. Currently, most organizations

[2]John A. Fossum et al., "An EDP Monitoring System for a Compensation Plan," *Compensation Review,* Second Quarter, 1974, pp. 28–29.

maintain only promotion and transfer data, but in the future, as organizations spend more time and effort in training and developing employees, they will develop more complete career planning files. It is likely, however, that these files will not be easily computerized. The extent of the responses to some sections could be so broad and comprehensive that the data base would be prohibitive. It is possible, however, to computerize certain sections.

4. Recruitment files maintain records of job applicants, recruitment activities, and indicators of high-risk and low-risk persons newly hired. (Low-risk persons are those individuals whose profile characteristics on an average are most stable. They stay with the company and seek advancement. High-risk persons are those who tend to have the highest job-hopping rate.) Organizations must take great care not to discriminate in favor of one group or another when actually using such indicators to restrict recruiting or hiring practices. If these practices violate Equal Employment Opportunity regulations, they are illegal. Any practice that permits an employer to discriminate in favor of one employee over another must be proved through historical records to have job relatedness and be valid and reliable. This holds true in hiring, pay, promotion, training, layoff, or discharge practices. The entire area of equal employment requires great diligence in maintaining accurate and valid records about practically every area. This gathering of employee statistics not only holds true for EEOC requirements but also must meet the ever-increasing demands of a wide variety of other government agencies.

5. Turnover analysis includes data on organizational growth plans, retirement schedules, potential early retirement, and resignations. Exit interviews provide especially fruitful information when those employees who are leaving give accurate and honest reasons for their departure. Turnover data, when combined with pay structure and compensation survey data, are valuable for determining potential causes of turnover.

6. Attitude and preference survey files provide a data base that is most valuable when comparing surveys conducted over an extended period. These data, together with other compensation, human resource, and business data, provide indicators of both present and future problem areas.

Compensation Recordkeeping and Maintenance

The third area in which a compensation-focused CBIS can assist problem solvers and decision makers is the area of compensation recordkeeping and maintenance.

Information generated during payroll procedures enters into practically every payroll data file discussed in the beginning of this section. Specifically, payroll data files can be a source of such data as the following:

1. Gross and net pay for an individual employee.

2. Ratio of gross pay to net pay for the entire organization.

3. Comparison of budgeted pay to actual pay.

4. Breakdowns of compensation by (a) work group, (b) profit centers, and (c) grade or class.

5. Other pay statistics used for monitoring organization performance.

The following data and information also may be found in most payroll data file systems:

Employee identification number	Time worked	CPI factors (escalator clause)
Social Security number	Premium pay	Tax deductions
Work group account number	Incentive pay	Benefits (withholding),
Base pay	Bonuses	including nonoptional and optional contributions

This file can include data on all benefits and their costs. However, the benefits programs of most organizations are becoming so complex and costly that it may be wise to maintain a special benefits administration file that would include an analysis of the benefits, their total costs, and the amount of employee contributions. This data can also assist compensation and line managers in complying with various laws and regulations. By having this kind of file, organizations can then provide their employees with an annual employee benefits statement at a very reasonable cost. The payroll data file provides the data necessary to produce the gross and net pay amounts for each employee. The payroll data file generates compensation breakdowns by work groups, profit centers, and the total organization, as well as by grade or class, budgeted pay to gross pay, gross pay to net pay, and other pay statistics used for monitoring organizational performance. The items included in most payroll plans include employee identification number, Social Security number, work group account number, base pay, time worked, premium pay, incentive pay, bonuses, CPI factors (escalator clause), tax deductions, and benefits (withholding), including nonoptional and optional contributions. This file can include all benefits and their costs. However, the benefits programs of most organizations are becoming so complex and costly that it may be wise to maintain a special benefits administration file that would include an analysis of the benefits, their total costs, and the amount of employee contributions. This data can also assist compensation and line managers in complying with various laws and regulations. By having this kind of a file, organizations can then provide their employees with an annual employee benefits statement at a very reasonable cost.

Employee Benefits Statement—More and more organizations are using the computer to provide their employees with a statement that provides a wide variety of benefits, and pay information. This statement informs each employee of personal benefits accrued during the year. It summarizes the amount of financial protection afforded through the various health and accident programs as well as retirement benefits—either those earned through organizational programs or those derived from government agencies. The initial setup is fairly expensive, with costs ranging in excess of $20,000, depending on the size of the organization, the items described, the frequency with which the report is updated, and whether or not computer facilities and services are in-house or have to be purchased. Although the cost may appear to be prohibitive, the tailor-made information for each employee serves a valuable purpose and is practically unavailable through any other medium. Figure 14-3 is an example of an employee benefits statement.

Maintaining a Computer-based Compensation System—With decreased costs and increased accessibility, more and more organizations will be using the computer for storing, analyzing, computing, and disseminating compensation data and information. When using a computer for payroll preparation, the phrase "garbage in, garbage out" becomes of critical concern. To ensure prompt and accurate payments to employees, many potential opportunities for errors may, and frequently do, arise. Accurate paycheck disbursements require up-to-date information on:

1. Job changes.

2. Step-in-grade changes.

3. Hours worked.

4. Any earned differentials or premiums (particularly overtime hours worked and correct overtime rate of pay).

5. Paid time-off and correct rate of pay for paid time not worked.

6. Allotments deducted as requested.

7. Changes in dependents and marital status.

8. Correct deductions for FICA and Social Security.

Data inputs to payroll frequently come from the supervisors or the department head of the employee. Frequently, there are delays in the receipt of pay-related data, and the employee does not receive the proper amount of pay. It may be an overpayment or underpayment. When this occurs, the payroll administration must recalculate all affected pay disbursements and make the necessary adjustments. The major problem here is usually late or delayed arrival of critical pay-related data. There are also times when an employee receives some kind of retroactive payment. When this is the case, adjustments must be made to previously received wage payments. Another problem in this area relates to the design of the payroll software program. Some programs do not recognize changes in pay that occur within a pay period; others will accommodate pay changes made at anytime.

With the use of the computer for payroll administration, the need for special auditing activities also becomes imperative. Whenever money transactions occur, the possibility of criminal actions become likely. Vigilance is certainly a prerequisite for any computer-based compensation system. In addition to short-term auditing requirements, the following longer-term review and

Medical Benefits

FOR YOU
The plan pays for the following reasonable and customary expenses:

Hospital Expenses

100% of charges for semi-private room and board for up to 365 days.

100% of covered hospital in-patient charges for services and supplies for up to 365 days.

100% of covered hospital out-patient charges within 48 hours of an accident.

Surgical and Medical Expenses

100% of charges for surgery and anesthesia.

100% of charges for in-hospital doctors' visits.

Other Expenses

100% of diagnostic X-ray and laboratory expenses.
After a $2 deductible for each prescription,

100% of expenses for covered drugs dispensed by a pharmacist.

100% of expenses for local ambulance service.

Maternity Expenses

100% of covered obstetrical and hospital expenses. (Charges for doctors' office visits or complications may be covered under Major Medical.)

Major Medical Expenses

After a $100 calendar year deductible per person (maximum of $200 for a family),

80% of the first $5,000 of covered expenses not included above, then

100% of all other covered expenses in any one year.

Maximum Benefit

$1,000,000 is the maximum lifetime benefit for each covered person.

If You Are Disabled

Short Term

If you become sick or disabled and are unable to work, you will receive (depending on your accumulated sick leave):

$ 346 per week for up to 4 weeks, then

$ 346 per week for up to an additional 22 weeks.

Long Term

If you remain totally disabled after 6 months, you will receive:

$1,000 per month from the Long Term Disability Plan for as long as you are disabled to age 65. This includes Social Security benefits for you and your dependents.
In addition,

$ 45,000 Group Life Insurance continues at no cost to you.

PLUS you will continue to earn benefits in the Retirement Plan.

Benefits For Your Survivors

Lump Sum

In the event of your death from any cause, your beneficiaries will receive:

$ 45,000 Group Life Insurance

$ 255 Social Security

$ 45,255 Total.
In addition, the following benefits are payable in the event of accidental death:

$ 45,000 Accidental Death and Dismemberment Insurance.

$100,000 Travel Accident Insurance, if you die while traveling on Company business.

$ 40,000 Voluntary Personal Accident Insurance.

Monthly Income

In addition, your eligible dependents may receive the following estimated monthly Social Security benefits:

$ 891 for a spouse with two or more children, or

$ 764 for a spouse with one child, or

$ 364 for a spouse only, age 60 or over.

If you are age 55 or more with 10 years of service, you may elect a monthly benefit from the Retirement Plan for your surviving spouse.

Life Insurance For Your Dependents

Group Life Insurance

$5,000 for your spouse.

$1,000 for each dependent child over 6 months.
Voluntary Personal Accident Insurance

$ 20,000 for your spouse only, or

$ 16,000 for your spouse and **$ 2,000** for your dependent children, or

$ 4,000 for your children only.

FIGURE 14-3 COMPUTER PRINTOUT (THIS STATEMENT WAS PREPARED BY THE COMMUNICATIONS DIVISION OF JOHNSON & HIGGINS, AN INDEPENDENT EMPLOYEE BENEFIT CONSULTING FIRM.)

Your Retirement Benefits

Your Current Status

$ 47 is your accrued monthly Retirement Plan benefit as of 12/31/77.

You are now 0% vested in your accrued benefit.
YOU WILL BE 100% VESTED ON 06/30/78.
Your vested benefit is payable at age 65.

Retirement at Age 65

When you retire on your normal retirement date at age 65, you may receive an estimated monthly income of:

$ 316 Retirement Plan
$ 509 Social Security
$ 825 Total.

In addition,

$255 Social Security for your spouse at spouse's age 65.
The Retirement Plan amount shown is an optional form of payment, payable for your lifetime, but not for less than 10 years. If you die before receiving 10 years' payments, the remaining payments will be made to your beneficiary. Unless you elect otherwise, you will receive a reduced benefit if you are married, with one-half of that benefit continuing to your spouse when you die.

Early Retirement

You may retire as early as 55 if you have been in the Retirement Plan for 10 or more years.

The Value Of Your Benefits

As an employee of Volvo of America Corporation, you and your family enjoy these benefits:
- Medical Plan
- Sick Leave
- Short Term Disability Plan
- Long Term Disability Plan
- Group Life Insurance
- Accidental Death and Dismemberment Insurance
- Business Travel Accident Insurance
- Voluntary Personal Accident Insurance
- Dependents Life Insurance
- Retirement Plan
- Vacations and Holidays
- Social Security (the Company matches your contribution)

Volvo provides you with these benefits at a significant saving over what they would cost if purchased individually—and many of these plans would not even be available to you as an individual, at any cost.

Since Volvo pays most of the cost of these plans, your benefit programs form an important part of your total compensation.

$ 6,538 is the estimated total annual cost of these benefits.
$ 1,118 is your estimated annual rate of contribution ($ 1,070 for Social Security).
$ 5,420 is the estimated annual rate of contribution by Volvo.
Other benefits of significant value to you but not included above: Maternity, Military, Bereavement and Jury Duty Leaves, Tuition Refund, Recreational Activities, Purchase of Company Products . COMPANY CAR . LEASE CAR

Dear Employee:

This, your personalized Volvo benefits summary, is the pioneer of what we hope will be an annual publication.

Your benefit programs are a vital part of your total compensation as a Volvo employee. Volvo provides a wide range of benefits designed to protect you and your family against financial loss due to illness and injury and also to contribute to your financial security after retirement.

Over the years, the subject of employee benefits has become increasingly complex. Recognizing this, we have prepared this personal summary of the benefits Volvo provides for you and your family.

After you have read the summary and shared it with your family, we suggest you file it with your other important financial records.

Sincerely,

VOLVO OF AMERICA CORPORATION

Bjorn Ahlstrom
President

001
000-00-0001

SAMPLE, S.
95 WALL ST

NEW YORK,   NY10005

All information on this statement is as of **06/30/78**
Our records show your date of birth as **06/30/43** and your date of hire as **06/30/68** . Please notify your Personnel Office if this information is incorrect.

auditing activities will assist in maintaining a continuing viable compensation system:

1. An annual review of all jobs and their assigned grade levels.

2. A review, at least every five years, of the compensable factors or key method used to evaluate and classify jobs. This review should include (a) the validity of the factors, (b) their relevance to job requirements and the current operations of the organization, and (c) the weighting or value of job requirements and factors.

3. A review every two to three years of the performance appraisal system to ensure its valid relationship to job-required behaviors.

4. An annual review of market changes in the going rate of pay for the jobs of an organization.

5. Constant review of economic changes that affect the employee and the organization.

Interfacing with the Computer

The compensation specialists must recognize the opportunities available to them when interfacing with computer programmers and systems analysts. The major concern should be that the computer improve performance and make their jobs easier. There are a number of options available to compensation specialists to help achieve these goals. Following are three of these options:

1. Programs should be written so that an individual who understands the English language would require very little extra education to interact with the computer. This means that the procedures and the questions produced by the computer should be written in relatively simple and understandable English and should require brief answers (i.e., the use of the "primrose path" concept in which the individual interfaces with the computer by answering a series of "yes" or "no" questions and provides specific quantitative data upon demand).

2. The actual computer output should be produced in usable form. The data should have significant use and should be produced on paper in a convenient size. For example, a printout to be inserted into a personnel file should be on paper of suitable size for that file and not on typical printout paper.

3. The specialist should request that all files relate to a current data base.

The compensation specialist must also be aware that great masses of output data are usually unnecessary. Only the data necessary to meet specific requirements should be requested. Data should be presented in a form for quick and easy analysis. From the beginning, the compensation specialist should ask for as much flexibility as possible from the computer programs and should be aware of all costs, including hardware acquisition, software development, and even termination costs.

Granting employees access to accurate and timely compensation data can have a favorable impact on their attitudes and perceptions. These are difficult to measure, but the resulting employee behavior is easy to observe and measure (e.g., tardiness, absenteeism, turnover, low productivity, high material waste, and excessive maintenance costs).

A useful system will automatically retrieve only the data required and display it in a manner that facilitates understanding to those who have the right to know the requested data. Table 14-6 identifies some of the basic compensation data files that go beyond the payroll files existing in many organizations and the typical types of data in each file.

Communicating Compensation Information

If management is to develop an open and trusting climate, it must minimize secret, confidential information in the area of compensation. Developing trust depends on favorable comparisons and perceptions. To increase the chances that employees will make the most favorable comparisons and have the most favorable perceptions, employers must provide as much high-quality information as possible—that is, information that is valuable to the recipient. When the formal communication process restricts such information, it will then flow through the informal communication system—the grapevine. The quality of such information may vary considerably. Although this information occasionally may be accurate, it may also be either incorrect or inadequate and may lead to unsatisfactory comparisons that promote employee dissatisfaction. When there is a lack of good information, unsatisfactory comparisons are also made regarding promotions, transfers, and other reward areas that relate to individual requests and special privileges.

Suppressing compensation information may prevent discontent from surfacing. The issue then becomes whether it is better to keep discontent hidden from view to operate as an unidentified cancer that could destroy the organization or to permit it to surface and attempt to resolve and correct those issues responsible for perceived inequities. To establish trust and gain acceptable employee behavior at work sites where job interrelationships are becoming more complex and where employees are demanding opportunities for increased individual expression, it is imperative to provide more and better information regarding the employer-employee exchange process.

There is increasing recognition that if work and its related rewards are to be meaningful, employees must have more authority as to the who, what, when, where, and how of the job. This requires a much improved understanding of the why of the job. The ability to answer these six basic questions also requires that employees have more compensation information than has previously been provided.

The transfer of some compensation information certainly has an attached price and risk. However, if the organization wishes to reduce the manipulative

TABLE 14-6

EMPLOYEE COMPENSATION DATA FILES AND DATA ELEMENTS

1. *Basic Employee Data*
   Name
   Social Security number
   Birth date
   Race
   National origin
   Sex
   Veteran status
   Handicap status
   Date hired
   Time in current job
   Termination date
   Rehire date
   Separation allowance

2. *Employee Job Data*
   Job title
   Job code
   Department or work unit
   Job entry date
   Job evaluation rating
   Job evaluation date
   Exempt or nonexempt status
   EEO job category

3. *Employee Job Pay Data*
   Pay rate
   Pay period
   Pay grade
   Position in pay grade
   Pay minimum and maximum
   Date of last pay adjustment
   Date of next pay review
   Standard workweek hours
   Overtime rate and earnings
   Shift differential earnings
   Incentive earnings
   Cost-of-living adjustments
   Area wage differentials

4. *Performance Appraisal Data*
   Latest performance rating
   Date of last appraisal
   Performance pay adjustment

5. *Compensation Allocation Data*
   Percentage of total compensation
      spent on:
      Base pay
      Overtime
      Shift differentials

COLA
   Area differential
   Benefits (by each benefit component)
   Incentives (by type of incentive)

6. *Job Analysis Data*
   List of jobs by title
   List of jobs by evaluated points
   List of jobs by pay grade

7. *Work Force Pay Analysis Data*
   Number of employees on payroll
   Compa-ratio for each pay grade
   Compa-ratio for jobs in each pay grade
   Compa-ratio for jobs in each work unit
   Range index for each pay grade
   Range index for jobs in each pay grade
   Number of red-circled jobs in each pay grade
   Number of incumbents holding red-circled jobs
   Number of green-circled jobs in each pay grade
   List of incumbents holding green-circled jobs
   List of employees not receiving pay adjustments within standard time period
   Total overtime pay by pay grade
   Total overtime pay by job
   Tenure analysis by pay grade
   Tenure analysis by job

8. *Appraisal Data*
   Distribution of performance ratings by rates
   Distribution of performance ratings by jobs
   Distribution of performance ratings by EEOC categories

9. *FLSA Data*
   List of employees working overtime each week of pay period
   Overtime earnings

TABLE 14-6 (continued)

10. *EEOC Data*

Percentage of work force within each EEO job category by EEO protected groups

Percentage of EEO job categories in each pay grade by EEO protected groups

Percentage of EEO protected groups by EEO job categories and by pay grades receiving specific performance appraisal ratings

Percentage of EEO protected groups by EEO job category and by pay grades receiving performance pay adjustments

11. *ERISA Data*

Participation date

Benefits calculation date

Vesting date

Early retirement date

Normal retirement date

Termination date

Break-in-service dates

Benefit payment date under vesting termination

Break-in-service parity-return dates

Hours worked for vesting rights

Hours worked for benefits accrual

Eligibility periods

Eligibility computations

Total eligibility years

Total vesting years

Survivor option elective

Survivor option elective date

Survivor option effective date

elements, actual or perceived, inherent in any compensation program, it must open the system to employee involvement. Through such a system, employers transfer to workers much of the vital information of the organization for safekeeping. The transfer process has been practically a one-way street in the past with employees doing most of the transferring. It becomes a two-way street only when both employees and employers understand, agree, and accept the responsibility for the achievement of mutually shared objectives and goals.

Openness regarding compensation information calls for an analysis of two requirements: one, what the organization wishes employees to know about the organization and their jobs; the other, what employees want to know about their present and future opportunities. The integrating factor is job-related information. As more organizations post job openings to make employees aware of future opportunities, information on pay becomes a critical factor. Pay information could initially consist of only a starting rate for each job. This could soon escalate into providing significantly more information. There is no doubt that once an organization starts divulging pay information, demands for greater openness increase. There may be demands to know how pay is determined, who determines it, its relationship to pay in other organizations, and how the pay of one job relates to that of other jobs. In addition to pay information, employees then may want more information on benefits programs, how they are conceived, and what they offer.

Employers recognize that revealing even the starting pay of a job opens the door to requests concerning a wide variety of compensation information. It also may reveal inadequacies of the present compensation program and an inability to explain why compensation takes the form it does. Before opening a compensation system to employees, management must review its present program for adequacy, acceptability, and integrity. It then must develop training programs to assist operating managers in explaining this information to their subordinates. The final success of any compensation information program depends on how well supervisors can communicate pay and benefits information to their employees.

Money, pats on the back, status symbols, and so on are all motivators. It is up to each organization and each supervisor to identify the different ways that employees perceive each compensation component and the compensation-reward system as a whole. For this reason, it is critical that the organization be successful in communicating this message to its employees:

> We need your effort, energy, and contributions, and in turn we wish to compensate you adequately and fairly for your services.

SELECTED READINGS

Belcher, D. W., "The Changing Nature of Compensation Administration," *California Management Review,* Summer 1969, pp. 89–94. The basis of compensation management is the principle that money motivates people. Compensation is the price paid for employee contribution; thus, determining compensation means determining contributions.

Cook, Fred, "The Changing Goals of Compensation," *Business Management,* February 1970, pp. 23–24,55. Compensation planning can be brought into the mainstream of business planning if management will consider compensation as a major investment in the company's future. A properly designed compensation program will support organizational objectives and policy, establish standards of performance, and control and motivate employees.

Fossum, John A., William F. Jackson, Rachel Townsend, and Marlys Grantwit, "An EDP Monitoring System for a Compensation Plan," *Compensation Review,* Second Quarter, 1974, pp. 28–39. This article describes the design and the implementation of a personnel record and payroll system that monitored a wide variety of personnel, salary, and cost data by each section of the organization for each grade within each family.

Hulme, Robert D., and Richard V. Bevan, "The Blue-Collar Worker Goes on Salary," *Harvard Business Review,* March–April 1975, pp. 104–112. Based on a review of the experiences of five companies that now pay all employees by salary, the authors conclude that paying salaries to all employees is a worthwhile organizational objective, but without in-depth analysis and consideration of all factors involved in the success of such a program, more problems may be created than are eliminated.

Lawler, Edward E., III, "Secrecy about Management Compensation: Are There Hidden Costs?" *Organization Behavior and Human Performance,* vol. 2 (1967), pp. 182–189. The author reviews various behaviorist theories that influence the pay process in conjunction with surveys that focus on the perception managers have of their pay. He then develops some interesting hypotheses. In light of the comparisons managers make, it appears that organizational policy concerning the secrecy of pay rates has serious dysfunctional implications.

Meyer, Herbert E., "A Computer May Be Deciding What You Get Paid," *Fortune,* November 1973, pp. 168–176. Many executives are becoming increasingly concerned about the impersonality of the new salary administration program operated in computerized systems. There must be a trade-off, however, between the biases and the bad judgment of systems managed completely by people and the impersonality that arises when using computerbased operations.

Petric, Donald J., "Explaining the Company's Pay Policy," *Personnel,* November–December 1968, pp. 20–26. Good salary administration has to be flexible. In explaining salary policy, several points stand out: (1) salaries are important to all employees, (2) salary policy has a fascination to practically all employees, (3) employees want to know more about their salaries than organizations normally tell them, and (4) it is difficult to discuss salary policy because most issues do not have clear-cut answers.

Praz, Richard P., "Compensation's Fickle Future," *The Personnel Administrator,* May–June 1972, pp. 29–30. The three objectives for creating effective compensation programs are (1) recognizing that human needs differ, (2) using compensation programs to help achieve organizational objectives, and (3) implementing broad ranges of financial and nonfinancial incentives.

Robie, Edward A., "Compensation Administration in the Coming Decade," *Compensation Review,* Second Quarter, 1970, pp. 15–20. The compensation manager will have to respond even more vigorously in the coming decades to economic, political, and social realities and trends. To stay abreast of the rapid changes in compensation resulting from these diverse forces, the manager must be aware of and able to use the vast amounts of information available.

Rooney, Richard P., "The Right Way to Pay," *Administrative Management,* October 1972, pp. 75–77. The author contends that salary administration should accomplish five basic objectives: (1) reflect top management philosophy, (2) maintain a rational hierarchy of jobs, (3) assure internal equity, (4) enable the company to maintain a competitive position in the labor market, and (5) assure an orderly program of salary policy and control.

Scaletta, Philip J., Jr., "The Computer as a Threat to Individual Privacy," *Data Management,* January 1971, pp. 18–23. A discussion of the manner in which computerized data can be accessed illegally, thus jeopardizing the security of even highly confidential data. The author feels that under nearly all circumstances involving computerized files, the individual is deprived of both accuracy and access control. Thus, a real threat to individual privacy is developed.

Smith, Robert A., "Achieving Flexibility in Compensation Administration," *Compensation Review,* Fourth Quarter, 1970, pp. 6–14. Data processing techniques, together with new and improved evaluation tools and more accurate surveys, permit discarding grades and ranges and developing more flexible compensation programs. Management should establish ground rules that relate to the overall requirements of the program and take into consideration internal and external equity and opportunities for flexibility.

Tomeski, Edward A., and Harold Lazrus, "The Computer and the Personnel Department: Keys to Modernizing Human Resource Systems," *Business Horizons,* June 1973, pp. 61–66. A discussion of the key variables that influence the computerization of human resource systems. An effective computerized personnel system is one that permits the personnel department to be of true service to employees and management.

Torrence, George W., "Who Approves Salary Increases?" *Management Record,* July–August 1960, pp. 11–13. A discussion of how pace-setting firms in employee compensation tend to delegate responsibility for the approval of salary increases as far down the line as possible.

————,"The Budgeting of Salary Increases," *Management Record,* March 1961, pp. 2–7. Before developing a salary budget, organizations must first clarify their objectives in the compensation area.

————,"Individual vs. General Salary Increases," May 1961, pp. 18–20. To prevent pay inequities when instituting general salary increases, some firms find it both essential and beneficial to use a salary budget before granting general increases.

————,"Explaining Salary Programs to Salaried Employees," *Management Record,* July–August 1961, pp. 15–17. A review of what companies tell their employees about their pay program as well as how they get the message out and when they do it.

————,"Administering Merit Increases for Salaried Personnel," *Management Record,* November 1961, pp. 9–12. A review of the way some companies reward their outstanding performers and the way these companies attempt to use merit increases to motivate their employees to achieve higher levels of performance.

Part 4

Managerial and Professional Compensation

The first three parts of this book analyzed and developed compensation packages and systems for the operative employees of the organization. Although ability to pay and management philosophy were recognized as important determinants of pay policy, governmental influence—the influence of legislation on employee rights and job security—was always of paramount consideration. In part 4, ability to pay and management philosophy continue to be dominant considerations, but legislative influence switches from job rights to tax obligations.

As organizations design compensation packages for their key officials and for the other managers and professionals who direct, coordinate, and provide highly specialized services, many varying federal and state tax requirements become of critical importance. Although compensation for these managers and professionals continues to involve techniques and procedures related to internal equity and external competitive demands, sheltering earned income from the tax collector becomes a significant issue. Here, at the top level of the organization, every possible course of action is identified, analyzed, and developed to promote the life-style of the affected employee both today and into the short- and long-term future. Innovative techniques are continuously being explored and developed to assist these top-level employees accumulate capital, build estates, and defer tax obligations to some future date.

Compensation programs for top-level managers are frequently designed by a group of consultants who specialize in executive compensation. These consultants combine knowledge of basic compensation practices with knowledge of tax laws, insurance, accounting practices, and financial investments to provide their clients with the maximum benefits possible from the organizational funds available for their total compensation.

Of particular interest to all compensation practitioners and, for that matter, to all employees, is the fact that many of the compensation components that in the not-too-distant past were found only in the compensation packages of top-level executives are now drifting fairly rapidly to the lower echelons of the organization. A preview of the future compensation for lower-level managers and even nonexempt employees is found in the current compensation package of the key officials of the organization.

Part 4 describes the compensation received by the members of the board, the chief executive officer and other members of senior management, the operating managers, professionals, and sales personnel. Chapter 15 first looks at the compensation provided to those responsible for reviewing the strategic operation of the organization and ensuring its effective operation—the board of directors. This analysis includes a brief description of the compensation committee of the board and its responsibilities.

The chief executive officer is hired by and reports directly to the board. The reward for achieving this position is the big payoff—normally the best salary in the organization, a wide variety of short- and long-term bonuses, stock options, extremely generous retirement plans, and other highly desirable benefits and services. At each successively lower level of the organization, these compensation components are scaled down. Many eventually disappear by the time the ranks of operating management are reached. For lower-level managers, the extremely lucrative compensation packages offered to top management become a highly desirable but most elusive "golden carrot" that is available to the few who perform exceedingly well and are selected to be the potential leaders of the organization.

Chapter 16 analyzes the compensation packages of operating managers and professionals and the very special programs designed for sales personnel. The compensation packages for these groups are influenced top-down by the packages offered to top officials of the firm and bottom-up by the compensation plans designed for the operative employees. It is at this level in the organization where, in recent years, the problem of pay compression has been a serious issue. In analyzing the compensation components made available to the operating managers, particular attention will focus on the compression issue.

15

Board of Directors and Senior Management Compensation

CONTENT

Chapter 15 identifies and describes the major components of the compensation package of the board of directors, chief executive officer, and senior managers of the organization. Particular attention focuses on the highly desirable and increasingly visible components of their compensation packages. There is a discussion of the relationship between current and past tax legislation and compensation practices. The issue of how reverse discrimination impacts on top management compensation and the actions organizations are taking to minimize this negative influence are also discussed. This chapter describes the various compensation components that are combined to provide the short- and long-term rewards that establish a motivating workplace environment that both stimulates and rewards superior performance.

GOALS

Upon concluding this chapter, you should be able to recognize what organizations offer to those individuals whose leadership and direction enable the organization to achieve its mission. You should also be aware of the compensation components available to reward these managers. It is necessary also to understand how organizations combine various kinds of stock acquisition plans, stock-based (phantom stock) plans, short- and long-term bonuses, special retirement and annuity plans, and other highly desirable benefits and services (frequently called perquisites), into the compensation package for these key individuals.

A small and select group of knowledgeable and skilled individuals is responsible for the overall management of the organization. These people determine the mission of the organization and set the objectives that direct the actions of the work units and employees. To be successful in this role, not only must these key officials have a knowledge of the products of the organization, the technologies it uses, the customers it serves, and the legislative and social mandates that limit or restrict its action, they must also be fully aware of the resources available to the organization that will enable it to achieve its mission and objectives. These leaders of the organization are the board of directors and senior management.

BOARD OF DIRECTORS

The board of directors usually consists of between 10 to 20 members who are elected by the shareholders of the corporation. These members, in turn, are classified as inside and outside members. *Inside* members are those individuals who are also employees of the corporation—normally, the chief executive officer and other key senior staff officials. *Outside* members are usually knowledgeable and skilled individuals who have considerable business experience or who represent an important segment of society or who are major shareholders in the corporation. These individuals may, at times, represent suppliers of inputs to or receivers of outputs from the corporation. (Care must be taken that individuals coming from these areas do not represent a conflict of interest as board members.)

In recent years, there has been considerable interest in increasing the number of outside board members while keeping the total membership the same or even decreasing it in size. This kind of action has frequently resulted in an outside-inside membership ratio of approximately 70 to 30, with 70 percent being outside members.

The outside members bring knowledge and information about the external environment to the board. This knowledge and information assist the board in implementing policies and strategies that lead to current and long-term success. The inside directors, meanwhile, provide a broad perspective of what the organization is doing and what it is capable of doing. The knowledge-and-skill mixture of the two diverse groups enables the board to make decisions that protect the investments of the shareholders in the corporation and that ensure their receipt of a proper return on their investments.

In performing their fiduciary obligations, boards of directors provide certain services. Among the more important are:

1. Establishing policy for key internal and external operations that permits effective use of organizational resources while complying with social and legal mandates.

2. Ensuring that senior management is properly structured and staffed.

3. Identifying the mission of the organization and preferred practices to accomplish the mission.

4. Reviewing senior management actions to ensure that actions are congruent with established policies and plans and that these managers are making best use of available resources and achieving desired results.

To accomplish these major requirements and other collateral assignments, members of the board are being required to spend more and more time preparing for and executing board business. Not only are board members required to have a broader knowledge of business-related activities, they are also being held increasingly liable and financially accountable for what they have done, what they have undone, and what they have not done.

Among the increased responsibilities being accepted by the board, a major area that has aroused considerable interest is board-of-directors review and approval and, in some cases, design of compensation programs. To facilitate board action on compensation issues, a special committee of the board—the compensation committee—is formed. This committee exercises almost total authority over the compensation practices of the organization and is currently recognized as one of the most powerful and prestigious committees of the board.

The *compensation committee* usually consists of from three to five outside directors who may perform all or a select group of the following activities:

1. Periodically review and appraise the performance of the chief executive officer and top management.

2. Set compensation for the chief executive officer.

3. Review compensation of competitive companies.

4. Review and approve proposed increases in compensation for officers and directors.

5. Monitor executive perquisites and expenses.

6. Review general policies and procedures relating to director and officer compensation and total compensation for all employees.

7. Ensure compatibility of the long-term strategic goals of the corporation and the performance goals used as a base for determining long-term incentive awards.

8. Develop special supplemental awards in cash, stock, or a combination of both for extraordinary accomplishments.

9. Review and approve labor budgets.

10. Report findings to the full board.

Like most people, members of the board recognize the honor bestowed upon them by being offered the position, but they also expect to be compensated for the services they provide. The compensation package for members of the board is fairly simple. (Normally, only outside members receive compensation for being a board member and attending board and committee meetings. Very few corporations pay inside directors for board services.) Outside board member compensation usually consists of an annual retainer or a fee for each board and committee meeting attended. The average retainer for an outside board member is approximately $12,000 annually, with a range of between $2,000 and $30,000. The average fee per meeting is approximately $500, with fees ranging between $100 and $1,500. Many corporations pay both a retainer and a fee.

In addition to the retainer and the fees for attending meetings, most organizations reimburse outside members for all incurred travel expenses and provide director and officer liability insurance (D&O) to indemnify board members for personal losses sustained from legal action arising out of their activities as board members.

Some organizations now provide their outside directors with (1) group travel insurance, (2) group life insurance, and (3) accidental death and dismemberment insurance. A few are offering group medical and hospitalization insurance.[1]

SENIOR MANAGEMENT

Senior management is responsible for the proper organization and operation of the firm. To accomplish this critical assignment, qualified and competent people are appointed to key positions. These individuals have the responsibility for developing long-term plans and implementing strategies to achieve the established objectives of these plans. They must also allocate organizational resources (human, capital, and technical) in a manner that facilitates the accomplishment of both short- and long-term desired results. Finally, they are responsible for identifying levels of performance and, underlying this critical responsibility, they must approve performance standards that relate desired to actual results.

In the great majority of cases, individuals appointed to these key positions in an organization have demonstrated their skills in a wide variety of assignments. These people are the chosen few who survived the many challenges facing managers in the world of work. Their success in performing senior management assignments reflects directly on the survival and the continuing growth of the organization. The future of all who have a vested interest in the organization (employees, shareholders, customers/clients, and the public in general) is influenced by how they perform. What to many may appear to be an exciting, possibly easy, assignment is in reality a 24-hour-a-day, 7-day-a-week, 52-weeks-a-year risk-taking assignment in which stress-related issues appear with every decision-making requirement. For these reasons, the chief executive

---

[1] Detailed information on corporate compensation practices for outside members of the board of directors is found in Jeremy Bacon, *Corporate Directorship Practices: Compensation 1979, Report No. 778* (New York: The Conference Board, Inc., 1980).

officer and the other members of senior management are usually rewarded in a very generous manner.

Chief Executive Officer (CEO)

Attracting and retaining the kind of talent that is willing to expend the effort and the energy necessary to lead the organization successfully requires a well-designed compensation strategy. This strategy must recognize, stimulate, and reward superior performance. When a person reaches the rank of CEO, the terms *competent* or *acceptable* as adjectives describing performance are unacceptable.

Rewarding superior performance at this level does not involve promises of future opportunities. Rather, it requires payments of significant size today and guaranteed future payments predicated on the achievement of well-identified and specifically described results. An analysis of the short- and long-term compensation packages and the variety of components offered to these key individuals assists in describing why the development of chief executive compensation programs requires the effort of skilled professionals.

In many organizations, those who reach the top position have the opportunity to become wealthy. The lure of wealth, in addition to the trappings of status provided by the "top job," is a major motivating factor for working and making the many personal sacrifices necessary to gain this position in an organization. A major objective of compensation plans for chief executive officers is to assist these individuals with substantial incomes to become wealthy. To gain this objective in current society, the impact of taxes and inflation becomes especially critical. With the highest tax rates now at 50 percent, the issue is not *what is paid* to, but *what is kept* by the CEO and how the life-style of this person can be maintained through the expenditure of pre-tax dollars rather than after-tax dollars. To assist the chief executive officer accumulate wealth and, at the same time, enjoy the good life, compensation specialists use all of the tax, accounting, and financial knowledge at their command to design the CEO's compensation package.

The first compensation component normally considered in achieving the good life and building an estate is base pay. After establishing an acceptable base pay, interest focuses on establishing performance-based bonuses, equity components, and retirement plans. The design of these components must consider the procedures that receive the most favor under current tax laws and the opportunities available to recycle earnings so that capital can expand on a tax-free basis.

Tax Legislation and Senior Management Compensation

Following the 1913 passage of the federal income tax law, the next piece of legislation that influenced corporate compensation practices was the Revenue Act of 1918. This act permitted corporations to deduct as an expense "reasonable" levels of compensation. An additional influence on executive compensation came in 1921 when tax exemption was granted to profit-sharing and bonus plans.

Until the late 1920s, however, executive compensation was basically a private affair between the board of directors and the involved executives. It was not unusual for the full board to delegate to the chairman complete authority to determine executive bonuses with shareholders having practically no voice in any such actions. Executives in major corporations would often have relatively low base pay but extremely high annual bonuses. An example is the 1929 managerial profit-sharing plan for the president of Bethlehem Steel. Eugene G. Grace, president, received a salary of $12,000 and a bonus of $1,623,753.[2]

The influence of the federal government on executive compensation began to evolve with the passage of the Revenue Act of 1934. This act required corporations subject to federal income tax regulations to submit the names and the salary amounts of all the executives who earned more than $15,000 a year. This salary disclosure figure was raised to $75,000 with passage of the Tax Revenue Act of 1938.

Chapter 3 lists and briefly describes the major pieces of tax legislation passed by the United States Congress that are of particular interest to CEOs and other highly paid employees. It must also be noted that a wide variety of state and local tax laws also impacts directly on executive compensation. These laws identify kinds of income and applicable tax rates that are included within earned income, capital gains, and ordinary income. Tax planning in conjunction with the development of an executive compensation plan must consider all tax consequences and the opportunity for reducing tax obligations. Tax consequences and tax savings are not only important to the employee but also to employers when calculating corporate income tax obligations. Any kind of deferred compensation plan requires sophisticated tax computations.

Tax Features—Tax consequences quickly become complex because of the impact of the maximum tax on earned or personal service income (currently, the maximum tax rate is 50 percent), minimum tax on items of tax preference, ordinary income tax, alternative minimum tax, income tax averaging opportunities, capital gains taxes, and special averaging rates on pension distributions.

In 1921, the Treasury Department adopted a capital gains tax rate. For the first time, different kinds of income were identified and defined. From 1921 until the present time, the tax rates on various kinds of income have moved up and down, and descriptions have varied as to what is to be included or exempted from specific kinds of tax obligations.

To relate tax legislation to executive compensation, it is essential to understand the following terms:

Earned or Personal Service Income. Employee income gained from direct wage payments, professional fees, cash or stock bonuses, pensions, annuities, and some forms of deferred compensation. The maximum tax rate on earned income is currently 50 percent.

---

[2] "Salary $12,000, Bonus $1,623,753," *The Literary Digest*, August 9, 1930, p. 10.

457
**Board of
Directors and
Senior
Management
Compensation**

Ordinary Income. That income gained from dividends, interest, rent, and some forms of deferred compensation. The maximum tax rate on ordinary income is currently 50 percent.

Capital Gains. Profits made from sale of an asset that appreciated in value since time of purchase. Net short-term capital gains are those net gains assets held for one year or less. These are taxed at ordinary income tax rates. Net long-term capital gains are net gains on those assets held for more than one year. These are taxed at 40 percent of the ordinary income tax rate (maximum long-term capital gains is 0.40×0.50 or 20 percent).

Minimum Tax. This is a 15 percent add-on tax imposed on some deductions, such as accelerated depreciation and certain income tax preference items.

Qualified Plans. Those compensation components such as pension plans, savings and thrift plans, and certain deferred plans that meet specific IRS regulations or rulings. By meeting these requirements, employers can deduct any contribution to the plan as business-related costs and the recipient employee does not have to declare the employer-made payments as earned income until actual receipt of the contribution. Interest and dividend equivalents gained from employer contributions (such as "qualified deferred" plans) are normally considered as earned income, not ordinary income.

Deferred Payment. Normally an unsecured promise of a payment that will be made at some future time.

Stock Options as a Compensation Tool

Prior to World War II, personnel administration was just beginning to evolve as a distinctive staff function in the larger and more progressive organizations in the nation. Compensation administration, however, was barely a gleam in the eyes of some of the more innovative leaders in the fields of personnel administration and industrial engineering. Although the entire field of personnel administration received a huge boost from the employee rights and protection legislation of the 1930s, the influence of legislation on senior management compensation practices was negligible. Prior to 1945, the major impact of government legislation on senior management compensation was how stock options were classified and taxed. At this time, there were two classes of stock options: *proprietary options* and *nonproprietary options*.

Proprietary options provided no income to recipients at the time of exercise; and at the time of sale, gains were treated as long-term capital gains. Nonproprietary options created immediate income for the recipient and were treated as ordinary income upon exercise of the option (maximum ordinary tax rate then was 90 percent).

In 1945, IRS took the position that all options were compensation and effectively eliminated proprietary stock options and almost eliminated the use of stock options as a compensation tool. During the period between 1945 to 1950, corporate leaders claimed that there was a need to expand proprietary interest to corporate leaders by providing opportunities for acquiring equity interests at nominal cost. With the passage of the Tax Revenue Act of 1950 and subsequent amendments to the Internal Revenue Code, profits from *restricted* stock options were recognized as long-term capital gains, which then had a maximum tax rate of 25 percent. The 1950 restricted stock option plans had the following features:

1. Options could be granted only to employees.

2. Recipients must be employed for a lengthy period of time on a continuous basis.

3. Option price could be as low as 85 percent of fair market value at time of grant.

4. Options could be exercised up to 10 years after grants.

5. Sale of stock could be 2 years from the date of the grant or six months from time of exercise.

By 1964, the IRS, Congress, and corporate shareholders felt that top executives who were the recipients of restricted stock options had betrayed the intent of the 1950 Code change. Therefore, the Revenue Act of 1964 replaced restricted stock options with qualified stock options. The 1964 qualified stock option plans had the following features:

1. Options must be granted within 10 years of the date of the plan adoption.

2. Option price of the stock is 100 percent of fair market value at date of the grant.

3. Stock option plans must be exercised within 5 years of the grant.

4. Stock options must be exercised in order of grant unless the earlier granted option has expired.

5. Stock options must be in possession of the recipient for 3 years in order to obtain long-term capital gains treatment.

6. After making a grant, the recipient cannot own more than 5 percent of the outstanding corporate stock unless the equity capital in the corporation is less than $2 million.

7. The right to shares terminates at death or three months after resignation.

The Tax Reform Act of 1969 did not change the requirements for a qualified stock option, but it did raise the maximum tax rate on capital gains to 35 percent. It also introduced a 10 percent minimum tax on preference items, and the untaxed half of the capital gains was identified as a preference item. This change in the tax law reduced the value of the qualified stock option.

Then, the Tax Reform Act of 1976 killed qualified stock options. The act forbade the granting of any more qualified stock options and set the date of May

20, 1981 as the last day any previously granted stock options could be exercised and take advantage of qualified stock option tax provisions. This act then set into motion great interest in and expanded use of nonqualified stock options.

459
**Board of
Directors and
Senior
Management
Compensation**

The major features of a nonqualified stock option are:

1. Options must be granted pursuant to an approved corporate plan, and the purpose of the plan must be clearly identified.

2. An option can be granted at any price.

3. There is no limitation on the duration of the option.

4. There is no sequential exercise restriction.

5. There is no restriction on the amount of stock a recipient can own.

6. After exercise, shares must be held for six months to receive long-term capital gains treatment.

At the time of writing this book, because of the influence of tax legislation, concern for improvement in productivity, and the necessity to be competitive on a world-wide basis, corporations currently design their long-term executive incentive plans to include (1) nonqualified stock options, (2) restricted stock grants, and (3) phantom stock plans that use some kind of corporate performance measures to determine the value of the option to the recipient. With the passing of the Economic Recovery Tax Act of 1981, a new kind of stock option—the incentive stock option—was provided. This stock option is a substitute for the recently eliminated qualified stock option, but returns those wishing to use stock options almost full circle to the restricted stock option program of 1950.

Some of the major features of an incentive stock option are:

1. The option holder must be an employee from the date of the grant of the option until 3 months before the date of the exercise. (A disabled employee has 12 months after leaving employment to exercise the option.)

2. Option price must equal or exceed the value of the stock.

3. Option must be exercised within 10 years after the grant.

4. To be eligible for capital gain tax rates, the stock must be held for at least 2 years from the date of the grant and at least 1 year after exercise of the grant. (No tax consequence results at the time of the grant or exercise of an incentive stock option)

5. Outstanding stock options must be exercised in order of grant.

6. Maximum value of stock option granted to an employee in any calendar year generally shall not exceed $100,000.

7. Terms of the option must forbid transfer other than at death and must be exercisable only by the optionee and during that person's lifetime.

8. Recipients of an option must not own more than 10 percent of the combined voting power of the employer or its parent or its subsidiary immediately before the granting of an option.

9. The option plan must be approved by the stockholder within 12 months before or after the adoption of the plan.

10. The option must be granted within 10 years of the date of adoption or date of approval.

Senior Management Compensation Plan

To lure and retain competent leaders, a compensation plan normally includes three parts: (1) base pay, benefits, and services; (2) short-term incentives; and (3) long-term incentives. A practice that is becoming more common is to offer an incoming chief executive officer (CEO) a contract in which all three of the above-mentioned parts are negotiated.

Executive Contracts.—Although not commonly offered to every CEO or key official, employee contracts are provided by a number of organizations to attract certain individuals and to retain key personal. The executive contract may include specifications for front-end bonus, salary, pension, life and medical insurance, cash and deferred bonuses, stock acquisition opportunities, a variety of other benefits and services, widow's pensions, and severance payments. These contracts normally stipulate the number of employment years and the option opportunities for renegotiation at the end of contract period.

Key personnel who may be reluctant to leave a secure job are requesting and receiving the protection offered by an employment contract. In fact, some organizations now use these contracts to retain personnel by making it more difficult for them to be attracted to recruiting offers from other organizations.

A rather recent innovation is the front-end bonus. The front-end bonus is a "no strings attached" offer to a key individual for recruiting purposes. Normally, this kind of bonus replaces the value of stock options, accumulated bonuses, and other benefits the individual must give up when moving to the new employer. In recent years, highly desired individuals have received front-end bonuses that have exceeded $1 million.

Base Pay, Benefits, and Services.— Over the past 30 years, behavioral scientists have been researching how chief executive and top management base pay compensation decisions are made.[3] Among the variables identified and investigated by these individuals, the ones that appear to be extremely valuable

[3] Among the more notable investigations in this area are David R. Roberts, "A General Theory of Executive Compensation Based on Statistically Tested Propositions, *Quarterly Journal of Economics*, May 1956, pp. 270–294; Herbert A. Simon, "The Compensation of Executives," *Sociometry*, March, 1957, pp. 20–35; Kenneth E. Foster, "A Different Perspective on Executive Compensation," *Compensation Review*, Third Quarter, 1980, pp. 47–54; and Noresh C. Agarwal, "Determinants of Executive Compensation," *Industrial Relations*, Winter 1981, pp. 36–45.

in determining or predicting the base pay of CEOs and other top executives are size of the organization, profitability of the organization, number of levels in the organizational hierarchy, location of the executive's job in the hierarchy, and worth of the job to the organization. Because of their availability, the statistics most often used when investigating the compensation of the CEO are annual base pay and annual bonus. Other compensation-related data, such as benefits and services, and compensation components provided within long-term incentive plans are usually omitted.

461
**Board of
Directors and
Senior
Management
Compensation**

The extensive analysis performed by many organizations concerning CEO compensation indicates that:

1. CEOs of large firms receive higher base pay and larger annual bonuses than CEOs of smaller firms—doubling an organization's size normally results in nearly a 20 percent increase in the CEO's pay—(size is usually measured by annual sales in dollars, although the number of employees and the total assets may be used to indicate the size of the firm).

2. CEOs of more profitable firms are paid better than those leading less profitable firms (profit is usually measured as net profit before taxes).

3. CEOs who are better performers receive higher pay and annual bonuses than the less effective performers (effectiveness of performance is measured by return on assets, return on equity, return on sales).

In addition to these three factors, the worth of jobs below that of CEO impacts directly on the incumbent's pay. Although the level in the organizational hierarchy appears to influence pay, from the third level and below, jobs at the same level are paid differently because of job worth—job content.

Although the pay of the job immediately adjacent to the CEO (normally, the chief operating officer—COO) varies according to the kind of industry, the size of firm, and its profitability, there is a fairly consistent relationship between the pay provided for these two jobs. The COO will usually earn between 75 to 85 percent of what the CEO earns. At the third level, functional responsibilities appear (e.g., finance, marketing, manufacturing), but in addition to the functional description of their work, a common title is executive vice president. Incumbents at this level will earn between 50 to 75 percent of what the CEO earns. At this third level, employees will receive significantly different amounts of base pay and annual bonuses based on the established comparable worth of jobs of the organization.

The size of the business, as measured by sales, affects the entire pay structure of an organization. It is not unusual to find the following pay ratios between highest to lowest paid employees:

Small business (under $25 million)	15:1
Moderate size business ($25 million to $100 million)	20:1
Large business ($100 million to $1 billion)	30:1
Giant business (over $1 billion)	50:1 to 100:1

At the present time, the cash compensation—base pay and annual bonus—for CEOs averages around $400,000. The annual bonus will range between 50 to 60 percent of the annual cash compensation for the CEO.[4] In addition to the base pay and annual bonus, the CEO receives the various benefits and services provided to all other employees and, frequently, a very select group of benefits and services that are not granted to other employees.

When comparing the basic benefits received by the CEO and other key officials of the firm, a bias against these senior jobholders becomes evident. The problem frequently comes under the title of *reverse discrimination* in compensation practices. The discrimination occurs primarily because of the necessity for organizations to comply with IRS rules and regulations when designing "qualified" retirement plans (pension, savings and thrift plans), group life insurance plans, and long-term disability plans. In order for the company to be able to receive a tax deduction for the cost of these plans and for the employee to be able to defer any tax on employer contributions, the plans must be "qualified." A qualified plan must be (1) in writing and in effect in the tax year in which qualification is sought, (2) communicated to all employees, (3) established and maintained by the employer, and (4) operated for the exclusive benefit of the employees and their beneficiaries. A qualified plan must not discriminate in favor of officers, shareholders, or highly compensated employees (the prohibited group). A plan may, however, discriminate in favor of employees not in the prohibited group.

Under ERISA regulations, qualified plans may be either defined benefits or defined contribution plans. A defined contribution plan is one in which the employer provides a specific contribution to the account of each employee in the plan. In a defined benefits plan, the employee's benefits are first determined and the employer makes contributions sufficient to provide these benefits.

The 1974 ERISA legislation established a $25,000 limit to a defined contribution plan and a $75,000 limit to a defined benefits plan. In addition, the legislation permitted an annual increase in the limits of the plan based on a change in the Consumer Price Index (CPI). The 1981 limit on a defined contribution plan is $41,500, and the top benefits payable to qualified plan participants are $124,500. Because of these and other limitations, qualified plans actually discriminate in favor of the lower-paid employees.

Some of the ways qualified plans discriminate against the highly-paid employees are:

1. By integrating the pension plan payment with the tax-free primary Social Security payment, the lower-paid employee receives a much higher percentage tax-free benefit in the pension payment.

2. The maximum qualified benefit payment of $124,500 restricts the amount of pension payment to a highly-paid employee. (For example, an employee earning $300,000 per year and retiring under a 50 percent pay plan

---

[4] Edwin S. Mruk and James A. Giardina, "Executive Compensation 1980 Update," *Financial Executive*, October 1980, pp. 42, 44, 46.

would receive only 83 percent of entitled pension payment: 50 percent of $300,000 = $150,000; 124,500/150,000 = 83 percent.

3. Long-term disability (LTD) plans that have a cap or limit to maximum monthly payments will severely restrict the monthly income of a disabled highly-paid employee. (For example, in the third year of a disability, a typical LTD plan may call for the disability payment to be 50 percent of base pay to a maximum of $4,000 per month less Social Security. A $300,000 per year executive earning $25,000 per month would receive only 4,000/25,000 or 16 percent of base pay.)

4. Group life insurance plans frequently provide each employee with a benefit of two times base pay to a maximum of $250,000. (For example, the beneficiary of an employee who earned $25,000 per year would receive 200 percent of base pay, while the beneficiary of a $300,000 per year employee would receive 250,000/300,000 = 83.3 percent of base pay.) In addition, section 79 of the Internal Revenue Code limits tax-free life insurance to $50,000, and premium costs for insurance exceeding $50,000 are considered as imputed income to the employee.

To prevent discrimination against their more highly-paid employees, many organizations develop executive benefits plans that permit the highly paid executives to be treated as well as the lower-paid employees. It is in the design of these kinds of executive benefits plans that knowledge of tax laws, insurance programs, estate building, and organizational compensation practices are skillfully combined.

To maximize the time available to key executives for business-related purposes and, at the same time, enhance the quality of their lives, many highly desirable and special benefits and services are made available. These benefits and services are frequently grouped under the title of perquisites (perks). Perquisites are usually restricted to the CEO and that small group of key officials who comprise the senior management of the organization. In addition to the status relationship, perquisites provide benefits that either are not considered as earned income to the recipient or are taxed at a very modest level. The amount of tax liability incurred by the recipient depends to a significant degree on the design and the structure of the specific perquisite plan. The Tax Code definition of income includes moneys, property, and services received for services provided.

A brief description of some of the more common perks assists in identifying their desirability:

Company-provided car The employee is able to use the car for both business and personal use. (According to IRS, the employee must pay a flat monthly maintenance charge or a mileage charge for personal use.)

Parking. Special no-cost, readily accessible to work site parking services.

Chauffeured limousine. Normally provided only to the CEO or key officials. The chauffeur may also act as a bodyguard.

463
Board of
Directors and
Senior
Management
Compensation

Kidnap and ransom protection. A service of recent vintage aimed at protecting key officials who may be victims of such action.

Counseling service. Includes financial and legal services. Tax-related expenses are tax deductible; cost of nonbusiness-related services is considered taxable income.

Attending professional meetings and conferences. Opportunity to enhance professional knowledge and enjoy activities at selected sites.

Spouse travel. The company pays for expenses incurred in taking a spouse to a convention or on a business trip.

Use of company plane and yacht. Opportunity to mix use of company plane and yacht for personal enjoyment and business purposes.

Home entertainment allowance. Executives who do considerable entertaining are frequently provided with a domestic staff or given a home servants allowance. The allowance may include cost of food and beverages and payment of utility bills.

Special living accommodations. Executives required to perform business activities at odd hours or at a considerable distance from home are provided with an apartment or permanent hotel accommodations.

Club membership. Country clubs and luncheon club memberships are provided to executives who use such facilities in the performance of their jobs (personal use is recognized as imputed income by IRS).

Special dining rooms. The business provides special dining facilities for key officials and their business guests.

Season tickets to entertainment events. The executive has free use of season tickets for family and business associates to a variety of entertainment events.

Special relocation allowance. A variety of relocation allowances is provided only to key officials. This includes low interest loans to purchase a new home and complete coverage of all relocation expenses.

Use of company credit card. No waiting period for reimbursement of company-related charges and use of card for personal service and delay in repayment to the company.

Medical expense reimbursement. Coverage for all medical care.

College tuition reimbursement for children. Special programs that provide for college tuition.

In addition to these perks, many organizations provide additional insurance and retirement benefits to their key officials. As mentioned earlier, executive benefits plans supplement coverage for executives that is limited by some kind of government regulation (i.e., the 1964 limit of $50,000 on life insurance and the 1974 limits on defined benefits and defined contributions plans). Additional supplements to life insurance are described later in this chapter.

Although "reverse discrimination" may be a valid concern when analyzing and designing the compensation program for CEOs and other key officials, it appears that the specialists working in this area have done an exceptional job in keeping their "clients" whole (i.e., maintaining their real income and standard of living—current and future).

Short-term incentives—The short-term incentive plans designed for the CEO and other key officials usually provide payments on an annual basis. The awarding of the payment, normally a bonus, is predicated on the achievement of short-term measurement of a specified result. The basic criteria used for determining the size of the award are some kind of indicators of corporate performance such as net income, total dividends paid, or rate of achievement of some predetermined corporated objectives (e.g., a specific return on investment as determined by net profits divided by net assets).

The size of short-term bonuses received by CEOs who work in bonus-paying corporations averages between 50 to 60 percent of base pay. Most short-term bonuses are paid immediately in cash, although many companies do provide their bonus recipients with the opportunity to defer receipt of payment.

It is not unusual for an organization to recognize the full bonus award in computing annual pension earnings. However, only a minority of firms recognize short-term bonus awards when computing profit sharing, matching savings or thrift payments, or determining the amount of group life insurance the executive may have or the amount of earnings covered by a long-term disability plan.

In moving down the organizational hierarchy from the CEO, short-term bonuses as a percentage of base pay drop rapidly. Whereas the CEO's bonus will frequently be over 50 percent of base pay, the COO (second level) will receive approximately 40 to 45 percent of base pay, the executive vice presidents, 35 to 40 percent, and the vice presidents at the fourth level, 30 to 40 percent. The design and the development of short-term bonus plans are discussed in much greater detail in chapter 16 in the section that describes the compensation program for operating managers.

Long-term Incentives— In recent years, a number of professionals working in the area of executive compensation have been claiming that the compensation plans for these key officials are being improperly designed.[5] The concern of these professionals is that these top leaders are being rewarded for short-term results while the very nature of their jobs requires that they ensure the long-term survival and nurture the long-term growth of their organizations. To improve short-term results, these key officials can reduce the flow of funds into such areas as purchasing new and improved equipment, building more efficient facilities, maintaining current plant and facilities, providing adequate employee training, fostering research and development, and implementing proper marketing programs. Restricting the amount of money spent in these areas may have minimal or no influence on current earnings and, by reducing current spending, significantly improve certain critical financial measures. However, these kinds of actions may have a significant influence on the future ability of the firm to

[5] David J. McLaughlin, "Surging Executive Pay: Where Is It Going?"*Management Review,* January 1978, pp. 8–16. Edward Meadows, "New Targeting for Executive Pay," *Fortune,* May 4, 1981, pp. 176, 177, 180, 184.

compete in national and international markets. In addition, various accounting procedures such as the use of first in–first out (FIFO) instead of last in–first out (LIFO) costing of inventory provide higher profits in times of relatively high inflation, but may also inflict greater tax burdens. Leasing facilities and equipment, instead of purchasing them, to decrease assets and increase return on investment (ROI) percentages may increase business costs in the long term. These examples all provide opportunities to improve current financial records, but they may hurt future stability and growth.

As mentioned in chapter 2, the central purpose of senior management (executives and senior managers) of the organization is effectiveness. The primary measure of effectiveness for most organizations is long-term survival and growth. To promote this kind of behavior, the compensation program must provide rewards to those officials who take the kinds of action and make the decisions that attain these kinds of results.

Conceptually or theoretically, there is little argument with this approach operationally, but many issues quickly emerge. As mentioned briefly in chapter 13 (Performance Appraisal), measurement of individual performance is a most difficult assignment because of the problem related to developing and using credible performance standards. Performance standards are already difficult to develop at lower levels in the organization where the elapsed time between work performed and observable and measurable results is minimal. Moreover, the problems increase in a geometric proportion when measuring the results of current decisions two to five or even more years in the future. This is the heart of the problem facing professionals who design long-term compensation reward programs for the top officials of corporations.

In addition to measurement, long-term executive compensation programs very quickly become complex. Each component of a long-term executive compensation plan is, in itself, fairly simple. However, combining all the components into an executive plan that satisfies many individual needs, meets external demands, and relates to various other contingencies requires skill in development and care in administration. Identifying major organizational and key personnel considerations assists in further explaining how executive compensation plans become complex:

Organizational Considerations

1. Need to retain key personnel (golden handcuffs).

2. Desire to link interests of key personnel with those of the shareholders.

3. Identification of those performance measures that best indicate organizational success.

4. Time frame for measuring results and granting subsequent awards.

5. Ability of organization to afford awards to be granted in both the short- and long-term.

6. Influence of uncontrollable economic, political, social, and environmental forces on organizational outputs.

7. Tax deductions available to the organization.

8. Influence changes in tax laws may have on the organization.

9. Accounting procedures required in producing balance sheets and profit-and-loss statements.

10. Influence of future changes in accounting procedures on the compensation plan.

Recipient Considerations

1. Assistance in developing an estate (wealth building).

2. Enhancement of status and current standard of living.

3. Long-term financial security.

4. Recognition of superior performance.

5. Tax deduction and deferrals available.

6. Impact of changes in tax laws.

7. Protection of future earnings in case of merger or buy-out (golden umbrella).

To integrate long-term corporate growth goals with both personal and corporate tax obligations, many varying compensation components have been developed over the past 40 years to be a part of an executive compensation plan. Among some of the more widely used classifications of components are:

1. *Long-term bonus plans.* The major variations among kinds of bonus plans are in (1) the amount of cash received, (2) the time of receipt, and (3) the measures or indicators used to determine the amount and the timing of the award.

2. *Stock acquisition plans.* These include stock options, stock grants, and stock purchase plans. Among these three major stock acquisition programs are a wide variety of components with unique design features to serve specific purposes.

3. *Stock-based awards.* These plans may provide cash or shares of stock, or some combination of the two, using various performance measures to determine the size and the timing of the award.

4. *Special retirement and insurance plans.* These unique long-term protection plans, normally made available only to key officials, supplement the "qualified" plans provided to all employees of the organization.

5. *Tax shelter supplemental income investment, and wealth-building*

programs. This general category includes compensation components that vary as much as imagination, ingenuity, tax laws, and economic benefits permit.

Long-term plans are designed to provide awards that are earned over a specific period of time—2 to 5 or even 10 years into the future. The size of the bonus normally relates to the achievement or the continued achievement of certain well-defined results. The annual future awards may increase proportionally to the consistency and the improvement made in performance as measured by specific outcomes.

Organizations are now tying together their long-term bonuses with the long-range plans. The strategies established for achieving the long-range plans have specific corporate objectives. These corporate objectives, in turn, become the measures that determine the amount and the timing of the awards to be granted. The objectives may relate to some internal financing figures such as real growth in earnings per share (total growth minus allowance for inflation) or to some figures that compare results achieved with those of other organizations in a similar competitive environment.

Just as with short-term bonus plans, payment of an earned bonus increment can be deferred until some later date (e.g., after retirement) and can be paid in cash, shares of stock, or both. Compensation experts have frequently stated that they feel that bonus plans are often insensitive to corporate performance.

Stock acquisition plans permit corporations to achieve five goals. These are: (1) permitting employees or select groups of employees to advantageously acquire shares of stock in the corporation; (2) promoting substantial ownership rights among employees or select groups of employees; (3) establishing a motivational work environment that stimulates superior performance; (4) enhancing employee willingness to save for the future; and (5) assisting employees to develop a substantial estate.

These plans vary significantly as to eligibility, tax obligations to employer and recipient, and accounting treatment for corporate financial records. The following review and brief description of some of the more common stock acquisition plans, their unique features, and the purposes they serve will assist in gaining an appreciation of the variety of stock-related compensation components available and their relationship to tax legislation.

Stock purchase plans are the most common kind of stock acquisition plans. A "qualified" stock purchase plan is one that permits almost all employees of an organization to acquire corporate stock. Internal Revenue Code 423 defines the requirements a corporation must meet to "qualify" a stock purchase program. A qualified stock purchase plan, similar to a nonqualified stock purchase plan, permits the purchase of corporate stock over a relatively short period of time. A qualified stock purchase plan, however, requires the recipient to purchase the stock within five years from the date of grant of the purchase option. The price of the stock can be as low as 85 percent of the market price at the time of offer or the market price at the time of purchase, if lower. No employee may be permitted to purchase more than $25,000 worth of stock at the fair market value in any one year.

If the employee meets IRS employment regulations (is employed by the corporation granting the option at all times during the period starting with the date of the grant and ending on the date three months before the option is exercised), no tax liability results at the time of the exercise. If the employee does not sell the stock within two years after the granting of the option or within one year after acquiring the stock, the difference between the option price and the fair market value of the stock at the time of sale is considered ordinary income and the remainder is capital gains.

Because of the limitations inherent within qualified stock purchase plans, some corporations use nonqualified stock purchase plans for executives. The various kinds of executive stock purchase or nonqualified stock purchase plans provide corporations with the flexibility of blending specific organizational requirements with key personnel demands. Depending upon the specific features of the plan, recipients of the nonqualified stock purchase plans are able to acquire stock at prices ranging from full market value to a flat one dollar per share for stock having a fair market value ten, twenty, or more times that amount. In addition, the corporation may provide special loan arrangements so that the recipient has minimal financial burden when purchasing the stock. These stock purchase plans normally carry some restrictions. Typical restrictions are: (1) the stockholder must be employed for a certain period of time; (2) the corporation has the right to buy back the stock; and (3) stockholders cannot sell for a definite period of time. There is, normally, no waiting period to purchase the stock. Among the various kinds of executive stock purchase plans are (1) full market value, (2) earn-out or performance, (3) discounted, and (4) formula value.

Full market value stock purchase plans require the recipient to pay the full market price for the stock, but, normally, the corporation provides favorable loan or pay arrangements to assist in the purchase of the stock.

Earn-out or performance stock plans permit key employees to receive a loan to purchase the stock. The employee then satisfies (does not have to repay) the loan by meeting certain performance requirements such as (1) continued employment or (2) specific organizational performance measures.

Discounted stock purchase plans are plans in which the purchase price is less than the fair market price of the stock. A typical restriction with this kind of plan is that the corporation has the right to repurchase the stock if the recipient leaves the firm within a specific period.

Formula value stock purchase plans relate the price of the stock to some special formula and not to the fair market price. Two commonly used formulas are (1) book value and (2) price earnings multiple. To establish the book value or stockholder's equity, the corporation must (1) determine net worth (total assets less total liabilities) and (2) divide net worth by number of shares of outstanding common stock.

A special kind of formula value stock purchase plan is the *book purchase plan*. In this plan, the corporation provides the recipient with low- or no-interest loans to purchase the stock. The recipient can, after a specific period of time, sell the stock back at the then-existing book value.

Stock purchase plans grant the recipients immediate ownership. They enable the recipient to pay capital gains on all appreciation. Stock dividends are taxable at personal service income tax rates (50 percent maximum). The stock offer is a capital transaction for the corporation, not a compensation expense. Thus, it is a business expense and not a profit-and-loss charge (charge against earnings).

Stock option plans are similar to stock purchase plans with one major variation: stock options are granted to key personnel over a period of time that exceeds the time periods granted for stock purchase plans. Just as with stock purchase plans, the employee receives the right to purchase a specific amount of corporate stock at a stipulated price within a specified period of time. The employee is under no obligation to purchase the stock. In working with stock options, two important words to recognize are "exercise" and "window." The word *exercise* means the time when the stock option recipient actually acquires or purchases the stock. The word *window* refers to the specific period of time set by government regulation after the granting of the option that the recipient has the right to purchase the stock (this may also be called the *exercise period*). Under certain kinds of stock options, the recipient is required to report any difference between the fair market price of the stock and the price of exercise and is subject to tax at personal service income rates and must pay tax on that amount during the applicable tax period. When meeting capital gains time requirements, all other appreciation at the time of sale is taxed at long-term capital gains rates.

In May of 1981, tax legislation ended the use of qualified stock options and the need to comply with section 422 of the Internal Revenue Code which identified requirements to be met for qualifying stock options. Therefore, at this time, all stock options are, in fact, nonqualified stock options. Tax laws do not impose any limitation on the amount of the stock a corporation can option to an individual or individuals. The limitation relates to practical business considerations. The shares of stock authorized for stock options are usually functions of (1) the size of the corporation, (2) the shares outstanding, and (3) the number of employees provided stock option rights. The actual size of an option granted to a specific employee usually depends on that individual's base pay and level in the hierarchy.

A wide variety of nonqualified stock option plans has been designed over the years to meet various employee and employer demands. The nonqualified stock option plans are very similar to the previously described stock purchase plans. The major kinds of nonqualified stock option plans are:

1. Full price stock option plans.

2. Discounted stock option plans.

3. Variable price stock option plans (including the nonqualified "yo-yo" plan).

4. Tax offset stock option plan.

5. Formula value stock option plan.

The *full price*, *discounted*, and *formula value stock option plans* have features comparable to the stock purchase plans with the same titles. The *variable price stock option plan* permits the price of the stock in the option to vary according to some stock market determined value, financial performance measure, or other indicators of corporate performance. A particular kind of variable-priced plan is the *"yo-yo" plan*. The unique feature of this plan is that each dollar increase in the market price of the stock reduces the option price of the stock by an identical amount. The initial option price is usually 100 percent of the fair market value.

The *tax offset stock option plan* requires the corporation to pay the recipient upon exercise of the option an amount of money sufficient to offset assessed tax liability. As in all nonqualified stock option plans, the corporation is able to declare a tax deduction equal to the amount the recipient declares as income at the time of the exercise of the option. By granting the recipient money sufficient to pay incurred taxes, the corporation, in effect, returns the tax savings to the employee.

A special kind of stock option plan is the granting of *stock warrants* to an employee. A warrant is a right to buy a specific number of shares of stock at a specified price within a definite time period. Warrants are normally transferable, can be sold by the warrant holder, and have a fair market value.

A third kind of stock acquisition plan is the *stock grant*. A stock grant provides selected employees with stock at *no* cost. Stock grants take two basic forms: stock appreciation grants and full-value grants.

Stock appreciation grants entitle the recipient to receive payments that equal the appreciated value of the stock (or number of shares or units of stock granted) over a designated period of time. A *full-value stock grant* entitles the recipient to receive the total value of the worth of a share of stock (or number of shares or units of stock granted) over a predetermined period of time. Total value includes base value of stock at time of initial grant, dividend, and appreciation of stock value during the period when the grant is in force.

Most stock grant plans take place over a period of time in excess of five years. Usually, the recipient or the firm must meet certain predetermined performance standards.

Some of the more common kinds of stock grant plans are the (1) restricted stock plan, (2) performance share plan, and (3) phantom stock plan. Each of these three kinds of plans may have a number of different features.

In a *restricted stock plan*, the corporation awards a specified number of shares to certain individuals who have demonstrated continued superior performance. In some cases, the employee may be required to pay a specific amount for the stock. When this occurs, the restricted plan becomes, in essence, a nonqualified stock option. The recipient has stockholder voting privileges and rights to all dividends, but, during a stipulated (restrictive) period, may not sell, transfer, or use the stock as a pledge or security for a debt. When a restriction is not met, the recipient may be required to sell the stock back at a penalty. The restrictive period may be any substantial period of time; a common period is 10 years. Normally, restrictions lapse following retirement or involuntary termination.

471
Board of
Directors and
Senior
Management
Compensation

With all stock grant plans, the recipient must pay at personal service income tax rates the fair market value of the acquired stock. Dividends are also taxed at personal service income tax rates. All gains realized from the sale of the stock are taxed as long-term capital gains. Dividend payments made by the company on restricted stock may be charged as a business expense, and it can amortize the value of the stock on the restricted period. The amortized value is a charge to earnings. The corporation receives a tax credit for any increase in the value during the restricted period.

Restricted stock plans can be modified to have not only certain time restrictions, but may also include the meeting of certain performance measures before the actual granting of the restricted stock. The size of the grant may also be predicated on the reaching of certain goals or measures. This kind of grant is called a *restricted stock performance plan.*

A *performance share plan (PSP)* is similar to the restricted stock performance plan except that there is *no* holding period determining when the stock can be sold. These PSPs usually set grants for medium time periods—3 to 5 years. However, the holding periods for some plans may range from 6 to 10 years in length.

When reaching certain predetermined performance goals, the recipient has the right to specified shares of stock. The performance goals may be earnings per share over a specified time period or return on assets. The actual amount of stock granted may relate to some formula such as the price of stock at the time of payment and the actual goal achieved by the recipient.

Another kind of stock grant plan that gained popularity in the 1970s is the *phantom stock plan.* In this plan, stock or stock appreciation awards are made in artificial units. These units become a credit to the recipient against an equivalent number of shares of stock in the corporation. The actual payment value, which can be made in stock or cash or a combination of the two, is established by some predetermined formula that relates to either the market or some nonmarket value of the stock.

A typical phantom stock plan may take this form: In five years, it grants a specified number of units which are equal to shares of stock in the firm. The value of the units may equal the price of the stock at that time or the appreciated value of the stock from the time of the grant to that predetermined future date. It may also include the value of all declared dividends earned by the equivalent shares during the waiting period.

A special kind of phantom stock plan is a *stock appreciation rights (SAR).* An SAR may take one of two distinct forms. An SAR may be linked directly to a stock option plan, or it may be freestanding. A stock option linked in tandem with an SAR permits the optionee to receive a stipulated payment that can be made in cash, stock, or a combination of the two in lieu of all or a designated part of the option. The amount of the option covered by the SAR may be a specified number of, or a certain percentage of, the option shares and be payable only in money. The value of the SAR may be limited to the appreciated value of the stock option from the time of the grant of the option to the time the SAR is available. Or the SAR value may be the full value of the stock at the time the option can be exercised and all dividends earned since the stock option was granted. The SAR may have a limit such as a certain percentage of the initial value of the option. A freestanding SAR is similar to the previously described phantom stock plan.

A plan that combines the features of a phantom stock plan with a performance share plan is a *performance unit plan (PUP)*. Similar to a phantom stock plan, the grant is made in some number of artificial units with each unit usually being the equivalent of one share of company stock. The actual dollar payout of these units is equivalent to the value of the stock at some future date stipulated in the plan.

Like the performance share plan, the recipient or the corporation must meet certain performance measures in order for the recipient to acquire the grant units. While the PUP unit awards are made at the time of the grant, the units acquire a cash value only at the end of a stipulated period and upon the meeting of prescribed performance measures. The major difference between a PUP and a PSP is that a PUP has a prescribed and definite limit while a PSP is open-ended.

A *formula value appreciation rights plan* is a phantom grant plan in which the actual number of stock units used for determining appreciation gains is based on a predetermined formula rather than on the fair market value of the stock. The predetermined formula may be based on the number of years of continuous employment or on certain performance criteria.

A *formula value stock grant* is another kind of phantom grant plan in which the value of the stock unit awards does not relate to the stock's fair market value, but rather to some other evaluation procedure. A specific kind of formula value stock plan may grant the recipient a specified number of units equivalent to the book value of the stock at some specified future date (five years, upon retirement, etc.). This kind of grant is called a *book unit plan (BUP)*.

An offshoot of the phantom stock plan is the *phantom convertible debenture*. This kind of plan grants phantom corporate bonds that pay interest and, upon maturity, will pay the recipient the face value of the bond or be convertible to shares of stock.

Securities Exchange Commission and Senior Management Compensation

In addition to the Treasury Department regulations concerning the acquisition of corporate shares of stock by employees, the valuation of the stock and its disposition and taxation, the Securities and Exchange Commission (SEC) issues regulations regarding the communication and the acquisition of stock by certain key personnel. Under the Securities Act of 1933 and the Exchange Act of 1934, the SEC has the right to require corporations listing stock on national securities exchanges to disclose information about stock ownership and remuneration received by certain individuals.

Remuneration is a term used by the SEC to identify specific compensation components. These components include salary, fees, commissions, bonuses, stock and property payments, executive insurance, personal benefits, pensions or retirements plans, annuities, deferred compensation plans, short- and long-term incentive plans, stock purchase plans, and profit-sharing and thrift plans. The key personnel whose remuneration must be documented on corporate proxy statements are the five highest-paid executive officers and/or directors if they each earn over $50,000 in total remuneration. This group of key officials is frequently called "insiders." The remuneration disclosure report must identify these insiders by name and job title. The corporation must also report all remuneration paid by the corporation and its subsidiaries to all directors and officers as a group without naming them.

Under sections 16(a) and 16(b) of the Exchange Act of 1934, officers, directors, and those individuals holding 10 percent or more of the stock in the corporation must disclose their stock ownership and provide monthly reports of changes in amount of ownership.

Some of the special SEC requirements regarding the stock transactions of insiders are:

1. Insiders cannot buy and then sell stock on the same day.

2. Insiders must comply to a ten-day window (i.e., they can buy and sell only for a ten working-day period beginning on the third day following the end of a quarterly or annual financial reporting period.

3. Insiders are effectively prohibited from selling stock within six months of a purchase that includes the exercise of a stock option.

ESTATE BUILDING AND MAINTENANCE

By the time most individuals reach key policy-influencing and organizational leadership positions, they are giving considerable thought to acquiring sufficient funds to allow them to continue after retirement their current life-style and to protect their families in case of their own death. Relatively high levels of base pay, bonuses, and a wide variety of stock acquisition or phantom stock plans provide sufficient income for most key personnel of modern corporations to afford a highly desirable standard of living. To develop an estate that permits a continuation of this living pattern involves the use of various compensation components (1) that defer income and provide income continuation after retirement or in the event of permanent disability, or (2) that ensure a flow of income to the family of the deceased executive. In planning the estates of these key individuals, estate taxes as well as income taxes play an important role.

Because of the continued high income of many key personnel after retirement, variations in the rates of ordinary income, personal service income, and capital gains become more critical than prior to retirement. This occurs because of the declining percentage of income that is recognized as personal service income versus that recognized as ordinary income. To individuals who have acquired estates of considerable size, federal and state estate taxes, probate charges, and estate administration costs become important considerations. Protecting the family of a deceased executive from substantial financial burdens becomes a part of this phase of compensation planning and implementation.

In addition to the stock acquisition plans previously described, a number of different kinds of retirement, deferred income, and income continuation plans have been developed and used by corporations to protect their highly compensated employees.

Retirement Plans

Key personnel certainly may take advantage of the same retirement opportunities provided to lower-level employees. However, because of federal restrictions on qualified plans, there are limits to the amount of contributions and benefits any one individual may receive. As mentioned earlier, it is important whenever possible to "qualify" profit-sharing or stock bonus-based retirement plans. By using qualified plans, the employer may deduct amounts currently contributed to the plan. Employees may defer the receipt of income and the consequent taxation of the employer contributions. Income earned by the plan is tax-free. Briefly, qualified plans must not discriminate in favor of the highly-paid employee, and restrictions must be imposed that limit the *constructive receipt* (made available to employees) of employer contributions.

To supplement qualified retirement plans and escape burdensome qualification requirements, organizations use a variety of nonqualified unfunded programs. An unfunded program is simply based on a promise to selected individuals that the corporation accepts the obligation to pay certain deferred benefits from the general assets of the corporation at a specified time. An unfunded salary continuation program may use insurance contracts purchased through the use of the general assets of the corporation. Various kinds of insurance policies are used by corporations to fund supplemental retirement programs. Among the more commonly used are "Section 79" plans, split-dollar life insurance, and retired life funding contracts.

Section 79—Section 79 insurance is a group permanent insurance normally offered by the corporation to a select group of employees. It has a whole life feature, with stable costs and no possibility of cancellation. Both employer and employee contribute to the plan. The employer contribution pays for the "risk assumption" portion of the premium; the employee contribution builds the cash value of the policy. Upon retirement, the employee can select either (a) a lump-sum cash payment, (b) an annuity income, or (c) reduced paid-up death benefit, or (d) elect to continue insurance at the full face amount of the policy and pay premiums at the original age rate.

Advantages of Section 79 insurance are that (1) it is a less expensive way to provide post-retirement insurance than through normal corporate group insurance; (2) premiums are tax-deductible to the corporation; (3) income upon retirement is taxed as personal service income; (4) death benefits are income-tax-free; and (5) the employee can borrow on the cash value of the policy. The employee must pay tax on the premium value of insurance protection as calculated by using IRS Tax Table 79.

Split Dollar—Split-dollar life insurance plans involve both employer and employee in the purchase of a cash value or permanent life insurance policy. The employer usually pays that part of the premium that equals the increase in the cash value of the policy for the current year. The employee pays the balance, which is the term element of the premium. The resulting cash value of the policy can be used for funding a deferred compensation agreement. The cash value is retained or assigned to the employer while the employee designates the beneficiary for the remaining part of the death benefit—that amount which exceeds the cash value. At death, the insurance proceeds are received tax-free by the employer and the employee's beneficiary. The beneficiary may escape paying estate taxes if the employee makes an absolute assignment of the proceeds to the beneficiary.

The employee gains by being able to purchase insurance at a lower price than if the purchase has been made by the employee alone. The employee pays taxes on any amount by which the term value of the benefit and any dividends received exceed the employee's premium payment. The Internal Revenue Service P.S. 58 rate table identifies the premium value of the insurance protection for the year.

Retired Life Funding Contract—A retired life funding contract can be designed to provide a large amount of life insurance coverage after retirement to a select group of employees. The corporation pays the cost of the premium for active employees. The premium is determined to be actuarially sufficient to pay term premiums for the remainder of the employee's life. The premium must not exceed the amount needed to allocate the cost over the remainder of the working life of the covered employee.

For tax purposes, the plan is similar to a qualified plan. The cost of the premiums of the plan are tax-deductible to the employer but are not considered as earned income to the employee. Interest earnings are tax-free. Term life insurance premiums paid by the fund after retirement are tax-free to the retiree, and death benefits are income-tax-free. This kind of plan provides money to cover estate taxes and other charges upon death.

Deferred Compensation Plan—A deferred compensation plan involves the deferral of a certain amount of current pay (either a decrease in existing salary or deferral of a proposed increase) until retirement. Upon retirement, the employee receives a stream of payments over a designated period or for life. If the individual dies before retirement or before the payment of installments as set forth in the plan contract, the beneficiary of the employee receives the amount owed. Because most retired top personnel will be paying maximum income tax rates after retirement, deferred compensation plans may provide minimum tax benefits.

Salary Continuation Plans—Another approach available for providing key personnel with a stream of income for a period of years after retirement, or

477
**Board of
Directors and
Senior
Management
Compensation**

for the life of the individual, or to the widow, beneficiaries, or estate of the employee (if death occurs prior to retirement), is through the use of a salary continuation plan.

A salary continuation plan may involve an agreement between the key executive and the corporation whereby the executive agrees to be available for advisory or consulting services after retirement and also to refrain from entering the employment of a competitive company while receiving continued salary payments. The contract terminates if the executive is discharged for a cause as defined in the employment agreement.

Another plan used to provide salary continuation is the *supplemental income plan (SIP)*. A SIP is a future income contract between employer and employee. Like a deferred compensation plan, it provides supplemental income payments for a specified period of time or until death or upon incurring permanent disability. The amount of the payments can be based on some formula using years of service, final salary, certain performance goals, or any combination of the preceding.

The employer can either fund the contract or can let it be unfunded and make payments out of future earnings. A funded SIP commonly uses some form of life insurance for financing the payment. A special kind of multipurpose life insurance policy has been developed to fund SIPs. A policy is issued on the life of each employee participating in the SIP, and the policy is owned by and payable to the corporation. The policy covers the expenses incurred in case of preretirement death of the employee. Or, after the retirement of the employee, the company can surrender the policy and use the funds collected or the loan value of the policy to offset the cost of installment payments for the employee. The company may also maintain the policy and upon the employee's death recover the face amount of the policy. The company pays no taxes on the face amount of the policy. Employee-received payment is considered earned income, and the employee is taxed at personal service income tax rates in the years the payments are received.

In addition, split-dollar insurance plans can be used to fund salary continuation plans to escape income taxation upon the employee's death and remove any proceeds from the estate of the deceased for estate tax purposes.

The corporation can use its share of the anticipated proceeds from the split-dollar policy to fund the cost of providing salary continuation benefits. When using split-dollar insurance for this purpose, the plan should be executed separately from any other split-dollar plan to eliminate any suggestion that the employee has an interest in the employer's investment and to prevent current taxation based on constructive receipt.

Insurance–related Information—When developing a supplemental benefits plan for key personnel and using insurance to provide the additional benefits, answering the following questions will assist in making the wisest and most useful insurance selection:

1. How is the current group life insurance plan structured?

2. What are the differences between the pay of key personnel and the maximum insurance available through the group life plan?

3. What amount of extra life insurance should be offered to key personnel?

4. Is group life coverage provided after retirement? If yes, what is the amount?

5. Do the laws of the state in which the company is incorporated place a limit on group life insurance? If yes, what is the amount?

6. What opportunities are available to eliminate use of personal after-tax dollars to provide additional life insurance coverage?

7. How can group life insurance plans be utilized to give extra benefits on a tax-favored basis to select groups of employees?

8. How can group life insurance plans be redesigned or rearranged to reduce long-term costs to the company and also provide substantial benefits to select groups of employees?

SELECTED READINGS

Bacon, Jeremy, *Corporate Directorship Practices: Compensation 1979, Report No. 778.* New York: The Conference Board, Inc., 1980. A review of a survey of over 1,000 companies that presents a comprehensive analysis of compensation practices of inside and outside directors. It includes a comparison with a similar survey conducted in 1977.

Baker, John C., "Are Corporate Executives Overpaid?" *Harvard Business Review,* July–August 1977, pp. 51–56. The board of directors with an outside-dominated compensation committee must restrain the large salaries and the liberal benefits paid to top executives

Balkcom, John E., "Executive Compensation: A History of Imbalance in Public Controls, Shareholder Interests and Executive Rewards," *Directors and Boards*, Spring 1977, pp. 4–28. A comprehensive review that places in perspective the major factors influencing the evolution of executive compensation and the continuing involvement of the federal government in this area.

Crystal, Graef S., "The New 10 Commandments—Plus 1—of Executive Compensation," *Financial Executive*, July 1974, pp. 36–47. A review by a foremost consultant in executive compensation of the motivational aspects of money. He discusses individual perception, relating rewards to performance, recognition, and status as areas that must be considered in designing an executive compensation plan.

Ellig, Bruce R., "Corporate Objectives and the Executive Compensation Package," *Industrial Management,* September 1973, pp, 5–6, 11. One of the top compensation practitioners stresses the need to focus attention on corporate objectives when designing an executive compensation plan. He looks particularly at type of industry, degree of risk, importance of technology, and stage of development of the business.

Foote, George H., "Performance Shares Revitalize Executive Stock Plans," *Harvard*

Business Review, November–December 1973, pp. 121–130. Tax reforms of the past decade have brought performance share plans into the limelight. This approach rewards executives more on earnings improvement than do the vagaries of the stock market. These are "phantom" plans that require no financial investment on the part of the recipient. The author reviews participative limits, award provisions, payout stipulations, impact on company earnings, and cost.

Forseter, Bernard, "Designing Deferred Compensation Plans," *Taxes*, November 1974, pp. 675–679. Deferred compensation must primarily consider the overall financial plan selection, but it must also recognize the importance of such unique elements as eligibility requirements, integration with Social Security, actuarial assumptions, methods of funding, and vesting.

Lerner, Robert J., "Long-Term Incentive for Management, Part 5: Formula Value Incentive Plans," *Compensation Review*, Second Quarter 1981, pp. 42–50. A useful analysis of some of the basic performance measures, including earnings per share, dividends, net assets per share, average stock price, and price earnings ratio, as used by leading corporations in their formula based long-term incentive plans. (The other four articles on long-term incentives that preceded this article may also be of interest.)

Miller, Ernest C., "Compensating A Company's Board and Top Management—An Interview with Courtney C. Brown, Corporate Director, " *Compensation Review*, Fourth Quarter 1976, pp. 14–18. Brown, author of "Putting The Corporate Board To Work," stresses that the board's compensation committee should play a strong role in setting compensation for the president and CEO. The board, as a whole, should set its own compensation.

Mruk, Edwin S., "And How Would You Like Your Compensation, Sir?" *Management Review*, August 1974, pp. 15–23. Perquisites and other benefits are taking on increased importance as tax changes limit the value of deferred compensation. Executives want cash now in the form of higher salaries and larger bonuses. Effective compensation planning requires flexibility in the design stage.

Parham, John C., "The Expanding World of Executive Perks," *Dun's Review*, September 1973, pp. 64–67. Executive compensation is growing more diverse and complex as companies strive to attract and retain topflight executives. A list of perquisites compiled by Hewitt Associates and adapted by *Dun's* shows some 80 different benefits available to executives.

Rappaport, Alfred, "Executive Incentives vs. Corporate Growth," *Harvard Business Review*, July–August 1978, pp. 81–88. The author contends that most forms of executive compensation direct executive behavior toward the attainment of short-run goals. The challenge in executive compensation "lies in designing incentive systems that induce executives to make decisions congruent with the long-term economic interests of the company."

Thomsen, David J., "Executive Compensation Gimmicks—Look Out!" *Financial Executive*, August 1973, pp. 58–62, 64, 66. One of the foremost professionals in the compensation field analyzes various compensation components and notes how businesses use them. Stock appreciation rights, seesaw options, split-dollar insurance, cafeteria compensation, and performance shares have been used well by some businesses. However, these components have been adopted indiscriminately by others to circumvent regulations. The long-term consequence of such "fads" and actions frequently is the unequitable compensation of executives. This leads to misinforming stockholders on the worth of key officials.

16

Compensation for Exempt Employees and Overseas Staff

CONTENT

This chapter describes the influence of nonexempt, lower-level compensation and the top-down influence of senior management compensation on the group of managers who provide the "here-and-now" direction to the organization's daily operation. Particular attention focuses on the pay compression problem that has existed for some years at this level in the organization. This chapter also includes descriptions of special kinds of compensation opportunities that recognize the individual efforts of professional and sales personnel. The chapter concludes with a review of the unique elements of compensation practices for personnel in foreign operations.

GOALS

Upon concluding this chapter, you should recognize the opportunities available for compensating the employees who provide front-line direction to the production of organizational goods and services. You should also understand the productivity dangers inherent in pay compression at the lower levels of the managerial and professional hierarchy and be able to design special programs for minimizing this dangerous problem. Another goal is to provide assistance in designing compensation plans that recognize the individual contributions of professional and sales personnel and employees who work in foreign assignments.

The employees who occupy positions in the middle of the organizational hierarchy frequently find that their compensation program is critically influenced by the compensation system designed for their subordinates. They are also the beneficiaries of a trickle-down of some of the compensation components offered to those at the top level in the organization. However, the true golden carrot placed in front of this group of employees is the information that, through faithful service and superior performance, the compensation opportunities provided to top-level employees can one day be theirs. In differentiating the compensation provided to the subordinates of this group of employees, efforts must be made to identify and measure contributions and to recognize achieved results through the compensation program of the organization.

OPERATING MANAGERS

This group of managers holds positions with a wide range of titles and also an extremely wide range of pay, although the total compensation package includes fairly comparable components. The employees in the lowest group of operating managers often have the title of foreman, first-line supervisor, and, possibly, groupleader. Moving further up the hierarchy, there are unit, department, or branch managers or functional unit managers such as sales, personnel, accounting, data processing, and, finally, at the highest levels of operating management, plant managers or superintendents and store managers. Interspersed among these managers are administrators who perform highly specialized services and who may, at the same time, act as supervisors of subordinate administrative staff workers. As discussed in chapter 2, this group of managers is responsible for meeting daily quality, quantity, and timeliness standards in the goods and the services produced by their units.

The base pay of the employees at the lowest levels of operating management is frequently much less than that paid to the highest level of operative employees. Furthermore, the managers responsible for the operation of large facilities, stores, and major service-producing units receive base pay and have pay-for-performance opportunities that exceed those received by some members of senior management. A brief review of the major compensation components provided to operating managers identifies the similarities and the differences between their compensation programs and those offered to their subordinates and superiors.

Base Pay

The base pay of operating managers is determined in a manner like that used for their subordinates. If an organization uses a formal plan to evaluate operative jobs, there is a good chance that operating manager jobs will also be evaluated by a structured, formal procedure. A major added compensable factor for managerial jobs is recognition for supervisory responsibilities. This factor could include such elements as the number of people and kind of work supervised and the scope and closeness of supervision offered. Organizations also make extended use of surveys to determine the going rate of pay for comparable jobs in the market place. The same mixture of considerations (ability to pay, traditional and historical relationship of job and pay, evaluated job worth, market information, and various subjective considerations) meld and result in a rate of pay for each job.

Many organizations establish in their compensation policy a minimum difference between the pay of a supervisor and of his or her highest-paid subordinate. When this is the case, the most commonly found difference is 15 percent, with a minimum difference ranging between 10 and 20 percent. The failure to establish a minimum difference and the occurrence of certain compensation decisions may result in subordinates receiving annual earnings far larger than that of their supervisors. This problem will be discussed later in this chapter under the topic of pay compression.

Benefits

The major benefits received by the operating managers are similar to, if not identical with, those provided to their subordinates. Time off with pay relates more to tenure with the organization than with the job level. Medical, hospital, and surgical plans vary minimally among all levels of employees. A number of important benefits do vary relative to base pay. These are group life insurance (a certain proportion of base pay), disability and pensions (monthly payment based on some calculation related to annual earnings), and savings and thrift plans (maximum amount contributed by employee is usually a specified percentage of base pay with the percentage of employer contribution usually the same for all levels). Corporations that have qualified stock purchase plans offer them to all employees, but the number of shares an individual may buy frequently varies according to base pay.

Some major differences in benefits and services do appear, however, in the ranks of operating management. Employees in operating management jobs may receive a larger amount of life insurance as a proportion of base pay than that offered to operative employees (i.e., managers, two to three times base pay; operatives, one to two times base pay). The opportunities to attend professional meetings at desirable locations and to receive paid-for subscriptions to professional journals, magazines, and newspapers begin to appear at this level in the organization. The right to use a company car also becomes increasingly evident at the operating management levels. Special parking places, even club memberships and free tickets to entertainment events, also begin to appear as part of the total compensation package. The higher levels of operating management are often granted the right to use special corporate entertainment facilities.

Pay-for-Performance

Possibly the most significant and, if properly designed and administered, most important difference between the compensation package provided to operative employees and that offered to operating managers is the addition of pay-for-performance awards to the latter's package. In recognition of superior contributions, organizations are including some kind of performance-based awards in their operating management compensation programs. As mentioned when discussing pay-for-performance programs, the great barrier to success with these plans is the inability to identify workable and acceptable performance standards and then to measure demonstrated workplace behaviors against these standards. When done poorly, pay-for-performance plans can actually be a disincentive to improved organizational productivity. When done well, they aid in establishing the kind of motivating workplace environment that all top managers desire.

Short-term bonuses—Since operating managers operate in the here and now, there is no reason not to provide rewards based on the quality of current performance. Short-term bonus plans for many operating managers are similar, if not identical, to those offered to operative employees. These comparable short-term bonus plans include profit-sharing, Christmas bonus, and year-end bonus plans. Each of these plans usually relates the size of the bonus to the weekly, monthly, or annual earnings of the employee. The bonus may be calculated as a percentage of annual earnings; or it may be equivalent to one, two, or possibly four weeks of pay. The Christmas and year-end bonus plans are usually informal and discretionary. The profit-sharing plan is usually formal and structured. The profit-sharing plan and, usually, the year-end bonus plan are linked directly to the profitability of the firm, while the Christmas bonus relates closely to the firm's ability to pay.

The one plan offered to operating managers that is seldom offered to operative employees is a short-term bonus that uses some kind of formula for determining the size of the bonus pool and the actual amount allocated to each eligible participant. The bonus plan will define eligibility requirements.

The actual size of the bonus pool may depend on some policy determinant that sets aside (1) a certain percentage of annual profit for the bonus or, possibly, (2) a certain percentage of annual pay. The profit-related calculation in (1) can be very complex. A more simple and commonly used calculation for the bonus is to base it on a percentage of profit after taxes. This calculation should be done after deducting a certain amount for stockholder dividends and after setting aside a certain amount for retained earnings. It is not unusual for this latter kind of calculation to result in an allocation equaling ten percent of net profit after tax and after setting aside a specific amount for dividends and retained earnings.

The individual allocations are commonly a percentage of annual earnings or base pay. For lower-level operating managers, the percentage will usually range from 5 to 10 percent, with higher-level operating managers receiving as much as 20 percent of base pay.

Many bonus plan administrators are attempting to link participant awards to some kind of performance measures. Performance appraisal ratings are being used more often to determine the award's actual amount. Some plans are being designed to combine the size of the bonus pool and the actual individual allocation to the achievement of certain organizational or unit performance goals such as sales, shipments, or profit center earnings, and individual performance ratings. Effort is focusing on designing bonus plans that relate awards to performance and provide a large-enough award to modify behavior so that organizational goals can be achieved.

EFFECTS OF COMPRESSION

In the past decade, with increasing union bargaining strength, government pay-influencing legislation (minimum wage changes, Equal Pay Act requirements, EEO affirmative action plans, ERISA, etc.), inflation, and unchanging personal service income tax rates at the middle income levels ($20,000 to $75,000), many operating managers have found their relative compensation shrinking dramatically in comparison with that received by the workers they supervise. This results in the "inequity" or "compression" problem that has been a source of irritation and growing dissatisfaction among management and other professional personnel.

David Kraus of McKinsey & Co. conducted a number of analyses of compensation and disposable income data on chief executive officers (CEOs), middle-level personnel, and lower-income factory workers. The data and the information provided in his writings offer valuable insights into reasons for unrest among the people in many of the middle- and lower-level management jobs and their professional counterparts.[1]

A review of some of the analyses developed by Kraus identifies the issues facing both compensation designers and professionals and operating managers. Using data generated by the American Management Associations (CEO and mid-level personnel) and the Bureau of Labor Statistics (factory workers), Kraus compares the average pay for the years 1964, 1974, 1976, and 1980 of the following:

1. CEOs of businesses having annual sales of $118 million in 1964 and, with an adjustment for inflation, $225 million in 1976.

2. Controls in businesses of the same size.

3. Lower income factory workers.[2]

These statistics have been further updated to 1980 using the same procedures as indicated above. The 1976 sales volume of $225 million would be $310 million in 1980, adjusting for inflation between 1976 and 1980. See tables 16-1, 16-2, and 16-3 for a comparison of pay practices from 1964 to 1980.

[1] David Kraus, "The 'Devaluation' of the American Executive," *Harvard Business Review,* May–June 1976, pp. 84–94.

[2] The 1964 and 1974 data are in Kraus, "The 'Devaluation' " and the 1976 data in Kraus, "Compression."

TABLE 16-1

1964–1976 PAY PRACTICES FOR REPRESENTATIVES OF THREE MAJOR GROUPS

Group	1964	Percentage Increased 1964–1974	1974	Percentage Increased 1974–1976	1976	Percentage Increased 1964–1976	1980	Percentage Increased 1964–1980
CEO	100,000	30.0	130,000	11.5	145,000	45.0	244,000	144.0
Controller	31,000	35.5	42,000	4.8	44,000	41.9	69,400	122.6
Lower-income Factory Workers	5,400	70.4	9,200	17.4	10,800	100.0	15,000	177.8

Another way to analyze pay changes of representatives of the three basic pay groups is to review changes in the relationship of multiples of pay (as in table 16-2).

To gain additional insight into the relative change in pay between operative employees and mid-level personnel, a review of data presented in the Employment Cost Index of the Bureau of Labor Statistics reinforces the presentation made by Kraus (see table 16-3).

From a review of the data developed by Kraus, it appears that the pay of mid-level personnel has kept up with that of senior management. Comparing senior management pay to that of mid-level personnel, however, can lead to inappropriate conclusions. This analysis of pay presents only a partial, and in many ways inaccurate, picture of what is truly happening with regard to total compensation and disposable income.

An analysis of total compensation gives a much better insight into the actual differences in the compensation received by senior management and that received by operating managers. During the 15-year period between 1964 and 1979, the best talents available to businesses have used their innovative abilities to develop new compensation components or to vary the application of the existing ones. Through these changes, it has been possible to:

1. Minimize the immediate tax burden liabilities of the executives and senior managers.

2. Provide business-paid compensation components that senior management officials—for that matter, most people—desire for improving their lifestyles.

3. Expand opportunities to defer ownership of compensation rewards to delay incurring tax liabilities.

4. Grant ownership opportunities that permit a select group to expand their wealth as the value of the business increases (ownership of stock in a business that pays dividends and whose fair-market value increases in worth).

These changes in the design and the implementation of the compensation package have, for the most part, been restricted to the top half of 1 percent to 3 percent of the business.

TABLE 16-2

PAY MULTIPLES

Group	1964	1974	1976	1980
CEO to Controller	3.2	3.1	3.3	3.5
CEO to Lower-income Factory Workers	18.5	14.1	13.4	16.3
Controller to Lower-income Factory Workers	5.7	4.6	4.1	4.6

TABLE 16-3

EMPLOYMENT COST INDEX DATA[a] (PERCENT INCREASE)

Group	Sept. 1975 to March 1976	March 1976 to March 1977	March 1977 to March 1978	March 1978 to March 1979	March 1979 to March 1980
Managers and Administrators	2.6	6.3	6.5	7.2	7.5
Clerical and Kindred Workers	4.0	6.6	7.5	7.4	9.6
Blue-collar Workers	4.1	7.4	7.8	8.3	9.4
Workers, Occupations Covered by Collective Bargaining Agreements	4.1	7.8	7.8	8.2	9.5

[a]Straight-time hourly earnings including production bonuses and cost-of-living allowances.

Because of increasing communication of top management pay figures, resulting in stockholder unrest over the pay of these key individuals, and the impact of IRS tax regulations and SEC restrictions, changes are occurring in pay practices for top management. More of the compensation of executives and senior managers is going into long-term pay components. The wide variety of deferred stock acquisition and cash bonus plans and the extensive array of perks have substantially improved the total compensation package of these senior officers. Those at the middle- and lower-levels of operating management, however, have very few opportunities to receive these lucrative rewards. Many of those occupying operating management and professional jobs have witnessed an actual decline in their purchasing power. At the same time, an analysis of employee pay leaves little doubt that production workers represented by the more powerful unions are doing extremely well relative to most operating manager, professional, and nonrepresented operative employees.

Top-down influences in an organization that lead to the compression of the pay of middle- and lower-level operating managers are:

1. Stockholder unrest over the continuing escalation of executive and senior management pay.

2. Use of various deferred and incentive plans plus perquisites to sweeten senior management compensation without large increases in their base pay.

3. Budgetary limitations on the funds available for compensating management employees.

Bottom-up pressures come from:

1. Rapid increase in entry-level rates of pay to new college graduate hires.

2. Negotiated annual pay increases to union-represented employees.

3. Increase in the government-established minimum wage level.

The maintenance of a viable compensation structure is a major force for minimizing compression. Extending the spread of operating management pay grades has been one approach used by organizations to maintain the 10 to 30 percent difference for internal equity purposes. More firms are turning to overtime pay for operating management personnel. Organizations providing overtime pay to management personnel will pay overtime on a straight-line rate or at the conventional time-and-a-half rate. To receive overtime payment, overtime work must be scheduled and approved in advance. Very few firms provide payment for casual overtime. Some firms are now providing overtime pay to all exempt personnel with annual earnings up to $35,000 to $40,000. In most cases, overtime payments do not begin until the exempt employee has worked 45 hours per week.

Other organizations with formalized cost-of-living adjustment plans for nonexempt personnel or for members of a bargaining unit now grant their lower- and mid-level operating management personnel similar increases. Such increases normally become progressively smaller when moving upward through the hierarchy of an organization and disappear entirely by the time an employee reaches a base pay of $50,000.

All of these approaches add to the labor budget—specifically, the budget for operating management—at a time when budget formulators are trying to limit the size of budgetary increases.

EFFECTS OF INFLATION

With the movement of inflation from a traditional one to three percent annual increase to one moving into double-digit figures, employees have demanded that their employers keep them "whole." The unsatisfactory effects of inflation have had their greatest impact on operating management personnel.

These employees have not received pay increases commensurate with those received by their subordinates. Furthermore, pay raises received have resulted in greater tax liabilities, further compounding the ill effects of inflation. Since 1964, there have been large increases in the Social Security (FICA) taxable earnings base and tax rate (taxable earnings 1964, first $4,800; 1981, first $29,700; tax rate, 1964, 3.625%; 1981, 6.65%). In addition, many state and local governments have legislated some form of local income tax and others have increased their income tax levies. Until 1981, there had been *no* decrease in federal income tax rates, although during this period, there were some increases in standard deductions and individual exemptions. However, lower-paid workers usually received the greatest benefits from liberalized personal exemptions or increase in standard deductions with regard to federal income tax.

Social Security taxes appear to consume a fair share of each boost in pay given to operating management employees. The additional earnings, whether gained from a cost-of-living adjustment, a merit increase, or promotion, have resulted in the employee moving into progressively higher income tax brackets (tax-bracket creep).

The deductions, the exemptions, and the credits available to these employees have not increased proportionately to increases in pay. This situation, in turn, results in a larger percentage of gross pay being subject to higher rates of income tax. During this same period, executives with very high incomes have benefitted from the reduction in the maximum personal service income tax rate from 70 to 50 percent. The combination of increases in various tax liabilities, erosion in purchasing power caused by inflation, and relatively small increases in pay has often resulted in reduced purchasing power and investment opportunities available to operating management personnel. Table 16-4 identifies changes necessary in pre-tax income to maintain the same purchasing power in 1975, 1980, and 1981 as in 1970.

TABLE 16-4

**Pretax Income in 1975, 1980 and 1981
Necessary to Equal 1970 Aftertax Purchasing Power**

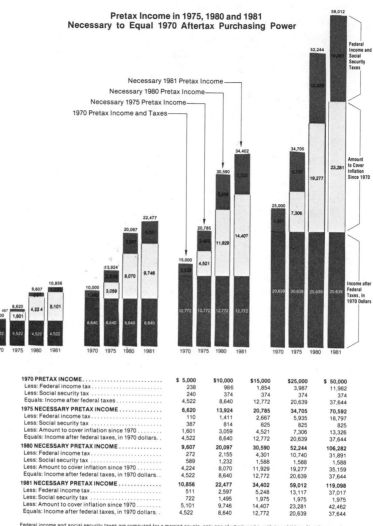

1970 PRETAX INCOME	$ 5,000	$10,000	$15,000	$25,000	$ 50,000
Less: Federal income tax	238	986	1,854	3,987	11,982
Less: Social security tax	240	374	374	374	374
Equals: Income after federal taxes	4,522	8,640	12,772	20,639	37,644
1975 NECESSARY PRETAX INCOME	6,620	13,924	20,785	34,705	70,592
Less: Federal income tax	110	1,411	2,667	5,935	18,797
Less: Social security tax	387	814	825	825	825
Less: Amount to cover inflation since 1970	1,601	3,059	4,521	7,306	13,326
Equals: Income after federal taxes, in 1970 dollars	4,522	8,640	12,772	20,639	37,644
1980 NECESSARY PRETAX INCOME	9,607	20,097	30,590	52,244	106,282
Less: Federal income tax	272	2,155	4,301	10,740	31,891
Less: Social security tax	589	1,232	1,588	1,588	1,588
Less: Amount to cover inflation since 1970	4,224	8,070	11,929	19,277	35,159
Equals: Income after federal taxes, in 1970 dollars	4,522	8,640	12,772	20,639	37,644
1981 NECESSARY PRETAX INCOME	10,856	22,477	34,402	59,012	119,098
Less: Federal income tax	511	2,597	5,248	13,117	37,017
Less: Social security tax	722	1,495	1,975	1,975	1,975
Less: Amount to cover inflation since 1970	5,101	9,746	14,407	23,281	42,462
Equals: Income after federal taxes, in 1970 dollars	4,522	8,640	12,772	20,639	37,644

Federal income and social security taxes are computed for a married couple, only one of whom works, with two children. No allowance is made for any other taxes. Calculations use the tax laws in effect each year. Deductible items are assumed to equal 17% of pretax income in 1970, 20% in other years. For calculating maximum tax and earned income credit, all income is assumed to be earned, personal service income. Inflation is calculated from the deflator for personal consumption spending, with a 10% rise assumed from 1980 to 1981.

Source: "The Two-Way Squeeze, 1981," Economic Road Maps Nos. 1900–1901, New York: The National Conference Board, Inc., April 1981.

COMBINED EFFECTS OF COMPRESSION AND INFLATION

Of great importance to policy makers is the psychological impact compression and inflation have on operating management personnel. The concept of equity was presented in chapter 1. Very briefly, this concept states that each employee develops a work-related, perceptual model of equity. The equity model is a ratio, with the rewards received from doing the work as the numerator and the inputs and efforts or investments provided by the employee as the denominator. The ratio values primarily have this effect:

$$\frac{\text{Reward Received}}{\text{Inputs Provided}} = \text{less than 1 (Job dissatisfaction quite likely)}$$

$$\frac{\text{Reward Received}}{\text{Inputs Provided}} = \text{1 or more (Job satisfaction possible)}$$

Employees seldom compare only their own inputs with rewards received. Normally, they compare their reward-inputs ratio with that of one or more other employees. When the value of the ratios does not favor the individual, job dissatisfaction is again likely to occur as shown in the Employee Equity Perception Ratio:

$$\frac{\text{Rewards Received by A}}{\text{Inputs Provided by A}} = \text{or} \neq \frac{\text{Rewards Received by B}}{\text{Inputs Provided by B}}$$

When employees perceive a ratio to be less than acceptable, they normally take some action to correct any imbalance. There are two major steps open to employees to correct equity imbalances at the workplace. The first step is to request an increase in rewards (increase in base pay, cost-of-living additions, merit increase, promotions). If this step yields little or no results, a second step is to reduce inputs or investments into the job.

The validity of this theory becomes evident when management has trouble convincing operatives whom they feel to be most qualified to accept first-level management jobs. A remark often voiced with the refusal to accept a promotion is "The job doesn't pay enough for me to accept these additional responsibilities and headaches." Or, in other words, the ratio between the rewards provided and the inputs required in performing job A are out of line with the rewards and the inputs of job B.

The compression problem is having an unsatisfactory impact on the equity perceptions of operating management employees. In addition, loss of real income is resulting in an inability to improve a standard of living and, at times, is even causing a decline. This significantly reinforces dissatisfaction among operating management jobholders.

These dissatisfactions are occurring at a time when organizations are facing declining levels of productivity. Is it not possible that a major reason for the decline in productivity is the refusal of lower- and mid-level operating managers to provide the enthusiastic, innovative, risk-taking leadership necessary for an organization to accomplish its missions and objectives?

When people refuse to accept promotions, there is a chance that there are troubles in the numerator (rewards) part of the ratio. When effort and enthusiasm decline, there is an equally good chance that employees are, on their own, improving the equity balance by reducing their inputs and attempting to equalize them with rewards.

OVERCOMING INEQUITIES — IMPROVING PERCEPTIONS

An approach used by organizations to increase the pay of their operating management personnel has traditionally been through the use of promotions and merit budget increases. Problems are now arising from the widespread use of these techniques. In the recession of the mid-'70s and with the lowering of improvement in productivity rates (at times, actual decline from quarter to quarter), organizations have recognized that, in some cases, they have too many managers and have worked at reducing their numbers. Increased use of quality-of-work-life and job enrichment programs that delegate more authority to lower-level employees further reduces the need for managers and promotional opportunities. Promotions in name only were and still are common. Giving an employee a new title and an increase in pay with the same or comparable responsibilities and duties is a phony promotion that has limited incentive value. The negative point here is that the employee realizes that the employer is playing games with the job hierarchy. This jeopardizes the entire formal internal equity system that compensation management spends so much time and effort in establishing.

In many other cases, merit increases have had little to do with individual employee performance. With from 95 to 98 percent of all employees receiving "merit" budget pay increases, and with these "merit" increases ranging from six to eight percent, the validity of the word "merit" becomes highly suspect.

Promotion without significant changes in job responsibilities and "merit" increases that do not relate to superior performance are having an adverse impact on profitability. These issues further compound the problem of compensation for operating management personnel. A viable answer to this problem is the development of incentive plans that significantly reward those whose performance is truly beyond acceptable stated standards.

PROFESSIONAL COMPENSATION

Professionals are those employees who regularly perform nonroutine assignments requiring originality, discretion, independent judgment, innovative abilities, and analytical skills. Their jobs normally require specialized and prolonged courses of intellectual instruction. They normally hold, at a minimum, an undergraduate degree in some specialized area such as science, engineering, accounting, finance, medicine, law, etc. Laws or existing practices may require them to have a certification or license to practice. Their work normally involves the solution of complex, technical problems that vary widely and may have a broad range of interpretation. They devote a minimum amount of their time to directing the work of others.

The design of compensation programs for these professional employees is a problem area for many organizations. These employees are easily able to identify with other professionals who have similar credentials and work for themselves or for other organizations. They develop fairly accurate perceptions of the kinds and the quality of work their peers are performing in other kinds of work settings and of the compensation and noncompensation rewards these peers are receiving. From their perception-based measurements (see equity theory discussion in chapter 1), either they achieve greater satisfaction from their current jobs or they become dissatisfied with their jobs or work environment.

The compensation of professionals normally follows the same route as that provided for operating management personnel. In fact, their pay opportunities usually "top out" and equal those of jobholders in the middle levels of operating management (currently between $35,000 to $70,000). Frequently, to obtain greater income, professionals move into positions of management that are related to their own areas of specialization. Much to the dismay of many organizations, the result is the loss of a good researcher or engineer and the gain of an incompetent manager. In many of these cases, not only does the organization suffer from the twin losses, but also the individual does not enjoy the managerial assignments and would much prefer to be working in the professional specialty area.

Although the compensation programs for professionals are similar to those provided to operating managers, there are some differences. These are discussed in the remainder of this section.

Base Pay

A major variation in the compensation program for professionals may begin with the technology used for evaluating professional jobs. Chapter 8 includes a description of the maturity curve method of job evaluation. The maturity curve method has gained popularity for evaluating professional jobs because it emphasizes individual qualities rather than the job content focus of the more commonly used point-factor methods. The maturity curve method uses a graph with the x-axis (horizontal) indicating age, years of professional experience, or years since last degree. (Linking age to pay determination, however, may be a dangerous practice since it may place the employer in violation of the Age Discrimination in Employment Act.) The y-axis (vertical) indicates median pay. A typical maturity curve may appear to be similar to a learning curve with a rapid rate of increase in the left-hand side or early stages in the range at the x-axis measurement and then level off or slightly increase in the middle of the curve. In some cases, the curve may bend slightly downward in the latter stages of measurement. This drop downward may be interpreted to mean that professionals who have spent over 20 to 25 years in their field receive reductions in their pay. A better answer may be that the higher-paid professional in that particular time measurement has moved out of the field (into private consulting or a management job) and the group mix whose pay is being identified in the latter stages of the curve is different from the one in the earlier stage.

The philosophy that underlies the development and the value of maturity curves is that age or years since last degree relate directly to increased levels of knowledge and greater professional value. Typically, the recently graduated professional works on parts of projects or major assignment areas, performs fairly detailed or routine work, and receives fairly close supervision. At the next step, the employee assumes responsibility for a significant portion of a project and works independently. The third stage finds the professional designing projects, performing an entire assignment, or teaching subordinate professionals how to perform their assignments. The fourth step of the career of a professional may find the individual in a management or advisory position.[3]

Benefits and Services

Benefits that are highly valued by professionals relate to professional development and growth. The opportunity to attend professional meetings, write a paper to be presented at such a meeting, take a spouse at company expense to those meetings, and receive professional journals and magazines is most desirable. Time off to prepare a paper for submission to a professional journal or for delivery at a professional meeting contributes to enhancing the individual's stature. The opportunity to attend special courses that provide new knowledge or update existing knowledge is also highly prized. Possibly most important is the opportunity to work on challenging assignments. Other on-the-job noncompensation rewards include better office space and equipment, increased technical or clerical assistance, and more influence over budget decisions.

The professional employee frequently looks outside the organization for growth and reward opportunities. Additional education, visibility at professional meetings and in professional journals, opportunities to participate in unusual or critical projects—all have very definite monetary value to professionals. This kind of professional growth may not only influence pay increase and promotion opportunities on the present job, but also lead to offers of better jobs in other organizations.

Pay for Superior Performance

Most professionals, like most other employees, want to be recognized for what they do. Possibly, for professionals, bonuses or merit awards for exceptional contributions are more important than for almost any other group of employees. As discussed earlier in the description of the maturity curve method of job evaluation, the individual professional truly makes the job. Professional jobs can be described only in fairly general terms; but the results achieved relate significantly to the competency, interest, and effort of the jobholder. Considering the opportunities available for the professional to truly make the job, rewarding demonstrated performance must be an important part of the pay package of the professional.

[3]The four stages in the career of a professional are identified and described in Paul H. Thompson and Gene W. Dalton, "Are R & D Organizations Obsolete?" *Harvard Business Review*, November–December 1976, pp. 105–116.

Special Performance Awards—Over the years, a number of short-term performance awards have been developed for professional employees. Awards are made for outstanding technical contributions or performance of a truly outstanding nature. The awards include a variety of both noncompensation and compensation awards. The noncompensation awards include certificates, plaques, jewelry (pins, rings, etc.), and pictures placed in special locations. Compensation awards range from a sabbatical at full pay with all expenses paid to pursue a special course of study, to an all-expense paid attendance at a technical meeting, to a paid trip to a national conference that results in a paid vacation at a highly desirable location. Special one-time money bonuses may range from $25 for a suggestion to $100,000 or more for a specific technical contribution.

For the professional who works in the research and development field, awards are provided for filed and issued patents. Patent awards may range from $100 to $500 at the time of filing for a patent to an additional $100 to $500 at the time of issuance, to an amount that may vary from a few hundred dollars to as much as $10,000 for a patent that has commercial value to the company. Some organizations provide special awards for the number of patents issued to an employee. These awards may range from $200 to $1,000. A few firms are now offering the scientists who develop patentable ideas a percentage of all royalties generated as long as the individual remains with the company or into retirement. Royalty earnings could easily exceed $100,000.

Formal cash awards offered to outstanding contributors may range from $500 to $100,000. The number of prizes offered annually depends on corporate policy and the size of the prizes awarded. The special awards are usually granted to a small number of employees on an annual basis.

Some organizations reward their members who are elected to office in professional organizations or who publish articles in respected professional journals. Awards of this nature frequently range from $100 to $300.

Awards of significant size usually require approval of key officials, including the president. Some even require approval of the board of directors. Rewards of $1,000 or less may require the approval of only a divisional leader. In some cases, an immediate supervisor or the next higher level supervisor can approve an "instant" award that recognizes a specific valued behavior. This instant reward may equal $100 to $200 or two weeks' or one month's pay. These kinds of awards not only assist in establishing a motivating work environment and retaining key personnel, but they may also be helpful in attracting hard-to-recruit specialists.

SALES COMPENSATION

The acceptance and the use of the output of an organization normally require the talents of a special group of people. These individuals present the output to potential consumers, then influence the consumers to use it. Output can be a product, a service, or both. It can be tangible (an automobile) or intangible (life insurance). It can be a service provided by a business in a highly competitive industry (time-sharing and data processing) or electricity from a monopolistic public utility. It can be the output of a profit-making business (General Motors) or a nonprofit organization (the Salvation Army).

In most cases, those responsible for the sales of the product or service are members of a sales or marketing unit. There are numerous examples, however, of individuals from the chairman of the board, CEO, down through the management ranks who perform sales activities. This section, however, focuses on those individuals whose major responsibilities require contact with buyers whom they must influence to purchase the goods or services.

Sales Personnel Job Responsibilities—Although the basic duties of a salesperson normally are to make sales, these individuals perform many other assignments. They may identify potential customers, review current products on the market, and identify the degree of competitiveness of major suppliers and their products. They may report on product quality (their own and their competitor's). Market analysis, including present and possible future consumer demands, is another kind of information-gathering mission they may perform.

Some sales personnel do not directly sell anything. Their sole responsibility may be to contact potential consumers or those who direct consumer activities (the doctor who writes a prescription for a patient requiring a particular medicine) and inform them of the strengths and the benefits to be derived from using their product or service. Their main responsibility may be to acquire preferred space in the area where their purchaser is displaying the product for sale.

Sales personnel may set up displays, direct promotional campaigns, provide instruction to customer sales personnel, and give technical advice. They advise on size, color, and style to order; acceptable order quantities; and delivery and reorder date expectations, warranties, and other guarantees.

Most sales personnel have to maintain extensive records; and many make frequent, detailed reports on factors that influence sales. They do this to accomplish company sales goals and to meet customer demands.

Sales Objectives of the Organization

From the brief description of some of the varied activities performed by sales personnel, it becomes obvious that, although the primary objective of the sales force is to transfer ownership of organizational output to the consumer or to the sponsor of the consumer, there are many ways of performing this transfer and sales operation.

Some of the major sales objectives of a business are:

1. Selling a specific amount of output at a price sufficient to guarantee a certain profit.

2. Establishing and maintaining a certain share of the market.

3. Penetrating a particular consumer market or territory.

4. Generating a particular annual growth rate by units of output sold, sales dollar volume, profits generated, share of the market, etc.

5. Maintaining satisfied customers.

In meeting these objectives, short- and long-range targets should be identified so that the attainment of objectives in one time-span does not adversely influence similar attainment in another. Time references should be considered. Another consideration is the fact that sales competition among different units can have unwarranted effects on a specific product or service line. Additionally, a sales program that generates an acceptable level of profit in both the short and long-run must be compatible with the requirements of those responsible for supplying inputs into the production process: producing, storing, and distributing the output; and maintaining the records and reports necessary for efficient operation.

Organization of a Sales Department

Because of the variety of objectives an organization expects to accomplish with its sales force, and the responsibilities and duties assigned its personnel, a sales department usually requires more than just salespersons. If an organization produces a variety of products for different kinds of consumers in various locations, requirements for segmentation and specialization begin to arise.

Many changes have occurred in the way organizations inform their customers about their product or service. The heart of this change is the twentieth century phenomenon known as the marketing expert.

The skills involved in designing, styling, and merchandising a good or service have become so important that, in many cases, sales has become a subsidiary of marketing. The senior salesperson for many organizations is frequently the marketing manager or vice president of marketing. Reporting to this senior marketing manager is a general sales manager. Then, depending upon product differentiation and sales requirements, there may be a product sales manager or a division sales manager. At the next level is the regional sales manager, whose subordinates are district sales managers. The final level of sales management is the sales supervisor. Reporting to this individual are those responsible for direct sales activities.

Many businesses do not have six levels of management in their sales structures, but this kind of structure may be found in the large, complex businesses that consider the continued and aggressive sale of their products the difference between death or mere survival and continued growth and prosperity.

Sales Personnel Assignments and Personal Characteristics

The large business that spends much of its sales dollar or gross revenue on presale advertising of its product requires a different kind of salesperson (and sales compensation plan) than the organization whose major, if not sole, sales expense is the money allocated to the compensation of its sales personnel.

A certain type of salesperson is required when the major challenge is to inform others of the product or service and what it can do for them. At the other end of the spectrum are sales personnel who must search for and identify potential customers and then make contact with them, persuade them of the potential benefits of the goods or service, and finally, convince them to purchase. In all cases, sales personnel must know the qualities both of their own products or services and those of their competitors.

Oral communication skills are in more demand in some cases than in others. Sales personnel who must find their own prospects and set up their own work schedules must have different planning and self-discipline abilities than those whose work schedules are set, to a large degree, by a sales manager. It takes one kind of effort to discuss a service or product with a person who is unfamiliar with the output of the company and another kind to discuss a nationally known product or service that has a substantial reputation.

Some sales jobs require voluminous reports; others require nothing more than a signed or acceptable order form that can be read and understood by those who must record and complete the order.

Designing a Sales Compensation Plan

There are two basic methods available for paying sales personnel. The first is salary. The salary method provides a specific amount of pay each pay period to the salesperson regardless of quality of performance. The salary-only plan includes a program in which the organization covers all expenses incurred by the salesperson in the performance of assignments.

The second method is the sales commission. In this method, the salesperson receives a commission that is usually a percentage of the net sales price of the product. If no sales are made, the commissioned salesperson receives no money. Success in selling a product, on the other hand, can result in the salesperson becoming extremely wealthy.

Another approach combines expenses and commissions. In this case, the business covers all expenses incurred by the salesperson, ensuring at least that there is no out-of-pocket loss. The salesperson must still depend on commissions to provide the necessities and the luxuries of life for self and dependents. In some cases, the expense payment can be increased to cover expenses incurred in maintaining a family. (In reality, this would be a salary plus commission plan.) The salesperson still relies on the commission to provide a higher quality of life and desired luxuries.

An incentive supplement to a salary or commission plan is made available through a bonus. Bonuses can be combined with a salary-only plan, a commission-only plan, or a commission-plus-expense plan to direct sales efforts toward a certain goal. The bonus is normally a cash payment. Businesses provide bonuses to employees who meet or achieve certain quotas. The amount of the bonus usually depends on the goal's importance and on how well an individual or group of salespersons meet a particular quota.

Quotas are normally set as a percentage of sales or may relate to some other well-defined goals that have easily recognizable and observable quantitative measures. Other kinds of common bonus-related quotas are larger-than-average orders, full-line selling, sales of a new product or particular product, and calls per week. Quota plans may be directed toward the sales efforts of individuals or the results of a group of sales personnel.

Many quota plans require the development of a formula for determining the actual size of the bonus earned. The variables in the formula may be the percentage of quota sold by a specific salesperson, the total bonus as determined by collective efforts of all sales personnel, the maximum size of bonus pool, and other appropriate variables.

A modification of the bonus plan is the contest or prize program. The prizes available through the winning of a contest are usually in-kind or non-cash. They may consist of desired merchandise, a vacation to a resort area, a trophy, or a plaque. In reality, businesses use bonuses and prizes for the same purpose—to stimulate performance.

Features of Sales Compensation Plans

Establishing a *salary-only sales compensation plan* requires the same effort as that necessary for determining the pay of any employee. The first step is job analysis—a careful review of job requirements and identification of the specifications or incumbent qualifications necessary to perform the job. Then, through some form of job evaluation, a determination of an appropriate ranking of the job must be made. The final step is to set the pay, which requires market survey data to determine what other businesses are paying their personnel who are performing comparable responsibilities and duties in similar areas. These job analysis–evaluation activities take a considerable amount of time and effort and must be reviewed routinely.

Once established, a salary-only plan is the simplest to operate and the easiest to understand. Since the salary-only plan pays the salesperson the same rate of pay without regard to sales volume, the business can demand that the employee perform marketing activities other than direct sales and expect a minimum amount of complaint. A salary-only plan provides the employee with a steady income during periods of low demand for the product or service and protects the business from making excessive commission payments when the salesperson had little or nothing to do with the increased volume. The salary-only plan emphasizes that the salesperson is an employee who must follow directives established by the business. (In many cases, the commissioned salesperson develops the attitude of an independent contractor and pays minimum attention to the employer's request.)

A salary-only plan provides minimal monetary stimulation for performing superior sales activities. It places increased burdens on performance appraisals for determining in-grade pay increases, transfers, and promotions. The salary-only plan is especially valuable where sales require extensive technical expertise and where the final closing of a sale may require considerable time and the efforts of more than one individual. It is useful also for paying trainees or those who must perform a series of marketing activities other than direct sales. Some businesses find a salary-only plan most satisfactory when those who have final responsibility for the purchase of a product are in one control location and those who directly influence or control final sales are dispersed over a wide geographical area. Salary-only plans are also useful when the initial sale or continuing sales are not possible without the support of the many local users who must also be contacted, or when purchases made in one territory have an impact on the sales in another territory.

Paying a salesperson a percentage of the dollar volume of the sale is probably the oldest form of sales compensation. From a motivational point of view, this is a superior pay plan. The employee recognizes an immediate reward from sales effort. The consequence of a salesperson's behavior is the commission, which reinforces and strengthens desired behavior.

The pressures resulting from a *commission-only plan* rest directly on the salesperson. Sales result in an earned commission; the more sales, the greater the earnings. No sales—no income; no income leads to a very unsatisfactory life-style. The commission-only plan relieves management of much of its regulation and direction responsibilities. Commission-only sales personnel must assume almost complete responsibility for their success. The planning of calls, job knowledge, customer contact, and closing skills are all individually controlled factors that *directly* influence sales success.

Some of the weaknesses of a commission-only plan are:

1. Commission sales personnel may suffer financially during periods of declining consumer demand.

2. When commissions are identical for all products or services sold, sales of high-profit or hard-to-sell items may suffer as the salesperson will naturally focus on the item easiest to sell.

3. Management finds it difficult to direct the efforts of salespersons toward activities that do not have an immediate influence on obtaining additional sales.

Commission-only plans have had historical use in particular industries (garment, door-to-door selling, insurance) where the resistance to product purchase is high. Commission-only plans are useful for companies that use sales representatives who are independent contractors and may sell for more than one firm.

The first activity required in designing a commission-only pay plan is the establishment of a commission rate or a commission formula. A commission rate varies according to the dollar value of the product sold, the amount of product a salesperson could normally be expected to sell in one year, the amount of profit a company realizes from the sale of the product, and customer acceptance or resistance to the product. These commission-influencing factors vary from product to product and from industry to industry. It is not unusual for an insurance salesperson to receive 90 percent of the first year's insurance premium, a door-to-door salesperson to realize a 40 percent commission on all products sold, a garment salesperson to receive a 7 percent commission, and a person selling a costly piece of equipment to receive a 2 or 3 percent commission on sales. It is not uncommon for each type of industry to have traditional practices concerning commission size. Other factors that may be considered in designing a commission-only plan are (1) frequency of commission calculation, (2) timing of commission payment, (3) kind of payment if other than cash, (4) any amount of commission to be withheld, and (5) opportunity to draw against future commission earnings.

Some firms vary their commission rates in line with changing sales volume. A progressive commission rate is one that increases as sales volume increases. A regressive rate is one that declines as sales volume increases.

Companies that produce products that provide different margins of profit may vary the rate of commission by item sold. Some firms vary commission rates according to the difficulty of selling a product in a specific territory. Any type of variation in a commission rate structure makes a commission-only plan more difficult to administer.

Salary–Only and Commission–Only Supplements

A supplement to any kind of sales compensation that has a high incentive potential is the bonus. Bonuses can be designed to fit almost any sales requirement. The kind and the size of a bonus can vary almost infinitely.

The first bonus-related decision a company must make is whether or not a bonus would stimulate and reinforce desired sales behavior. The company then must decide the size and the timing of delivery of the bonus. At the same time, the standard to be used for determining the bonus must be set.

Bonus attainment may relate to such standards as:

1. Total units sold.

2. Total dollar sales volume.

3. Dollar volume or quantity of specific item sold.

4. Profitability of the company.

5. Number of new accounts sold.

Although most bonuses are money-oriented, more firms are turning to an in-kind bonus to stimulate additional sales efforts. These in-kind bonuses are often grouped under the category of contest prizes. The dollar and incentive value of such prizes often exceeds that provided by a cash bonus. A new automobile, a no-expense ocean cruise or trip to Paris for the winning salesperson and his or her spouse are kinds of contest prizes or in-kind bonuses that many people find highly desirable.

Although companies have much flexibility in designing a bonus, they still must be careful that those who earn the bonuses have truly outperformed those who did not receive them. Everyone who has the opportunity to earn a bonus should know the requirements for winning and that those who earn bonuses do so because they have met standards and provided highly desirable behavior. Subjectivity in determining the kind, size, and timing of a bonus is an acceptable business prerogative. Subjectivity in determining the winner of a bonus can have a devastating effect on morale and can destroy any benefits a bonus may provide.

In addition to cash bonuses and prizes, many companies find that the combination of salary and commissions provides the most satisfactory type of sales compensation plan. When combining the two, the salary component varies drastically. It can be sufficient to cover only traveling expenses, or it can be designed to cover some travel and family expenses.

Some firms also supplement a commission-only plan with a "draw." A "draw" is a certain amount of money a firm advances to its employees to cover their expenses and enable them to meet subsistence requirements until they receive their commission payment. Sales personnel repay this advance or draw from commissions earned.

Performance Appraisal

When the pay of sales personnel is primarily by salary, any merit increase or other reward may be determined through an appraisal of performance. Performance appraisal issues and methods for sales people differ little from those facing other employees. Some standards are easy to identify while others are quite nebulous; it may be difficult to identify and set quantitative performance measures. In fact, a major reason for moving from commission to salary is the difficulty in measuring performance against important sales-related criteria other than dollar or unit sales. The need for assessing performance of sales personnel is as critical as it is for any other employee. Management by objectives (MBO) has been used successfully for appraising the performance of sales personnel.

Sales Manager Compensation

The problems relating to the compensation of those who manage sales personnel are similar to those found in developing a compensation plan that relates manager-subordinate compensation. The one principal difference is that commissioned sales personnel and bonus winners may be earning considerably more money than their supervisors.

The ideal situation is for the base pay of a sales manager to be from 15 to 50 percent higher than that provided to immediate subordinates. As in the case of most plans, pay differentials are greatest at the highest levels and the difference decreases in moving down the organizational hierarchy. When everyone is on a salary, this type of program is possible to establish and maintain. But in commission-based pay plans, there is a great likelihood that a small group of sales personnel will have higher earnings than even the highest-level sales manager.

Although it is not always desirable to have sales personnel make more than their managers, this situation is not intolerable. It is not always true that the best salesperson will make a good manager. The best use of individual talent may lie in selling, not in managing sales people.

Establishing pay grades and ranges of pay for sales management personnel is the same as in the procedures discussed in part 2 and in particular chapter 10.

Compensation Components Other Than Pay

Sales personnel, again like all other employees, normally receive a wide array of compensation components in addition to their base pay or commission, bonus, and prize earnings. Pension plans; health, accident, and dental insurance for self and dependents; major medical insurance; long-term disability insurance; life insurance; vacations; and holidays are all provided. Complete car and entertainment expenses (paid for by the business or written off as a tax deduction) are additional benefits.

Sales management personnel also enjoy the benefits and the perks provided to their peers.

INTERNATIONAL COMPENSATION

Compensation managers of many organizations are now facing an entirely new set of issues—designing and managing the compensation of employees who work for the company in a foreign nation. The unique compensation issues are in these general areas:

1. Incentives provided to stimulate movement or expatriation to a foreign location or host country.

2. Allowances for repatriation to home country.

3. Additional tax burdens placed on employees working in a foreign location.

4. Labor regulations in both the host country and the home country.

5. Cost-of-living adjustments in the host country.

6. Home country and host country currency fluctuation.

7. Formal and informal compensation practices unique to the host country.

8. Determining home country for setting base pay of third country nationals.

Home Country of Employee

An organization operating in one or more foreign nations may draw employees from three different places of residence: (1) the specific nation or host country where the operation is located; (2) the home nation of the parent operation; and (3) foreign countries other than the site of the operation.

In most cases, manual laborers and those employees who perform semi-skilled and skilled trades that can be quickly learned come from the host country. A major variation in this general rule currently exists in the Middle Eastern petroleum-exporting nations where manual laborers come from such labor-rich countries as Pakistan, India, and Korea. Skilled technicians, craft-workers, professionals, administrators, and managers initially come from the home nation of the present operation or from other foreign countries that have qualified people willing to work in the host country.

The title given to those employees whose basic residence or home is the host nation is *nationals* or *locals*. Those who come from the home country of the operation are *expatriates* and those whose nation of residence is neither the host country nor the home country are *third country nationals (TCNs)*.

The compensation provided to locals, expatriates, and TCNs can vary considerably. Normally, the total compensation package provided to locals is the least costly while that provided to expatriates is most costly. From strictly a cost point of view, the more locals employed at the work site, the less the labor cost and the greater the return on invested capital. The expenses involved in stimulating an employee to move to a foreign site, the payment of relocation costs (both to the new site and return to the home base at the end of the foreign assignment), and, finally, the additional tax burden incurred by having expatriates and, at times, TCNs in foreign operations are substantial. These expenses often result in an excessive drain on the profitability of the foreign operation.

There are five basic reasons for hiring nonlocals to staff a foreign operation. The first reason is that the talent (knowledge and skills) to operate the foreign operation is not available among the local population. This is especially true where the kind of operation is new to the country and the technological skills have not yet been developed. A less common reason may be that there is not sufficient available labor (the Mid-East example of importing manual labor). A third reason is that the organization has certain information that it considers highly secret, sensitive, and confidential and trusts only those employees who have had extensive employment with it and have established a reputation of loyalty and dependability. Since many foreign operations are new ventures, the home nation may not have had time to develop a cadre of locals whom it trusts with sensitive and confidential information. The fourth reason is that often as firms train locals in certain skills, these workers become in such great demand that they can earn more money either working for themselves or for the host country. The fifth reason is to provide employees with an opportunity to gain experience in a foreign assignment.

Identifying Able Individuals Willing to Move

When first establishing a foreign operation, a certain number of employees who are thoroughly familiar with the way the company functions and its technology must come from already existing operations. If the firm has no foreign subsidiaries, or if locals in already existing foreign operations cannot be transferred to the new site, then employees must come from the parent company in the home country. It may also be possible to recruit and hire individuals working for other companies who have the required knowledge and skill. These people may either be from the home nation or be TCNs.

Recruiting new employees with the requisite knowledge and skills, or influencing current employees to move to a foreign site, requires a wide array of compensation-related incentives. The kind of compensation components offered and the amount or quality of components available vary according to the desirability of the location.

Site Desirability—Each site has its unique strengths and weaknesses, and these vary according to the way each individual perceives them. Some of these strengths or weaknesses relate to geographical location and climate. Others relate to social and political conditions. Working in an extremely cold or frigid region of Siberia, or the desert areas of the Sahara or Saudi Arabia, or a malaria-ridden jungle or coastal area of equatorial Africa requires more extensive incentive-to-move compensation components than a move to Paris or Zurich.

A person with a family that includes school-age children would be concerned with educational opportunities. A person who likes to travel may look at the accessibility of other countries from the site of the foreign operation. A person interested in leisure-time pursuits may consider the rewards available through hunting, fishing, beach and water sports, or skiing and mountain climbing.

Finally, countries with unstable political systems require inducements that compensation managers would not have to overcome when sending employees to a site where security of property, even life, is not an important concern.

Transfer Incentives——Usually, the first compensation issue that confronts the compensation manager is the amount of additional pay required to induce an employee to move from the present job site to the new one in the foreign country. In some cases, the site may be so desirable that almost any job candidate would find it sufficient if the organization guaranteed that the individual would be as financially well-off in the host country as at home (keeping the employee "whole"). In most cases, however, the person asked to move to a foreign site will demand some premium over that earned in the present assignment.

The next set of compensation issues revolves around present housing. In many cases, the employee owns a house and looks to the employer to cover some or all of the expenses involved in selling it. These sale-of-residence expenses may include sufficient money to guarantee the employee no financial loss in the house sale or even some percentage of the profit. Because a house, in many cases, is currently one of the best investments a person can make, organizations now provide home rental assistance and absentee ownership management services for the homeowner who rents rather than sells while on foreign assignment.

After taking care of the existing house concerns, the movement of the family and the personal property to the host country comes into focus. In most cases, the organization again takes care of all moving expenses to the new site. In those cases where it is impractical to move the family, special consideration must be granted for their maintenance at the present residence. In cases where spouses or families do not make the move, the transfer will probably be for a limited period—a two-year contract, with at least one extended, completely paid leave at home at the end of the first year or at the end of the contract, or even a couple of completely paid holidays with the family in addition to the leave.

To maintain the employees' present standard of living in the foreign location, organizations provide a number of allowances to keep them "whole." A major one provides money for additional living costs (food, housing, transportation, and other consumables in the host country). Compensation managers obtain "ball park" figures on additional living costs to be incurred in moving an employee to a foreign location from various sources. These include (1) *U.S. Department of State Indexes of Living Costs Abroad and Quarters Allowances* on a quarterly basis, published by the Bureau of Labor Statistics, and (2) reports available from other organizations. Living costs may include special allowances for utility expenses, servants, operation of the living quarters, and educational allowances for the children.

Many organizations provide a set of travel and holiday benefits to employees in foreign locations. These benefits provide paid holidays to some desirable vacation site for the employee and family.

With the completion of the employee's contract at the foreign location, the employer then picks up repatriation expenses—those incurred in returning the employee to the home site. In addition to covering transportation and moving costs, some firms allow repatriates an allowance for house-hunting; some grant returning employees money to redecorate their homes. Repatriates who purchase new homes may find that their employers will assist in securing a homeownership loan and some provide money toward purchase of a new residence.

To ease the burden connected with moving to and from a foreign site and to assist in living at the new location, many companies now provide in-depth educational and counseling programs. Such programs inform employees on preferred ways of doing things when making moves, the accepted customs and norms at their new work locations, and things to do to make life more enjoyable in the host country. They may also cover the expense of having the entire family learn the language of the host country.

Establishing a compensation plan for a job in a foreign location begins with the determination of base pay. The market or "going" rate of pay for a comparable job in the *home* country at the time of expatriation is normally used for setting this rate.

After setting base pay comes the determination of a *Foreign Service Premium* (FSP), which is an incentive bonus for performing the assignment in the *host* country. The FSP is usually expressed as a percentage of base pay and is part of the total pay received by the employee each pay period.

Some organizations are now granting expatriates lump-sum bonuses in lieu of FSPs. These lump-sum payments are made at the time of expatriation and repatriation.

In host areas where conditions (climatic, political, social) are undesirable, a "hardship" or "location" allowance is added to base pay. Most pay plans include a cost-equalization allowance that includes cost-of-living and housing allowances. The equalization allowance consists of the *difference* between the costs of food, other consumable items, services, and housing in the home country and the costs of those items in the host country. In some cases, the cost-of-living allowance (COLA) is tied to a change in the currency exchange rate between home country and host country. (It must be remembered that compensation *computations* are made in *home* country currency while actual *payments* are made in *host* country currency. This requires the use of some equivalency formula between home and host country currency.)

Many organizations also provide a tax equalization allowance. In computing such an allowance, the first step is to determine the hypothetical tax liabilities incurred by the employee. This is done by assuming that the employee is still working in the home country and receiving the established base pay (excluding all allowances and premiums for working in the foreign assignment) for a comparable job. Using the base pay and appropriate home base income tax rates, a hypothetical tax liability is established. Then the organization computes all tax liabilities (both those of the home and host countries) of the expatriate for all income earned on the job (base pay plus premiums plus all living cost adjustments). From these total tax liabilities, the hypothetical tax the expatriate would normally have paid on a comparable job in the home country is subtracted. This is the amount of tax burden assumed by the employer on the tax equalization allowance. Next to base pay and premiums, the tax equalization allowance until 1982 had been the highest cost incurred in sending an American to a foreign location. The tax burdens for Americans employed abroad was considerably lightened by the Economic Recovery Tax Act of 1981 which allowed the first $75,000 of their income to be excluded from taxation.

To minimize problems related to exchange of currency and to protect the employee, many organizations now "split" an expatriate's compensation between home country and host country compensation packages. A split-pay plan is one in which a certain amount of the total pay received by the expatriate is paid in home country currency and credited to a designated account in the home country. The expatriate receives the remaining pay in the host country in host country currency.

A procedure often used for determining the amount of the split that goes into the home country or domestic account and the amount that goes into the host country or foreign account takes this approach. First, a spendable income for the employee in the home country must be established. Spendable income is that amount of pay spent on goods, services, and housing. It represents total pay minus taxes (income and FICA), savings, investments, health and life insurance premiums, and any contributions made by the employee to benefit components.

Supplementing the spendable income are housing and cost-of-living allowances to ensure the expatriate the same standard of living in the host country as that enjoyed in the home country at the time of expatriation. These disposable income and living adjustment allowances are further supplemented during the period the expatriate is in the host country by the spendable portion of any pay increase granted and by any cost-of-living changes that occur (in the host country, using host country cost-of-living adjustment figures).

The domestic account consists of pay plus premiums minus spendable income and amount set aside for hypothetical income tax. It also includes that part of any pay adjustments (merit and general increases) granted to the individual or all employees of the organization not set aside for spendable income or additional tax liabilities.

Expatriate, TCNs, and Host Country Personnel Trade-offs

As already mentioned, from a labor cost point of view, the ideal approach is to have the foreign site completely operated by personnel who are natives or citizens of the host country. Even when desired, however, this is not always possible for the reasons already mentioned. When locals are not available, the choice is then between expatriates and TCNs.

In recent years, with rapidly increasing levels of knowledge and expanding technological skills among citizens of the industrialized nations, the TCNs have become more popular candidates for foreign assignments. In many cases, these TCNs reside in nearby countries (reducing relocation costs), and they are more fluent than expatriates in the local language. They are more familiar with social norms of the host country (reducing cost-of-living adjustments and additional costs incurred through unexpected resignations). Often, TCNs receive the same compensation that would be provided to a local, or a compensation package equivalent to what they would receive in their native countries.

Developing a Foreign Location Compensation Plan

Although it is normally necessary to tie expatriate compensation and, at times, that offered to TCNs, to that currently available at the home location, the total compensation plan should relate to accepted host country patterns as much as possible.

Base rates of pay should consider host country market requirements. Cost-of-living adjustments should relate to indexes developed and published in the host country. The total compensation package should integrate host country Social Security and pension programs into any benefits package offered.

In many nations, health plans, pension plans, and survivor insurance programs are far more liberal and costly to the employer than those in the United States. Before finalizing any compensation program for a foreign operation, it is imperative to identify all required and expected benefits, cost them, and integrate them with what the firm wishes to offer employees in its host country operation.

Finally, when formalizing a compensation plan, the employer must be extremely careful in translating the description of the plan and all of its components from English to the language of the host country. Many a costly and unacceptable slip can happen in the translation process. Following the translation, each component must be reviewed with a translator to ensure that the translated copy carries the same meaning the plan was originally designed to carry. The same care and consideration given to the design of a compensation program at the home base must be given to that of a foreign compensation plan. In addition, local economic, tax, and compensation requirements must be integrated into the final design of the compensation package.

SELECTED READINGS

Foote, Marion R., "Controlling the Cost of International Compensation," *Harvard Business Review,* November–December 1977, pp. 123–132. The incremental costs (those costs beyond base pay and bonus) incurred in sending expatriates to foreign operations consume 3.7 percent of the total corporate profit before taxes and 8.6 percent of the pre-tax profit contributions from international operations. The skyrocketing costs of sending expatriates and TCNs to foreign work sites are requiring international compensation managers to take a hard look at the compensation components offered and their value.

Gonik, Jacob, "Tie Salesmen's Bonuses to Their Forecasts," *Harvard Business Review,* May–June 1978, pp. 116–123. Compensating sales people according to how much of their quota they can achieve can be an effective motivator. This system takes into account unequal territories and provides payoff for good forecasting, actual results, and relationship to business objectives.

Johnson, M. C., "Should You Ask for A Raise?" *Industry Week,* June 14, 1976, pp.32–37. Although managers, especially those with a good record, should feel free to ask for a raise, a survey of managers reveals that few ask questions and even fewer (out of anxiety, intimidated by the company policy, etc.) ask questions concerning pay raises.

Kassen, M. Sami, "The Salary Compression Problem," *Personnel Journal,* April 1971, pp. 313–317. Each year, as new college graduates receive higher salaries for entry-level positions, the salary compression problem becomes more severe. In order to solve this problem, organizations should review and update their compensation programs, relate pay to performance, and set goals.

Kraus, David, "The 'Devaluation' of the American Executive," *Harvard Business Review,* May–June 1976, pp. 84–94. The changing relationships among executive, mid-level, and factory workers' pay are examined. Solutions for these problems are developed.

Miller, Ernest C., "Setting Supervisor's Pay and Pay Differentials," *Compensation Review,* Third Quarter 1978, pp. 13–27. An excellent discussion with sufficient examples that describe how organizations design the pay programs for their first- and second-level supervisors. For this group of employees, the author discusses pay structure design, overtime and shift differential programs, and bonus plans.

Sbarra, Robert A., "How to Meet the Compensation Needs of Middle Management," *Business Management,* January 1969, pp. 35, 40–42. Although over 10 years old, this article provides keen insight into the problems encountered when designing a compensation program for employees in the middle of the organization. Sbarra identifies typical problems and provides a number of suggestions that are useful today in developing a program that assists in establishing a motivating work place environment.

Steinbrink, John P., "How to Pay Your Sales Force," *Harvard Business Review,* July–August 1978, pp. 111–122. An examination of the 19th Biennial Survey of Compensation of Salesmen conducted by Dartnell Corp. reveals that each of the three basic types of compensation plans—salary, commission, and combination (salary plus commission)—have certain advantages and disadvantages. The author identifies these strengths and weaknesses and gives reasons for selecting each type of plan according to the needs of the business.

Teague, Burton W., "Extra Pay for Executive Culture Shock," *The Conference Board Record,* January 1975, pp. 18–27. The payment of foreign service premiums is still a commonly used bonus offered to employees willing to take foreign assignments. Premium pay varies by geographic area, with the size of premiums dependent upon the actual deprivation imposed by the work location. Some organizations distinguish between a premium for service abroad and an allowance for hardship.

Young, David, "Fair Compensation for Expatriates," *Harvard Business Review,* July–August 1973, pp. 117–126. Cultural dislocation, differing customs, and additional costs oblige employyers to adjust the pay of managers in foreign countries. The extensive additional costs incurred in sending an employee to a foreign work site are a sound investment when the right person is assigned to the job and the compensation is adequate and fair.

Action Words

The following words are valuable for precisely identifying and defining the functions of a job. Through the use of concise terminology, it is possible to minimize ambiguity or misunderstanding relative to what is being done. It is not a complete list, however, and job description writers may find other verbs to be more suitable.

Accept.   To receive as true; to regard as proper, normal, inevitable.

Account.   To give a report on; to furnish a justifying analysis or explanation.

Accumulate.   To collect; to gather.

Achieve.   To bring to a successful conclusion.

Acknowledge.   To report the receipt of.

Acquire.   To come into possession of.

Act.   To perform a specified function.

Activate.   To mobilize; to set into motion.

Adapt.   To suit or fit by modification.

Adjust.   To bring to a more satisfactory state; to bring the parts of something to a true or more effective position.

Administer.   To manage or direct the execution of affairs.

Adopt.   To take up and practice as one's own.

Advise.   To recommend a course of action; to offer an informed opinion based on specialized knowledge.

Advocate.   To recommend or speak in favor of.

Affirm.   To assert positively; to confirm.

Align.   To arrange in a line; to array.

Allot.   To assign as a share.

Alter.   To make different without changing into something else.

Amend.   To change or modify for the better.

Analyze.   To separate into elements and critically examine.

Answer.   To speak or write in reply.

Anticipate.   To foresee and deal with in advance.

Apply.   To put to use for a purpose; to employ diligently or with close attention.

Appoint.   To name officially.

Appraise.   To give an expert judgment of worth or merit.

Approve.   To accept as satisfactory; to exercise final authority with regard to commitment of resources.

Arrange.   To prepare for an event; to put in proper order.

Ascertain.   To find out or discover through examination. To find out or learn for a certainty.

Assemble.   To collect or gather together in a predetermined order from various sources.

Assess.   To determine value of; to evaluate.

Assign.   To specify or designate tasks or duties to be performed by others.

Assist.   To help or aid others in the performance of work.

Assume.   To undertake; to take for granted.

Assure.   To give confidence; to make certain of.

Attach.   To connect; to bind or affix to.

Attain.   To come into possession of; to arrive at.

Attend.   To be present.

Audit.   To examine officially with intent to verify.

Authorize.   To approve; to empower through vested authority.

Award.   To confer or bestow.

Balance.   To compute the difference between the debits and credits of an account; to reconcile accounts.

Batch.   To assemble into a group for one operation.

Budget.   To plan expenditures.

Build.   To construct.

Calculate.   To make a mathematical computation.

Call.   To communicate with by telephone; to summon; to announce.

Cancel.   To mark out; invalidate. (Printing – to delete.)

Certify.   To confirm as accurate or true.

Chart.   To draw or plot data (as on a graph). To make a detailed plan.

Check.   To verify; to compare with a source.

Circulate.   To pass from person to person or place to place.

Clarify.   To make easier to understand; to explain.

Classify.   To arrange or organize according to systematic groups, classes, or categories.

Clear.   To gain approval of others; to free from obstruction; to authorize; to get rid of.

Close.   To bring to a conclusion; to bar passage; to shut; to suspend or stop operations.

Code.   To use symbols (letters or numbers) to represent words.

Collaborate.   To work jointly with; to cooperate with others.

Collate.   To organize or assemble in a predetermined sequence.

Collect.   To gather.

Communicate.   To impart a verbal or written message; to transmit information.

Compare.   To examine for the purpose of discovering resemblances or differences.

Compile.   To put together information; to collect from other documents.

Complete.   To finish; to fully carry out.

Comply.   To act in accordance with rules, requests.

Compose.   To make by putting parts together; to create; to write (an original letter, report, instructions, etc.).

Compute.   To determine or calculate mathematically.

Concur.   To agree with a position, statement, action, or opinion.

Condense.   To make more compact.

Conduct.   To carry on; to direct the execution of.

Confer.   To compare views; to consult.

Confirm.   To give approval to; to assure the validity of.

Consolidate.   To bring together.

Construct.   To make or form by combining parts; to draw with suitable instruments and under specified conditions.

Consult.   To seek advice of others; to give professional advice or services.

Contact.   To communicate with.

Contribute.   To supply or give something; to submit for publication.

Control.   To measure, interpret, and evaluate actions for conformance with plans or desired results.

Convert.   To alter the physical or chemical nature of something; to alter for more effective utilization.

Convey.   To move from one place to another; to transport; to communicate.

Convince.   To persuade; to cause others to believe something, using evidence and/or argument.

Coordinate.   To regulate, adjust, or combine the actions of others to attain harmony.

Copy.   To duplicate an original.

Correct.   To make or set right; to alter or adjust to conform to a standard.

Correlate.   To establish or demonstrate a causal, complementary, parallel, or reciprocal relation.

Correspond.   To communicate with.

Counsel.   To advise; to consult with.

Create. To bring into existence; to produce through imaginative skill.

Debug. To detect, locate, and remove mistakes from a routine of malfunctions from a computer.

Decide. To arrive at a solution; to bring to a definitive end.

Delegate. To commission another to perform tasks or duties which may carry specific degrees of accountability and authority.

Delete. To strike out or remove.

Deliver. To set free; to convey; to send to an intended destination.

Demonstrate. To illustrate and explain, especially with examples.

Describe. To represent by a figure, model, or picture; to trace the outline of; to give an account of in words.

Design. To conceive, create, and execute according to plan.

Determine. To resolve; to fix conclusively or authoritatively.

Develop. To disclose, discover, perfect, or unfold a plan or idea.

Devise. To form in the mind by new combinations or applications of ideas or principles; to invent.

Dictate. To read or speak information to be recorded or written by another.

Direct. To guide work operations through the establishment of objectives, policies, rules, practices, methods, and standards.

Discipline. To penalize individuals or groups whose behavior is contrary to established rules and regulations.

Discuss. To exchange views for the purpose of arriving at a conclusion.

Dispatch. To send off, or forward, to known destination or on specific business.

Display. To show; to spread before the view.

Dispose. To sell or get rid of.

Disseminate. To spread or disperse information or ideas.

Distribute. To deliver to proper destination.

Divert. To turn from one course or use to another.

Draft. To prepare papers or documents in preliminary form.

Draw. To compose or write up, following a set procedure or form (as in a contract). To pull or move something.

Edit. To revise and prepare material (written, film, tape, sound track) for publication or display.

Elaborate. To work out in detail; to give details.

Elect. To choose or select carefully.

Eliminate. To get rid of; to set aside as unimportant.

Employ. To make use of; to use or engage the services of; to provide with a job that pays wages or a salary.

Encourage. To inspire with spirit, hope; to give help or patronage to.

Endorse.   To support or recommend.

Engage.   To interlock with; to mesh; to provide occupation for; to arrange to obtain the use or services of.

Enlist.   To engage for duty; to secure the support and aid of.

Ensure.   To make sure, certain, or safe; to guarantee.

Establish.   To bring into existence.

Estimate.   To forecast future requirements.

Evaluate.   To determine or fix the value of.

Examine.   To inspect closely.

Exchange.   To give or take one thing in return for another.

Exclude.   To shut out; to bar from participation, consideration, or inclusion.

Execute.   To put into effect; to carry out.

Exercise.   To exert influence; to train by drills and maneuvers; to use repeatedly in order to strengthen and develop.

Expedite.   To accelerate the process or progress of.

Extend.   To total columns. (Bookkeeping term)

Extract.   To draw forth; to withdraw; to separate; to determine by calculation.

Facilitate.   To make easier.

Feed.   To move into a machine or opening in order to be used or processed; to furnish with something essential for growth, sustenance, maintenance, or operation.

File.   To arrange in a methodical manner; to rub smooth or cut away with a tool.

Finalize.   To put in finished form.

Find.   To encounter; to come upon by searching or effort.

Follow up.   To pursue closely in order to check progress.

Forecast.   To predict; to estimate in advance.

Formulate.   To develop or devise.

Foster.   To promote the growth or development of.

Function.   To act or operate as. To serve.

Furnish.   To provide what is needed; to supply.

Gather.   To collect; to harvest; to accumulate and place in order.

Generate.   To bring into existence; to originate by a vital or chemical process.

Govern.   To exercise continuous sovereign authority over; to control and direct the making and administration of authority over; to hold in check; to have decisive influence.

Guarantee.   To secure; to answer for the debt, default, or miscarriage of.

Guide.   To show or lead the way to; to manage the affairs of; to influence the conduct or opinions of.

Help.   To be of use to; to relieve; to remedy; to serve.

Hire.   To engage the service of for a set sum.

Identify. To establish the identity of; to associate with some interest.

Implement. To carry out; to execute a plan or program.

Import. To bring from a foreign or external source.

Improve. To make something better.

Indicate. To show, demonstrate with precision.

Inform. To communicate information to.

Initiate. To start; to introduce; to originate.

Innovate. To exercise creativity in introducing something new or in making changes.

Insert. To put (something) into, between, or among other materials.

Inspect. To examine or determine; to critically analyze for suitability.

Install. To place in office; to establish in an indicated place, condition, or status; to set up for use in office.

Institute. To establish in a position or office; to originate.

Instruct. To teach; to coach; to communicate knowledge; to direct or order.

Integrate. To unify; to make whole by putting all parts or elements together.

Interpret. To give the meaning of; to explain to others.

Interview. To obtain facts or opinions through inquiry or examination or various sources.

Invent. To think up or imagine; to create.

Inventory. To catalog or to count and list.

Invest. To spend or use time, money, or effort to achieve a future benefit.

Investigate. To observe or study by close examination and systematic inquiry.

Issue. To put forth or to distribute officially.

Itemize. To list; to write down in detail.

Join. To put or bring together.

Justify. To prove or show to be right or reasonable; also, to align words such that both left- and right-hand margins are in line (typing term).

Keep. To hold or retain; to maintain.

Lead. To guide or direct on a course or in the direction of; to channel; to direct the operations of.

Lend. To give for temporary use on condition that the same or its equivalent be returned.

Let. To allow; to rent or lease; to assign, especially after bids.

List. To enumerate; to enter into a catalog with a selling price.

Load. To place in or on a means of conveyance; to increase the weight of by adding something heavy.

Locate. To find, determine, or specify by means of searching, examining, or experimenting. (To seek and find.)

Look up.   To search for and find.

Maintain.   To continue; carry on; or keep in an existing state.

Make.   To cause to happen to; to cause to exist, occur, or appear; to create; to bring into being by forming, shaping, or altering material.

Manage.   To handle, control; to alter by manipulation; to succeed in accomplishing.

Map.   To make a survey of for the purpose of representing; to plan in detail.

Market.   To expose for sale; to sell.

Match.   To set in competition with; to provide with a worthy competitor; to cause to correspond.

Mediate.   To interpose with parties to reconcile them; to reconcile differences.

Merge.   To combine items from two or more similarly ordered sets into one set that is arranged in the same order.

Model.   To teach by personal example; to instruct by demonstration.

Modify.   To make less extreme; to limit or restrict the meaning of; to make minor changes in.

Monitor.   To watch, observe, to check for a specific purpose.

Motivate.   To arouse or stimulate to action.

Move.   To go from one point to another; to begin operating or functioning or working in a usual way.

Name.   To nominate; to speak about.

Negate.   To deny the existence or truth of; to cause to be ineffective or invalid.

Negotiate.   To confer with others with a view to reaching agreement.

Neutralize.   To destroy the effectiveness of; to nullify.

Notify.   To make known.

Nullify.   To make of no value or consequence; to cancel out.

Observe.   To see, notice, or watch something or someone.

Obtain.   To acquire or gain possession of.

Occupy.   To take possession of; to fill.

Omit.   To leave out; to disregard.

Open.   To make available for entry or passage; to make accessible; to expose to view; to disclose.

Operate.   To perform an activity or series of activities.

Oppose.   To resist; to withstand; to place opposite or against.

Organize.   To arrange; to systematize or methodize.

Orient.   To cause to become aware of, familiar with, or adjusted to facts, principles, procedures, or situations.

Originate.   To create; invent.

Oversee.   To watch; to superintend, supervise.

Participate. To take part in.

Perform. To fulfill or carry out some action.

Permit. To consent to; to authorize; to make possible.

Persuade. To move by argument or entreaty to a belief, position, or course of action.

Pinpoint. To locate or aim with great precision or accuracy; to cause to stand out conspicuously.

Place. To locate and choose positions for.

Plan. To devise or project the realization or achievement of a course of action.

Post. To record information in ledgers or other forms from another source.

Practice. To perform or work at repeatedly in order to gain proficiency.

Predict. To declare in advance; to foretell on the basis of observation, experience, or scientific reason.

Prepare. To make ready for a particular purpose.

Prescribe. To establish as a rule or guide.

Present. To introduce; to bestow; to lay as a charge before the court; to offer to view.

Preserve. To keep, guard, observe; to keep safe, protect; to keep free from decay; to maintain.

Prevent. To stop something from occurring; to take advance measures against.

Price. To fix, to establish, or to find out the value of.

Proceed. To begin to carry out an action.

Process. To subject to some special treatment; to handle in accordance with a prescribed procedure,

Procure. To obtain possession of; to bring about.

Produce. To grow; to make, bear, or yield something; to offer to view or notice; to exhibit.

Program. To arrange or work out a sequence of operations to be performed.

Project. To throw forward; to present for consideration; to communicate vividly, especially to an audience.

Promote. To advance to a higher level or position.

Propose. To form or declare a plan or intention.

Provide. To supply what is needed.

Pull. To haul, tow; to remove, as in filing.

Purchase. To buy or procure by committing organizational funds.

Qualify. To moderate; to alter the strength or flavor of; to limit or modify the meaning of.

Quantify. To make explicit the logical amount of; to determine or express the amount of.

Question. To interrogate; to doubt; to dispute; to inquire.

Rate. To assess the value of; to appraise; to arrange in sequence of rank.

Read.   To interpret; to scan; to study the movements of; to understand the meaning of; to utter aloud the printed written words of.

Receive.   To acquire, come into possession of.

Recommend.   To advise or counsel a course of action; to offer or suggest for adoption.

Reconcile.   To adjust; to restore to harmony; to make congruous.

Reconstruct.   To rebuild; to reorganize or reestablish.

Record.   To register; to set down in writing.

Recruit.   To seek out others to become new members or personnel.

Rectify.   To correct by calculation or adjustment; to remedy; to set right.

Reduce.   To narrow down; to diminish in size or amount; to abridge; to lower in grade or rank.

Refer.   To send or direct for aid, treatment, information, or decision; to direct attention; to make reference to.

Refine.   To improve or perfect; to free from impurities.

Register.   To enter in a record.

Reinforce.   To strengthen with additional forces or additions.

Reject.   To refuse to have, use, or take for some purpose; to refuse to hear, receive, or admit.

Release.   To set free as in releasing information; to permit the publication or dissemination of.

Remit.   To send money in payment of; to submit or refer for consideration, judgment, decision, or action.

Remove.   To change the location, station or residence of; to dismiss from office.

Render.   To furnish an opinion; to answer.

Represent.   To act in the place of or for.

Report.   To give an account of; to furnish information or data.

Requisition.   To ask in writing for something that is needed.

Rescind.   To make void; to repeal; to abrogate a contract by restoring preexisting conditions.

Research.   To inquire specifically, using involved and critical investigations.

Respond.   To make an answer; to show favorable reaction.

Restrict.   To confine within bounds; to restrain.

Retrieve.   To regain; to rescue.

Review.   To consider; to reexamine.

Revise.   To rework in order to correct or improve; to make a new, improved, or up-to-date version.

Route.   To forward; to schedule or dispatch.

Salvage.   To rescue or save (as from wreckage or ruin).

Satisfy. To carry out the terms of (a contract); to meet financial obligations; to make reparation to; to please.

Scan. To examine; to search a series of punched cards, tapes, or a memory bank to locate specific data (computer usage).

Schedule. To plan a timetable; to fix time.

Screen. To examine in orderly fashion to determine suitability or acceptability (as in appraising potential employees); to cull.

Search. To examine; to probe; to make a thorough examination or investigation of.

Secure. To gain possession of; to guarantee; to make safe.

Select. To choose the best suited.

Sell. To give up property to another for money or other valuable consideration.

Send. To dispatch by a means of communication; to convey.

Serve. To assist; to be of use; to hold office.

Service. To adjust; to repair or maintain.

Sign. To formally approve a document by affixing a signature.

Simplify. To clarify; to reduce to basic essentials.

Solicit. To approach with a request or plea; to strongly urge.

Solve. To find a solution for.

Sort. To separate or arrange according to a scheme. To rank by kind, class, division, etc.

Specify. To state precisely in detail or to name explicitly.

Spend. To use up or pay out.

Standardize. To bring into conformity to something established by authority, custom, or general consent as a model or criterion.

Stimulate. To excite to activity; to urge.

Structure. To give arrangement or form to; to arrange or organize.

Study. To contemplate; to carefully examine or investigate; to deliberate.

Submit. To present data for the discretion or judgment of others.

Summarize. To restate material (facts, figures, etc.) briefly.

Supervise. To personally oversee, direct, inspect, or guide the work of others with responsibility for meeting with certain standards of performance.

Supplement. To add to.

Supply. To furnish something that is needed; to provide; to equip.

Survey. To examine as to condition, situation, or value.

Synthesize. To form new product by combining different elements.

Systematize. To arrange methodically.

Tabulate. To put in table form; to set up in columns, rows.

Take. To assume possession of; to grasp; to gain approval of; to undertake or perform.

Tend.   To act as an attendant.

Tender.   To present for acceptance.

Test.   To put to proof; to examine, observe, or evaluate critically.

Total.   To add up; to compute.

Trace.   To locate something by searching or researching evidence.

Trade.   To give in exchange for another commodity; to make a purchase.

Train.   To teach, demonstrate, or guide others in order to bring up to a predetermined standard.

Transact.   To carry on business; to negotiate.

Transcribe.   To transfer data from one form of record to another or from one method of preparation to another, without changing the nature of data.

Translate.   To turn into one's own or another language.

Transmit.   To transfer or send from one person or place to another; to send out a signal either by radio waves or over a wire.

Turn.   To make rotate or revolve; to cause to move around so as to effect a desired end (as locking, opening, shutting); to reverse the sides or surfaces of.

Type.   To write using a typewriter; to arrange by categories.

Uncover.   To expose to view by removing a covering; to reveal.

Understand.   To grasp the meaning of; to have thorough or technical acquaintance with or expertness in the practice of.

Update.   To bring current.

Utilize.   To make use of.

Verify.   To confirm or establish authenticity; to substantiate.

Weigh.   To ascertain the heaviness of; to consider carefully.

Withhold.   To hold back; to refrain from granting, giving, or allowing.

Withstand.   To stand up against; to resist successfully.

Write.   To set down letters, words, sentences, or figures on paper or other suitable material; to author; to draft.

Glossary of Terms

Compensation specialists frequently must use the words and terms in this glossary in performing their assignments. To facilitate its use, it has been divided into three major sections:

1. Compensation administration.

2. Data processing.

3. Industrial engineering.

COMPENSATION ADMINISTRATION

Accountability.   A term used in job analysis to denote the end results to be achieved by the employee.

Across-the-board increase.   An increase in wages given to the majority of workers. Sometimes known as a general increase.

Actual hours.   The actual number of hours worked in a period by an employee.

Actuarially sound.   A pension fund is considered "actuarially sound" when the amount in the fund and the current levels of contributions to the fund are sufficient, on the basis of assumptions made concerning interest and other factors, to meet the liabilities already accrued and accruing.

Actuary (pensions and insurance).   A person trained in mathematics, statistics, and legal-accounting methods, and the sound principles of operation of insurance, annuities, and pension plans.

Administration.   Commonly used term indicating the top levels of management in industry and business, or its functions. Occasionally used in an opposite sense to mean the routines of lower management levels.

523

Administrator (pension). The trustee of a jointly administered labor management pension (for purposes of the Federal Disclosure Act). In its usual meaning, it denotes the person or organization that performs the routine clerical operations of the plan.

Aggregate funding method. A method of accumulating money for future payment of pensions whereby the actuary determines the present value of all future benefit payments, deducts from this value whatever funds may be on hand with the insurance company or trustee, and distributes the cost of the balance over the future on a reasonable basis.

Agreement increase. An increase in pay given to all workers or to a majority of workers as a result of contract negotiations.

Amortization. Paying off an interest-bearing liability through a series of installment payments.

Annualize rate. Transforming an investment rate of return for a period greater than or less than one year to a rate in terms of 12 months.

Annuity. Periodic payments made to a pensioner over a fixed period of time or until his death. *To purchase an annuity* means to pay over a lump sum or make periodic payments to an insurance company. In return, the insurance company guarantees to provide certain periodic payments to the participant as long as he lives beyond the first due date of the annuity.

Annuity, joint and survivor. An annuity payable as long as the pensioner lives and continued either in whole or in part after his death to a named survivor or contingent annuitant, if living, until the latter's death. Also called *contingent annuity.*

Annuity, modified refund. An arrangement commonly used under a contributory pension plan. If an employee dies after retirement, his beneficiary or estate will receive a sum equal to the accumulated value of his own contributions to the pension fund, with or without interest up to his retirement date, less the total retirement benefits he received prior to his death.

Approved pension plans. Those plans that qualify for certain tax exemptions under provisions of the Internal Revenue Code and regulations of the Commissioner of Internal Revenue.

Authority. (1) The right to take independent action. (2) The right to direct the actions of others. As applied to functional or staff authority, it is the right to direct another unit of the organization *only* with regard to the functional specialty of the directing party.

Automatic wage adjustment. Automatically increasing or decreasing wages in accordance with some specific plan.

Automatic wage progression. Automatically increasing wages after specified periods of service (also *length-of-service increases*).

Automation. A combination of several machines or other automatic devices performing a coordinated sequence of operations.

Average earned rate. An hourly rate arrived at by dividing hours worked into the equivalent earnings paid for a calendar quarter for use in the next quarter. Excludes overtime bonuses and other payments not considered to be earnings.

Average hourly earnings. Hourly pay determined by dividing hours worked per period into the total wages paid for the period.

Average straight-time hourly earnings.   Hourly pay determined by dividing the hours worked per period into the total straight-time earnings for the period (excluding overtime).

Balance sheet.   An organization's financial statement showing assets, liabilities, and capital on a given date.

Base wage rate or base rate.   The hourly money rate paid for a job performed at standard pace. Does not include shift differentials, overtime, or incentive premiums.

Benchmark.   A standard with characteristics so detailed that other classifications can be compared as being above, below, or comparable to it.

Beneficiary.   A person named to receive benefits from an insurance policy, pension plan, will, or other source.

Blue-collar workers.   These include skilled, semiskilled craftworkers, and unskilled laborers, and their immediate supervisors, who are usually paid on an hourly basis.

Board.   A committee of considerable rank or importance in an organization (e.g., board of directors or executive board).

Board of directors.   A governing body of a corporation that is elected by stockholders to represent them.

Bona fide occupational qualification (BFOQ).   The phrase used in Title VII of the Civil Rights Act of 1964 to allow an exception to the equal employment law. BFOQ exceptions are rare and do not include race or color.

Bonus earnings or bonus.   Extra compensation in addition to regular wages. See text for further explanation.

Bootleg wages.   Wages above market rate that an employer must pay in a tight labor market to attract and hold skilled workers.

Budget.   A definite plan for sales, output, and expenditures that imposes goals and limitations on various activities of an organization or an individual.

Call-back pay.   Payment given to an employee who is called back to work after his regular working hours.

Call-in pay.   Guaranteed pay for workers who report to work at the usual time and for whom there is no work.

Cash.   Ready money; payment for goods or services in money.

Cash equivalents.   Payments easily and quickly converted to money.

Centralized.   The condition in which a firm is organized so most authority for planning and decisions is retained by top management.

Check-off.   The deduction of union dues or assessments from employees' pay for the purpose of turning them over to the union.

Chief.   The head of an activity. In an organization, it is usually coupled with the name of a department or activity (e.g., chief engineer).

Class of positions.   A group of positions, regardless of location, that are alike enough in duties and responsibilities to be called by the same descriptive title, to be given the same pay scale under similar conditions, and to require substantially the same qualifications.

Class-series. A grouping of job classes, regardless of location, having similar job content but differing in levels of skill, responsibility, knowledge, and qualification requirements.

Commission. A form of compensation for the sale of products or services; usually an amount figured as a percentage of the sale.

Committee. A group that meets as a body or through communication, usually in an advisory capacity. Some high-ranking committees have authority to direct action.

Communication. Generally refers to the transmittal of thoughts, ideas, instructions, orders, etc., from one person to another. Within an organization, it often applies particularly to relations between superior and subordinate.

Comparable worth. The concept of measuring a job's value to the firm. This value is important to determine rates of pay for jobs having dissimilar job content and making different requirements on the jobholder.

Compa-ratio. The ratio showing the relationship of total actual pay in a pay grade to the midpoint of that pay grade. A ratio of 1.0 normally indicates adequate distribution of employees in that grade.

Compensable factors. Elements that describe and differentiate among jobs. Used to analyze jobs to develop their worth to the organization.

Compensatory time off. Time off given in lieu of overtime. Under the Fair Labor Standards Act, it must be given in the same workweek.

Conglomerate. A large collection of enterprises, often dissimilar, combined by merger or purchase by a parent or holding company.

Constant. A fixed or invariable value or data item.

Consumer Price Index. A listing of price changes in a selected list of products and services in representative cities that is prepared by the Bureau of Labor Statistics. Sometimes mistakenly called the "cost-of-living index."

Consideration. A legal term meaning the compensation to be realized by a party to a contract for performing contract provisions.

Contingent annuity. *See* Annuity, joint and survivor.

Contributory pension plan. A pension plan in which the employee contributes part of the cost.

Control. In management, the function of seeing that policies and plans are carried out. Can be a specialized activity, e.g., production control, inventory control.

Controller. An executive who is responsible for accounting and the control of expenditures. (Also, *comptroller.*)

Corporation. A business that exists by charter from a government, is owned by stockholders, and is subject to control by those who possess the majority of voting shares.

Cost-of-living adjustment (COLA). Pay adjustments devised to bring wages and salaries in line with changes in the cost of living. Generally based on changes in price indexes published by the Bureau of Labor Statistics.

Cost-of-living index. A measure of the average changes in the cost of goods purchased by consumers against the cost during some base period.

Coverage. The number of jobs or the number of personnel whose jobs have been assigned a standard during the reporting period.

Criterion. A standard or measure used to appraise an employee's job proficiency or effectiveness.

Death benefit. Amount paid or payable to the beneficiary of a pension plan or insurance policy on the death of the employee or insured.

Decentralized. The condition in which authority, responsibility, facilities, or work are dispersed among several units or locations.

Deferred full vesting. A plan in which the employee retains a right to all accrued benefits of a pension plan if he is terminated after he reaches a certain age and/or after he completes a certain period of service or participation in the plan.

Deferred graded vesting. A plan in which the worker acquires a right to a certain percentage of accrued benefits of a pension plan when he meets the requirements set down in the plan.

Department. An individual or a group that operates as a distinctly separate unit, usually one of considerable size or importance.

Direct labor. Labor performed on a product that advances it toward its ultimate specifications.

Director. (1) A member of the board of directors. (2) Title given to the head of an important activity, e.g., personnel director.

Disassemble. To separate two mating parts.

Discount. A selling price below an established price.

Discount stock option. Rights to a stock option at a price less than 100 percent of fair market value.

Dividend. A proportion of a business' net earnings paid to its stockholders.

Division of labor. In general, the assignment of tasks or responsibilities to an individual or a group within an organization. Often applies to dividing work into relatively small tasks among individuals, as in mass production.

Document. Any record that has permanence and that can be read by man or machine.

Downgrading. The demotion of an employee to a lower-rated job.

Earnings. Total wages of compensation received by an employee for time worked or services rendered (includes all compensation, overtime, premium pay, etc.).

Earnings per share. Net income less preferred dividends divided by share of common stock outstanding.

Effort. The will to perform productive work, either mental or manual.

Efficiency. (1) In an energy-consuming apparatus or process, the ratio, output/input, expressed as a percentage or a decimal. (2) A ratio that compares actual performance with a standard, as in performance rating.

Employee benefits. Tangible compensation given to employees other than wages.

Employee stock ownership plan (ESOP). A stock bonus plan that allows employers to take advantage of certain tax privileges while encouraging employee ownership of the company by granting stock to employees.

Environment.   The external conditions affecting an individual or a group.

Equal pay for equal work.   The principle that regardless of age, sex, color, or religion, an individual should be paid the same wage for the same type of work.

Equities.   Ownership of property.

Equity funding.   The funding of a portion of a retirement plan by investment in equities. It affects the employer's contributions but not the employee's benefits.

Escalator clause.   Provision in a labor agreement for making wage adjustments upward or downward in accordance with cost-of-living fluctuations.

Exempt employees.   Executive, professional, and administrative employees and others who perform specific duties, earn above a specified minimum and are exempt from the overtime pay requirements of the Fair Labor Standards Act.

Exercise price.   The price at which a seller must sell a share of stock at a given time to a specific purchaser.

Factor comparison.   A job evaluation plan in which relative values for each of a number of factors of a job are established by direct comparison with the values established for the same factors on selected or key jobs.

Factor Evaluation System (FES).   A method developed by the U.S. Civil Service Commission (now Office of Personnel Management) to evaluate and classify positions. Nine well-defined factors, with multiple levels in each factor, are basis for the position analysis.

Factory manager.   Head of a manufacturing division or plant of an enterprise.

Fair day's work.   The amount of work performed by an operator or group of operators that is fair to both the company and the operator, considering wages paid.

Family.   The grouping of two or more class-series in an organization that have related or common work content.

Fiduciary.   Any person who (1) exercises any discretionary authority or control over the management of a plan or the management or disposition of its assets, (2) renders investment advice for a fee with respect to the funds or property of a plan, or has the authority to do so, or (3) has any discretionary authority or responsibility in the administration of a plan.

First-line supervisor.   The manager closest to nonsupervisory employees in the organization's hierarchy. Also called front-line supervisor.

Fixed benefit retirement plan.   A type of plan providing retirement benefits in a fixed amount or at a fixed percentage.

Flat-benefit plan.   A plan providing benefits unrelated to earnings. For example, a certain amount per month per year of service.

Foreman.   Head of a department in a factory.

Finge benefits.   *See* employee benefits.

Function.   (1) In industrial operations, an activity performed by a machine, an individual, or a group, (2) a specific purpose of an entity or its characteristic action in communications, (3) a machine action such as a carriage return or line feed.

Functional.   A classification of an activity.

Fund. Money and investments held in trust, or share of insurance company assets for payment of pension benefits. (Verb: to accumulate money necessary to pay off a pension benefit.)

Funding method. Manner of accumulating money for future payment of pensions.

Garnishment. A legal action whereby a portion of an employee's wages are attached by a creditor to pay a debt.

General foreman. A foreman in charge of several activities in a factory and to whom subordinate foremen may be responsible. A superintendent.

Golden handcuffs. Compensation components earned over a period of time that assist in retaining an employee.

Golden umbrella. Compensation components payable to an employee upon dissolution of the organization or termination of the job.

Goods. The tangible products of the economic system that can satisfy human wants or desires.

Green-circle rate. Rate of pay less than the minimum for that pay grade.

Group annuity. A type of pension plan designed by insurance companies for a group of persons, usually employees of a single employer, covering all qualifying persons under one contract for the benefit of the members of the group.

Group bonus. A bonus payment based on the performance of a group of workers operating as a unit.

Group permanent insurance (pensions). A retirement plan that usually combines life insurance with retirement benefits and uses the level premium method, under a contract between the employer and the insurance company.

Guaranteed annual wage. A plan that guarantees a minimum income to employees annually.

Guaranteed wage rate. The rate of pay an employer guarantees to his employees on incentive work.

Halo effect. The tendency of one factor to influence the rating of other factors in job evaluation and in personnel rating.

Health maintenance organization (HMO). An independently or federally funded organization that provides comprehensive health care service at a fixed monthly fee for a specified group of members.

Heredity. A psychological or physiological factor that establishes the inherited traits, characteristics, or tendencies of the individual.

Human factors. The physical, mental, and emotional constraints that affect operator performance.

Human resources. All employees of an organization.

Human resource accounting. An approach to placing a dollar value on the organization's employees and its customer goodwill. (Also called human asset accounting.)

Immediate full vesting. A provision that entitles employees to all the retirement income that has been accrued by employee on company contributions during their years of service with the company.

In-basket exercise. A specific type of work sample test often used in managerial selection. Individual is given "basket" of work to respond to, using all possible resources.

Incentive. A reward, financial or otherwise, that compensates the worker for high and/or continued performance above standard. Also, a motivating influence to induce effort above normal (wage incentive).

Incentive stock option. A stock option defined in the Economic Recovery Tax Act of 1981 that is similar to a restricted stock option.

Indirect labor. Labor that is necessary to support the manufacture of a product but does not directly enter into transforming the material into the product.

Individual contract pension trust. A pension plan under which a trust is created to buy and hold title to individual insurance or annuity contracts for those covered under the plan. The trust receives the premium payments from the employer and transmits them to the insurance company, receiving in turn the individual policies.

Inflation. A phase of a business cycle characterized by abnormally high prices and a decrease in the purchasing power of money.

Insured plan. A plan funded with a life insurance company. The life insurance company guarantees the payment of annuities purchased.

Job. A collection of responsibilities and duties that, considered as a whole, constitute the established assignment to one or more individuals.

Job analysis. The process of carefully observing and appraising a job and then recording the details of the work so that it can be evaluated. (Also referred to as *job study.*)

Job bidding. Method of allowing employees to bid for (apply for) job vacancies. (Also called job posting and bidding.)

Job description. A summary of the most important features of a job in terms of the general nature of the work involved and the types of workers required to perform it efficiently. It describes the job, not the individual who fills it.

Job duties. A group of employee work activities or tasks which, taken together, describe a major purpose (i.e., responsibility) of that job.

Job evaluation. A procedure for determining the relative worth of various work assignments.

Job responsibility. A major purpose or end result of an employee's work activity; one of the primary reasons for the job's existence.

Job specification. Normally that part of the job description that includes the requisite qualifications of the jobholder. Frequently called *man specification.*

Keogh Plan. A retirement plan designed for self-employed individuals and their employees. (Also referred to as H.R. 10 Plan.)

Key class. Selected occupations about which data may be gathered from other employers to provide the basis for setting pay.

Key-man insurance. A health and/or life insurance policy taken out on essential employees, usually to benefit the employer and compensate for employee's lost services.

Learning curve. A graphic presentation of the progress in production effectiveness as time passes.

Level annual premium funding method. A method of accumulating money for payment of future pensions under which the level annual charge for a particular benefit is determined by the actuary for each age of entry, and is payable each year until retirement so that at that time the benefit is fully funded.

Life expectancy. The average number of years an individual of any given age may be expected to live, based on averages obtained from a mortality table.

Line. Employees directly involved in producing and/or selling the products or services of the organization. Compare line vs. staff.

Management by exception. Confining an executive's attention to matters commensurate with his rank and ability. Accomplished by delegation of authority and detail responsibility to subordinates.

Management by objectives (MBO). A formal planning, operations, and control program in which supervisor and subordinate mutually discuss and agree on the achievement of certain desired results and in which the performance of the subordinate is measured by the relationship between goals set and results achieved.

Manager. A person engaged in management functions. A title usually applied to a position of considerable rank and often coupled with an adjective or phrase to define areas of responsibility (e.g., factory manager, sales manager).

Man specification. *See* job specifications.

Manning tables. Classifications of all employees by job, age, sex, skill, experience, etc., to provide information concerning manpower requirements.

Market price. The last-reported price at which a security (stock or bond) is sold.

Mechanization. In industry, the use of machines to perform labor.

Median. The middle value in a distribution, with an equal number of values above and below it. An important statistic in evaluating groups of salary figures.

Merit increase. A wage increase granted because of the individual worker's merit.

Merit rating. A method for appraising the worth of an employee with respect to his job. Serves as a basis for pay rating, promotion, or reassignment of work.

Method. A term used to signify the technique used for performing an operation.

Midpoint. The salary midway between the minimum and maximum of a pay range.

Modified refund annuity. *See* annuity, modified refund.

Money-purchase benefit formula. A type of plan under which contributions of both the employer and the employee are fixed as flat amounts or flat percentages of the employee's salary. Either at retirement, or as contributions are paid, a benefit is provided for the employee of whatever amount the accumulated contributions, or current contributions, for him will produce according to the premium or actuarial tables adopted.

Mortality experience. The rate at which participants in a pension plan have died or are assumed to die. Also, the financial effect of the actual deaths that have occurred on the operation of a plan.

Mortality table. A listing of the mortality experience of individuals by age. A mortality table permits the actuary to calculate, on the average, how long a male or female of a given age may be expected to live.

Mutual rating. The rating of each person by everyone in his immediate working group.

Noncontributory pension plan. A plan in which the employer pays the entire cost of the premiums or of building up a fund from which pensions are paid.

Nonexempt employees. Workers subject to the provisions of the Fair Labor Standards Act.

Nonfinancial incentive. Any incentive to reward increased productivity other than monetary remuneration.

Occupation. A generalized job common to any industries and areas.

Office manager. Head of office activities. Often applies to management of the general office handling stenographic and clerical work.

Option. An agreement or privilege which conveys the right to buy or sell a specific property (security) at a stipulated price in a stated time period.

Ordinary life pension trust. A trust-funded pension plan that provides death benefits through the purchase of ordinary or whole life insurance contracts for covered employees. The trust pays premiums on the insurance coverage until the employee reaches retirement age. The trust also accumulates, in an auxiliary fund, the additional sums necessary to purchase the retirement benefits of the plan for the employees, using the paid-up cash value of the life insurance policy for each employee as part of the purchase price of the annuity.

Organization. (1) A systematically grouped body of individuals assembled for the accomplishment of a common objective. (2) The process of arranging units of the group and assigning responsibilities to each.

Organization chart. A diagram depicting an organization's structure including the names of the units, titles and names of individuals, their relative ranks, and interrelationships as to authority and responsibility.

Organization structure. The relative rank and relationship between organization units as defined in an organization chart.

Output. The total production of a machine, process, or worker for a specified unit of time.

Overtime. Time worked by an employee in addition to his regularly scheduled hours and in excess of the legal maximum hours of work.

Package. A term frequently used to describe a combination of benefits received by workers as a result of collective bargaining. A package may include wage increases as well as fringe benefits.

Par. The value that appears on the face of a certificate (stock, bond, etc.). The value the issuing company promises to pay on maturity.

Par value. Price set by either the articles of incorporation or the corporation's directors below which a share may not be originally issued by the corporation.

Pay adjustment. A general revision of pay rates. May be either across-the board, such as "cost of living," or spot adjustments for revisions in prevailing rates.

Pay compression. Upward movement of pay rates which reduces the differentials between jobs having dissimilar levels of responsibility, knowledge, and skill requirements.

Pay grade. The designation assigned to a pay range.

Pay plan.   A schedule of pay rates or ranges and a list showing the assignment of each class in the classification plan to one of the rates or ranges. May extend to rules of administration and the benefit package.

Pay policy line.   The trend line, or line of best fit, that shows the middle pay value of all of the jobs plotted on the scatter diagram.

Pay range.   A sequence of salary rates having minimum, maximum, and intermediate rates, and assigned for pay purposes to a particular position or class of positions.

Pay step.   The levels within a pay range. See text for further explanation.

Pay survey.   The gathering of data on wages and salaries paid by other employers for selected key classes or positions. See text for further explanation.

Pension.   The amount of money paid at regular intervals to an employee who has retired from a company and is eligible under a pension plan to receive such payments.

Pension trust fund.   A fund consisting of money contributed by the employer and, in some cases, the employee, to provide pension benefits. Contributions are paid to a trustee who invests the money, collects the interest and earnings, and disburses the benefits under the terms of the plan and trust agreement.

Performance.   The ratio of the actual production produced by an operator to the standard production.

Performance appraisal rating.   A method for appraising the contributions of an employee with respect to his or her job. This rating serves as a basis for merit increases, promotions and/or reassignment of work.

Performance shares.   Grant of stock units that entitle the recipient to actual shares of stock or their cash equivalent value at the time of payment and contingent upon prescribed performance criteria.

Performance share plan.   A stock grant plan that requires the achievement of certain predetermined performance goals before the recipient has the right to the stock.

Periodic review.   A plan of regularly reviewing the status of an employee or reviewing the contents of a job.

Perquisites.   Also called "perks." Usually noncash compensation for top-level executives; extra benfits above regular salary such as club memberships, cars, and legal/financial counseling.

Personnel department (division).   A staff concerned with securing and maintaining the manpower of the organization. Functions may include employment, compensation, training, safety, health, and other activities that contribute to satisfactory employer-employee relations.

Personnel manager (director).   Staff executive in charge of personnel administration. Head of personnel department.

Phantom stock.   An award of artificial shares of stock that have a value equal to an equivalent number of shares of stock in the corporation. The units' actual cash or stock payout value is set by some predetermined formula that relates to either the market or nonmarket value of the stock.

Pink-collar workers.   These are workers who occupy jobs in which 70 to 80 percent of the incumbents are female.

Plan. A basic division of accomplishment involving the mental process of determining the next action.

Point rating system (point system, point method). A method of job evaluation in which a range of point values is assigned to each of several job factors. The wage rates for specific jobs are then determined by comparing the total points each receives with the point values and wages of key jobs.

Policy. A code or guide for action that stipulates, in a general way, the preferred method of handling a situation or responsibility.

Portability. In a pension plan, an arrangement under which the contributions of employers who are parties to the plan pool their pension contributions in a central fund, where they are earmarked for the individual employees to whom they are credited. In this way, the employee doesn't lose his pension rights because either (1) he leaves the job before he has service enough to acquire rights or (2) he hasn't stayed long enough for his benefit to become vested.

Position. (1) An element of work consisting of locating an object so it will be properly oriented in a specific location. (2) A job performed by a particular employee.

Premium. A selling price above an established price.

Premium pay. Extra pay over the regular wage rate for work performed outside or beyond the regularly scheduled workday (Sundays, holidays, night shifts, etc.).

President. Head of an organization. May act as general manager, or may assume more limited duties of importance to the organization as a whole. In the corporation, elected by the board of directors and responsible to them.

Prevailing rate. The amount paid for like work by others in the labor market.

Price earnings ratio. The current stock market price of stock divided by its current or estimated future earnings.

Process. Any arrangement of machines, methods, resources, and/or personnel put together to accomplish a predetermined goal or produce goods and services.

Production control department. The staff concerned with production control. Usually subordinate to *factory* management. May serve under *general* management for matters of company-wide interest.

Production manager. Usually the head of production operations. Occasionally the staff supervisor over production control.

Profit sharing. A method of compensation to employees based on the profit realized from the organization.

Program. A series of actions proposed in order to achieve a certain result.

Promotion. The upgrading of an employee to a higher job classification.

Qualified pension plans. *See* approved pension plans.

Quality control. A function of management, the object of which is to maintain a quality of product in line with established policies and standards. Broader in scope than inspection.

Range spread. The difference between the minimum and maximum pay rates of a given pay grade expressed as a percent of the minimum.

Ranking method.   In job evaluation, a method in which jobs are listed in order of rank or relative value without attempting exact numerical rating.

Rate range.   The range between the minimum and maximum hourly rates for a particular job classification.

Real wages.   The purchasing power of the money received as wages.

Red-circle rates.   Rates that are above the maximum rate for a job (also *ringed rate*).

Restricted stock plan.   Recipient of stock grant does not receive right of full ownership until certain predetermined conditions are satisfied.

Right-to-work laws.   State laws prohibiting any type of union security arrangement between an employer and union which make union membership a requirement.

Routine.   An ordered set of instructions that may have some general or frequent use.

Rule of 72.   A technique used to identify the number of years required for an investment to double in value. In this case, a rate of return of 7.2 percent will double the investment in 10 years.

Salary.   Compensation for a given period of time, such as weekly or monthly, rather than hourly.

Scientific management.   The type of management that employs principles derived from research, from analysis of extensive records and other pertinent data, and from objective study of methods and results. A concept developed by F.W. Taylor in the late nineteenth century.

Secretary.   (1) A company officer in charge of corporate records, by-laws and minutes of meetings, the corporation seal, meeting notices, and lists of stock- and bondholders. In smaller concerns, often combined with the job of treasurer. (2) A title usually applied to the assistant of an executive or organization unit.

Self-administered trustee plan.   A retirement plan under which contributions to purchase pension benefits are paid to a trustee, generally a bank, which invests the money, accumulates the earnings and interest, and pays benefits to eligible employees under the terms of the retirement plan and trust agreement. This plan is administered by the employer, or by a committee appointed by him under the terms of the plan, and the trustee.

Seniority.   Rights and privileges accorded employees over other employees based on length of service.

Service.   Work done for others.

Share.   In a corporation, a unit of ownership interest. *See* stock.

Shareholder.   The owner of one or more shares of stock. *See* stockholder.

Shift differentials.   Extra pay allowance made to employees who work on shifts other than the regular day shift.

Sign-off.   The requirement that union officials approve job description, job classification, etc. by signing their names.

Single premium funding method.   A method of accumulating money for future payment of pensions under which the amount of money required to pay for each particular benefit, or each year's unit of benefit, without any further contribution requirement, is paid to the insurance company or paid to the trust fund.

Skill. Proficiency at following a prescribed method.

Sliding scale. Automatic wage adjustments (upward or downward) according to some specified agreement.

Social Security option. An option under which the employee may elect that monthly payments of annuity before a specifed age (62 or 65) be increased and that payments thereafter are decreased to produce as nearly as practicable a level total annual annuity to the employee, including Social Security.

Soldiering. The premediated, deliberate waste of productive time by a worker.

Source document. A record prepared at the time, or place, a transaction takes place.

Speed-up. Forcing workers to increase production without extra compensation.

Staff. Employees who provide assistance or services to other employees rather than producing the basic good or service of the organization. *See* line.

Standard deviation. A measure of dispersion of a set of numbers around a central point.

Statistical quality control. A type of quality control that makes use of mathematical statistics in sampling inspections and in the analysis of quality control data.

Stock. (1) In corporation financing, the form in which an owner's interest is represented; (2) in an industrial enterprise, the stored finished goods ready for sale.

Stock appreciation rights (SARs). A phantom stock plan that normally provides a recipient with the cash equivalent to the appreciation of the stock and declared dividend during a stipulated period.

Straight time. Regular wage rate for work performed at a nonpremium time (i.e., regularly scheduled workday).

Subsystem. A part of a larger system, which in itself forms an organized whole.

Superintendent. The manager of a factory or one of its divisions. May be equivalent to factory manager or general foreman.

Supervisor. In general, any person who directs the activities of immediate subordinates. Often a title applied to a group leader who heads a section within a department.

Synthetic feature. A composite, not naturally related to job content, used for identifying and defining job worth. *See* compensable factor.

System. An assembly of methods, procedures, or techniques united by regulated interaction to form an organized whole. An organized collection of men, machines, and methods required to accomplish a set of specific functions.

Systems analysis. The analysis of an activity to determine precisely what must be accomplished and how to accomplish it.

Take-home pay. Wages minus any tax deductions or other deductions that the employee is required to make.

Task. A task is created whenever human effort must be exerted for a specific purpose.

Top management. The directors and top executives who control the major divisions and the enterprise as a whole. The chain of command including the board of directors from the heads of primary divisions.

Treasurer. The company officer responsible for financing, banking, relations, disbursements, and the like. Responsibilities may include records of and payments to holders of stocks and bonds of the company. May have direct or staff authority over, or parallel with that of the controller.

Trust fund. *See* pension trust fund.

Turnover. (1) In general labor terms, turnover is the number of persons hired within a stated period to replace those leaving or dropped; also, the ratio of this number to the average work force maintained. (2) In pension plans, turnover refers to the ratio of participants who leave employment through quits, discharge, etc., to the total of participants at any age or length of service. Also called *withdrawal* or *withdrawal rate.*

Underutilization. The term used especially by federal EEO agencies meaning an employer is employing minorities and/or women at a rate below their percentages in the relevant labor market.

Unit benefit plan. A type of pension plan providing retirement benefits expressed as a definite amount of percentage for each year of service with the employer. The plan may define the benefit as a small unit of annuity for each year of membership in the plan, usually a percentage of the employee's earnings, such as 1 percent. The total of these units is the amount he will receive each year upon retirement. Sometimes referred to as a unit-purchase type of plan.

Universal compensable factor. Certain qualities which might be considered common to all jobs, such as mental, physical, and skill requirements. *See* compensable factors.

Upgrading. The advancement of an employee to a higher classification (commonly called a promotion).

Validation. Verification, by means of EEOC approved methods, that an employment test or other selection procedure actually predicts job performance.

Variable. A quantity that can assume any of a given set of values.

Variable annuity. An annuity under which the benefit varies according to the investment results of the funds set aside to provide it.

Vesting. In pension plans, vesting means that a participant who leaves the employ of the company for any reason not excepted by the plan does not lose all of the equity built up on his behalf, but may, at a designated time, receive either a stated lump-sum payment or payments, or a reduced or pro rata pension at the time he reaches retirement age.

Wage curve. A series of wage rates shown graphically.

Wage differentials. Differences that exist in wage rates for similar jobs because of location of company, hours of work, working conditions, or type of product manufactured.

Wage level. The average of all the wage rates paid to workers in an occupation, an industry, or a group of industries.

Wage rate. The money rate expressed in dollars and cents paid to the employee per hour.

Wages. Compensation paid to hourly workers (including those on incentive pay) for service rendered.

White-collar workers. "Nonmanual workers," like office, clerical, sales, or administrative personnel.

Withdrawal.   See turnover.

Work physiology.   The specification of the physiological and psychological factors characteristic of a work environment.

Work station.   The area where the worker performs the elements of work in a specific operation.

Workers' Compensation.   State laws that require most employers to provide employees with insurance protection from employment-related disabilities.

Works manager.   Head of a plant. Responsibilities usually confined to physical plant, manufacturing, and allied functions. A factory manager.

Worth.   The value of something measured by its qualities or by the esteem in which it is held.

DATA PROCESSING

Access time.   The time interval from the instant data are called for from a storage device to the instant delivery begins. Usually a computer term.

Address.   A computer term indicating where a piece of information can be found in the memory storage.

ALGOL (algorithmic language).   A language primarily used to express computer programs by algorithms.

Algorithm.   A prescribed set of well-defined rules or processes to solve a problem in a finite number of steps.

Alphanumeric.   Pertaining to a character set that contains letters, digits, and usually other characters such as punctuation marks. Synonymous with *alphameric.*

APL (a programming language).   A mathematically oriented computer language.

Arithmetic unit.   That part of the computer processing section that adds, subtracts, multiplies, divides, and computes.

Assemble.   The act of bringing two mating parts together.

Base.   The number of characters used in a digital numbering system.

BASIC (beginners all-purpose symbolic code).   A programming language used in time sharing.

Batch processing.   The execution of computer programs serially. Pertaining to the sequential input of computer programs or data.

Baudot code.   A code for transmitting data in which five equal-length bits represent one character.

BCD (binary coded decimal notation).   Positional notation in which the individual decimal digits expressing a number in decimal notation are each represented by a binary number.

Binary notation.   A fixed-base notation where the base is two.

Bit.   Contraction of "binary digit." The smallest unit of information in a binary system. A bit may be either one or zero.

BPS (bits per second).   The instantaneous bit speed within one character, as transmitted consecutively by a machine or a channel.

Buffer.   A routine or storage used to compensate for a difference in rate of flow of data, or time of occurrence of events, when transmitting data from one device to another.

Byte.   A sequence of adjacent binary digits operated upon as a unit and usually shorter than a computer word.

Cathode ray tube (CRT).   A display device that presents data in visual form by means of controlled electron beams.

Central processing unit (CPU).   A computer unit that includes circuits controlling the interpretation and execution of instructions. Synonymous with mainframe.

Character.   A letter, digit, or other symbol that is used as part of the organization, control, or representation of data on a computer.

COBOL (common business-oriented language).   A business data processing language.

Coding.   Converting instruction into language commands that can be processed by a computer.

Computer.   A device for performing logic operations or mathematical calculations. An electronic machine for computations that would otherwise require many hours of human effort. The analog computer projects its results as a graph. The digital computer operates on discrete data, delivering output in numbers or letters.

Console.   That part of a computer used for operator-computer communication.

Control unit.   Those parts of a digital computer that effect the retrieval of instructions in proper sequence, the interpretation of each instruction, and the application of the proper signals to the arithmetic unit and other parts in accordance with this interpretation.

Data bank.   A comprehensive collection of libraries of data.

Data cell drive.   A random-access storage device holding millions of characters on magnetic material strips filed in groups called cells.

Data collection.   The act of bringing data from one or more points to a central point.

Data processing.   The variously required selections, classifications, computations, tabulations, and recording of results of accumulated data. Often refers to the work of the electronic computer.

Debug.   To detect, locate, and remove mistakes from a routine or computer malfunctions.

Decimal notation.   A fixed-base notation, where the base is 10.

Decoder.   A device that decodes.

Digit row.   One of the horizontal rows of bits on a punched card, generally referring to the rows 1–9.

Disk pack.   A direct access storage device containing magnetic disks on which data are stored. Disk packs are mounted on a disk storage drive.

Display.   A visual presentation of data.

Flip-flop.   A computer circuit or device containing active elements capable of assuming either one or two stable states at a given time.

Format.   The arrangement of data.

FORTRAN (formula translating system). A language primarily used to express computer programs by arithmetic formulas.

Full duplex. In communications, pertaining to a simultaneous two-way independent transmission.

Half duplex. In communications, pertaining to an alternate, one way at a time independent transmission.

Hardware. Physical computer equipment like mechanical, magnetic, electrical, or electronic devices, as opposed to the program or method of use.

Hexadecimal notation. A numeration system with a base of 16.

Hollerith card. *See* punched card.

Housekeeping. Operations or routines that do not contribute directly to the solution of the problem but do contribute directly to the operation of the computer.

Initialize. To set counters, switches, and addresses to zero or other starting values at the beginning of or at the prescribed points in a computer routine.

Input. Pertaining to a device, process, or channel involved in the insertion of data.

Input/output. Commonly called I/O. A general term for the equipment used to communicate with a computer. The data involved in such communication. The media carrying the data for input/output.

Instruction. A statement that specifies an operation and the values or locations of its operands.

Instruction cycle. The phase in the CPU operating cycle during which an instruction is called from storage and the required circuitry to perform that instruction is set up.

Integer. A natural, or whole number.

Integrated circuit elements. A combination of interconnected circuit elements.

Job. A specified group of tasks prescribed as a unit of work for a computer. All necessary computer programs, linkages, files, and instructions to the operating systems.

K. An abbreviation for the prefix kilo, that is, 1000, in decimal notation. Loosely, when referring to storage capacity, 2 to the 10th power, 1024 in decimal notation.

Keypunch. A keyboard-actuated device that punches holes in a card to represent data.

Label. One or more characters used to identify a statement or an item of data in a computer program.

Language. A set of representations, conventions, and rules used to convey information.

Line printer. A device that prints all characters of a line as a unit.

Loop. A sequence of instructions that is executed repeatedly by the computer until a terminal condition prevails.

Magnetic core. A configuration of magnetic material that is used to concentrate an induced magnetic field to retain a magnetic polarization for the purpose of storing data, or for its nonlinear properties as in a logic element. It may be made of such material as iron, iron oxide, or ferrite and in such shapes as wires, tapes, toroids, rods, or thin film.

Magnetic disc. A flat, circular plate with a magnetic surface on which data can be stored by selective magnetization of portions of the flat surface.

Magnetic drum. A right circular cylinder with a magnetic surface on which data can be stored by selective magnetization of portions of the curved surface.

Magnetic ink character recognition (MICR). The machine recognition of characters printed with magnetic ink.

Magnetic tape. A tape with a magnetic surface on which data can be stored by selective polarization of portions of the surface.

Mainframe. *See* central processing unit (CPU).

Manual data processing. Data processing procedures using pencil, paper, adding machine, calculator, etc.

Mark sense. To mark a position on a punched card with an electrically conductive pencil for later conversion to machine punching.

Master file. A file that is either relatively permanent, or that is treated as an authority in a particular job.

Memory storage. That section of the computer that files or holds facts.

Microsecond. One-millionth of a second.

Millisecond. One-thousandth of a second.

Minicomputer. A small, desk-top, digital computer, with a CPU, a least one I/O device, and primary storage capacity of 4K bytes.

MODEM (modulator-demodulator). A device that modulates and demodulates signals transmitted over communications facilities.

Multiplex. To simultaneously transmit two or more messages on a single channel.

Nanosecond. One-thousand-millionth of a second.

Object program. A fully compiled or assembled program ready to be loaded into the computer.

Off line. Pertaining to equipment or devices not under control of the central processing unit.

Online. Pertaining to equipment or devices under control of the central processing unit. Pertaining to a user's ability to interact with a computer.

Operand. That which is operated upon. An operand is usually identified by an address part of an instruction.

Operating system. Software that controls the execution of computer programs and that may provide scheduling, debugging, input/output control, accounting, compilation, storage assignment, data management, and related services.

Optical character recognition (OCR). Machine identification of printed characters through use of light-sensitive devices.

Output. Computer results, such as answers to mathematical problems.

Peripheral equipment. In a data processing system, any unit of equipment distinct from the central processing unit, that may provide the system with outside communication.

Picosecond. One-thousandth of a nanosecond.

PL/1 (programming language 1). A high-level programming language.

Primary storage. The main internal storage.

Processor. In hardware, a data processor. In software, a computer program that includes the compiling, assembling, translating, and related functions for a specific programming language.

Production run. A computer run, involving actual data, as contrasted with a test run, using data for checking purposes.

Punched card. A data card with holes punched in particular positions each with its own signification for use in electrically operated tabulating or accounting equipment or computers.

Random access. Pertaining to the process of obtaining data from, or placing data into, storage where the time required for such access is independent of the location of the data most recently obtained or placed in storage.

Real time. Pertaining to the actual time during which a physical process transpires.

Register. A device capable of storing a specified amount of data, such as one word.

Remote access. Pertaining to communication with a data processing facility by one or more stations that are distant from that facility.

Run. A single, continuous performance of a computer program or routine.

Search. To examine a set of items for one or more items that has a desired property.

Secondary storage. Auxiliary storage.

Sequential access. Pertaining to the consecutive transmission of data to or from storage.

Software. A set of computer programs, procedures, and possibly associated documentation concerned with the operation of a data processing system.

Statement. In computer programming, a meaningful expression or generalized instruction in a source language.

Storage. Pertaining to a device into which data can be entered, in which they can be held, and from which they can be retrieved at a later time.

Subroutine. A routine that can be part of another routine.

Telecommunication. Pertaining to the transmission of signals over long distances, such as by telegraph, radio, television, or satellite, or any combination.

Teleprocessing. A form of information handling in which a data processing system utilizes communication facilities.

Terminal. A point in a system or communications network at which data can either enter or leave.

Time sharing. Pertaining to the sharing of the time of a device by various computer users.

Transitor. A small, solid-state, semi-conducting device, ordinarily using germanium, that performs nearly all the functions of an electronic tube, especially amplification.

Turnaround time. The elapsed time between submission of a job to a computing center and the return of results.

Word. A character string or a bit string considered as an entity.

Word length. A measure of the size of a word, usually specified in units such as characters or binary digits.

X punch. A punch in the second row from the top on a Hollerith punched card. Synonymous with eleven-punch.

Y punch. A punch in the top row of a Hollerith punched card. Synonymous with twelve-punch.

Zone punch. A punch in the eleven, twelve, or zero row of a Hollerith punched card.

INDUSTRIAL ENGINEERING

Abnormal time. Time values taken during a time study that are either higher or lower than most observations. Also known as "wild values."

Accelerating premium. A wage payment plan in which the percentage of premium rises as the production level rises.

Activity sampling. *See* work sampling.

Actual time. The average elemental time a worker takes to perform a task during a time study.

Allowed time (or allowance). An amount of time added to the normal time to provide for personal delays, fatigue, and unavoidable delays. *See* also standard time.

Avoidable delay. Cessation of work caused by the operator.

Base time. In time study, the time it takes a particular worker to perform an operation or one of its elements as determined from a series of time recordings (observed times).

Bedaux plan. A constant sharing wage incentive plan. Provides that the bonus for incentive effort be distributed between the employee and management.

Controlled time. Elapsed elemental time, depending on the facility or process.

Cycle. A series of elements that occur in regular order and make an operation possible. As the operation repeats, the elements repeat.

Daywork. Pay for work on the basis of time rather than output, exlusive of incentives or other bonuses.

Decimal hour stopwatch. A stopwatch used for work measurement, the dial of which is graduated in 0.0001 of an hour.

Decimal minute stopwatch. A stopwatch used for work measurement, the dial of which is graduated in 0.01 of a minute.

Differential piecework. Compensation for labor in which the money rate for each piece is based on the total pieces produced during the period (usually one day).

Differential piece rate. A piece rate that increases in value at one or more standard task points.

Downtime. A period of time in which a machine or process is inoperative due to breakdown or lack of material.

Elapsed time. The actual time that has transpired during the course of a study or an operation.

Element. A division of work that can be measured with a stopwatch and that has readily identified terminal points.

External element. An element usually beginning with "stop machine" and ending with "start machine" performed by the operator outside of the machine cycle.

Fatigue. A lessening in the capacity for the will to work. Weariness from labor or exertion.

Fatigue allowance. An amount of time added to the normal time to compensate for fatigue.

First piece time. The time allowed to produce the first piece of an order. It is adjusted to allow for the operator's unfamiliarity with the procedure and for delays resulting from the newness of the work. It does not include time for setting up the work station.

Flow process chart. A graphic representation of all operations, transportation, inspection, delays, and storages occurring during a process or procedure.

Frame counter. A device that automatically tabulates the number of frames that have passed the lens of the projector.

Gain sharing. Any method of wage payment in which the worker participates in all or a portion of the added earnings resulting from his production above standard.

Gain-sharing plan. A wage payment system that pays the worker a bonus for output above standard in less than direct proportion to said output.

High task. The amount of production derived through time study that a normal person can accomplish without emotional or physical harm.

Idle time. Time during which the worker is not working.

Industrial engineer. An engineer concerned with factory operations. May apply particularly to responsibility for operation standards, perhaps to production control.

Industrial engineering. A branch of engineering concerned with coordinating human organization with physical plant for the purpose of production or service, and with control of those activities.

Internal element. An element usually performed while the machine is operating automatically.

Leveling. A term used synonymously with performance rating. It assigns a percentage to the operator's average observed time to adjust his time to the observer's conception of normal.

Loose rate. An established allowed time that permits the normal operator to achieve standard performance with poorer than average effort.

MTM (methods-time measurement). A procedure that analyzes a manual operation and the basic motions required to perform it. A predetermined time standard is assigned to each motion and is determined by the nature of the motion and the conditions under which it is made.

Machine cycle time. The time required for the machine in process to complete one cycle.

Machine idle time. The time when the machine or process is inoperative.

Man-hour. The standard amount of work performed by one man in one hour.

Man-machine process chart. Process chart showing the exact relationship in time between the working cycle of the operator and the operating cycle of his machine or machines.

Maximum performance. That performance which will result in the highest obtainable production.

Measured daywork. A daywork method of wage payment in which the wage rate is periodically revised to reflect output records. Work for which performance standards have been established but where the worker is compensated on an hourly basis with no provision for incentive earnings. Also, an incentive system in which hourly rates are periodically adjusted on the basis of worker performance during the previous period.

Merrick differential piece rate. An incentive wage payment plan having three different piece rates established on the basis of operator performance.

Methods study. Analysis of an operation to increase the production per unit of time and consequently reduce the unit cost.

Microchronometer. A specially designed clock devised by Frank B. Gilbreth capable of measuring elapsed time in "winks" (0.0005 minute).

Micromotion study. A motion study or time study in which motion pictures are taken to analyze detailed operation elements.

Minimum time. The least amount of time taken by the operator to perform a given element during a time study.

Motion study. The analysis and study of the motions constituting an operation to improve the motion pattern by eliminating ineffective motions and shortening the effective motions.

Normal performance. The performance expected from the average trained worker when he is following the prescribed method and working at an average pace.

Normal time. The time required for the standard worker to perform an operation when working at a standard pace without delay for personal reasons or unavoidable circumstances.

Observation. The gathering and recording of time to perform an element, or one watch reading.

Observed time. In time study, the time actually observed for the worker to perform a complete operation of one of its elements.

Observer. The analyst taking a time study of a given operation.

Occurrence. An incident or event happening during a time study.

Personal allowance. A percentage added to the normal time to accommodate the personal needs of the worker.

Piece rate. A wage rate for each piece or other quantity unit produced by the worker (e.g., a wage of $1.25 per 100 pieces).

Piecework. Work paid for according to number of pieces produced or operations completed.

Point. A unit of output identified as the production of one standard man in one minute. Used as a basis for establishing standards under the Bedaux system.

Rate. A standard expressed in dollars and cents.

Rate cutting. A practice of the arbitrary reduction of established rates on piecework.

Rate setting. The act of establishing money rates or time values on an operation.

Selected time. An elemental time value that is chosen as being representative of expected performance of the operator being studied.

Standard. An established norm or accepted model applying to structure, measurement, method, performance, or other characteristics of things, individuals, or actions. An accepted basis for comparisons and appraisals (e.g., a standard of length measurement such as the inch, or a standard of performance such as standard time).

Standard hours (or time). The amount of time established in a wage incentive plan for performing a specific task (referred to as standard task). The measure of a "fair day's work" for a particular operation.

Standards department. In an industrial organization, usually the staff concerned with the development and maintenance of standards relating to production methods and times—time and motion studies.

Standing committee. A permanent committee, often specified in the organizational structure (e.g., policy committee or finance committee).

Synthetic basic motion times. A collection of time standards assigned to fundamental motions and groups of motions.

Synthetic time study. A time study in which no operator is actually observed at work. The time elements are derived from various other sources of time data (e.g., methods-time measurement).

Temporary standard. A standard established to apply for a limited number of pieces or limited period of time to account for the newness of the work or some unusual job condition.

Therblig. One of the basic elements of work operations. A concept developed by the Gilbreths. (Examples are search and grasp.)

Work factor. Index of additional time required over and above the basic time as established by the work-factor system of synthetic basic motion times.

Work sample test. A typical work task, which must relate to observable job behaviors, used to predict an individual's success or aptitude for success on the job.

Work sampling. Method of analyzing work by taking a large number of observations at random intervals to establish standards and improve methods.

INDEX

551

ORGANIZATIONS: